LWICH COLLEGE.

DULWICH COLLEGE
A HISTORY, 1616–2008

BORN SEPT. 1ST, 156... ...DIED NOV. 25TH 1626

Edw: Alleyn

DULWICH COLLEGE
A HISTORY, 1616–2008

Jan Piggott

with contributions from

Graham Able, Allan Ronald & Terry Walsh

DULWICH COLLEGE

London, 2008

British Library Cataloguing in Publication Data.
A record for this book is available from the British Library.

ISBN 978-0-9539493-2-8

Published in 2008 on the order of the Governors of Dulwich College by
DULWICH COLLEGE ENTERPRISES LTD
Dulwich College, Dulwich Common, London, SE21 7LD

To purchase a copy, please contact
THE COMMISSARIAT, DULWICH COLLEGE
Phone 020 8299 9222 · *Fax* 020 8299 9222
E-mail the.commissariat@dulwich.org.uk
www.dulwich.org.uk/shop

Designed and typeset in Monotype Bulmer by
Strathmore Publishing Services, London EC1
www.strathmorepublishing.co.uk

Origination by David McLean and Dulwich College
Print management by David McLean

Printed in China by Everbest Printing

CONTENTS

PREFACE &
ACKNOWLEDGEMENTS

'Vivit Fundatoris nomen, Unicae virtutis omen'. The school song of Dulwich College vows to keep alive the name of its Founder, and claims the benefits of his legacy as uniquely virtuous. This history shares similar aims; beginning at the height of the reign of Elizabeth I, it concludes in the autumn of the reign of Elizabeth II.

The first two chapters offer a detailed account of the life and fame of the extraordinary man who founded Dulwich College and his skills as actor and entrepreneur in the colourful London of late Tudor and early Stuart days. They also attempt to restore the balance of Edward Alleyn's reputation for his 'bad shillings' earned from entertainment enterprises by demonstrating his charitable works for the underprivileged as Churchwarden in Southwark; I have found no documentary evidence for the allegations (published from the 1970s onwards) that he profited from brothels. With much of the enormous fortune that he amassed in London, and the property and manorial rights in which he invested, he endowed 'Alleyn's College of God's Gift at Dulwich' to benefit the poor and to perpetuate his name. Of relatively humble birth, among playwrights and courtiers he was conscious of his lack of university education; once he had bettered himself at an early age, married but childless, he returned his bounty to London for the education of orphans. He directed that the 'Poor Scholars' at Dulwich were to be drawn from the very parishes that formed the arena of his great career in entertainments and properties, his stated intention to help them towards better lives; the cleverest of the boys were expected to take up the closed Scholarships he endowed by which the College were to pay fees and maintenance at Oxford and Cambridge.

The next three chapters recount the disappointing but interesting fortunes of his College of God's Gift over the two-and-a-third centuries following Alleyn's death, together with glimpses into the daily life of the 'Society' formed of the Master, Warden and Fellows and their charges, the Poor Scholars; in 1857 the reforms of the Dulwich College Act were to sweep away this comfortable and mostly neglectful and outmoded establishment, making radical changes to the constitution of the College and its by then very wealthy Estate. Apart from the services in the Chapel, the Old College in Dulwich Village is now a largely silent historic site; these chapters aim to revive the voices of its forgotten *dramatis personae*, together with the school-rooms, the Hall, the Chapel and the surrounding meadows, woods and messuages.

The latter half of the book concerns the 'Second Foundation' of Dulwich College from 1857 until the present. Alleyn's ideal of academic and social improvement in the first College drove the second, in that 'exhibitions' [scholarships] and low fees made available an expensive academic and liberal education to clever boys from poor, or relatively less affluent, middle-class homes. Dulwich College, in the space of only a few decades, with an enlightened curriculum and scholarly teachers, grew into a large and a great urban day Public School (with some boarding pupils, as Alleyn originally intended); shaped by the different educational ideals of those early Masters with very different personalities, Canon Carver, J. E. C. Welldon and A. H. Gilkes, and overcoming fearful opposition and setbacks, it was to achieve extraordinary success and fame.

The College nurtured its Alleynians, who in turn animated the life of the metropolis and the nation. The prosperity and the fame of Old Alleynians resulted from the high cultivation and sense of service that many of them carried away; they were characterised by enterprise, courage and rectitude in the 'professions', in the Armed Forces, in other kinds of public service and in the Arts where they showed marked eloquence in literature, painting, and music. To Dulwich College as their Alma Mater they were usually loyal; they were also grateful to the nourishing mother, many of those who could afford to giving generously to the College Mission, to Memorial Funds, to Bursaries and to appeals for new buildings. Clearly, very many adult Alleynians that are to be met with today, bred by the College in a rich cultural environment, were also fashioned in virtuous and gentle discipline, recalling the Renaissance ideal of the education of courtiers.

Christison's two volumes of the *Dulwich War Record* give the names and details of Alleynian servicemen in both World Wars, with photographs and poignantly short biographies of those who died, memorialising their actions and the fields of battle where they fell. Boys who stand silent and marshalled at the War Memorial on Remembrance Day cannot possibly apprehend the full measure of the sacrifices their Alleynian predecessors made, the heroism and gallantry of the Victoria Cross holders and of the hundreds of other Alleynians who fought; these include the young Battle of Britain pilots in the skies above the College's classrooms and its catchment area, and the boys and masters who withstood aerial bombardment and its fears with such fortitude.

A school takes a great deal of its character from its headmaster (even by reaction). I have perhaps given too much space to the lives and characters of the great Victorian and Edwardian Masters of Dulwich College, Carver and Gilkes, who between them created the modern College. Canon Carver, with his apparently mild and genial manner, was victor in an intense battle to establish the College not only as a 'first grade school' but as a serious competitor with the great ancient public school foundations; Gilkes had perhaps as noble an ideal of the pedagogue as can be imagined (although in recent times Stephen Howard came close to it) and it was Gilkes who transformed an extraordinarily good new school into a great school, with its glories of academic supremacy, sporting triumphs and alumni both eminent and individual. His son Christopher, Master of Dulwich College in turn, saved the College from death during the Second World War and its aftermath; shrewdly adapting to the times, he altered its character, bettering a whole generation of the sons of suburban households susceptible to lower expectations, narrow outlooks and few books.

Dulwich College still fosters the best qualities of character-building of the traditional schools, at the same time as infusing a critical faculty, a sense of worldly wisdom and a spirit of practical enterprise. Unselfish *esprit de corps* and involvement in the College Mission (in the spirit of Edward Alleyn) were inculcated by Gilkes and his staff by addresses from the platform in the Great Hall, but also by example. More testing perhaps in its way than the lively discussion of texts in the classrooms of Charles Barry's *palazzo*, with its grass swards, fine trees and Victorian clock-chimes, is a 'streetwise' consciousness among College boys of metropolitan, social, political and commercial issues; this is undoubtedly part legacy of the Revd William Rogers, Carver's antagonist and the formidable early Chairman of the Governors, who intended a more utilitarian school at Dulwich, and was himself a noble champion of education for the poorer classes of the parishes which Alleyn himself intended to benefit. The persistence of the early Masters, all of whom faced hostile criticism and fought against bureaucracy, apathy and vested interests, contributed to the robust character of the College we have inherited.

One might argue that it does not really signify all that much where a man went to school, that nature determines more than nurture. In countless examples, however, the College can be shown to have developed the defining interests and characteristics of boys at the determinant age who were equal to the stimulating transformation; these qualities are as likely to have been sparked outside the classroom as in it, and this history takes seriously the contribution of extra-curricular activities, with a particular interest in drama and music, in the societies, and in the College magazines. A separate chapter by Terry Walsh covers Games and Sports. This book has therefore treated the various careers of selected Alleynians as a matter of great interest; the question, as in H. M. Bateman's cartoon of the suburban day-boy sketched on his unwilling way to school in 1912, is still 'Dulwich. The Boy – What will he Become?'

Unhappy modern testimonies of life at Dulwich are to be found from boys who disliked the prevailing atmosphere; at times poor teaching, petty, hollow conventions, over-emphasis on Sports, and the cruder elements of the boys' own power-structures obtained. On the other hand, there is the testimony of P. G. Wodehouse, known to his contemporaries in the 'Golden Age' of Dulwich under Gilkes as someone whose participation at school (sporting, literary and cultural) was extraordinarily full and wide: he maintained contact with the College, and could write in 1945 to S. C. 'Billy' Griffith (the Alleynian cricketer), 'I believe a boy has a much better time at Dulwich than anywhere else. I don't know why it is, but we seem to turn out such an awfully nice type'. Happy schoolboys often become happy students, and in 1923 the famous writer C. S. Lewis, Fellow and Tutor of Magdalen College, Oxford, wrote that Dulwich (under George Smith's Mastership) of all schools was sending up to Oxford the best scholars, the best men and the best gentlemen.

The chronicle necessarily involves the history of the Dulwich Estate while it played an integral role at the College; the Estate was administered by the Master, Warden and Fellows until 1858. Although the Dulwich College Act of 1882 created a separate Board for Estates Governors, the Dulwich Estate, as was Alleyn's intention, still subsidises the College (and the other Foundation Schools). The history of the Picture Gallery until its recent independence is a further and significant part of the College's rich story. I have peopled the second half of the book with characters, anecdotes and voices (in actual quotations where possible) in an attempt to revive impressions of the daily life at the College as well as describing its essential developments and reforms.

Love of an institution can develop slowly, and even against the grain. I joined the English Department in 1972 in an era of high academic excitement, teaching questioning pupils who took little on trust; many were on 'free places', their fees paid by local councils, inheriting in its maturity the scheme of the so-called 'Gilkes Experiment', which was the forerunner of the government Assisted Places scheme. Retired from the class-room in 2001, I worked until 2006 as the Keeper of Archives (a post I had held since 1992). Chapter Ten covers the history of the College since the last war; its latter half, which is synoptic, offers a subjective and partial view of my own times. My greatest anxiety is that individuals who served the College faithfully (or their families), or those who attended it, will find unjust omissions and false emphases. For such omissions, as for mistakes and muddles, I ask to be forgiven.

It is a pleasure to acknowledge the use I have made of resources and ideas contained in the previous College histories: the two volumes of *The History of Dulwich College* (1889) by William Young, a Governor of the College in Queen Victoria's latter years; *God's Gift* (1981) by Sheila Hodges, from David Emms's era; and the unpublished typescripts by R. J. Mackenzie of A. H. Gilkes's day (1909–12) and by William Darby, an Assistant Master at the College (post-1945). Lieutenant-Colonel T. L. Ormiston, an intensely loyal Old Alleynian, in his *Dulwich College Register, 1619–1926* accomplished a staggering project of detailed research about Alleynians and their careers which has led me to some very interesting discoveries. Harding Dunnett's booklet *Eminent Alleynians* (1984), although (as he recognised) very limited in selection, was also useful. I have compiled no Bibliography: the list of Abbreviations placed before the Notes records the major sources, and the others are to be found in their context within them.

I warmly thank Graham Able with Colin Niven, Allan Ronald and Terry Walsh, for the three chapters they have contributed with their special knowledge. Susan Cerasano and Grace Ioppolo were particularly generous to me with information and comments on Edward Alleyn's career and the theatres of his day. Colin Niven, Simon Northcote-Green and Allan Ronald patiently read all I had written in draft; I am enormously grateful to them for their comments and corrections, which I greatly enjoyed discussing; similar thanks and appreciation are due to Graham Able, Christopher Field, Gardner Thompson and Terry Walsh for the care and attention with which they made detailed comments on Chapter Ten. The selection and interpretation of events is my own, however, and I must of course take the blame for surviving errors and omissions.

My greatest debt is to my former pupil, now my mentor, Nick de Somogyi of Cambridge, who with tireless patience meticulously edited the text, and by his questions and suggestions improved the thinking, the expression and the shaping of the book, as well as saving me from a number of *bêtises*. Nicholas Jones and Patricia Saunders of Strathmore Publishing worked heroically on my behalf; for a third time now I am indebted to David McLean for his excellent and congenial work as designer of my books.

At Dulwich College I must thank Graham Able and the Governors for commissioning this book, and the Deputy Master, Ralph Mainard (of Dulwich College Enterprises) for publishing it. Warm thanks are also due for information and for many kind favours to: Calista Lucy (Keeper of Archives) with her patience and resourcefulness, Terry Walsh (Senior Fellow and Archivist), with his phenomenal memory, knowledge and loyal affection for the College, together with their colleague in the Archives, Soraya Cerio; Deirdre Young, Dorothy Wright, and Alexandra Fabian of the Alleyn Club and Development Office; Marianne Bradnock (Head of Information Services and former Head of Libraries) and Paul Fletcher of the Wodehouse Library; Peter Titmarsh (School Staff Instructor, CCF); Rosemary Weavers (the Master's Personal Assistant), Sarah Betts (Registrar), and Mette Turner (Co-ordinator of the Music Department). Among my former colleagues, I thank the following for information and discussion: Nick Black, Ian Brinton, John Carnelley, Garth Davidson, Fergus Jamieson, Michael Hart, John Heath, Peter Jolly, Gardner Thompson, the Revd Robin Turner, Anthony Verity, Jonathan Ward, Mark Whittaker, and the Revd Stephen Young.

I have received much kind and willing help from representatives and archivists of institutions; these include Simon Bailey (OA), Keeper of Archives at the University of Oxford; Elizabeth Boardman, Brasenose College, Oxford; Rita Boswell, Harrow School; R. A. D. Chappell, Churchwarden of St Michael's Millbrook, Ampthill, and the Vicar, Michael Trodden; Shirley Corke, Charterhouse School; James Cox, Caius College, Cambridge; Robert Elwall and Valeria Carullo, RIBA Photographic Collection; Geoffrey Fisher, the Courtauld Institute; Colin Gale, Bethlem Royal Hospital; Bernard Horrocks, National Portrait Gallery; William Ingram, University of Ann Arbor, Michigan; Patricia McGuire, King's College, Cambridge; Janet McMullin, Christ Church, Oxford; Beverley Matthews, Tonbridge School; Simon May, St Paul's School; Peter Meadows, the Ely Dean and Chapter; Katie Mooney, Institute of Education, University of London; Peter Morris, Old Tonbridgian Society; Elaine Mundill, Glenalmond College; Susannah Schofield, Alleyn's School; Xavier Saloman and Fulvio Rubesa, Dulwich Picture Gallery; Lisa Wells, the Headmasters' and Headmistresses' Conference; Thomas Woodcock, Norroy and Ulster King of Arms, and Robert Yorke, the College of Arms.

I am also indebted to the very many Old Alleynians I have approached, and to the alacrity with which they have offered information and recollections; they include Derek Akers, Bernard Battley, Vivian Bazalgette, Peter

Branscombe, Ian Bristow, Brian Capon, the late Sir Colin Cole, Patrick Darby, Peter de Bolla, Brian de Looze, Peter Edgley, Alex Hemming, Ian McCallum, Douglas Pinnock, Gavin Stamp, Jeremy Tambling, A. F. 'Pat' Thompson, Andrew Wilton, and Anthony Woods.

Writings in copyright are reproduced by kind permission of the P. G. Wodehouse Estate, of the Raymond Chandler Estate (Charlie Campbell of Ed Victor Ltd), and of the Michael Powell Estate. Papers of Oscar Browning, J. E. C. Welldon and Sir Jack Sheppard are quoted by kind permission of King's College, Cambridge; an extract from *The Caian* is quoted by kind permission of the Master and Fellows of Gonville and Caius College, Cambridge. Other acknowledgements are given in the Notes.

Among many friends and acquaintances to whom I am indebted for various generosities I would like to thank the following, with thanks also and apologies to others whom I may have carelessly omitted: Sir Edward Cazalet, Jonathan Cecil, Ian Christie, David and Gill Cooper, Tony Cox, Katherine Duncan-Jones, Susannah Fiennes, Michael Gilkes, Jeremy Gotch, John Gowar, Brian Green, Andrew Gurr, Crispin Hodges, Sheila Hodges, Gordon Higgott, John Ingamells, Liz Johnson, Cas Piggott, Thelma Schoonmaker, the Hon Alexandra Shackleton, Margaret Slythe, Ann Savours Shirley, Giles Waterfield, and Trudy Wilson.

Sydenham, March 2008

J. R. P.

Jan Piggott, MA, PhD, FSA, is the author of

Turner's Vignettes (1993)

Shackleton, the Antarctic and Endurance (2000)

Palace of the People, The Crystal Palace at Sydenham (2004)

He also contributed to

Wodehouse Goes to School (1997)

TO ALLEYNIANS

past, present
and future

and in memory of

McCulloch Christison, OA
1880–1972

William Duff Gibbon, OA
1880–1955

Stephen Howard
1928–78

William Kip after Stephen Harrison, 'The Device called Londinivm', from *The Archs* (sic) *of Triumph*, 1604. Edward Alleyn stands with raised arm in the central niche of the Arch set up at Fenchurch Street, where on 15 March 1604 the *The Magnificent Entertainment* and the procession began. Alleyn (in lines written by Ben Jonson) welcomed the new King, James I, on behalf of the City of London, performing as 'Genius Urbis': 'a person attyr'd rich, reverend, and antique: his haire long and white, crowned with a wreathe of Plane tree, which is said to be *Arbor genialis*, his mantle of purple and buskins of that colour. He held in one hand a goblet, in the other a branch full of little twigs, to signifie increase and indulgence'. The recumbent figure below is old Thamesis. (© British Library, G. 10866)

EDWARD ALLEYN

… others speake, but onely thou dost act.
Weare this renowne. 'Tis just, that who did give
So many *Poets* life, by one should live.

– BEN JONSON, 'To Edward Allen'

Bishopsgate: Alleyn's birth and family – Alleyn's acting career – Alleyn's acting style – The Magnificent Entertainment, 1604 – Philip Henslowe – The Alleyn and Henslowe papers – Henslowe's Diary – Bankside and Clerkenwell: Henslowe's and Alleyn's theatres – Master of the Royal Game of Bears, Bulls, and Mastiff Dogs – The Earl of Arundel and Inigo Jones – Death of Henslowe – Joan Alleyn – From actor to gentleman armiger

Bishopsgate: Alleyn's birth and family

Edward Alleyn, the Founder of Dulwich College, is said to have been born in Bishopsgate Street, just beyond the actual walls and gate of the Tudor City of London, on 1 September 1566; he was baptised the following day at the parish church of St Botolph without Bishopsgate.[1] Alleyn was in the habit of noting his birthday in his diary. The one surviving volume, running from 29 September 1617 to 1 October 1622 by which time he was living at Dulwich, shows that he celebrated his birthdays by feasting with his pensioners at the College. Christ's Chapel at Dulwich was consecrated on his fiftieth birthday in 1616. He was to die at the age of sixty in 1626.

The family name was pronounced in the same way as it was often spelled: *Allen*. He usually signed himself *Alleyn*, but in contemporary documents we also find *Allin, Alen, Allein*, and *Alleyne*. The Founder's father, also Edward Alleyn, was a 'yeoman' [a middle-class farmer or owner of a small estate] from Willen in Buckinghamshire who had settled in London by 1555, and his mother was Margaret Townley of a Lancashire family.[2] Edward Alleyn senior, according to Thomas Fuller's *History of the Worthies of England* (1662), kept an inn 'near Devonshire house, whyre in now is the sign of the Pye'. The inn stood up from the church of St Botolph on Bishopsgate; the mansion of Devonshire House was built across the road in the later years of Queen Elizabeth, on the east side of Bishopsgate above Houndsditch, with pleasure gardens and bowling alleys. It was a lively quarter of London in which to be brought up: Bishopsgate Street passed through the surviving medieval Gate to the main north road; behind the gardens and orchards of the houses to the west lay the open Moor fields with cattle and horses, a dog-house and men practising archery or the new art of musketry.[3]

Edward Alleyn must have taken the measure of London from his early days; his father had served the court and had been in charge of a charitable institution. A copy of a report of 1567 calls him 'one of the Queens Maiesties porters'.[4] From 1546 to 1561 he was also the first Keeper, and the first to be appointed by the City of London rather than the Crown, of the nearby Bethlehem Hospital for lunatics.[5] This was the original madhouse that gave us the word 'Bedlam'; it was relocated in 1812 to the domed premises in Kennington that now house the Imperial War Museum. Innkeepers used to lodge and to care for elderly and insane people. As 'Keeper of Bethlem', Alleyn, who presumably was victualler to the Hospital at first, was a kind of steward to no more than about twenty 'lunatic people'. The post was not made a medical appointment until 1619: Edward Alleyn senior was followed as Keeper at Bethlem Hospital by a draper and a grocer. The Alleyn family probably lived in the Master's house until 1570: 'Edward Allen, citizen and innholder, and Margaret his wife' held the lease of it, together with two walled gardens, a monks' cemetery and a chapel.[6] The Hospital declined; in December 1598, twenty-eight years after the elder Edward died, it was 'loathsomely and filthily kept, not fit for any man to come into'.[7]

The very many London properties assigned in 1619 by Edward Alleyn to his College of God's Gift when he became a magnate included the former 'sign of the Pye' itself in Bishopsgate; it is assumed but not proven that Alleyn's father actually ran the public house.[8] In 1678 the College was involved in a dispute over tenement walls between Pye Alley and Bedlam.[9] That the College had a special regard for the Pye as the birthplace of the Founder is suggested by the payment in 1681 for '2 stones with the Colledge armes at Pye alley'.[10]

Young Edward Alleyn had brothers: John, his elder by nine years, became a 'cyttysen & Inhoulder of London' [11] and an actor; he died at the age of 39 in 1596.[12] William, Oliver and Percival died in their youth. His father left his 'lands and tenements' to his wife and divided his 'goods, leases and ready money' between his wife and surviving sons. When his father died, Edward Alleyn was four years old. By the age of thirteen he had known two step-fathers: from when he was five to eight his mother (described as 'illiterate') was married to one Richard Christopher, also known as Grove, who was buried on 11 March 1578; in the following year she married a haberdasher, John Browne. Browne sued Edward's brother John over the possession of some Bishopsgate leases of his father, claiming he had stolen them from the house.[13] There is no evidence that either of Alleyn's two step-fathers were actors, as has been claimed.[14]

Alleyn was to maintain close relations with the church and parish of St Botolph, building ten alms-houses at nearby Petty France in 1614,[15] and reserving places for their pensioners and orphans at the College; it is very likely that in his boyhood he sang in the church choir and owed the church his education and his love of music. It is possible that he saw theatrical performances at his father's inn or at others in the neighbourhood. Open-air stages were put up in the courtyards of inns on barrels or trestles. This was a boom period for the theatres: five inns were converted into playhouses; four of these were located near to, or in Bishopsgate, and the other was at Newington Butts where Alleyn later played.[16] The arched street entrance of the larger inns, with their great doors for horses, coaches and drays, their yards where the 'groundlings' stood to see the play, and the open galleries round the yard with their staircases and balusters, influenced the design of Elizabethan and Jacobean public theatres. The usual agreement was that the takings for performances from the galleries went to the innkeepers, and from the yard to the actors – the coins from that audience being collected into padlocked wooden boxes; we still speak of a 'box office'. James Burbage, whose son Richard (1568–1619) was to become Edward Alleyn's main rival as an actor, set up a new playhouse called the Theatre (short for Amphitheatre) in Finsbury Field in the adjacent parish of Shoreditch in 1576, when Alleyn was ten years old, one of the two playhouses in the neighbourhood outside the walls of the City. In 1598 the 'sharers' (the actors who were part-owners) of the theatre quarrelled with the landowner and after a violent affray dismantled their theatre and carried its timbers, most likely across the river Thames which was frozen, to set up the Globe on Bankside.[17]

Alleyn passed his early days among playhouses and public houses, the enterprising arena of popular entertainment and leisure. He must have heard about the court entertainments in connection with his father's post under Queen Elizabeth. There was the also St Botolph's church itself, with its spacious nave and choir for ritual, singing and rhetoric, serving a parish that devoted compassion and relief to the poor and the suffering. These two polarities – entertainment and charity – determined the career of this passionate and loyal Londoner, who through his famous talent as an actor, his ventures on Bankside and at the Fortune theatre, his speculation in property and all his other enterprises, raised himself to become a very wealthy man, recognised at court and in the streets, a gentleman and lord of manors in South London, and the Founder of the College of God's Gift at Dulwich.

By 1580 Edward Alleyn's elder brother John was a member of the company of actors called 'Lord Sheffield's men', and was later described as 'servant' to the Lord High Admiral Charles Howard (1536–1624), second Baron Howard of Effingham and Earl of Nottingham, who was cousin to Sheffield. He held, in fact, the post in which his more brilliant younger brother Edward succeeded him as the leading actor and the manager of his theatrical company. Howard, the Queen's cousin, was a very prominent courtier, Knight of the Garter and Privy Councillor, and moreover commanded the victorious fleet against the Spanish Armada in the magnificent flagship *Ark Royal*. John Alleyn was said at one time to be living in Howard's household; in the late 1580s he appears to have been involved in the same acting troupe as his brother Edward, but by 1592 he had left the stage.[18] Edward advanced him £11 with the security of a 'Scarlett cloake wt Sylver buttons faced wt purple' and other garments on 24 August 1592.[19]

After their mother died the brothers mortgaged a house in Bishopsgate to buy a job lot of costumes and stock, 'suche Share parte and porcion of playinge apparrelles, playe Bookes, [musical] Instrumentes and other commodities' at the cost of £37 from Richard Jones, a member of the theatre company known as 'Worcester's Men'.[20] They also paid Isaac Burges of Clifford's Inn £16 for just two items: 'one cloke of velvet with a cape Imbrothered with gold pearles & redd stones, & one Roabe of cloth of golde'.[21] Such costumes were very expensive, and of course a central investment for theatrical companies. A surviving inventory of costumes in Edward Alleyn's hand, made between 1590 and 1600, mentions items worn by Faustus ('Faustus jerkin, his clok') and other characters in Marlowe's plays, and lists 14 cloaks, 16 gowns, 16 'Antik Sutes' [fancy dress or clown's costumes], 17 jerkins and doublets, 11 French hose and 8 Venetians [breeches].[22]

Alleyn's acting career

Alleyn was reported, some 36 years after his death (and in a not very reliable source) to have been 'bred a Stage-player, a calling which many have condemned, more have questioned and some few have excused, and far fewer conscientious people have commended.' [23] Whether this is true or false, it is possible that in the convention of the day he played women's parts before his voice broke. The first documented record of his career is in March 1584 at the age of 17 when he was named among the actors from Worcester's Men in trouble with the Mayor of Leicester for defiant and aggressive behaviour, playing the drums and trumpets in the street to announce a performance when they were refused a licence to play. [24]

Alleyn's patron Worcester died in 1589; and by 1592 he was playing with the majority of what had been Lord Strange's Men, whose patron was the courtier and poet Ferdinando Stanley (?1559–94), at the Rose theatre. The company was by then a leading one, whose actors and tumblers often played at court. The Lord Chamberlain had divided the company into two in 1594. Old James Burbage and the Alleyn brothers had apparently quarrelled at the back of the Theatre in May 1591 about takings held back from when their company played there for some months. One of these companies formed the Lord Chamberlain's own, with Shakespeare and Burbage, and the other was in the name of his son-in-law – the Lord High Admiral; Edward Alleyn was to wear Howard's livery for ten years.[25] The owner of the Rose on Bankside where the Lord Admiral's Men performed was the financier Philip Henslowe (c. 1555–1616). On 22 October 1592 Alleyn married Henslowe's

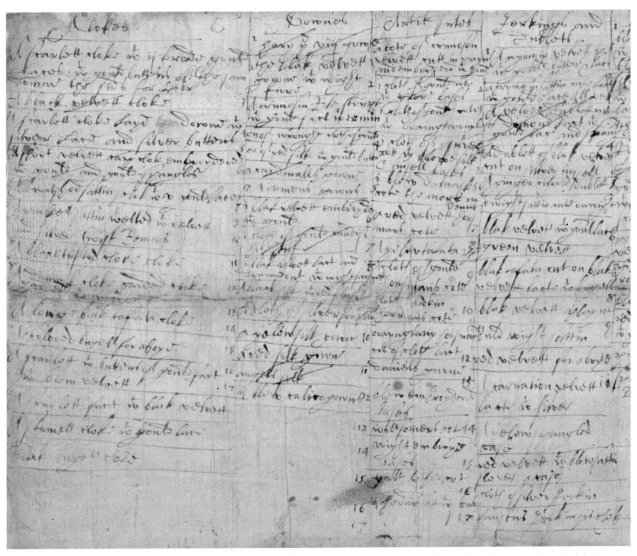

Costume inventory for the Lord Chamberlain's Men in Edward Alleyn's handwriting, 1590–1600 (detail). Note 'Faustus Jerkin, his cloke' at foot of column 4 ('Jerkings and Dublets'), item 17. John Payne Collier in the 1830s made forgeries in spaces: in column one (under 'Clokes') to the authentic 'scarlett cloke' (item 1) he added 'for Leir', and next added 'Romeos' to the authentic 'purpell sattin' (item 6). The costumes would have been worth a great deal of money. (Dulwich College)

step-daughter, Joan Woodward.[26] The marriage was full of love, but childless. Joan was the daughter of Agnes Woodward, a wealthy widow who had married Henslowe in 1579. We learn from a court case that Henslowe had been at one time her first husband's servant; it was said in a court of law after his death that he acknowledged that he had been 'wholly advanced by her'.[27] Though Joan Woodward may have been illiterate – she signs documents with a mark [28] – we may assume that she was well bred. Agnes Woodward was the widow of the bailiff of Viscount Montague, who had a house in Southwark before 1577.[29] This man, Henry Woodward, was buried in the church of St Saviour on 8 December 1578. Agnes managed her own fortune and her own business affairs.[30] Henslowe, who had arrived in Southwark from his native Sussex by 1577 and became an important citizen of 'the Liberty of the Clink' on Bankside, was the most influential figure in Alleyn's career and early took him into partnership; as will be seen, he had a remarkable range of interests in property and entertainments in addition to other financial and mercantile enterprises.

Burbage and Alleyn became the two most famous actors of the day. Their contemporary Sir Richard Baker (1568–1645) named the two of them as supreme in *A Chronicle of the Kings of England* (1643), published at the Restoration and dedicated to Prince Charles; in one page he lists the most celebrated statesmen, seamen, writers, divines and academics of the Jacobean period; of dramatists he records just a pair, Shakespeare and Ben Jonson, balancing them with two actors:

> After such men, it might be thought ridiculous to speak of Stage Players; but seeing excellency in the meanest things deserves remembring and *Roscius* the Comedian [actor] is recorded in History with such commendation, it may be allowed us to do the like with some of our Nation. *Richard Bourbidge* and *Edward Allen*, two such actors, as no age must ever look to see the like.[31]

Burbage, the son of the theatre-owner, created Shakespeare's most famous roles at the Globe; Alleyn, the leading actor of the Admiral's Men and the son-in-law of the proprietor, performed at the Rose the title roles in plays by Christopher Marlowe (1564–93), some of which may even have been written with him in mind. Burbage, Alleyn and the comedians Richard Tarlton (d. 1588) and Will Kempe (d. 1603) were the first 'celebrity' actors, whose performances audiences would attend for the sake of the actor. Burbage, unlike Alleyn who retired at the peak of his powers and fame, was on the stage for 35 years. He left £300 in land at his death; his estate was worth less than Shakespeare's (d. 1616).[32]

Alleyn was a favourite of Queen Elizabeth; this can be documented from two Privy Council warrants preserved at Dulwich authorising Alleyn, against opposition from local residents, to finish constructing the new Fortune theatre in Golden Lane (see below). The first, signed by Lord Admiral Howard in 1599, mentions the Queen's 'speciall regarde of fauor in their proceedinges' towards the Company and her 'greate lykeinge and Contentmt' at Christmas and on many occasions.[33] The second, dated 8 April 1600 and sent to the Justices of Middlesex, says that the Queen has 'sondrye tymes signified her pleaseur' with Alleyn and wishes him to 'revive' his services again – in other words to return to the stage.[34] Alleyn was paid the large sum of £28.10s for his court performances at Christmas 1600.[35] That he was capable of great charm is shown by some touching verses addressed to 'sweete Nedd.'[36]

From the titles of plays, as well as the names and signatures, recorded in Henslowe's papers, we know that the company's playwrights included not only Christopher Marlowe but also Ben Jonson, George Chapman, Thomas Dekker, Thomas Nashe, Michael Drayton, Thomas Middleton and John Webster. In Henslowe's famous diary Ben Jonson signed contracts, and one entry for 1597 records that he read the actors the outline of a new play.[37] By 1597, however, Alleyn had retired from being a 'sharer' in the Company, taking a payment of £50. The evidence is an entry by Henslowe in his diary: 'a not of all suche goods as I haue Bowght for playnge sence my sonne edward allen leafte [p]laynge.'[38]

Alleyn was a 'musicion' as well as an actor, and is so styled in a document when he was 29.[39] His accounts mention the purchase of musical instruments and printed music, as if for his own use. A letter from John Poyntz offers to mend his lute.[40] Alleyn's own diary of his later days at the College at Dulwich records several times the visit of a 'noyse' [group] of trumpeters who 'came and sownded', and were paid 2s.6d.[41]

Alleyn's acting style

Although there are forceful tributes to Alleyn's acting, and important references to his style and technique, there are no detailed contemporary accounts of what it was like. He was early a great success on the stage, but ended his own career abruptly. In 1587, at the age of 21, he played the title role in the first performance of Marlowe's *Tamburlaine the Great, Part One*; this was a part calling for such dynamic action and such 'astounding' language in the actor that (as Marlowe boasted in his Prologue to the play) it would amaze the audience:

> Where you shall heare the Scythian *Tamburlaine*
> Threatning the world with high astounding tearms
> And scourging kingdoms with his conquering sword.

Tamburlaine, traditionally considered a portrait of Edward Alleyn. Richard Knolles, *The Generall Historie of the Turkes*, 1621. (Dulwich College)

It was Alleyn who first gave life and breath, probably in 1589, to Marlowe's Doctor Faustus; by magic he summoned up Helen of Troy and implored a kiss, for her lips to suck forth his *anima*, both soul and his breath together, and to make him immortal:

> Was this the face that Launcht a thousand ships,
> And burnt the toplesse Towers of *Ilium*?

Alleyn also first declaimed Faustus's midnight agony of damnation and death:

> *O lente lente currite noctis equi*:
> The Stars moue still, Time runs, the Clocke will strike.
> The deuill will come, and *Faustus* must be damn'd.
> O I'le leape vp to heauen: who puls me downe?
> See see where Christs blood streames in the firmament,
> One drop would saue my soule, halfe a drop, ah my Christ.

Faustus was Alleyn's most frequent and famous part; to this play, a Puritan legend suggests, we owe the foundation of Alleyn's College of God's Gift, in a vision of the Devil experienced by Alleyn that drove him to repent; there may be something in the story. The scene where Faustus steps inside a circle drawn on the stage floor to conjure up spirits was very famous; from a poem of 1600 we know that Alleyn played it dressed in a surplice with a cross upon his breast. The performances seem to have released some black magic hysteria in Elizabeth's reign. The Puritan William Prynne, in *Histrio-Mastix, The Players Scourge* (1633), recalled an apparition of a real devil on the stage among the actors, the 'visible apparition of the Devill on the stage at the Belsavage Playhouse' while the actors were 'profanely playing the History of Faustus'. The fearful sight left some spectators 'distracted' [mad].[42] He does not mention Alleyn by name, but when the biographer John Aubrey visited the College in 1673 he was told of the tradition that in the middle of *Faustus* Alleyn was 'surpris'd by an apparition of the Devil [among six actors playing devils], which so work'd on his Fancy, that he made a Vow, which he perform'd at this Place'.[43]

Playing the triumphant conquering hero in *Tamburlaine* Alleyn made a famous entrance pulled in a carriage by the kings of Trebizond and Syria with bits in their mouths; he scourges them with his whip, crying out:

> Holla, ye pampered jades of Asia,
> What, can ye draw but twenty miles a day?

Alleyn made the roles of Tamburlaine, Faustus and Barabas famous.[44] By 1594 he was so well known that the title-page of *A Knack to Knowe a Knave* describes the play 'as it hath sundrie tymes been played by Ed. Allen and his Companie', rather than the proper title of his company,

the Lord Admiral's Men. Alleyn was said at the time, as was Burbage, to have the power to make even inferior parts and plays interesting: he was 'able to make an ill matter good'.[45] Certainly he must have had extraordinary physical and mental stamina – he had to memorise over 800 lines for many of the plays, and at the Rose he may well have acted in as many as fifteen a month. He was a skilled fencer – in Greene's *Orlando* a stage direction reads, 'they fight a good while and then breathe'.[46]

Alleyn's style was said by a contemporary to be convincing and natural: 'so acting to the life that he made any part (especially a majestick one) to become him'.[47] In the eighteenth century he was remembered for his agility, liveliness, memory and elocution and also for having a 'flexanimous genius', meaning that he had the ability to move the soul.[48] It is likely, however, that we would think that he over-acted. There is a tradition that when Shakespeare wrote the lines in *Hamlet* (1600) telling the players how not to act – to avoid sawing the air with the arm, strutting, bellowing and 'tear[ing] a passion to tatters' – he was condemning, through the mouth of Burbage, the less subtle gestures and delivery of the old rival Alleyn. Ben Jonson (in his ode to Shakespeare set at the head of the First Folio in 1623) paid tribute to 'Marlowe's mighty line'; and an exaggerated histrionic style of language and action for Marlowe's heroes was exactly what Shakespeare satirised in the scene in *Henry IV, Part Two* set in a pub (perhaps in teasing allusion to Alleyn's origins) when Pistol bursts in, spouting phrases burlesqued from some of Alleyn's most famous parts – or brilliantly nonsensical phrases inspired by them. We can see exactly what amused Shakespeare about Alleyn's orotund lines and manner of delivery:

> Pluto's damnèd lake, by this hand, to th' infernal deep, with
> Erebus and tortures vile …
> Hollow pampered jades of Asia … let the welkin roar …
> Why, then, let grievous, ghastly gaping wounds
> Untwine the Sisters Three! Come, Atropos, I say!

Doll calls Pistol bombastic – a 'fustian rascal' – for this. Alleyn's resonant speech, perfectly suited to Marlowe's extravagant heroes or the Revenge heroes of Thomas Kyd, was certainly popular – over two thousand packed the Rose. The phrase describing a 'robustious periwigpated fellow' of an actor mocked by Hamlet certainly seems to indicate Alleyn's Tamburlaine: *robustious* means 'violent, boisterous, self-assertive'; Alleyn played the part in a wig.[49] Ben Jonson also mocked the 'Tamerlanes and Tamerchams of the late age' with their 'scenical strutting and furious vociferation' to the 'ignorant gapers' in the audience; a later writer said that the poets of the Fortune 'had always a mouth-measure for their Actors (who were terrible teare-throats)'.[50] Doubtless the 'garlic-breathed

*Thomas Nashe, Pierce Pennilesse,
his Supplication to the Devil, 1592.*

stinkards', in Dekker's phrase, loved this style. In spite of
Shakespeare's satire, many rhetorical echoes from Marlowe or quotations from him are to be found in his plays.

Alleyn retired from full-time acting at the age of 31,
although he came out of retirement to launch the new
Fortune theatre in an unknown role in 1600. [51] Perhaps his
retirement was a shrewd move, as his style of acting was
beginning to seem out of date. It is, however, difficult to
agree with John Payne Collier, who doubted whether
Alleyn ever really liked his profession. [52] Ben Jonson,
despite his jeering at strutting Tamerlanes, was a colleague
of Alleyn's in the production of court masques and presumably a friend; he wrote a short poem in which he said
that Alleyn outstripped the great Roman actors, praising
his vocal powers and his generous range of characters. It
has the ring of sincerity. Although their acting styles were
so different, both Burbage and Alleyn were several times
compared to Roscius, the manly, famous and wealthy
Roman actor (born a slave) praised by Cicero in the *Pro Q
Roscio Comædio* for his 'elegant pronunciation and formal
gesture'. John Weever (1576–1632), for example, wrote in
1598 an epigram about Alleyn asserting that while Rome
had her theatre, her dramatists and her Roscius, Phoebus
Apollo had now transferred their brilliance to London;
and now the god of poetry rated the contemporary London stage and its star as better than classical Rome:

Then t'*Allen Roscius* yeeld, to *London Rome.*

Jonson's testimonial epigram to Alleyn, published in
1616, is praise of an actor's skill of a very serious order:

To Edward Allen

If *Rome* so great, and in her wisest age,
Fear'd not to boast the glories of her stage,
As skilfull ROSICUS, and grave ÆSOP, men,
                                        [Claudius Æsop, tragic actor]
Yet crown'd with honors, as with riches, then;
Who had no lesse a trumpet of their name,

Then Cicero, whose every breath was fame: [*Then* = than]
How can so great example dye in mee,
That ALLEN, I should pause to publish thee?
Who both their graces in thy selfe hast more
Out-script, then they did all that went before: [*then* = than]
And present worth in all dost so contract,   [concentrate]
As others speake, but onely thou dost act.
Weare this renowne. 'Tis just, that who did give
                                    [i.e. by Edward Allen's acting]
So many *Poets* life, by one should live. [53]
                             [*live*, i.e. by Ben Jonson, in this poem]

Alleyn specialised in roles that were outlandish and
larger than life, such as the title-heroes of Marlowe's
plays, all of them 'over-reachers': Faustus, who gratifies
his fantasies of power and knowledge by the black arts;
the bombastic vaunting Tamburlaine; Barabas, the lurid
Jew of Malta, whose death in the boiling cauldron is
punishment for his pastimes of murdering 'sick people
groaning under walls', or poisoning wells and an entire
nunnery; the Duke of Guise, another murderous Machi-
avel, in *The Massacre at Paris*. Alleyn also played the
ranting jealous hero of Robert Greene's *Orlando Furioso*
whose wits are crazed by loss of Angelica; Muly
Mahamet in George Peele's *The Battle of Alcazar*; and
Cutlack the Dane. [54] While Burbage and Alleyn were
famous for their range of characterisation – their contemporaries compared both of them to Proteus, the mythological Greek shape-shifter – scholars generally concur
that the Marlovian Alleyn must have lacked subtlety
compared to the Shakespearean Burbage. It is tempting,
but probably glib, to think of Alleyn as Laurence Olivier,
and of Burbage as John Gielgud.

Thomas Heywood in his Dedication to a text of the
revival of *The Jew of Malta* at the Cockpit theatre in 1633,
seven years after Alleyn's death, called him 'so vnimitable
an Actor'; his Prologue declared Marlowe 'the best of
Poets in that age' and 'Allin' the 'best of Actors', who

wan   [won]

The Attribute of peereless, being a man

Whom we may ranke with (doing no one wrong)

Proteus for shapes, and *Roscius* for a tongue,

So could he speake, so vary.[55]

Braggadocio and swagger seem to have characterised Alleyn's art, his voice capable of thunder. Young gallants in the streets of London imitated his theatrical mannerisms of speech, eyes and walk:

Clodius, me thinks, lookes passing big of late

With Dunston's browes, and Allen's Cutlacks gate.   [*gate* = gait]

His eyes are lightning, and his words are thunder,

Stalking and roaring like Iobs great devil.   [Job's]

These lines show that Alleyn favoured roles in plays where the hero is fired by encounters with devils, like *Faustus*: 'Cutlack' is probably St Guthlac, the warrior who became a hermit and like St Anthony fought with devils. 'Dunston' is St Dunstan who calls up devils in *A Knack to Know a Knave*.[56]

It may be wrong to polarise Alleyn's acting as tending to the bombastic, turgid and blustering and Burbage's as discriminating and finely modulated. The understated acting fashionable nowadays would hardly have registered in the large open-air theatres such as the Rose and Globe, and one should think of the great performances there as closer to Verdi than Chekhov. The audiences of the day should not be romanticised. Theatres were sometimes rowdy, the scenes of affrays, brawls, pranks, horseplay, duels and murders. Disgruntled audiences disrupted performances; gangs broke furniture, cut costumes to pieces, and burnt playbooks. Feuds in the audiences might develop between groups such as butchers or feltmakers and the gentry, gallants or law students; the actors themselves might become involved. There was much tobacco smoke. Cutpurses, trolls, and doxies mingled with the audience; lewd jigs were danced at the end of the plays. Alleyn and Burbage had to stamp their presence over such turmoil, and, like Old Hamlet, 'to threaten and command' their audience. Prince Hamlet's speech to the players stresses enunciation and the suiting of the action to the word. Such practices were taught as part of the curriculum in schools and universities as 'Rhetorick', or public speaking (the word could also mean literary composition). Rhetoric was thought to

After Isaac Oliver,
Henry, Prince of Wales.
(© Dulwich Picture Gallery)

be useful in cultivating 'audacity to the bashfull', and included recitation, declamation, with breathing and appropriate body, face and hand language. According to Thomas Heywood in *An Apology for Actors* of 1612, boys and young men were taught to act 'not like a stiff starched man' and to avoid 'violent absurdities'; at Cambridge this public exercise was thought to 'embolden' their junior scholars. [57] Alleyn's Poor Scholars put on performances on Twelfth Night in 1620 and 1621, as he recorded in his diary: 'yᵉ boys playd a playe'; [58] it would be wonderful to know what play it was, and to have been present at the production; surely he must have coached them himself.

The Magnificent Entertainment, 1604

Following Queen Elizabeth's death in 1603, King James became patron of the Lord Chamberlain's Company of actors, re-named the King's Men, and the Lord Admiral's Servants were assigned to his very young heir, the magnificent Henry Frederick, Prince of Wales (1594–1612), the dashing hope of the Stuarts: Alleyn was now described as 'servant to the highe and mightie prince of Wales' and Master of the King's Games; along with the eight other principal actors he was given four and a half yards of red cloth for livery to take part in the King's ceremonial progress on 15 March 1604. [59] However, his name does not figure in the official list of Prince Henry's actors. In 1619 his diary records that '4 of yᵉ prince's men' (now Prince Charles's, after the Prince Henry's tragic early death in November 1612) dined at the College on 20 June. Alleyn would certainly have benefited from Prince Henry's patronage, as he mentions ruefully in a draft letter to Sir Francis Calton: 'I know yᵉ Princ at that tyme my most excellent mr: whose love to all his servants wase such that I knowe he would have protected me in my right'. [60] Alleyn owned a splendid portrait of the athletic Prince Henry brandishing a lance; it is still in the Dulwich collection.

In 1604 Alleyn came out of retirement from the stage to welcome King James I on behalf of the City of London in an out-of-doors pageant, *The Magnificent Entertainment Given to King James*; the text was a collaboration between Ben Jonson and Thomas Dekker. On 15 March the King, with the Court and the City dignitaries, processed from the Tower through the streets to see and listen to scenes from an allegorical play performed in the open air at a series of temporary triumphal arches, some 42 feet high, carved and gilded with statuary and set up at crossroads. The arches, designed by Stephen Harrison, had been erected on behalf of 'the Lord Mayor and Aldermen, the Council, Commoners and Multitude', together with the Italian, Dutch and Belgian communities. From a series of detailed engravings made at the time by William Kip for

Of all which perſonages, *Genius* and *Thameſis* were the only Speakers : *Thameſis* being preſented by one of the children of her Maieſties Reuels : *Genius* by M. *Allin* (ſeruant to the young Prince) his gratulatory ſpeach (which was deliuered with excellent Action, and a well tun'de audible voyce) being to this effect :

That London may be prowd to behold this day, and therefore in name of the Lord *Maior* and *Aldermen*, the *Councell, Commoners* and *Mulsstude*, the heartieſt Welcome is tendered to his Maieſty, that euer was beſtowed on any King, &c.

Thomas Dekker, Introduction to *The Magnificent Entertainment*, 1604, describing Alleyn's performance as 'Genius Urbis'. (Dulwich College)

Harrison's *The Archs* [sic] *of Triumph Erected in Honor of the High and Mighty Prince James the First* (1604) we know exactly how they looked. Tall and imposing as *Genius Urbis* [Spirit of the City], Alleyn was presumably chosen to speak for London as owner of the most famous lungs of his day. (Burbage, two years younger than Alleyn, was chosen six years later in 1610 to star in a water pageant for Prince Henry, and delivered his speeches from the back of an artificial fish in the river Thames.) The introduction to Dekker's printed text of *The Magnificent Entertainment* (1604) declares that 'Master Alleyn (servant to the young Prince)' delivered his 'gratulatory speech' with 'excellent action, and a well-tun'd audible voice'. [61] The flattering opening address by the Genius of the City, in rhyming couplets by Ben Jonson, was given by Edward Alleyn, wearing a purple mantle and buskins; it declared that, in the course of its long history, London had undergone various regimes, but was all the time waiting for the moment that the Stuarts set foot in the City for its real happiness and prosperity to come about. Alleyn is clearly shown at the centre of the engraving by Kip of 'The Device called Londinivm'. This first Triumphal Arch was set up at Fenchurch, and Alleyn is pictured striking an attitude in a niche, 'sawing the air with his hand' in the very style that Hamlet mocked. *Tamesis the River*, played by a boy actor, whom *Genius* awakens to tell the triumphant news of the house of Stuart, reclines drowsily at his feet, and there are musicians above him. Before the King's arrival the Arch was 'covered with a curtaine of silke, painted like a thicke cloud'; at the King's approach it was drawn to reveal on the pediment models of the 'houses, towres and steeples' within the City, 'set off in prospective'. The allegorical meaning of the cloud, Jonson explained, was to signify 'the clouded face of the City' which was longing to see their new monarch, and by its removal the sun flooding the City. [62] Alleyn appeared in a second scene by Ben Jonson in *The Magnificent Entertainment*, performing on the seventh Arch, the Temple of Janus, set up at Temple Bar, presumably running ahead down back streets in between. Here he confronted a Flamen [Roman priest] standing at an altar: abruptly dismissing him and his superstitious fumes, he presented James with the heart of London, in a perpetual flame never to turn to ashes, which he promises to tend with his prayers, wishes and vows:

> My cities heart; which shall for ever burne
> Vpon this altar, and no time shall turne
> The same to ashes: here I fixe it fast,
> Flame bright, flame high, and may it ever last.

A flaming heart is a traditional emblem of charity. In heraldry a crest is a separate addition to a coat of arms and a symbol set above it; Alleyn chose for his crest 'from a ring of flames, an arm with a hand holding a heart', or in correct heraldic terms 'on an esquire's helmet, an Arm couped at the elbow and erect, issuing out of flames of fire, and holding a human heart, all proper [in natural colours]'.[63] When Alleyn the childless actor came to found his charity of God's Gift in 1619, he settled his heraldic crest on the College, and his seal to the Foundation Document clearly shows the arm holding aloft the heart out of flames, impressed above his coat of arms. By this esoteric heraldic symbol Alleyn surely indicated that what he had received from the streets of London in fame and fortune he was returning to the city by his philanthropic scheme: to raise up poor orphan boys from the streets to 'godliness and good learning', in the words of the Founder's prayer. With this emblem he associated for ever his College of God's Gift with the flaming heart of charity, alluding to the speech to King James that might be said to be the high point of his career.[64]

Lines in Ben Jonson's *The Magnificent Entertainment* (1604), delivered by Edward Alleyn as the Flamen, offering the flaming immortal heart of London to James I.
(Ben Jonson's *Workes*, 1640. Patrick Spottiswoode)

Philip Henslowe

At the age of 26, Alleyn strengthened his theatrical and business partnership with Henslowe by marriage with his step-daughter, Joan Woodward, on 22 October 1592, as detailed above. Because of many references to Henslowe as 'citizen and dyer' in legal documents, this is usually given as his profession, and indeed his purchase of 60 and 153 dozen goatskins to dress and sell is recorded in covenants from the early 1580s preserved at the College.[65] Henslowe's enterprises were, however, very varied, and he was a prominent figure in the heady London world of enterprise and speculation, more particularly the public and court entertainments of plays, presumably the splendid court masques, and certainly the crude and cruel entertainments of animal baiting and fights. He managed the famous Lord Admiral's Company (Howard had no financial interest in the company)[66] while Alleyn selected and produced the plays and acted the leading parts. Henslowe was much involved at court among the great figures of the day, being a 'Groom of the Chamber' to Queen Elizabeth in 1592–3, a high rank of court servant, who dressed in scarlet for royal processions. He was known as a 'Gentleman Sewer', and documents of 1603 call him 'one of the sewers of the King's chamber' at Greenwich;[67] a *sewer*, a word deriving from [as]*seoir*, to seat, was a kind of court *maître d'hôtel*, who presided at banquets and supervised the seating of guests and the tasting and serving of food. An acrostic on his name among the Henslowe papers praises his services to his 'roiall Princes'.[68] This post involved travel and periods from home; Joan Alleyn wrote to her husband in 1603 that 'my father is at the Corte, but where the Court ys I know not'.[69] At Queen Elizabeth's funeral both Henslowe and Alleyn were given an allowance of black cloth to wear. Henslowe was paid a court annuity in 1606–7.[70]

The Alleyn and Henslowe papers

Much extraordinary documentary evidence about the material aspects of Alleyn's career and the theatre of his day survives in the Alleyn and Henslowe papers in the

Archives at the College, such as the building contracts for the Rose in 1587 and the Fortune in 1600,[71] and accounts, letters and signed agreements with actors and playwrights. Uniquely among libraries in the world, there are examples of the three documents essential for a stage performance of Alleyn's day: his own learning 'scroll' of lines for the title role of Greene's *Orlando Furioso* of 1591–2 with alterations in his own handwriting;[72] a fair handwritten copy of the full text of a play, *The Tell Tale* (almost certainly a later play from the years immediately following Alleyn's death), which would have served as the unique complete version of the play to hand at rehearsals and which was then held at performances by the 'book-holder' or prompter;[73] and thirdly a 'platt' [plot], which is a large sheet of paper listing the scenes with the actors' entrances and the properties to be ready; this is for a play of which the text is lost, called *The Secound Parte of the Seuen Deadlie Sinns*. It names actors as well as characters, including one called 'Ned' (as the young Alleyn was known) and another 'R. Burbadge' (Richard Burbage). This extraordinary document survived only because it was folded and recycled to form a book-cover; it has an oblong hole to hang over a peg backstage in the theatre. It gives no text for the allegorical and mythological play but lists the scenes in order with their entrances and exits, and contains stage directions. Two of these – *Sloth Passeth ouer* and *Lechery passeth ouer the stag*[e] – would make excellent mime exercises for drama students today. The props include a severed head in a dish, and there are sound and musical cues. David Kathman, a theatre scholar, recently re-identified the Company who put on this play from the actors' names on the document, and showed that the *Platt* may in fact belong to a play in the repertory of the Lord Chamberlain's Men in 1597–8; the sheet formed a wrapper to *The Tell-Tale*, which did not belong to Alleyn but instead came into the College's possession as part of a bequest to the College in 1687 from the Restoration actor, William Cartwright (1606–86; see Chapter 3), that happened to include some much earlier theatrical material.[74] 'Ned', traditionally taken for evidence that Alleyn and Burbage played together in this play, is now thought to be a possible reference to Shakespeare's younger brother Edmund.[75] There was probably no special intention or motive to preserve the theatrical papers at the College except perhaps as the personal archive of the Founder; they were kept in the Treasure chamber above the porch, and survived the porch's collapse in 1703, and later neglect, damp and decay.

Cartwright, a famous performer of Falstaff in his day, was the son of an actor of the same name who had been an associate of Alleyn; he presumably knew of the survival of the collection of Alleyn's and Henslowe's theatrical papers at Dulwich. Alleyn's own written or printed playbooks were probably lost in the fire at the Fortune theatre in 1621. The collection lost some of its integrity at the end of the eighteenth century and in the early nineteenth century: Cartwright's collection of playbooks was pillaged by David Garrick (1717–79) for his own collection 'in exchange for some more modern publications'.[76] Some of the manuscripts were lost by the scholar Edmond Malone (1741–1812), including further 'plats' of Alleyn's plays, *Dead Man's Fortune*, *The Battle of Alcazar*, and *Frederick and Basilea*, which are now in the British Library; *Tamar Cam* is now lost but was transcribed. Malone also made some dubious swaps: 'The late Mr Malone was lucky enough to induce the Master, Warden and Fellows to exchange the Old Plays [from Cartwright] for old Sermons, and the Old Plays form the bulk of the Commentator's collection at Oxford'.[77] A manuscript copy of Simon Baylie's *The Wizard* now in the British Library has a note (in an eighteenth-century hand) saying that Garrick took it from the College.[78] John Payne Collier (1789–1883), a brilliant scholar and shameless forger, made extensive use of the theatre papers in the 1830s, cutting out and stealing some items. Wishing to back up spurious scholarly 'discoveries' about Shakespeare, he forged entries where there were empty spaces of half-lines or so on the paper; for example, in Alleyn's costume inventory (mentioned above) he added to the document, already romantic enough by its genuine mention of Marlowe's *Faustus*, and using a fairly convincing imitation of Alleyn's handwriting, that a 'scarlett cloke' with gold buttons was 'for Leir', a purple satin cloak was 'Romeos' and the spangled hose were 'for Pericles'.[79] A lost *Ld. Admirals Enventary* of 1598, copied out by Malone, a respectable textual scholar, from the Dulwich papers, has a most romantic list of properties and costumes kept by Alleyn's company: a lion skin, a white hat, a tree of golden apples; 'the clothe of the Sone and Mone', 'owld Mahemetes head'; a pope's mitre, a hell mouth, a chime of bells; a snake, Neptune's fork, Mercury's wings and caduceus; the tomb of Dido; 'Tamberlynes cotte, with coper lace' and his crimson velvet breeches; 'Tamberlyne brydell' with which the conquered kings pulled the tyrant's chariot on all fours, and Bajazeth's cage for the same play; the 'dragon in fostes' [*Faustus*] and the cauldron for *The Jew of Malta* from which Alleyn, acting the death of the wicked Barabas who is boiled alive, howled at the end of the play.[80] Collier removed a page of Henslowe's diary, claiming he had found it marking a place 'in a volume of old plays', and it is now in the British Library.[81]

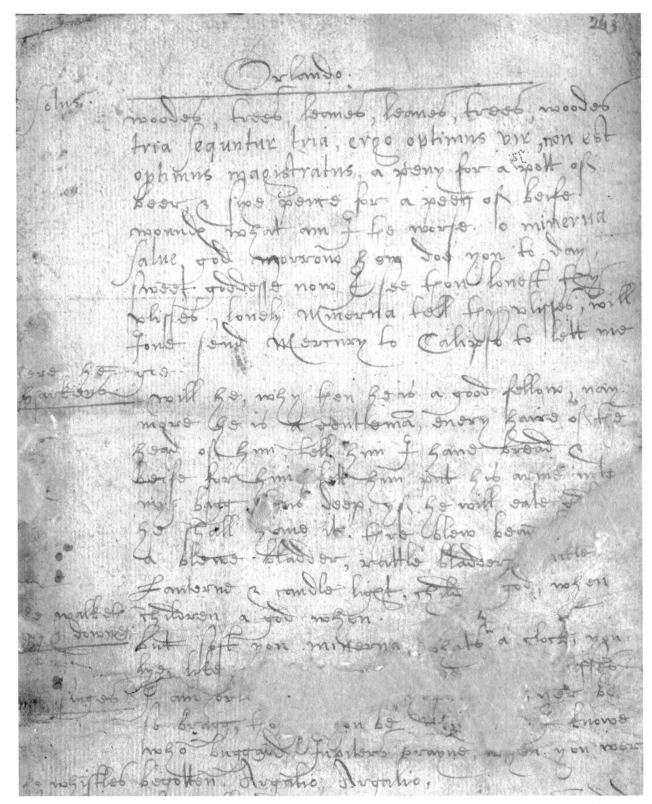

A section of Edward Alleyn's learning script for the mad scene as the hero of Greene's *Orlando Furioso*, *c*. 1591–2, originally part of a roll. Stage directions in the margin read: 'Solus'; 'here he harkens'; 'he walketh up and downe'; 'he singes'; 'he whistles'. (Dulwich College)

Henslowe's Diary

Philip Henslowe's Diary was among Alleyn's papers left to the College at Alleyn's death in 1626. The 'Diary' is an account book (1576–1609), first used by his brother John to record mining and forestry enterprises in the Ashdown Forest. It records among many other items the expenses and revenues for the years 1592 to 1604 of the Rose theatre, together with his investments in the Fortune theatre and in acting companies. As such it is the most important single surviving theatrical document of the great age of English drama. From it we learn the titles of the plays which were performed at the Rose and which of these were the most popular: at the height of Christopher Marlowe's fame and fortune, over a period of 18 weeks in 1592, Henslowe's share of the daily takings at the door for named performances varied from seven shillings to three pounds, thirteen shillings and sixpence. *Doctor Faustus* was conspicuously the most popular play. Henslowe records in the diary over 325 performances;[82] over half of the plays are now lost.

The Rose had no artificial lighting; the matinee performances at two o'clock were often restaged at court in separate evening productions. There are detailed records of Henslowe's contracts with actors, playwrights and others involved in the business, including the censor. These bind the actors, for example, to work exclusively for his company for two or three years; Henslowe advances them money and acts as their banker. Writers sign contracts to finish their plays. Playwrights submit 'foul sheets' – their first drafts – and their 'fair copies'. Robert Daborne is rewriting a scene in Act III of *Machiavell and the Devil*.[83] Ben Jonson was advanced 20 shillings in 1597 'vpon a Booke wch he was to writte for vs before crysmas next',[84] and was twice advanced £4, once with Alleyn as witness. Jonson figures several times in the Alleyn and Henslowe papers, perhaps most vividly in a manuscript of two poems written out in his own exquisite formal italic handwriting for a patron, and in a reference in a letter from Henslowe to Alleyn about Jonson killing an actor from the Lord Admiral's Company in a duel. In September 1598 Edward Alleyn was on tour with a play in the provinces, and Henslowe told him that 'benjemen Jonson bricklayer' (a common taunt at his original trade, about which Jonson was touchy) had killed Gabriel Spencer, a member of his company, 'in hogesden fylldes' [fields], which 'hurteth me greatley'.[85] Jonson and Spencer had recently been imprisoned together for four months for their part in the satirical play *The Isle of Dogs*, and a quarrel had led to a duel; Spencer had earlier killed a man with a rapier. Jonson was lucky not to have gone to the gallows for manslaughter, but his goods were confiscated and he had his thumb branded.[86]

Henslowe's Diary is also a curiously personal document, and includes revolting dotty recipes to cure wind in the stomach; other medical and herbal remedies involve bat's blood, boy's urine, ants' eggs and swine's grease, and earthworms fried in goose-grease. He records his accounts for the used clothing trade, with pawn-broking and lending money at 40 per cent interest. As pawn-broker he advances money on cloaks of black velvet and taffeta [a lustrous silk fabric], and capes and robes of cloth of gold. His great fortune incorporated many small pawning transactions of domestic objects in Southwark – silver buttons, looking-glasses, scissors, a new comb, wedding rings, 'apostle spoons', a set of three ear-pickers, silk stockings of sea-water green – the objects sometimes bundled up in curtains or tablecloths; all these were stored in his house on the Bankside. From such petty dealings, as well as receipts from the most lucrative partnership in the entertainment world (with bear-baiting and plays at the theatres and at court), and from rents from public houses, the Southwark fortune of Henslowe and Alleyn grew, to be invested in time in the Dulwich estate and to endow the College of God's Gift. The Bear Garden – on the days when it was open – could bring in much more revenue than the theatres: Henslowe records for St Stephen's Day one Monday in 1608 receipts of £4, and on the Tuesday £6, while the Fortune brought in on the same days £1.5s.0d and £2.5s.0d. However, this comparison is not so telling nor so sure as it might be, in that the Bear Garden was not necessarily open on the same days directly in competition with the theatres, and the players were often at court on St Stephen's Day while some other entertainment took place at the Fortune.[87]

'My sonne edwarde allen' often figures in agreements in the diary,[88] and his letters address him as 'my wealbeloved sonne'.[89] Alleyn personally signs as a witness to loans to the actors in the company, and is recorded as selling texts of plays to the company.[90] Henslowe enters details of the building of Alleyn's house on Bankside facing the river.[91] He enters the payments he made for fabrics, cloaks, doublets, costumes, hats and playbooks, such as one to 'lettel [a surname] tayller [tailor] to taffty [taffeta] sasenet [soft silk] to macke a payer of hosse [hose] for nycke [Nick] to tvmbell in be fore the quen' on Christmas Day 1601;[92] amounts paid to the Master of the Revels for licences for plays; the cost of a dinner of venison at the tavern with members of his company; and of wine after a read-through of a play. Henslowe's father Edmond for a long time was Master of the Royal Game in Broil [Brill] Park in Sussex and in Ashdown Forest, where he also held mining rights. His brother John first used the diary to record the interests he kept up in Sussex in cutting woods, making charcoal, and mining. Joint enterprises of Alleyn and Henslowe included a house in which to make starch, and buying ground for hogs.

Henslowe also used to bail actors and playwrights out of the nearby prisons, the Clink or the King's Bench, usually for debt, as he did for Thomas Lodge,[93] and in response to charming letters in an elegant hand from a young actor, Nathan Field (1577–1633). Field had been head chorister at Queen Elizabeth's chapel, in 1600, and was in turn boy actor, adult actor and playwright; he addresses Henslowe as 'Father Hinchlow'.[94] Henslowe often sent money to Dekker, who was in the King's Bench

Nathan Field to Philip Henslowe ('Mr Hinchlow'), begging for £5 in advance on a play script, to release himself, Robert Daborne and Philip Massinger on bail from debtor's prison. A receipt on the verso shows that Henslowe obliged. (Dulwich College)

prison on Bankside from 1612 to 1619. No doubt such actions bound these men to Henslowe. He acted both as paymaster and banker to his company; on one occasion, the players wrote to Alleyn complaining about the hold that his father-in-law had over them: 'the reason of his often breaking with us, hee gave in these words. Should these fellowes Come out of my debt, I should have noe rule with them'.[95] It seems that in his latter years Henslowe became difficult and exacting; in around 1615 the company complained to Alleyn that in the last three years Henslowe had 'broken and dismembered' five companies of players, and that he regarded theatre property as his own: he had taken 'right gould and silver lace of divers garments to his owne use'.[96]

Bankside and Clerkenwell: Henslowe's and Alleyn's theatres

Bankside, on that part of the south bank of the Thames immediately facing St Paul's Cathedral, was the quarter of pleasures for Londoners, where public houses with gardens, playhouses and the pits for bear-baiting were to be found. The Bankside public houses called 'the *barg*, *bell* and the *cocke*', standing next to the site of the Rose theatre, were leased by Alleyn in 1589;[97] they are assumed to have been of ill repute, though there is no documentary evidence that Alleyn profited directly from prostitution. Earlier in the sixteenth century Bankside had certainly been a louche neighbourhood with its notorious 'stews' or bordellos; the venereal diseases caught there – nicknamed 'Winchester goose' from the adjacent palace of the Bishop of Winchester – are the subject of jokes in Shakespeare. Twelve brothels were licensed, and the Bell certainly figured in the list of a row of such houses facing the river; they were governed by strict rules, were whitewashed and had hanging signs. However, in 1546 the brothels were put down, as was 'proclaimed by Sound of Trumpet'.[98] E. J. Burford, writing in the 1970s, referred to Alleyn as 'the grand-whoremaster'; he also calls Joan Alleyn 'a well-known actress', and since most people know that there were no actresses on the stage in those days we can discount his scholarship; this prurient fantasist says that the taverns called The Unicorn, The Bell, The Barge and The Cock belonged to Alleyn and 'all four were active brothels at that time', without giving any evidence whatsoever.[99] 'Bawds' rents' – perhaps we should not be shocked to learn – often supported charities. Thus it is not inconceivable (but seems unlikely) that in his will Alleyn would settle four notorious brothels on his second wife, Constance Donne, who was the daughter of the Dean of St Paul's. There is some ambiguity about this issue: Lord Hunsdon as official Lord of the Paris Garden (another name for the Bear

British School, *Nathan Field*, c. 1610. (© Dulwich Picture Gallery)

Garden) issued leases for brothels in Elizabeth's day, and well-to-do 'Bawds of the Banke' were named in subsidy lists.[100] John Stow writing in his *Survey* in 1598 says of Bankside, 'Whoredom still prevails', but that 'the Sin was no longer allowed in this Place'. Stow quotes Bishop Hugh Latimer mentioning in a sermon to King Henry VIII that the brothels had gone elsewhere from Bankside, and that the new ones must be put down.[101]

The City officials in general seem to have deprecated the stage and strictly kept the playhouses outside their boundary, fearing their influence on idleness, disorder and political excitements among the young. Meanwhile at the court, however, plays and extravagant masques were most popular entertainments, and were promoted by the Lord Chamberlain. During one season in 1613 as part of the nuptial celebrations of King James's daughter Princess Elizabeth and the Elector Palatine, twenty plays were performed at court, including eight by Shakespeare.

Philip Henslowe, as already mentioned, was the owner of the Rose at Bankside, which he also managed. He had had the theatre constructed on the site of a former rose garden, which was leased to him as early as 1584; this was where Alleyn's fame as an actor was to flourish. Alleyn joined Henslowe in partnership here in 1592, the year of his marriage with Joan. Henslowe's contract of

1587 with the carpenter John Griggs survives for the Rose, a playhouse 'now in framing'; the contract is an agreement between Henslowe, 'dyer', and John Cholmley, grocer, who was to build a small tenement next to the theatre for 'victualinge'.[102] Originally the profits were to be divided equally between Henslowe and Cholmley.

During the plague in 1593 the Privy Council at Croydon licensed Alleyn to play seven miles outside London; among the actors mentioned in the company are Will Kempe, the famous clown, and John Heminge, later a leading actor of the King's Company and one of the joint editors of the posthumous First Folio, *Mr. William Shakespeares Comedies, Histories and Tragedies*, of 1623. When the plague was over the following April the Council gave Alleyn permission to leave the theatre at Newington Butts and return to the Rose.[103] A petition from Henslowe and the Thames watermen – who owned the river-taxis and were losing trade from the embargo – saying that 'the sickness' is over in 1593, was a factor in this decision.[104] One of the signatories was the master of the Queen's barge. In 1604 Charles Howard signed a licence from the Privy Council requiring the justices of Middlesex and Surrey to open once again the Globe, the Fortune and other playhouses unless more than thirty people died in a week from the plague.[105] Despite refurbishments, after 13 years the

structure of the Rose, with its yard open to the elements, had deteriorated. The Globe theatre had been built near the Rose in 1599, and here the Chamberlain's Men (and their principal playwright Shakespeare) performed. For these reasons Alleyn and Henslowe presumably determined to build an improved style of playhouse on the north side of the river, though the building of the 'rival' Globe may not have been at the time as much as a 'threat' to the Rose as theatre historians since E.K. Chambers have assumed. Within a year of the opening of the Globe the Privy Council agreed that only two London playhouses should be licensed: the Globe for the Lord Chamberlain's Servants, and a new 'howse of Allen' in Middlesex to replace one on Bankside. Performances were to be only twice a week, and not on Sundays or during Lent or a plague.[106] The Rose was no longer a playhouse but was used for prize-fights and other entertainments. Henslowe and Alleyn together commissioned the new theatre, the Fortune, in Golden Lane, Cripplegate, and it was constructed in 1599–1600. Eighty feet square on the outside, 55 feet square on the interior and three storeys high, it had a plastered wooden framework on bricks over piles. The site of the theatre, then next to open fields,[107] was just outside the north wall of the City, on the present Fortune Street, off Golden Lane, and close to the Barbican.

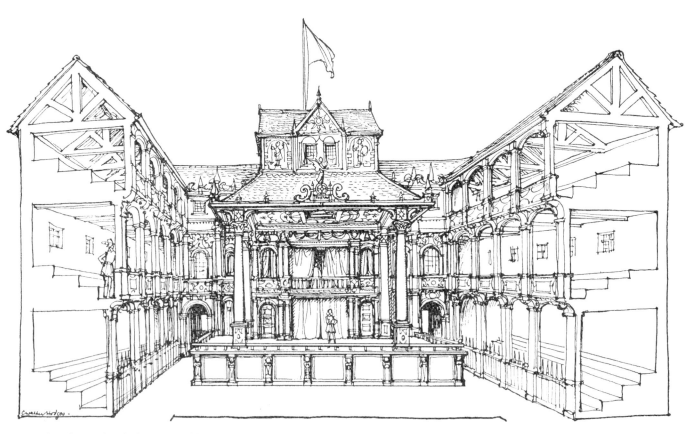

C. Walter Hodges (OA), Interior of the Fortune Theatre, 1600. (*The Globe Restored*, 1953; © C. Walter Hodges Estate)

It was a large theatre for its day; Howard's Privy Council ordered the Justices of Middlesex to allow the building of the Fortune in its place, since the Rose was now 'dangerous' and 'verie noysome to the resorte of people in the wynter tyme'. Howard, as quoted above, mentions the 'speciall regarde of fauor' of the Queen towards Alleyn and his actors. [108] In Cripplegate lived many poor citizens, and Alleyn is recorded as having paid the parish church of St Giles without Cripplegate, next to the Fortune, 'a very liberall porcōn of money weekelie towards yᵉ relief of our Poore'. [109] This parish was to become one of the beneficiaries of Alleyn's Foundation of the College of God's Gift, sending both pensioners and boys. Alleyn appears to have owned the Fortune himself (but not to have managed it) until 1618, when he leased it to a group of 24 actors as shareholders, including William Cartwright the elder, for 31 years for a rent of £200 per annum and 'two rundlettes of wyne, the one sack and the other clarett'. [110] He dined at the Mermaid with five of the actors on 18 September 1618. [111]

The Fortune was totally destroyed in a great fire on 9 December 1621; John Chamberlain wrote in a letter to Sir Dudley Carleton that it was 'the fairest playhouse in this town'. He reported that 'it was quite burned down in two hours, and all their apparel and playbooks lost, whereby these poor companions are quite undone'. [112]

Alleyn's own entry on the disaster in his diary, written at Dulwich after the foundation of the College, is stoically laconic: 'this night att 12 of yᵉ clock yᵉ fortune was burnt'. [113] He built it up with a new design, polygonal and in brick. [114] He records in his diary that he took the architectural drawings for the second playhouse, 'yᵉ Fortune plott', to show the great connoisseur, the Earl of Arundel (see below), on 12 June 1622. [115] Leases from 1623–4 show that Alleyn granted a number of twelfth parts in the ownership of the Fortune and its taphouse for forty-nine and a half years. [116] Alleyn in his last months dedicated his income from the playhouse to the support of his Foundation; it was, moreover, 'intended as a considerable part of yᵉ Revenue of this Colledge'. [117] At that point this amounted to £120 per annum, but the benefit was short-lived. [118] Alleyn's theatre fell on bad times: in 1628 some sailors stormed the stage and beat the actors; the Plague closed it down in 1636; in 1639 the actors set up an altar with a 'basin' and candlesticks and bowed down before it, and although they argued that they were performing part of an old play at a heathen altar, they had to pay an enormous fine of £1,000. [119]

The site was still in the possession of the College when the theatre fell into ruins after the Puritans closed it in 1641 and set its interior on fire in 1649. By 1656 the Fortune was decayed and falling to ruin; its timbers were

said to be rotten and the building a threat to pedestrians, 'in greate danger of falling, to yᵉ hazzard of passengers liues'. In 1660 the materials from the demolition were sold for £75, and by 1661 it was quite deserted. [120] Later on, 23 crowded shops and tenements were built, and a street cut from Whitecross Street to Golding Lane. [121] The College posted bills and paid for advertisements in 'newesbookes' to find a tenant prepared to build tenements. The building materials were 'divers times stolen away'. The Sale offered the playhouse, a taphouse together with the adjacent buildings and a second hostelry, 'Mr Rivers howse and sheds, yᵉ Kings head' and some 'bricke tenements' on the site. In 1661 the remaining structure was demolished and eight new houses or tenements were built, which were later increased or divided into twenty. 'W[illia]m Beavan citizen, tiler and bricklayer' next bought the site and laid it waste; he applied for a 45-year lease, but the College said the Founder had placed a maximum of 21 years on leases. Non-payment of rents from the site was to bring frustrating and expensive litigation to the College. Thirty-five years after the death of Alleyn the defendants received the rents and profits, sublet the properties, and meanwhile had deviously got hold of 'evidences and wrightinges' of the playhouse. [122] Curiously, in spite of the demolitions, a portion of the Fortune front with a pargeted royal coat of arms was still standing in 1811, when it was sketched and engraved. [123]

The site of the Fortune across the Thames, including Golden Lane and Play House Yard, figures on nineteenth-century maps of the Dulwich Estate as a puzzling insertion on the margin. At the Charity Commissioners Inquiry in 1854 it was said to be 'the greatest receptacle of vice in the whole parish', on a long lease with many hutch-like houses in it. [124] In 1860 the Governors were told, with ten more years of the lease to run, that there were 77 houses, 'abodes evidently of the lowest and most abandoned classes of society'; there was only one water tap, and the privies had doors opening onto the paved way. The rent was £230 per year, and the lessee made twice that amount. When a church, St Mary Charterhouse, was put up at this period, the Governors gave a portion of a site for it. A Report to the Governors of 1871 suggests that the site might best be sold at auction. There was a 'dangerous structure' and the College was required by the Sanitary Inspector to carry out works. [125] It was not sold until 1955, and is now part of the Barbican complex.

Alleyn's and Henslowe's papers record details of the construction and the materials of the Rose and the Fortune theatres, itemising the wooden boards, the 'turned ballysters', the lime, nails, thatch, and tiles. Accounts also mention breakfasts and drinks for the workmen.

John Griggs, the builder of the Rose, was a neighbour and friend of Henslowe and Alleyn.[126] Peter Street, the builder of the Fortune, signed with his initials the contract to build the three-storey theatre in 1600; he also rebuilt the Bear Garden and its stables in 1606.[127] The Fortune contract specifies details for the galleries, windows and chimneys, and that 'the saide Stadge [is] to be in all other proporcons Contryved and fashioned like vnto the Stadge' of 'the saide late erected Plaiehowse on the Banck in the saide parishe of Ste Saviours Called the Globe' put up by Street only a year previously.[128] Griggs had also earlier worked on Henslowe's house and he was the builder of Alleyn's house on the Bankside with deal boards, lead guttering, and tiles rather than thatch. The house had features suiting the prosperous burgher and churchwarden of Southwark such as a wainscoted hall and a 'court cupboard' for display of plate and other items.[129]

One of the Bankside properties jointly owned by Henslowe and Alleyn was the wharf where the royal barges were kept, and for which the crown paid rent; Old Barge House Alley is still today on the site.[130] Paul Hentzner, a German who visited London in 1598, described Queen Elizabeth's state barge which he saw here with its 'two splendid cabins beautifully ornamented with glass windows, painting and gilding'.[131] On 19 December 1618 Alleyn recorded in his diary that he 'bought off Mathewe all ye upp. pt off ye quens barge'. He possibly used two painted panels from the saloon, showing *Pietas* and *Liberalitas*, for a splendid chimney-piece for the College, which is now in the Masters' Library; the timbers are of the same period. There is a pleasing oral tradition from the nineteenth century that the panels from the Queen's barge were formerly with Drake on the *Golden Hind*.[132] The provenance of the panels has been questioned by Susan Foister,[133] who said that it was not proven that the panels on Alleyn's chimney-piece came from a royal barge, and also that the barge in question had presumably belonged to James's Queen Anne, whose funeral Alleyn attended. This is possible, in that although Alleyn made his purchase before Queen Anne died the following year on 4 March, she had been ill since 1615 and for many months had been unable to leave Hampton Court. Alleyn in 1622 petitioned Lord Cranfield, the Lord High Treasurer, for arrears of rent for the barge-house since 1615, 'little use having been made thereof since the death of her Matie [Majesty], only one Dancer that was Master of her Maties Barge keepeth possession thereof, your supplicant having these three years been importuned by one Kellock Master of the Princes Barge to have had it for his highness use'.[134]

Peter Street died in 1609, and in 1613 Henslowe contracted with Gilbert Katherens, a Southwark carpenter, to pull down the Bear Garden and replace it as part playhouse 'for players to plaie in' and part arena 'for the game of Beares and bulls to be bayted in';[135] the stage and tyre house [dressing room] was a temporary structure on trestles. The playhouse here was now called the Hope theatre. Bear-baiting took place on Tuesdays and Thursdays and stage performances on the other days apart from Sunday. In the 'Induction' to Ben Jonson's *Bartholemew Fair* the Scrivener names the Hope as the theatre where it is being performed and complains of the animal stink; the Book-keeper mentions the sweeping up of apple cores from the audience for the Bears 'within'.[136] The building contract mentions 'turned cullumes' [columns] 'upon and over the stage'. This new bear garden was a later venture of Henslowe's, and Alleyn was to receive one quarter of the daily receipts from the galleries after Henslowe's death in 1616.[137]

Master of the Royal Game of Bears, Bulls, and Mastiff Dogs

Alleyn's motives for retiring from the stage at the peak of his powers and at the age of 31 in 1597 might have been to concentrate on his investments and on a more lucrative career as impresario in the entertainment enterprises with Henslowe, possibly compounded as well by the feeling (mentioned above) that his style of acting was now old-fashioned. The names of 468 actors in this period are recorded; of these only six became really wealthy men, through investment in theatres, land and property. (As well as Alleyn, conspicuously the wealthiest, these names included Richard Burbage and the two actors who edited the memorial volume of the Shakespeare Folio, John Heminge and Henry Condell, and Shakespeare himself).[138]

The particular enterprise coveted by Alleyn and Henslowe was to become the joint keepers of the royal menagerie and organisers of animal entertainments at court. The post of 'Maister, Guyder and Ruler of all our Beres and Apes' was established by Richard III in 1484; the royal title was now styled as 'Cheefe Master, overseer and ruler of our beares, bulls & mastiffe dogges', as it is phrased in a draft of the Patent at the College. They failed to secure the post in 1598: the Lord Admiral let them down by failing in his promise to speak to Queen Elizabeth at Windsor when the previous Master lay very sick, and the Queen had already given the position to Sir John Dorrington, who thereupon appealed to Alleyn for help with bears. A friend, Arthur Langworth, a landed proprietor of the Brill in Ringmer, wrote to Alleyn blaming him for this failure: 'My L[ord] of Nottingham told you what to do, therfore blame yor selfe'. [139] They might have expected the appointment when James I came to the throne, but it went to Sir William Stewart, a friend of the King and a Scot. They managed to buy the position from Stewart for £450 in November 1604, and father and 'son' held it until Henslowe's death in 1616. In the account for King James's funeral expenses in 1625 Alleyn appears as 'Master of Bears and Bulls' just below the King's Players. [140] There was an allowance of 14 pence a week to keep and exercise twenty mastiff bitches. They were expected to 'take up and kepe dogs' for the King throughout the realm and to control the export of dogs. [141] The licence for compulsory purchase of dogs for the King throughout the country (the most vicious dogs, apparently, came from Lancashire and Cheshire) was probably open to corruption. Naturally this royal commission was unpopular. Alleyn and Henslowe sent out agents who were lucky to escape with their lives in several violent affrays in Cheshire. Their warrants with the Great Seal of England demanding sale on the spot were said to be counterfeit and their agents were imprisoned; owners wrote angrily to Alleyn hoping to reclaim their dogs.

During the second week of James's residence in London following his accession, and only a few days before Alleyn's performance in *The Magnificent Entertainment*, he had organised for the King an indoor lion hunt at the Tower of London. Reading the accounts of the early months of James's taking up his residence in London, it is striking just how prominent Edward Alleyn must have appeared to the new monarch as citizen, actor and impresario. Edmund Howes (*fl.* 1602–31), who was to be a signatory at the Foundation of the College, published a detailed description in his continuation of John Stow's *Annales* (1631). For this sport Alleyn had got together the 'fellest' [most cruel] dogs that he could find:

> Whereupon the king caused Edward Allen, late servant of the Lord Admirall, now sworne the Princes man and Maister of the Beare Garden, to fetch secretly three of the fellest dogs in the Garden; which being done, the King, Queene and prince, with 4 or 5 Lords, went to the Lions Towre , and caused the lustiest Lion to be seperated from his mate, and put in the Lions den with one dog alone, who presently flew to the face of the Lion, but the lion suddenly shooke him off, and graspt him fast by the necke, drawing the dog vp staires and downe staires. The King now perceiving the Lion greatly to exceede the dog in strength, but nothing in noble heart and courage, caused another dog to be put into the den, who prooved as hotte and lusty as his fellow, and tooke the Lion by the face, but the Lion began to deale with him as with the former; whereupon the King commanded the third dog to be put in before the second dog was

The Paris Garden. (John Payne Collier, *English Dramatic Poetry and Annals of the English Stage*, Vol. II, 1831)

spoiled, which third dog, more fierce and fell than either of the former, and despight either of clawes or strength, tooke the Lyon by the lip. But the Lion so tore the dog by the eyes, head and face, that he lost his hold, and then the Lion tooke the dogs neck in his mouth, drawing him vp and downe as he did the former, he being wearied could not bite him so deadly as at the first, now whilest the last dog was thus hand to hand with the Lion in the upper roome, the other two dogs were fighting together in the lower roome, whereupon the King caused the Lion to be driven downe, thinking the lion would have parted them, but when he saw he must needs come by them, he leapt cleane over them both and, contrary to the King's expectation, the lion fled into an inward den, and would not by any means endure the presence of the dogs, albeit the last dogge pursued egerly, but could not finde the way to the Lion. You shall vnderstand the two last dogs, whilst the Lion held them both under his pawes, did bite the Lion by his belly, whereat the lion roared so extreamly that the earth shooke withall, and the next Lion rampt and roared as if she would have made rescue. The Lion hath not any peculiar or proper kind of fight, as hath the dog, beare or bull, but onely a ravenous kinde of surprising for prey. The first 2 dogs dyed within few dayes, but the last dog well recovered of all his hurts, and the young Prince commanded his seruant, E. Allen, to bring the dog to him to S. James, where the Prince charged the said Allen to keepe him and make much of him, saying, he that had fought with the King of Beasts, should never after fight with any inferior creature. [142]

Bears, many of which came from Russian explorers and huntsmen in Greenland and Germany, appeared from time to time in stage plays. Alleyn was the proprietor of a male lion and a tiger, and also from 1609 he took care of two polar bear cubs, captured on an arctic sea-voyage the same year, which were housed separately. He asked for the payment of two shillings per day for keeping '2 white beares and a Lion' belonging to the King in

1615; it is very likely that these two bears were the same as those which were set to pull a chariot with Prince Henry (playing the ruler of the Fairy kingdom) in Jonson's elaborate emblematical masque *Oberon* in January 1611.[143] Alleyn's agents took the bears on provincial tours. The bears had names, which appear in the documents, such as 'Littel Besse of Broml[e]y' who performed a 'greatt victorie' over the dogs in twenty matches in a day, killing some but most of which were sent halting away; other famous bears were given names which seem to parody Alleyn's heroic roles: Harry of Warwick, Sampson, Black Ned, Don John, Ned of Canterbury.[144] Polar bears are amphibious, and in July 1623, three years before the death of Alleyn, a polar bear from the Paris Garden swimming in the Thames was baited by dogs to entertain the Spanish Ambassador.[145] 'White Bear Alley' is marked on a map in Stow's *Survey* of Southwark of 1598.

The post, however, seems to have disappointed Alleyn and Henslowe, and they sent a bitter petition to the King complaining of their financial losses and of fatalities among their beardogs and bulldogs, the death of 'a goodlye beare called G[e]orge Stone' and in particular their loss of income from a new ban on baiting on Sunday afternoons after divine service; under Elizabeth 'fre Libertie was permited withowt restrainte to bayght them' at that time of the week.[146]

Even during the period from 1616, when Alleyn was presiding at his College of God's Gift at Dulwich, and up until 1625 he was organising baiting for the court; for example his diary for 6 June 1620 reads, 'ye bayghting wase at greenwiche this daye & ye king sent a young tyger to ye garden'.[147] Alleyn and Henslowe owned and managed the Bear Garden, on Bankside, which had been used as an animal baiting house, a 'Game place', since 1526; Alleyn

Wenceslaus Hollar, 'Long View' of London, Antwerp, 1647 (detail), taken from the tower of St Saviour's, Southwark (Southwark Cathedral), showing the Bear Garden, Bankside and the second Globe Theatre. (*Note:* Hollar has mistakenly transposed the names of the Globe and the Bear Garden.)

took out a lease of it after the Plague in 1594. An outlay of £450 brought in £60 a year, [148] and Alleyn finally bought it from Henslowe in 1610. Here audiences of two to three hundred watched 'a great mastyffe dog and foule ouglye bear', fight 'with terrible tearings, a ful ouglye sight'. [149] The famous engraved panorama of London from the South Bank by Wenceslaus Hollar published in 1647 shows the theatres and the 'Beere bayting' house next to a field of sheep and horses. At the Paris Garden Alleyn would have kept as many as 120 mastiffs, three bulls, twenty bears, two polar bears and the lions; a leopard is mentioned, and once 'my lord' sent a wolf. The appalling noise of the animals was notorious. [150] Alleyn's accounts include meat for the bears. Records survive of trade in the animals: Sir William Fawnte wrote to Alleyn lamenting the feebleness of his favourite bull, 'Star of the West', but offering to sell Alleyn his aggressive one-eyed bull Beves [Bevis], with a caution that he would 'throo vp your do[g]ges in to the loftes oreles [or else] ding out theare braynes agenst the grates [metal bars]'. [151]

Animal sports of the day were brutal, a theatre of cruelty. The bears were more valuable than the bulls, and were better protected. In a later copy of a contemporary poster for the Bear Garden, found in the Alleyn and Henslowe papers, dogs are advertised to weary a bull dead at the stake at the Bear Garden. Spectators are invited to see and bet on dogs baiting a single bear, a comic interlude with the droll behaviour of a monkey baited on horseback by dogs, followed by the 'plasent sport' of 'whiping of the blind bear. Vivat Rex'. [152] John Stow in 1598 in his *Survey* of Southwark complained about the 'Foulness of these rude Sights and beastly Combats' of the bears, bulls and mastiffs and the 'terrible tearings' that occurred, and the gambling that went with them. [153] Paul Hentzner described sadistic performances in Henslowe's pit on Bankside for the Londoners, constantly smoking their pipes:

> Whipping a blinded bear, is performed by five or six men standing circularly with whips, which they exercise upon him without mercy, as he cannot escape from them, because of his chain: – he defends himself with all his force and skill, throwing down all who come within his reach and are not active enough to get out of it, and tearing the whips out of their hands, and breaking them. [154]

The monkeys on horseback were not attacked by the dogs, but their grotesque shrieks of fear when dogs hung from the ears and neck of the pony highly amused the spectators; the bulls indeed tossed up the dogs with their horns. The baitings were interspersed with circus or carnival acts, such as actors dancing, fighting and throwing white bread among the crowd, or fireworks and fruit falling on them from above. Samuel Pepys later in the century was at the Bear Garden several times and enjoyed 'good sport' there, although he calls the bulls tossing the dogs in the air a 'very rude [rough] and nasty pleasure'. In 1653 when bearbaiting was suppressed by law, Cromwell's soldiers shot seven bears to death next to the Hope theatre, two years after they set the Fortune theatre on fire. [155]

The Earl of Arundel and Inigo Jones

Alleyn was part of the circle of courtiers and professionals involved in masques; two of the most interesting of the men whom he knew through his professional life were to be signatories to the Deed of Foundation of Alleyn's College of God's Gift in 1619. [156] Thomas Howard, the 14th Earl of Arundel (1585–1646), a scholarly and energetic figure, was one of the most influential noblemen of England and a privy councillor, created Earl Marshal in 1621. One of the three wealthiest Stuart peers, a kinsman of Alleyn's patron Charles Howard, Lord High Admiral, Arundel was a cosmopolitan figure, a lover of Italy and continental culture, highly important in the history of English collecting and taste. [157] Together with Inigo Jones (1573–1652), the brilliant architect and designer of masques and his companion in Italy, he introduced a pure form of Italian Renaissance architecture that eventually drove out the native Jacobean manner. He established the aristocratic fashion for collecting classical sculptures, and Alleyn records in his diary for 1618 a tour round his galleries at his palatial mansion in the Strand: 'I wase att Arundell Howse wher my Lord showed me all his statues and picktures that came from Italy'; [158] Arundel's classical statues, the famous 'Arundel marbles', some of them excavated for him in the Roman forum, are now in the Ashmolean Museum at Oxford, but his collection of seven hundred paintings has been dispersed. [159] Arundel was briefly imprisoned in the Tower in 1621 for refusing to apologise for an insult to Lord Spencer in the House of Lords: he retorted to a reminder that members of his family had been condemned for treason, that at the time his own family were serving king and country, Lord Spencer's were keeping sheep; Alleyn paid him a visit in the Tower. [160] Arundel was a member of the circle of Prince Henry from 1610 to 1612; athletic and a lover of horses, in January of that year he took part in an elaborate jousting Arthurian masque with text by Ben Jonson and scenes and costumes by Inigo Jones, *Prince Henry's Barriers*. Jones and Arundel travelled together to arrange court entertainments; Arundel accompanied Princess Elizabeth to Heidelberg in 1613, after her marriage to the Prince Palatine. Arundel and Jones were both state Commissioners for New Buildings, which meant that they had to authorise all new projects; this as well as their court association may well have been a factor in their presence as signatories at Alleyn's inauguration of the College. Inigo Jones had joined Arundel in 1613 on the continent, and returned late the following year. Inigo Jones was appointed Surveyor to the King in 1615. [161]

Death of Henslowe

When Henslowe died in January 1616 Alleyn immediately took over the direction of his enterprises. The validity of Henslowe's will and his legacies to Alleyn was the subject of Chancery litigation between Alleyn and Henslowe's nephew John, who claimed that Alleyn with the connivance of Agnes Henslowe forced Henslowe to bequeath all he was worth – £10,000 to £12,000 – to Agnes in a new will drawn up by Alleyn himself just a few hours before Henslowe's death from a 'palsy'. John claimed that formerly all his uncle's estate was to pass to him. The litigation went on for a number of years eventually reaching the Star Chamber. Alleyn admitted that he had put a pen 'into [Henslowe's] hand' to make his mark since he was too weak to sign, and the will was proved next day. Judgement was given in favour of Alleyn, and interesting evidence was taken of Alleyn's probity and the 'industry and care of the defendant'. Several witnesses declared that Alleyn was a main reason for Henslowe's successes, and that it was always intended that the estate was to pass to him. The joint lessee of the Bear Garden, Jacob Meade, testified that Alleyn was 'the chief means of bettering the estate of the said Philip Henslowe'. [162] Agnes died a year later, and was interred in the north side of the choir of the new College chapel. [163] The Papers give glimpses of Alleyn's daily life; one document illustrates how inheriting Henslowe's estate and affairs brought troubles: as late as 1621 Alleyn was accosted by an embittered courtier in the Strand over a financial agreement of Henslowe's. [164]

Joan Alleyn

Among the Papers now at the College there is an extraordinary survival of personal letters between Alleyn and Joan written in the first year of their marriage which shows their relationship in a touching light. Alleyn, so boisterous on stage, writes tender and teasing letters to 'my good sweetheart & loving mouse', and she in turn styles herself 'your mousse' in reply. She could not write, and her letters are actually written out by her step-father, or a professional scribe. [165] Alleyn teases Joan that he has heard she and her friends have been 'carted' by an officer of the Lord Mayor in the street in Southwark, a punishment for whores. The letter ends with nicknames, that tease her and her sister Elizabeth: 'Farewell mecho

[meek, tame] mousin and mouse, and farewell bess dodipoll' [doddy, from the root dote; cf. dotty = simpleton, easily taken in; poll, head]. [166] These letters were written when Alleyn was on tour during the Plague in the summer and early autumn of 1593 and when the London theatres were closed; he was making the 'long journey' of the theatrical companies in the provinces to Bristol, Shrewsbury, Winchester, and York. At this time Joan writes that they have heard that when very sick at Bath an understudy played Harry of Cornwall; [167] she complains that he has not written when the families of other members of the company have had letters. About a sixth of the population of London died during the great plague that year; at its worst a thousand died every week in the city and five hundred in the suburbs. The actors were forbidden to perform within a seven-mile limit of London; neither bowls nor bear-baiting were allowed. On tour in the provinces the actors took a half-cut in pay. A member of the company who was also a member of the household was Alleyn's page and apprentice actor, John Pyk (Pyge/Pig); he got Alleyn himself to write out for him a jolly letter home to Joan while on tour, which gives a homesick glimpse into the Bankside house in 'lovly London' with the inglenook by the fire and the larder. He signs himself 'your petty pretty pratlying parlying pyg'. This letter also shows that Alleyn was capable of laughing at himself for his famous persona as a swaggering 'majestic' actor: Pyg is made to swear 'by the fayth of a fustyan kinge'. [168] The house where Henslowe and Joan were then at home on Bankside near the prison of the Clink faced the river, increasing their chances of survival from the plague because of the better air. Alleyn reminds her to pray, and sends practical advice, to wash the front and back doorsteps and plant rue and herb of grace in the window-boxes. He asks father and step-daughter to sow parsley in his spinach beds, as he would himself; they reply that the beans have grown up into high hedges, and are producing good cods [pods]. Alleyn asks Joan to dye his 'orayng tawny stokins of wolen' a very good black for the winter. The family write that 'the sickness' has taken the wife, children and entire household of another actor, Robert Brown, and his doors are shut up. Joan is glad to hear that he is enjoying 'hauckinge' [hawking] on tour. A true voice of feeling animates her concern and her longing to see him: 'thoughe you have worne your appayrell to rags, the best ys you knowe where to have better and as well-come to me shall you be with your rags, as yf you were in cloathe of gold or velvet. Trye and see'. [169]

A portrait of Joan was painted, dated 1596, giving her age as 22; she is pictured with a modest face and expression, wearing a hat and red gloves that match the red leather of the Bible she holds. [170] At the College where

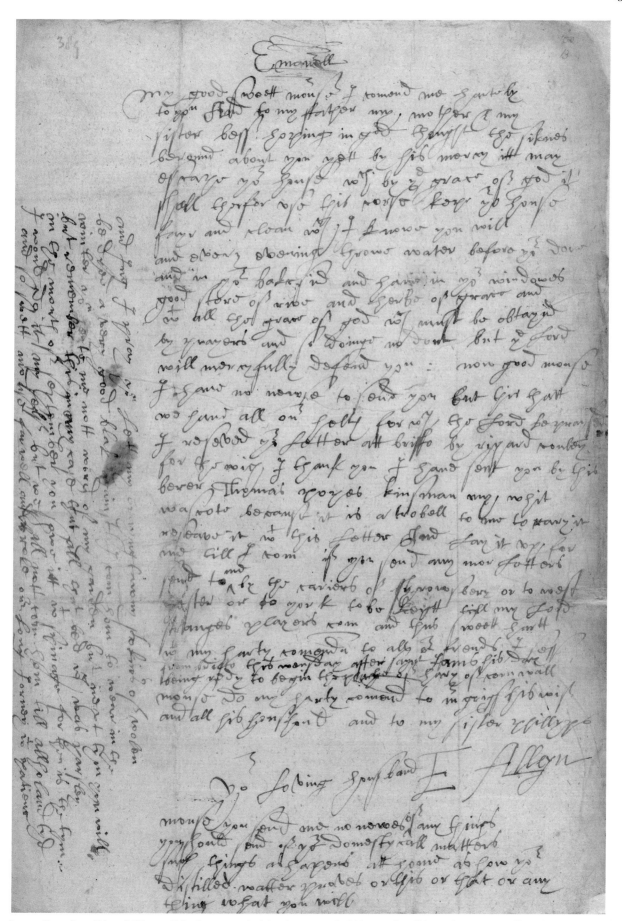

Letter of 1593 from Edward Alleyn at Bristol, on a provincial acting tour and within months of his marriage, to Joan Alleyn, his 'good sweet mouse', at home on the Bankside, striking domestic and pious notes; severe plague had closed the theatres. (Dulwich College)

she spent six years among the Poor Scholars before her death she seems to have taken an active pastoral role. She was praised for her piety in some rough verses by one of the Poor Scholars from St Botolph's at the College from 1617 to 1621, Richard Meridall. They declare that, embraced by virtue, she is the 'Patrones[s] of vertue and vnderstandinge'; she 'keepes foule vice from this most heavenly place'; she relieves the twelve orphans; she does 'in love & charitee excell'. In 1619 Alleyn records in his diary that he and Joan stood in the street at Cheapside 'at mr gosens ye Gowldsmith' to see the Lord Mayor's Show together.[171] Joan Alleyn died on 29 June 1623, and on 1 July she was 'solemnely interred in the Quier of the Chapell' on the south side near the altar.[172] The Painters' Work Book at the College of Arms (1619–34) contains a record of six 'Escochions in metall for Alleyns wife' for the obsequies, made by the Herald painter Richard Mundy.[173] Her mural tablet in the chapel (now lost, but transcribed in 1814) called her 'religious and loving', and referred to the couple's thirty years of 'uninterrupted comfort and harmony'.[174]

From actor to gentleman armiger

Actors until the age of Alleyn had little social status; Tudor statutes classified them with 'masterless men', i.e. vagabonds. Alleyn was probably the object of Ben Jonson's envious satire in his *Poetaster* of 1601, where actors 'grow rich' and like Alleyn 'purchase' lands.[175] An anonymous Cambridge play of 1605, *The Second Part of the return from Parnassus*, features two Cambridge scholars who are forced to become actors at the Globe for a while. They mock the rise of successful actors from 'ragges' to 'galland', swaggering upstarts becoming 'glorious vagabonds', and who are, like Alleyn, attended by pages. For Studioso it is a 'vile world, that lifts them vp to hye degree':

> England affordes those glorious vagabonds,
> That carried earst their fardels on their backes,
> Coursers to ride on through the gazing streetes,
> Sooping it in their glaring Satten sutes,   [sweeping]
> And pages to attend their maisterships:
> With mouthing words that better wits have framed
> They purchase lands, and now Esquiers are made.[176]

From the Lord Chamberlain's Company Shakespeare, Burbage and four other actors achieved the status of gentlemen with coats of arms. It is not known if and when Alleyn paid for a coat of arms, giving him the right to be called a squire, or esquire; it is possible that he was

Pedigree of Edward Alleyn from the Visitation of Surrey, 1623. (© The College of Arms, London. MS. C. 2, p. 143)

armigerous by birth. As already noted, both the arms and the crest of the heart upheld from flames were in use on his seal in the Deed of Foundation of the College of God's Gift in 1619; the coat of arms was illustrated and confirmed in 1623 when the College of Heralds made their Visitation of Surrey, including Dulwich, and Alleyn signed the document showing the pedigree of his family. The familiar coat of arms is properly described as 'Argent a chevron between three cinquefoils gules'. The visitation also shows Alleyn's arms impaled with Henslowe's from his marriage with Joan: 'Gules a lion passant guardant or with a chief azure semée of fleurs de lis'.[177]

The award of the coat of arms and possession of so many properties and rights marked of course Alleyn's worldly success in the world of his day. While his contribution to the drama of his age is now largely the preserve of specialist historians, not least on account of the priceless archive he left behind, his benefaction, in the second half of his career, as Founder of the College of God's Gift, has kept his name bright and high. The word 'Alleynian' would eventually stand as perpetual testimony to his charity, connoting both educational enterprise at the College and the service rendered in turn to society and to civilisation by its pupils.

Opposite: British School, *Joan Alleyn.* Her age is inscribed as 22 years, and dated 1596. (© Dulwich Picture Gallery)

EDWARD ALLEYN &
'GOD'S GIFT COLLEGE'
1616–26

I like well that Allen playeth the last act of his life so well.

– FRANCIS BACON, LORD VERULAM

Churchwarden of the Liberty of the Clink in Southwark – Purchase of the Manor of Dulwich – Dulwich village – Christ's Chapel – The Letters Patent – Precedents – The Foundation ceremony – Alleyn's Statutes – The Chapel and the College – The Master, Warden and Fellows – The Poor Scholars – The Poor Brethren and Sisters – The 'Assistants' – Edward Alleyn and the Estate – Marriage to Constance, daughter of John Donne – Alleyn's will and death

As has been seen, from 1597 Alleyn turned his extraordinary energy and enterprise from acting to the management of theatres and of animal entertainments and to speculation in property, either in partnership with Henslowe or on his own initiative; from 1600 he began to spend great sums on extensive land and manorial rights south of the river, eventually concentrating on the hamlet of Dulwich, set among many acres of meadows lapped in the valley between Herne Hill and the bosky North Wood (Norwood) of the Surrey hills. In the early nineteenth century the area could still be called 'the prettiest of all the village entrances' in the environs of London, set in the vale with its cornfields and pasture meadows, elms and sycamores, and its 'pleasant lawns and blooming gardens, with bursts of the fine distances'.[1] As a result of Alleyn's strictures about running the Estate, and in spite of some development, it retained its rural and natural charms, and even something more transcendent. In 1824 the artist Samuel Palmer noted in a sketch-book his affection for its 'sweet fields' with a 'mystic glimmer' behind the hills; Dulwich was 'the gate into the world of vision', giving a promise of paradise over the hills with their ancient woods.[2] Charles Dickens, considering pleasant spots near London to reward the eupeptic Mr Pickwick in retirement, chose for him a villa in Dulwich, the 'quiet pretty neighbourhood', with a lawn in front, a large garden and a miniature conservatory. In Edwardian days, by which time of course housing developments had spoiled many fields, the schoolboy P. G. Wodehouse could still respond to the sub-urban charms of the Dulwich College estate, which he later used as a setting in *Big Money* (1931) and other novels and which he renamed 'Valley Fields'; although he cast a satirical eye on the 'fragrant backwater' and the rows of 'Neo-Suburbo-

Gothic' villas of jaundiced yellow bricks with their small gardens – 'bijou bowers of verdure' – his affection for the area is also obvious.[3]

Alleyn chose the manor of Dulwich as the ideal rural domain to live in and to govern; here he was to bring about the Foundation of his ideal community, intending both thanks to God for his good fortune and a practical return to London for its bounty by setting up Christ's Chapel (1616) and the College of God's Gift (1619). Meanwhile his experiences as churchwarden in the parish of St Saviour must have schooled his charity. His enduring legacy of the pleasant suburb of Dulwich and its famous schools is incalculable.

Churchwarden of the Liberty of the Clink in Southwark

In the second phase of his career Alleyn by no means retired from public life: he is thought to have managed the Fortune theatre until 1612; on Henslowe's initiative the two impresarios were developing a Blackfriars property called Porter's Hall to turn into a small private playhouse. This was almost completed in 1617, but was successfully opposed for a while by the wealthy residents.[4] Later it became famous as a theatre run by 'men of grave and sober behaviour'.[5] While Alleyn was directing the baiting and animal entertainments at the Bear Garden and at court and moving in court circles, he undertook a less worldly and less well-known but active role as churchwarden at St Saviour's, Southwark (from 1905 Southwark Cathedral). This was his own parish, the arena of the greatest period in English drama where the Rose and Globe theatres, the Bear Garden and his own house on Bankside lay. Shakespeare's younger brother Edmond had been buried in its churchyard in 1607. On the south bank of the Thames lay the (recently dissolved) Bermondsey Abbey of Black Monks, the original proprietors of the Dulwich estate, and also charitable 'hospitals' for the poor and Lazar houses for lepers.[6] There is documentary evidence that Alleyn was closely involved in much parish relief among the poor and distressed. No doubt what he learned here influenced him to establish the College of God's Gift in perpetuity as the heart of his great estate, and thus to keep the name of Alleyn alive. Before his death the 'eleemosynary' (or charitable) community at Dulwich was built and peopled with the deserving poor, both young and old, and appeared to be set to flourish. St Saviour's responded in an almost feudal way to Alleyn: they said that one of the Poor Brethren from their parish who was sent to live at the College would serve as a 'poore elected Beadesman' to pray for his soul.[7]

Alleyn's sector of Southwark was known as 'the Liberty of the Clink'; it was at that time home to 560 households, rich and poor together. Southwark, the somewhat unruly suburb across London Bridge, was originally a village; for centuries malefactors from London had taken refuge there, and the 'Stews' or bordellos had prospered. It was the site of no less than five prisons, including the King's Bench, the Marshalsea (immortalised in Dickens's *Little Dorrit*) and the Clink. Alleyn's house facing the river was said to be 'harde by the Clinke', which was the prison 'for such as should brabble [squabble], frey [fight], or break the peace on the said bank', and was originally intended for those who caused trouble in the brothels.[8] From the debtors' prison, the King's Bench, the playwright Thomas Dekker wrote to Alleyn with a poem in his praise and a heavy hint about his own need for charity.[9] Behind Bankside were winding lanes and tenements. Two hundred and fifty watermen lived in the Liberty, dependent on the taverns, theatres and the Bear Garden for their trade in ferrying pedestrians over the Thames (preferable to crossing the congested single London Bridge) for which they charged fourpence. Stow lists the people as 'Woodmongers, Timber Merchants, Shipwrights, Bargemen, Watermen and such whose living depended upon the river', including 'Stewholders'.[10] A census in the Alleyn and Henslowe papers describes 150 of the inhabitants as following 'handye trades'; there are the same number of 'verie poore people, widows and others'.[11] Philip Henslowe became a vestryman at St Saviour's in 1607, and a churchwarden in 1608; Edward Alleyn was churchwarden from 1610 to 1617. In 1616, he brought about the building of parish almshouses on the site of the old Soap Yard, Deadman's Place. By 1843 these were 'dilapidated, stale and scarcely waterproof', and the College contributed £100 towards their demolition and

rebuilding.[12] Henslowe left a bequest to the poor of the parish in his will of 1616; he had been a governor of the Free Grammar School attached to St Saviour's, founded in 1562 with a charter from Queen Elizabeth and given a further charter from James I in 1612. This school would seem to be a model for Alleyn's school at Dulwich, as its staff consisted of Schoolmaster, Usher (assistant teacher) and Chaplain.[13] St Saviour's grammar school, later combining with St Olave's, was to be much more successful than Alleyn's Foundation, until the latter was reformed in 1857; the vestry clerk of St Saviour's referred to the grammar school as 'an exceeding good school' in 1855. In 1894 new premises were built for it with money from Alleyn's College.[14] Alleyn in his Dulwich days was apparently on friendly terms with his local vicar in Camberwell, the Revd Edward Wilson, who in 1615 founded a successful Grammar School there (Wilson's School, since resettled in Wallington). Edward Wilson had been appointed to the living at Camberwell by Queen Elizabeth in 1577. He preached on two occasions at the Chapel, and seems to have given Alleyn encouragement in the foundation of God's Gift College: he was Alleyn's guest twice at dinner during the crucial weeks in 1619 when Alleyn was in difficulties obtaining the royal Letters Patent.[15]

The Alleyn and Henslowe papers include many parish documents: as churchwardens at St Saviour's their responsibilities included distributing to the poor the small royal pensions called the King's subsidy,[16] together with the takings at the church door and the offertory at the communion table. They were 'seasors' or assessors for taxation among the parishioners towards relief of the poor by pensions and contributing to rents; they themselves head the list, with only two other names taxed in the highest bracket of sixpence weekly, the next being fourpence.[17] Alleyn and his father-in-law appear from the documents and letters to have been truly enlightened burgesses with a sincere interest in the poor.[18]

A list addressed *c.*1609 to Alleyn of 'thinges necessary to be considered of, and which may tend much to the orderly and peaceable gouernment of this Libertye' lists problems such as the lodging of strangers, particularly newcomers who may be 'lewd and ill disposed people', and strife and drunkenness among the poor.[19] A sidesman (assistant churchwarden) brought up before Alleyn a resident guilty of allowing dicing and bowling in his house at the time of divine service.[20] Letters from parishioners appealing to Alleyn show what he was expected to interest himself in: Thomas Kellocke complains of the 'wrongs and iniures' done to him by Alis Dought;[21] Anne Poyntz writes of her 'vnkind husband';[22] Mawdlyn

Foord complains of wrongs offered her by Christopher Horsebrook and his wife;[23] the sidesman reports to him that William King and Sisly his wife are 'keping of a house suspected for bauderies'.[24] There are of course requests for loans and appeals for relief from desperate parishioners.[25] The churchwardens were also responsible for public health, seeing to it that no bedding was brought into the parish from plague-houses.[26]

Alleyn's turning from the stage to philanthropy at the height of his powers, culminating in the foundation of the College of God's Gift, was celebrated in a eulogy of four stanzas written to him by an associate, Sir William Alexander, later the Earl of Stirling (who wrote *Monarchicke Tragedies* and an elegy on Prince Henry, *Paraenesis*) in a poem inscribed 'To his deservedlie honoured frend Mr. Edward Allane, the first founder and Master of the Colledge of God's Gift'. Alleyn, the rich and famous actor, will earn immortality for his princely Christian charity,

Who at the height of that which thou profess'd
Both ancients, moderns, all didst farr exceede …
And when thy state was to a better chang'd,
That thou enabled wast for doing goode,
To clothe the naked, give the hungrie foode,
As one that was from avarice estrang'd:
   Then what was fitt thou scorn'd to seeke for more,   [than]
   Whilst bent to doe what was design'd before.
Then prosecute this noble course of thyne
As prince or priest for state, in charge though none,
For acting this brave part, when thou are gone,
Thy fame more bright, then some's more high, shall shyne. [than]
   Since thou turn'd great, who this worlds stage do trace
   With whom it seemes thou hast exchanged thy place.[27]

Purchase of the Manor of Dulwich

By the time Alleyn bought the Dulwich estate he was lord of the manor of Lewisham. He had paid £1,000 in December 1600 for land there amounting to 1,100 acres including the manor and parsonage, and there he sat as magistrate; a letter of 1624 makes it clear that he was still the landlord.[28] He had become lord of the manor of Kennington by 1604. He still held property in his native Bishopsgate, and (since 1599) land (with a parsonage) at Firle and at Ringmer in rural Sussex. Alleyn's Memorandum Book lists some of these properties and others, and the price that he paid for them, including houses and shops in White Cross Street and Goulding [Golden] Lane with houses, taverns and wharves at Bankside.[29] Journeys to Sussex may have taken Alleyn through Dulwich and over the North Wood to Croydon. One of the traditional pilgrim routes, incidentally, ran from the Thames ferries through Lambeth by way of 'Crokestrete', Croxted Lane (now Road) over the hill to Penge, and thence by Otford to Canterbury.[30]

During the summer of 1605, at the age of 38, Alleyn began to negotiate with Sir Francis Calton, who was from a prominent City goldsmith's family, for the manor of Dulwich including 'the wodes vpon the waste'.[31] On 3 October he bought it for £5,000 (£717,568 in today's money), agreeing payments over seven years; on the back of the document Alleyn wrote notes of his financial resources, including his share of theatrical wardrobe, worth £100.[32] A Deed of Sale of 1606 includes Camberwell and its advowson [the right of choosing the vicar].[33] In 1606 he is styled Lord of the Manor of Dulwich; he sold the manor of Kennington to Calton for £2,000 in 1609.[34]

Calton's grandfather Thomas had been given a lease of the manor at Dulwich by Letters Patent from Henry VIII in 1544, and Calton had inherited it at the age of ten in 1575. Calton was knighted in 1605, and became Lord Mayor in 1612. He writes charming and gentlemanly letters, but seems an improvident character. He complained often of Alleyn's 'hard dealing',[35] and repeatedly wrote to Alleyn for advances and loans on large and small pretexts: he was buying and building onto a large new house at Greenwich; he must pay the baker and brewer when he left the house; or he needed to increase a dowry for his second daughter.[36] Alleyn in his will not only forgave him a debt of £20, 'due long since', but left him a considerable legacy of £100.[37] Alleyn seems on his part to have imagined constant plotting by Calton to recover the estate with 'secret conveyances' and holding back of important 'deeds, evidences and munymentes'; he spent a great deal of money on legal fees in bills in Chancery against Calton in the early years of the College as well as a great deal of time, becoming what he called the 'daylie Orator' [petitioner] to the Lord High Chancellor.[38] From his letters to Calton it is clear that Alleyn felt that he had been denied the opportunity of advanced education: a draft letter apologises that he cannot reply in the same style, saying that he writes himself 'not with so much scholarship for I Have none at all'.[39] He bought further acres and messuages [houses] on the Dulwich estate from Sir Edmond Bowyer, a Dulwich resident who was sheriff of Surrey in 1600 and its Member of Parliament in 1603, and more from Calton in the years 1606–14.[40] Until about 1612 Alleyn is believed to have remained resident at Bankside, where letters are addressed to him, but after this date he began to be habitually styled as 'Edward Alleyn of Dulwich, Esquire'; a letter of 1617 is directed to Alleyn at the manor house (Hall Place in 1541) at Dulwich and another letter 'at his house dullige court'.[41]

Dulwich village

Dilwihs – so named for its cultivation of the herb dill – was granted by King Edgar to a thane in 967. *Dilwich* was granted by Henry I to Bermondsey Abbey (founded in 1083) in 1127: 'Henricus rex primus dedit monachis de Bermundseye Retherhithe, Dilwich &c.'.[42] Alleyn indeed refers to the estate in a document as the 'Abbey lands'.[43] In 1530 the Abbot of Bermondsey and 15 named monks gave a 50-year lease of the manor to John Scott, Baron of the Exchequer, for services to the Abbey.[44] The Abbey possessed the lands for four centuries until its suppression and voluntary surrender to Henry VIII in 1537–8 when they became crown property, thereafter passing to the Caltons. When Alleyn became owner of the estate, Sir Francis Calton eventually passed on to him its muniments and Court Rolls dating as far back as 1333, when Edward III was on the throne.[45] Many of these (still in possession of the College) are dull legal documents, leases, bonds, rentals, mortgages and assignments, but the people mentioned in them recall the forgotten inhabitants of Dulwich village: innkeepers, haberdashers, woodmongers, leather-sellers, dyers, watermen, oar-makers, basket-makers, weavers, shoemakers and 'one of the cookes of her Maisties kitchen'. There are records of disputes over the price of beer, over hedges, ditches, cattle, and fences, and over pigs and biting dogs; problems recur with drunkenness, assaults and affrays, trespass, illegal wood-cutting and saw-pits. The Dulwich estate contained the woods and common and the two substantial 'messuages', Dulwich Court and Hall Place. Alleyn at some point settled at the moated Hall Place, once a country residence of the Prior of Bermondsey,[46] in its demesne of about thirty acres south of what is now Park Hall Road and between Alleyn Park and Rosendale Road,[47] and lived there even after the College was built; as magistrate he held 'Court Baron' at the house in 1608.[48] In 1814 this manor house could still be described as among 'romantic shades, surrounded by gentle acclivities on all sides, and diversified by wood and lawn'.[49]

Christ's Chapel

In May 1613 Alleyn settled with John Benson of Westminster to construct 'a certaine building of brick' for 'a chappell, a scholehowse and twelve almshowses'.[50] The chapel was built before the rest of the College as if for its symbolism as the heart of the College, and was consecrated and dedicated on his fiftieth birthday, 1 September 1616. George Abbot, Archbishop of Canterbury (1562–1633), who had been a political ally of Prince Henry, officiated for the consecration, since the post of Bishop of Winchester, the appropriate see for Dulwich at the time,

was vacant; he licensed the chapel, to be known as Christ's Chapel, for Holy Communion, baptism, marriage (which clause lapsed from 1754 until the last century) and burials. The form of the service of consecration was written out in full in Abbot's register; it was printed in 1737 in Wilkins's *Concilia*.[51] Abbot later agreed to become Visitor [inspector] of the College, and moreover enjoined this duty on 'his heirs for ever'; the Archbishops of Canterbury indeed were to hold this office for centuries, and when in 1857 the Act dissolving the old corporation became law, its second clause confirmed that the Archbishop should continue as the Visitor of the New College for ever. Eight injunctions [authoritative orders], major and minor, were to be made by the Primate: in 1664, four times in the 1720s, in 1742, and finally in 1819 and 1851. Alleyn inscribed Abbot's letters licensing the Chapel as 'The Instrument off Consecracon for yᵉ Chapple dedicated to the Honore off Christ in Dullwich with yᵉ churchyard therevnto belonging'.[52]

Edward Alleyn's Chalice, 1599. Silver-gilt.
(Dulwich College. Photograph by John Hammond)

The Latin text held at Lambeth Palace records sonorously how the 'venerabilis vir Edwardus Alleyn, armiger', with the King's approval intends a College for the poor and has built a chapel or oratory also to serve the hamlet of Dulwich, seeing that the parish church of Camberwell is too far off to visit, and perilous in winter. Only part of the consecration service was in English. Five knights were present, including the local magnates Sir Thomas Grymes of Peckham and Sir Edmond Bowyer of Camberwell, sheriff of Surrey and Sussex and the Member of Parliament for Surrey. After the Archbishop had read the instrument of consecration in Latin, he prayed in English for the hallowing of the building in the tradition of places of prayer in the Old Testament, especially Solomon's Temple, alluding to Psalm 84: 'For shall the sparrow have an house, and the swallow her nest and shall we not find out an house for thee, O Lord our redeemer?' He invoked God to listen to the prayers of children. Alleyn's first Chaplain, Cornelius Lymer, who had been Chaplain of Christ Church, Oxford since 1604, had been appointed the day before, and read Psalms 84 and 122 and the tenth chapter of John's Gospel.[53] A procession from the Chapel through the village to the foot of Court Lane to consecrate the Burial Ground (to be closed in 1859) was led by the Archbishop, who then sat on an outdoor throne.[54] Archbishop Abbot was himself planning to found an almshouse in Guildford, the Hospital of the Blessed Trinity; this was to house twelve brethren and eight sisters and his nephew as Master. Like Alleyn's College of God's Gift, it was to be formed of a quadrangle, with a chapel and quarters for the Founder. He laid the Hospital's foundation stone in 1619, and it was given a charter in 1622.[55]

For Alleyn 1616 was also the worrying year of litigation over Henslowe's will described in the last chapter. When making his annual accounts in his diary two years later, next to an amount of £67.5s.6d he adds a comment (which is unusual), writing resentfully that it is for 'Lawe yᵉ worst of awe' [all].[56] Within a year of the consecration of the Chapel, his mother-in-law Agnes Henslowe died, at a very advanced age (though not perhaps at a hundred years old as some contemporaries said), and was buried there on 9 April 1617.[57] Her gravestone, now lost, and recorded in 1814 as much defaced, read that she was the wife of Philip Henslowe, Esq., 'one of the ordinary Sewars of the chamber to Queen Elizabeth and King James the 1st'.[58]

The Letters Patent

Alleyn found great difficulties in his way to obtain the royal licence, the Letters Patent, necessary to found the College and to consign his property to it. He needed the support of the Lord Chancellor, Francis Bacon (1561–1626), who was eventually to attend the Foundation ceremony and to sign the charter in the Chapel in 1619. Bacon initially opposed the scheme on the grounds of tax evasion and with what seems a rather callous attitude towards such charitable enterprises. When Solicitor General in 1611 he had opposed the founding of the Charterhouse by Thomas Sutton, arguing that the salaries of university lecturers in the 'universities of this realm, which I take to be of the best endowed of Europe', were the best endowment for education to flourish rather than investing in the teaching of children.[59] He was also against settling estates in 'mortmain', avoiding death duties, because of the loss of revenue to the state. Magna Carta forbade the conveyance of property to corporations without royal sanction. Bacon was thus a formidable obstacle to Alleyn's College; Alleyn rode from Dulwich four times in five days to see him. He must have been in a state of high anxiety, as the College was already built, with the Poor Scholars, Brethren and Sisters in place, although it had not yet an official licence or a ceremonial Foundation. The first Poor Brethren and Sisters had arrived in October 1616 – John Jones, Alice Foster and Margaret Chapman – and the first Poor Scholars in the summer of 1617. Edward Young, Schoolmaster, was appointed on 20 June. In 1613 Alleyn had told Edmund Howes at the Chapel consecration that he intended his poor scholars to arrive between the ages of four to six and stay until they were fourteen or sixteen; he added that the Foundation was to include 'thrice two poore folks lodgings' in three separate parishes to be built within two years. The first boy to arrive was Henry Layton from the parish of St Saviour's, admitted on 29 March; another eleven followed from the parishes on 11 September.[60] Bacon pressed Alleyn to spend at least part of his bounty to endow two new lectureships, one at Oxford and another at Cambridge, but Alleyn held fast to his deliberated and specific charitable scheme, behind which lay no doubt his desire to benefit the deprived from the parishes of London where he had lived and gained his fortune. Alleyn noted in his diary for August 1618 that he called on the 'Lo: Chancellor … about staying [delaying] yᵉ pattent'.[61]

The next day, 18 August 1618, Bacon wrote to George Villiers, Marquis of Buckingham and King James's favourite, and mentioned Alleyn's appeal for a 'license to give in mortmain £800 land, though it be of tenure in chief [tenancy by perpetual ground-rent], to Allen, that was the player, for an hospital. I like well that Allen playeth the last act of his life so well; but if His Majesty give way thus to amortize [alienate in mortmain] his tenures, the Court of Wards will decay, which I had well hoped should improve'. Bacon appears to have failed to see the point of Alleyn's charitable intentions: 'hospitals [almshouses or schools, as in 'Chelsea Hospital' and 'Christ's Hospital'] abound, and beggars abound never a whit the less'. [62]

It is easy to be cynical about Alleyn's motives for founding the College; even his contemporaries suggested that in a sense he was laundering what Thomas Fuller (1608–61), writing in his *Worthies of England*, called his 'bad shillings':

> He got a very great estate, and in his old age, following Christ's counsel, (from what *forcible motive* belongs not to me to enquire) 'he made friends of his unrighteous mammon', building therewith a fair college at *Dulwich* in *Kent*, for the relief of poor people.
>
> Some, I confess, count it built on a foundered foundation, seeing, in a spiritual sense, none is good and lawful money save what is honestly and industriously gotten. But perchance such who condemn Master Allin herein, have as bad shillings in the bottom of their own bags, if search were made therein … Thus he, who out-acted others in his life, out-did himself before his death. [63]

Alleyn finishes off his annual accounts in his diary with the flourish 'Blessed bee yᵉ Lord god Euer Lasting yᵉ giver off all. Amen'. [64] Modern cynics may question whether Alleyn's religion was compromised by his capitalism, but this is to ignore its ring of honest piety, though it is true that the formula is common in contemporary accountancy. Each year he ends his diary with this axiom thanking God for his prosperity, suggesting perhaps the motto '*Detur Gloria soli Deo*' [Let glory be given to God alone], which was to be adopted for the College in the nineteenth century by Canon Carver and Welldon. [65] Of the list of Alleyn's books at his death 12 out of 26 were theological. [66] Alleyn's devotion does seem genuine, however. The Memorandum Book of his property deeds and values begins with a prayer, the phrasing of which seems to be influenced by the opening soliloquy on the theme of *memento mori* from his most famous role, Marlowe's Faustus, whose play also features a parade of the Seven Deadly Sins, led by Pride. Alleyn's prayer may likewise reveal something of the man: his list begins with Gluttony, which suggests that he found the pleasures of the table too attractive:

> Lorde God prosper me
>
> Grace and Pece
> be wt vs all   [with]
> then be nere so hie   [*nere* = never]
> regard Thy fall
> Rember thou must Die   [Remember]

> Beware of sinfull Gluttonie
> Fly alwayes filthie Lecherie
> Regard no worly Treasurey   [worldly]
> Sett prid both from thy hart & ie   [heart and eye]
> thie buisines do nott Slothfully
> tread downe all present envie
> veng nott thie quarell wrathfully [67]

Some have suggested that Alleyn's charity might have been partly motivated by his ambition for honours. It is true that Alleyn thought he deserved a knighthood, and solicited his friends at court late in his life to that end. In 1624 Henry Gibb, a Groom of the Bedchamber to the King and an associate of Alleyn's from Prince Henry's circle, wrote to him about 'your desire to have some further dignetie Conferd vppon you', and promised to speak to courtiers 'when the king returns'. He received a promise from Sir John Hungerford to approach King James. [68] A social prejudice against actors persisted until the days of Garrick; in 1764 Horace Walpole wrote of the disgrace of Lady Susan Strangways who ran off with 'O'Brien the player', saying that 'even a footman were preferable'. [69] It was not until 1895 that Sir Henry Irving became Britain's first theatrical knight.

One would have to be very cynical, however, to deny the signs of Alleyn's religious devotion and charity, together with his almshouses, his practical interests in the poor in Southwark and in the other parishes to whom he was such an extraordinarily generous benefactor, and perhaps most of all his active paternal involvement in the College once it was founded. He hoped, no doubt, to perpetuate his memory and to foster children, so to speak, down the ages; when Cornelius Lymer wrote to him to accept the invitation to preach at the consecration of the Chapel, he commended Alleyn's ostensible motive, a 'crowne of immortall glory'. [70] Alleyn could not have been blind to the effect of education and culture on his successful contemporaries; it is even possible that he was inspired by the glittering theatrical career of the playwright Christopher Marlowe, the author of Alleyn's most celebrated roles, in spite of what we now know about his dubious political and social circles and his death by stabbing in a house in Deptford at the age of 29 in 1593 and his subsequent burial in an unmarked grave. Marlowe rose by the type of charitable patronage envisaged by Alleyn, which was not only intended to school his Poor Scholars but to send them to university with scholarships from the College: from being the son of a shoemaker in Canterbury, Marlowe became a graduate of Cambridge in 1584 and hence a 'gentleman' and a learned writer; this occurred because he won a scholarship, as one of 50 poor boys, for classical education at the King's School, Canterbury;

he was next maintained at Corpus Christi College at Cambridge by a scholarship endowed by Archbishop Parker.[71] A panegyric in *The Actor's Vindication* by Thomas Heywood (added to the second, posthumous edition of 1658 and probably written by the actor William Cartwright the younger), describing Alleyn's latter days, is persuasive not only for its tribute to Alleyn's gifts as an actor, but for its testimony to Alleyn's later piety:

> Among so many dead [English actors; he names Tarlton, Kempe and William Sly] let me not forget the most worthy famous Mr. *Edward Allen*, who in his life time erected a Colledge at *Dulledge* for poor people, and for education of youth: When this Colledge was finisht, this famous man was so equally mingled with humility and charity, that he became his own Pensioner; humbly submitting himself to that proportion of diet and cloathes, which he had bestowed on others; and afterwards were interred in the same Colledge.[72]

From the entries in the diary from 1617 to 1622 we know that Alleyn dined with the Poor Brethren and Sisters not only on his birthday but also on feast days. Even after Alleyn's visits to Bacon, there was a year's delay before the granting of Letters Patent with the royal seal, with a licence for the College addressed to Alleyn as 'Chief Maister Ruler and Overseer of all and singular our games of Beares, Bulls, Mastive Dogs and Mastive Bitches', dated 21 June 1619. 'Yᵉ great Sealle' cost him a total of £18.16s.11d., including the vellum and strings (to rule the lines on it invisibly while it was being written out by the scribe) at seventeen shillings and sixpence.[73] Alleyn had to pay more visits to see the business through: to Sir Henry Yelverton, the Attorney-General, and a horse-ride to Wanstead to see Villiers: 'I rode to wansted wher yᵉ markques off buckinghame vndertooke yᵉ K[ing]s hand for me';[74] he also took wine with Bacon's gentlemen, and gave gratuities to those around Buckingham and Bacon. Alleyn received the Patent on 26 May 1619; the day after, he rode to Greenwich for the King's signature. The licence confirms the constitution of the College with the Master, Warden, four Fellows, six Poor Brothers, six Poor Sisters and twelve Poor Scholars. Both branches of the charity – the educational and the 'eleemosynary' [the

charitable almshouses] – were to be combined in 'one body Corporate and Politiq and one perpetual Coyminallty [commonwealth, self-governing community] to have perpetuall succession for ever to endure', and Alleyn was given 'full power and lawful authority to visit, order and punish'. The document also testifies that all Alleyn's property was to be transferred in mortmain to 'The Colledg of Gods Guift in Dulwich' – and specifies the manor of Dulwich, Hall Place, Ricotes (or Rigates), 18 acres of pasture in Lambeth, property in St Botolph's, Bishopsgate, the Fortune theatre on Whitecross Street and Golden Lane, and all his other lands. Alleyn meanwhile for his lifetime was to enjoy all the revenues from these properties as a life interest. The Archbishop of Canterbury was inscribed as Visitor of the College.[75]

Precedents

For the architecture and constitution of the College of God's Gift Alleyn followed a Dutch prototype, that of the *Orphanocomium* and *Gerontocomium* at Amsterdam, a group of almshouses for young and old founded in 1530 and formed around a courtyard; he had a transcript of their statutes.[76] It appears that Alleyn may have had some reciprocal dealings with this institution, for he records in his diary that on 30 June 1619, Lord Caron, Ambassador to the Dutch, came to Dulwich with three parliamentarians from the States General of the Low Countries 'to see this place'.[77]

The Chapel services were to be read and sung in 'the manner and forme, as neere as may be, as is usually observed in the King's Chappell [Chapel Royal], or in the Collegiate church of Saint Peter at Westminster [Westminster Abbey]', indicating a 'High Church' ritualist model similar to that promoted by William Laud (1573–1645), later Archbishop of Canterbury, and hence in antipathy to Puritanism. The stipulation of two candles on the altar may not now seem significant, but it was consistent with Laudian High Church practice.[78]

Alleyn visited schools and 'hospitals' in England to study statutes and syllabuses, and also the catering arrangements. The course of instruction was to follow that of the 'free grammar Scholes of Westminster and St. Paules'.[79] He investigated the syllabus at Dean Colet's St Paul's, which he visited twice. The speech days he wished to be modelled on those at Westminster and Merchant Taylors'. 'Mr doctor Love', the Warden at Winchester from 1613 to 1630, sent Alleyn suggestions for rules and statutes based on those at Winchester; he questioned the wisdom of Alleyn's proposal of election of Poor Scholars by lottery, and offered to revise the statutes of God's Gift College. Alleyn made notes on 'the order in Eaton Colledge bakehouse and brewhouse'.[80]

Among fo many dead let me not forget the moft worthy famous Mr. *Edward Allen*, who in his life time erected a Colledge at *Dulledge* for poor people, and for education of youth : When this Colledge was finisht this famous man was fo equally mingled with humility and charity, that he became his own Penfioner; humbly fubmitting himfelf to that proportion of diet and cloathes, which he had beftowed on others; and afterwards were interred in the fame Colledge. To omit

Thomas Heywood, *The Actor's Vindication*, 1658. (Dulwich College)

The Foundation ceremony of God's Gift College, with menu for the Dinner, and showing a section of the costs, recorded by Edward Alleyn in his diary for 13 September 1619. (Dulwich College)

The Colledge of *Gods-Gift*, at *Dulwich*, in the County of *Surry*: founded, raised, and builded, at the cost and charges of Master EDWARD ALLEYNE, Esquire, in *Anno Dom.* 1614.

THe thirteenth day of September, being Munday, *Anno* 1619. the Colledge of *Gods-gift* in *Dulwich*, consisting of one Master, one Warden, and foure Fellowes; three of which are persons Ecclesiasticall, and the fourth a skilfull Organist. Moreover, twelve aged poore people, and twelve poore children; Master *Edward Alleyne*, publikely and audibly, in the Chappell of the said College, did reade and publish one Writing Quadrupartite in Parchment, bearing date the day and yeere forementioned. Whereby he did make, create, erect, found, and establish the said Colledge, according to the power and liberty given him by his Majesties Letters Patents, under his great Seale, bearing date at *Westminster* the 21. of Iune, in the yeere abovesaid. When he had read and published the said Writing, he subscribed it with his name, and then fixed his Seale to every part of the Quadrupartite writing, in the presence and hearing of these witnesses:

Frances Lord Verulam, Lord Chancellour of *England*, and one of his Majesties Privy Councell.

Thomas Earle of Arundell, Knight of the Garter, Earle Marshall of *England*, and one of his Majesties Privy Councell.

Sir *Edward Cecill*, Knight, *alias* Generall *Cecill*, second Sonne to *Thomas Excester*.

Sir *Iohn Howland*, Knight, and high Sheriffe of the Counties of *Suffex* and *Surry*.

Sir *Edmund Bowyer* of *Cammerwell*, Knight.

Sir *Tho. Grymes* of *Peckham*, Knight.
Sir *Iohn Bodly* of *Stretham*, Knight.
Sir *Iohn Tonstal* of *Cashaulton*, Knight.

And divers other persons of great and worthy respect. The foure Quadrupartite Writings forenamed, were ordered to foure severall Parishes.

viz. {
Saint *Botolphs* without Bishopsgate.
Saint *Giles* without Cripplegate.
Saint *Saviours* in Southwarke.
And the Parish of Cammerwell.
}

A briefe recitall of the particulars.

Recitall of King *Iames* his Letters Patents.

Recitall of the Founders deed Quadrupartite.

Ordination of the Master, Warden, &c.

Ordination of the assistant members, &c.

The Master and Warden to bee unmarried, &c.

The Master and Warden to bee one and twenty yeeres of age at the least.

Of what degrees the Fellowes ought to bee.

Ttt   Of

The very first entry in Alleyn's diary, for 29 September 1617, records a visit to Sutton's Hospital, the Charterhouse, which he paid with his wife, Edward Young (the Schoolmaster) and two friends.[81] Sir Thomas Sutton (1532–1611) was another philanthropist, a soldier who made a vast fortune in land, coal, copper, and money-lending, and who in 1611, the year of his death, gave a huge endowment of £50,000 for the Charterhouse, a 'hospital' such as Alleyn's for both young and old.[82] In 1594 Gregory Fiennes, Lord Dacre, like Alleyn a childless public-spirited rich proprietor, had founded Emanuel School, with almshouses for twenty poor folk, both men and women, where he intended twenty 'poore children' to be brought up 'in vertue and good and laudable artes'. This had a courtyard and a chapel, but in fact until 1736 only housed one or two children a year.[83] Both Sutton and Dacre died in the very year of their endowments, but Alleyn was able to put his great scheme into action and to preside over it himself; just as the entry on Alleyn in the

Biographia Britannica (1747) put it, since the College was 'not trusted to the execution of others', his active participation in his own charity added 'a great lustre in the act'.[84]

The Foundation ceremony

On 13 September 1619 the great actor read aloud his Deed of Foundation[85] in the College Chapel. He must have enjoyed this performance. The chronicler Edmund Howes was present as a signatory; when he published a continuation of John Stow's *Annales* in 1631 he added an account of the ceremony, saying that Alleyn 'very publiquely and audibly' read the document, and 'did subscribe his name and fix his seal'.[86] Alleyn set down in his diary: 'They first Herd a sermond, & after ye Instrument of Creacion wase by me read, & after an anthem They went to dinner'. Alleyn had ridden to the Palace at Croydon twice in August to dine with the Archbishop of Canterbury and discuss the arrangements, although on the actual day the Archbishop was indisposed and did

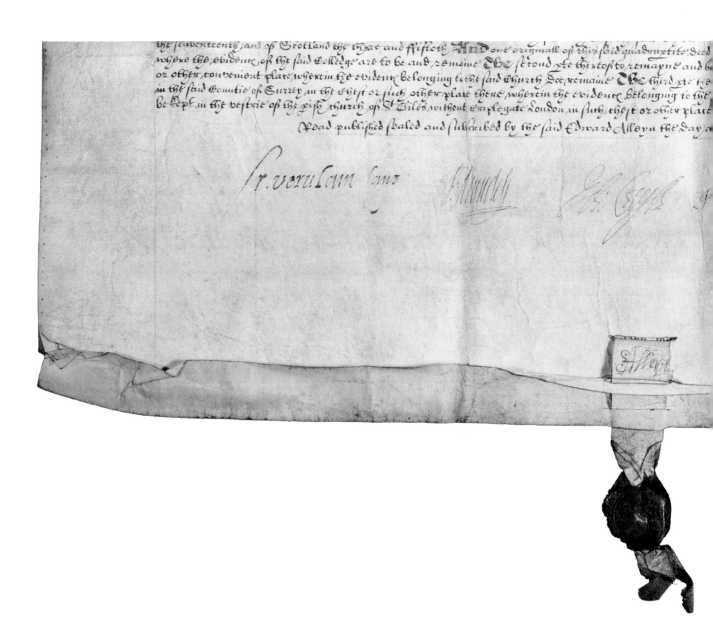

not attend. Alleyn's accounts of expenses for his horse, incidentally, are frequent in the diary, and at this season he had made much use of it: he issued invitations at short notice across the river in person: 'I rode to London to Envit Lordes to yᵉ Creacion'.[87]

The 'Instrument' casts an interesting light on the title 'God's Gift College', in that Alleyn clearly intended the phrase 'God's Gift' to record his perpetual gratitude for what he had received, dedicating it 'to the honour and glorie of Almightie God, and in a thankfull remembrance of his Guift and blessings bestowed on me the said Edward Alleyn'. In 1858, by Act of Parliament under the new Scheme to convert the College into a 'public school', it was renamed 'Alleyn's College of God's Gift'; by further Act in 1882 it became 'Dulwich College'.

The menu for the elaborate banquet is itemised in the diary; it included beef, capons in white broth, pigeons, venison, mutton, roast beef, green salad, oysters, neat's tongues [ox-tongue], a Florentine [meat in pastry], duck,

eels, partridges, rabbits, anchovies and artichoke pie.[88] The mutton, beer, wheat and butter were produce from the Estate.

The signatories to the Deed of Foundation on this momentous day included three famous Jacobean Londoners: Francis Bacon (Lord Verulam), the Lord Chancellor, who signs himself 'F. Verulam Canc'; Thomas Howard (Earl of Arundel), Knight of the Garter; and Inigo Jones 'Suyᵒʳ' [the King's Surveyor]. The other signatories were local landowners – Sir Thomas Grymes of Peckham, Sir Edmond Bowyer of Camberwell, Sir John Bodley of Streatham, Sir J. Tonstall of Carshalton – together with Sir Edward Cecil (General Cecil and later Viscount Wimbledon), Lord Lieutenant of Surrey; Sir John Howland, High Sheriff of Surrey and Sussex; and a notary public from Gray's Inn. 'Many others' were present. Alleyn himself signed and sealed the Deed, and copies on vellum were signed for each of the four parishes. His signature seems the stiffest and the least

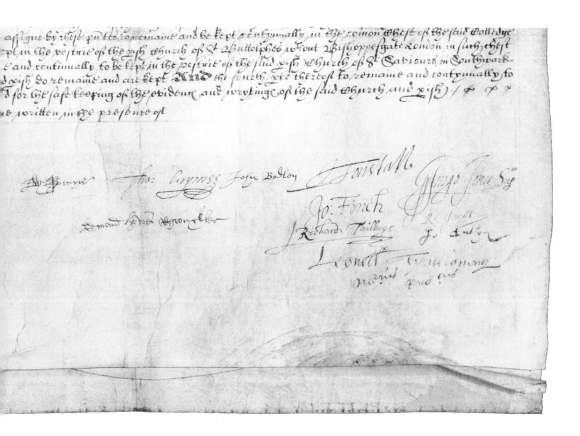

The Foundation Document of the College of God's Gift (detail) with signatures of Francis Bacon (Lord Verulam) as Lord Chancellor, the Earl of Arundel, Inigo Jones as King's Surveyor, and other witnesses, inscribed after it had been read aloud by Edward Alleyn in Christ's Chapel on 13 September 1619; his own signature and seal with crest appear below. (Dulwich College)

polished on the document, particularly among the elegant new 'Roman' hands of Arundel and Jones. Arundel and Jones were present as associates of Alleyn from court entertainments and, as mentioned in the last chapter, also perhaps as the official Commissioners for New Buildings.[89] It is possible that Alleyn and Jones were involved in 1613 in the court celebrations involving masques, feasts and revelry for the marriage of James's daughter Princess Elizabeth to Frederick, the Elector Palatine, at Whitehall Palace Chapel. The actors at the Fortune theatre, Alleyn's colleagues from the Admiral's (and subsequently the Prince's) Men, were adopted from 1613 by the Elector Palatine in London as his Company, and as such played at court. It is tempting to speculate that Alleyn accompanied the players, Arundel, Jones and Edward Cecil (who was Treasurer to the Princess) in the suite of 41 that accompanied the Princess to Heidelberg in April 1613 after the wedding for further entertainments. Were that the case, then Alleyn might have visited the Hospital at Amsterdam en route. The Elector and his wife were for a winter King and Queen of Bohemia in 1619 at the outset of the Thirty Years War; on 9 April 1620 Alleyn entertained four actors from 'ye King of bohemes men' at Dulwich, including William Cartwright the elder. Ten years after the marriage celebrations, and just three years before Alleyn's death, with Arundel and Inigo Jones he was to be involved as a prominent organiser in similar court activities in preparation for the reception at Southampton of the Infanta of Castile as bride of Prince Charles (which in the event was called off); on 5 June 1623, one Dr Meddus wrote to Revd Joseph Meade telling him of the abortive journey by Arundel and the third Earl of Pembroke (1580–1630): along with

Allein (sometime a player, now 'Squire of the Beares'), and Inigo Jones, surveyor of the King's works, [they] rode hence on Tuesday towards Winchester and Southampton to take order for his Majestie's entertainment, with the Prince's and Ladie Marie's, for shows.[90]

The 1619 Deed of Foundation addresses greetings to all true Christian people, and refers back to the Letters Patent from James I of 21 June of that year, licensing Alleyn to consign his property to relieve and maintain poor men, women and children and to educate the children. The Deed repeats the terms of the Letters Patent, but includes an organist among the four Fellows. Alleyn consigns his property to the College, and seems to take pleasure in the recurrent resonant phrase 'for ever'. He names the first officers (including his two cousins, Thomas and Matthias, as Master and Warden) and the first Poor Brethren, Sisters and Scholars. Four copies of the document were signed, and one was to remain in the common chest of the College.

The College of God's Gift was designed by Alleyn to benefit the four parishes associated with his career: St Botolph's, Bishopsgate (where of course he grew up, and where he still owned property and had endowed almshouses); St Giles, Cripplegate (where the Fortune theatre lay just outside the City), which from 1773 by a boundary change became St Luke's, Finsbury;[91] St Saviour's, Southwark, near the Bankside (the site of his house, the Rose, the Bear Garden and the Hope); and St Giles, Camberwell (which included the manor of Dulwich). Three poor scholars were to join the College from each parish, along with three poor brethren or sisters.

Alleyn's Statutes

Alleyn's statutes are fascinating in what they show of the imaginative foresight of his philanthropic idealism and his practical sense in organising rules and conventions for his community. They show the experience he had gained as a churchwarden, and also skills learned as manager of a theatre and repertory company and producer of plays. Fuller wrote confidently that 'sure I am, no hospital is tied with better or stricter laws, that it may not *sagg* from the intention of the founder'.[92] The phrase 'for ever' which recurs throughout the Statutes, just as it does in the Foundation Document, may have been a reassuring vaunted motif, but ambiguities and contradictions were soon apparent in later years. The statutes were comprehensive, even as to clothing and catering.

Alleyn completed his Statutes within two months of his death, after seven years of experience at the College; they were dated 29 September 1626, and were finally signed on 20 November, less than a week before he died. He put in a clause inviting changes and new ordinances, but in fact the Statutes were the cause of laissez-faire, and of endless mischief and harm and of expensive litigation over the years, until they were swept away by Act of Parliament in 1857. As late as the eighteenth century, lawyers were seriously questioning whether Alleyn had any right in formulating his Statutes to diverge from the terms of foundation as originally spelled out in the Letters Patent. For all Alleyn's good intentions and foresight, the principal causes of trouble were two: first, the status of the parishes and their representatives, elected as 'Assistants', and the extent of the part they played in the government and finances of the College; and secondly the complicated and rather crude system known as the 'Dividend'. Alleyn introduced the latter as a means of dividing up the surplus revenue from the Estate when income exceeded expenditure. By the early nineteenth century the surplus reached colossal amounts. By a depressing irony, Alleyn's generous ideals of community, fairness and relief were dissipated in greed and quarrels.

The College's Statutes, plate and ready money were to be kept in Alleyn's massy oak 'comon chest', dated 1616, clamped with great iron bands and studded with great iron nails, in the treasure chamber above the 'great porch' in the tower. Restored in 1879, it stands today in the Lower Hall at the College. Both the chamber door and the chest were fitted with three padlocks and keys, so that six officers, two from the College and two churchwardens each representing St Botolph's and St Saviour's had to be present to unlock them. The College 'evidences' [property documents], plate and money were to be checked each year. The lengthy Statutes were to be read aloud four times a year in full assembly. We learn that Alleyn's personal papers were kept 'in a chest at the bed's feete in the yellow chamber, the keye whereof is in the till of my deske'. [93]

At the heart of the community were to be the daily services in Chapel. These were held on weekdays at 10.30 a.m. and 5 p.m., and on Sundays and holidays, when surplices were to be worn, at nine in the morning and two in the afternoon. Alleyn clearly enjoyed the stage management of the procession into Chapel: first the Poor Brethren and Sisters, then the Poor Scholars two by two, the Junior and Senior Fellows two by two, then the Warden and Master alone. Four days were set annually for Communion, followed by a feast for the poor brethren and sisters. Death also had its prescriptions: only the Master, Warden or Fellows were to be buried in the Chapel, with vaults in the middle of the upper end of the Choir for the Master and Warden, and for the Fellows to the side.

Edward Alleyn's oak Treasury Chest of the College of God's Gift, dated 1616. (Dulwich College)

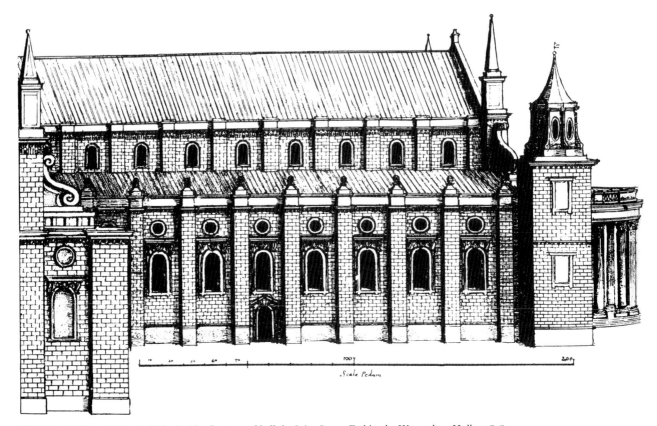

Old St Paul's Cathedral, embellished with pilasters and balls by Inigo Jones. Etching by Wenceslaus Hollar, 1658.

The Chapel and the College

The Chapel and the College were constructed by John Benson of Westminster, Inigo Jones's builder who also worked on the masques and other projects for Prince Henry, as noted above. One would like to believe what James Allen, the Master of the College of the day, told the author of the article on Edward Alleyn in *Biographia Britannica* (1747), not much more than a century after the event, that the buildings were 'after the design and direction of Mr. Inigo Jones, who was a witness in his deed of settlement'.[94] Benson's contract of 17 May 1613 proposes the first turning of the earth, a trench 'on Dulwiche Greene for the foundacon to be digged and made fitt', and then to erect 'a certaine buildinge of brick', the rest finished white, to serve as 'a chapell scholehowse and twelve almshowses' with a Tower and a Porch 'beautified'.[95] According to an account book of 1712 there were stone Figures [statues] that originally stood in the porch, possibly the '4 figuers of ye seasones' bought by Alleyn in 1619.[96] The bricks came from Lambeth.[97] A gate room was to be ornamented with frieze, cornices and 'piramides'. Jones was kept extraordinarily busy with his work as the King's Surveyor with very little time for private commissions, and 1619 was the year when the Banqueting Hall in Whitehall was begun, but it is possible that he made at least a sketch of

elevations for Alleyn. Certainly when Jones worked later at Old St Paul's from 1633 to 1642, recladding or recasing the outer elevations of the clerestories and aisles of the medieval nave and transepts, he embellished them with pilasters, ball finials and obelisks ('piramides') in a style remarkably similar to the courtyard of Dulwich College. The 'dorick pilasters with petty stalls [plinths], bases, capitals and the cornishe' of Benson's contract, seen in early prints of the courtyard of the College, are sophisticated for their day, but the segmentally headed windows of the College do not accord with Jones's new Italianate style. The dimensions of the original ground-plan of the chapel are given in Wilkins's account of the consecration, 47 feet by 24, suggesting not the conventional Tudor Gothic proportions of a chapel but the ground-plan of a Vitruvian double-cube space, the hallmark of Jones's new chapels, such as the Queen's Chapel of 1623–5 at St James's. The Chapel was, however, most likely a hybrid rather than a new style building, as Jones's chapels do not have the open-timbered roof of a late Gothic type found at Dulwich.[98]

In 1890 the architect Ewan Christian wrote a report on the Chapel for the College Governors. He noted that the later changes to the Chapel, 'so barbarously treated' by the College, spoiled the 'once fair proportions' of

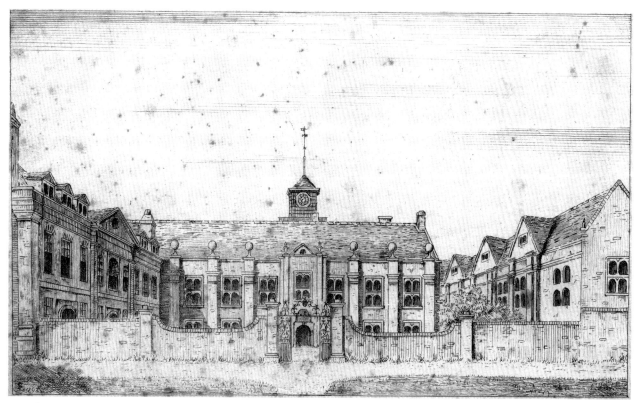

Main elevation of Dulwich College, 1792. Daniel Lysons, *The Environs of London*, Vol. I. (Dulwich College)

'what must have been a comely structure' with the addition of the trumpery south aisle and gallery by George Tappen in 1823 and 'the anachronistic mid-Victorian woodwork of the screen, stalls and pulpit'; these features, a pastiche of the early sixteenth century, he judged 'handsome of their kind', but in a quite incongrous style taken from more than a century earlier than the Chapel. In his view the original Chapel must have been 'a truly noble structure'.[99]

Alleyn bought a 'p: [pair] orgaines' on 27 April 1618, made by 'm^r. gibbs of powles', most likely a portable organ.[100] There was originally a cloister, a passage from the porch through to the other side of the Chapel, as one was pulled down in 1670.[101] Descriptions of the interior of the Chapel are lacking, but an eighteenth-century source mentions organ pipes decorated (as for a family chapel) with the Founder's arms impaled with those of Henslowe, 'Azure, a wolf Rampant, Ermin'.[102] Alleyn's accounts mention a pulpit, a cushion, a font and a communion table. After his death the College commissioned in 1641 a 'new glasse windowe of divers coloured glass … of same worke and fashion as the east windowes of the Parishe Churches of St. Martin in the fields and St. Clement Danes'. This cost them £11 [£957].[103]

For the layout of the rooms in the College and its fittings we have only clues in Alleyn's accounts and in later descriptions. The Hall abutted onto the chapel, as in an Oxford or Cambridge college. The Master's lodgings included a great chamber above the Hall, and another chamber over the parlour. In 1807 these were said to contain very noble old furniture.[104] The Warden was accommodated above the servants' hall. The six Poor Sisters had rooms on the ground floor on the west wing opening onto the quadrangle, the Poor Brethren facing them on the east wing. Upstairs on the east wing was a long chamber for the Poor Scholars. The twelve of them slept here, in six bedsteads, and their lessons also took place in 'ye schole chamber' adjacent, mentioned by Alleyn in his Diary.[105] On the first floor of the west wing was a 'great chamber', like an Elizabethan long gallery; this measured, according to Samuel Lysons in 1792, 77 feet by 15 feet 6 inches, and was 'richly ornamented in stucco' but 'very ruinous'.[106] Lysons mentions paintings, presumably those of Alleyn's own collection. Horace Walpole in 1791 was dismissive about these decorations: 'an hundred mouldy portraits among apostles, sybils and kings of England', and also about the Gallery 'with a very rich ceiling' then being pulled down.[107] Alleyn's Diary mentions purchases of paintings: he bought eight 'kings

Sibilla Delphica. Oil on panel. (© Dulwich Picture Gallery)

Sibilla Europea. Oil on panel. (© Dulwich Picture Gallery)

picktures' in October 1618 and a few days later eight more. Christ, the Virgin Mary, and twelve apostles were bought from Mr Gibkin 'at a noble [6s.8d] a peece'. The existence of portraits of Calvin and Luther and of two other Protestant divines in the College's collection would seem to call into question the view of Alleyn as a follower of the traditionalist Archbishop Laud, and indeed of the College as a conservative (i.e. High Church) institution in the seventeenth century; it has been assumed that these pictures were part of Alleyn's own collection, but there is no surviving evidence. Paintings may well have been added in the early days by the Fellows or well-wishers of the College without record, in the same way as books were added to the Library.[108] Other details of the building are lacking, but probably the rooms already had the disposition noted by E. W. Brayley in his *Surrey* (1842): in sequence after the Chapel and the Hall in the main south block to the west – extending further than it is today – were an ante-room, the Library, the Master and Warden's apartments, the Audit Room, the Treasury Chamber and the College kitchens. The First, Second and Fourth Fellows had their rooms on the first floor of the East Wing, and the Third Fellow his next to the boys' dormitory and school room in the

West Wing.[109] In the Audit Room was hung after his death the great portrait of the Founder.[110] Alleyn's diary mentions the paved great kitchen and a Music Room. By 1620 there were six tenor viols and a bass viol; 'a newe pair of Virginals' was bought in 1630.[111] A second organ, the 'schoole organ' presumably in the Music Room, figures in an account for 1635.[112]

The records of Alleyn's library, probably misleadingly, are modest. He listed 41 titles of books or pamphlets – theology, demonology, politics and history (with some of King James's speeches and his book on the Divine Right of Kings) and a book by the playwright Robert Greene – on the back of a torn draft petition to the King.[113] Also surviving is 'a note of those Bookes which yᵉ Worp. [worshipful] Edward Alleyne, founder of this Colledge, left after his death', in all 26 items.[114] In 1609 Shakespeare's sonnets were published, and Alleyn records buying the book for 5d that year. He wrote down this purchase under some rough accounts of 'Howshowld stuff' on the back of a letter from Sir Thomas Bowker asking for a mastiff whelp to be sent to him; as with almost all of Alleyn's own listed books the volume does not survive.[115] As well as following the literature of his day, he seems fascinated by magic and the occult,

Doctor Faustus's special skill, and marks in his diary astrological signs by each date; the volume of Cornelius Agrippa's *De Occulta Philosophia* (1533) in the Fellows' Library has annotations that may be in his hand. In 1617 he commissioned verses for a 'silver book' which he had specially illuminated and decorated with crimson satin lining and 'glass work'; he presented it to the Countess of Suffolk at Suffolk House on 31 December, and it had cost him the great sum of £15 [over £1,900].[116] Looked at more closely, the gift loses its charm, and was at best a political token. Lady Suffolk (d. 1638), presumably known to Alleyn for her part in dancing in Stuart court masques, was the glamorous, wanton, avaricious and pro-Spanish wife of the Lord Treasurer, Thomas Howard (1561–1626), Earl of Suffolk. Suffolk was prosecuted before the Star Chamber in October 1619 for corruption, fined and imprisoned; a large bribe to Lady Suffolk was often necessary before creditors who were owed money by the Exchequer were paid.[117] Alleyn had dealt with the Earl of Suffolk before this; as Privy Councillor he had signed the request in 1613 to Justices of the

Peace in Cheshire and Lancashire to examine and punish a landowner and his servant who beat and abused Philip Henslowe's deputies for taking up dogs.[118] Alleyn went to see Suffolk on business in 1617; in 1619 Suffolk became the Lord Treasurer.

Out of doors stood a malt house, a barn, and a great garden house.[119] Land to the south of the College was designated for recreation with a garden and an orchard, and there were three home fields, the Howlettes. There were ponds for fishing, both on and near the Common. Inside the College Alleyn seems to have taken most pains over the joinery, carving, painting and gilding of an elaborate chimney-piece in 'yᵉ great chamber', put up in 1618; this was made from 'yᵉ barge stuff',[120] and presumably included the two painted panels of *Pietas* and *Liberalitas* he had bought from the Queen's barge, as described in the first chapter. (The great chamber served later as 'Audit Room'). In 1870 the Master, Dr Carver, found workmen about to demolish the chimney piece; on his initiative it was installed in its present setting: the Masters' Library at the New College.[121]

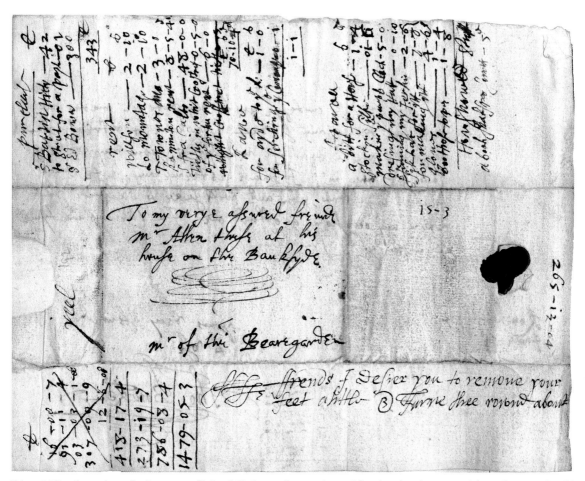

Edward Alleyn's purchase, for fivepence, of 'a book Shakesper Sonnetts', noted (last item in column, top right, under 'Howshowld stuff') on the back of a letter of 1609. Other expenses are for property, rent, law and apparel; they include payments to Sir Edmond Bowyer and Sir Francis Calton, and rent for the Fortune theatre. (Dulwich College)

The pair of panels represents two emblematical female figures appropriate to God's Gift College, symbolising as they do different types of giving. *Pietas* offers up a flaming altar with one hand, while the other rests on the neck of a pelican, a traditional symbol of Christ (from the ancient belief that it wounds its own breast to feed its young with its blood). *Liberalitas* holds two cornucopias, symbols of the generosity with which monarchs reward their subjects; from one horn flow the fruits of the earth, from the other costly artefacts. Were Alleyn's two panels to be extended to a triptych, the third would surely present the fickle goddess Fortuna, who is traditionally pictured standing on a sphere, the iconography figuring the most powerful secular force to hold sway over our globe: a capricious 'Lady Luck', as it were. This goddess was as liberal a patron to Alleyn's career as either Queen Elizabeth or King James; his naming of the Fortune theatre honours her bounty, and at the same time declares his ambition to out-perform the rival Globe. A statue of 'Dame Fortune' graced the exterior of the

Pietas, presumably part of 'ye queens owld barge' bought by Alleyn in 1618, now set into the chimney-piece in the Masters' Library at the New College. Oil on panel. (© Dulwich College)

Liberalitas, a pair to *Pietas*. (© Dulwich College)

Fortune, as we are told by Thomas Heywood in *The English Traveller* (1633), in the same way that the Globe's flag is thought to have shown 'Hercules and his load' – the world. Contemporary reports (quoted above) describe the Fortune as the finest playhouse in London – overshadowing even the Globe at Fortuna's feet. From the fortune Alleyn earned from the prosperous theatre named after her, he piously endowed the College of God's Gift. Four centuries later it still could be said that Alleyn's horn of plenty strews the gifts of prosperous London at the feet of the young; in response, with their own profuse gifts, Alleynians serve London (and the globe) with true liberality.

The Master, Warden and Fellows

A Fellow in Latin is called a *socius*, and the Fellowship of all the College officers together was often known as the 'Society'. Alleyn presided at the College until the time of his death, although he was never named as Master. Thomas Alleyn (d. 1631), his cousin, a citizen and barber-surgeon of London, was named in the Deed of Foundation as Master, but he did not actually assume the office until Alleyn's death. The first Master, Warden and Fellows were appointed by Alleyn, but he set up elaborate regulations for their election in the future. At the start the College was strongly headed by 'Founder's kin': as well as Thomas Alleyn the first Master, Alleyn's cousin Matthias Alleyn (d. 1642) was the first Warden and succeeded as the second Master. The second Warden was Thomas Alleyn (d. 1669), son of the first Master, who became in turn the third Master.

Neither the Master nor the Warden was an academic appointment; Alleyn stipulated genially that they should be 'of learning, judgement, and understanding, sufficient to discharge their places in the College'. Over the years, however, their lack of qualifications had two grave consequences: they took too little interest in the education of the Poor Scholars, and the Fellows at certain periods are known to have treated their superiors with contempt. The Warden was essentially a bursar, responsible for the estate, disbursements, profits and pensions; he could also act as proxy for the Master, and normally succeeded as Master on the Master's death. The Warden had to deposit a surety to avoid peculation – by the early nineteenth century this was increased to the colossal sum of £8,000, usually divided into four payments, and paid by guarantors. A new Warden also had to pay for a dinner at his expense – in 1831 this was accompanied with music in the Picture Gallery. The Master and Warden ideally were to be 'of my blood and sirname', or for second choice 'of my sirname only'; though eccentric, this was perhaps an excusable vanity to keep God's Gift College in the name of an Alleyn. Moreover, they must be 'of honest lives and conversations [behaviour]'. Over the years the candidates who presented themselves included a wonderful range of professions: malt-factor, vintner, soldier, foundryman, hosier, peruke-maker, linen-draper, dyer, carpenter, grocer, weaver, timber merchant, distiller, doctor, cooper, troop-of-horse man, stay-maker, sea-captain, attorney-at-law, Gentleman Usher to the Queen, and mathematical-instrument maker.[122] When a series of candidates applied, they were reduced to two by the Fellows and the 'Assistants'; next an election between these two was made by drawing of lots, the elder applicant to draw first from 'twoe equall small rowleses of paper to be indifferently made and rolled up' after the box was shaken three times. The successful candidate would draw the one paper roll with the words 'GODD'S GUIFT' written on it. The runner-up was given the amount of salary that had accrued for the post since it fell vacant.[123] In the nineteenth century this ritual took place in front of the altar at the Chapel; the tin box was placed in turn on the crown of the head of each of the candidates, the Master then taking the box, and shaking and turning it three times.[124] The Master's function in God's Gift College was 'to governe all the persons thereof, and admonish, correct and punish them according to the statutes', but Alleyn added in a characteristic note that the Master was to take a special care to see that the Poor Brethren were not wronged nor the Poor Scholars abused. In 1678 Elias Alleyn, who claimed to be of 'Founder's kin', was appointed but was 'voided' by the Archbishop of Canterbury. The monarch himself, Charles II, was appealed to and reaffirmed the appointment, only to annul it when Elias Alleyn was shown to be a fraud.[125] When the Master or Warden was installed there was a service in chapel, a sacrament with the Fellows 'to express the mutual love and concord which is between them'. The entire community was to be celibate, though not only Alleyn himself but also his cousins the first Master, Thomas Alleyn, and the first Warden, Matthias Alleyn, were already married when the College was founded. In 1620 the Revd John Harrison, Usher, ran away with Anne (Nan) Allen, a niece and ward of Edward Alleyn who was employed as a servant at the College, and then wrote to justify his action. When he wrote again asking Alleyn to stand godfather to their child, Alleyn angrily refused. Harrison's next response seems to refer to the short temper of the Alleyn family: 'my wife had gott a Scribe as gott some of yoᵘ spiritt but I by chance prevented it least evill wordes should corrupt good manners'.[126] Alleyn however, left her £20 in his will.[127] Rumours of secret marriages troubled the College down the ages. Dr John Alleyn, the Master from

1668 to 1686, was said by the Fellows to be secretly married to a 'madame Nye' and to have had children by her. Joseph Allen, the Master from 1746, resigned in 1775 to marry Mrs Plaw of Thurlow Lodge. A Bill was presented to the House of Lords in 1814 to allow the Master to marry, but was withdrawn, and Launcelot Baugh Allen (who was promoted to Master from Warden in 1811) accordingly resigned in 1820 as he had recently married a local lady.[128]

As will be seen, the College as ordained by Alleyn's Statutes down the years until the reforms of the New Scheme of 1857 was sometimes in the hands of conscientious and worthy Masters, Wardens and Fellows, but there was also a good deal of torpor and fecklessness or worse; it has to be said that superior personal qualities of the Master, Warden and Fellows such as might have raised the College out of its academic mediocrity or failure were not much in evidence. The First Fellows stayed hardly more than two years on average, and left to better their careers. The Mastership by comparison was more of a congenial near-sinecure, and all who held the office (except the two who left to marry) died in office. There was good living but little real incentive of work and salary for the Fellows, and in the first year of the College when Richard Barlow was offered the Ushership, he wrote to Alleyn refusing it; he said that there was no security after a year's trial, and that he was surprised at being expected to buy his own bed, gown and commodities out of his own pocket.[129] There were some remarkable exceptions to the mediocrity of the Master, Warden and Fellows, particularly in the eighteenth century with a formidable and erudite Scot, the Revd James Hume, who was Second Fellow from 1706 to 1730. In the early nineteenth century there appeared the one really distinguished figure of national importance and influence in the history of the College, Dr John Allen of Holland House, who was Warden from 1811 and Master from 1820 until his death in 1843. In that year John Gay Newton Alleyne (1820–1912), later to achieve distinction in iron and steel manufacture and construction and in civic life, was appointed Warden; he resigned in 1851. In both the latter cases, however, their gifts were not really suitable or directed towards the proper education of the poor scholars of the College of God's Gift.

The first two Senior Fellows were originally to be graduates of Oxford or Cambridge and to act as Preachers, giving morning and evening sermons on Sundays and on the Founder's birthday, 1 September. They were also to sing parts in the choir. The actual teaching was to be shared by the Second Fellow, an 'approved' schoolmaster, and a Third Fellow, a 'sufficient' Usher, who was to be responsible to the schoolmaster. The Fourth Fellow was the Organist, sometimes referred to in the documents as the '*pulsator organorum*'. Alleyn's second Organist, from 1622 to 1624, was Benjamin Cosyn (*c.* 1580–1653) a composer and the compiler of the celebrated manuscript anthology of 1620 (which includes his own work) *Benjamin Cosyn's Virginal Book*, now in the British Library.

Alleyn's *Statutes* made just before his death would have added to the original senior members of the College six resident 'junior ffellowes'; as 'six chaunters for musique and singing' they were to boost the Chapel choir. Alleyn intended what amounted to a daily full cathedral choir service in his chapel.[130] Two of these Junior Fellows were to be music teachers, 'men of approved skill to sound the organs in the chappell, and singe their partes in the quire' and to 'instruct boys in singing', playing upon 'the violls, virginalls, organs, and other instruments as they shalbe found capable'. The other four Junior Fellows – tailors, glovers, embroiderers, and shoemakers, for example – were to teach useful trades or handicrafts in the afternoons to the less academic boys, and were expected to make the clothing for the Poor Scholars. This later addition to the Society perhaps represents Alleyn's disappointment; he may by that time have admitted to himself that many of the orphan scholars were not up to his original academic ambitions for them. In fact these Junior Fellows were never appointed, as in 1627 soon after Alleyn's death legal advice was taken by the College: additional appointments and emoluments were ruled to be contrary to the original Foundation. Alleyn may have had a further motive to strengthen the power of the College in its own government. A mischievous result of the six Chaunters not being appointed was that the Assistants from the four parishes were empowered for centuries to outvote the College. Meanwhile an attempt was made to teach Latin to 'grammarians' among the boys. However, over the years the real or assumed lack of ability of the poor scholars became an excuse for not teaching them properly. The Visitor, the Archbishop of Canterbury, by Statute was to nominate and send a learned man to examine the poor scholars annually and to observe the chapel arrangements, but this also soon lapsed.

Provision was made for servants and labourers: a man each for the Master and Warden, a porter, a cook, a kitchen boy, a maltster and brewer, a butler, a bayley [bailiff], a ploughman, a plough boy, and a mole-catcher; these again were all to be single men. Joan Alleyn had a maid, and there were three women servants. Liveries were provided. The porter was to be present in the lodge or in the forecourt yard and open the gate from 5 a.m. until 10 p.m. in summer and from 6 a.m. until 9 p.m. in winter.

He had also to wait on the Master and Warden at dinner and toll the bell for the services. Dogs figure in the College papers – in 1660 two puppies were bought for 3s.; in 1686 an entry in the accounts reads, 'pd. a man for keeping yᵉ Dogg and teaching him, though he learnt nothing'. In 1660 there was a mastiff called 'Lyon' and in 1724 a 'Venture' and a 'Thunder'. At the end of the eighteenth century there were pet ravens, with bells round their necks. [131]

A common diet was to be taken, although the Master and Warden and Fellows might take their meals in the Parlour if they wished in cold weather, and not in the Hall. The Hall had two tables, one the 'high table'. The College 'gave eare unto a chapter of the Bible', read by one of the Poor Scholars after grace. Three of the Poor Scholars took it in turns to fetch and serve the food. At 8 a.m. a twelve-ounce loaf was quartered for each member and served with a cup of small beer. For dinner on Mondays, Tuesdays and Thursdays a good 'mess of pottage' [stew or soup] was served together with boiled beef, more bread and 'beer without stint'. On Wednesdays, Fridays and Saturdays there was a half-pound of butter and two pounds of cheese among all, or fish, with pies of pear or apple. On Sundays and holidays, 'gawdy days', roast beef and mutton were served.

The clothing of the Poor Scholars was determined as a white calico surplice, a long coat (such as is worn by Christ's Hospital boys today) of good cloth of 'sad' [dark and sober] colour, a bodice lined with canvas, skirts with cotton lining, canvas shirts, white cotton drawers, knitted stockings, shoes and belt, a girdle and black cap. Thus the boys were clothed until 1857, and as such indeed they are shown in the Victorian painting 'Old Time Tuition at Dulwich College' (illustrated in Chapter Five). Alleyn's diary records purchases of surplices for the boys, of musical instruments, lute-strings, '5 songe bookes' and paper with ruled lines for music, stationery, pens and ink, and pewter chamber pots. [132]

The College was to be managed by meetings on Friday evening with the Master, Warden and Fellows, reviewing the accounts and business; what Alleyn called 'Private Sittings' were to be held monthly. Three days a week could be spent away from the College by the Master, two by the Warden, and one by the Fellows; Alleyn set penalties for breaking this limit, including expulsion from the Society. [133] As early as 1619 Alleyn's Preacher was absent for two weeks and was fined two weeks' salary. Later on there was collusion among the Fellows to extend their absences, and in 1695 Archbishop Tenison instituted an Exeat Book. A tour to assess the state of the College buildings and the Estate in March was to be an annual feature. Proper records of accounts in 'faire ledgier bookes' and of entrances and changes in the community, of christenings, marriages and burials, complaints, controversies and appeals against expulsions were to be kept. Alleyn wrote out the title page of the Register himself. [134]

W. D. Caröe, a collegian of Alleyn's day, holding a model of the Chapel. Mosaic and oil, with gilding, 1911. Reredos (detail), Christ's Chapel, Dulwich.

Preface inscribed by Edward Alleyn in his *Register* for God's Gift College, 1616. (Dulwich College)

The annual expenditure was reckoned at £600 including wages, pensions, food, clothing and sundries. If the College income reached £15 over expenditure, the 'divident' would come into effect, an elaborate system that became open to abuse. The amount of the excess was to be split into 600 parts, of which 120 parts, for example, were to be spent on an improvement in diet, while the rest mostly would be a monetary bonus for the members, including the Poor Brethren and Sisters.

The Poor Scholars

The Poor Scholars from the parishes where Alleyn derived his fortune were selected at the age of six to eight years old and were to stay at the College until eighteen years old, and then 'put forth either for Schollers or Trades as their capacity will fitt'. Candidates were initially selected by the churchwardens, and the Master and Warden chose two from the boys sent by each parish, but in the case of the local Camberwell and Dulwich boys the College was to choose them. Preference was to be given to 'orphants', then to sons of almspeople. Alleyn's word for the Poor Scholars, as written in his own hand in the Register, was the 'collegians'; other

early documents call them 'colledgiantes'. Lord Arundel, ignorant perhaps of the policy of the limitations of residence in the admissions statutes, wrote to 'his louing frend' in 1616 recommending a 'poore fatherless boy'. [135] The lessons given to the poor scholars were to be shared with boys from Dulwich Village; the Fellows were directed 'freely, without recompense or reward, [to] teach and instruct the children of the inhabitants within Dulwich aforesaid in wrytinge and grammar'. Their parents would pay an admission fee of two shillings; there were levies of sixpence a quarter for brooms and the rods to beat the boys and a pound of good candles at Michaelmas. Alleyn was hoping, significantly, to have boarding scholars, whom he referred to as 'forreyners'; he made provision to include many more boarders than the Poor Scholars, but the total number of pupils was never to exceed four score. From this clause for boarding pupils it looks as if Alleyn hoped for a Winchester of the London suburbs, but in effect it was a disaster in his own day. Alleyn was able to refer to 'ye 4 borders' in his diary, [136] but hardly for long: Mr Rogers sent his three sons 'at board and schooling' for twelve pounds 'a peece' on 15 June 1620, but they left on 21 October;

Mr Woodward sent his son at twenty shillings a year on 12 September 1620, but the boy had left before the following January.[137] During the bitter 'War of Dulwich' in the nineteenth century over the reform of the College, the supporters of the New College as a 'public school of the first rate' were to make great capital out of this and other clauses to contradict the claims of the Parishes that Alleyn's bequest was strictly for the poor; in 1875 an article in *The Alleynian* managed by a careful selection of this Statute from the others (and by editing out the Poor Scholars) to make a good case that Alleyn's real intention for his Foundation was 'a great public school in embryo'.[138] The aim was for the Collegians to become proficient in 'good and sound learning, wryting, reading, grammar, musique and good manners'. The syllabus was conventional: 'the rules and precepts of the grammar allowed in England', and to teach and instruct in such other books 'as are commanded by publique aucthoritye', and such as were used at Westminster and St Paul's.[139] A 'fair hand' in writing was to be taught. Lessons took place from six in the morning until nine-thirty and from one to four in the afternoon from March to August, and from seven in the morning until nine-thirty from September to February; there were roll-calls. It was Alleyn's intention for boys to be 'streamed' or placed in a class according to ability, and not according to the teachers' favouritism.

Four boys were to be maintained at College expense at Oxford or Cambridge. The scale of failure of Alleyn's plans for this enlightened clause was to prove one of the saddest aspects of the first College; the Founder's ideal of educating boys to enter Oxford or Cambridge whose parents would not necessarily aspire to send them there nor could afford the fees was not achieved on a proper scale until the 'Dulwich Experiment' that started in 1946 and finished in the 1970s and with the Assisted Places scheme of recent memory and the Bursary schemes of our own days. Alleyn's generous ideal of actually supporting his Collegians at Oxford and Cambridge was seldom effected. Dr Carver and A. H. Gilkes in the earlier days of the New College fought hard for College exhibitions to Oxford and Cambridge; while many were actually awarded during that era, they were not sufficient to cover all the fees.

Music sessions took place between 9.30 a.m. and 3.30 p.m. Alleyn wished the boys of the highest form to attend the 'Elections' at Westminster or 'Marchant Taylor's schole' to observe the boys 'exercises' and orations each year, but this was soon dropped, apparently to spare the feelings of inferiority of the Dulwich boys, as was admitted by John Allen in 1828 to the Archbishop of Canterbury when, as Visitor, he asked why it was not

done. We know little about the daily experiences of the Poor Scholars; that young Will Ashby ran away in Alleyn's own days does not prove much about their general welfare.[140] It is uncertain how much contact Alleyn himself would have had with the Poor Scholars, but the Twelfth Night play, which seems to have been a tradition of his own days at the College, surely was of his own production, recorded in laconic diary entries for January 1621 and January 1622: the first year 'att night ye 12 poor supt and ye boys made a shoe [show]', and the following year 'ye boyes playd a playe'.[141] There are a number of bleak entries in the weekly accounts for coffins for Poor Scholars, sometimes anonymous.[142]

The Poor Brethren and Sisters

Not content with his new charitable provision for pensioners at Dulwich, Alleyn founded almshouses at Bath Street, City Road, in the parish of St Giles, Cripplegate in 1620, the year after the Foundation; he recorded in his diary for 13 July that he 'layde ye first brick of ye foundacion of ye almes howses in Finsburie'. Three men and seven women were installed at the new almshouses on 30 April 1621.[143] Alleyn left money in his will for more almshouses for ten persons in both the parishes of St Botolph's and St Saviour's within two years of his death, but they were never built; the almsfolk were to have been part of the Foundation of the College of God's Gift. The Vestries (the elected parish representatives), brought an action against the Master in 1633, but had to be content with a payment of £120.

The Poor Brethren and Sisters at the College of God's Gift were appointed by churchwardens of the beneficiary parishes. Folk from 'my almshouses at London' could be included in those put forward to come to Dulwich. They should be over 60, religious, and of 'sober lives and conversation [behaviour]', neither 'infected with any noisome disease' nor 'decrepit in limbes and members'. In the nineteenth century there was some protest from St Saviour's that candidates had been turned down who suffered from rheumatic gout or had been run over by a cart.[144] Marriage or fornication would lead to expulsion. Alleyn held in mind the possibility of the return of the plague. His pensioners were not allowed to visit local houses, nor indeed the kitchen and buttery. There was the threat of the stocks if fines did not keep them in order. They brought their own goods with them, and had to declare monthly how their pension was spent. Their effects were sold at death and the proceeds divided into twelve among the others, a statute that was not rescinded until 1814.[145] They had responsibilities: by turn they had to sweep and keep clean the inner and outward courts and cloisters (or pay another to do it if they were too infirm) and weed the garden in the forecourt. The Sisters were to make the beds of the Fellows and sweep their chambers. The Master was to choose a Matron for the boys; her reward was rather dismal: she received a double share of proceeds of the effects of a dead pensioner. In 1728 Dame Pomfrey repeatedly refused to wash and comb the boys

before school in the morning, and was expelled.[146] They might keep cats, but no dogs or poultry, and were not to spoil the inner and outward courtyards with laundry or dust, water or filth. No weapons, cards or dice were allowed. A fourth offence of visiting a tavern would result in the stocks. Obedience to the Master was axiomatic.

'Ye boys played a play'. Edward Alleyn's diary entry for Twelfth Night (6 January) 1622. (Dulwich College)

Some of the Poor Brethren and Sisters in the early days failed to be picturesque charitable folk, obliged as they were to wear pensioners' gowns outside their rooms. The men were found drunk, and the women guilty of 'unquietness'; as early as 1617 John Muggleton from St Botolph's, Bishopsgate, aged 60, who had been chosen by the Rector, the Revd Stephen Gosson (the playwright and satirist turned priest and polemicist against the theatre and acting), was expelled for being drunk and marrying.[147] Alleyn records in his diary on one occasion in 1620 that all the poor except Alice Man, who was 'put by' for 'incharitye', received communion.[148] However, he was spared the sight of John Allanbee in 1631, who must have fooled the churchwardens and the Master and Warden on his admission: he was noted as a 'disorderly person', drunk and lewd, scolding and railing, abusing the Fellows, and running drunk into the Chapel at the time of Divine Service; he was quoted as 'wishing God to confound all prowd prests'. He 'would have lain with a poor sister persuading her that fornication was not a sin if both parties agreed'.[149]

The 'Assistants'

Alleyn decreed the appointment of two churchwardens of each parish as non-resident 'Assistants' to the Warden and Fellows in governing the College, bound to attend meetings and monitor the accounts every March and September and review leases on the estate, presumably to avoid the risk of inbred corruption at the College. From early days this initiative engendered animosity between the parishes and the College; the Assistants constantly suspected that the College conspired to ignore Alleyn's intentions to distribute excess monies to the parishes and to support the local almshouses there. There was also the legal complication that the Assistants were an additional feature of the Corporation added by Alleyn in the Statutes in 1626 which had not been specified in the original royal Letters Patent of 1619.

Edward Alleyn and the Estate

Alleyn plainly enjoyed the seignorial responsibilities for his lands. The fields were to fill the College larders by husbandry: milk, butter and cheese from their own cows, and mutton from their sheep; crops for bread, with barley for beer; fruits from the orchards; chickens with other domesticated fowls, and pigeons. Twenty acres of wood and coppice were to provide fuel. Controlled woodfalls [cutting] were decreed, twenty acres of coppice of ten years' growth to be cut yearly; the faggots were to be stacked in the yard and the bailiff was to issue the fuel to the members of the College. Alleyn's love of trees is shown in a tender Statute: 'Item, I especially prohibitt

and forbid, for all succeeding times to come, that any timber trees fitt for shadow or shelter, be cutt and felled in any of the groundes adjoining or lying neere to the west, south, and south-west p[ar]tes. of the said College'.[150]

The diary and other papers show Alleyn's interest in the details of running the estate. A Memorandum Book gives expenditure for a tile-kiln, mentions sawyers and thatching, and lists the cut wood used as fuel.[151] The documents show his pride in the new part he played as a country squire; the running of the estate was another element of his ideal community for him to direct and to a certain extent to initiate. The poetry and power of the stage gave way to the pleasures of farming, of supervising the harvest and the ranged sheaves of corn: 'this daye by night ther wase 140 shock [group of sheaves] sett vp and 4 acres off oates bownd & shockt bleased be ye Lo: god Amen'.[152] The reapers, often tenants obliged to help as part of their lease agreement (known since the fifteenth century as the 'bidreap'), dined with him. Their work was not always satisfactory; he writes about a certain group of ten of their 'so fowle work'.[153]

There were two teams to plough, one of five horses and the other of six oxen. Sheep were shorn, and the diary records a visit to Croydon fair to sell and buy horses, the purchase of 'implements and tools of husbandry', the stock of cows and oxen, and lists the expenses of improvements: fences, buildings and footpaths.[154] He mends glass and buys hay-rakes, seeds, a gnomon for a sundial and a 'Pewter Lymbeck 8s' for distilling. The Bankside vegetable garden that figures in his correspondence with Joan thirty years before has given way to an orchard and pleasure garden (now the site of the Gallery garden, College Gardens, Butterfly Walk and the Lawn Tennis Club); he buys roses, 'piony', asparagus, pear and pippin trees to plant.

Alleyn was undoubtedly genial and gregarious, and entertained on a lavish scale at the College, founding its reputation for open hospitality; by the time of James Hume in 1706 this 'publicke table' had become something of a scandal. Although he may not have been thought quite worthy of a knighthood, Alleyn still moved in high circles, dining with the bishops of London and Winchester, and the Archbishop of Canterbury; two Spanish Ambassadors, the famous Count Gondomar and the Marquis Inijosa;[155] Sir Julius Caesar, the Master of the Rolls, and Montague the Lord Treasurer; and Lord Admiral Howard's daughter, the Countess of Kildare. On 4 September 1622 five titled people dined with him at the College including Sir Thomas Grymes of Peckham – together with his niece Constance Donne, 'ye dean of Pales dahter', Alleyn's future second wife. The 'Waterpoet', John Taylor (1578–1653), also dined, and Alleyn subscribed a pound for his publishing venture of an intended picaresque journey to Scotland.[156] Actors from the Fortune company and others, but no playwrights, dined. Shakespeare's friend and fellow-actor John Heminges (1566–1630) visited in June 1622, possibly in connection with the First Folio edition he was compiling. Another famous guest at dinner was William Harvey (1578–1657), physician to King James and Charles I, who discovered the circulation of the blood; he prescribed some purgative pills for Joan.[157] Guests brought gifts such as a pig, a capon or cakes. Alleyn's leases often included with the rent 'good fat and sweet capons at Easter', or once 'upon the last daye of August one good and sweete Buck of the Season'. A relative from the country, Elizabeth Socklen, sent 'a littel cheise' in 1612.[158] That he still enjoyed ceremonious entertainments is shown by his visit with Joan to the Lord Mayor's Show in the City and his paying sixpence to attend the tilting at Whitehall.[159] He records frequent gifts of money to the needy or the imprisoned.

Marriage to Constance, daughter of John Donne

On 28 June 1623, after 30 years of marriage, Joan Alleyn died at the age of 52. She was buried in the Chapel two days later, on the south side, near to the high altar, as recorded in the College Register.[160] Within six months of the death of Joan, on 3 December 1623 at the age of 57 Alleyn married at St Giles, Camberwell, the 20-year-old Constance, eldest daughter of John Donne (1572–1631), Dean of St Paul's, the famous poet and divine. The rediscovery of this connection between two famous lives was made by Daniel Lysons in the late eighteenth century.[161] Alleyn heard Donne preach at Camberwell three times between 1 January 1619 and 14 July 1622. They went together to dine with the Grymes family at Peckham on the second occasion, and met at dinner with the Archbishop of Canterbury at Croydon Palace on 21 September 1622.[162] The marriage was thought a peculiar alliance, particularly as Alleyn was six years older than his bride's own father. John Chamberlain wrote to Dudley Carleton, 'the straungest match in mine opinion

Funeral Certificate of Joan Alleyn, with arms of Alleyn and Henslowe, July 1623. (© College of Arms, London. MS 1.22, f. 81v)

is that Allen the old player hath lately married a young daughter of the Deane of Paules, wᶜʰ I doubt [suspect] will deminish his charitie and devotion towards his two hospitals'. [163] Chamberlain made a serious point about the marriage being a potential distraction from Alleyn's fortune and income being spent on his endowments, as marriage settlements and legacies were very costly.

Donne had a 'peculiar tenderness' towards Constance, his eldest child; since the death of his wife Anne when Constance was 16, she had acted as his housekeeper. Donne referred to her as his 'Con', and a letter of his to Sir Henry Wotton of 1611 calls her an 'affectionate companion above stairs and servant below stairs'. [164] Alleyn's neighbouring Lord of the Manor in Peckham – today's 'Lordship Lane' recalls the boundary between the two estates – was Sir Thomas Grymes (d. 1644), 'haberdasher and citizen', whom we have already met as a signatory of the Foundation Deed. Grymes was married to Margaret, the sister of Donne's wife Anne; they were daughters of Sir George More of Loseley Park. Grymes was Member of Parliament for Surrey in 1623. He and Alleyn seem to have enjoyed cordial relations: in a letter Grymes refers to him as 'his very loving Nephew', and writes to him offering 'the best friendly office', in other words his influence with the Commissioners for New Buildings. He also seems to have trusted Alleyn financially. [165] He and his wife are known to have been kind to Donne's children when he died. Constance was perhaps a favourite, as they called their younger daughter after her. Donne's will of 1631 calls Grymes 'my very worthy friend and kind brother-in-law'. [166] Grymes most likely gave away Constance in the wedding at Camberwell on 3 December 1623, as Donne lay desperately ill, his own subject in *Devotions* (1624), the book of meditations in sickness in which he hears the bell toll rather than peal.

Donne urged the couple to marry speedily as gossip was spreading, saying that, 'yᵉ world took large knowledge of itt'. At dinner at the Deanery at St Paul's on 21 October Donne had met with Alleyn and Grymes to discuss the marriage settlements; Donne agreed to pay £500, and Alleyn the same amount on his death. Grymes urged Alleyn to increase the amount. [167] We know little about the marriage, but there is no convincing evidence for Edmund Gosse's assertion that it 'was a match into which sentiment did not enter', nor for Gosse's description of Alleyn as 'an eccentric and grasping old widower'. [168] However, there is certainly evidence that Alleyn quarrelled with Donne about money, and that Donne looked down on him. Constance appears to have become estranged from her father, who begins to call her 'my poor daughter' in his correspondence. Alleyn drafted a long and bitter letter to Donne in 1625, on the

John Donne, dressed in his shroud to deliver his last sermon. Frontispiece engraved by Martin Droeshout for *Deaths Duell*, 1632. (Dulwich College)

back of another letter to himself recommending a Poor Brother. [169] It is hard to say, but as the draft was much revised and was preserved by Alleyn, the letter was probably sent. Gosse calls it 'boisterous' and a 'stormy reproach'. [170] It expresses Alleyn's puzzlement at Donne's 'hard dealing' towards him, and complains of his own 'so grav a cause of discontent' and 'many unkind passages' [exchanges] between the two men in the first year or so after the marriage took place; Donne had apparently let him down in a promise to lend him money, and Alleyn recalls a violent quarrel at Donne's house. He recounts how Donne, after dinner in his parlour on 21 October 1623, told him it was his intention to bestow 'all yᵉ benefet of yʳ pryme Leas[e]', worth £500, on Constance, and that Alleyn on his return home promised Constance to make this settlement up to £1,500. Alleyn pressed Donne to show 'the comon curtesie afforded to a frend' in lending money that was not in use. Alleyn refers to this as 'unuseful monies'; such loans among families and friends were common at the time. Alleyn, 'presently [immediately] being inflamed', lost his temper, speaking 'passionat words', claiming that that he must 'bee branded either for a foole or a knave'. Donne next, also 'enflamed', said of his promise of his five hundred pounds, 'itt was false & a lye!' Alleyn thereupon told Donne that were he not in holy orders and that were they both thirty years younger (hinting at Donne's rakish early career), the affair would have ended in a duel. Alleyn complains how he has been denied the courtesy of the Dean's household on his visits to the City. As for Donne, the prejudice of the day against actors may have influenced him, although he had been in his youth 'a great frequenter of plays'; he presumably saw Alleyn in *Tamburlaine*, as he mentions the Scythian shepherd (Tamburlaine) and Bajazeth's cage in a poem, 'The Calme'. [171] Alleyn's letter also mentions grievances of Constance against her father: childbed linen, interestingly, was promised but was not forthcoming; a 'little nagg' she wished for had been sent to her brother, young John Donne, an undergraduate at Oxford; a diamond ring with three stones in it, given to her father at his request, was promised to be returned, but had not been. It seems that Alleyn and Constance did expect a child, as Alleyn tells Donne that his daughter Lucy has come to help as nurse, and Alleyn suggests that Donne should be paying her upkeep. If so, however, the child in question did not survive.

The most interesting detail of this extraordinary document, perhaps, is Alleyn's assertion that – in the light of the many parts he played on the stage – he is the 'playn man' that Donne called him: 'I desire allways so to be for I thank god I never could disgwise in my life'. Alleyn refers to his own 'illiterat playn[n]ess' and appears to attack Donne's intellectual sophistication, his love of elaborate and learned English: 'I am too ould now to lerne retorick of yᵉ curioust schoole in Cristendom, my hart and tong must goe to gether'; this vaunt of his own sincerity and trustworthiness also betrays a sense of his inferior education. [172] By 1626, however, after Alleyn assigned to Grymes for Constance before his death the leases of the Unicorn in Southwark, and the Barge, the Bell and the Cock on Bankside, there appears to have been some measure of reconciliation between father and daughter. [173] After Alleyn's death Constance remarried, to Samuel Harvey, a man of roughly her own age and of good family who lived at Aldborough (or Albury) Hatch in Essex; she gave birth to three sons. Here John Donne died in 1630, and Constance herself was dead by 1636. Donne's funeral report gives Constance's name, but mentions only her second husband, not Alleyn. [174]

Alleyn's will and death

As well as being the proprietor of the Bear Garden and mounting his horse to ride to Greenwich to discuss the day's baiting with the King, Alleyn frequently rode to London, crossing the river by boat; in town he visited the Red Bull theatre at the upper end of St John's Street (where he appears to have had a financial interest in the

takings) [175] and taverns such as the Cardinal's Hat and the famous Mermaid in Bread Street, where he dined with five actors from the Fortune after Queen Anne's funeral in 1619. [176] An intimate friend whom he often visited was a Lady Clarke, whose second husband had died in 1607, and to whom he took silk stockings. [177] The diary records, among the College items of sugar loaves and copies of the catechism, payments for luxurious items to silk-weavers and goldsmiths and for bottles of muscatel. He was something of an aesthete, buying 'crymson sattine for yᵉ lining off a boke', and also something of a dandy, in spite of Cartwright's testimony about his dressing like one of his pensioners: his new clothing in these years included a beaver hat with taffeta lining, a satin embroidered hat-band, orange-tawny silk for a nightcap and pairs of silk stockings 'which Hath bene knitt for me': 'watshod' [waterproof], 'rose collored', 'popinjay' [(parrot) green], 'ash-colourd', and 'se[a]water green'. [178] After 1622 the entries in the College Register are no longer in Alleyn's hand, suggesting perhaps some withdrawal from direction of the College. He seems to have been a healthy man, though he sickened once at Lady Clarke's and occasionally records examination of his water by doctors. [179]

In 1626, the second year of Charles I's reign, Alleyn bought from George Cole, who was probably a London barrister, [180] an extensive estate in remote Yorkshire at Simondstone, Aysgarth, near Hawes. [181] Buying an estate with several farms and houses so far north at this stage of his career, even for investment, seems capricious; perhaps it represented a wish to associate himself with his maternal latitude in the north of England, although the ancient seat of Margaret Townley's great family in Lancashire lay further west. On a visit on horseback to take possession of this estate he was taken ill. On 14 October 1626 he was said to be 'towardes a recovery'; [182] however, on 13 November, being 'sick in body but of sound mind', at the age of 60 he wrote a will:

> first and principally I commend my soul to Almighty God, my merciful Creator, and to Jesus Christ, my most loving Saviour and Redeemer, in whom and by whose merits I only trust to be saved, and made partaker of everlasting life: and my body I will to the earth, from whence it came, without any vain funeral pomp, or show, to be interred in the quire of that chapel, which God of his goodness hath caused me to erect, and dedicate to the honor of my Saviour, by the name of Christs Chappell in Gods Gift College, hereto by me founded in Dulwich aforesaid.

He made provision for ten new almshouses at St Botolph's and St Saviour's; in his mind these and the City Road almshouses were to be three satellite houses to the College. Most of his property went to the College, including his books and musical instruments,[183] but a sizeable legacy of £1,500 in ready money went to his widow Constance, more than originally promised, together with an extra £100 and jewels. He changed his mind about the taverns, the Barge, the Cock and the Bell, and left them to his executors Sir Nicholas Carew and Sir Thomas Grymes, who in fact sold them to raise the money for Constance's bequest. His cousin, Thomas Alleyn, the first Master, received £50.

The list of bequests to the College begins with a fine piece of symbolism, giving in trust to future Masters and to the College two heraldic objects: the first was his signet ring with his coat of arms, 'to be worn by the Master and his successors', consigning the responsibility for the immortality of the name of Alleyn and for the Alleynian ideal for ever – in the words of the Victorian school song,

> *Quotquot annos, quotquot menses,*
> *Fertur principum memoria.*
>
> [Let the memory of our founder
> be carried the months and years to come]

The second was the metal College seal, on which Alleyn's crest, surmounting the arms, is also engraved. The crest (described in Chapter One) flourishes a human heart, held aloft by a 'cubit arm' (the forearm, in heraldic terms), said to be 'issuant from flames of fire'; in other words compassion and charity were to flame high and bright in perpetuity. The will specifies wainscots, hangings (possibly the Flemish tapestries bought in 1619), linen and the furniture of the College, including the six bedsteads and pewter chamber pots of the Poor

Edward Alleyn, 1626, detail of hand over heart, with signet ring. (© Dulwich College)

Scholars. The rents of old Blew House were dedicated to the poor of St Botolph's, Bishopsgate. His executors received all his new Yorkshire properties.[184]

The College commissioned a splendid full-length portrait of Alleyn, soberly dressed but with some style: the large black felt hat, a ruff with lace-edged vandykes, gloves and elegant shoes; the right-hand glove has been removed to emphasise the red sardonyx intaglio signet ring on his little finger with the coat of arms conspicuous towards us.[185] The tradition voiced in the eighteenth century was that this was a posthumous portrait: 'the resemblance of his face is said to have been drawn when he lay dead in his coffin';[186] it has been remarked, however, that he does not look as old as his 60 years.

Alleyn died on 25 November, and was buried two days later in the choir, at the heart of his chapel, and close to his choristers.[187]

3

THROUGH COMMONWEALTH
& RESTORATION
1626–1704

… the slender prologue of poor annals.

– F. R. MACKENZIE, 1912

Founder's kin: 'of my blood and sirname' – The Civil War and the Commonwealth, 1642–59 – The Restoration and after: the Fellows – John Reading, Organist – Bequest of William Cartwright junior – The Poor Scholars – The Poor Brethren and Sisters – Income and expenditure: the Estate – The Sheldonian Visitation – The beneficiary parishes

From the first decades after Alleyn's death until the end of the seventeenth century – and in effect up until the reforms of 1857 – the history of God's Gift College can hardly be said to be inspiring, nor does it have a great deal of antiquarian or romantic appeal. Considered strictly as an institution, Alleyn's College did not prosper significantly. Alleyn's generous hope was for the quiet good progress of the cleverest of the Poor Scholars to follow up the education they received at the College with a university degree, subsidised by grants from the income from the Fortune theatre and from his investments in land, to better themselves and society with 'godliness and good learning'.[1] There is significantly little information about the Poor Scholars and the education they received, but plenty of records of spite, bickering and worse among the officers of the College. Alleyn by a statute set up the College Register to record (in addition to the routine Chapel entries of christenings, marriages and burials) crises or difficulties rather than positive attainments; since bad news is perhaps historically more interesting, and since mostly negative events at the College were written down or passed down over the years in perhaps distorted memories, we have a chronicle of symbolic calamities such as the College steeple and tower falling to the ground and of Cromwell's soldiers making bullets out of the lead coffins below the Chapel floor. Alleyn must have hoped for a chronicle of serene decades of an ideal charitable community living in mutual harmony, with devout and musical ceremonies in Christ's Chapel at the heart of his Foundation; our next three chapters must struggle to point to more progress than what Mackenzie described as the 'slender prologue of poor annals' to the larger history of the new Foundation that began in 1857.[2]

*

Founder's kin: 'of my blood and sirname'

The chronological list of Masters of the College, inscribed in gold on a panel above the mantel of today's Board Room at the New College, is headed exclusively by 15 men called Alleyn or Allen up until the year 1858; this can still cause surprise by its reminder of Alleyn's original dictate that the Master and Warden were in perpetuity to be of his blood and surname, or of his surname alone if this was not possible. Four of the five first Masters were of Alleyn's own family; this dynasty ended in 1686, though the issue of 'Founder's kin' continued to complicate elections.

The first major problem faced by the Founder's kinsmen Thomas Alleyn (the Master) and Matthias Alleyn (the Warden) after he died in 1626 was the Statute providing for resident 'Chanters', to be Junior Fellows, as described in the last chapter: the College's income alone would not support them, and it is possible that the Senior Fellows also resented the idea. Educationally, however, it would surely have benefited the boys. The Fellows took legal advice in 1627, and were told that since the Letters Patent did not specify Junior Fellows, they could not be appointed.[3] The rules for Alleyn's 'Dividend' – his stipulation that after £100 per annum had been placed in the treasure chest for contingencies, any surplus income was to be divided up once a year – were not strictly followed; the income almost at once declined, although there was to be one single distribution in 1628.[4] This Dividend was not to come properly into force until the next century. The failure of the rents from the Fortune theatre, which Alleyn presumably anticipated would provide a considerable revenue, explains the shortfall: Alleyn calculated the annual income of the College at £800, but by 1637 the arrears from the Fortune were £128.5s.7d. and by 1649 were

£1,041.1s.5d.[5] The theatre continued to decline, and rents were unpaid or came in late; with the collapse of the entertainment industry under the Puritans in 1644 and the death of King Charles I on the scaffold in 1649, the situation worsened. New tenants absurdly sought to justify their non-payment of rents by claiming they were due not to the College but to Edward Alleyn himself and his other heirs, which it took an expensive law case to overturn. The College meanwhile paid twice for paving at the Fortune site in the 1650s. It was not until 1666 that rents from properties on the site began once again to support the College;[6] by 1662 there were nineteen new 'messuages' on the site.[7] Shortly after Alleyn's death, portions of the Dulwich estate previously assigned for farm land to support the College were leased, violating the Statutes; it is thought that this may have been on the advice of Archbishop William Laud, in his capacity as Visitor.[8] Leases continued to be issued with a clause including a day's work on the College land with a team of plough and men, and thus some College fields were still in cultivation.

Alleyn himself had been litigious – it was a litigious age – but the years of depressing and expensively protracted drawn-out law cases that marked the College's early centuries began in earnest in 1632, when the Churchwardens of St Botolph's, Bishopsgate, and St Giles, Camberwell, took the College to court for non-payment of allowances to their thirty 'out-members' (pensioners whom Alleyn had intended to share in the foundation, and whom he had intended to receive sixpence a week with a gown every two years), and for the failure of the College to build the stipulated ten new almshouses. It was shown that the College could not afford the building work, and the parishes settled for £120.[9] St Botolph's also complained that their Assistants had been opposed by the College Fellows when they attended the two annual meetings, and had even been refused payment for their horse hire and dinner. They said that the Fellows kept horses at the College's expense, and that by their selfishness the poor of the parishes were utterly defrauded and wronged; thus began a wrangling dialogue that was to continue until the 'New Scheme' of 1857, and which rumbled on for a half-century after that.

It is easy to see rights on both sides of the argument over the intentions of Alleyn's bequest, and especially easy to sympathise with the parishes' resentment when the College became so wealthy from the end of the eighteenth century, with the increasing value of suburban dormitory estates. The Assistants and the Corporations of the parishes questioned the College's actions and accounts, and brought lawsuits. Archbishops issued injunctions and counter-injunctions. In this early instance, William Laud in 1636 decreed that the Churchwardens should attend each Audit of the accounts, reminding the officers of the College of 'that duty which your ffounder hath laid upon them'.[10] The Fellows themselves could be very difficult on the occasions of these joint meetings with the Assistants, held in March and September; on several occasions during the rest of the century some of them refused to sign the accounts, whether from principle or contrariness is unknown, and were suspended and even expelled for refusing to do so.

The career of a College Fellow tended to be both brief and unsatisfactory. The First Fellow, the Revd Joseph Reding, left on Alleyn's death, and the College was thus without a resident Preacher until September 1628. The first one to be appointed under the two Alleyns, the Revd Robert Welles, was expelled in 1629 after hardly more than a year for 'divers misdemeanours' and for not following the Statutes. Truculence among the Fellows was quite common over the next centuries: the Revd Simon Mace, who was elected First Fellow in 1635, left the following year to be chaplain on the royal pinnace *Greyhound*; on his return to the College in September 1637 he made trouble for Matthias Alleyn, calling him a 'hypocrite' and 'Cussener' [cheat]; he was expelled on 30 May 1639. It was recorded against Mace that he took some boys to the alehouse, where they got drunk, and told them that Latin and singing would do no good for them; he challenged John Alleyn to a fight; moreover, at dinner he scandalised the company by saying that the Lord Archbishop of York was the most 'devilisht plotter of villainy in the world' and would make a 'brave pope'.[11]

Of Thomas Alleyn, the first Master, we know little; he was a barber-surgeon, and must have still on occasion practised his profession, as a document records that he supplied medicines to Lord Conway in 1626–7.[12] When Thomas died in 1631, he was succeeded by Matthias. At the same time a second Thomas Alleyn (another cousin of Edward Alleyn, this one from Willen in Buckinghamshire) was elected Warden without a lottery (see Chapter One); he was now the nearest in kin to the Founder except for John Alleyn, son of Matthias. John Alleyn, however, was a married man, and so by Alleyn's statute was barred from the post. In 1643 Thomas, after eleven years as Warden and one as Master, agreed to resign in favour of this John Alleyn, and signed a weary declaration that he was prepared to give up 'the great burthen, care and government of the said Colledge'. King Charles I sent a warrant from Oxford to accept the resignation and to elect John Alleyn in his place. In the event, though, John Alleyn did not take up the position at that time, preferring to follow his calling as a surgeon,[13] and Thomas Alleyn kept his post as Master until his death in 1668. Raph [*sic*] Alleyn, another surgeon, became Warden in 1642, claiming Founder's kin, which was unproven; he succeeded Thomas as Master on his death, and held the post until his own death in 1678. Together, Thomas and Raph Alleyn, as Master and Warden, stood their ground at the College through the very troublesome years of the Commonwealth.

The same John Alleyn, the son of Matthias, re-appeared at the College after the Restoration in 1668 with a royal 'mandamus' [written command] from Charles II dispensing with the objection to his married status and commanding his election as Warden. [14] To this the College dignitaries assented, but despite written assurances by the Visitor, Archbishop Gilbert Sheldon (1598–1677), that he would not interfere to prevent it, [15] they would not allow Alleyn's wife, Lucia, to be admitted. The lady in fact withdrew, and indeed died the following month; she was buried in the Chapel. Thereupon the King wrote to say that John Alleyn had obtained the mandamus on the basis of his statement that the first Master and Warden had been married men, but he had since taken advice and found out that the statute prescribing celibacy had been subsequently instated. The King therefore declared the election void, and recommended one Elias Alleyn, a maker of mathematical instruments. Meanwhile, however, the 'court' of the College, had already elected John, as he was of Founder's kin. [16]

John Alleyn, who in turn became Master in 1678, was said to be skilled in music; he received an Hon. DCL [Doctor of Law] degree at Oxford in 1670, presumably on the recommendation of Archbishop Sheldon, who was Chancellor of the University until 1669. [17] In 1673 John Alleyn was accused of embezzling thirty shillings, and the receipt of the Archbishop's letter to the Master on the subject in a meeting produced a 'thunderclapp of ill language and opprobrious terms … fitter for a Billingsgate shrew than for a master of a colledge'. [18]

The same Elias Alleyn (Charles II's preferred candidate) was in fact elected Warden in 1677 – and proved a bad hat: accused of defrauding the College of £10 in 1680, he refused to appear at the Audit, and it was later discovered that he had razed out the entry from the Register, 'surreptitiously' taking the book out of the Treasury chamber. [19] The Archbishop, appealed to by the College, ruled his original election as Warden void, but Elias Alleyn produced an order from the King, later proved to be a forgery, calling for his reinstatement, which was temporarily effected. The Archbishop was astonished, and a letter from the King, which scarcely concealed his royal impatience at being 'often troubled in this matter', endorsed Elias's dismissal. [20] In the same year (1680), the Revd James Alleyn was appointed as Preacher, but

turned out to be a notorious drunkard and base 'whore-master'; the next year he appealed to the Visitor to remove himself without the scandal of expulsion; his resignation was allowed. [21] Alleyn's noble bequest had deteriorated into tawdriness and turbulence.

In 1635 the zealous ritualist Archbishop Laud made his formal 'Visitation' (the official report as Visitor) to the College. He sharply criticised the Chapel services and decreed that the boys were to wear surplices. The Fellows were also to wear their surplices, and moreover were to sing; or if they would not sing, they must pay someone to sing for them. The same year Richard Crane was paid five shillings for a quarter of a year's singing in the Chapel, but this was a practice that does not seem to have been continued. [22] The Master, Matthias Alleyn, was openly admonished for lowering the High Church tone of the Chapel: Laud ordered that 'the Bason and two candlesticks which the Master confesseth hee tooke away from the altar and keepeth at his chamber in the said Colledg be placed there again'; Matthias Alleyn was no longer to keep a horse at the College's expense; it was not 'seemly'. [23] In 1637 the College Fellows had had to borrow money at interest to maintain the Poor Brethren and Sisters. [24] The collapse of the Chapel steeple in 1638 must have seemed symbolic.

Laud, noting the 'sad ruine and decay' of the buildings, took the admirably drastic step of closing the College for six months from 10 October, dissolving the 'Society' to pay for repairs. The Fellows received no emoluments, but for the half year the pensioners were paid two shillings a week. [25] Matthias died in 1642 and the second Thomas Alleyn, thought to have been a capable Warden, succeeded him. By 1642 he had brought the College to a credit balance of £44. [26]

The Civil War and Commonwealth, 1642–59

Written records of the College during the Civil War are very sparse, and some details come from perhaps not very reliable hearsay a hundred years later. Though the Master and Warden remained at the College throughout, all the Fellows, except for the Revd James Mead, departed at the outset of the war; they were styled 'delinquents' by Parliament, and were said to have left to join the King's army, or so Daniel Lysons was told by the Fellows much later when he recorded his visit to the College in his *Environs of London* (1792). The Master and Warden were summoned to the Bear Inn in Southwark by the Committee of Safety for the County of Surrey on 25 March 1644, in order to supply an account of the College, and were then prohibited from electing Fellows. [27] However, receipts survive from 1646 for taxed contributions from College funds to the King's cause: ten shillings for Sir Thomas Fairfax; three shillings for the relief of Basing House (where Inigo Jones had taken shelter with other Royalists and was eventually captured); and two shillings towards the disbanding of forces after the Battle of Newbury.[28] Lysons wrote as follows:

> During the civil wars, Dulwich College had its full share of the general confusion; the Master and Warden did not take an active part, but the fellows were in arms for the king; in consequence of which, their fellowships were sequestered, and a school-master and usher only (Stephen Street, and Edmund Colley) were appointed by the ruling powers … In 1647, Fairfax's army being then at Putney and Fulham, a company of soldiers, under the command of Capt. Atkinson, was quartered in the college, for which they received the sum of 19s. and 8d., a poor recompence for the destruction of their organ, and other outrages which the soldiers committed. There is a tradition yet current in the college, that they took up the leaden coffins in the chapel, and melted them into bullets.[29]

Ten soldiers were billeted under Captain Atkinson.[30] In 1645 Parliament, under a scheme called the Committee for Plundered Ministers, appointed two teachers for the Poor Scholars, as mentioned by Lysons; in fact there were in turn three Parliamentary Preachers, including John Crofts, described as a 'godly and orthodox divine',[31] and a Schoolmaster, the Revd Edmund Colby, but no Usher, to replace the four 'deserted' Fellows. As will be seen, the teaching of the Poor Scholars under this regime must have been in fact the most effective between Alleyn's death and 1857 – certainly if we measure it by the number of boys admitted to Oxford and Cambridge for this period. For obvious Puritan reasons no Organist was appointed, and the post lapsed until 1669, after the Restoration. Lysons mentions the successful appeals that the two Parliamentary appointees made to the College for a grant for 'double diet', on the grounds that there were formerly four Fellows.[32] Thomas and Raph Alleyn (Master and Warden, respectively) refused, however, to pay salaries to the Parliamentary non-Fellows, and were arrested by the Serjeant at Arms (following threatened arrest) and brought before the Committee of the House of Commons on 20 September 1644, and forced to give in.[33] On trial the two were accused of 'alienating' [transferring] lands worth £200 per annum for their own use, of aiding and abetting the late King, and of putting up the Fellows to serve in the Royalist army; both were subsequently released. The Revd Colby, falsely accused by one Poor Sister of an affair with another, was dismissed in 1658. The third Preacher appointed by the Committee was the Revd John Skingle, who served from 1649 and, like Colby, was 'discharged' in 1658, in the month of his death, when his goods and books were listed in an inventory.[34]

By 1658, then, the College's Parliamentary appointees had all disappeared. The Master and Warden had petitioned the Committee to restore their personal right to elect Fellows; their request was firmly rebuffed, the Lord Protector replacing the Commission of 'the late Archbishop of Canterbury' by one of his own,[35] and the College now reverted to the electoral process of Alleyn's original formula.[36] The College plate was pawned between 1644 and 1652;[37] Young surmises that this was from prudence rather than necessity, but also records a tradition that much if not all of it was sold to support the King.[38] An Audit was made, and the Fellows were disallowed horses and 'double diet'. It was at this time that the Dulwich villagers complained to the Parliamentary Committee that the College had long been without an able minister and a 'painfull [painstaking] scholmaster'.[39] The College's problems did not abate with the Restoration of the monarchy.

The Restoration and after: the Fellows

Unlike the era of Alleyn's own days at the College, for which the Diary serves as record (for a limited number of years) and for which there are many surviving letters and documents, the latter part of the seventeenth century is by comparison obscure from lack of documentation. The Register and the Weekly Accounts record premature decay of the fabric of the College: in 1656 a surveyor reported alarming damage and rot to buttresses and beams, and 'a great part of the Colledge brick wall of the lodginge chambers in the fore court fell downe'.[40] Worse was to follow in 1661: 'five chimneys, the garret, the picture gallery and fower of the old women's roomes fell downe'.[41] In 1703 'the Colledge porch with ye Treasury Chamber, &c. tumbled to ye ground'.[42] The Plague struck in 1665–6, and the Register notes the deaths of one Poor Scholar, a cook and a kitchen-boy.[43] However, in 1689 after William of Orange's victory in Ireland at the Battle of the Boyne the College celebrated 'the Kings return' with a bonfire and beer.[44]

The Fellows in the Restoration period at God's Gift College tended to be colourful but deplorable. The Revd Benjamin Bynes, appointed Preacher in 1689, was originally a Poor Scholar from Southwark, whom the College had awarded in 1675–6 part-maintenance at Queens' College, Cambridge, with an 'exhibition' of £18 per annum for four years, and £20 for the four years following until he took orders.[45] This return of pupil as Fellow, elected as a former Poor Scholar without a lottery, realised Alleyn's hopes for the Poor Scholars to serve the College in turn when they graduated. However, Bynes was expelled after just fourteen months, for refusing to sign the Warden's accounts and the order for payments,

British School, *John Reading*. (© Dulwich College)

by the Visitor, Archbishop William Sancroft.[46] As mentioned above, refusal by the Fellows to sign the accounts and accusations of 'missaplication [sic] of yᵉ revenue'[47] were common occurrences down the years, and this seems to indicate that there was reason for suspicion in the conduct of the accounts rather than just contrariness in the Fellows who refused to sign.

The Revd Francis Brockett, who was the Schoolmaster from 1662 until his death in 1680, was an unruly man in holy orders. According to a warrant for his arrest on evidence given against him by Thomas Bowdler of Camberwell in October 1677, he used the Poor Scholars as if they were his bloodhounds: the deponent 'doth goe in feare of looseing his life or receiving some bodily harme'. Bowdler had been 'violently assauted & wounded by severall of [Brockett's] schollers', and

Brockett was alleged to have threatened 'to teare the man in pieces or words to that effect', and indeed to have actually set some of the boys on him. Brockett somehow managed to retain his post.[48] In 1695 the Preacher, the Revd Richard Prichard, was suspended by Archbishop John Tillotson for refusing to sign the accounts; he had been at the College for five years – evidently an unhappy experience for all: the Warden, Thomas Alleyn, threatened to pull him 'out by yᵉ Heels' if he ever again mounted the pulpit.[49]

The Master made a formal complaint about Prichard, and when the Archbishop asked Prichard for a statement, he sent in a petition of twenty articles, pointing out the failures of the Master and Warden to follow the Statutes, many of them very petty, and deposing that the Warden, Thomas Alleyn, was a man of 'mean education'. The Library at the College, he said, contained few books and 'would not yield to be sold for ten shillings'. The 'articles' Prichard sent to the Archbishop represent at their nadir the antagonism and petty squabbles between the Fellows on the one hand and the Master and Warden on the other; they make unpleasant reading.[50] Prichard's taunt about the College Library may have been provoked by the Master's refusal to allow the Fellows a key to the room where some of the most valuable books were shelved.[51]

John Reading, Organist

The Fourth Fellow or Organist from 1700 to 1702 was the composer John Reading (1686–1764).[52] John Reading's father of the same name, who was the Organist of Winchester College, was also a composer. Surprisingly, his son was only 14 or 15 when he was appointed. He was one of the famous Children of the Chapel Royal, singing for the great Dr John Blow, with whom he also studied; it was quite normal for the boys after their voices broke to leave with a testimonial pledging their ability to undertake the musical duties of any cathedral. The Chapel Royal was formerly the King's Chapel, whose services Edward Alleyn decreed were to be the model in his own day for Christ's Chapel.

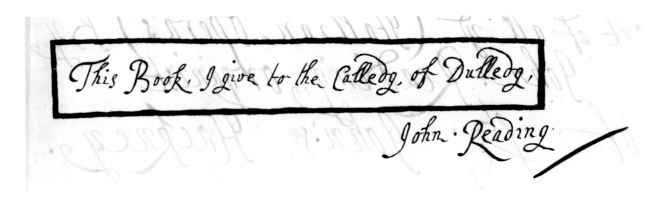

This Book, I give to the Colledg. of Dulledg.

John . Reading

Aria in John Reading's hand: 'In the Opera of Calypso, sung by Mrs Margaretta', for two violins and a Tenor, by J. E. Galliard, 1712. (Dulwich College, MS 86)

Reading left the College after just two years to become choirmaster at Lincoln Cathedral, and spent most of a long and successful career as organist in London churches. He must have held affectionate memories of the College where in his youth he had his first post and thought more highly of the institution at that period than historians of the College, since he bequeathed to it twelve bound volumes of manuscript music. The manuscripts included twenty unpublished organ voluntaries of his own composition, a mode he developed with conspicuously greater sophistication; there are also many transcripts of works by his contemporaries and immediate predecessors, including Henry Purcell. These precious volumes, with their calligraphic musical notations, contain anthems, airs from operas, music for the theatres, and popular songs. Each book he inscribed, 'This Book I give to the Colledg of Dulledg. John Reading'. The bequest included two remarkable printed books of music – his own publication, *A Book of New Songs (after the Italian Manner)* of 1710, and Handel's *Atalanta* of 1736.[53]

*

Bequest of William Cartwright junior

In 1687 a famous Restoration actor, William Cartwright the younger, who published the description of Alleyn's humble way of life among his pensioners quoted in the previous chapter, died at the age of eighty. His father, William Cartwright the elder, had been an actor; as a member of the Lord Admiral's and Prince Henry's Men, he had of course been a colleague of Edward Alleyn.[54] On four occasions between 1617 and 1622 Alleyn recorded in his Diary the name of the elder Cartwright as his guest to dinner at the College. Cartwright was also one of ten actors who in 1618 rented the Fortune from Alleyn as 'sharers', for £200 per annum and 'two rundlettes [small casks] of wyne, the one sack [Spanish white] and the other claret' of a stated value each Christmas.[55] His son became in due course from 1663 an actor in the His Majesty's Company at the Theatre Royal, Drury Lane, where his great roles included Shakespeare's Falstaff, Brabantio in *Othello*, heroic roles in Dryden, and three of Jonson's most enjoyable characters: Sir Epicure Mammon in Jonson's *Alchemist*, Corbaccio in *Volpone*, and Morose in *Epicæne, or the Silent Woman*; he was admired by

John Greenhill, *William Cartwright the younger*, c.1665.
(© Dulwich Picture Gallery)

Pepys.[56] To the College he bequeathed the income from an estate, but also a considerable number of paintings, mostly by contemporary London or Dutch painters, and of uneven quality. The 77 canvases now at Dulwich Picture Gallery are in fact the sole surviving collection of a middle-class man of his day. In 1752 the pictures were said to have been 'neglected in a garret' and havoc made among them by a College butler. In the nineteenth century, after the New College was built in 1870, they were kept in the Master's apartments in the South Block, and Canon Carver referred to them as the 'House Collection'.[57]

Cartwright's collection consisted of religious paintings, landscapes, seascapes, still-lives and portraits. The latter included the poets Michael Drayton and Richard Lovelace (and other members of his family); members of the royal family, including the admired portrait by Marcus Gheeraerts the younger (DPG 389) said to be of Elizabeth, 'the Winter Queen', eldest daughter of James I, wife of the Elector Palatine and thus Queen of Bohemia (see Chapter Two); and the famous series of theatrical portraits. Among this latter group was Richard Burbage, identified in Cartwright's handwritten catalogue as 'mr burbig his head',[58] possibly a self-portrait; a romantic image of Henslowe's actor Nathan Field; and a colourful three-quarter portrait of Cartwright's own father. There was also an interesting album of drawings and an engraving of London with the 'City Cavalcade on the Lord-Mayor's Day'.[59]

Cartwright had pursued a second career as a prosperous bookseller in Turnstile Alley when the theatres were closed, and left the College a number of Quarto playtexts and some of the most valuable books in the Fellows' Library, among them the Mercator's *Atlas* of 1635 and two of the three volumes that make up the First Folio of Shakespeare's Works, the *Comedies* and *Histories*.[60] The bequest also included his silver tankards, a Turkey carpet and damask linens. The books were catalogued by the Warden, and were originally arranged on special shelves in the locked chamber next to the Dining Room, with the pictures. The legacy was vexed by problems over Cartwright's will or 'Resolucion', and appeal was made to the Archbishop of Canterbury; lawsuits were filed against Cartwright's servants, Francis and Jane Johnson, who were found to have pawned some playbooks from the collection (such as would of course now be priceless) for twenty shillings, and to have made off with other articles.[61] Francis Johnson was imprisoned in the Fleet.[62] Cartwright asked to be buried in the Chapel, but the College had to insist that this was contrary to the statutes, and he was buried instead in St Paul's, Covent Garden.[63] His bequest should probably be interpreted as an affectionate tribute to Alleyn himself and to his father's friendship; there is no evidence of the younger Cartwright having any contact with the College of his day, nor indeed of a continued connection of the College with the theatrical world.[64]

The Poor Scholars

When the diarist John Evelyn visited the College in 1675 he perhaps sensed a pervasive low morale, the consequence of wrangling Fellows and of education that became more cavalier as the century drew to a close, which jaundiced his account of the College; significantly, he makes no mention of the Poor Scholars:

> I went to see Dulwich Colledge, being the pious foundation of one Allen … The Chappell is pretty, the rest of the Hospitall very ill contriv'd; it yet maintains divers poore of both sexes. 'Tis in a melancholy part of Camerwell parish.[65]

One wonders, in the light of thin documentation for this period, how the Poor Scholars coped with the poor quality and rapid turnover of many of the Fellows. A solitary boarder arrived in 1630: 'Sr John Rivers broughte his sonn to the Colledge to be commoner';[66] no further record is made of him. The Register lists grants of shoes and shirts to the boys; it records mending their shoes, but not their academic progress. It is true that there is an entry in the Register giving 'the fform of Westminister [sic] School' with the course of lessons followed there 'as declared by Mr ffrowick that had been Usher under

Dr Busby for severall yeares 29th of May 1684', which could be taken as evidence that ostensibly they were aware of their responsibilities.[67] Medicines, including purgatives and curatives for 'ye Itch' for the boys, figure in the accounts, and there are gloomier expenses for coffins and for a shroud. Green rugs were obtained for their beds in 1674, a gross of brass buttons for their coats in 1678, and three dozen flat caps with bands in 1683.[68] A Latin grammar costing eightpence figures in the accounts for 1632, and between 1679 to 1702 editions of Homer, Phaedrus, Virgil, Cicero and Ovid were bought. There were further purchases of anthologies and word-books, and of a Wingate's *Arithmetic* in 1689.[69]

As mentioned earlier, a surprising fact is that during the Parliamentary and Restoration periods the Poor Scholars for the first time began to achieve Alleyn's aim of entering Oxford or Cambridge colleges with a grant from God's Gift College, at first under the Parliamentary teachers who were appointed without Alleyn's ritual or the approval of the Master or Warden. From 1650 to 1690 twelve boys from the College are recorded as entering Oxford or Cambridge. Not a single boy followed them between 1690 and 1714; from 1714 to 1770 there were six. In spite of the affluence of the College after 1770, to its shame, not a single Poor Scholar entered a university until the New Scheme of 1857. While the undergraduates were awarded an exhibition of £20 per annum by the College (following Statute 81), they did not all complete their courses: neither one of the first two to be sent, John Brooke (Christ's College, Cambridge, 1650) nor Thomas Woodall (Exeter College, Oxford, 1658) graduated. Alleyn had provided for a further payment of £5 to any College boy who gained a BA or MA degree. Queens' College, Cambridge, housed four former Poor Scholars from Dulwich in 1678, during the reign of Charles II. Payments of quarterly allowances were made to Charles Allington, a Fellow of Queens'; for Thomas Richardson, who graduated in 1678; for Benjamin Bynes (who graduated MA in 1683 and, as noted above, was elected Preacher at the College in 1689 but expelled); and for William Stuart.[70] Roger Bailey graduated at Wadham College, Oxford, in 1666, and returned the following month to the College as Usher for a year, but resigned after only eight months, after noting in the Warden's weekly accounts that he had only signed them on the Visitor's orders; John Small graduated from Wadham in 1671.[71] Isaac Dismarrits, sent to Balliol at Oxford in 1690, received payments for clothing, a lexicon, furniture and coach hire to and from Oxford.[72] No further information has been found about William Greenhaugh sent to Oxford between 1657 and 1662, or William Waite, admitted to Wadham in 1667.[73]

There was criticism that the grant of £5 to boys going into trades, as set down in Statute 81, lowered their expectations.[74] Records show that during this era they were apprenticed to such masters as a merchant tailor, a box-maker and a glazier.[75] The College helped them to find work, and paid for their 'articles' [binding apprenticeship agreements].[76] The Poor Scholars were the cause of those perennial anxieties experienced by adults in institutions responsible for the young people in their care, such as when a runaway was reported in a newspaper in 1687:

> Went away from Dullidge School the 3d. Instant, Richard Goulding, a fresh coloured Lad, about 13 years old, very dark curled Hair, a light coloured Suit on, and a white old Hat. Whoever gives notice of him to Mr Goulding in Sheerborn lane near the Post Office, shall have two Guinea's Reward; and the youth shall be kindly received by his Parents.[77]

In 1704 young Edward Jinks was whipped and expelled for theft.[78] In 1759 the College were to bring a pederast attempting to prey on a Poor Scholar to trial: the *Private Sittings* record how a stranger named Richard Branson was to be tried at the Quarter Sessions for attempting to corrupt the morals of the boy 'by endeavouring to commit Acts of Uncleanness as an Introduction to commit Sodomy upon the said Fosset, who detesting the crime has made ample Discovery, and has given Information upon Oath'.[79]

The Poor Brethren and Sisters

We hear even less in the records about the pensioners than about the Poor Scholars during this period. A sensational case, however, was the expulsion of a presumably demented Poor Sister, Dorothy Jenks, in 1650 for 'horrid and detestable Oathes and curses' and for slandering another in the courtyard in the presence of strangers: she said her fellow Sister had been the mistress of a Mr Colby, had had a child by him and burnt it; she accused Mr Colby of inviting boys to watch his exploits.[80] Though Alleyn anticipated problems with alcohol and fornication among his devout pensioners, some truly awful men and women appear to have been admitted from those sent by the parishes. The corrective 'stocks' and 'cage' stood first of all on 'the outer court-yard', which was still the unenclosed village green in front of the College, and were then moved to the burial ground; they were certainly used, mostly for drunkenness. At least by the eighteenth century they carried a board inscribed with a sententious motto: 'It is a sport for a fool to do mischief – thine own wickedness shall correct thee'.[81]

*

Income and expenditure: the Estate

The College weekly account books for the seventeenth-century period, and indeed up to 1775, survive.[82] They show that at best a quiet even life at the College obtained at intervals in this era. A College bell was cast in 1634.[83] For the recreation grounds eighty red rose plants and one hundred tulips were bought in 1632, and a hundred damask roses in 1662; mouse-traps were bought, and six dozen tobacco pipes in 1679.[84] The kitchen gardens were stocked with apple, peach, apricot and pear trees, gooseberries and currants, onions, lettuce, spinach, radishes, parsley, sweet marjoram and rosemary. From these account books we learn how the College ate: the fare followed Alleyn's prescriptions, but with a few flourishes, such as fritters on Shrove Tuesday, 'piggs petty toes', and a chicken for the Warden when he was ill.[85] The College archives hold some records of the management of the woodlands, of tithes, lawsuits, and the leases on the Dulwich estate of mansions, messuages and meadows. There are also leases of properties inherited in the Bishopsgate and Cripplegate areas.[86] The College kept a much smaller group of labourers than in Alleyn's day. In 1630 they had to expel the maltster, who was also the servant to the Master, for fraud and theft of malt.[87]

The College itself had of course inherited the lordship of the manor; in the seventeenth century 'our lordship' in College documents refers to the Estate. Intruders were whipped by law in 1668 for unauthorised cutting of wood in 'Peckarmans copies [coppice]'. In 1667 there were still 268 acres of woodland on the estate;[88] the rest of the Estate mostly consisted of fields and houses with grounds, but land was licensed to be broken for clay and a kiln put up for making tiles on Dulwich Common in 1663, and another for tiles and bricks in 1667 on 'Ling's field'.[89] Rocque's map of 1762 shows a 'Brick kiln' on the Common. A windmill once stood on the Common on the site of the lawns near to the North Block of the present College, on the other side of College Road from the Mill Pond, which was never a mill pond, but rather a fish-pond adjacent to a mill. That mill was stated by Matthias Alleyn in a document of 1627 to have been built by Edward Alleyn himself; it was leased to Nicholas Weekes at the time when he, his wife and four children died of the plague in 1663.[90]

The Sheldonian Visitation

The most important event of the later seventeenth century at God's Gift College was undoubtedly the formal Visitation begun in 1664 in the reign of Charles II, made by the formidable Gilbert Sheldon, Archbishop of Canterbury from 1633 to 1677, and the astringent 'injunctions' that followed on 9 October 1667. Sheldon was the Warden of All Souls College at Oxford University; at Oxford in 1668 his gift to the University, the great Sheldonian Theatre (designed by Christopher Wren) was completed. A rich philanthropist, he donated £72,000 for charitable purposes. However low the College was to sink after this Visitation, it received an excellent disciplinary shock from Sheldon's prescriptions and his forthright reminders to uphold Alleyn's intentions, even though in many important respects what the College was told to do was not carried out.

The Fellows had continually wrangled over such matters as the distribution of income and whether the Schoolmaster should keep his hat on in the presence of the Master. Sheldon's committee rightly focused instead on the educational aspect of the College, and the verdict was damning: 'Yᵉ school is not so well governed as it ought, nor in so good reputation as it might be wished'; 'we do not find that the orders by statute for the manner and houres of keeping schoole and teaching yᵉ poore schollers and Foraigners are observed'. In particular the Schoolmaster, the Revd Francis Brockett, who has already figured in these pages, was condemned for 'passion and indiscretion', and was formally admonished. He was not to use blows against the boys any more, only 'Rod or Ferula & the same with Mildness and Moderation'.[91] Brutal treatment of schoolboys by their teachers was of course by no means uncommon down the centuries.

The 'society' of Fellows was reported to have been conducting an unseemly campaign by the 'priests and University schollers' against the Master and Warden, who were laymen: 'they think they have advantage thereby to despise them'. The academic Fellows were condemned as 'petulant and sawcy'. Sheldon intended that the Master and Warden were to have their authority boosted in College meetings. They were to be marked with more dignity by their dress: 'whereas the fellows come to the Chapel in surplices and hoods according to their degrees and the Master and Warden barely in surplices … [this] makes them appear to these young fellows but as singing men'. Sheldon's remedy, 'for greater reverence in their outwarde appearance', seems now a touch cosmetic: in Chapel the Master and Warden were to replace their plain surplices with gowns and a 'civil hood', distinguished by 'a long tippet of Taffety or Sarcaneth [soft silk]'. Owing to the 'iniquity of the late times' the Communion table had been turned 'end ways East and West' and was now righted. Sheldon, undoubtedly to the College's dismay, ordered the retention of the six 'Assistants' from the parishes to join in discussion of the College's business and to be present at the Audits, and revived the cause of the thirty 'out-member' pensioners to be restored: they were to receive sixpence a week from the College. Sheldon's secretary wrote from Lambeth Palace to ensure that at least one injunction was being carried out promptly: that the poor brethren and sisters in the parish almshouses should 'have their gownds against [*in advance of*] this Christmas'.[92]

Sheldon thought the Estate was not being properly managed, and ordered a formal 'terrier' – a rent roll showing acreage and boundaries – to be made of the lands, tenements and woods, setting out all the leases on the estate, and to be submitted to him; this document survives and lists the fields, houses, barns and stables.[93] The rents were increased, and in a short time the College was solvent again, with an income of £660.10s. per annum to cover diet, pensions, clothing and horses. Sheldon was told that the College ploughs and carts had decayed or perished since 1637 when the husbandmen and ploughmen still worked the land for the College; he recommended that more land should be released to rent. For Christ's Chapel he demanded that a 'good organ' be installed 'forthwith', and a new instrument was indeed constructed by the eminent organ-builder George Dallam in 1669. The Weekly Account Book for 23 November 1668 records payments for this work: Dallam 'examined all our old organ pips and layd them in order',[94] proving that the organ was not totally destroyed by the Cromwellian soldiers as Lysons reported; there were payments for a new case and an organ loft. Four horses were to be kept. The previously withheld rents from the Fortune and the many shops and tenements on its site, that amounted to a loss reckoned at £2,400 over 25 years, and which had led the College into debt, were at last forthcoming, as noted earlier in this chapter; they were now increased. Sheldon's injunctions became in theory the law of the College until 1724.[95]

Alleyn the Founder, perhaps from a mixture of vanity and of loftier ideals, had persuaded George Abbot, the Archbishop of Canterbury, to agree to act as Visitor to the College and for his successors to hold this position. For over two centuries this in effect proved a considerable vexation for successive Primates. The constant appeals to Lambeth Palace from the ailing College and its disgruntled satellite parishes, the pettiness of many of these complaints, together with Sheldon's account of the poor performance of the College and its squabbling 'society', gave the College of God's Gift a very bad name at the Palace. When William Sancroft succeeded Sheldon as Archbishop in 1677, his kinsman Dr Peter Mew, Bishop of Bath and Wells, wrote to him warning that

'yᵉ coll of Dulwich will I fear give you as it did your predecessor a great deal of trouble … I hear they are embroiling themselves in their old disputes'.[96] Sancroft's successor Tillotson received a petition from the College Organist, Charles Garraway, who had been elected in 1678 following the installation of the new organ; he complained of the 'slovenly manner in which the singing in the Chapel is carried on, especially that the Master and Warden & Fellows will not or cannot sing, and the boys for want of judgement and mutual assistance follow one another in such a confused manner as renders it very absurd to the auditors'.[97] The Archbishop replied that choristers must be hired if nobody could sing, as indeed had earlier been prescribed. Garraway, who also complained about his meagre salary, was expelled in 1696 at the same time as Richard Prichard – presumably a pair of bachelor malcontents.[98] The 'old disputes' rumbled into life again towards the end of the century, when the Fellows would frequently grant each other two or three days' absence, and manage to get round the Master and Warden.

The beneficiary parishes

It has been seen how the beneficiary parishes early after Alleyn's death complained about their treatment at the twice-yearly Audit and about the amount of money they received from the College; in 1695, during the reign of William III, the issue of the thirty out-members, Alleyn's other almsfolk, and their pensions recurred. The 'Assistants' elected by the parishes never were welcome at the College, perhaps understandably; one of the clauses in the querulous petition Richard Prichard sent to Archbishop Tillotson in 1695 told him that the six Assistants from the Parishes should not be allowed a say in the government of the College by the Master and Warden, as the Assistants were 'men of small Insight in Laws and Constitutions and slender Abilitys for yᵉ Government and Regulation of a Corporation to wᶜʰ they pretend [claim] authority'.[99]

In 1680 the Master had complained to Archbishop Sancroft that the Schoolmaster was absent for two or three days a week, since he had taken a second job as a curate, and moreover that he refused to teach the local boys, which he was enjoined to do, without extra salary.[100] Overall, from the reign of William and Mary to that of Queen Anne the College of God's Gift failed dismally to hold aloft the heart of charity, and failed to take their teaching seriously; the flame burnt dimly.

4

THE EIGHTEENTH CENTURY

1705-1805

by Allan Ronald, MA, FSA Scot

A fruitful fund of quarrels and disorders.

– REVD JAMES HUME to WILLIAM WAKE,
ARCHBISHOP OF CANTERBURY, 1728

Revd James Hume, Second Fellow, 1706–30 – Hume's reforms – The Estate – Charges against Hume – The Poor Scholars – Archbishop Wake's Injunctions, 1724 – Memorials – James Allen, 1712–46 – Joseph Allen, 1746–75 – Thomas Allen, 1752–1805

With the death of the Revd Job Brockett on 2 January 1705 his duties as Preacher passed to the Schoolmaster, the Revd Joseph Billington; Billington's classes in the school were in turn assumed by the Usher (or assistant schoolmaster), the Revd Rupert Sawyer. When Sawyer himself died at the end of May in that year the school was left without a full-time master. Into the gap stepped the Revd James Hume, described by William Young as 'without doubt the most able and remarkable of the Fellows, either before or since his time' and 'the ruling spirit of the College for nearly 24 years'. [1]

Revd James Hume, Second Fellow, 1706–30

James Hume was born about 1679, the only son and eldest child of the Revd James Hume, minister of Kirkmahoe, near Dumfries. His father was a clergyman of the Episcopal Church of Scotland, established in the face of Presbyterian opposition after the Restoration of Charles II in 1660. From the Reformation in 1560 the Church of Scotland had been Calvinist in doctrine and order, led by ministers. Throughout the seventeenth century various monarchs imposed bishops on this body, without changing its parochial administration or worship. The Scottish Episcopal Church of Hume's father was not Anglican, save that it derived its mode of Episcopal succession from the Church of England. Worship was moulded by no prayer book, and the Calvinist disciplinary system continued to flourish. The intense animosity between Episcopalians and Presbyterians after 1660 stemmed from the brutality with which the Episcopalian Church and the state had attempted to enforce uniformity on the extreme Presbyterians. This opposition was particularly fanatical in the south west of the country where Hume was born and grew up. After

1690, with the establishment of a Presbyterian church order in Scotland, Hume's father was turned out of his living. In spite of this troubled upbringing, Hume was able to attend the University of Edinburgh, from which he graduated in 1697 or 1698. He seems to have made his living in Edinburgh as a schoolmaster before heading for London in late 1704. [2] For many of his fellow Scots Episcopalians, London was the sole hope of ordination and employment. The Bishop of London, the Rt Revd and Hon. Henry Compton, was favourable to Scots who were willing to take the oath of allegiance to the monarch and ordained one hundred and eighty of them between 1690 and his death in 1713. [3] For many of these men he found employment in America and the West Indies, over which colonies he held spiritual rule. A few others found curacies in his own diocese, then covering Middlesex and Essex, and some even found places in London itself. Hume used his employment as a schoolmaster in the city to make himself known to a sufficient number of clergy to support his request for ordination, and once successfully ordained deacon in June 1705 he was in a position to look for a church living. The vacancy at Dulwich occurred at this point and he would have had the qualifications required (a university degree and Holy Orders), plus the bonus of some years' experience of teaching. He was taken on, at first on probation for a year, and then, in October 1706, by an unusual practice, was appointed Second Fellow and Schoolmaster by order of the Visitor of the College himself, Archbishop Thomas Tenison. [4]

Later writing to Tenison's successor as Visitor, Archbishop William Wake, in 1728, Hume declared, 'I should think it the greatest honour and happiness of my life could I contribute anything to the furthering of so good and charitable a work' as the settled and purposeful ordering of the College as a whole.[5] To this end, and from the first, he concentrated his efforts on better financial control and management, especially in relation to hospitality and the letting of College property, and on the statutable division of surplus revenues thus raised. In particular, he therefore cut off both the drain on resources and the unhelpful external control represented by the thirty Out-Members of the beneficiary parishes (those aged men and women supported by the College funds) and the Assistants, or churchwardens, of those parishes. While it may strike us as odd that his 'memoirs' focus on the kind of legal and administrative work more suited to the Master or Warden than to the Schoolmaster, it would seem that those officers – certainly at the outset of Hume's time at the College, and even during the reign of James Allen (1683–1746), Warden and Master from 1712 – were willing to let this active and determined figure have the lead in College business. Although his conduct of the school itself was criticised by his enemies, he appears, as we shall see, to have managed it at least as well as most of his predecessors and better than many.

Hume's reforms

By Statute 117 (as described in Chapter Two) a Dividend was to be paid to all members of the Foundation if there chanced to be over fifteen pounds surplus at the end of the financial year; there had, however, been only one such payment, in 1628. Hume saw that this extra income was one way of increasing the salaries of the Fellows, and thus making them more attractive to worthier candidates. When he claimed that 'some of our places have been often ill-supplied',[6] he was repeating a truth contained in the petition of the four Fellows of the College to the Visitor, Archbishop Sheldon, which had been made in 1676. They had pointed out that places among the Fellows had been vacant for as long as two years 'because no persons fitly qualified could be procured to accept of them – by reason of the smallness of the salaries'.[7] In order to create the necessary surplus of funds for a Dividend payment Hume first of all called for 'industry and frugal management'[8] on the part of the managers of the College's internal economy. In particular he sought to cut down the conspicuously lavish expenditure on hospitality that flourished at the time of his arrival at Dulwich. The College kept open house for all comers at dinner every day of the week and Hume noted that even some of the guests had commented on the indiscretion of doing so 'when at the same time we [Fellows] have hardly salary enough to find us clean linen'.[9] In spite of its possession of a garden, orchard, pig-run, poultry-yard and pigeon-house, the College was indeed spending prodigal amounts on food at this time, as the Weekly Account Books show. On 1 May 1708 a salmon

and a sturgeon were bought, and in one week in 1710 thirty-one pounds of beef and three pounds of suet were purchased; on a single occasion in 1714 one hundred and nineteen pounds of Suffolk cheese were bought in. Although Hume was successful in putting an end to habitual and excessive hospitality, the College still did itself rather well on special occasions. In 1731 when William Allen, appropriately enough a grocer, was elected Warden the bill of fare – admittedly, and as statute ordained, paid for by the successful candidate – was as follows:

> Two Hams, 2 dishes of Boyld Fowls with Cabbage, Carrots, French beans and artichouk.
> 2 Veneson Pastys.
> A large sirloin of Beef.
> 3 Dishes of Turkeys larded & Ducks.
> 2 Codlin Tarts Creamed.
> 2 Geese, gravy & apple sauce.
> 2 Marrow puddins.
> 3 Dishes of Fruite.
> 2 Dishes of Lobsters.
> 2 Dishes of Custards & Florentines.
> 4 plates of Mellon.
> 3 plates of Pickles.
> 3 plates of Prawns.
> 2 plates of Lemons.
> 2 plates of Salads.
> 4 large fouls and sauce for ye old people.
> A plumb pudding for the 12 boys.
> A Gallon of white wine, 6 Gallons of red, and 3 quarts of sack.
> Musick and wine in the Gallery.[10]

Eventually Hume won over the opposition to his scheme for a Dividend, and the first payment, of a £200 surplus, was given out in March 1715. By the year Hume left the College in 1730, the Dividend was £300; that sum had doubled by 1733.[11]

The Estate

To maintain this increase in the income of the College it was also necessary to ensure that its property be let out at the highest possible rents that the market would bear. At the time of Hume's arrival on the scene there were three abuses which actively reduced this income from rentals. The most serious of these was the system of 'recommendams': this involved the leasing of a property with a built-in recommendation that it should be extended, usually for 21 years, at no increase in the rent. Obviously, as the values of property rose, this was a clear way of keeping down the amount that should have accrued to the landlord. Secondly, and equally deleterious in terms of income, was the underletting of valuable property. Hume noted in the early 1720s that the Bull inn at Dulwich had been underlet at a loss to the College of £294.[12] Thirdly there was a danger from an increase in the number of copyhold leases. This was a form of tenancy which gave greater rights to the tenant than a normal leasehold arrangement and therefore obviously threatened the College's power as landlord. The matter became particularly urgent in 1722, when Mr Samuel Hunter, Extra Commissioner of the Navy Board 1712–14, and others with property adjoining the Common, sought to have small tracts of the common land leased to them under copyhold. Hume recognised that to grant their suit would mean that the College as landlord would lose control over the land leading up to its own houses, effectively rendering them unlettable to anyone save the holder of that land. In a series of consultations, in which Hume seems to have been the sole negotiator for the College's interests, 'recommendams' were, for the time being, discontinued, market rents more generally set, and the threat of copyhold tenancies on the common land was averted. The College income from rentals rose from £592 per annum in 1706 to £1,465 per annum in 1726.[13]

Charges against Hume

In crossing an important tenant such as Mr Hunter, however, Hume brought down upon himself and the College an act of revenge. According to Young, Hunter's aim in instigating a Visitation of the College by Archbishop William Wake was simply to gain a revision of the statute restricting leases such as his to a term of 21 years.[14] It would appear, however, that he also sought the elimination of the Dividend payments, the intrusion of the 'Junior Fellows' who had been legally dispensed with in 1628, and, above all, the dismissal of the Schoolmaster. Hume was accused on five grounds: there were not four boys at the university, as the Statutes demanded; he was deliberately holding back scholars from university to save charges to the College and gain thereby from the Dividend; he refused to teach freely the children of the inhabitants of Dulwich – there were twelve local boys, aged ten or under – as the Statutes prescribed; although he was Second Fellow he did not carry out the duty of the post by preaching on Sunday afternoons; and, finally, he did not have the qualifications for his post required by the Statutes. Hunter must have considered Hume a very serious obstacle to his ends to have concerted such a powerful attack against him; and for this we do not have to rely on Hume's evidence alone. An anonymous letter, possibly by Hunter, among Archbishop Wake's papers is directed against the Schoolmaster's failure to carry out the preaching role assigned to his post, and promises to go beyond the Archbishop to Parliament, the Lord Chancellor and, if necessary, the Crown to attain this end.[15]

The Poor Scholars

Hume refuted the charges in a letter to the Vicar-general, the Archbishop's 'right-hand man', Dr Bettesworth. First, he writes, there had only once been a time when four boys were at university, between 1674 and 1677. In his own time Hume had sent two boys to Trinity College, Cambridge.[16] Secondly, he admits to believing that a poor scholar ought not to be devoted to a learned profession without 'pregnant parts and a promising genius': 'it is much better for a poor heavy boy to be put to a good trade,' he argues, in a memorable turn of phrase, 'to learn to make a pulpit rather than to preach in one'.[17] Moreover, he goes on to suggest that it is in his own interest to send boys to university and by this advertisement of his ability to attract fee-paying pupils to the College. Thirdly, he claims that to take in the children from Dulwich and teach them English and arithmetic as demanded would be demeaning both to his role and the standing of the school itself: such elementary tuition was the function of a dame-school,[18] not a College which had been patterned on Eton, Winchester and St Paul's. The fourth and fifth charges arose from the disastrous confusion of Alleyn's Foundation documents, and Hume easily showed that the role he filled, the Second Fellow described in the Letters Patent and not that of the Statutes which had been legally abrogated, did not include the requirement to preach and did not have to be performed by a graduate of Oxford or Cambridge.

Archbishop Wake's Injunctions, 1724

In addition to seeing off these personal attacks, Hume set out his own wishes for the coming Visitation, and it is perhaps a measure of the weight of his opinion with both Bettesworth and Wake that these were embodied in the latter's Injunctions of 1724 almost in their entirety. The most important referred to the school. Injunction One demanded that candidates for election as Poor Scholars must be 'instructed in the catechism … able to read well in the New Testament … and be well qualified and likely to make a proficiency in the said school'. For the first time in over a century, then, the school had some kind of entrance qualification to be overseen by outside inspection at the hands of the Archbishop's chaplains. By Injunction 7 those boys unfit for university were to be taught 'vulgar arithmetick and a good hand' and then, 'at a competent age', to be apprenticed to a suitable trade rather than kept on at Latin and Greek as had previously been the case. Injunction 13 limited the number of boys from the hamlet of Dulwich to twelve, and stipulated that they must be under ten years old on entry, able to read the New Testament and subject to expulsion at the discretion

Parish Keys to the College
Treasury Chest, 1784.
(Dulwich College. Photograph
by John Hammond)

of the Schoolmaster. They were to be distinct from 'Founder's Boys' but were still expected to assist decently at Divine Service. All of this should have meant an improvement in the results of the school; that it did not is no fault of Hume, who was only on hand to supervise the school for the next five years.

A great deal of his time over these years was taken up with the complicated litigation that arose from Injunction 17 whereby the Assistants, elected from among the churchwardens of the parishes associated with the Founder, were reduced in number from six to three. The parishes fought this case from 1725 to 1729 (the year before Hume left the College), and he seems to have once more led the College in its dealings with Bettesworth and Wake. At the heart of the case was the confusion inherent in the two sets of 'Foundation documents': as Hume put it, 'multiplicity of laws, and those obscure, inconsistent and defective, have always been and cannot fail of being, a fruitful fund of quarrels and disorders'.[19] The case was taken not only against the College but also against Archbishop Wake himself, who found himself caught up in wearisome litigation when there were larger matters –such as organising the coronation of George II – to occupy his time.[20] To cut a very long story short, the Assistants, or Churchwardens, were restored to their original number of six, and the College lost £149 in costs.[21]

Memorials

In his quarter-century at Dulwich Hume had indeed done much for the good running of the College, for the increase of its income and for the better ordering of the school. By 1729 he had also made another major contribution: the first catalogue of the Library, by now comprising 1,082 books. This had been ordered by Wake's Injunctions and was to have been carried out by the First Fellow, or Preacher; it is a further tribute to Hume's abilities that the task was given to him. When he resigned his post early in 1730 to take up the living of St Lawrence, Bradwell, in Buckinghamshire, Hume made his second addition to the fabric of the College Chapel. The first of these, dating from 1710, had been the inscribed memorial tablet – in Latin – to the Founder, which can still be seen above the north door. It refers to Alleyn as 'the Roscius of his age' and elegantly renders his official title under King James of 'Master of the Royal Game of Bears, Bulls and Mastiffs' as *Theriomachiæ Regiæ præfectus.* Archdeacon, later Bishop, Edmund Gibson evidently objected to the splendid original ending of Hume's inscription as 'insufficiently suited to the gravity of the matter'. It ran as follows:

> *Postquam annos aliquam multos Collegio suo praefuisset*
> *Vitae tandem Fabula pulcherrime peracta*
> *Scaenae subductus est – Plaudite!*

[After heading his own College for a considerable number of years, and having at last admirably acted out the drama of his life, he was taken from the stage. Applaud him!] [22]

The fact that Hume was chosen to compose this memorial must reflect the regard his colleagues had for his latinity; indeed the more personal pages of Hume's surviving papers, now held in the British Library, show him conducting a series of correspondences on scholarly subjects, all in Latin, ranging from the philosophy of Locke to discussions of linguistic difficulties in Greek poetry. In this he was very much part of that Scottish Latin culture whose contemporary eminences were Archibald Pitcairne and Thomas Ruddiman. [23]

On his departure from the College, Hume donated to its Chapel the elegant font of variegated marble we see today, a fluted oval basin on a baluster designed by his fellow Scot, James Gibbs (1682–1754), architect of St Martin-in-the-Fields and St Mary-le-Strand. The font is notable for the palindromic inscription [reading the same both forwards and backwards], *NIΨON ANOMHMA MH MONAN OΨIN*, meaning 'Cleanse away sin, and not just its appearance'. This lustral epigram was possibly seen by Hume on the font of 1673 at St Martin's, Ludgate. The marble rim carries a Latin inscription recording its status as a gift from James Hume, 'Scoto-Britannicus', and therefore represents a pleasing and permanent reminder of this tireless benefactor of the College.

James Hume left Dulwich in 1730 and served as vicar of the parish of St Lawrence, Bradwell, Buckinghamshire (now part of Milton Keynes) until his death in 1735. While there he maintained his literary correspondence with his fellow expatriate clerical friends in London, always in Latin, and often sent Horatian verses accompanying gifts of chickens and smoked hams from his bucolic retreat. At his own expense he paved, wainscoted and railed the chancel of his parish church and donated a new chalice. When he died, he emulated Edward Alleyn by providing annual doles in his will for deserving aged and infirm parishioners and bursaries for promising schoolboys; these charitable donations are still maintained in the parish. He left his library to the neighbouring parish of Willen, by coincidence the native village of Edward Alleyn senior, where an extensive library, lost in a fire in the middle of the twentieth century, had been established by another schoolmaster, the great Dr Busby of Westminster.

James Allen, 1712–46

Hume's time at Dulwich coincided with the tenure of another powerful and opinionated personality in high position, James Allen, who was elected Warden in 1712 at the age of 29. He signed his name 'Alleyn', but on his

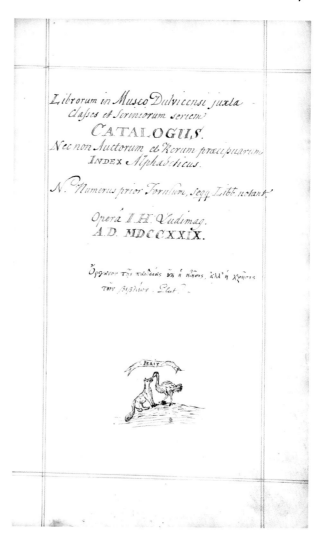

James Hume's title-page to his manuscript Library catalogue, 1729. The design of the heron and the wolf alludes to Æsop's Fable XXIX: the heron, having removed an obstruction from the wolf's mouth, asks for a reward, only to be told by the wolf that the reward was to escape alive; together with the motto ('in vain') Hume registers bitterness in receiving no payment from the College for his labours. (Dulwich College)

election as Master in 1721 changed it to 'Allen'. His portrait by John Ellys (now at James Allen's Girls' School) shows him in a silk gown with shirt and gloves; it has a contemporary inscription describing him as 'Six feet high, skilful as a skaiter and a jumper, Athletic and humane'. He certainly saw to it that the fabric of the College was well maintained, overseeing the rebuilding of the east wing in 1738–9 at a cost of just over £3,000. This large outlay was made possible in part by the increase in rental income achieved by Hume. Allen's other great innovation was the establishment of a separate school for the boys and girls of the hamlet of Dulwich, financed by the rents from a gravel pit at Kensington and six adjacent houses, now on the site of Kensington

Church Street, bought in 1737 from Isaac Ware and Charles Carne for £500, which at that time generated £21.6s per annum. He established this school in 1741 in an attempt to have the local children taught those rudimentary subjects, reading for the boys and reading along with sewing for the girls, which the Schoolmaster Fellows who succeeded Hume seem to have considered to be too undignified or too onerous. The School initially stood across the road from the College in two rooms at the Bricklayer's Arms, and on the site of the house now called Rokeby, adjoining Woodyard Lane.[24] It is this establishment which later became James Allen's School for Girls.

Silver flagon by William Gamble, 1654. Given to the College by James Allen in 1712 on his election as Warden. Inscribed 'Jacobi Alleyn 1712', spelled thus in deference to the Founder; on becoming Master, he reverted to 'Allen'.
(Dulwich College. Photograph © Len Cross)

James Allen improved the aspect of the College Estate in a series of ways, planting chestnut trees in avenues, and adding 'rare and exotic trees'. He thought of the College's acres in terms of landscape gardening as well as of agriculture, and created in 1740 a formal 'canal', the Long Pond. This ran for 500 feet along the east side of Dulwich Village (between the modern Gilkes Place and East Dulwich Grove) until 1861, when it was filled in with spoil from the main drain. In spite of James Allen's straight lines newly imposed on the estate, the poet and physician John Armstrong (1709–79), writing in praise of fresh air in *The Art of Preserving Health* (1744), recommended the pleasures of leisurely walks in the Dulwich woods and fields to those who toiled for 'power or gold' in the 'rank' city; here one could

> lose the world amid the sylvan wilds
> Of Dulwich, yet by barb'rous arts unspoil'd.[25]

Allen, the son of a wealthy merchant, began his professional life as a 'cursitor', one of the clerks attached to the Chancery Court, an office whose duties he fulfilled during his free days from the College. He came from a line of tradesmen, including officers of two City livery companies, the Skinners' Company and the Fishmongers' Company, who had become 'gentrified' in the seventeenth century; one of his ancestors, Sir Thomas Allen (1602–81), had been knighted.[26] As one might imagine, the co-existence of two such strong-willed and dynamic figures as Allen and Hume was not an easy one, and there is no doubt that Hume left Dulwich under a cloud after a squabble with the Master over his absences while seeing to the accommodation in his Buckinghamshire living. While the Hume papers leave us in no doubt that he had a waspish and arrogant side to his nature, we can be sure from other sources that the fault did not lie all on one side; Allen was by no means an easy man to work with. In 1735 there was a dispute with the then Warden, Thomas Allen, over dancing in the Long Gallery on the first floor of the College; the Master, oddly perhaps for one so accomplished at skating and jumping, was firmly against it. 1743 saw more acrimony between the Master and Warden on one side, and the Fellows on the other, this time over the scarcely vital matter of the appointment of College servants. The Fellows took their case to the Visitor in an appeal, and in March 1743 he had the whole set of College officers to see him at Lambeth Palace. Archbishop John Potter now had the opportunity to find out about these embroilments at first hand. Obviously exasperated by this petty squabble, he issued a set of Injunctions which supported the Master and Warden but which were sharply critical of the school and demanded 'a greater proficiency among the scholars'.[27]

Charles Stoppelaer, *James Allen*, 1737.
(© Dulwich College)

Finally, in 1744 Mr Tutty the Usher resigned, having been fined, unjustly as he thought, for absence, leaving a sting in the tail of his letter of resignation: '[I] hereby permit the Master, Warden and Fellows of the said College to proceed to a fresh election and do heartily wish that they may elect such a person who will advance the happiness of the College by promoting the peace and unanimity thereof'.[28] More serious as a charge against James Allen as a competent man of business is his failure to keep a strict eye on the College books as presented by the Wardens of his time. William Allen, who held that office between 1731 and 1735, was found guilty of peculation and fraud,[29] while Thomas Allen, his successor, resigned in 1740, a departure not unconnected, perhaps, with a deficiency in his accounts of just over £170.[30]

James Allen's last year of life, 1745–6, was notable for the appearance of his sister's husband, Alexander Forbes, fourth Lord Pitsligo, as the commander of a force of cavalry in the Highland army of Prince Charles Edward Stuart. Pitsligo, one of the models for Baron

Bradwardine in Scott's *Waverley*, was by now 67 years old and an asthmatic, yet he remained a convinced Jacobite who had been 'out' in the Rising of 1715 and was not now going to miss the chance to draw his sword again; after the Battle of Culloden in 1746, in which he fought, he remained in hiding until his death in 1762.[31] Whether the embarrassment caused by his brother-in-law's supposedly treasonable actions hastened the Master's end or not, history does not tell us.

Allen left his furniture, linen and china to Elizabeth Wakeham of the old Blew House; when she died her maid and companion was to inherit the house. This was Elizabeth Plaw, and it was for her that the next Master, Joseph Allen, was to resign his position in order to marry, leaving the College to set up home at Blew House.

In James Allen's last year a glowing testimonial to the College appeared in the pages of the *Gentleman's Magazine*. The anonymous writer of this conservative article gives his readers a tour of the College and its gardens, 'in the old taste' with orchards and vegetable plots. The Library, he reports oddly, 'has but very few manuscripts (if any)'. The Master is said to be 'a man of fortune' and 'entirely well beloved'. He gives the text of some encomiastic verses inscribed on a tablet (now lost) set into the outer wall of the College:

> Written on the wall of the College of GOD'S GIFT at Dulwich,
> founded by EDWARD ALLEYN Esq: who died 1626
>
> *Quod petis hic est.* HORACE
>
> Attend, vain shade of *Ægypt*'s mighty lord, [Cheops]
> For sumptuous walls, and tow'ring piles ador'd;
> Whose hand laborious taught their pride to rise,
> To spurn afflicted earth, and threat the skies.
> Own you mistook the road to real fame;
> And view these humbler roofs with conscious shame.
> Say to what end you rear'd each mighty tow'r,
> Each fond effect of too luxuriant pow'r.
> Say, to what end thy lab'ring subjects groan;
> And load whole regions with a mass of stone?
> Say, where the praise whole millions to consume,
> And lie, magnific in a splendid tomb?
> See for the poor, these friendly walls appear;
> Want finds relief, and charity is here.
> Here, let the honest, and distress'd repair,
> And with their *maker's* bless the founder's care.
> Survey the joys that charity can bring.
> And see the *player* far excel the KING.
> Courts to the dead thy mighty fabrics give;
> These walls receive, and nourish those who live.

Praising the officers of the College, since he claims that at Dulwich (unlike other institutions) the endowment does not constitute the means for 'luxury to overseers and governors', the journalist goes on to record something very close to Edward Alleyn's ideal:

> in my opinion very few charitable designs have been preserved from the innovations that interest and power introduce, or better answer the end prepared, to relieve the distress'd with judgement, and establish a lasting name without vanity.

'Were the Founder to rise from the dead,' he claims, he 'would not make one alteration'. The twelve boys are 'educated in the principles of religion and literature', and Prayers are held twice daily. The Pensioners are neither 'deficient in limbs or senses' nor suffer from 'chronical disorders'. If his conclusion is overly sentimental, it at least gives a pleasant glimpse of 'the spirit of devotion' in Christ's Chapel, and stands as a useful corrective to the many negative descriptions of life at the Old College from this period. The writer approved of the service he attended, which showed

> the hearty, the unaffected piety of the pensioners, the plainness, and simplicity of the place, the universal decency, the sober and religious behaviour of the congregation (respectable citizens of country retirement, honest farmers and their families).[32]

Joseph Allen, 1746–75

Despite the *Gentleman's Magazine*'s glowing praise, however, by the time that Joseph Allen succeeded as Master in October 1746 the pattern which had been set since the very foundation of the College of God's Gift showed no signs of changing: the school continued to fail, the Master and Fellows pursued a series of petty feuds, and the church-wardens of the associated parishes remained a source of trouble in and out of the courts. To be fair, four boys were sent to university during the period 1746–75, but this was hardly an improvement on the numbers sent previously, especially in the light of Wake's Injunctions and the higher standards of entry they had set. Indeed, the Visitor continued to complain about poor achievement in the class-room. In 1758 Archbishop Thomas Secker sent a Dr Hall to report on the school, who found that it was 'twelve years since any boy was sent … to the university'.[33] The Master justified the failure of the school on the grounds of the 'incapacity or want of genius in the poor scholars', and the then Schoolmaster, William Swanne, himself a former Poor Scholar who had gone up to Christ Church, Oxford, supported this claim, stating that the youths 'have been found incapable of ever making any proficiency either in Greek or Latin'. Furthermore, he added the telling point that the academic judgement passed on the boys was not his alone, nor simply that of the Master and Fellows, but had been endorsed by 'the opinion and sentiments of

George Romney,
Joseph Allen, c. 1778.
The statuette of
Æsculapius indicates
his medical profession.
(© Dulwich College)

your Grace's predecessors' chaplains, who in this case are always our judges'.[34] In spite of this lack of potential candidates, two more boys from among the Poor Scholars did proceed to university: William Cotton went up to Christ Church, Oxford, in 1764 and George Long followed him to New College in 1770. Regrettably, these were the last boys ever to go from God's Gift College to either of the universities[35] until the old College was swept away by Act of Parliament in 1857. For the remaining 87 years of the old College's existence all the poor scholars were put out as apprentices to various trades: to carpenters, plasterers, joiners; tailors, vintners, coopers, clockmakers; drapers, silk-dyers, seal-engravers; to makers of harpsichords, tea-chests, gloves, harnesses, coaches and buttons.[36] Edward Pruden was expelled for truancy in 1784; his parish returned his gown.[37] Perhaps the saddest entry of all is that for John Watson, apprenticed to a blockmaker [maker

of pulleys for ships] in 1791: 'disgrace and so he died'.[38] After Wake's Injunctions permitted expulsion from the College, only four boys are listed as suffering this fate in just over a century.

Was it just bad luck that the College's 'intake' of boys was so academically limited in its nature? Did the dead hand of the Founder and his lottery of an entry system, more appropriate to a day-time television quiz show than to a place of learning, condemn the school to failure? Certainly the entry requirements, even after Wake's intervention of 1725, were minimal. Other schools were better provided in this regard: from its very beginnings Merchant Taylors' School had stipulated a knowledge of the Catechism in 'English or Latin' and an ability to 'read perfectly and write competently'.[39] At Charterhouse, founded at much the same time as God's Gift College, only those boys whom the Schoolmaster found to be 'well

Dulwich College. Drawn and
engraved by William Ellis,
March 1792. (Jan Piggott)

entered in learning' were to be admitted. [40] A school which
Edward Alleyn must have known well as a vestryman of
St Saviour's, Southwark (as noted in Chapter Two), was
St Saviour's Grammar School: on entry to this establishment, founded in 1562 to give free tuition to the children of
the parish, the pupil had to be able to read both English
and a modicum of Latin. [41] 'Incapacity' and 'lack of genius'
seem to have been inevitable given the sheer luck involved
in the entry procedure and the inadequate demands made
of those seeking an education at the College. Things were
made worse by the fact that no single Schoolmaster had
stayed long enough to stamp his own character on the
school; between 1619 and 1705 there had been 21 Schoolmasters, the most notable of whom, James Hume, had
perforce spent much of his time on administrative affairs.
In addition, as we have seen, the energy of the Master,
Warden and Fellows was too frequently dissipated in litigation and internal strife. This continued to be the case
during Joseph Allen's period as Master.

Before becoming Warden of the College in February
1745 Allen had been a ship's surgeon, and it was in this
capacity that he had taken part in George Anson's great
voyage of circumnavigation from 1740 to 1744. He must
have been a hardy customer to survive the appalling
rigours of this voyage: by the time Anson's little fleet of
six ships had rounded the Horn only 335 survived out
of an original company of 961 boys and men; over half of
the crews died of scurvy. [42] There were two principal
disputes between the new Master, Joseph Allen, and the
Fellows during his time in office. In 1749 the Usher,
Thomas Waterhouse, was the subject of a petition
presented to the Visitor by Dr Allen: not only had he
been negligent and lacking in punctuality, but he had
also 'rudely and repugnant to the aforesaid Statutes
disobeyed and withstood the lawful commands of the
Master, and has often abused him'. [43] Waterhouse was
accused of calling Allen 'a vile despicable fellow, telling
him he looked like the devil', and it was further alleged
'that he was perjured and said many other reproachful
speeches, grinning in the Master's face, and using the
most provoking gestures'. [44] Waterhouse replied to this
petition by claiming that 'his behaviour was stigmatised
by the most reproachful terms and that truth had suffered
an equal violation with his character'. [45] Further papers
now flowed from the Fellows, several of whom had been
in office for decades, supporting Waterhouse against
what they termed the 'illegal exercise of power by the
Master of Dulwich College'. [46] According to these papers

Dulwich College, 1790 (detail). Engraved by Taylor after anonymous drawing. *The European Magazine*. (Jan Piggott)

the Fellows 'have lived in perpetual terrors and apprehensions of his threats and censures (which are generally delivered in the roughest terms) and have hitherto submitted to mulcts [fines] and punishments which they deem to be irregular and oppressive'. No record remains of Archbishop Herring's decision, but Waterhouse remained in office until his resignation in June 1751.

The second dispute occurred in 1768 when the Master fined the organist, Mr Richard Randall (1736–1828; at the College 1763–82), ten shillings for absence without leave and then inflicted more fines of increased sums for further unofficial absences. Randall was a celebrated tenor as well as an organist, and the 21 volumes of his engagement diaries (presented to the College in 1914) show that he was much in demand for singing at oratorios and operas in the London theatres and in City churches; he was indeed often absent from Dulwich as a 'lay-clerk' [singing man] at Oxford or Cambridge college chapels and at cathedrals in the south of England. The Audit Court of three Churchwardens and three Fellows heard Randall's complaint and thought 'it right to remit the said fine'.[47] Naturally the Master objected and protested to the current Visitor, Archbishop Secker; unfortunately the Primate died before coming to a decision. His successor,

Dr Cornwallis, did not have to act upon the Master's protest, since it had meanwhile been withdrawn.

In June 1775 Dr Joseph Allen resigned as Master of the College in order to marry the widowed Elizabeth Plaw of Blew House.[48] In spite of his often stormy relations with his colleagues, Dr Allen was not only presented with handsome compliments from them when he retired but, at their expense, had his portrait painted by George Romney, with a sculptured figure of Æsculapius, the Greek god of medicine, in the background, alluding to his earlier career as a ship's surgeon. This painting now hangs in the Board Room at the College.

Thomas Allen, 1752–1805

Thomas Allen, who succeeded Dr Joseph Allen as Master in 1775, had been a malt factor when he became Warden in 1752. Young remarks, almost with surprise, that following his succession there were 'scarcely any quarrels among the Fellows'.[49] This may have had something to do with his diminutive frame – he became known locally as 'The Little Old Master' – but surely also with the fact that he had been a member of the College for 23 years before succeeding to the Mastership. Thomas Allen lived at Sycamore Cottage in the village with 'certain female relations or connections'; a broad white line was chalked on the garden wall of the College to guide him home on dark, foggy nights after his dinner and bottle of port wine.[50]

Experience of a College such as Alleyn's College of God's Gift was a quality his predecessor had sadly lacked, and something of Thomas Allen's practical character may be seen in the restraint he showed over one particular instance of internal friction, itemised in a letter to him of August 1782. The then Warden wrote to the Master, Allen, complaining that the Schoolmaster, the Revd Nevile Stow, had 'left off instructing the poor scholars in Latin, a thing unheard of since the foundation'. Following the Warden's accusation of neglect of duty and breach of his oath as a fellow, furthermore, Stow had been 'pleased to call me … a dirty scoundrel!' Despite this alleged behaviour, Stow's career continued unimpeded – he went on as Schoolmaster until his death in 1810. His failure to provide the teaching of a subject essential to any grammar school, is, however, further evidence of the deplorably low academic standard of the College at this time.

If it was a case, more or less, of 'all quiet' within the College, there was strife enough outside it, mainly relating to grievances regarding tenants and leases, a perennial problem it would seem. Trouble began almost at once when the College brought an action of ejectment against Robert Bulkeley, a tenant who held leases on, among other properties, the Crooked Billet, later the King's Head and subsequently the White Hart. According to the College, he had felled about two thousand trees and 'filled up sundry ditches and a draining pond'.[51] The case dragged on until 1778 but at least the College won this time, being awarded damages of £150, plus costs. A far more complicated case was that of Charles Maxwell, who filed a bill in Chancery against the College in 1782. This also involved the Green Man, the inn where Dulwich Common to the east joins Lordship Lane.[52] Maxwell had bought the lease of the property and expended a considerable sum of money on improving it. Nonetheless, when it came up for renewal he asked for a further 21 years at the old rent. The College not only upped the rent by half, acknowledging the fact that the property had been so improved, but changed the lease to take away certain rights of access. Maxwell demanded that the terms of the original lease should apply and took his case to Chancery. The Warden and Fellows were all for complying with their tenant's demands but the Master forthrightly declared that 'he would sooner die in Newgate than suffer the seal to be put to this lease'.[53] Judgement was given in 1783 and the College had to allow Maxwell the original lease. In a later case, that of William Kay in 1788, the College did rather better.

Kay was another tenant who had expended vast sums in improving property that he rented rather than owned, in his case some two thousand pounds 'and upwards'.[54] After much argument and further expenditure on the approaches to the property, the exasperated Kay published an open appeal to the Visitor, in which he asserted that the College authorities not only 'rule the tenants with the most absolute and despotick authority' but also by 'taking advantage of other men's improvements, they have doubled and trebled the income of their estates, which though given for charitable uses, is squandered in connections of evil example and immoral tendency'.[55] Rather than waste money on a writ, the College, under Thomas Allen's pragmatic mastership, simply refused to grant Kay any further lease until he apologised, which he accordingly did.

A glimpse of the College at this period – a significantly less rosy portrait than the *Gentleman's Magazine*'s from nearly fifty years before – can be had from a letter written by Horace Walpole to his friend Mary Berry on 8 June 1791:

> This morning I went … to see Dulwich College, founded in 1619 by Alleyn a player, which I had never seen in my many days. We were received by a smart divine, *très bien poudré*, and with black satin breeches – but they are giving new wings and red satin breeches to the good old hostel too, and destroying a gallery with a very rich ceiling; and nothing will remain of ancient but the front, and an hundred mouldy portraits, among apostles, sibyls and Kings of England.[56]

The College was able to restore its fabric as a result of improved income from rents. When Thomas Allen became Warden in 1752 the surplus funds for the Dividend amounted to £950; by the year of his death, 1805, it totalled £3,875. In 1776 Sarah, Lady Falkland (from her second marriage; first the widowed Countess of Suffolk) bequeathed three hundred pounds to the Master and Warden to be invested to provide a dole to be paid to the twelve old Almspeople every Christmas Day. Lady Falkland inherited the fortune of her father Thomas Inwen of Southwark: a churchwarden of St Saviour's, he had been one of the Assistants of the College, and signed protests to the Visitor about the increased salaries of the Fellows in 1728. The Governors in the 1890s placed a portrait, of obscure provenance, in the Board Room at the College believed to represent her (DPG 498), but it is now considered to have been painted too early to be authentic.

The last years of the reign of the 'Little Old Master' saw revolution in France and fears of invasion. On 1 May 1798 a meeting, with the Warden in the chair, was held to 'form an armed association of infantry in the hamlet for the better defence and security of the neighbourhood at this critical juncture'.[57] Indeed, Dulwich Common was used as a training ground for volunteers and militia; the Clump on the present playing fields, so frequently 'attacked' by the College Combined Cadet Force at the culmination of Annual General Inspections in the recent past, may well have echoed to the rattle of Brown Bess muskets over two hundred years ago.

Two significant improvements were made in Christ's Chapel during the course of the eighteenth century. A new organ was installed in 1759, built by George England and Thomas Whyatt for £260 and the exchange of the old one; its oak case and front gilt pipes survive.[58] In 1796 Thomas Mills (1749–1834) of Saxham Hall in Suffolk bought for £50 at Christie and Manson's auction a very large oil painting, a fine sixteenth-century Italian copy of Raphael's *Transfiguration*, and presented it to the College. What connection, if any, Mills may have had with the College has yet to be established; soon after, he wrote to complain that he had heard of his gift's neglect and of its lying folded in the gallery at the College, and asked for

its return for a church of his own he was building.[59] The painting was thereupon placed above the altar, where it remained until its removal to the north wall of the choir in 1878.[60]

One hundred years after James Hume arrived at Dulwich, most of what he had reasoned, schemed and argued for had come to pass. The Dividend was not only a regular occurrence but was ten times what it had been when he left the College in 1730; income from rents had increased, and the College had greater success in ensuring that leases reflected the value of its property; only in the most important field of all, the school, had his aims remained unfulfilled, in spite of the efforts of his successors and the regular inspections by the Archbishop's chaplains. When Thomas Allen died on 20 July 1805, he had been a member of the College, as Warden and then Master, for 53 years. The institution over which he had presided so genially and, in financial terms, so successfully had barely another 53 years to run before a government inquiry into the activities of the Estate and the College weighed them in the balance and found them wanting.

John Nixon, 'A Visit from the Founder', 1797. Pen and wash, for engraving. The cause of Alleyn's imagined rising from his grave in protest at a sermon is unknown. The figure in the pulpit on the left is the Master, Thomas Allen. (© Jeremy Gotch)

5

DECLINE & REFORM

1806–58

PART I

… you might as well make dirt-pies or build houses with cards.

– WILLIAM HAZLITT, 1822

Masters and Wardens – John Allen (1771–1843) – John Allen at Dulwich, 1811–43 – The Fellows – Ozias Linley – John Vane – John Lindsay – The Estate – The Old College – The Chapel – The Bourgeois Bequest and Picture Gallery – The Fellows' Library

The saddest annals of God's Gift College concern the first half of the nineteenth century when Alleyn's noble ideals to encourage and enable the orphan boys to better themselves through education were badly betrayed. The 'Society' of the Masters, Wardens and Fellows could be said to have turned their posts into sinecures and to have held down the Poor Scholars rather than advancing them. Their charity towards the Almsfolk, selected during this era more for picturesque than deserving qualities, became cosmetic. Privilege and class division obtained; the Fellows enjoyed leisured ease and good living, while the Poor Scholars almost all left the College to find menial jobs. A. H. Gilkes's judgement of 1905 that the preceding Masters, Wardens and Fellows were 'a poor set of people', and 'often somewhat rotten at heart',[1] seems generally true to the surviving evidence, although of course it is also true that the evil that men do lives after them, and the good 'is oft interred with their bones'.

In 1810 the 'Society' was served by a household consisting of a butler, cooks, a scullion, and gardeners; the 1841 census adds a footman, a groom, housemaids and a clerk.[2] The College now resembled a great country house – for celibate Fellows. At the Inquiry before the Charity Commissioners in 1854 George John Allen, the fifteenth Master of the College, testified that there were eight servants, though Sir Charles Barry reminded the committee that Alleyn's Statutes actually allowed for as many as ten.[3] The same year the anonymous author of a pamphlet, *Dulwich College; or a Model for Free Grammar School Reformation in a Letter to Lord Cranworth*, complained (with some exaggeration) that what in the eighteenth century had been but modest accommodation for the Master had now been turned into a mansion.[4] Taken altogether, the evidence points to this being the worst epoch for the Founder's boys but

the most comfortable for the gentlemanly scholars in positions of responsibility.

The College became something of a byword in the outside world for its failings; in Charles Kingsley's 'The Dulwich Gallery', a chapter of his novel *Alton Locke* (1850) set in the late 1840s, the hero's cousin regales him on their way to visit it,

> with sneers at the fellows of the college to which we were going – their idleness and luxury – the large grammar school which they were bound by their charter to keep up, and did not – and hints about private interest in high quarters, through which their wealthy uselessness had been politely overlooked, when all similar institutions in the kingdom were subject to the searching examination of a government commission.[5]

Even if the members of this establishment heeded these criticisms, which is doubtful, they did little to redeem the old order of the College or to prolong their own livelihoods by moving with the spirit of the age; indeed, the great reforms of the proposed 'Schemes' from the Charity Commissioners and the Dulwich College Acts of Parliament during the 1850s and 1880s to establish a new College developed so strongly in direct reaction to its abiding decadence.

William Hazlitt, on a visit to the Gallery in 1822, taken by 'something affecting and monastic in the sight of this little nursery of learning, simple and retired as it stands, just on the verge of the metropolis, and in the midst of modern improvements', nonetheless had spoken pessimistically of its failings as if they were inevitable: 'nothing comes of these endowments and foundations for learning, – you might as well make dirt-pies, or build houses with cards'.[6]

This half-century remains of great interest, however. An important reason for this is the development of the

J. C. Varrall after H. Gastineau,
Dulwich College, Surrey, 1819.
The Picture Gallery, the Chapel and
the East Wing from the meadows
(now Dulwich Park).
(Dulwich College)

Estate, which came to provide the means for the New College and conditioned its character. An unusual feature of God's Gift College as landowner, compared with almost all schools with great endowments of property in cities, or the Oxford and Cambridge Colleges, was that it presided physically in the centre of the source of its nourishing wealth at Dulwich, governing the surrounding property. Alleyn's endowment became of course extraordinarily valuable when commons were enclosed, meadows were given over to housing footage, and new roads were made. Also this is the era of the most interesting and distinguished individual in the larger life of the nation to serve at Dulwich, and after Edward Alleyn the most famous, John ('Holland House') Allen (1771–1843), who was Warden and Master for a total of 30 years. The Picture Gallery, an architectural masterpiece containing paintings of world fame, was moreover built in 1811.

Dulwich Village, where much natural and historical charm was preserved, thanks to the protection of Alleyn's conservative strictures, such as those designed to protect the trees he is known to have loved (and also, doubtless, thanks to the laissez-faire of the officers of the College), became favoured both as a dormitory for London, only five miles from Charing Cross, and as the object of a genteel excursion; what the College had lost in revenue by resisting developments the Fellows had preserved in beauty, wrote Anthony Highmore, in his book *Pietas Londinensis* (1814). Highmore spent his childhood and most of his life in Dulwich, on intimate terms with the Master, Warden and Fellows, and wrote enthusiastically about its amenity and its attractions for 'opulent and respectable tenants'.[7] Even as late as the

1860s the odour of hay in June from hundreds of acres still not yet given over to housing could be smelled from miles away.[8] An essay by Leigh Hunt of 1834 describes taking the Dulwich stage-coach from Fleet Street to the Greyhound inn, and notes with pleasure that the village was still full of trees. After a hearty supper, Hunt awoke in the morning to a window giving on to 'rich meadows, where the haymakers were at work in their white shirts'.[9] Another writer in the early nineteenth century wrote satirically of the milieu of the Village:

> I doubt if there is a more snobbish suburb than Dulwich in the whole of the outlying districts of London. Here is a summary of the place: Poverty (genteel), Pride (heaven knows what for) and Pianos (badly played), the hallmark of the village proper where they hand round afternoon tea and ask one another to Soup and Fish dinners and don evening dress for a chop.[10]

Masters and Wardens

In 1805 William Allen, Warden for 30 years and the third of that name, succeeded 'the Little Old Master', Thomas Allen. William Allen had been a civil servant in 'Lord Dartmouth's Office', the Board of Trade. He had a reputation as a good administrator, but we know little about him except that he had pretensions as a writer: he had published (at his own expense) the fruit of his leisurely meditative life at the College, a poem called *Hymen* in 1794 (which calls him 'W.A.W.' on the title-page, the final 'W' standing for 'Warden of the College') and in 1798 a 'Sacred Drama', *Hezekiah, King of Judah; or, Invasion Repulsed and Peace Restored*. The rhyming couplets of *Hymen* (by the celibate writer) point youthful men towards the path of nuptial happiness and calm domestic joys, and warn against 'unequal' marriages such as giddy girls running off with their footmen. Conservative, patriotic and a loyal monarchist, his laboured *Hezekiah*, claiming to be 'of National Application at this awful crisis', draws a parallel between Israel as England and Nineveh as France, in which a cruel invasion by a modern Sennacherib is extinguished by Providence, who takes account of our superior virtue and religion. Rather daringly, the King is given a dissipated son like our own heir to the throne, young George. The quality of the writing may be judged from part of a Chorus:

> Armies of a savage race,
> Big and strong and fierce of face,
> Come with hostile steps around,
> While their horses paw the ground.

Lancelot Baugh Allen, a barrister of the Inner Temple, replaced William Allen as Warden in 1805 and himself succeeded as Master in 1811, whereupon John Allen began his long tenure at Dulwich by winning the election for Warden. In 1820 he became the Master when Lancelot Baugh Allen resigned to get married, and this office he held until his death on 10 April 1843.

The attraction of the positions of Master and Warden seemed well known to all who were surnamed Allen. The *European Magazine* in August 1791 published a pleasant article about the College (which hardly mentioned the Poor Scholars):

> The master of this College is Lord of the Manor for a considerable extent of ground, and enjoys all the luxurious affluence and ease of the prior of a monastery ... Great interest is constantly made by the unmarried men of the name of Allen to obtain the post of warden. [11]

The Masters and Wardens of this period tended to be indulgent rather than rapacious landlords; they were slow to capitalise on the potential of the Estate, resisting the first proposal by the South Metropolitan Railway to cut a railway line through it in 1846; in 1853 four separate lines were proposed, but all were rejected, although the College did express interest in an approach from the Direct Southern Railway Thames Terminus Company. [12] They meanwhile continued to entertain celebrities, rather like a genial and wealthy Oxford or Cambridge College, and once again kept open house in the way James Hume had complained of in the previous century: in 1830 Cyrus Redding rode to the College with Thomas Campbell, 'the poet in high spirits, talking of the many times he had been entertained there, of the kindness of the brethren, and of the valuable collection of pictures of Sir Francis Bourgeois'. [13]

The educational weaknesses of Alleyn's scheme became increasingly apparent in this period as society evolved. Alleyn's 'College of God's Gift' was a closed corporation without disinterested and enlightened Governors; the Archbishops of Canterbury, who had held their position as 'Visitor' since 1619 and who were beset with their responsibilities to the nation, now grew even more impatient of settling petty squabbles between the Dulwich Fellows and the Churchwardens or of having to read Memorials asking permission to cut down a few trees. College meetings, with their factions and voting with the power of veto, led to craven and lazy decisions. Alleyn's vanity in perpetuating the Founder's name by the absurd method of appointing men as Master and Warden who happened to be surnamed Alleyn or Allen naturally meant that poorly qualified and inferior men took office. As Mackenzie pointed out, this statute 'must have deprived the College of the services of a better man, and the use of the lot in deciding between the two selected candidates must have often resulted in the success of the less qualified candidate'. [14] The poor salaries and the 'monkish' restriction of celibacy, said to be *contra bonos mores* [immoral] in modern times, [15] were perhaps a discouragement in applying for appointment as Schoolmaster or Usher; but the living was generous, and there was the additional lure of the large annual distribution of surplus revenue under the terms of Alleyn's Dividend clause (see Chapter Two). Under John Allen's Mastership a less quarrelsome society of comfortable old bachelors formed, with convivial or eccentric cultivated Fellows who seem to have had little or no real interest in teaching the boys. The manuscript book of *Private Sittings* 1805–29 (MSS(2), 56), which records the minutes of College business, contains not a single reference to the teaching of the boys, but many to the ordering of wines, the leasing of fields (with clauses for them to be properly manured), or the renting of pews in the Chapel. When the boys are referred to, it is either to register their permission to fish in the mill pond, or else to document the leaving arrangements for their apprenticeships mostly for fairly 'humble' occupations. The Revd William Rogers, a Governor of the new Foundation who became its famous Chairman of the Board, recalled for example an encounter with a former Poor Scholar who drove a cab, bought for him out of College funds. [16] The College records, together with the evidence given in the Inquiry of 1854, show that in fact the Poor Scholars made, in their way, a wide and important contribution to Victorian society: as farmer, builder, printer and chemist; as law stationer, lapidary [cutter of precious stones], gun-case maker and engraver; as bookbinder, oil- and colour-man; as watchmaker, silversmith, gold-beater, and ship insurance-broker; as tailor, barber, silk-weaver and auctioneer; as cooper, carpenter, coachbuilder, and boot-and-shoe-maker; as 'Chronometer Escapement and Compensator Balance' maker and Peckham butcher. Two boys became organists at Norwich. One signed up as an artillery-man in the East India Company's service.[17] William Sheppard 'rose to be master of a large business' in the City, and Henry Joseph Hartley (1829–1924), an orphan from St Luke's, Finsbury, and in 1854 a journeyman printer,[18] became prosperous enough to leave printing and embark on a higher career as a journalist and art critic. One of the last of the Poor Scholars from Bishopsgate was a highly successful Londoner, whose career Alleyn would surely have commended: Sir Horatio Davies (1842–1912), after being apprenticed to an engraver at the age of 14, entered the hotel and catering business and made a fortune. A Freemason, he served as Councillor, Sheriff and Member of Parliament, and became Lord Mayor of London in 1897–8, the year of Queen Victoria's Jubilee, and when 'there had never been such lavish expenditure'. In 1897 he returned to the new College to give the prizes, arriving in his splendid coach.[19] There is some justification perhaps for the cynical rationalisation of those Fellows who claimed that if the Poor Scholars had been crammed and subsidised by the College to go to Oxford or Cambridge, they would simply have ended up as wretched and poverty-stricken curates, rather than following some learned profession. George John Allen defended himself and the Fellows at the Inquiry by saying that they had found no boy suitable to go to university; it was 'improbable' that 'they would acquire at our school sufficient learning to obtain that success at Oxford or Cambridge which would be of advantage to them in after life'.[20]

In 1820 thirteen unmarried Allen candidates put themselves forward for the post of Warden; they included a Captain of the Bengal Service, two second-year undergraduates from Oxford and Cambridge, three barristers, an indigo broker and a bookseller. Jeffrys Thomas Allen was elected, but from 1835 was an invalid; he died in 1841. Thereupon the eldest son of the Bishop of Ely, George John Allen (1810–83), a barrister, was elected, paying securities of £8,000 himself and four securities of £2,000 from friends – a new clause thought necessary to prevent opportunist embezzlers.[21] In 1843, on the death of John Allen, he was duly promoted to Master; John Gay Newton Alleyne (1820–1912), the talented heir to a Baronetcy, won the subsequent election for Warden.[22]

The *Illustrated London News* of May 1843 published an account of the election (as has already been referred to in Chapter Two); the journalist was intrigued by the antiquated ceremony: standing before the altar, the Master held aloft the box containing two very long strips of paper, shook it three times, then distributed the strips between the two candidates, who with 'great difficulty' unravelled them, the words 'God's gift' being written on the winner's.[23]

John Allen (1771–1843)

John Allen's 30 years at Dulwich as Warden and Master seem almost a minor aspect of his career and fame. His first post was in Edinburgh as a highly qualified surgeon at the Royal Infirmary and he was then appointed Lecturer in Physiology at the University in 1799. Early in his life he was a 'free-thinker', and his friends were Edinburgh radical intellectuals who formed the nucleus of the Scottish liberal party. In 1792 he joined the Speculative Society, of which Walter Scott was the Secretary. Allen's associates, in particular Francis Jeffrey and Sydney Smith, founded the *Edinburgh Review*, to which he was to make 35 contributions on historical and political subjects.[24] Allen was in London by February 1798, when he was a founder member of the King of Clubs, a dining club that became the congenial focus for many prominent figures of liberal Whig dissent. In 1802, at the age of 30, his life was given new direction by the third Lord Holland (1773–1840). Holland had been much influenced by his uncle, the brilliant Whig politician Charles James Fox, who had brought him up. He reportedly asked Lord Lauderdale to find him a clever young Scottish surgeon to accompany him and his wife, who was in delicate health, to the Spanish Peninsula after the Peace of Amiens. Allen travelled with them for three years, beginning with two lively months in Paris, where the Hollands were presented to Napoleon, and a much longer sojourn in Spain during an unsettled period of harsh negotiations with France. The actor John Philip Kemble (who at a later date was said to have played a part in the bequest to the College of the famous Bourgeois and Desenfans Collection of paintings) was on a tour of the continent at that time and stayed with the Hollands in Valencia.[25]

On his return to London, Allen became a member of the inner circle of the Whig aristocracy and of fashionable wits at Holland House in Kensington, 'one of the most brilliant centres of political and literary society in all Europe',[26] where he 'had the opportunity of becoming acquainted with all the distinguished men of all countries'.[27] Given the notoriously enduring sympathies of Holland House with Napoleon,[28] it is interesting that Allen was already disenchanted with him by 1800, later writing from Spain that he would rejoice at Bonaparte being dethroned and hanged. When Napoleon was crowned Emperor in 1805, Allen's hopes for France were crushed: 'great was then his despair and indignation'.[29] Allen made no secret of his Republican sympathies nor of his hatred of royal prerogative and hereditary power, and considered the subsequent return of the Bourbon monarchy to France, instead of an honest and philanthropic republican government, 'an event never too much to be deprecated'. He prized a miniature he owned of Oliver Cromwell, and when he sat to Edwin Landseer for his portrait, the bronze bust of Cromwell[30] placed pointedly at his elbow declared his politics. As an observer of contemporary British politics, he was disappointed that Prince George deserted his liberal views on becoming Regent, and as George IV he considered him 'in all respects a good-for-nothing dog'. Allen was particularly bitter about the rise of the 'Ultra Tories' at home, 'and thereafter seldom devoted his time to modern politics', turning instead to a study of history, particularly that of the Anglo-Saxons;[31] his *Inquiry into the Rise and Growth of the Royal Prerogative in England*, published in 1830, however, was a political polemic as well as an academic study. It was republished with a Memoir after his death in 1849.

Allen, of course, followed James Hume as the second proud Scot at the College. A patriot, he published a pamphlet in 1833 called *Vindication of the Ancient Independence of Scotland*, contradicting British historians by asserting that Scotland was independent of feudal domination by English monarchy from the seventh century until the time of Edward I. The Scots were to him champions of liberty; Wallace he thought of as 'an imperishable name' like William Tell, and modern Scots were eminent 'owing to the sentiments and spirit' Wallace inspired.[32]

From his position as family doctor Allen became in time an indispensable confidant of the Hollands. He was given comfortable quarters at Holland House, where he acted as an honorary steward, carving at the head of the table and keeping the lists of guests. He travelled again with his patrons to Spain and Portugal in 1808; during his Dulwich years he was also with them in France, Italy and Germany in 1814; in Italy again in 1815 and 1816; and then in Paris in 1825. During his Mastership the number of days the Master was absent from the College increased from 40 to 196 days in the year. Holland House would only 'allow' him 'a few hours in each week' at the College when it was absolutely necessary, according to Charles Greville.[33] In 1834 the Charity Commissioners were to insist that the Founder had only intended to allow the Master forty days' absence.[34]

For forty years Allen played a major part in the success of Holland House, influencing and influenced by its ethos, and famous as 'a man of vast information and great conversational powers'.[35] Particularly it was said that he was the 'oracle' of Holland House on all literary subjects.[36] The poet Byron wrote in his journal for 13 December 1813:

> Allen (Lord Holland's Allen) – the best informed and one of the ablest men I know – a perfect Magliabecchi[†] – a devourer, a Helluo [glutton] of books, and an observer of men, has lent me a quantity of Burns's unpublished, and never-to-be published, Letters. They are full of oaths and obscene songs.[37]

Allen's friendship with Lord Holland – a tolerant, urbane and kindly man, according to the statesman Henry, Lord Brougham – lasted for 38 years, until Holland's death in 1840: 'for the latter and more important part of his life [Allen] shared all his thoughts and was never a day apart from him'. It was Allen who carried out the research and criticised the text for many of Lord Holland's speeches and writings. He also wrote the historical portion of the *Annual Register* for 1806–7. Brougham admired Allen's sterling integrity and other qualities: 'his indignation was never more easily aroused than by the aspect of daring profligacy or grovelling baseness. His feelings too were warm; his nature kind and affectionate'. Brougham wrote that 'he had the genuine Whig spirit excited and confirmed by his deep study of our former history',[38] an allusion in part to the excellence of his Anglo-Saxon scholarship.[39] Allen was for a short while Undersecretary to the Commissioners treating with America; but for his low birth, wrote Brougham, Allen would have been a natural candidate for high office in politics: but a line had been drawn by the high aristocratic habits of the current government – those 'monopolists of political preferment' – between the ruling caste and the rest of the community. Allen was not a patrician; the 'fruit and shade' were to be reserved for the Establishment.[40]

Allen's bold contempt for Christian tenets and for the Church was notorious. This was consistent with the ethos of Holland House, which Greville said 'went on as if there was no such thing as religion'.[41] On one occasion Allen 'got into such a fury against the *charlatanerie* of the Apostles and Fathers and the brutal ignorance of the early Christian converts' that it made Lord Holland laugh aloud.[42] He was widely known as 'Lady Holland's atheist'.[43] That lady (Elizabeth Vassall, 1770–1845) would reportedly tease him by saying, "Now, Doctor, can you assure me there is not another world?" "Pooh! pooh!, madam," said Allen. In answer to this she said, "Now, Doctor, will you give me your word of honour that there is not?"[44]

---

† (1633–1714), librarian to Cosimo III de Medici, whose memory was 'like wax to receive and marble to retain' and who did not undress at night, 'life being so short and books so plentiful'.

S. W. Reynolds after C. R. Leslie, *Lord and Lady Holland, Dr Allen and William Doggett in the Library at Holland House*, *1839* (detail). John Allen standing between Lord and Lady Holland; on the right, the Groom of the Library. (Jan Piggott)

A Dulwich legend holds that Allen caused oval windows from his study to be let into the Chapel on the west wall, on either side of the organ, so that he could fulfil his statutory attendance of communion services while sitting at his desk – a fact he did not like to be broadcast. However, the windows were actually in place by 1814 when Allen was Warden, and Highmore says the point of them was that they were to be used when sickness prevented attendance at chapel. [45]

Allen's interests included the history and literature of Spain and Portugal; he was said to be assembling materials for 'a historical and statistical account of Spain'. [46] What he lacked in imagination, we are told, he made up for with 'the most capacious understanding memory': he was able to give full details of any book that had made an impression on him. A review he wrote of a book of Napoleon's letters from St Helena turned into an extraordinarily detailed account of his early career, which, remarkably, profoundly impressed the exiled Napoleon himself. [47] That Allen did not finish his academic projects or publish more was ascribed by his contemporaries

to his sociable habits and 'Lady Holland's exigencies'. Allen was obviously devoted to both the Hollands, although Lady Holland, according to Greville's memoirs, 'worried, bullied, flattered and cajoled him by turns'. [48] Macaulay said she treated him 'like a Nubian slave': [49] "Mr Allen, go into the drawing room and bring my reticule"; "Mr Allen, take a candle and show Mr Cradock the picture of Napoleon". [50] She always took Allen with her on her drives. [51] After Lord Holland's death he lived at her house in Westminster, and here he died of jaundice on 10 April 1843.

The eloquent text of Allen's memorial tablet in the country church of Millbrook, near the Holland country retreat of Ampthill Park in Bedfordshire, was composed by Colonel Charles Richard Fox, the Hollands' son, who presented his copy (DPG 447, now missing) of the Landseer portrait of Allen to the College. Fox praised his 'strong understanding and great learning and his earnestness and simplicity of character', combined with his 'kindness of heart, and a steadfast love of liberty and truth'.

Allen's mind was clearly a fascinating one, and he inspired great affection. Fox wrote of him in a memoir that he was

a stout, strong man, with a very large head, a broad face, enormous round silver spectacles before a pair of peculiarly bright and intelligent eyes, and the thickest legs I ever remember. His accent Scotch; his manner eager but extremely good-natured ... the most liberal of men towards others of all opinions, provided he deemed them honest in their profession of them. Violent often in language, and uttering the most terrifick expressions towards those he believed to be either hypocrites, or cruel, or bigoted, he was in acts and deeds most gentle and kind-hearted.

This verbal sketch goes well with his portrait painted by C. R. Leslie in 1839 in the conversation piece *Lord and Lady Holland, Dr. Allen and William Doggett in the Library at Holland House* (RA 1841; private collection), in which Allen's genial figure is shown standing between the seated Hollands. Charles Fox recalled that at six years old he was amused by the Doctor's behaviour on their travels in Spain with a *cortège* of three large English carriages:

he used to be constantly reading, and also kept a very exact and minute journal of all he observed and heard, which was his practice whenever travelling. Whilst the post-horses were changing, he used to walk on at a rapid pace with his book ... He sometimes ran, an operation which was a great amusement to me, as, though active and buoyant, his gait was most extraordinary, and he used to move from side to side in running in a manner not a little laughable.[52]

John Allen at Dulwich, 1811–43

Intelligent and erudite as he was, John Allen does not appear to have interested himself much in the education of the Poor Scholars. From rather selfish remarks in his letters it might wrongly be assumed that he also administered the College in a cavalier way. On his appointment as Warden, for example, he wrote to an Edinburgh friend, John Thomson, from Holland House on 9 May 1811:

The duties of the office are to see, in conjunction with the trustees, that the other officers do their duty, and that the persons supported and maintained by the Establishment behave themselves properly; and more particularly it is the duty of the Warden to manage and superintend the pecuniary concerns of the Establishment. It will be necessary for me to have my nominal residence at the College, and to be actually there at least twice a week, and when the Master is absent, still oftener. On the whole it is a very pleasant situation, and to a literary man gives perfect independence of the world.[53]

The impression at Holland House was (not unnaturally) that he was a model Master of the College, 'where he occasionally went to stay': Charles Fox averred that 'his zeal for the good of the college, and his judicious management of it, ... his attention to the schools and charities depending on it, will be long remembered with gratitude'.[54] In a letter of 1820, following his promotion to Master, Allen complained that he had more to do than usual at Dulwich, and hoped 'to have little to do there in future, except to superintend and see that other people do their business'. He added that he was lucky in his new deputy, the Warden, Jeffrys Thomas Allen.[55]

There is thankfully little evidence of wrangling and pettiness among the Fellows under Allen's benign rule: he was more concerned to foster a convivial society of cultivated gentlemen (even if they were in Orders) than to consider educational benefits, as can be shown amusingly from the letters he wrote to a protégé of Holland House, the talented, restless and melancholy Revd Blanco White (1775–1841), encouraging him to apply for the post of organist at the College. White had been the unwilling tutor of Henry, son and heir of his patron Lord Holland, from 1815 to 1817 during Allen's time at Holland House. Of Spanish and Irish blood, Blanco was a refugee from Spain, a renegade Catholic priest who turned to the Church of England and then to Methodism, a political journalist and propagandist, and an author in Spanish and English.

March 6, 1831

Dear Blanco,

Poor Linley, 4th Fellow and Organist of Dulwich College, died this morning. Some years ago, you had thoughts of offering yourself for the situation, if it should become vacant, and therefore I hasten to inform you of the event, that you should announce yourself as a candidate without delay, in case you are still of the same mind. You are aware of the nature of the office. The organist is a Fellow of the College, and the late Mr Linley was a clergyman. The duties are to play the organ on Sundays, and instruct the children in music – twelve in number. The emoluments are at present about £160 per year, besides apartments, commons and wine. As the organist is completely on the same footing with the other Fellows, we wish, of course, to avoid common musicians, and to have a man of education, with the manners and feelings of a gentleman.

The Revd John Lindsay, Third Fellow and Usher, also wrote to White about the vacancy in 'the little monastery here', encouraging him to apply. White's response was to offer to pay someone else to play and teach the boys for a few months, saying he could not possibly accompany the Psalm tunes 'at this moment'. Allen wrote again:

March 8, 1831

Dear Blanco,

I am very glad you propose to stand, and with your knowledge of music I have no doubt you will learn to play the organ in much shorter time than you mention. [56]

In the event, White drew equal votes but lost the 'lot' at election to the Revd R. G. Suckling Browne (resigned 1836). [57]

In 1829 Allen requested a meeting with the new Archbishop of Canterbury, the conservative William Howley (1766–1848), at Lambeth Palace; he took with him his Warden (Jeffrys Thomas Allen), and the formidable Second Fellow and Schoolmaster, the Revd John Vane. They had a session of an hour, and the *Private Sittings* book records a 'long explanation' about the 'education afforded to the Poor Scholars and the provision made for them when they quitted the College'. The Archbishop 'appeared to be satisfied', and declared his wish that the College of God's Gift should be administered 'in the manner which had given satisfaction to his Predecessor'. [58] The meeting ended with an urbanely vague gesture by John Allen:

The Master assured His Grace that if any measures could be suggested tending to increase the usefulness of the College or to add to the comfort or happiness of any individual member of it, it was his wish and he would venture to add, the desire of every other member of the College to carry them into effect to the utmost of their ability.

A further insight into this disreputably evasive interview was given in Allen's evidence to the Charity Commissioners in their Inquiry of 1834; it transpired that, at the outset of his Dulwich days, Allen may have more or less conspired with his predecessor as Archbishop, the aristocrat Charles Manners-Sutton, in return for being left in peace:

We were informed by the present Master, that when he became Warden in 1811, he communicated to the Visitor his desire to make the school as efficient as possible, and that the Visitor intimated in return that the school had engaged much of his (the Visitor's) own attention; but he found so many obstacles to any alteration in the course which had been long pursued, that he recommended the college to go on as they were then doing, and qualify the boys for becoming respectable tradesmen. [59]

In 1829 Allen bought for the College, out of its surplus funds, a £100 share in the new free-thinking London University, which entitled him to 'present' one student per annum, with the stated intention of sending one of the Poor Scholars after his apprenticeship; but nothing came of this arrangement. [60]

Allen wrote firm letters to tenants on the estate, which were copied into the *Private Sittings* books: one to Lancelot Baugh Allen (following his resignation as Master) complaining that he had pulled down without permission an old stable and coach-house on the land he leased (he was fined £10); another was written to George Grote (1794–1871), the famous classical historian and politician. Grote had pollarded and thinned a belt of trees screening his house from the road, an 'ornamental appendage'; Allen regretted that his 'first intercourse' with a gentleman, and one, moreover, 'whose literary attainment and public character I respect', should be on so disagreeable a subject, and said that he had harmed both the property and the beauty of the estate. Both tenants were told (as he wrote to Grote) that 'a gentleman of your rank and fortune' should set a better example to poorer tenants and not encourage the caprice of others. [61] Grote appears to have paid the £20 fine with a good grace. In the year of Allen's death the College wrote to Colonel Fox thanking him for his gift of a copy of Landseer's portrait of him (see above), saying that Allen had 'endeared himself to every member of the Society'. [62]

Significantly, Allen broke with a Dulwich tradition, electing to be buried not in Christ's Chapel together with his predecessors at the College, but with the Holland family at Millbrook, 'as near as possible to the spot where the remains of my beloved Georgina and those of her lamented father are laid'. [63] The death in 1819 of the lively ten-year-old daughter of the Hollands, after a driving accident, had greatly grieved Allen; her marble head by Sir Richard Westmacott, set beside those of her parents in the country church, taken together with the mural tablet to Allen (quoted above), tenderly evoke his devotion to the Hollands. His wealth at his death was thought to be large, about £7,000 or £8,000; it is hard not to wonder to what extent Alleyn's Dividends contributed towards it. [64]

The Fellows

Three of the Fellows during this period had such original characters that they left a strong impression in memoirs of the period, as is shown below. The Revd Robert Corry (1771–1838; BA Oxford, 1791), on the other hand, is a tantalisingly obscure figure who is presumed to have been an important link in the bequest to the College of the Bourgeois and Desenfans collection of paintings (see below). A fashionable clergyman, the Morning Preacher of St George's in Bloomsbury for twenty years, he became Usher at the College in 1806, was promoted to Schoolmaster in 1812, and resigned the following year. From 1822 he was Rector of Tarrant Hinton in Dorset. The three new Fellows of the final decades of the old Foundation who were still in office at its dissolution in

1857 – the Revd Charles Howes (d. 1880), the Revd William Fellowes (d. 1867) and the Revd William Chafy (d. 1878) – by contrast seem to have been bland and conventional; while perhaps slow to recognise their doom, by then so clearly written on the wall, they were quick to defend their interests at the Inquiry.

Ozias Linley

The atheist John Allen's Fellows were all clerics. The eccentric Revd Ozias Thurston Linley (1765–1831) won the election for Organist in 1816 by 'drawing against the celebrated bass singer Mr Bartleman',[65] and held the post until he died at the age of 66. Both his theology and his behaviour were peculiar and dogmatic. Once arrived at Dulwich, he gave the texts of his old sermons to his maid at the College, Betty Slaughter, to kindle his fire. Linley's sisters from Bath, Elizabeth and Maria, are pictured by Gainsborough in the famous double portrait of 1771–85 at the Picture Gallery (DPG 320), which Linley lent in 1822. His brother William gave the College this painting and three more Gainsborough portraits, together with other Linley family portraits, in 1835. His sisters were the darlings of concert audiences, and the dramatist Sheridan was his most unsatisfactory brother-in-law. Linley was highly strung, and when excited would beat the table in Hall with his fist, making all the glasses and decanters jump, while his expressions of contempt, usually directed at bad clergymen, became more and more ripe. At musical performances he was overheard to mutter such comments as "Mercy on my ears! A chorus of bull-frogs; a chorus of warming pans; a chorus of bagpipes!" He would twist his snuff-box between his fingers and pull his wig awry and back to front, revealing his bald head. Linley stood at odds with the Preacher, the elderly Revd Thomas Jenyns Smith, who had received Horace Walpole, 'a *petit maître* in his dress, language and habits'; Linley said he was 'all primroses and violets'. The Third Fellow, the Revd John Lindsay, once delivered a sermon on the subject of anger, which he directed at Linley; Linley was in the organ-loft behind a curtain, and when asked his opinion of the lecture claimed he had heard nothing of it: he had been busy reading *Robinson Crusoe*.[66] Linley was the last Fellow to be buried in the Chapel.

John Vane

The Revd John Vane (1792–1871), a fearsome teacher, was illegitimate; he was rumoured to be the son of the politician, Viscount Castlereagh (1769–1822), War Minister during the Napoleonic Wars and Foreign Secretary from 1812, but his father seems in fact to have been Henry Vane (1771–1813), a wealthy landowner of County Durham. After graduating MA from Trinity College, Cambridge,

in 1817, he was Schoolmaster and Second Fellow from 1818 until he resigned in 1848. While at Dulwich he was also the first incumbent of the new church of St George at Camberwell from 1824. He was also appointed Chaplain in Ordinary to King William IV and later to Queen Victoria (he brought the Prince Consort to visit the College in 1843); from 1835–9 Vane was Chaplain to the House of Commons. He maintained his own man-servant in the College, and paid the College £5 a quarter for his board.[67] Henry Joseph Hartley, the former Poor Scholar who published a series of reminiscences in the *Alleynian* in 1905, recalled him as manly and lordly in manner, but also as overbearing and vindictive. In the schoolroom he would conduct long discussions with the Housekeeper about their guests at meals and the menu – John Allen liked steak pudding, Hartley recalled, which was withheld from the boys – or he would read the *Morning Chronicle* while deputing a monitor to hear the lesson. He looked up the answers to the sums set for the boys, and referred difficult passages in Latin to the Usher.[68] A bully of highly strung boys, his eyes would flash and his mouth twitch when crossed; he enjoyed using the birch, and would routinely flog boys, interpreting his victims' inability to supply correct answers as a deliberately contrary refusal to do so – on more than one occasion he flogged a boy four mornings in succession for leaving out a word in a repetition exercise. Once a boy had to stand in the middle of the chapel during a whole service with his coat turned inside out, and 'as the body and sleeves of the coat were lined with white, he presented a very ridiculous appearance'.[69] Vane left the College in 1828 to become Rector of Wrington and Vicar of Burrington in Somerset; he founded three of the four schools in the parishes and supported them generously.

John Lindsay

After the New College had been established for almost fifty years, an oil painting was exhibited at the Royal Academy in 1906 depicting a lesson with the Poor Scholars of this era. The point of *Old Time Tuition at Dulwich College, 1828*[70] was to congratulate the reformers by the implied contrast it presented to the enlightened tuition of the New College. The artist, Walter Charles Horsley (1855–1934), pictured the low ebb teaching had reached in John Allen's days, called by Dr Carver 'a long period of lethargy more perilous still' than the early difficulties of the College.[71] The artist's own father had supplied an eye-witness description of the scene: the Usher who sits up luxuriously in bed, wearing a floral dressing gown and a nightcap, smoking the churchwarden clay-pipe that (according to Horsley *père*) was scarcely ever out of his mouth, his slippers on the floor beside him, while the Poor Scholars in their long coats stand to repeat their Latin or else sit in dejection over their slates – this extraordinary figure is the Revd John Lindsay (MA 1812; d. *c.* 1875), Usher at the College of God's Gift from 1814 to 1834. According to Hartley's reminiscences, corroborated as 'thoroughly authentic' by Carver in a speech at an Alleyn Club dinner in 1904, the Fellow in the picture might just as well have been John Vane as John Lindsay, since Vane also took the first lesson of each day smoking his pipe in bed.[72] The painter's father, John Calcott Horsley (1817–1903; the artist who designed the very first Christmas card), was a friend of the College whose name appears in a list of guests at the laying of the foundation stone at the New College in 1866; his family were tenants of the College in a house at High Row, Kensington. The elder Horsley was invited at the age of eleven to stay with Mr Lindsay to copy pictures in the Gallery; he recalled that Lindsay 'was not an early riser, so he arranged that his class should come up to his bedroom for their lessons at eight o'clock every morning'. The young Horsley took dinner with the Fellows and their guests, 'a rather long perform-

ance'; the hall opened on to 'delightful gardens harmonious with nightingales'. He wrote of Lindsay's dressing gown and nightcap lesson that 'the contrast between this primitive class and the present college, now with its hundreds of boys and its modern methods, is eloquent of the changes', which confirms the intention of his son's picture as a compliment to the reformers and to the work of the great first Masters of the New College, Alfred Carver, James Welldon and Arthur Herman Gilkes.[73]

Lindsay seems to have regarded his post at the College as a privileged living in a kind of 'mutual household' in a country mansion, as in 1831 he was allowed to have constructed (at his own expense) a new staircase to his chambers, extending from the north face of the east wing with an oriel window showing the Lindsay coat of arms above it. On his resignation the College repaid him for the work,[74] but it was removed *c.* 1864 at the same time as an additional eight almshouses were constructed.[75] The oriel is to be seen in the engraving of the College in Brayley's *Topographical History of Surrey* (1842). Lindsay left the College in 1834 to become Vicar of Stanford on Avon and Swinford near Rugby.[76]

W. C. Horsley, *Old Time Tuition at Dulwich College, 1828*, (RA 1906). The Revd John Lindsay, Third Fellow and Usher, and the Poor Scholars at eight o'clock in the morning. (© Dulwich College)

T. A. Prior after D. McKewan, *Dulwich College* (detail), engraved for E. W. Brayley's *Surrey*, 1842. Lindsay's oriel window to left. (Jan Piggott)

The Estate

From 1800 until the building of the New College in 1866–70 the value of Alleyn's manorial estate was increasing fast while London grew ever more populous and prosperous. The College benefited from the Enclosure Acts, specifically from a new Act of Parliament to develop the Dulwich fields into villas, and from compensation for cutting the new railway-lines through the estate. The colossal Crystal Palace, twice the size of its parent building at Hyde Park, rebuilt in 1854 crowning Sydenham Hill, dominated the College, with its glass cliffs and great barrel-vaults. The Palace's permanent displays served as a three-dimensional encyclopaedia of natural history, architecture and sculpture; there were concerts with vast orchestras and choirs, and a bizarre variety of other entertainments, such as the firework nights in the Park with grand tableaux and moving pictures (such as battles and gladiator fights) outlined in fire. The Palace made the suburb even more attractive as a dormitory. The estate was, of course, not yet disfigured by the development of close housing; in 1900 the local Estate Agent still offered for sale large houses set in four and a half or even 15 acres of grounds. [77]

In 1805 the new Act for Inclosing Lands in the Manor of Dulwich made it possible for about 130 acres of common and wasteland on the southern part of the Estate to be enclosed; [78] ancient bridleways and footpaths could be stopped or diverted, and grazing forbidden. The subject of the Fellows' discussions changed from housekeeping and the mundane daily issues of their charitable and educational responsibilities to estate management on a formidable scale, with proposals for railway lines and their stations, tunnels, raised embankments and bridges, and for parks and cemeteries. [79] As early as 1788 the College had employed a Steward and Solicitor, Charles Druce (1762–1845), who appears to have been forceful and utterly loyal to their interests. [80] After his prodigious service of 57 years, he was succeeded by his equally energetic son, also Charles (1792–1881, the father of 21 children), until the old Foundation was dissolved in 1857. The College had commissioned work from a respected architect, George Tappen (*c.*1771–1830), of John Street, Pall Mall. On Tappen's death (Sir) Charles Barry (1795–1860) was chosen as Architect and Surveyor to the Estate, to be paid two guineas a day for his attendance. [81] Barry had already made his mark as the architect of the

Travellers' Club (1829). John Allen, the Master, was making use of his Holland House connections in appointing Barry, and came close to making Dulwich a colony of the great house. Barry's second son Alfred (1826–1910, Headmaster of Leeds Grammar School and Bishop of Sydney) wrote a biography of his father which described his three youthful years on an architectural grand tour. At Rome he became friendly with the Marquis of Lansdowne, and 'through him he was introduced to Lord and Lady Holland and became a not unfrequent visitor in the society for which Holland House was then famous. There he first met many noblemen of the Whig party, who showed him great kindness, and many of the distinguished literary men and artists of the day'.[82]

Under the Dulwich College Building Act of 18 June 1808 Parliament was involved in the Estate for the second time, granting the College the right to modify Alleyn's statutes such as to allow building on the fields, and to extend leases in the manor by 21 years from 63 to 84 years; previously there had been no security for tenants

anxious about their short leases. Two hundred acres of the woods or coppices, however, were not to be let by the College. At this time the 'Society' may have seriously discussed pulling down their decaying premises: a clause in the Act provided for rebuilding the College 'upon any other Scite', subject to the Visitor's approval.[83]

Tappen built substantial villas on the north verge of the Common: The Willows, Northcroft, and Glenlea (now Tappen House). Earlier mansions still stood, such as Belair with 46 acres, Kingswood (where Charles I had hunted stags) with 27 acres[84] and Toksawa with 22 acres. The Casina (or Casino) at Herne Hill (1796–7, demolished 1906), was designed by John Nash with a domed rotunda, and had charming grounds of 17½ acres, laid out by Humphry Repton; a small portion of the landscape garden and 'fish pond' survives, now the municipal 'Sunray Gardens' of Southwark Council, below Red Post Hill. The Common itself was leased to a Mr Lett in 1812 and he made plantations there, including clumps of trees, one of which, 'The Clump', formed of elms, is well

William James and George Tappen, 'Plan of the Manor' for 'the Award under the Act of Parliament for Inclosing Lands', 1809 (detail). James Allen's Long Pond, fish-ponds; the Crown, Greyhound and French Horn; outbuildings on site of the future Picture Gallery. (Dulwich College)

Drawn and lithographed by T. M. Baynes, *Hern Hill*, 1823 (detail). The verge of the Dulwich Estate; John Ruskin lived at nos. 28 and 30, Herne Hill, and later at 163, Denmark Hill (with seven acres of grounds). Signposts indicate Brixton and Dulwich. (Jan Piggott)

known to Dulwich sportsmen.[85] The avenues of chestnut trees on the Estate date from this period.[86] In 1815 the Mill on the Common, supposedly built by Edward Alleyn himself (see Chapter Three), was pulled down.[87]

Where the Common came to an end at Lordship Lane stood the Grove Tavern (formerly the Green Man, and now the site of the Harvester), which was advertising its 'Great Breakfast Room' in 1762. Lysons in his *Environs of London* (1792) said that it was, partly on account of its grounds, 'a place of much resort for parties of pleasure from London'.[88] Dr Alexander Glennie leased the large hostelry and grounds for a school, which became famous for its having Lord Byron as a pupil for three years from 1799 (when he was eleven). The boy is said to have taken part in mock footpad attacks on strangers. His mother's fits of temper in interviews with Dr Glennie, when he remonstrated with her about the boy's absences, used to reach the ears of the other boys. The house was demolished in 1825, and boards were put up advertising it as land for building; since no one responded, it reverted to pasture. However, Bew's Corner, a wooden inn kept by a former College servant, remained in place there for many years.[89]

The fields and woods of Dulwich became a favoured spot for metropolitan duels: in *The Adventures of Captain Blake* (1838), a novel by W. H. Maxwell (1792–1850), Regency bloods do not hesitate to cross a stile into the fields for their feud, nor to summon a surgeon from the inn after the event: '"There is not a prettier shooting ground in Britain than the Dulwich meadows" … "Where shall our rendezvous be? Oh, the Greyhound. Capital house that! Civil people, excellent wine, and if a man's nicked, the greatest attention".'[90]

In 1854 at the Charity Commissioners' Inquiry (see below) there was discussion of a possible development of the whole Estate, to be laid out in villas, as Thomas Cubitt had done at Clapham New Park. Barry was said to have a scheme ready, but Sir Joseph Paxton, the architect of the neighbouring Crystal Palace, had on an earlier occasion quashed the idea, saying that he would dislike seeing the Estate covered with houses; he was teased that he might feel differently if they were all to be made of glass.[91]

Despite the 1808 Act, the College continued to offer low rents and allowed little building to take place. While the rich took houses on the Estate, there was still poverty in the hamlet of Dulwich, as is shown in the bequest of

1829 by John Whitfield (still commemorated in Christ's Chapel prayers) of almost £700 for bread and potatoes to be distributed every winter among twenty poor widows. [92] The revenue from the Estate meanwhile increased from £3,760 in 1808 to £6,500 in 1818, rising to £8,100 in 1828. Account books survive, variously detailing income from rents, from felled timber and from the lease of pews to parishioners in the Chapel. [93] The Kensington estate bequeathed by James Allen in 1741 to support 'such and so many boys to read and poor girls to read and sew', brought in an annual income of £150 by 1810. [94]

William James, a surveyor, prepared a map and a report in 1809. He described the Dulwich Estate, 'embosomed in a rich and fertile vale', as 'scarcely to be equalled' in the environs of London, 'secluded from the bustle and activity of Trade and Commerce, from the noisome air of manufactories and the busy hum of many men'. [95] His opinion was that 'the mansions and villas built by some of the tenants may vie with any in the kingdom for Beauty, Elegance and Substantiality', and he foretold that 'the neighbourhood will become most genteel and select'. Some of the older properties plainly irritated him – they were 'only fit to be pulled down'. The College turned down James's recommendations, however, when it was found that much drainage was necessary, and that just two of the five roads he proposed would cost between £3,000 and £4,000. [96] They would not have appreciated James writing in his report that favouritism from the College to certain tenants was unfair, and that there was 'a liberality in their Landlords bordering on weakness'. [97] Properly managed and developed, the surveyor said, the Estate could bring in £15,000 in annual rents. [98] The 200 acres of woods and coppices assigned by Alleyn for the provision of faggots for fuel were no longer necessary since coal was cheap, and the College was now allowed to assign part of the woods for building leases. The *Private Sittings* minutes record a decision in 1809 to advertise by putting up 'painted boards' in the fields for 'charming spots to build upon'. [99] Surprisingly, the Charity Commissioners' Inquiry was told in 1854 that many of these boards stood for years with no takers. [100] Toll gates and roads with 'fingerposts' for directions were developed. [101] By 1814 Manning and Bray reported that 'Merchants and rich traders of the City of London' had taken 'a great many good houses', [102] as was echoed in 1841 by Brayley's *Surrey*, which recorded a great increase in the leases taken by this social class. [103] In 1843, after much negotiation, the College presented a freehold half-acre of land for the building of a new church to cater for this influx of new residents: St Paul's church at Herne Hill (G. Alexander, archt.; rebuilt after a fire by G. E. Street in 1858). [104]

The Old College

The really significant enterprise in the last decades of the Old College is the building of the Picture Gallery, described below; meanwhile, additions and alterations were made to the ailing Stuart building of the College and to its East Wing, refaced in 1739 as part of James Allen's refurbishment of the Estate (see Chapter Four). [105] The remaining red brick was by stages covered with stucco: the Tower by 1810, the front elevation by 1815, and the rest by 1832. [106] The square Tower retained a weathercock on its wooden turret, dated 1772. [107] It can be seen from a Ground Plan of 1811 [108] that the Hall had now been split equally into a Boys' Hall and a Dining Room, physically dividing the Poor Scholars from the 'Society', and contrary to Alleyn's notion of the community as a family, sitting at a Common Table for meals. When, four days a year, the boys feasted with the Poor Brethren and Sisters in the Hall, the 'Dons' looked in and partook of a glass of wine and a sandwich without sitting down. [109] The long gallery with pictures was converted into dormitories in 1818 by George Tappen, as the old heavy and elaborate plaster ceiling was deemed hazardous; [110] Alleyn's and Cartwright's pictures were meanwhile dispersed into the Dining Room, Audit Room and the apartments of the Master and Fellows. The powerful seventeenth-century painting *The Judd Marriage* (DPG 354), a *memento mori* showing a couple with the corpse of a young man, was hanging in the Audit Room in 1814. [111] In 1815 a new stable and coach-house were built, and in 1821 Tappen repaired the West Wing, described in 1814 as 'ruinous', with barge-boarding on the eaves. [112] The Warden's apartments were much enlarged and new kitchens built at the same time, at a cost of 3,000 guineas; [113] a special building fund had grown to £5,800. The Warden, Lancelot Baugh Allen, wrote a letter to John Allen, then absent with the Hollands, in which he doubted Tappen's estimates for this work, offering the view that the whole West Wing should be pulled down and the main body of the College instead continued to the west; he joked that the College would be reduced to a poor house and Tappen would run off to America. [114]

The Charles Barrys in turn added Gothic features to the Old College: in 1832 the West Wing was converted by the father into a schoolroom, a dining room for the boys, and a dormitory in the former Gallery upstairs, and both Wings were 'embellished' with flourishes deriving from foliated finials such as at King's College Chapel, Cambridge. [115] In 1858 his son Charles Barry junior (1823–1900) was appointed Surveyor and Architect by the new Governors, when his father's post was made invalid with the old constitution. In 1866 he built

The Grammar School. Rock & Co, 1849. (Dulwich College)

a new clock tower, added the cloister and designed elaborate terracotta (literally 'cooked earth') chimneys for the East Wing. The elder Barry devised a brilliant unexecuted scheme to enclose the courtyard with a screen and a lodge like a Cambridge college, with a pillared loggia as a playground for the boys in wet weather; the style can only be guessed at from a ground plan in the Archives, as there is no drawing of its elevation.[116] The Grammar School of 1841, across the road to the west, commissioned by John Allen in response to criticisms of the education of the Poor Scholars by the Visitor (see below), was designed by the elder Barry, and is the most important memorial of his tenure for 28 years of the post of College Architect and Surveyor: an elegant, rather plain hall in a simple version of the Tudor Gothic style which Barry made world-famous at the Palace of Westminster from 1835[117] after an earlier essay (in collaboration with Pugin) at the King Edward VI Grammar School at Birmingham (1837, now demolished). The Grammar School cost £900.[118] The College had a pleasant approach from the north 'through a venerable grove', and a bench had been set to encircle a very large elm.[119] To the south the old-fashioned garden still extended, Alleyn's original pleasure grounds, described in 1791 as 'adorned with walks and a great profusion of fruit-trees and flowers'. There was a 'fish-pond' (where the boys were permitted to angle) until 1872, when it was filled in.[120]

The Chapel

Brayley's *Surrey* (1841) informs us that the Chapel 'may be regarded as a kind of parish church to this hamlet.... All the parochial duties, except marriage, (which has not been solemnized here since the year 1754), are performed by the senior fellow, gratuitously'.[121] There are few records of services and events in this period, but significant alterations were made to the interior. In 1823 the south-side aisle with gallery was built by George Tappen to cope with the increased population of the Village.[122] A Judas tree had been planted in 1816 by the Chapel wall. In the same year Alleyn's original worn tombstone was removed, and a 'handsome black Marble Grave with the Founder's Arms' was commissioned from Henry Westmacott.[123] Sir Horatio Davies, speaking at an Alleyn Club dinner in 1898, recalled how when a Poor Scholar he witnessed the actual remains of Edward Alleyn being taken up, presumably when the Chapel was altered in 1850–51 and Alleyn's tomb was lowered to ground level.[124] The original tombstone was later found by the landlord of the Half Moon Tavern in Herne Hill serving as a cover or break-water for a parish sewer, and he saved it in the tea-garden or skittle alley of his inn.[125] In 1925 the Governors mounted the old slab in the wall of the Cloister. Thirty-one bodies are said to lie below the floor: Edward Alleyn, his first wife Joan, his mother-in-law Agnes Henslowe, seven Masters, five Wardens, and sixteen Fellows.[126]

The pulpit on a slender column, the rood-screen with impish carved animals in motion, and the pews with poppy-heads, all of oak, were designed by Joseph Clarke (a minor architect with a large practice in restoration and in building churches or schoolhouses) in 1850. Clarke also designed the stone-carved panel with the College arms above the porch.[127] These alterations, as well as some repairs to the Chapel, cost the College £2,000 in 1851. In 1878 some of Clarke's figures on the stalls were removed; it was objected that their shapes were too fantastic.[128]

In the 1840s the College funerals for the pensioners were described as 'papistical':

> it was the custom for the Master, fellows and choristers, after walking in procession through the College cloisters, to precede the coffin and mourners through the village, singing verses of the 140th Psalm and the well-known chorale of 'St Ann'.[129]

The Bourgeois Bequest and Picture Gallery

In 1811 the College accepted a bequest from Sir (Peter) Francis Bourgeois, RA (1756–1811) of a collection of some 370 paintings. A large number of these paintings, it was claimed, had been intended for a royal collection commissioned by the King of Poland, Stanislaus II Augustus Poniatowski, a scheme abandoned when the King was forced to abdicate in 1795. The collection included masterpieces by Poussin, Watteau, Reynolds and Van Dyck, by Rembrandt and other Dutch painters. A Picture Gallery designed by Sir John Soane (1753–1837) was built to house the collection, and is of course now world-famous. This surprising endowment could not be said to be of obvious benefit to the objects of Alleyn's charity, his Poor Scholars or the Almsfolk, but it became an extraordinary boon to the neighbourhood and to the nation; it is now the first connotation of 'Dulwich' to the majority of cultivated visitors.

The College was offered the legacy by Francis Bourgeois on his deathbed, two weeks after falling from a horse. Four years earlier his friend and associate had died, Noël Joseph Desenfans (1744–1807), towards whom, as his protégé and heir, Bourgeois felt a 'filial veneration'.[130] The two men were collectors, and they also dealt in paintings, taking advantage of the sale of the great collections being sold in France and Italy during the Revolution and the Napoleonic wars, and both had settled in London from the continent, advancing themselves in the art world among the rich and famous.

Francis Bourgeois, the son of a watchmaker from a 'considerable' family in Switzerland and an English mother, had been 'designed' for the Army, but 'he quitted it for the pencil [paint brush], in which he had received

some lessons from a Foreigner'.[131] An artist of modest ability, he is also known to have added fake signatures to paintings.[132] King Stanislaus Augustus of Poland gave him a knighthood (l'Ordre du Mérite) and the title of Painter to the King of Poland, shortly before his abdication; George III permitted him to be addressed in England as a knight, as a 'courtesy title'.

Noël Desenfans was born near St Quentin in Northern France and educated at the Universities of Douai and Paris. At the age of 17 he published a novel, L'Elève de la Nature (1763), which attracted the attention of Rousseau. He had come to London in 1769, initially as a language teacher. Later, on the strength of his novel, a comedy and some pamphlets, he styled himself as a 'man of letters'. At the suggestion of his friend Michael Poniatowski, the Prince Primate of Poland and brother to the King, he was appointed 'his Polish Majesty's Consul-General in Great Britain' in 1794, and at the same time was asked to get together a Polish royal collection.[133] The paintings were left on his hands; after unsuccessful attempts to sell them to the Tsar of Russia and to dispose of them at an auction in 1802, Desenfans tried to interest the British government in acquiring them. He was concerned about the lack of public galleries, and in 1799 had published a plan for a free National Gallery and National Portrait Gallery (for heroes such as Nelson and prominent figures of the current reign).[134] The government declined Desenfans's offer to take the collection, which was conditional on their finding premises for it and making it the basis of a National Gallery.

At the age of 31 Desenfans had married Margaret Morris (1731–1813), a wealthy lady from Swansea who was 14 years older than him and the aunt of two of his pupils. Bourgeois willed that the collection made by himself and Desenfans, including 21 pictures by himself, was to be given to the College when Margaret Desenfans died, to be known as 'the Bourgeois Collection'. In the event, however, Margaret Desenfans very soon after his death consigned the collection to the College, and interested herself in the construction of the Gallery at Dulwich.

The details of the bequest and the reasons why Francis Bourgeois chose Dulwich to house the collection are complicated. He was aware that the College already had a gallery (of a sort) founded by Alleyn and augmented by Cartwright; that the Fellows 'were not shackled with any onerous duties to divert them from the due care of the paintings'; and that the country air would 'operate favourably in preserving them from the atmospheric and other evil influences of the metropolis'.[135] Additional factors were the association of Lancelot Baugh Allen and John Allen, Master and

Paul Sandby, *Sir Francis Bourgeois and Noel Desenfans*. Watercolour. (© Dulwich Picture Gallery)

Warden, with the world of art and literature and their affluent hospitality at the College. The bequest raised a few eyebrows: the *Somerset House Gazette* declared in 1824 that the collection was bequeathed to Dulwich 'almost unaccountably'.[136]

Bourgeois was 'in the habit of visiting' the College, and was said to be fond of it.[137] Lancelot Baugh Allen was furthermore on intimate terms with both Bourgeois and Desenfans, and a frequent guest at their house, nos. 38 and 39 combined, Charlotte Street, Portland Place, where the pair (minus Margaret Desenfans) entertained *cognoscenti* in a setting closely hung with pictures; after dining in a room with fourteen Poussins, the guests sat in the 'Cuyp Room', a library.[138] A further connection between Dulwich and Charlotte Street was the College's Usher, the Revd Robert Corry, who 'occasionally officiated at Sir Francis's private chapel' at the house. This was in fact the mausoleum designed by Sir John Soane to house the tomb of Noël Desenfans following his death in 1807; 25 feet long, it was built in the back yard where they had pulled down a coach-house.

According to one tradition, it was Corry who first suggested that the collection be given to the College.[139]

A memorandum by Lancelot Baugh Allen at the Soane Museum[140] tells how Corry brought Allen, to his delight, the news of the intended bequest at his chambers in the Temple in December 1810; Allen and Corry promptly called on Bourgeois, together with his solicitor. This document shows that Bourgeois was concerned for the integrity of the collection and that he was already planning a commemorative dinner for the Royal Academy to be held every year among his pictures at Dulwich. He thought that a staff of two people would be adequate to run the new Gallery. A further bequest, 'to the poorer part of your society' (which Corry told him they did not need), was suggested. Bourgeois then requested that his remains, and those of Desenfans, be interred in sarcophagi above ground 'in some little nook of the chapel'; to the latter Lancelot Baugh Allen agreed, disingenuously or in apparent ignorance of Alleyn's strictures about banning outsiders from sepulture in the College Chapel. Soane was urged as architect since he was a friend of Bourgeois, and since he also understood how to work economically. Style was discussed: Soane was said to object to the 'Gothic' style suggested by Allen as the most compatible with the existing buildings of the Stuart period.

Another tradition holds that the offer of the collection to Dulwich was influenced by John Philip Kemble (1757–1823), the great actor and manager of the Drury Lane and Covent Garden theatres, who was (as we have seen) friendly with Lord and Lady Holland and is known to have been a guest at the College; Kemble was also later among the guests invited to the dinners for the Royal Academy held at Dulwich.[141] Corry also was an associate of Kemble, and is a documented guest at one of his dinners as early as 1798.[142]

There is only hearsay for either theory about who may have prompted the bequest. The antiquary John Britton, who was reporting a conversation with Lancelot Baugh Allen and with Corry a few days before writing, said that Bourgeois himself was 'the real and ostensible founder of the Dulwich Gallery', and that 'the Members of the College entered into his views with great spirit'.[143] Bourgeois on his death-bed asked to see his fellow Academician Joseph Farington, and told him that he had earlier thought of leaving the collection to the British

Museum. An elaborate scheme for private collectors to contribute pictures to the British Museum at Montague House had been part of his proposal of a National Gallery.[144] Although saying that he himself was 'an Aristocrat both in feeling & principle', Bourgeois told Farington that he disliked the aristocratic government of the Museum, and in particular a clause that would allow them to sell pictures left to them to buy a stove; by contrast, Dulwich was an institution 'of unpretending merit' dedicated to an excellent purpose, at a moderate distance from London in delightful countryside.[145] It is likely that the same motive as Alleyn's, that of perpetuating his name, influenced him; the collections of paintings in London at this time, housed in aristocratic *palazzi*, were known by the name of their owners, and indeed the College in early days referred to 'the Bourgeois Gallery'. Leigh Hunt (who remembered seeing Bourgeois in dandy's buskins and boots) said that there was certainly vanity in the bequest, 'though attended with touching circumstances'.[146] From 1857 by Act of Parliament the

Left: Exterior of the Mausoleum.
(© Martin Charles)

Right: Interior of the Mausoleum.
(© Martin Charles)

collection was called 'Dulwich College Picture Gallery' with a separate endowment fund; in 1979 amongst other changes to the Foundation its title was abbreviated to 'Dulwich Picture Gallery' (see Chapter Ten).

When the will was read, Bourgeois had left his collection to the College with £2,000 towards the repair or rebuilding of the West Wing picture gallery. He specified Soane as the architect. Soane was also to design a Mausoleum at Dulwich for Bourgeois himself and for Desenfans; his executors gave a further £1,000 from his estate to build it. Soane said at once that the West Wing was ruinous and must come down. He prepared for the College an elaborate series of drawings of alternatives, with ground plans and perspective drawings, including a grand scheme which was essentially a rebuilding of the College around the (preserved) Chapel; these drawings survive at the Soane Museum.[147] His own preferred option shows the two West and East Wings demolished and a proposed Great Quadrangle to the south, with an arcade of 13 bays, a loggia reminiscent of an Oxford or

Cambridge College, and an entrance lodge; the positions of the present Gallery and Chapel represent two sides of this scheme. A memorandum in the *Private Sittings* book on 14 July 1814 in John Allen's handwriting records a feeble decision that the idea of this arcade 'be postponed to some future period'.[148] The Mausoleum was originally to have been a prominent feature within this quadrangle, but it was decided to move it to its present position outside on the west after building on the top-lit Gallery was started.[149] Soane's estimate for the lesser scheme, which the College accepted, was £11,270, including £1,000 for the Mausoleum. Soane, out of friendship for Bourgeois, neither asked for nor took any fee for his designs; indeed he offered to make up a deficit in the building expenses from his own pocket, though this was politely declined. The College's resources were £5,800 in their building fund, marked for the West Wing, the £2,000 left by Bourgeois, and a further £4,000 given by Margaret Desenfans.[150] Soane surely knew of the great potential resources of the College, and perhaps hoped to excite their building ambitions, but he found himself having to write reassuring letters to the College authorities, who were cautious, and even alarmed, about costs, 'to economise the expenditure as far as is consistent with solidity and durability of construction'.[151] John Allen, the Warden at that stage, was involved in meetings, and (as bursar) visited Soane personally to convey the College's decision not to pull down the West Wing but to build a new wing for the Gallery that would also house the Poor Sisters, indicated on plans as 'apartments for old women'.[152] Soane's wife wrote later in a letter that Lancelot Baugh Allen was 'a time serving vain hypocrite', and the College must have proved in many ways vexing clients; however, a friend thanked Soane in September 1812 for a sketch of what he referred to as 'your favourite subject, the Mausoleum and Gallery'.[153]

The Mausoleum was close in style to the earlier one in Charlotte Street, as Bourgeois requested in his will, a chamber with a Greek Doric peristyle of eight columns and a dome with an *oculus*; there were rectangular recesses for sarcophagi. An *ouroboros* serpent motif, symbol of eternity, is figured on high, and Soane extended necropolitan flourishes on the exterior of the Mausoleum with *acroteria* [ornaments above the pediment] of cenotaphs and cinerary urns. For the Mausoleum, as in his own house at Lincoln's Inn Fields, he made use of amber glass, high up in the four voids of the lantern.

The dinners for Royal Academicians were intended by Bourgeois to be held on St Luke's Day (18 October), the patron saint of artists; Mrs Desenfans endorsed this date for the dinners in her own will, with a bequest of the interest on £500 to pay for them.[154] Soane in a florid passage in his *Memoirs* (1835) tells how the guests, after inspecting the collection and dining in the brilliant light of

the Gallery among the paintings, were to rise to view the Mausoleum, and would thus appreciate the theatrical effect of the contrast whereby the 'dull, religious light shews the Mausoleum in the full pride of funereal grandeur, displaying its sarcophagi, enriched with the mortal remains of departed worth'. The guests would be dining in communion with the dead Academician and his friend: 'calling back so powerfully the recollections of past times that we almost believe we are conversing with our departed friends who sleep in their silent tombs'. Soane's Memoirs also record his intention, at one point, 'to have followed the example of my much esteemed friend Sir Francis Bourgeois, and to have left my Library and Collection of Antiquities to the College';[155] the Soane Museum might have stood today at Dulwich, an adjunct to the College. The empty extra sarcophagus in the Mausoleum is thought to have been reserved by Soane for himself should he have carried out this bequest.

A letter from Soane to Druce transcribed in the *Private Sittings* book offers to design the Gallery in a 'plain and substantial manner' for reasons of economy;[156] ironically it is the austerity of the building that commands its great prestige among modern architects; in John Summerson's judgement it is 'the quintessence of the Soane style and the apex of his achievements'.[157] Compared with Soane's more elaborate manner used on the grander public buildings in the metropolis such as the Bank of England, it is austere with eloquent restrained ornamentation. Soane used the cheapest London stock bricks, 'fine yellow bricks', rather than the stone facing typical of the period, but used Portland stone to enrich the lantern of the Mausoleum and the frieze with a Greek key-pattern.[158] Summerson's brilliant analysis of the spaces, intersections and the tensions of

the Gallery justifies his claim that 'it reaches a level of emotional eloquence and technical performance rare in English, or indeed in European architecture'. [159] Both Lancelot Baugh Allen and Corry were executors of Bourgeois's will (with a legacy of £1,000 each). [160] A codicil of £19,000 in further bequests was never executed, and the residue of the estate all came to the College. £5,470 was found from this residue to pay the shortfall on the building, and Margaret Desenfans gave another £3,000. Mrs Desenfans herself had died on 16 May 1813 when the Gallery was almost complete; she bequeathed her own fortune, with busts and statues of Bourgeois and her husband by Richard Westmacott, marquetry and Boule tables and chests, other furniture, a clock and vases to the College. [161] The total cost of the Gallery was £14,222 of which the Bourgeois estate and Mrs Desenfans contributed nearly two-thirds. George Tappen oversaw the construction from 1813. The 'apartments' for the Poor Sisters occupied what is now the smaller enfilade of rooms on the west side of the Gallery, which were not to be converted for pictures until 1884 and 1886 under Charles Barry.

The coffins of the two connoisseurs were placed in the Mausoleum in March 1815. The paintings had been moved from Charlotte Street in September 1814, but the public were not admitted until 1817 until the problem of heating the gallery was solved. Steam heating from a coal boiler was installed, and was extended to the Chapel; the stoves, peculiar large, squat, green cylinders (supplied by the firm of Bolton and Watt) are to be seen in a drawing of the interior. The very next year leaking pipes had caused dry rot. The floor was covered with a green oil cloth; the walls were originally painted a heavy 'burnt Oker' colour recommended by Benjamin West, the President of the Royal Academy. [162]

The Bourgeois Gallery was always intended to be open to the public; the collection of Desenfans and Bourgeois at Charlotte Street had been declared as not exclusively 'for persons of rank and affluence', and had been open to students. [163] Margaret Desenfans specified in her will that the Gallery was to be open without admission charge on Tuesdays. Tickets had to be applied for north of the Thames, at certain auctioneers and print-sellers: Colnaghi, Ackermann, Clay and Boydell. In 1814 John Britton protested in print that since the Gallery was intended 'for youthful students' the opening hours were 'utterly inadequate'. [164] By 1817 the Gallery was open daily except for Fridays and Sundays. [165] The Fellows almost immediately began their practice of borrowing pictures for their rooms: John Lindsay took a Poussin and a Van Dyck. [166] Sometimes the privilege worked in reverse: John Vane presented a copy of a painting by Rubens to the Gallery, *Night Scene, a Woman and a Boy with Candles* (DPG 403), in 1830.

Opposite: The West Façade of the Gallery under Construction, c. 1815. Soane Office drawing for a Royal Academy Lecture. (© Trustees of Sir John Soane's Museum) · *Above:* Interior of the Picture Gallery. Rock & Co, 1849. (Dulwich College)

John Bonham was appointed as 'a servant to have care of the Picture Gallery' for £80 per annum and his lodging.[167] The first Keeper was Ralph Cockburn (d. 1820), at a salary of 200 guineas per annum.[168] Stephen Pointz Denning (c. 1787–1864), a minor painter, followed him in 1821, and his duties were to include instruction for the Poor Scholars in drawing.[169] In 1834 he was reproached for the 'intemperate manner' in which he stopped an engraver taking a drawing from one of the pictures without permission.[170]

Bourgeois feared the College might ignorantly allow the paintings to be 'injudiciously cleaned and injured',[171] and John Allen, acting on the wishes of Margaret Desenfans, approached the President and Council of the Royal Academy to superintend the Collection. This was the start of a long association with the Academy, who were to appoint a Governor to the Board of Dulwich College until as recently as 1994.

Margaret Desenfans made a further bequest for Academy dinners: a fine set of silver plates, pierced silver bread-baskets and cutlery (all of which survive), together with decanters and linen; the servants were to wear her deceased husband's livery. On 10 September 1814 the College held the first dinner at the College and the Academicians were shown the newly cleaned seventeenth-century portraits.[172] Joseph Farington records in his Diary the painters, sculptors and architects who attended these dinners, their position on the seating-plan of the long table, and also the menu. Only on this occasion were candles allowed in the Gallery.[173] As well as the Academicians, some of the richest proprietors in the country attended, together with Holland House celebrities such as the pair of wits, Samuel Rogers and Henry Luttrell. It is obvious that John Allen enjoyed presiding as host, and Farington wrote that the menus in 1817 and 1820, which included nine quarts of turtle soup and haunches of venison with champagne, Moselle and Madeira, were 'very handsome'.[174] In 1811 a ground plan of the College shows a wine cellar half as large again as the kitchens,[175] and the College accounts show lavish purchase of wines.

Benjamin West, William Mulready, Henry Fuseli and Kemble were among the thirty guests in 1817; J. M. W. Turner, Soane and Francis Chantrey attended in 1820.[176] In 1821 John Allen told the President that the dinner must lapse that year, as they had overspent on the previous dinner; the interest on Margaret Desenfans's capital for the dinner was only £15.2s.4d. and the College had spent £62.18s.9d. The Academicians must have felt that this occasion was worth continuing; they complained that the College had invited too many of their own friends, and they asked to have a close look at the wills of both Bourgeois and Margaret Desenfans.[177] Lancelot Baugh Allen

and Corry remonstrated with John Allen.[178] Eventually the dinners took place roughly every three years, followed by a garden party. When there was no dinner, there was usually a garden party. This tradition persisted into the next century; the Revd William Rogers, Chairman of the Governors, and his friend, the Governor Charles Roundell (1827–1906), invited distinguished company from town; a band played, and 15 four-in-hand carriages lined Gallery Road. Among the guests was the novelist Henry James, who in 1903 wrote recalling one such occasion:

> Even though, as I hope, these hospitalities still take place for new generations, I view them afar off, in a mellow social light which is one with the sweet-coloured glow of the long picture gallery of that fortunate institution, a vista of Dutch and other of the minor masters, looking down upon tables of tea and heaped strawberries and ices, upon smiling pilgrims from town, amiable women and eminent men, upon individuals and couples detached and absorbed, preferring eagerly the precious pictures even to the strawberries, nowhere else so big, upon high doors opened, to the ripe afternoon, for adjournment to beautiful grounds.[179]

The tradition continued until the Second World War. In 1914, together with famous artists and architects, Sir Ernest Shackleton was a guest only a few weeks before leaving on the *Endurance* expedition. In the early days, the select Academicians, as they were required to, viewed the pictures before the dinners; they also selected four to borrow for the students at the Painting School to copy.[180] This led to problems when the students sold the copies they made, or made surreptitious copies for engraving.[181]

The Gallery soon made Dulwich famous; writing in 1832 John Britton said that as the object of an excursion it 'forms one of the most delightful intellectual trips which the neighbourhood of the metropolis affords'.[182] It also prompted Hazlitt's essay and critique of the paintings, 'The Dulwich Gallery', quoted above.[183]

The Fellows' Library

In 1811, the same year in which the College received Francis Bourgeois's bequest for the Gallery, the book of *Private Sittings* records that 'presses' [cupboards] were to be prepared in the Treasury chamber to receive the 'Records',[184] Alleyn's papers and the College muniments, a sign that their significance was beginning to be appreciated. The first public mention of the survival of these documents appears to be one referring to the Founder's Diary in the entry on Edward Alleyn in *Biographia Britannica* of 1747.[185] The glory and pride of the Dulwich College library, the Henslowe and Alleyn papers (described in Chapter One) are the most important record of the great period of Elizabethan and

Jacobean drama to survive; Henslowe's Diary in particular, together with letters, contracts and deeds, shows in detail the enterprises of Alleyn and his father-in-law. By the end of the eighteenth century they began to be recognised as an invaluable historical source for the drama, but also for social and economic history. Presumably the manuscripts were originally kept with the College's cash, the Statutes and property deeds in Alleyn's great chest or elsewhere in the Treasury Chamber. Following the Stratford jubilee of 1769, a bardolatrous fever to discover old texts and facts about the Shakespearean period possessed scholars. The visits to Dulwich and the misbehaviour of David Garrick, Edmond Malone and John Payne Collier have been touched on in Chapter One; no record in the College papers survives of Garrick's crafty exchange of playbooks for theology. In 1792 the Master received a letter from Malone asking him 'to do Mr. M. the favour to breakfast with him' and to put the Founder's Diary, '(if it be so small as not to be an incumbrance) in his pocket'.[186] Malone was lent Henslowe's Diary along with a mass of Alleyn and Henslowe papers 'in a trunk and a basket' on 26 March 1806.[187] Henslowe's Diary was actually mislaid for a considerable period of time and was not returned to the College until Malone's death in 1812 by his executor, the younger James Boswell.[188] Malone transcribed and published from the Dulwich collection the texts of the *Platt of the Secound parte of the Seuen Deadlie Sinns* and the four similar cue-scripts which disappeared from the College Library to end up in the British Library.[189] The British Museum Trustees bought Garrick's collection, which included printed play quartos with Dulwich College shelf-marks.[190] In 1819 the Archbishop of Canterbury, Charles Manners-Sutton, asked to borrow Henslowe's Diary, and Lancelot Baugh Allen delivered it to him.[191]

The Revd Daniel Lysons, the antiquary, describing the College and its history in his *Environs of London* (1792) tells us that,

> adjoining the audit-room is a small library, in which are the books bequeathed to the college by Mr Cartwright. This library formerly contained a very valuable collection of old plays, which were given by the college to Mr Garrick, when he was making his theatrical collection, in exchange for some more modern publications. There still remain some scarce editions of books in various departments of literature, as it may be imagined would be found amongst the stock in trade of a bookseller, who lived in the middle of the last century. The college is likewise in possession of a few curious MSS.; among them is the Founder's Diary.[192]

The depredations made in the collection began to attract notice: John Britton wrote that the majority of Cartwright's plays and romances were 'long ago exchanged for ponderous tomes of controversial Divinity &c. at the repeated solicitations of our most early modern collectors of dramatick entertainments'.[193] In 1843 the College was able to buy back 36 letters and papers from James Orchard Halliwell that had not been returned by Malone.[194] In 1886 the Librarian of the British Museum was 'somewhat embarrassed' to have bought two documents from the papers, but his Trustees refused to return them.[195]

John Payne Collier first visited the College after he wrote to John Allen on 8 March 1830 asking to see Edward Alleyn's diary, saying artlessly, 'I do not like to leave any stone, however small, unturned'.[196] He spent long hours at the College examining and transcribing the theatre papers; some of his most outrageous forgeries have been noted in Chapter One. In blank spaces between lines as he turned the pages in Alleyn's Diary he wrote in two references to Alleyn attending performances of Shakespeare's *Romeo and Juliet* and *As You Like It* on specific dates.[197] In October 1840 he was given a loan of Henslowe's Diary for two months to transcribe it; he kept it for five years. The College prudently noted that the Diary contained '239 folios of which 22 are mutilated' before lending it to him. In all he added 16 forgeries to Henslowe's Diary and 23 forgeries among the papers, four of them naming Shakespeare or his plays.[198] Two other forgeries were made to 'prove' points about Shakespeare's career: that he was a resident of Southwark in 1596 and that when he retired to Stratford he had sold the Blackfriars theatre property to Alleyn.[199] Sir George Warner of the British Museum, who published his *Catalogue of Manuscripts and Muniments of Dulwich College* in 1881, rather generously summed up Collier in the *Dictionary of National Biography* by saying that 'to one fatal propensity Collier sacrificed an honourable fame won by genuine services to English literature'.[200] By 1857 the manuscripts were kept, as was the College plate, in oak chests in an oak-panelled Treasury, opening out of the Master's drawing room.[201]

Almost two-thirds of the Fellows' library consists of theological works. The College received bequests from the Fellows and from obscure well-wishers, and we read that every Master was 'expected to add to it'.[202] The Fellows in earlier days followed current affairs, and there is a remarkable collection of chronicles, broadsheets, proclamations and pamphlets, particularly those about the Popish Plot of 1678. John Allen bought books for the Library in Brussels and Paris as well as London,[203] and at his death he left Spanish books, some with Holland House book-plates, to the College. How the wonderful copy of the *Nuremburg Chronicle* (1493), with its wood-engraved illustrations, came into the collection remains unknown.

PART II

The work was finished today as the clock struck twelve …

The Crystal Palace Company and the Estate – The Dividend – The Churchwardens, the Charity Commissioners and the Master of the Rolls – The Grammar School – The Poor Brethren and Sisters – The Poor Scholars – The Archbishop, the Charity Commissioners and the 'Schemes' – The Charity Commissioners' Inquiry, 1854 – The Dulwich College Act, 1857

At mid-century two dynamic forces swept away the old Foundation and created the new College. The first and most important was conceptual and political: a new consciousness of the role of education in society and the zeal to reform charity schools brought about the exhilarating new constitution of 'Alleyn's College of God's Gift' in 1857. Even so, the reform had taken twenty years: an Inquiry and censure from the newly formed Charity Commissioners in 1834 were followed by a law case brought by the Churchwardens in 1841, and by a further and devastating Inquiry in 1854.

The effect of the second force on Dulwich was physical and economic: the second Crystal Palace, relocated from Hyde Park, was rebuilt in 1854 on its new site on Sydenham Hill. Proposing to educate as well as to entertain the People, it gradually garnered a remarkable increase of population to the Estate, in addition to the general suburban development, and brought a dramatic access of wealth to the Foundation. In 1866 the Chairman of the Governors declared in public that the receipts from the railway developments on the Estate had paid for the building of the noble New College buildings.

To place the enquiries and the reforms in their context it is first necessary to understand the changes to the Estate and to the College's finances and their management that made its position even more vulnerable to charges of conservative selfishness and contempt for educational progress. Loud allegations of malpractice in the College's deals with the Crystal Palace Company were made both locally and by the representatives of the beneficiary parishes, and the details of the negotiations and the amounts of money involved figured largely in the Charity Commissioners' Inquiry of 1854, whose main aim was reform of the school.

The Crystal Palace Company and the Estate

In May 1853 by an Act of Parliament the Crystal Palace Company were authorised to buy land belonging to the old-fashioned estate below it for the frontage of the Palace on Sydenham Hill, as well as part of the woodland opposite, and to make the broad carriageway now called Crystal Palace Parade. A second Crystal Palace Company Bill of 1854, which ordered further compulsory purchase of land and the widening of roads, was 'strenuously' but unsuccessfully opposed by the College, the Churchwardens and Sir Charles Barry, possibly to send up the price. Eventually the College received £12,500, a colossal sum, for the Palace Road (now Crystal Palace Parade) and land opposite the Palace. Here it was proposed to build three grand hotels, but in 1865 the Crystal Palace High Level Railway Station (demolished 1961) was built on the site.[204]

The Crystal Palace developments brought 'a very large increase' to the College revenues. George Wythes, a housing developer and a major Crystal Palace Company shareholder, took a lease for £1,871 per annum of seventy acres of woodland in Dulwich Wood Park. Wythes shortly afterwards sublet this land to the Crystal Palace Company, who paid him £3,200 per annum.[205] Sir Charles Barry, by now for 18 years the College Surveyor and (as architect of the Palace of Westminster) an eminent figure in Victorian architecture, himself acted as broker to the deal, advising the College that this proposal was for a 'most eligible letting'; he joined the Master, Warden and Fellows at the Private Sittings, along with the College solicitor Charles Druce, which was unprecedented.[206] The Company were displeased that Wythes had to pay Barry a fee of £400 per annum for services which had not been forthcoming for a year, and that they would have to submit all plans and designs for the elevations of villas to him, which he had the authority to veto. Wythes undertook to spend £40,000 on roads and planned to build 149 large villas over four years.[207] Further Crystal Palace Acts of July 1854 and July 1856 allowed for roads to be made to the Sydenham [Hill] Station and for compulsory purchase of a portion of the Dulwich Wood Estate for the railway. Paxton, the Palace's architect, negotiated in person with the College in 1854 over boundaries. He told the Charity Commission Inquiry that by 1854 the Company had already spent

£16,000–17,000 on difficult roads over the Estate,[208] including the steep wooded road now called 'Fountain Drive' and the magnificent serpentine 'Victoria Road' (after 1876 renamed 'Dulwich Wood Park') which served as a dramatic formal carriage sweep up Sydenham Hill to the Palace. This road also was 'strenuously' opposed both by Barry and the College.[209]

The College was next involved in the territorial expansion planned by the Crystal Palace Company closer to the Palace: the trading quarter of the Crystal Palace was to be kept to the south, as it is today, and the area along the top of Sydenham Hill to the north-east was to be leased from the College as a private speculation by Francis Fuller, their Managing Director and Surveyor, and developed as an exclusive neighbourhood. A new church was planned for the top of the hill to attract respectable tenants to this area, towards which Fuller offered £5,000 in 1852. Barry acted as intermediary for the contract, to lease 105 acres of woodland for large villas, which brought the College £2,009 per annum.[210] It was to be called the Sydenham Palace Estate. The houses were to be designed by Fuller's agents, Charles Barry junior and Robert Richardson Banks, who were partners in a new architectural practice; Sir Charles argued for and won better terms for them.[211] The press showed an interest in the transaction over the Dulwich Wood lease, and *The Times* on 3 July 1854 thundered of 'embezzlement' by the Fellows of £9,000–13,000 per annum as a result of these transactions 'in point of fact if not of law'. The plan failed, as Fuller got into financial difficulties.

On 4 June 1854, some ten days before the Grand Opening of the Palace, the Company recklessly and illegally took over a small portion of College land, leased to Fuller – Rockhills' Corner, at the top of the hill – and demolished two cottages on it, in order to improve the road giving onto 'the private apartments appropriated to the Queen', a dining room and a drawing room. There followed a long battle with the College, who demanded in compensation for this small triangle of land a proportion of what was said to be £20,000 per acre. Paxton claimed that he had been misled by a man from his own solicitor's department, who had assured him that what was actually a last-minute annexation of an old and tiresome obstruction in their way, made impatiently on a royal pretext, had been authorised by Druce himself. Four years later the College accepted a lesser payment of £365.[212]

The Palace wanted to ensure that no licences for new public houses near the Palace should be issued on the Estate to compete with their own licensing or catering. No doubt the College was happy to agree; John Ruskin, a tenant of the College at Herne Hill, was to complain bitterly of the excursion riff-raff drawn to the neighbourhood (see Chapter Six).

The Crystal Palace Company was impatient for the College to develop building on a large scale. They also complained to the Charity Commissioners' Inquiry that the College had acted greedily and against the public interest in all these transactions, especially since, as Paxton had declared, the re-siting of the Palace had doubled the value of the Estate, and would bring a 'fixed' population. The Company also deprecated the profit made by the College on the tolls to the turnpike road, as 'an amazing tax' on their visitors. They said that, since so many of their employees would be looking for schools for their sons, they had an interest in the quality of the education to be provided by the Foundation. Fuller, who had a major role in the building and management of the Palace, proposed to put himself forward as a Trustee of the New College, but his speculations had broken him and he was suddenly declared bankrupt.[213] In 1863 the West End of London and Crystal Palace Railway Company proposed a line and tunnel at the south-west corner of the estate to run from Gipsy Hill to the Lower Level station at the Palace; by a new Act of Parliament they became entitled to compulsory purchase of woods and land.[214]

The boys of the New College were to benefit, in due course, from the excitements associated with the colossal neighbouring Palace. The displays in the Palace, in effect a museum of civilisation, were truly inspiring. In 1913 Bishop Welldon, former Master of the College, wrote to *The Times* to say that he had 'learnt to appreciate the beauty and the value' of the Crystal Palace during his tenure in the 1880s; by 1913, however, the Palace was in decline, and Gilkes at Speech Day told parents that it had brought Dulwich College nothing but harm, and that the worst mischief they could give their sons would be a season ticket for it.[215] The boys of Dr Carver's New College were nevertheless impressed by the famous and fashionable visitors the Palace attracted: on Garibaldi's visit in 1864 they asked to draw his carriage themselves through the Village; although this was refused, it was agreed that Garibaldi's procession should drive slowly past the College, 'for a favourable view'. One Old Boy, Major-General Sir A. M. Stuart, recollected seeing 'the road from the College to the Palace full of carriages, on the occasion of a Handel Festival, and in some cases postilions with white beaver hats, in the procession'. Events attracted 'myriads' of carriages; the procession of Abdul Aziz Khan, Sultan of Turkey, (including practically the whole British royal family) in 1867 took six hours to pass.[216] The Palace traffic contributed sixpences to the tolls, amounting in 1860 to £375 for nine months.[217]

The Palace on the hill above the Estate also expressed new architectural ideas. The splendid High Level Station was designed by Edward Middleton Barry (1830–80), the youngest and most gifted son of Sir Charles. Its style of red brick with buff enrichment established a colour scheme followed by the New College, and might be said to have created a kind of livery, or family style, for many of his elder brother Charles's buildings on the Estate, such as the North Dulwich railway station built the following year in 1866 for the London Brighton and South Coast Railway.[218] Charles Barry designed some of his most pleasant houses in this livery in both Italianate and Gothic styles in the former Dulwich Wood sector of the Estate, in 'the valley in the hollow' between the Palace and Gipsy Hill, which was now, in deference to the new arrangement, called the Dulwich Palace Estate.[219] When Barry proposed works to the Governors, such as grand new villas, railway bridges and viaducts, a characteristic epithet of his, which recurs in the minutes of their meetings, was 'ornamental': he was anxious to set a standard of superior architecture for the Estate, drawing on a wider range of historical sources than most Victorian architects.

With monies from the land bought and leased by the Crystal Palace Company and their associates, the College also extended the Estate; in 1859 they bought the adjacent Knight's Hill estate of 59 acres, formerly the mansion and demesne of Lord Thurlow, for £13,000 from the executors of a Governor, Charles Ranken.[220] Meanwhile the College still resisted the East Kent Railway's proposal to cut a further line through the Estate.[221] When three separate railway lines were finally given permission to cross the Estate, the compensation was indeed sufficient to build the magnificent New College in the late 1860s.[222]

In 1866 Charles Barry designed the New College with arcading in cloister and turrets (see Chapter Six), and he also added a mansard roof to the tower at the Old College; in both buildings he was echoing motifs from his brother's Crystal Palace High Level Station, which added the flourish of a mansard roof to each of its 16 turrets. Visitors to the Palace passing the main elevation of the New College in their carriages would have been impressed by its architecture, a telling advertisement for the College itself, just as to the west Barry's raised embankment of the London, Chatham and Dover railway, then as now the main railway line to the Continent, passing through West Dulwich station, gives a panorama of the College set in its grounds.

*

The Dividend

By 1855 the question of radical reform of antiquated charitable institutions, the almshouses and endowed schools, had meanwhile animated the newspapers and periodicals; in that year Trollope's *The Warden* was published, in which Dulwich is named as a 'hotbed of peculation [embezzlement]', well overdue to be put down.[223] Writing after the College was reformed, a journalist in 1873 recalled the old order as 'a mere nest of sinecurists, in close connection with a joyless almshouse and a feeble and ineffective charity school'.[224] The main charge of embezzlement was directed at the bonus, or 'Dividend' (the annual distribution made among the Fellows and others when the income from the Estate was more than the expenditure on the College), which had by now reached a very large amount. James Hume had persuaded the Society to implement the benefit to attract better staff; since salaries remained low, the Dividend had become something of a scandal.

The actual salaries of the Master, Warden and Fellows in 1832 amounted to only £141.2s.4d.[225] When the Parishes involved in the Foundation did not receive what they thought they deserved from the surplus income, they appealed to the Charity Commissioners and set in motion the end of the old regime. At Alleyn's death the income from the estate was £800, intended to balance the expense of running the College. By 1738 it was £1,368, but by 1832 the Warden had £7,893 at his disposal. In 1775 the Dividend was £950; in 1805 it had increased to £3,875 and in 1821 to £5,571. From 1821 onwards stock and exchequer bonds were bought, particularly during the 1840s.[226] In 1832 John Allen received from the Dividend his quota as Master of forty of its six hundred parts (following Alleyn's Statute 117), just under seven per cent, which amounted to £590; Jeffrys Thomas Allen, as Warden, received thirty parts, five per cent, amounting to £442. The twelve brethren and sisters did well from the Dividend in 1832, getting £134 each. Indeed, the Churchwardens of St Saviour's thought the sum excessive, writing in a pamphlet that 'the old men and women receive benefits quite disproportioned to their condition, and inconsistent with the objects of the founder'.[227] An annual sum of £5 was set aside for the Library.[228] The Warden made shrewd investments.

It is said that the economist John Maynard Keynes used to telephone his broker from his morning bath at King's College, Cambridge, and thus richly endowed his college; at Dulwich, by contrast, the annual benefit by-passed the educational needs of the Poor Scholars entirely: in 1854 alone the Master received £640 for his salary and Dividend, on top of his excellent board and lodging.[229]

The Churchwardens, the Charity Commissioners and the Master of the Rolls

In Alleyn's scheme Churchwardens from the beneficiary parishes were to elect 'Assistants', who were to keep an eye on the affairs and finances of the College; they continued to attend, unwelcome, twice a year at the Audit. A symptom of their dissatisfaction was that in 1829 Alleyn's will was printed as a pamphlet to stir up feelings of injustice and resentment. The almshouses at St Botolph's, Bishopsgate, and at St Saviour's were by now ruinous and dilapidated; the College claimed they were not legally responsible for their repair. The College was only too obviously irritated by the claims of the parishes; they sent coals to the almsfolk, perhaps to salve their consciences. In 1842 they declined to uphold or contribute to the repair of almshouses at St Luke's, but the following year they paid £1,000 for the repair of Alleyn's Southwark almshouses in Soap Yard.[230]

The Charity Commissioners were established in 1832. Two years later, exasperated at being refused their gown allowances, the Churchwardens prompted them to enquire into the College. A full report was published. The demeanour of the almsfolk was noted as 'decent and obedient'. The Commissioners reviewed the procedures for sending the Poor Scholars, and the Assistants were criticised for no longer selecting three or four boys as candidates for election whenever a vacancy occurred, as Archbishop Wake had insisted in 1724. They were critical of the Fellows, and found the arrangements for their leave lax; John Allen should tear himself away from Holland House and restrict his annual quota of absences from 196 days to 40. Their strongest criticism, however, was reserved for the education of the Poor Scholars. The Revd Mr Vane, they reported sharply, 'does not think he is called upon to give the boys a good Latin education'. They were taught Reading, Writing, Arithmetic, History and Mathematics. Only two of the twelve were actually being taught Latin, and that at an elementary level and out of the Eton Grammar rather than texts; the Fellows were reminded that the Founder intended a Classical education. The boys' diet and clothing was much better than that prescribed in the Statutes, but the Commissioners pointed up the betrayal of Alleyn's aims, damningly concluding, 'the superior sort of education contemplated by the Statutes, if it ever was in fact afforded, has for many years ceased to be so'. Anthony Highmore in 1814 had already demonstrated the humbug of ignoring the needs of the more able scholars: he wrote that it was sheer nonsense to claim that there had been and would be no 'extraordinary talents' among the Poor Scholars, as so many churchmen came from 'no better, or not so good foundations' and that universities took young men 'of any station in life'.[231] Recalling Wake's injunctions that at fourteen the boys should be separated into a class for university and a class for apprentices, the Commissioners deplored that not a single boy had gone on to university since 1770. Moreover, fewer than two boys a year were even being apprenticed: 'the prime object of the education given to the Poor Scholars should rather be to qualify them for becoming intelligent and respectable tradesmen than to advance them far in Greek and Latin'. They found on examining the boys in the presence of the Assistants that what they were taught they seemed to know well. All the boys except one were being taught music by the Organist. For many years past there had been no boarders, or so-called 'foreign scholars', and though as many as three Dulwich boys had been taught without any fees since 1811, 'the rich are not willing that their children should associate with boys of such habits as parish boys usually have'.[232] William Young in his history of the College prints the full report, and notes that the official College minutes include only one reference to it, and one to the case in the Court of Chancery which ensued, which records that an eminent barrister was retained.[233]

Following the Report, the Commissioners, in the name of the Attorney-General, filed against the College in 1836 for the Founder's intentions to be properly carried out; for the extension of the Charity to more projects among the parishes; for increasing the number of scholars and securing the benefits intended for them; and for a proper scrutiny of the Revenues. The Commissioners had examined the accounts, and reported that the Members received too large a share of the Dividend, some of them receiving not only 'more than they were intended to receive, but something which they were expressly intended not to receive'.[234] The Attorney-General asserted that the stock bought in the name of the Master and Warden must not profit them personally but the College, in particular its building fund. The College replied by claiming that they were not entitled to make alterations to Edward Alleyn's statutes – contrary to Alleyn's express clause directing that necessary changes should be made in altered circumstances in the future – nor were they entitled to divert revenues from their nominated ends. The College were quick to protect their interests: they appealed to the Visitor and paid him his expenses; at the same time they bought a piece of silver at Garrard's for their solicitor, Charles Druce.[235] The Churchwardens and the Camberwell vestry lodged their complaints with the Archbishop.

The Master of the Rolls, Lord Langdale (1783–1851), delayed a judgement for five years until 1841. Perhaps surprisingly, he decided in favour of the College, on the grounds that it was not right 'to make alteration or diverge' from the original Letters Patent. He backed the distribution of the surplus income as being within Alleyn's statute, and implied that anything regulated by the Archbishop of Canterbury as Visitor must be correct.[236] He ruled that the endowment was intended for the College, and that it was not a Trust obliged to maintain the thirty 'out-member' almsfolk, as the Attorney-General had argued.

After a pause of seven years the Churchwardens and Association of St Saviour's in 1848 sent a 'memorial' or petition to the new Archbishop, John Bird Sumner (1780–1862), which resulted in an Injunction in 1851. The College retained a Queen's Counsel in 1849; according to a report in *The Times* the College protested disingenuously through their silk that this was the first time that they had heard criticism of the education offered to the Poor Scholars, reminding his Grace that Archbishop Wake in 1724 had ruled that the number of Assistants should be reduced to three, but that he had bowed to pressure and withdrawn the ruling. They also claimed that the Assistants had no right to suggest that more land should be let to build rows of houses to increase the income of the estate.[237] The Primate, formerly an Assistant Master at Eton, at last ruled in his Injunction that a percentage of the College's surplus income was to be allocated to improving the education of the Poor Scholars. They were all to be taught Latin up to the age of 14. Religious Knowledge, he noted, had been the least regarded subject in the last 25 years at the College; this may well have been a legacy of John Allen's days as Master. Sumner appears to have been influenced in his ruling by the new theories of education associated with the Prince Consort (1819–61), who was shocked by the narrow classical syllabus and the lack of scientific knowledge among English schoolboys, and also by the spirit of the Great Exhibition, with its vision of a more comprehensive grasp of both the modern world and the realities of Nature. He said that four boys were to stay at the College up to the age of 15 or 16 to be prepared for university. Classicists of 'superior talent' should stay on until they were 18 to be prepared for 'higher positions in society'. For this they would need to study Surveying, Chemistry, Civil Engineering 'or any of the applied sciences', to be taught by professors brought in from King's College in the Strand or the London University for two days a week.[238]

The Assistants were to complain in 1854 at the Charity Commissioners' Inquiry that not all the accounts had been made available to them, and that they had not been made aware of the considerable purchase of investments in the Funds. At the Audit, in a scene worthy of a Rowlandson cartoon, the Master sat in a high chair, and the Assistants said they were 'very much awed' by the heavy atmosphere, and that they lacked the courage to ask questions; they felt as if they were going to be examined rather than examining. When they did pluck up the courage to ask whether the full accounts were on view or what exactly the Poor Scholars were being taught, their questions were abruptly quashed. If the Assistants refused to sign the accounts – as they did on several occasions – they were denied the conspicuously over-generous allowance given by the College for 'horse hire' to attend the Audit originally prescribed by Alleyn, which (rightly or wrongly) they referred to as 'a little screw to produce the signature'. The Master of the day, George Allen (see below), told them that any criticisms or complaints would have to be addressed through the House of Lords. The Assistants claimed that, if the Master was truly zealous in following Alleyn's educational ideals, a thousand children could be educated for the equivalent of the College's monthly expenses. It was also pointed out that an independent auditor for the accounts was needed to avoid corruption, particularly when the College dealt with the new Railway Companies.[239] The failure of Alleyn's system to provide disinterested and powerful Governors to ensure good schooling became more drastic with each succeeding year.

The Grammar School

The College had got off lightly from the litigation of 1841. Lord Langdale, the Master of the Rolls, however, is reported to have told John Allen privately after the case that the poor education given to the boys was a matter of grave concern.[240] The College responded not by internal reform, but by opening in September 1842 an additional school for local boys, the Grammar School. Alleyn's Statutes had actually allowed for as many as 68 boys from the Village to join the Poor Scholars to be taught at the College. It was now hoped to attract to the Grammar School, from among the growing number of middle-class households in the area, those boys whose parents would not want them to associate with the parish boys.[241] Before this, boys from the neighbourhood had been provided for by the day-school, James Allen's school, which in 1812 was formed of 15 pupils;[242] by 1815 it had a new building (now demolished, on the site of the present Rokeby, Dulwich Village) and was called the Dulwich Free School, and by 1825 there were 60 boys and 60 girls on its roll. In 1842 a number of boys at the Free School left to join the lower Division of the new Grammar School. By 1854 James Allen's School was exclusively for girls.[243]

Within eight months of the opening of the Grammar School John Allen died. Its first Head Master was

Edward Baber, a graduate of the University of Durham, who was paid a salary of £150 per annum and all the fees. An Assistant Master was appointed in 1844. The prospectus described four graduated divisions; a fifth offered Greek and higher Mathematics. The fees ranged accordingly from 2d. to £1.4s. per quarter. Initially there was provision for a maximum of six boarders.[244] Baber was reprimanded by the College in February 1844 for violently beating the 'insubordinate and insolent' son of Dr George Webster, a prominent village resident, the founder and President of the first British Medical Association (who is commemorated by Charles Barry's drinking fountain of 1875 on the roundabout facing the Old College). The Warden examined the boy's back, but Baber would not accept the rebuke, and was sacked the following week.[245] His successor retired after only a year.

The Grammar School by 1856 numbered 30 boys in the Upper School, and 50 to 80 in the Lower School; there were 11 boarders. A wooden partition divided the building into the Upper and the Lower Schools. 'Upper' and 'Lower' referred not (as now) to the age of the boys, but to the level of the syllabus and the fees. The partition signified a social and an educational division: the Upper School, where Virgil and Cicero were studied,[246] was the origin of the modern Dulwich College, and the Lower School, specifically for poorer boys who left at 16, was in forty years' time to become Alleyn's School.

The Poor Brethren and Sisters

Throughout this period there are few mentions of the Almsfolk in the *Private Sittings* minutes; they appear in general to have been passive and, as far as the evidence goes, content. One pensioner, however, Bernard Ellis, was troublesome, introducing his 'niece' into his room and taking 'indecent liberties' with her in 1816 and later on causing a quarrel with 'violent language' in the Chapel with another Poor Brother, for which he was almost expelled, but instead forfeited his Christmas feast and a week's pension.[247] Not only the Society but the Almsfolk seem to have become more genteel: the Charity Commissioners in 1834 commented that, instead of the really needy, the Sisters were now 'decayed housekeepers of respectable character'.[248] Their new gentility can be shown from the fact that they resented the old Statute declaring that at death their chattels were to be sold and the proceeds to be split among the others; this was revoked in 1814.[249] They now dined in their own apartments. Charladies were hired to perform the chores of sweeping and bed-making to which Edward Alleyn had assigned the Poor Brothers and Sisters. The Statutes were ignored, in that they took in one Poor Sister at the age of 34 when 60 was the qualifying age.[250] The College

stocks had for a long time served more for antiquarian picturesqueness than use, and were finally done away with by 1814;[251] the punishment 'cage' was demolished in 1841. A set of iron railings had meanwhile been installed to enclose the lawns of the 'inner courtyard' (onto which the Poor Brethren and Sisters' apartments opened) in 1819.[252]

The Poor Scholars

While the mid-century debates over the College's future embittered the Churchwardens and threatened the comforts of the Master, Warden and Fellows, the sequestered life of the Poor Scholars doubtless continued in an even tenor. One Thomas Potter was noted in the *Private Sittings* for disorderly conduct and frequent absences,[253] but when the New College was constituted in 1858 he was given a place in the Lower School. The parish candidates for places were given a brief oral matriculation examination by one of the Fellows and then proceeded to the lottery described in Chapter Two. The case of Henry Joseph Hartley, a bright Poor Scholar and an orphan from St Luke's, whose reminiscences have been quoted above, is significant: his uncle, an attorney, asked for the boy to be transferred to the new Grammar School but was refused on the now familiar ground that 'the wealthy inhabitants of Dulwich did not like their sons to associate with the class of children of which the poor scholars were composed'. Whereupon in 1844, at the age of 14, Hartley sent his printed Petition, presumably his uncle's work, to the Primate, William Howley, pointing out that Alleyn intended 'a school of the first class, similar to those of Westminster and St. Paul's', and that 'the education given in the said College-school is of an inferior description (being little more than reading, writing, and arithmetic), and far from what it ought to be, and was intended by the Founder'.[254] Moreover, he continued, the new division into two schools, the College and the Grammar School, was contrary to the Founder's ideals. He asked for himself and all the 'Foundationers' to be transferred to the new Grammar School. Hartley, still a young man, later gave evidence to the Charity Commissioners' Inquiry in 1854, with a devastating indictment of the teaching of Latin and English by rote, which was, he said, 'perfunctory and unintelligent'.[255] The series of articles he contributed to *The Alleynian* in 1905 about his experiences tell us that when the Poor Scholars left, 'their scholarship was poor indeed', but that in many ways their days were content: 'lessons were easy and the holidays numerous'. He knew that Writing, Reading, Grammar and Music were on the Statutes for them to study. From 1836 they were also taught elementary Geography, and Arithmetic merely 'up to the rule of three': neither fractions nor decimals were taught. Latin lessons followed the Eton Grammar for repetition, and Latin versions of Æsop and a little Caesar were later used for translation exercises. There was no translation from English into Latin. On Saturdays the daily recitation of Latin grammar was replaced by the Catechism. They had 'much liberty with little supervision', and were well fed, clothed and lodged. The unchallenging life of the Fellows evidently extended to the Poor Scholars: Hartley wrote that the ruling principle of the College 'seems to have been that everything was to be made as easy and comfortable as possible for everybody'. On frosty winter mornings, on the other hand, at seven o'clock the younger boys lit candles from a tinder-box and practised writing for an hour. The schooling was so lax that the boys successfully begged for an hour off lessons to see one of the College pigs being killed. Hartley's memory of a kind of tacit apartheid between the Fellows and boys accords with the recollections of Sir Horatio Davies, Lord Mayor of London, who spoke of his eight years at the Old College in a speech at an Alleyn Club dinner in 1898: 'Our masters', he said, of whose 'luxurious nature' the boys were aware, 'liked to enjoy themselves. We boys liked to enjoy ourselves, and as a consequence of that mutual feeling, our masters went their way, and we boys went our way'. They were taught good manners, Davies said, and feasted on shoulder of veal on Sundays and on roast goose on Michaelmas Day.

Hartley in *The Alleynian* told a story of himself as a boy: when John Vane brought the Prince Consort on a visit to the College in the early spring of 1843, Hartley, dressed in his long blue coat, lifted a hand to his forelock and boldly accosted His Royal Highness with "A shilling apiece to pay, Sir, for walking on the College lawn". Albert muttered "What! What!" until Vane explained the situation to him, but he paid up affably enough. Hartley wrote generously that, in his view, the apathy towards education and towards change at the College reflected England's slow convalescence from the exhaustion of the Napoleonic wars; he welcomed the new religious controversies and the new scientific principles of education as a sign of intellectual recovery; and he ended by expressing delight that Dulwich College now ranked among the foremost public schools of England and of the world. [256]

The teaching was undoubtedly slack – the Visitor was told that although the College opened at six o'clock the Usher or Schoolmaster were never seen until nine. A dishonest arrangement furthermore existed between the First and Third Fellow to alternate their weeks of teaching, which was against the Statutes, and both were known to have been absent for weeks at a time. Boy monitors taught for whole weeks at a time. A story told at

an Alleyn Club dinner in 1926 was that one Poor Scholar was hauled up and punished for neglecting to take his cap off to his master in the street, and the boy pleaded that he did not know the man; the Fellow had been absent for three months. [257]

A 'Mark Book' from January 1839 to October 1841, kept when the Revd John Vane was Schoolmaster and the Revd William Chafy was Usher, has survived; laconically recording such daily schoolroom fare as 'the repetition generally well said', it mostly served to record bad work and behaviour. 'Parsing', Latin grammar and tables, History, and even English poetry are mentioned. One boy cribs his work from another; on one Saturday, 'King would not say his Catechism, obstinate and naughty'. Griffin (left 1842) and Hogan (left 1844) are the boys most disliked by the Fellows, and their idleness and obstinacy figure frequently. (In 1842 George Griffin's mother withdrew him with a pleasant and respectful letter to the College, transcribed into the *Private Sittings*.) [258] The book records frequent holidays for saints' days, for Queen Victoria's wedding, and one at Lady Holland's request; the school closes for cleaning. The *Private Sittings* volume reports periods of general ill health among the boys with outbreaks of scarlet fever; they were given vaccinations. James Outram, the son of a master baker, later apprenticed as a printer, was whipped in the 1850s. [259]

Once the Poor Scholars were placed in an apprenticeship they received in 1824 a donation of £25, which was increased to £30 in 1827. [260] The College mostly looked after their interests humanely after they left, investigating complaints against their masters, contributing to passages to Australia, and in 1841 giving a pension to a former Poor Scholar, Francis Holmes, who was destitute on account of his mental aberrations. [261] The story of Henry Webb, however, who in 1850 without his prior knowledge and consent was apprenticed by Charles Druce to a drunken carpenter who took away the clothes and allowance he was given by the College, reads like a dark chapter from Dickens. [262]

The Archbishop, the Charity Commissioners and the 'Schemes'

Twenty-five former Poor Scholars founded a 'philanthropic' Dulwich School Association on 6 April 1841, in effect an Old Boys' club, with John Vane as President, and John Allen, Jeffrys Thomas Allen and the other Fellows as Patrons. A dinner was held at the Greyhound inn attended by all the College authorities. [263] The printed Rules proposed an Association with quarterly meetings to cultivate friendship. 'Led by a grateful sense of the blessings received', their aim was to foster the apprentices from the College in a network of trades and to give financial help to those in distress. [264] However, the Association soon also began to voice complaints about the quality of their education. They made comparisons with Christ's Hospital, and called for French classes (which were instituted ten years later). [265] They called for the abolition of the separate dining room for the Master, Warden and Fellows. [266] The Master, Warden and Fellows immediately withdrew once the Association broadcast its opinion in 1845 that the teaching at the College was not even as proficient as those of the National Schools of Ireland, and they sent a Memorial to the Archbishop in protest. The Warden, by now John Gay Newton Alleyne (see below), is reputed to have called on former Founder's Boys who were new apprentices, forbidding them to join the Association, and the boys were now only given their leaving donation on condition that they did not join it. In 1851 the Association hammered home the failure of Alleyn's scheme: the Founder's boys were 'for the most part illiterate' and the majority lived in 'abject poverty' in manhood. They offered a prize for penmanship, which was accepted, but a later offer of prize for academic subjects was refused. [267] Robert Farmar, a former Poor Scholar, later a chemist and druggist, said that the letters written by the former pupils about the dinner of 1842 showed their 'miserable' education, but he admitted that it had improved since the days of the Revd John Vane. [268]

In 1851 John Gay Newton Alleyne resigned as Warden; he became involved in iron and steel works and in designing colliery plants, and was later the contractor for St Pancras railway station. The ensuing election for Warden, the first for seventy years, according to *The Times*, was declared invalid when the assistants outvoted the College over the four candidates named Allen, and went to law. *The Times* reported the election of 31 March: that morning, the Assistants selected a candidate not adopted by the College and there was a 'very stormy discussion in the Library', the Master 'assuming very high ground' and the St Saviour's man remaining firm; the service in the Chapel was delayed for twenty minutes. Richard William Allen, the Assistants' nominee, was elected and gave the customary Dinner. [269] The next month the Master and Fellows wrote to inform him that he was not after all to be admitted as they had taken legal advice that denied the Assistants any rights in the voting, and his bonds for £8,000 with further sureties of £8,000 from four guarantors, were rejected. Richard William Allen took the case to the Queen's Bench, and the Crown decided for him. [270] In spite of this litigation his tenure as Warden seems to have been a success. [271] Six years later he was to be pensioned off at £855 per annum. Preserving their interests was expensive: the College's legal costs for both the years 1851 and 1853 were £1,400.

The Charity Commissioners' Inquiry, 1854

In June and July 1854 a second official Inquiry by the Charity Commissioners signalled the end of the old Foundation. The College came under fierce public criticism from the former Poor Scholars and the Foundation parishes. A transcript of the first two of the eight days was printed, and a manuscript record of five of the six subsequent days of this Inspection survives, transcribed from a shorthand writer. The shrewd and fair Chairman was the Inspector of Charities, Thomas Hare (1806–91), the first proponent of the idea of 'proportional representation', who was a barrister and an associate of John Stuart Mill. [272] Evidence was taken for the College from the Master, Warden and Fellows, from Sir Charles Barry and Charles Druce; for the parishes from the representative Assistants. Sir Joseph Paxton and other Directors of the Crystal Palace Company, Samuel Laing, Francis Fuller and Charles Geach, also gave evidence.

It was said to be a common complaint at St Luke's that it was 'no boon' to send a boy to Dulwich as 'the children learn nothing'; the education 'would disgrace a workhouse school'. A vestryman from Camberwell testified that 'there was not a parochial school in the circle of the great metropolis' where boys did not receive a better education. A vicious circle also existed: it emerged that St Luke's deliberately put up their inferior boys for election. [273] The Assistants also accused the College of embezzling amounts due to the boys. They described many of the practices followed from Alleyn's Statutes, such as the rule of celibacy and too frequent services in the Chapel, as 'superstitious'. Sir Charles Barry was criticised for having too much personal 'interest' in his work as Surveyor. Some Assistants clearly hoped for large schools in their parishes to be built from the new wealth of the Estate. The Assistants were shown to be poor members of a governing body, as the Churchwardens were constantly changing. Moreover, the Inquiry showed that in general they were poor judges of education. The parishes were themselves at odds; Camberwell was particularly vocal at the Inquiry: its population had risen from 28,231 in 1831 to 54,668 in 1851, and the Vestry claimed that they had no proper schools; they asked for an 'Alleyne School' for boys. [274]

George John Allen, the last Master of the Old Foundation, told the Inquiry that his salary in 1844 was £40 and his share of the dividend £600. He echoed Vane's earlier testimony against the possible benefits of stretching the boys' minds in saying that he 'never thought it for the interest of any boy we have had there to send him up to the university'. [275] The Revd Charles Howes, who had been First Fellow or Preacher since 1841, gave evidence mostly about his privileges and comforts. He said that he shared in the large common rooms, the dining room, a good library, 'a large and even beautiful' garden, and enjoyed two good sitting rooms and two bedrooms of his own. He had formerly been a Fellow at Cambridge where he reckoned that his board and lodging were worth £100 a year, whereas at Dulwich his living was worth over three times that amount. He smugly resented criticism of the College, and robustly declared that as the heirs of Edward Alleyn the Fellows owned the Estate: 'let me add, that we are the absolute owners of the property, and do not hold it in trust'. He added unwisely that nobody had questioned their perfect right to live as they did, and that the Fellows used to joke about the ways in which they could spend the revenue to which they were legally entitled. 'We do not live in any absurd sumptuous style but only as private gentlemen', he added. Howes received £200 per annum, including a large share of the 'Dividend' (see above) once a year; the sum of his duties was to preach once on Sundays and to visit the sick.[276] The parish of St Saviour's issued another pamphlet, including a paragraph drawing attention to the presence of a large stock of wine laid down at the College;[277] in 1879 the Governors of the new College were to order that 31 dozen of Carbonell's port were to be auctioned off.[278]

Interviewed by Thomas Hare in June 1854, the Revd William Fellowes, Schoolmaster, also declared that he received £200 per annum. There were then ten Poor Scholars, of whom five studied Latin, but no Greek. No Roman authors were studied, however. One boy was studying French, and was taught by a Monsieur Grand-nom, who attended for four hours a week. There had been an attempt to modernise, as the Archbishop had directed: Scientific books, including those on Mineralogy, along with Euclid, and volumes on History, General Geography, Scripture and Accounting Book-keeping, were all now on the syllabus. He argued (with surreal logic) that as they were taught Euclid, there was no need to teach Greek. He further asserted that 'it has generally been, I think, considered by the college that the future prospects of the boys would be better consulted by putting them out to trades of a higher class, or to the professions, than by preparing them for the universities'. Music had once been taught in the afternoon, but the musical instruction was now left to the Revd Edward Giraud (1800–73), who had been in office for twenty years; the boys were taught to sing simple psalmody and to chant hymns and the 'Gloria Patri' after the psalm. Giraud meekly told the Inquiry that he was but an amateur organist and unable to control the boys; he relied on a former pupil, 'young Morley', who gave evidence, and was paid a pittance to keep the misbehaving boys in the choir in order.[279]

Thomas Hare told the Inquiry that he had attended a disappointing examination of the boys by the Archbishop's Chaplain. The case of William Cakebread, a recent Poor Scholar, was mentioned several times: he had left at the age of 16 to be apprenticed to a corrugated-iron house builder and was thought clever enough to have been prepared for university. Former Poor Scholars, such as Robert John Farmer who attended from nine to sixteen years old (1814–21), gave evidence. It seems that the witnesses who had been former Poor Scholars in the days of Vane and Lindsay were primed by the Churchwardens to give selectively the most damning evidence possible, but their accounts ring true. Their education was 'grossly neglected'; they carried out menial tasks for small wages from the Fellows, such as cleaning shoes, laying fires and making beds, according to Nicholas Edwin, a Poor Scholar from 1808 to 1815. It was claimed that in 1844 George John Allen showed a boy the Statutes to prove that the Poor Scholars were to act as servants to the Fellows.[280]

The spokesman for the parish of St Luke's, Mr Briscoe, claimed that the majority of the Founder's boys should be enrolled from there, as the parish was far the most helpless of the four, densely populated and destitute.[281] St Botolph's and St Saviour's admitted that they were satisfied with the arrangements of the education of the poor in their own parishes, but Camberwell and St Luke's hoped for new National Schools built with money from Alleyn's estate; a proposal to build three schools called 'Alleyn's Middle Class Schools' of 200 boys in the parishes was discussed, with the boys who were equal to university education being sent on to Dulwich.[282] A St Saviour's pamphlet of 1853 recalled that in 1850 the Archbishop had responded to their earlier Memorial by issuing an injunction 'securing to the boys an improved education' but had not answered their other demands. Hare ruled that although the College had distinctly failed to carry out the original intentions of the Founder, a failure compounded by their reaction to its increased endowment,[283] there had been no strictly improper practice but rather a culpable neglect of the boys' education. The Commissioners formally advised the suppression of the old Corporation.

One suggestion was to make education the priority by simply abolishing the Almshouse and the Picture Gallery; the paintings, it was airily suggested, could be disposed of 'to the National Gallery or elsewhere'.[284] Hare gave his own views on future reforms, proposing a 'great educational establishment' and the expansion of accommodation for the Almsfolk with 'ornamental gardens and pleasant residences', as part of the grand eleemosynary scheme. Rugby College [School] was held up as exemplary, its reputation a 'credit with the whole Empire', but it was the reorganisation and expansion of Felsted School in Essex by Act of Parliament in 1851 that Hare himself proposed as a model; it was noted that the Founder was said to have contemplated such a school as Merchant Taylors', Harrow, Rugby and Winchester. [285]

The debate on the future of the College was essentially between those who favoured a College offering a 'public school' education with boarding, and those who proposed a superior day school for a hundred poor orphans. New public schools were much in demand; many of the schools famous today and perhaps thought of as old foundations in fact originate in the nineteenth century, such as Cheltenham, Marlborough, Bradfield, Wellington, Clifton, Malvern, and Haileybury. [286] Mr Briscoe protested the danger of 'carrying the benefit of this very wealthy charity to another class of individuals'; St Saviour's commented uncomfortably in their pamphlet that a proposed division into an Upper and Lower School, on a principle of social class, was totally against Edward Alleyn's principles. [287] Reference was made to the Government report of Lord John Russell of 1853 in which there was a plan for the promotion of National Education, including an improved administration of charitable trusts. Birmingham Grammar School and Oundle were referred to as good models, and also the City of London School. The Headmaster of the latter school, Dr Mortimer, declared to the Dulwich Inquiry that the social mixture of the 600 boys in his care was 'pure Republican to the letter'. Reform might touch all aspects of the College, and there were strong feelings on both sides as to whether the boys should continue to wear their traditional seventeenth-century dress like the boys of Christ's Hospital. [288] As we have seen, two years before the Inquiry, St Luke's parish had published a pamphlet: *Dulwich College; or the Orphan and the Poor Defended from the Errors of the Charitable Trusts Board.* Referring to recent 'genteel embezzlement' and the 'sinecure to idle fellows', it warned that the reformation of old charities often meant spoliation. They mentioned the advantages of the newly built Crystal Palace to the locality of Dulwich, as it promised 'to advance all educational objects in a way difficult to be exaggerated, by becoming a real university of science, industry and the fine arts, to many surrounding schools'. The current scheme failed too obviously to do enough for the Poor Scholars or Almsfolk. [289] Neglected orphans were filling the gaols while their educated counterparts were benefiting out of all proportion from their support.

In 1856 Charles Dickens himself joined the public debate about the future of Alleyn's Foundation by chairing and addressing a meeting at the Adelphi Hotel,

canvassing for signatures to a petition for the support of 'Needy Actors' to be sent to the Charity Commissioners. Reminding his audience of its origins on the London stage, he proposed that a quarter of the revenue of the Foundation ought to be given over to supporting poor actors of both sexes and to the education of poor actors' children. Never had a former actor been given a home as a Poor Brother at the College, his supporters said. Their main argument – that Alleyn never specifically ruled out support to actors in his Statutes – was weak. They had heard from Sir Charles Barry that the annual income of the estate of 1,145 acres was worth £50,000 per annum, but through poor management was only producing £8,000. Dickens and his associates argued that the beneficiary parishes were the districts where the theatres were in Alleyn's day; since this was now no longer true, it was the indigent actors from all England that now needed relief from the old actor's charity. Dickens, who had been primed by his friend John Payne Collier, said that 'everything on and about [Alleyn] testifies to the truth and fidelity of his simple heart'. [290]

The Dulwich College Act, 1857

In January 1857 the College recorded in the *Private Sittings* petitions received from the Churchwardens of the parishes, from Camberwell residents, from certain leaseholders of Dulwich, and from the 'parties on behalf of the theatrical profession'. [291]

The College was forced by law to agree to the Scheme proposed by the Charity Commissioners, but they protested to the last: in a letter of December 1855 they wrote to the Commissioners declaring that the Government had no power to dissolve the Corporation nor to offer them 'allowances in lieu of their existing rights'; they greedily complained that the Scheme would lose them half a year's income for 1856, and that the generous figures proposed for their pensions did not take into account the real value of their 'vested interests', as they naturally understood that the revenue of the Estate was bound to increase. Their letter was not entirely selfish, since, as they pointed out, by the terms of the Scheme Dulwich itself was not to be given proper equality with the parishes, and they also said that it would be wrong that the now considerable funds from the bequest for the Bourgeois Gallery, including all the interest that had accrued, should be used for other purposes. [292]

At a College meeting in 1856 Charles Druce read aloud the draft of the House of Lords Bill, along with the Charity Commissioners' scheme for the new College. The Master, Warden and Fellows published a statement complaining that the Select Committee proposed to cut the pensions they had been offered by the Commissioners, and trusting

THE DULWICH COLLEGE CHARITY MEETING AT THE ADELPHI THEATRE.

At the Adelphi Hotel: Charles Dickens proposes that Alleyn's charity should support retired actors and educate their children. *Illustrated London News*, 22 March 1856. (Dulwich College)

that Parliament would prevent 'the confiscation of their property'. The Dulwich College Act became law on 25 August 1857. It provided that the Estate revenue would henceforth be split into four parts: three for education, and one for the almsfolk. The old educational foundation was to be dissolved after 238 years; 'Alleyn's College of God's Gift, at Dulwich' was to be re-established, with an Upper and a Lower School, these to be overseen by a Master and an Under Master. A Board of Governors with a permanent Chairman was to be appointed. Fifteen Governors were to administer both the College and the Estate, four of them to be appointed by the beneficiary parishes. The Master, for the first time, was to be a graduate. He was to have 'general control and superintendence of the educational branch of the charity', with much greater powers than formerly, and would be personally responsible for all appointments except that of Under Master. He was charged with the general direction and discipline of the school, of the boarding houses, and of the Almsfolk; he was to be a Trustee of James Allen's Girls' School. He would receive a basic salary of £400 per

annum, together with a set of complicated further allowances: thirty shillings for all boys above the number of 50; on top of that a 'capitation allowance' for each boy under 14 of £6 if they came from the four parishes, and £8 from elsewhere, and for boys over fourteen £8 if they came from the parishes, and £10 from elsewhere.

There were to be 24 Foundation Scholars on free places, drawn from the four parishes. The curriculum was to include Latin and Greek, English Literature, Religion, History, Geography, Designing, and the scientific subjects proposed by the Archbishop in 1852, together with the fashionable 'Industrial and Practical Arts'. The Lower School, located in the old Grammar School, was to offer schooling only until the age of 16, with a curriculum of 'an ordinary Secondary School of second grade'. The Poor Brethren and Sisters – their numbers now doubled – were to be overseen by the Chaplain, and to have improved residences with small gardens. The House of Lords proposed to add a clause for a new church to be built, but this was rejected, as were plans at this stage for a full boarding school. [293] The members of the existing 'Society' were pensioned off, with annual awards of £1,015 to the Master, £855 to the Warden, £500 to the Senior Fellow and £480 to the Junior Fellows. This was generous: according to the College Accounts for 1870, the pension paid that year to George John Allen (Master 1841–57) was almost exactly the same as the amount collected by the College from all parents for fees; moreover, Dr Carver, who had set up the new College as he wanted it and was running it with utter dedication and exhausting struggles to keep it from outside interference, was paid in the same year a total of £1,045 – hardly much more than the pension to his superannuated predecessor. These large pensions were a considerable burden on the College in Carver's day. The Commons Committee had wanted to reduce the Master's pension to £760, but this the House of Lords rejected. By 1873 these pensions had cost the College £60,000,[294] effectively leaving only £1,500 annual income from the Estate for the running of the College. 'Mr. Allen', the pensioned Master George John Allen, died at the age of 73, twenty-six years after retiring; his death was reported on the very day that Carver himself retired in 1883.[295] Up to eight scholarships at universities of £400 per annum were to be awarded to leavers.

The increased numbers of boys were to be housed by enlarging the Old College building, but it was three years before the New College, as we know it, was contemplated. The younger Charles Barry, appointed Surveyor and Architect by the new Governors after his father's post was made invalid with the old constitution, drew up plans in 1858 for the housing committee 'to adapt the present building for a Chaplain's residence and for the Master or Under-Master of the future upper and lower schools, and upper dormitories for the endowed scholars of each school' at a cost of £7,000.[296] As the College chapel, with its surrounding Picture Gallery, was now too small for the parish, a new church and vicarage were envisaged, and there was talk of building an enlarged chapel alongside the Old College on the lower school games field. A new chapel is shown as a mere outline on Barry's ground plans of the New College on Dulwich Common, engraved and printed for the Governors in July 1860; this was to be sited west of the Great Hall and on the same axis, roughly where the 'Clump' of elm trees is today. This excellent plan to build a chapel at the New College was raised again in 1882 and thereafter frequently by both Welldon and A. H. Gilkes during their mastership, but was not built for lack of the anticipated funds; this seriously harmed the College's corporate life.

The Act received the Royal Assent on 25 August 1857. The Schoolmaster, the Revd William Fellowes, and the Usher, the Revd William Chafy, kept a 'Day Book' during the last years of the Foundation. As with the surviving book from the 1840s, the Fellows record poor attainment and reveal their particular *bêtes noires*, writing entries such as: 'disgraceful work'; 'Cooper conducted himself very badly with jam at dinner-table'; 'I have today boxed Flin's ears for insolence!'; 'Powell warned today for making faces in Chapel'. The book concludes with the momentous day of the passing of the old regime. Shortly after midnight on 21 July 1858, the Revd William Fellowes wrote: 'The work was finished today as the clock struck twelve, and the old system passed away with it'.[297]

Mackenzie, almost always a wise historian of the College, wrote that 'the task of teaching twelve boys, drawn from the submerged class and varying in age from eight to eighteen, was a most discouraging one. The utmost industry and devotion could not have secured good results'. We cannot stand in the shoes of the Fellows of the day, but Mackenzie is surely too indulgent in his view of the old system: we know from the good results of Alleyn's scheme in the later seventeenth century, and from the later success in life of the Poor Scholars in the nineteenth century, that they should have been better served. The case of James Tatlock, a Poor Scholar of the Old Corporation, was called to the attention of the Governors of the New College in 1873: the boy had entered the College from St Botolph's in 1854, and had been transferred to the Lower School in 1858; he had recently been called to the Bar.[298] This surely corresponds to Alleyn's paradigm of social improvement, and it is clear that the Fellows, whether deliberately or unwittingly through their social prejudice, kept the Poor Scholars down. The Schoolmaster's formal record of the passing of College's 'old system' in its Day Book in 1858 is forcefully annotated in pencil by another hand: 'And a good thing too!'[299]

D? Carver.

'THE SECOND FOUNDATION':
CANON CARVER
1858–83

You leave Dulwich College, not as you found it, a small and struggling school of less than one hundred boys, but one of the greatest educational institutions of the country.

– Testimonial from THE COMMON ROOM *to* CANON CARVER *on his retirement,* 1883

PART I

The Revd Alfred Carver and his educational ideals – Early days of the New Foundation – The Lower School – The Governors – The Revd William Rogers – Building the New College, 1866–70 – Hume v. *Marshall, 1877*

Following the dissolution of the Old Foundation in 1858, the prospects for the College's new Corporation were exhilarating; few can have imagined, however, that within a mere 25 years, 'Alleyn's College of God's Gift, at Dulwich' would come to be recognised as a major public school. The task of creating a new College, and of protecting it against the formidable opposition that would arise, required a tenacious and cunning champion. The Revd Alfred James Carver (1826–1909), despite a mild and genial manner, met these requirements with such stubborn success that by the time of his retirement in 1883 he fully deserved his honorific cognomen as the College's 'Second Founder'. A later Master, George Smith, at an Alleyn Club dinner in 1919, praised the 'grim' austerity of Carver's business sense, as well as describing the 'genius' of his vision.[1] This chapter traces Carver's heroic struggles, and records the great achievements of the College under his rule, a period in which both the structure and aspect of today's Dulwich College were instituted.

The Revd Alfred Carver and his educational ideals

Carver came from a Norfolk medical family, proprietors of five manorial estates near Wymondham. His father was the evangelical Revd James Carver, well known for his philanthropic work in London, where he was Senior Chaplain to the Lord Mayor and to the Court of Aldermen of the City of London; he was also the 'Ordinary' (the priest who prepared condemned prisoners for death) at Newgate, where he devoted himself to the criminals and debtors. He sent Alfred to St Paul's School, where Dr John Sleath, the High Master, numbered nine Fellows of Trinity College, Cambridge, among his former

pupils. Carver duly graduated with First Class Honours in Classics at Trinity in 1849, and was also placed 'Senior Optime' in the Cambridge Mathematical Tripos. Queens' College, Cambridge, almost immediately appointed him Fellow and Classical Lecturer.

Carver was a remarkable prize-winner in his youth, for essays at St Paul's and then for undergraduate 'declamations' in the Hall at Trinity, and he kept his manuscripts of these early works.[2] They demonstrate his admiration for the ideal cultivated polity of Classical Athens and what he called the 'moral and mental energy' of Elizabethan England, a preoccupation reflected in his personal selection of the portrait gallery of heads, 'artistic modelled work in terracotta', that were later installed in roundels on the outer walls of the palazzo of the New College at Dulwich (1866–70); these consisted of sages and worthies from antiquity and from the Renaissance, together with a few later English luminaries (including David Hume, Doctor Johnson, Byron and Lord Macaulay, who had only recently died). Carver's own teaching was Socratic in theory and practice; Socrates and his disciple Plato from their roundels on high accost and overlook all who tread the gravel drive from the heraldic gates on College Road to affront the locked oaken valves of the palatial entrance to the Lower Hall. (Plato's terracotta head figures twice on the exterior of the New College: here, and again on the North Elevation of the South Block). One of Carver's Trinity speeches praises the female influence of Queen Elizabeth on the culture of the period and the 'hearty joyous vivacity' of Shakespeare's 'glowing scenes' with their 'elastic sprightliness and wit'. Among the heads in the same terracotta portrait gallery of philosophers, writers and scientists at the recently celibate College were

Opposite: Eden Eddis, *Alfred Carver*, 1867. Pencil and charcoal, heightened with white chalk. (© Dulwich College)

now placed 'fanciful and original female heads, taken from the most familiar characters of Shakespeare', together with the female Muses (now facing the South Circular Road) and a woman writer, Sappho, poetess of Lesbos. Ambitious productions of Shakespeare became an important feature of Carver's era, and he would entertain the boy players to supper afterwards in their costumes. [3]

Carver had to resign his fellowship at Cambridge, as was still the rule of the day, on his marriage to Eliza Peek of Clapham Common. His wife brought a share of the very large fortune her father and uncle had made supplying Victorian households (as what was in later years to become the Peek Frean company) with tea and biscuits. They had two sons and six daughters; the second son, Arthur Wellington Carver (1858–1925), joined the family firm, but later took orders in the Church, like his father. [4] Carver's private means were to be an important factor in aspects of the way he ran the College. In 1852 he was appointed as Surmaster of his old school, St Paul's. Dr Herbert Kynaston, the new High Master, wrote a warm testimonial to support his application to be Master at Dulwich, calling him 'the most amiable, the most high-principled, the most promising of my pupils at St Paul's', who was now his successful deputy. [5] Carver was ordained priest in 1854, and while working at St Paul's

undertook the curacy of St Olave's, Old Jewry, a post which he gave up on his appointment at Dulwich. Carver's application mentioned his teaching and his work in 'institutions for our working classes'. His referees wrote how the most refractory English 'seemed to melt at his touch into perspicuous and elegant Latin', and praised his zeal and principles as a Christian, several underlining his 'inward principle of right and ever present sense of duty'. [6]

Carver was 32 when he was appointed at Dulwich. Twenty years later, on 5 February 1878, his hostile Governors more or less forced him to agree to retire. He did so, but did not leave until five years later, after 25 years' service and at the early age of 57, once he felt that the College was at last securely and legally established on his principles. He doubtless understood his extraordinary opportunity to shape an essentially new school according to his own ideals, such as Victorian and Edwardian headmasters were sometimes given in the days before a Board of Education. He could write of the College in 1870 that it had 'fresh and vigorous life, with powers of influence and means of usefulness which few Foundations can rival', and of 'the well-grounded hopes for the future which far surpass the utmost hopes of its pious and munificent Founder'. [7]

Aristotle. Terracotta head on the New College, 1866–70, South Block, east elevation. (Dulwich College)

Among Carver's great qualities were his social vision and (while himself an outstanding Classical scholar) his belief in a wide curriculum. John Goodall, formerly an Assistant Master at the Grammar School, wrote in 1865 that the College 'may fairly aspire to become the leading middle-class school of England'; he remarked the social interaction and transformation that was taking place:

> wealthy men, who could afford to send their sons to Eton, are at this moment availing themselves of cheap schooling at Dulwich, while poorer men are expending sums which they can ill afford in qualifying their boys for forthcoming competitive ordeals for admission. A sprinkling of boys from affluent homes is a benefit to a middle-class school, by the superior type of their manners, demeanour, and tone of feeling. But a preponderance of rich boys is ruinous to hard work, economy, self-denial, and other homely virtues not yet out of fashion in families of moderate means.

Goodall agreed with Carver in seeing 'Exhibitions' [scholarships] to the College and Scholarships offered by the College to their leavers to attend university (such 'closed scholarships' as Carver himself had held from St Paul's at Cambridge) as factors 'absolutely necessary to sons of men of limited means'.[8]

'Mr Carver', according to an article in the *School World*

for 1891, 'was one of the first to see that the old, almost exclusively classical training of the Public Schools was inadequate to the requirements of this rapidly changing world'.[9] Carver was himself a polymath, and this was to be reflected in the signal success of his pupils in Modern Languages, Science, and in Art. Though St Paul's in his adolescence was essentially a Classical school, Science had been his hobby, and he carried out chemical experiments; he also made with his own hands a lathe and an orrery [a clockwork model of the planetary system]. At Cambridge he was interested in electricity and galvanism, and it was said that he could easily have qualified as a Civil Engineer.[10]

On Carver's first syllabus at Dulwich were to be found Chemistry, Mechanics, and Natural Science. The New College in 1870 housed one of the first Chemistry laboratories to be found in any English school, and shortly afterwards a Physics laboratory was added. Just five years after the New College was opened, a historian wrote that 'the public school spirit and high moral tone' that Carver had established at Dulwich placed it 'morally, socially and intellectually among the great public schools of England'.[11] An anonymous poem to Carver found among his papers expresses a frequent and proper compliment:

Francis Bacon. Terracotta head on the New College, 1866–70, South Block, east elevation. (Dulwich College)

What other schools, whose honour more appears,
Have done in ages, thou hast done in years. [12]

Carver himself said, 'I have always held it to be one great advantage which we have possessed at Dulwich over the old classical schools that we have been able to adapt our educational organisation to the long and more exacting requirements of modern times. Sooner or later all schools must follow. We at any rate have no need to fall back on a defunct or expiring system'. [13]

This breadth of approach would have delighted the Prince Consort, whose specific recommendations for a progressive school syllabus are quoted below. By stages up to 1880 Carver added to the standard subjects of the day – Divinity, English Language, Literature and Composition, Latin, Greek, French, History, and Mathematics – classes, taught by specialists, in German, Chemistry, Physics, Heat, Light, Electricity, Acoustics, Geology, Mechanics, Palaeontology, Botany, Anatomy and Physiology, Physical and Political Geography, Drawing and Designing, and Vocal Music. [14] At the same time, Carver strongly resisted both internal and external pressure to divide the College into Classical and 'Modern' sides, something he called a 'partial bifurcation', which made a boy specialise too young: boys should not have to choose between Greek and German. [15] The 'form subjects' taken by all boys were Religious Knowledge, Latin, French, and English. Four hours were assigned in which 'almost anything' could be taught according to the master's interests, and this included Science. [16] Carver took pleasure in expanding the choices on the curriculum; in 1872, when Prince Arthur gave the Prizes at the Old College, Carver announced the introduction of German and Chemistry. By now there were also special classes to prepare boys for careers in Engineering, for the India Civil Service, and for the Royal Military Academy at Woolwich.

Carver also introduced a series of voluntary evening lectures for the boys by visitors; from 1874 to 1879 the topics included Roman Archaeology, Animal Physiology, Astronomy, Plants, Voltaic energy, the Telephone and Telegraph, Memory, the Arctic Regions, the Zulus, and Afghanistan. John Sparkes (1833–1907), the Art Master at the College, lectured on Fine Art Theories in 1872, and Waterhouse Hawkins (1807–94), the zoologist and the sculptor of the dinosaurs in the Crystal Palace Park, on Natural History in 1879.

A broad curriculum best served both boys and society. [17] Carver believed in a 'sound liberal education' [18] and in identifying the right subjects for a boy rather than a shallow breadth of subjects for study. Looking back in 1881, he pointed with pride to the range of achievements of Alleynians, saying of himself and his staff:

Without neglecting classical learning, they took care to provide each boy with the means of preparing himself for the various occupations of modern life. To some extent their method was an experiment, but it had been justified by success. There was too much danger in the present day of making the curriculum too comprehensive and so frittering away the pupil's energies in getting a smattering of many subjects rather than soundness in a few. This danger could only be counteracted by careful study of the aptitudes of each boy, and by directing his course accordingly. [19]

Carver often said in public how much he resented the new public examination system, 'a real evil, against which all our schools ought to struggle'; it took up five or six weeks in a term of twelve or thirteen weeks. Excess examination he called 'pumping at the well'. [20]

Robert Mackenzie (1857–1912), who was commissioned to write a history of the College which was never published, and who knew Carver well, described him as having 'light-blue, short-sighted eyes that beamed in a very kindly fashion through spectacles. His movements were quick and eager and his general look told of innocence and energy'. This energy showed itself in his running up stairs two at a time, carrying piles of books; however, a loyal and level-headed Assistant Master, the Revd E. H. Sweet-Escott, who joined the College in 1879, in the course of some reminiscences in a speech at an Alleyn Club dinner fifty years later, associated Carver with what he described as a 'restless energy', particularly by comparison with his even more famous successor as Master, the god-like Arthur Herman Gilkes. [21]

Early days of the New Foundation

The first day of the new College of God's Gift, 5 November 1858, was recalled by Edward Everett (1848–1923), a loyal Old Boy and long-serving Assistant Master, in a speech at Carver's Golden Wedding celebration in 1903. On that day Everett had been a new boy of ten years old; he recalled that after prayers in the schoolroom, Carver said to the assembled 66 boys of the Upper School, "All boys who know any Greek, stand forward!" Eight or ten did so, and formed a Fifth Form, the oldest boy being 15 years old. Everett said that Carver's words, insignificant in themselves, 'started the great career of Dulwich College as an educational institution'. He declared that the grand old man of 1903 possessed 'that primal something without which no living person or institution can have any sort of success – *he called it into being*'. His unwearied and triumphant efforts, 'in the teeth of an opposition always violent, always unresting, often malignant', resulted in the great mark impressed by the College 'on the intellectual and athletic training of the youth of this country'. [22]

Carver's Under Master for the first two years was the Revd Alfred Povah, who had been the Headmaster of St Saviour's Grammar School in Southwark since 1850. By the end of the next year there were three Assistants, a part-time French teacher, and an organist. Carver at first took the Fifth Form for all work, Mr Povah taught the Thirds and Fourths, and Mr Watkins (the Writing Master) the Firsts and Seconds. One of the new Assistants was the distinguished art teacher John Sparkes, who had enrolled as a student at the Royal Academy Schools in 1852; from 1875 until 1898 he was Principal of the National Art Training School at South Kensington (from 1896 the Royal College of Art), appointed by Sir Edward Poynter (see below). Sparkes was later a figure of national importance who strove for the recognition of art in education and in life, and was a great pioneer of Art Schools and an authority on them; his obituary in *The Times* called him 'the most prominent art teacher in the country'. [23] The first Mathematics specialist was not appointed until 1864. [24]

When there was still much farm land towards Herne Hill and on either side of Dulwich Village there was still something of a country school about the Old College; in their delightful book *Memories of Dulwich College in the 60s and 70s*, published in 1919, Alleynians of that period recalled putting grass-snakes and birds from Dulwich Wood in their desks to disrupt French lessons. The boys robbed orchards and got up to other mischief, such as removing the villagers' front gates and exchanging them on their posts with others. In Back Lane (now Court Lane) they played with hoops and marbles. [25]

At Christmas in 1858 there were just 68 boys in the Upper School and 33 in the Lower School, including the former Poor Scholars. The very next year the Upper School had almost doubled to 130 boys, and the Lower School had more than doubled with 81 boys. By 1870, when the Upper School took possession of the New College, it was composed of 269 boys.

Carver's first days at Dulwich must have been dispiriting. On arrival at the Old College, he found a letter waiting for him from the Revd William Fellowes, the former Second Fellow or Schoolmaster, which expressed 'great feelings of regret': the boys had all left for their holidays; the Poor Scholars were with Fellowes in Ramsgate; the keys to the gates and the library were with the Butler; there was a large laundry bill outstanding, and 'a good deal of washing to be done'. [26] Despite Fellowes's stated expectations of a 'more hopeful state of things' to come, within his first two weeks at Dulwich, Carver had a furious public row with the Chaplain, the Revd John Oldham (1808–82), who was almost twenty years his senior and, as Minister at the East Dulwich Chapel since 1851, had a large local following. After Carver's very first

Sunday sermon in the Chapel he was 'violently attacked' by Mr Oldham, who declared, "I am an older man than you", and refused to accept his authority: this was a parish church, not a College chapel. [27] Such a conflict was more or less inevitable: Carver later put it to the Governors in 1859 that it was 'most undesirable' that the Chaplain of the College should also be the Incumbent of the Parish; the present Chapel was obviously going to be inadequate for the College once it developed, and a new Ecclesiastical District should be formed at once. [28] This was not to happen for a very long time, until the building of St Barnabas in 1895. The Governors in 1860 meanwhile directed that the Chaplain was to be subordinate to the Master, and that the Master and not the Chaplain was to instruct the boys for Confirmation. [29] Carver's contretemps with Oldham was the first of many such wrangles.

Although hugely popular with the boys throughout his tenure, Carver became involved in a series of tremendous feuds with adults who crossed him. He kept drafts of many bitter letters and memoranda of quarrels, in which his handwriting becomes erratic and inflamed, with heavy deletions when he decides he has gone too far. Eliza Carver seems to have entered with some zeal into her husband's conflicts. A memorandum in her hand says that when they first arrived they were told that the new schools were a nuisance and would ruin Dulwich; the inhabitants would no longer stand another Master 'lording it over them'; the last Master had always been 'pooh-poohed'; the College had never prospered, and never would do so. A draft letter from Carver to the second Duke of Wellington admits that in the early days at Dulwich they 'were by no means popular with the higher classes of society'. Carver believed that the Chaplain, Charles Barry junior (the Surveyor and Architect) and Charles Druce (the Solicitor) colluded to 'put down' the Master by confining his role to running the educational establishment; Carver, perhaps influenced by his seigniorial Norfolk background, caused a great deal of friction by expecting as Master to preside over the Estate as well as the College, as the Master had done under the Old Foundation. [30] However, these local feuds and an appalling slander and libel case between two of his staff in 1877 (see below) were not nearly so taxing as the superhuman struggle lurking for him against his Chairman of the Governors and the representatives of the Parishes.

One tends to imagine Carver presiding over the expansive New College and its grounds, but he and his family lived for twelve years, almost half his time as Master, at the Old College; here they brought up their family, entertained a great deal, and enjoyed the garden with its enormous catalpa tree on the south side of the Chapel, now the grassy forecourt of the Picture Gallery.

The Lower School

The 'Lower School', unlike today when it refers to a division of the College for the younger boys before they enter the Middle and Upper Schools, in the New Foundation was a separate school running parallel to the Upper School, specifically intended for the instruction and benefit of the industrial or poorer classes, with a bias towards commercial studies. The attempt to transform these boys into members of the middle class was not without difficulties: in 1867 the Governors recorded their censure of the Lower School boys for refusing to sing at Speech Day;[31] two years later, the Lower School examiner recommended improving the boys' pronunciation: the teachers should in particular inculcate the 'proper use of the aspirate'.[32] It was on the recommendation of the same examiner that Latin was dropped from the syllabus and Physical Science added.[33] Promising boys from the Lower School could be promoted to the Upper School, although when Latin was discontinued this became less likely.[34] In 1875 the Head Boy, Edward Robinson, son of a builder from Pond Cottages, was given a free place in the Upper School; he proceeded to Balliol College, Oxford, and then joined the India Civil Service as Head of a District, to be killed two years later at the age of 26 when a wounded man-eating tiger, whom he had shot 'in pursuit of duty', sprang at him.[35]

The Revd Henry Smith (1836–1918) succeeded the Revd W. F. Greenfield, who was in poor health, as Head Master of the Lower School in 1875; formerly a curate at St Botolph's, Bishopsgate (where the Rector was the Revd William Rogers, Chairman of the College Governors), Smith had been Head Master of Rogers's Goswell Street and St Botolph's Boys' Schools. Carver was nominally in charge of the Lower School, but he cannot be shown to have taken much interest in it. He is known to have declared that he did not want to be overwhelmed with parish scholars in the Upper School, preferring to enrol local boys who had won open College Scholarships; his ambition was to have two hundred boarders from elsewhere.[36] Indeed, the Lower School was to remain in the Old College buildings until Alleyn's School was built, after the final Scheme of the Endowed Schools Commission in 1882, despite the original intention that it share the New College with the Upper School. By 1870 its numbers had increased to 242 pupils. There were originally 24 Foundation scholars from the parishes in both schools, and they were fed, clothed and lodged in the village until 1882. Carver in 1863 decreed that the parish Scholars were to wear a 'short tunic buttoned to the chin, trousers of an Oxford mixture, an ordinary rifle cap with a broad band and narrow peak, and a dark-coloured Inverness cape for winter'.[37]

The Governors

In theory, the governing body of the College, which met for the first time on 1 January 1858, was magnificent. The Prince Consort himself, who is known to have taken an interest in the reform and reconstruction of the New Foundation, 'only declined the office [of Chairman] after fourteen days' consideration'.[38] The members of the Board in its early years bore all the marks of Prince Albert's industrial, educational and social concerns: as well as landowners and aristocrats, they included a famous builder of railways and bridges, a famous scientist, a metallurgist, two architects and a Royal Academician (the first such in an interesting series). These men were appointed by the Court of Chancery, but there was also an equal number of representatives of the 'Privileged Parishes', for example a pin manufacturer and a flour factor. The snag with these Governors was that soon after the inception of undoubtedly the most distinguished, intelligent, and cultivated group of Governors in the College's history, the most significant members, busy Victorians, became too much involved elsewhere and resigned, or else died shortly afterwards. The first Chairman, Lord Stanley, later Earl of Derby (1826–93), resigned before the year was out following his appointment as Colonial Secretary, and his successor, the second Duke of Wellington (1807–84), resigned in 1862. Lyon Playfair, later Baron Playfair (1818–98), also resigned in 1862 on taking up a chair in Chemistry at Edinburgh. An influential member of Prince Albert's circle of advisers during the Great Exhibition and its aftermath, Playfair represented the new age of scientific and intellectual enlightenment, and was a writer on broad social issues of political economy and public health. Albert's unwelcome view that the narrowness of British education left us behind our continental competitors made a slow but beneficial impact. In 1855, at the Birmingham and Midland Institute, the Prince had denounced the 'arbitrary selection of Maths and classical grammar, although they train and elevate the mind', and spoke of Science as a properly Christian object of study: it was our 'bounden duty', he said, to encourage the 'study of laws by which the Almighty governs the universe'. Pointing out that the current teaching of History and Modern Languages was inadequate, he also listed subjects that ought to be introduced in schools: Logic, Physiology, Psychology, Politics, Jurisprudence, Political Economy, and the Fine Arts.[39]

When Lyon Playfair delivered a lecture at the Society of Arts after the Great Exhibition, 'On the Chemical Principles involved in the Manufactures of the Exhibition', he declared that a Classical education was only useful for producing *literati*: 'how is it possible that dead literature can be the parent of living science and active industry?'[40] Playfair also drew up a broad proposal for the College, referred to in Carver's notes for 1858 as 'Dr Playfair's scheme'; it does not survive, but it evidently included a policy that 'the main facilities for study should be for Lower and Middle Classes. The Gentry should not in any way monopolise the resources of the school, but receive only a fair proportion'. It was Playfair who drafted the advertisement for the new Master of Dulwich.[41]

On the original Board was also Robert Stephenson (1803–59), the son of the railway pioneer George Stephenson, by now manager of his father's firm and one of the greatest of all builders of railways and bridges. He had earlier been the Chairman of Prince Albert's executive committee for the Royal Commissioners for the Great Exhibition of 1851. Stephenson died in 1859; a longer-serving member was the Revd Matthew Farrer (1816–89), a civilised churchman, who held, according to Carver, 'well matured views' which were discreetly and routinely ignored. He stepped down in 1879.[42] Two other members were John Percy (1817–89), an eminent metallurgist, until 1872, and, until 1875, the architect James Fergusson (1808–86). Fergusson had spent over ten years in India at the start of his career and was an expert on its architecture, becoming a well-regarded architectural historian and writer on aesthetics and mythology (as such even qualifying for Ruskin's admiration). He was also a minor architect, who designed the highly original Marianne North Gallery at Kew Gardens (1881) and was a Gold Medallist of the Royal Institute of British Architects. According to Carver, he also submitted a design for the New College.[43] Fergusson belonged to the circle of highly cultivated artists, writers and musicians who grouped around Sir George Grove (1820–1900) at Sydenham, together with the other artists and architects involved in the Crystal Palace, for the interior of which (with Sir Henry Layard) he designed the Assyrian Court; he was also the rather ineffectual General Manager of the Palace from 1856–8, at the time of his appointment to the College Board. By 1873 he appears to have lost interest, however, and was frequently absent from meetings.[44] An energetic architect Governor, by contrast, from 1861 until his death in 1873, was Sir William Tite (1798–1873), the President of the RIBA (1861–3); in addition to many more important buildings, he had designed in 1842 the main cemetery chapels, now demolished, and the surviving great walls and gates of Norwood Cemetery. He was also employed by the new railway companies in land valuation and purchase, and in the design of the new stations; as a Member of Parliament, he was in a useful position to speak for the College's interests in the House, during discussion of railway bills giving companies rights to compulsory purchases, as he did on the Brighton Railway Company's Bill in 1864 (see Chapter Five). Tite was famous for saying that he had inherited one fortune, married another, and earned a third; at his death, the Governors recorded his 'business-like qualities and honourable conduct', as well as his 'munificent liberality', especially in regard to the building of St Stephen's church at Dulwich in 1867.[45]

The Duke of Wellington (son of the late victor of Waterloo) was appointed Chairman on 14 December 1858,[46] and for a while the Governors met at Apsley House. He was thought to be an ineffectual Chairman, but was friendly to Carver, standing as godfather to Arthur Wellington Carver. The Duke said simply on his resignation, "I have been thinking it over, and I don't see why I should devote my time to looking after this estate and have to pay people to look after my own".[47]

The Revd William Rogers

Carver early came to understand the threat to himself and to the New College as he envisaged it when the Revd William Rogers (1819–96) was elected by the Board as Permanent Chairman of the Governors to succeed the Duke in 1862.[48] Carver's antagonist had been an original member of the Board on Prince Albert's particular recommendation,[49] as his son Edward, Prince of Wales, emphasised in his speech on the opening of the New College on 21 June 1870; he also said that Rogers had done 'more than any man living for the poor and middle-class education'.[50] Carver had naturally been led to believe that the terms of his own appointment were to set up a 'first grade' school, and moreover had ambitions to go further than the famous public schools in creating an ideal academy on the best educational principles, to prepare his boys to take a prominent part in public life. He was now up against a Chairman, with very powerful connections, who wanted to revise the essential nature of the College into a commonplace utilitarian school for industrial and commercial life, and planned to divert most of the copious funds from Alleyn's estate to schools in deprived London parishes. Carver would have preferred a public-spirited nobleman or a landed proprietor as Chairman, as was the case, he said, 'in all our great foundations'. Although Carver garnished the audience at plays and at Speech Days at the College with titled guests from London society, his ideal of such a Chairman was not simply snobbish; it was based on the idea that such men would be disinterested, in the true sense of that word: he believed that a Chairman 'ought to give *éclat*, not seek to derive importance or any personal advantages'.[51] There was a measure of paranoia in Carver's character, seeing enemies everywhere and collusion

Revd William Rogers. (Dulwich College)

between them against him; in this he was nevertheless sometimes right. However, there is no doubt that Rogers was the very worst enemy Carver could have imagined – a powerful and well connected man, with diametrically opposed ideals for the College, who came close to sabotaging its conspicuous success in sending boys to Oxford and Cambridge, and in nurturing so many important future public servants, famous academics, writers and artists.

As described below, Carver eventually took his grievances to the Privy Council, who, perhaps surprisingly, decided for him. The bitter personal and ideological quarrel between Rogers and Carver, and their rivalry for power as 'Head' of the College and Foundation, was nevertheless productive. In fact it engendered Dulwich College, defining the institution, and its strengths and success, for the next 150 years as a school not aloof from the streets of London, drawing its pupils from a very wide range of backgrounds, and bringing them up to appreciate, at least, the best traditional Public School values: a liberal education, good behaviour, culture and a strong sense of service. By the time Carver won his case,

however, he was exhausted, and the Governors were determined to punish him, popular and indeed famous though he was, by getting rid of him.

Following the early departure from the Board of so many of its distinguished intellectuals and prominent public servants, lesser members were appointed, and these tended to mismanage the Estate and lay the blame on others on the Board. The Parish representatives gathered behind Rogers, seeing their advantage; according to Carver, they tended to combine against the more interesting Governors, whom they called 'ornamental'. The eight Parish Governors developed an undue share of authority while the Chancery Governors, distinguished and busy men, were often unable to attend.[52] Charles Barry, who was not on the Board, emerges from Carver's private memoranda as an unscrupulous and ambitious figure, with 'absolute controul' over certain votes, colluding with the Parish men, even openly adopting 'extreme Parochial views' in return for votes for his building projects.

Carver sniffed another example of such widespread Dulwich 'jobbery' [taking advantage of influence] in a scheme by Barry and Druce, initiated in 1863, to build a new church in Lordship Lane, St Peter's, according to which the land would be donated by the College, which would also provide a grant towards its costs, and the Revd Arthur Druce, one of the solicitor's many sons, would then be installed as incumbent.[53]

Looking back at the period, the attitude of Rogers and the Parish men to the College probably deserves Carver's contemptuous play on words in calling them 'parochial'. Carver believed that the Governors envied the Upper School's success, and aimed to 'upset' it; it was also his view that a Board formed of 19 members was too large.[54] According to Carver, Rogers (who had been at Eton and at Balliol College, Oxford) actually began his years on the Board by saying that the College must look to Eton and Harrow for inspiration; indeed, at the laying of the foundation stone of the New College in 1870 he declared in public that Alleyn had always intended his College to resemble Eton, with 'oppidans' [town boys] and boarders.[55] However, within a few years Rogers had changed his tune entirely; Carver's interpretation of this *volte-face* was that, as an Etonian, Rogers 'had no desire to popularize the privileges of Eton'.[56] Carver's annual speeches at Alleyn Club dinners after his retirement always reminded his auditors (perhaps too often) that he gave himself to his battles in order to ensure them a 'first-grade school'; in 1898, for example, he said,

there was a powerful body of men both within the College and without, who insisted that the whole endowment of Alleyn's estate should be devoted to a school of an inferior grade, and that if Dulwich had a school at all, it should be only one of that description. I remember a favourite phrase, and it was a phrase that was uttered with authority more than once on the platform of our great hall: "we do not want an Eton or a Harrow here". The meaning that underlaid that remark had been repeated to me more than once, and I said: "Well, I do not want an Eton or a Harrow here, but if there be anything greater, better, and more useful than an Eton or Harrow, that I wish to have here". [57]

William Rogers may have had limitations of imagination and been extraordinarily stubborn, but he was by no means the demon that Carver would have us believe. He was, indeed, an admirable philanthropist, who devoted his career and his enormous energy and will-power to improve the condition of the London poor. Edward Alleyn would surely have approved of these activities, which were based moreover on direct experience of the very districts in which Alleyn himself had seen poverty, namely Bishopsgate and Golden Lane. A favourite of the Prince Consort and a Chaplain to Queen Victoria, a friend of Gladstone and the Archbishop of Canterbury, Rogers was well known and affectionately admired in London; he was also adept at using influential friends and his own skills to prise money from the City and other bodies to finance his projects. To the area of London that was his special concern, following his early service as Curate of St Thomas's, Charterhouse, he gave the name of *Costermongria*, from the costermongers who sold their daily wares from wheelbarrows, and he set himself the task of improving the welfare and education of those who got their living in the streets, in particular the 'ragamuffin' street children who remain familiar to us from Mayhew or Dickens. Rogers would of course have known that this same area of London still bore the bureaucratic imprint of Alleyn and Henslowe's seventeenth-century investments. He described the slum-dwellings of Golden Lane in his own day – where the Fortune theatre had once stood – as 'a disgrace to civilisation'. [58] Perhaps it was in part Alleyn's example that led Rogers to found a number of schools in the area in the 1850s, the government contributing £5,634. The intention was to provide schooling for the street children to attend after their jobs at the morning markets and before their basket deliveries in the evenings.

Prince Albert opened these schools in 1857 and made a speech about Rogers's 'noble and Christian-like exertions' which 'have attracted the notice and admiration of your Sovereign'; Rogers was, he said, 'an instrument under Divine Providence' to confer on the poor and the needy 'that greatest of all boons … the blessings of education'. [59] In the following year, the House of Commons proposed a Royal Commission on Popular Education, to which the Prince Consort himself appointed Rogers, who thereafter, in his own phrase, dedicated himself to 'national education, universal, compulsory, free'. Rogers's fellow Commissioners included the great educationalists Matthew Arnold and Mark Pattison, who travelled to France, Holland, Switzerland and Germany to report on popular schooling there. [60] By 1888, towards the end of his life, Rogers was able to reflect that education was in the reach of every English child, something that had looked unlikely when he began his career. [61]

From his early concerns for the poorest Londoners, Rogers later turned his attention to the children of clerks and tradesmen, for whom he intended to furnish 'Middle Class Schools': 'I dreamed a dream. It took the shape of an organised scheme of middle class education, and, for the money, my longing eyes were fixed upon the parochial charities of the City'. He determined to establish 'schools for the children of clerks, tradesmen *et cetera*' in London or its suburbs to prepare them, he wrote, for the 'industrial and commercial work of life'. [62]

This clash of the idealistic, academic, pious and forward-thinking Carver, striving for the College and for excellence against the broadly egalitarian and pragmatic Rogers, was of course characteristic of the age, and it is tempting, reading Carver's papers, to become his partisan. It would therefore be misleading to paint Rogers as wholly antipathetic to the spiritual aims and academic ambitions Carver held for the New College. In 1865, for example, Rogers founded a set of annual prizes in Divinity for both the Lower School and the Upper School – though his supervision of these prizes was not without irony, Rogers becoming well known to the public as ' "Hang theology" Rogers'. [63] This epithet, shocking for an Anglican vicar of his day, came from his own words in a notorious public outburst in 1866. He felt strongly that there was too much futile and mindless study by rote of scripture in schools, earned at the expense of a more secular and pragmatic education. Attacks were made in the press on his 'godless' schemes, though what he had actually said – in response to churchmen's demands for a larger share for religious studies in the syllabus of schools for the poor, and in opposition to the reluctance of many public bodies in funding those schools – was "Hang theology! Hang economics! Let us begin!"

William Rogers was a noble champion of education in the nineteenth century, voicing everywhere the view that education should be within reach of every child, and that schools should be paid for by taxes and county rates. [64] It is therefore perhaps unsurprising to learn that he eyed the Dulwich Foundation as a source of income for his schools when he joined the Board in 1856. [65] He strengthened his Alleynian hand in 1863 by being appointed

Rector of St Botolph's, Bishopsgate, from whose Rectory he continued to carry out educational schemes and other reforms, setting up schools, bath-houses, public toilets, soup kitchens, drinking fountains and – as a climax to a lifetime's philanthropy – the magnificent Bishopsgate Institute (1895). And yet these two great men, the Revd Rogers and Canon Carver, found themselves on a collision course from their earliest dealings. Mackenzie, Carver's friend and contemporary, vividly described the terms of their notorious combat of personalities as follows:

> Between [the Master] and Mr Rogers there could not but be antagonism. They stood for opposing interests and conflicting ideals. Other causes of difference were to be found in the dispositions of the men. Mr Rogers was a big, burly cleric of the 'squarson' [hybrid of squire and parson] type, who rode often with the Puckeridge hounds, and never let his cloth stand between him and his jest. The Master was an evangelical clergyman of courtly manners and scholarly tastes. Mr Rogers had been accustomed to lord it over half a dozen schools in Charterhouse. When he was chosen Chairman of the Dulwich Board, he imagined he would have things his own way. The Master, on the other hand, had a high opinion of the dignity of his office. He considered himself the natural guardian of the College's interests. In enthusiasm for their respective causes they were fairly matched. To the Chairman's masterful ways the Master opposed an extraordinary tenacity. The history of the next twenty years of College life is little more than the record of the duel between these two men. [66]

The first sign of difference between them appears in the minutes of the Governors' meetings in 1862: by a casting vote Rogers considerably weakened Carver's attempts to bolster his powers, when he 'negatived' a resolution to make Carver the 'resident representative of the Governors to administer [the College] daily', and refused to allow an amendment that 'the Master should be acknowledged and upheld in the full exercise of his functions and authority according to the terms of the act of parliament'. He even denied Carver a copy of these minutes, which Carver eventually had to secure from the printer. [67] At a subsequent Chapel service Rogers deeply offended Carver's ecclesiastical pride and precedence by arrogantly taking up a position on the north side of the altar opposite the Chaplain, thereby upstaging the Master. [68] According to a well-known story that first surfaced in a newspaper report in 1919, Carver used to pray not to lose his temper before meetings with the Governors. [69]

Rogers was to continue as Chairman of Governors until his death in 1896, thirteen years beyond Carver's retirement, seeing out Welldon's tenure as Master, and

The Revd William Rogers to Carver, 1876. (Dulwich College)

continuing into the early years of Gilkes's. This was in spite of the fact that, after injuring his spine in a hunting accident in 1880, he suffered from severe depression, and relied on being carried upstairs to the Board Room at the New College in a chair fitted with two carrying poles. He still entertained a great deal at the Rectory at Bishopsgate, where his dinners were famous, and entertained his friends annually to bacon and broad beans, followed by gooseberry fool, at the Greyhound. [70] In his *Reminiscences* of 1888, Rogers was publicly generous in retrospect about Carver, praising his 'wise management and great zeal'; Carver, on the other hand, wrote privately that Rogers was no nobleman, but a *commoner*, 'without scholastic attainment or intellectual influence'. [71] The antipathy between these two extraordinary men was never satisfactorily resolved; more remarkable to note is that, while forming a persistent background rumble, it never significantly hindered the great achievements of their time at Dulwich, chief among which must be counted the construction of Barry's New College.

Building the New College, 1866–70

The *palazzo* with a campanile on our South Circular Road, the New College designed by Charles Barry junior, arose because of the immense increase in the roll of Carver's successful Upper School, and was paid for with monies in compensation from the many railway earth-works on the Estate.

Barry drew up the first plans for the development in 1860, estimating the finished costs as some £40,000. An engraved ground plan was issued to the Governors on 4 July 1860, showing on the present site the outlines of a central hall and two flanking wings connected by a low single storey for classrooms and symmetrical 'play cloisters' open to the air towards the front; large rooms are designated for a library and a museum; a new Chapel to seat 500, and 32 Almshouses (each with a neat garden enclosure), are set on a western axis from the Great Hall onto the 'Clump' and the present games fields; a site is marked for an altogether new Picture Gallery, roughly where the present Science Block now stands. [72]

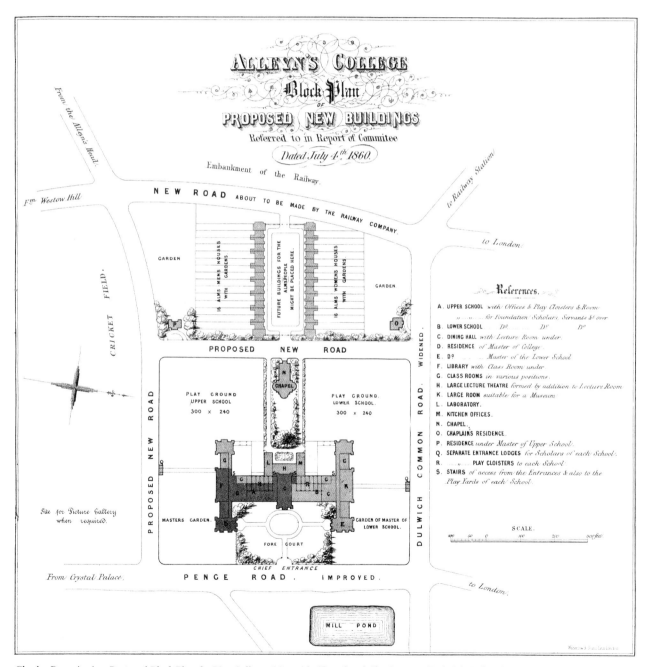

Charles Barry junior, *Proposed Block Plan for New College*, 1860, with Chapel and Almshouses. (Dulwich College)

In January 1863 the Governors seriously discussed the use of the railway monies for a New College building,[73] but the Court of Chancery initially withheld its consent to the use of this revenue for College buildings or for drainage. Meanwhile, therefore, between 1865 and 1867 the large amount of £6,154 was spent on improvements at the Old College.[74] However, the Governors decided against Barry's earlier plans of 1858 for further developing the Old College site, determining instead upon a New College. It was Carver's view that, following the Act of Parliament of 1857, the Upper and Lower Schools could not be severed, and he proposed that both establishments should be accommodated in any new building.[75] Barry made more detailed proposals in 1864 to accommodate 320 boys of the Upper School and 250 of the Lower School in opposite wings, with just eight classrooms in toto, and a clock turret separating the two. A very large 'school room ' with a 'lofty open roof' and a separate dining room were described, and Barry for the first time mentioned 'strings [horizontal bands], friezes, enrichments and carvings' of terracotta.[76]

Since he was already the College Architect and Surveyor, Charles Barry was awarded the contract without the usual open competition, a procedure the Governors adopted, they said, in order to have closer control over expenditure – an irony they no doubt later ruefully recalled when Barry's costs began to spiral out of hand.[77] Barry had made with his partner Robert Richardson Banks a dull design for the Middlesex Industrial Schools at Feltham in 1855,[78] and doubtless would have studied his father's work for the King Edward VI Grammar School at Birmingham of 1837. He was by no means a specialist designer of schools, however, his plans for Dulwich perhaps signalling a greater desire to make a splendid architectural statement, to which he might append his noteworthy signature. Rogers himself had proposed a central common hall for Upper and Lower Schools, and two wings.[79] Though there is evidence that Carver repeatedly consulted Barry at certain stages,[80] he later bitterly complained that he had far too little say in either the design or its relation to the needs of the school. He disliked an early plan for a complete quadrangle, 55 feet high, that was to be enclosed by lofty buildings up to 75 feet high. The classrooms were too small for 16 boys, he argued; there were too few staircases and urinals. A new Chapel was what Carver most desired, as the old one was already too small for the College to share with the Village; his earlier argument with Mr Oldham must also have continued to rankle. He had appealed for this before the New College was in view, but nothing had been done,[81] nor had the Governors adopted Barry's proposals of 1858 to extend the old Chapel with a large

first-floor gallery to the rear over the Audit Room, or even to 'throw the room into it'.[82] Carver also disliked the accommodation proposed for him and his family, originally to have been a separate residence on the site, 'treated externally in the same manner as the New College', but now to be incorporated in the South Block. The rooms were surely too small: he sent for statistics of the room sizes of the headmasters' houses at Wellington, Charterhouse, Marlborough and Clifton.[83]

In 1858 the surveyor and architect William Andrews Nesfield (1793–1881) prepared for the Governors a report, together with a delightful printed map,[84] showing a proposed development of the estate with new roads lined with trees and villas (of the first and second class), and recommending an elevated open site for the new College, either on what is now Beauval Road or on the present site of Alleyn's School. Nesfield designated three fields on Dulwich Common for six Second Class Detached Villas, but the Governors were inclined to site the College there; they confirmed their decision, which Carver approved of, in April 1863.[85] Every detail of plan and cost for the building had to be approved by the Charity Commissioners; Rogers in a speech to parents said that they could not lay a single brick without the Commissioners' assent, and that the resulting delays were very harmful.[86] At first the Commissioners decreed that the College must pay back the railway money spent on the buildings from income. Carver's memorandum with his criticisms of the building was not shown by the Governors to the architect until after the Commissioners had seen the plans, which seems absurdly high-handed. Carver, however, together with Barry, Fergusson and Tite, and with Rogers and some other Governors, met the Charity Commissioners on 27 February 1865. Barry agreed to increase the classroom space, and it was decided with regret that from economy the 'central hall' must serve for a Chapel until a separate Chapel could be afforded.[87]

On 16 January 1866 the Governors finally approved the plans for the College at an estimated cost of £61,993 (nearly £4m in today's prices).[88] The building was essentially as we know it, though a set of wonderful tall and slender 'streaky bacon' brick and terracotta chimney stacks, in his father's manner, were removed after a storm blew down one stack in 1913. This was done in stages over the years; a photograph of 1940 shows roughly a dozen stacks cut down to about one third in height still in place; the College Architect of the day, Austin Vernon, removed the stacks, no longer in use, over the Great Hall in 1944.[89] A large number of Barry's beautiful contract drawings survive in the Archives. The eventual cost, including the fittings, was £81,806.

Barry was asked to design the chapel, a fives court and a gym, none of which were to be built at that time. He was paid a salary of £300 and 5 per cent of the outlay.[90] The building was staked out on Midsummer Day, 1866, by William Downs, of Kennington, who had put in far and away the cheapest of twelve tenders.[91]

Progress was not smooth. Barry was cautioned by the Governors for initiating work without their sanction, and he wrote a long letter in his own defence. He said that he was surprised and sorry that they needed to make a decision on every small detail; the additions he owned to in this document, however, seem considerable: plate glass for the windows, and for the roof Taylor's splendid patent large dull-red tiles; he had improved the clock tower with an extra storey. Further embellishments were the ornamental turrets and finials on the roof of the Great Hall and the flourishes and iron cresting (removed during repairs after war damage) on the Lantern with its crocketed *flèche*,[92] the Devonshire marble pilasters in the Great Hall, and the polished granite pilasters on the external doorways and the windows of the Great Hall. Barry told the Governors ruefully that Downs the builder would probably make a loss, and that his own time and personal expense on the terracotta (described below), which had been freely given, had been considerable.[93]

Barry caused the Governors further anxiety by delaying his final accounts.[94] Meanwhile in a procession from the Old College on 5 July 1869 the Upper School, accompanied by Governors and former pupils, 'took possession' of the North Wing of the New College, originally intended for the Lower School. The Great Hall was still roofless,[95] and Alleyn's great chimney piece with the painted panels from the Old College was not installed in the Masters' Library until March of the following year. A boy who carved his name on a new desk in spite of a ban was caned in front of the whole school.[96] On 2 June 1870 Barry reported to the Governors that the College had cost £13,033 more than his estimate (£855,000 in today's terms), and he had discovered 'too late' a threat of litigation between Downs and John Marriott Blashfield (1811–82), the pioneering maker of the terracotta. £8,400 of this overspending, he claimed, was the amount of a 'serious miscalculation' by Blashfield. Blashfield had been an associate of Barry's in putting up great town mansions at Kensington Palace Gardens in the 1840s, when Blashfield had become bankrupt; since then he had developed his terracotta works. Barry asserted that Blashfield's was chemically 'the best terracotta at home or abroad', and unmatched for its 'finish and delicacy'. He admitted 'taking on a serious responsibility' in proceeding with the elaborate work, but claimed it was in 'the best interests of my

Charles Barry, Junior. (Dulwich College)

clients'.[97] In 1870 Blashfield also reneged on an agreement with the College to build six semi-detached houses in Croxted Road.[98]

In September of the same year the Governors investigated a complaint that Barry had been paid 'many thousands of pounds' by railway companies that should have been received by the College. Barry wrote acknowledging the payments, but claimed that they had been tendered independently of his post as Surveyor with the Governors and the College, and reminded them that the 'architectural appearance' of the New College should please them, as if he felt they had not shown their appreciation. The Villagers thought Barry was getting too big for his boots, and it was repeated everywhere as a common joke that Charles Hutton, the tenant of Belair, had received a letter purporting to be from the ghost of Edward Alleyn suggesting that Dulwich should be renamed 'Barryville'. Carver privately noted that Barry flattered the vanity of the Governors to consider themselves 'not as faithful Trustees of a noble Foundation', but as 'great landowners &c.' while they treated the Schools themselves as an 'encumbrance'.[99] The Governors doubtless still remembered how Barry in 1861, when surveying a proposed housing frontage on Sydenham Hill (carelessly, it is to be hoped, rather than dishonestly), left out a measurement, one whole tape long, of fifty feet; he wrote to them on 13 May protesting that 'my professional judgement – my zeal – and even my good faith with my employers' had been called into question.[100] A full report was ordered

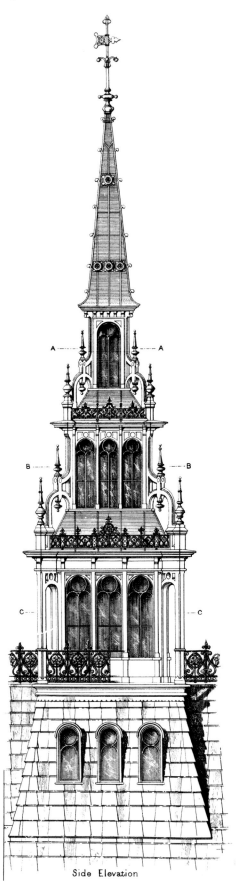

A ---- A

B ---- B

C ---- C

Side Elevation

Details of the Lantern above the Great Hall.
The Architect, 23 April 1870. (© RIBA Drawings Collection)

into the case, and on 4 November four Governors voted against him and eleven for him. In 1862 he wrote a disgruntled letter to the Executive Committee of the Governors complaining that he spent sixty days a year on his work for Dulwich, underpaid, and that was not worth his while, 'except for some professional position and new connections'. The Governors, he said, during this era were indeed 'in the position of large building speculators'.[101] Barry, of course, derived considerable income from designs for new houses on the estate for their tenants, such as Sir Henry Bessemer's mansion, described below, and for the fronts of the rows of houses on the new roads, which were made either by himself or by members of his office. He had most likely, however, forgotten his troubles at Dulwich by 1877, when he was awarded the triennial Gold Medal of the RIBA, specifically citing his design of Dulwich College.

The Governors were stunned at the final cost of the New College, but resolved at the same meeting, when Barry presented the accounts, to realise all possible capital to foot the bill.[102] It meant that plans to open local schools in the distant parishes were postponed, which further embittered the Churchwardens. Carver made a note of Barry's 'flagrant mistakes' in arrangements and plans, and also that his own house, now in the South Wing, was 'uninhabitable'.[103]

It is surprising to learn that Barry's first brief from the Governors of 4 July 1860 was for a brick-and-stone building 'without any great amount of ornamentation'.[104] Since he was closely involved with the railway negotiations and works, and familiar with the College's swelling finances, it is likely that he gambled on making use of the College's resources beyond the estimates, and decorated the palatial box of the College with the results of his and Blashfield's heady experiments with terracotta ornamentation; his uneasy admission of a serious 'miscalculation' of the expense when presenting the accounts seems disingenuous. His own account given to the RIBA of the architectural venture was that the Governors gave him 'no interference' as regards style or materials.[105]

The New College for its period is a very original building, eclectic in style: Barry described it, not very accurately, as 'Northern Italian of the thirteenth century, of which beautiful examples are seen at Milan, Verona, Pavia &c.'.[106] A strange marriage of neo-classical and Gothic styles, it has a Palladian ground plan, and is also Palladian in the relation of solids to voids and with its elaborate cornices; these are in the manner adapted by his father (based on his researches in Vicenza, in particular the study of the Palazzo Thiene of 1545) for his great London club-houses, the Traveller's (1829–32) and the Reform (1837–41).[107] In 1859 Edward Middleton Barry (see Chapter Five), the youngest son of Sir Charles and architecturally the most talented, had designed the Grammar School at Leeds in a conventional Victorian 'Decorated Gothic' style for his brother Alfred Barry (1826–1910), who was its Head Master from 1854. (Alfred Barry, incidentally, who became a Bishop and the Primate of Australia, was a Trinity contemporary of Carver and had been one of his referees for the post at Dulwich.) The Prince Consort was known to have disliked Gothic buildings for schools, with their 'monastic associations', and in 1852 his architect designed Wellington College in a French-Italian manner. [108]

Charles Barry avoided conventional Gothic at Dulwich. A mischievous, but not entirely hostile, reviewer of the New College in the *Building News* for 11 June 1869 said that Barry had tried to satisfy the current craving for a 'compromise' between the two rival styles, the Medieval and the Classic, but had failed. The reviewer praised the slender campanile, but thought that the towers destroyed the overall pyramidal form of the blocks. The details were better than the whole, but the critic made fun of the obtrusive chimney-stacks and the 'crowd of fussy erections which break the sky-line', calling them less 'temperate' than Chinese pagodas; they reminded him of 'bottles in a cruet stand'. He added that the buff terracotta was too pale, and the large chamfered panels beneath the ground-floor windows looked as if they were 'casts from boiler-plates'. The reviewer obviously thought the building miscegenated, wished the style had been more pure, and made a cautionary example of it for its mixture of styles. [109]

The red-and-buff colour scheme of the College owes much to a book on North Italian buildings by George Edmund Street (1824–81), *Brick and Marble in the Middle Ages* (1855), which commends their 'deep red hue … a most satisfactory effect of colour … when alternating with warm-coloured stone'. [110] The bricks for the polychromatic College are small and of a fine red colour. The dressings of unglazed terracotta in colour are mostly buff, but a few are red and duck-egg blue. The use of terracotta in place of stone was a novelty for the period, although E. M. Barry had used it (with white rather than red bricks) to embellish the palatial Charing Cross Hotel and Railway Station in 1864 (which originally flourished belvederes on the corners of its roof, just like the gables of the Great Hall at Dulwich). Barry claimed that terracotta would cost one-third of the price of Portland stone, and that heavy showers would wash it clean of dirt and soot. In a lecture at the RIBA he said that in the course of his architectural grand tour in Lombardy in 1847–8 he had set his heart on using the material in England, 'with so much of the old spirit as my powers would enable me to realise'. [111]

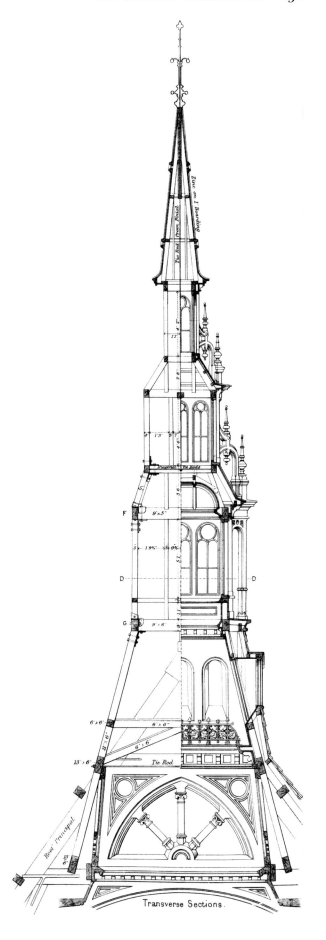

Transverse Sections.

The Entrance Gates of the College, as built. *The Architect*, 12 November 1870. (© RIBA Drawings Collection)

A 'large portion' of the terracotta, presumably the heads, Blashfield said, was 'partially' modelled by Barry himself.[112] Each terracotta piece was sculpted in clay, not moulded, and many of them, on arrival from Blashfield's kiln at Stamford, Lincolnshire, were found to be slightly too large or too small, as it was impossible to predict the shrinkage when firing.[113]

In a sense Barry overworked his designs; in Northern Italy he had filled his sketchbooks with details he liked and from which he quotes at Dulwich, like a young poet who uses too many adjectives. The main source, as he acknowledged, was the Certosa di Pavia (the Charterhouse, near Milan). Here Barry was inspired to imitate the cloisters and the elaborate façades, cornices, turrets, and cupolas. Ruskin, on the contrary, visiting the Certosa in 1849, was reminded of the art of 'inlaid cabinets and velveted caskets', of something 'painful and pitiful … exhausting and encrusting'. Even Barry's refined brother Edward, in a lecture at the Royal Academy, called the Certosa 'fantastic and not to be commended'.[114]

Barry's father, with whom he had worked at the Palace of Westminster, had died in 1860; the impress of the panorama of the Parliament buildings at Thamesbank on the younger Barry is clear in the minor Dulwich variation he created, which presents to the eye the same sequence: first a clock tower, next (at the heart of the Palace) an architectural 'lantern' crowning a great chamber, and finally a second, lower, tower (at Westminster, the Victoria Tower) on the North Block. With this triad of aspiration to the skies he quotes from his father's works; other features in the New College allude to them, such as the ceiling from Clumber Park, Nottinghamshire, duplicated in the College Board Room, and in the Great Hall the piers (originally of buff and light green terracotta, now covered with chocolate paint) for the pilasters, which are copied from the House of Lords chamber. Compared with his father's work, Barry's architecture has been described as 'derivative and synthetic',[115] and these repetitions might be seen as the work of a less inspired son parroting his father's work; on the other hand they could be thought of more kindly as a filial tribute to the great Victorian architect. The clock tower (copied from a campanile in Venice that collapsed in 1744),[116] resembles a finely sharpened pencil. Vertically it marks an aspiration; horizontally it marks a sublimation, progressing upwards from square to octagon to circle to fine vanishing point, where matter becomes spirit. The motive behind the Great Hall, a conscious

Prize-giving in the Great Hall, *c*. 1870. Water-colour and ink. (Dulwich College, gift of C.A.Barry, 1938)

variation on Westminster Hall with its hammer-beams, was presumably to remind Dulwich boys of English history and their political heritage: in Westminster Hall parliament first met, kings lay in state at their death, and state trials were conducted. The Great Hall also derives from the archetypal Anglo-Saxon hall, such as in *Beowulf*, and here the Alleynian tribal consciousness was

forged: outside the Hall was the darkness to be overcome, and the walls are decorated with names in gold recording heroic achievements of the tribe, academic, military, imperial and artistic. Barry was his father's General Superintendent in 1846–8 from the age of 23, when the Palace was rebuilt after the great fire, and designed some decorative details for Big Ben; he also helped to restore Westminster Hall. The Great Hall is another hieroglyph in homage to his father, whose first exhibited drawing at the Royal Academy at the age of 17 in 1812 was a study of the interior of Westminster Hall, the very building which, wrote Bishop Barry, was 'the key-note to his greatest work'.[117]

In the Great Hall the midday meal of the community was to be held; already a hundred took it daily in 1870.[118] Here tribal entertainments – music, drama, and debating – were held in the evenings; the boys joined hands to sing 'Auld Lang Syne', and Songs for the Meetings in the Great Hall, special little sixpenny books bound in Alleynian dark blue, generated esprit de corps. From this publication of Gilkes's days (1890 and 1895) we learn that these songs, unsurprisingly, were mostly patriotic and traditional; there were also one or two songs in Latin or translated from German, a few stirring or tender Irish, Welsh, Scottish or American numbers, and two songs from The Pirates of Penzance and HMS Pinafore by Gilbert and Sullivan. The notable School Songs were introduced in Welldon's era (see Chapter Nine). The Captain of a victorious Shooting Team would mount a ladder and hang up the coveted public schools trophy, the Ashburton Shield (won at Bisley in 1886 and 1900), while the organ played 'See the conquering Hero comes' from Handel's Israel in Egypt. In this Hall boys were transformed into Alleynians.

Barry's most transcendent feature, the Lantern with coloured glass, was set high at the apex of the Great Hall in the exact centre of the axes of the New College, north–south and east–west. Set where the Anglo-Saxons would leave a hole in the roof open to the skies in the centre of the Hall for smoke from the fire, the Lantern at Dulwich figures the descent of light into the College, God's primal Gift; the timeless enters a world of time. Not content with the theatrical effect from Westminster Hall of the hammer-beams, which terminate in carved wyverns [both eagle and dragon] and whose spandrels carry the College arms, Barry added a bravura touch to the roof with the barrel-vault and half wagon-wheels which he had admired in the church of San Fermo at Vicenza. The whole hall was originally much lighter in tone: the deal timbers of the roof and beams were originally their natural blond colour, varnished, with the principal lines of the mouldings picked out in a dark stain (as in an engraving); by 1911 these timbers had become dusty and grubby, and they were crassly stained dark all over, making the Hall too gloomy, at the same time as the panels on the roof, 'tastefully decorated' with elaborate coloured arabesques, were replaced with a dull stencilled design.[119]

As well as its antiquarian and historical associations the New College employed some of the latest technology, including 'fireproof' floors and 'speaking tubes' (a primitive internal telephone system). The Lecture Room, for Mechanics, Physics and Chemistry, constructed beneath the Hall where the front two compartments of the present Wodehouse Library are today, was a feature determined early on,[120] and something well in advance of other schools. This high auditorium rose from the deep basement with a well for the lecturer up to the ceiling directly below the Great Hall, and had ten rows of raked seats to hold up to 260 people. Carver had studied such rooms at the Royal Society and at the Chemical Theatre at London University. The Lecture Room was little used for academic purposes after the Great War, but Lower School assemblies took place here, and in 1927 it was converted into a Music Room, holding practices of the full orchestra and choir of 150 members, which must have been something of a trial of good humour. The laboratories had chemical troughs, sinks, and Bunsen burners; the boys themselves had to buy their own test tubes and glass rods.[121] Carver later asked for a workshop and appliances for Practical Mechanics to be put in at the New College.[122]

In 1871 the French Impressionist painter Camille Pissarro (1831–1903), in exile in Upper Norwood, chose Barry's New College for a subject, and made the fine colour study Dulwich College (Fondation Bemberg, Toulouse), where the red-brick buildings are seen from across the pond in autumnal afternoon sunlight. Lawrence Durrell, the novelist and poet (1912–90), lived as a boy for a while in Alleyn Park, and his brother Leslie attended the College; Durrell was to describe the New College as 'a fair candidate for the wildest Victorian building in the whole of London, with a crazy Dostoevskian gleam in its eye'.[123]

Dr Carver in the event probably did not eye his new buildings with simple admiration of their noble features; the Governors told him he should be satisfied with them, and stop asking for further developments or expenses. Carver calculated that the amount of money spent on Barry's terracotta embellishments cost the College the equivalent of ten years of the increases in salaries and Scholarships and further facilities for the boys that he was constantly refused by the Governors.[124]

The College gardens were originally laid out by a local resident and parent of three boys in the school, the garden architect Edward Milner (1819–84), Paxton's gifted assistant at the Crystal Palace; the Master's Garden was where the present Science Block now stands, and the Under Master's garden was to the north-east;[125] colourful plant bedding in the forecourt was soon replaced in 1872 with yews and turf.[126]

On 26 June 1866 William Rogers ceremonially laid the foundation stone of the New College on a platform

The New College, with scaffold to exterior of Great Hall, *c.* 1870. (Dulwich College)

hung with flags; beneath the stone he set in mortar a bottle containing a copy of *The Times* for the day and a set of 'coins of the realm', handed to him by Barry. It was the 250th anniversary of the signing of the Letters Patent of the College in 1616. Gladstone, then Chancellor of the Exchequer, was to have taken this part, but was called away at the last moment. Rogers, in an excellent speech, said that the two railways whose lines had already intersected the estate had put the College financially 'thirty years in advance'. He later wrote in his *Recollections* that 'thanks to the late Mr Charles Druce the Governors drove an uncommonly good bargain' with the railway companies.[127] Five hundred invited guests, including the two architects on the Board of Governors, Tite and Fergusson, sat in a specially constructed 'booth'. The Choir sang Mendelssohn's 'Let our theme of praise ascending'.[128] The occasion was marred by some expression of hostility towards Rogers from Carver's boys, and the Governors passed a resolution that 'public expressions of approval or disapproval on the part of the Boys of the Schools towards any of the authorities of the College' were not to be allowed.[129]

The history of how the College was paid for is complicated in detail, but simple in the source of the money: by 1873 the Crystal Palace and the railways had finally paid to the Governors about £100,000, more than covering the cost of the New College, the Schools Inquiry of that year was told. They listed the following payments: Crystal Palace Company £12,500 (1858); London, Chatham and Dover Railway, £21,800 (1863); West London and Crystal Palace Railway, £1,985 (1863); Crystal Palace and South London Junction Railway, £12,109 (1863); London, Chatham and Dover Railway, £30,000 (1865); London, Brighton and South Coast Railway, £1,270 (1865). In 1862 the London, Chatham and Dover Railway also agreed to construct Union Road (now Hunts Slip Road) and to give a half-fare concession to College boys.[130]

In 1860 Druce had reported that the Charity Commissioners would allow the College to borrow £40,000 in mortgages to build the New College, and also that the invested Picture Gallery Fund had reached £17,500 from which to borrow. The money from the London, Chatham and Dover railway was not yet to hand;[131] indeed the Crystal Palace Company and the property developer George Wythes were also seriously in arrears.[132] In 1866 they expected that the New College would absorb 'a very large proportion of the funded property of the College', which stood at £80,394.[133] In fact the College was partly paid for at the time from an invested 'Suspense Account' from Estate income. A 'Committee of Inhabitants of Dulwich and Camberwell' felt strongly that this should not be touched. They first appealed with accusations of 'gross misconduct' to the Charity Commissioners, who backed the Governors and warned the complainants against 'harassing the Trustees of Charities with vague and intangible accusations, which are easily made'; the Inhabitants were referred without avail to the Attorney-General.[134] This group was essentially the same body as the 'Dulwich Education Committee' of 1874, who were local supporters of Carver. In December 1868 Camberwell inhabitants protested that the Upper School fees in the New College were to double to £13.10s. per annum.[135] The *Building News* commented scornfully in 1869 that £10,000 was being spent on drains, and not on brains; they had heard that £120,000 would be required for the New College, while nine new schools, grammar or boarding public schools, including Framlingham and Bedford, had cost from £12,000 to £35,000. A deputation in protest had been received by the Home Secretary, and the magazine called for a parliamentary Inquiry, calling the expense a 'crying evil'; moreover, Barry's terracotta medallions were so high up that one needed to project one's head from a second-floor window or use a 'powerful glass' from the ground to look at them.[136] A London newspaper clamoured for the new building to be closed or converted into a lunatic asylum.[137] Representatives from the four parishes lobbied the Home Secretary. Carver made a reckoning that since the new Governors came into being in 1857, they had by 1869 received £92,253 from railways, and £132,131 from the Estate.[138] Between 1857 and 1881 the annual income of the Foundation increased from £10,771 to £19,853. Rogers claimed in his *Recollections* that although the income might be 'nearly £11,000 per annum, we were crippled for want of money';[139] as late as 1887 the College masters agreed to a temporary reduction of salary when the school had a deficit. There was a general principle adopted by the Governors in 1877 that the buildings and playgrounds should be provided and maintained from income, but the salaries and other purely educational expenses should be paid from fees.[140]

On 21 June 1870 the new *palazzo* for Edward Alleyn's boys was given perhaps the highest tribal accolade: the heir to the throne, Edward, Prince of Wales, attended the Great Hall with his bride of three years, Princess Alexandra, who was dressed in an amber tussore silk gown. The boys gave speeches in Greek, Latin, French and English, and sang; there was a prize-giving. Rogers caused lasting offence after the ceremony by drawing the Prince aside to smoke cigars in private during most of the elaborate reception planned for him by Alfred and Eliza Carver.[141]

Hume v. *Marshall, 1877*

Hardly had the New College been occupied than a very harmful libel case unsettled the school and brought bad publicity. Behind the ostensibly affable and orderly world of the masters assembled by Dr Carver for daily notices in the Masters' Library before morning prayers in the Great Hall lay ugly and boring back-biting and jealousies. A Common Room of schoolmasters may no doubt reveal the human failings of ordinary people, but it also has to be said that Carver did not excel at relations with his staff: he was autocratic, and held no staff meetings; he also had a tendency to think of people who had different ideas or ways of doing things from himself as demons, with sorry results. Readers of *The Times* and other papers in 1877 were given reports of devastating testimonies in the libel case between two Assistant Masters, held in Croydon before the Lord Chief Justice, revealing that behind the universal accolades for the success of the College lay the dreadful shame of its corporate life: that Carver and his deputy, the Under Master, communicated only in writing; that four of the Assistant Masters were not on speaking terms; that some of them drank spirits during the morning break, observed by the boys; and that the wives of members of the two rival factions in the College lowered their parasols on the street to avoid their enemies. The court was told that the teaching at the College was being seriously harmed by the animosities, disputes and grievances among the staff.[142]

The Assistant Master who brought the case, against Carver's wishes, was Andrew Hume, who was 43 years old and had been at the College since 1871. He objected to the Governors being told by the Under Master that he was frequently drunk in public, which he claimed was a false deduction from his weak knee and poor gait. The Governors had not reached any decision on the case before Hume brought the action. A graduate of Trinity College, Dublin, Hume according to many people did not have a particularly pleasant temperament and was certainly fond of liquor; he was said to be 'always excited' in manner. Carver had too much confidence in him, putting him in charge of the Rifle Corps, an unpopular appointment, and then appointing him the School Secretary in 1875. William Young, a Governor from 1872 (from 1891 also the Chairman of the Estates Governors) and the author of the great two-volume *History of Dulwich College* (1889), is said to have deliberately encouraged the libel case to damage Carver. Young was a prominent member of Lloyd's; like many of the Governors, he supported Rogers in his plans to divert income from the Estate to the Parishes. Mackenzie said that he was a cultured man with a good library, but 'prosecuted an enmity with bitterness'.[143] His 1896 obituary in the *Edward Alleyn Magazine* (of Alleyn's School) calls him 'a fine type of the business Scotchman, clear-headed and energetic, though somewhat brusque in manner'.[144] The Governors planned that Carver would resign after this trial, and indeed urged him to accept a 'liberal' pension of £1,200 per annum. The man whom Hume accused of libel in the case was Carver's fourth Under Master, the Revd James Marshall (1838–1926) who had been appointed from Clifton College in 1869; the appointment was made not by Carver, but by the Governors alone, as the constitution dictated. Marshall, an excellent teacher and Classical scholar (an editor of Horace), was disliked by Carver. A distinguished former pupil of the day, (Sir) Herbert Thirkell White (see below), praised Marshall's guidance and encouragement of the boys, but said that he did not suffer fools gladly, and had only a 'limited' popularity; his nickname was 'Beelzy'.[145] Carver kept a record of Marshall's failings, such as boxing boys' ears and leaving an examination unsupervised.[146] Marshall, summoned by the Governors to report on Hume, presumably told them what was later said in evidence at the trial: that Hume's nickname was 'B and S' [Brandy and Soda], that he was frequently drunk and incapable in the evenings, was drunk when announcing names of winners at a Sports Day, was drunk on trains and in the streets, and that his breath smelt of spirits in Chapel at nine in the morning. Young wrote letters to Assistant Masters asking if Carver had been told about Hume, and if he had done anything about it.[147] Young possibly had some grudge against Carver, as he had withdrawn his sons from the College to send them to Winchester: one was a Scholar, who had attended for five years, and who left from the Upper Fourth in 1871, and another left from the Upper Second form in 1875. Young printed some 'Notes by W.Y.' and posted them to the Governors, complaining that Carver had no knowledge of the boys generally and left the masters to run their own forms as they liked. Mrs Carver was sure that such behaviour was 'social jealousy' and arose from personal hostility to her husband. When Carver warned his third Under Master, the Revd George Bell (1865–1913), against Young, an anonymous letter on the same lines was sent to him, which he was sure was from Eliza Carver.[148] Carver was shaken by the lack of loyalty shown by his staff at the trial, and he kept many papers relating to it. In May he preached in the Chapel on

Elijah and commitment to the Cause, and the contest with the priests of Baal and their wicked King, in response to a 'pointed' sermon by Marshall on the evils of liquor. In consequence of the trial Carver suffered a 'severe illness' (acute inflammation of the lungs), his first and only one; this was brought about, he wrote, by the 'severe strain to strength and nerves to which I was cruelly and most unnecessarily subjected'.[149] The staff, the trial was told, were generally on good terms until the end of 1872, but when the Endowed Schools Commission threatened to split the school into two, they divided into hostile groups of Marshallites and Carverites 'at daggers drawn', and they were compared to the factions in medieval Italy, the Guelphs and Ghibellines.[150] Marshall, a severe man, was said in fact to have had few followers among the staff, whose nickname for him was 'J.I.', after Iscariot; however, when the Common Room was led to believe that Carver would resign and that Marshall would be appointed by the Governors to succeed him, some teachers 'turned to the rising sun'.[151] That the Under Master was the Governors' appointee, and could only be dismissed by them, was in itself a mischievous situation. Mrs Carver was rumoured to have sent more anonymous letters, warning of friendships with the enemy, which is more than likely.[152]

The Governors held an extraordinary series of 'Special Meetings'. At the Assizes it was Marshall who gave evidence that the masters drank spirits at 11 a.m. in the Buttery, witnessed by the boys. Shabby details emerged of talk at dinner parties, of malice and conflicts at the College, and of gossip by masters and former pupils, Villagers, and a chorister; all were recorded in the *The Times* and the *South London Press* for August 1877. Reports, with rumours and slanders, filled other newspapers.[153] It emerged in court that Marshall, who had living quarters with his family in the North Block, had refused five or six successive invitations to dine with the Carvers in the South Block, had often declared that much of the College endowment should go into new schools, and had ambitions to be Head of the Modern Side, a division which Carver opposed on principle. In the light of this situation it seems possible that Carver's educational principle was driven by the rationalisation of an ulterior fear of losing some of his own authority. Carver declared when summoned to give evidence that he was ill, and would hardly say anything, except that the evidence against Hume had been 'got up'. The verdict went against Marshall, but because the evidence was shown to be conflicting, a compromising and insulting award of forty shillings damages was made to Hume; the *South London Press* carried a statement subscribed to by most of the jurors in the case saying that they had actually recommended 'substantial' damages to him. The costs of almost £2,000 by law had to be paid by Marshall. The Lord Chief Justice in his summing-up expressed regret that this was the case, as Marshall had done 'his bounden duty' as a responsible schoolmaster; he added that the case should have been brought, if at all, against Hume's direct defamers, and that it should not have reached the courts before the Governors had deliberated the case. The Governors were eager to pay Marshall's costs, since his actions had been *bona fide* – but this they were forbidden to do by the Charity Commissioners. Hume was immediately dismissed by the Governors. A dissenting motion by George Turney, a Governor from St Giles, to dismiss Marshall came to nothing. [154]

Carver gave Hume a personal donation of £275 (which he said could 'scarcely be thought illiberal') to found a school, but he refused to pay Hume's costs for the trial, and referred later demands to his solicitor. Carver wrote a letter to Hume on 27 December 1877, saying that it would take him and his wife long to recover, if ever, from the gross misrepresentations and 'malignant persecutions' to which he had been exposed by the trial, and blaming Hume for bringing the action in the first place. [155] At a Governors' meeting, Rear Admiral Bedford Pim, MP (1825–86), the Arctic explorer who searched for Sir James Franklin, tabled the motion that it was 'a breach of trust' to induce the Master to retire 'in prime of life and unquestioned efficiency' by offering him a pension; in the interests of the College the 'chronic misunderstanding' between some of the Governors and the Master should instead be terminated at once by bringing against him a specific charge. This would lead either to renewed confidence or dismissal. The resolution was not passed. [156] Carver believed that two or three personal opponents had succeeded in poisoning the minds of many of the Governors and that he was mightily wronged: they 'sought to destroy the character and mar the life work of one whose only fault it has been to have been too successful in advancing the welfare and protecting the College at the sacrifice of his own interests and peace'. [157] More seriously, perhaps, Carver also believed that Rogers lied in court. The Lord Chief Justice in his summing-up referred to 'heats and animosities' among 'educated and honourable men'. In a private memorandum Carver regretted that he had backed Hume, as it had brought suspicions that he was shielding him. [158]

If possible, worse troubles hounded Carver the following year. 'A Marshall Defence Fund' in 1878 raised £1,628 for Marshall's costs, contributed by bishops, heads of Oxford and Cambridge Colleges, headmasters and very many assistant masters at the great public schools. The Committee of 37 men for this appeal

included five heads of Oxford colleges (among them Rogers's famous friend, Benjamin Jowett, the Master of Balliol), Rogers himself, the headmasters of Eton, Harrow, Rugby, Charterhouse, Clifton, and six other well-known schools. They printed two documents listing the subscribers and the amounts they gave: one, marked 'Private' in March, was followed by a 'Final Cash Statement' in July. The appeal was 'confidently' addressed 'to all interested in the welfare and moral tone of our Public Schools'. Carver was shamed by inference in the first paragraph for doing nothing about Hume's behaviour although he had been informed about it, and presumably also for protecting the man, while Marshall was painted as the honourable victim. Carver's feelings reading these documents and the names can be imagined: practically the whole of the educational establishment and prominent figures in the Church, two highly interwoven worlds in those days, were marshalled in censure against him. In December 1874 he had been the (sixth) Chairman and host to the Headmasters' Conference at Dulwich, entertaining them to dinner in the Great Hall and being thanked for the 'warmth and courtesy' of his hospitality, and here were seven of the eight members of the committee of the Conference elected in 1874, acting three years later as members of the actual committee of the Marshall Defence Fund and giving substantial contributions to it. What amounted to being 'sent to Coventry' by his peers for spoiling the moral tone of Dulwich and bringing the Public Schools into disrepute was compounded with the public hostility of people whom he had crossed in his career exposed in the columns of the Fund subscriptions. The latter could be measured by the significantly larger amounts given against their names: his former Under Master, Henry Roby; the first Chaplain, Cheetham; and a sacked Assistant Master, Edward Morgan. Rogers, Young and nine other Governors gave subscriptions of fifty pounds each, and two generations of the Druces, the Estate Solicitors, between them gave the enormous amount of 150 guineas. A good many Dulwich residents were listed and many assistant masters from great schools where Carver's name was presumably mud. [159]

Carver's intransigence had earlier done harm to the College and himself: after a quarrel he lost one of his most able and influential Assistant Masters to Wellington College in September 1875. This was a former favourite pupil of his, Charles Lane (1846–84), so prominent from his early days that he was the Captain of School from 1861 to 1865; he was also a College Exhibitioner at Cambridge. [160] Lane was a Dulwich hero: at the Old College in his last year he was set upon on the way home by six 'Lowers' [Lower School boys], as part of the 'deadly and ceaseless war' between the school's two parts, and he kept them at bay 'for a stricken hour by the College clock'.[161] Lane was the schoolboy editor and plainly the driving force of the short-lived forerunner of *The Alleynian*, the *Dulwich College Magazine* (see below). Returned from Cambridge to the College, his pupils admired him, thinking him 'straightforward and honourable'. Lane was also the prime mover of the Alleyn Club and its first Hon. Secretary; this was one of the very first Old Boys' associations. In June 1873 he wrote to *The Alleynian* with a proposal for an 'Edward Alleyn Club', for 'friendly intercourse between old pupils', for a dinner, prizes for sports and work, the exchange of information, and a benevolent fund. The club at Dulwich College was in fact called the Alleyn Club at its foundation; the Old Boys' association at Alleyn's School is called the Edward Alleyn Club.[162] The first dinner was held in 1874; by 1890 there were four dinners a year, with speeches and songs, followed by 'smoking concerts'.[163] In 1873, however, Carver called Lane a 'traitor' and a 'spy' over some unknown issue, and Lane sent Carver's angry letters to him to the Governors, who recommended that the two 'adjust their difference'.[164] A letter written by Lane to Salisbury James Price, a recent Old Boy, about 'the sickening sea of Dulwich

politics' and the 'low condition of Dulwich morality [morale]', saying that Hume, Carver's protégé, 'had poisoned the place', was quoted at the trial.[165] Although Carver was almost obsessive in keeping many drafts and records of his differences with people, he preserved no record about this quarrel, which is known to have grieved him sorely; he formerly described Lane as a 'dear friend'.[166] Lane left Dulwich after a farewell with a large gathering of well-wishers and a 'testimonial' held in the North Block.[167] Lane gave evidence against Hume at the trial, and for the Marshall Defence Fund he sent a sizeable cheque (conspicuous, that is to say, among the contributing Assistant Masters) of £10; many of his colleagues from Wellington also sent contributions, as did masters at Marshall's former school, Clifton. At Wellington in a short time 'nearly the whole management of that great school' was said to be in his hands. Lane died tragically at the age of 38, as a result of blood-poisoning after inspecting the school drains.[168] A famous trophy for a shooting competition between Dulwich and Wellington, the Lane Shield, (originally, and confusingly, the Allen Shield, but renamed after Lane by its donor, a Dulwich parent named C. A. Allen), preserved his memory for many years.

Assistant Masters, including Charles Lane and Edward Morgan, *c.* 1873. (Dulwich College)

Carver was not without some allies, however. In 1874 the Governors had been told by Young of general dissatisfaction with Carver and his management, but 18 masters signed a letter saying that 'we venture to assert our conviction that no Head Master in the kingdom more entirely carries with him, not only the thorough confidence, but the personal affection of his staff', and six men wrote individual letters of support. Carver went to the trouble in November of the same year of printing these testimonial letters, and in 1875 took legal advice about his position with the Governors. Carver was told that no body of gentlemen would forgive being upset by one under their

authority, and William Young was frequently to be heard on the train from West Dulwich asserting that Carver would find that a victory was worse than a defeat. [169]

James Marshall was the only master who did not sign Carver's farewell Testimonial on his eventual retirement in 1883. He was one of the eight candidates selected by the Governors to succeed Carver, presenting a most impressive printed testimonial with letters from Benjamin Jowett and Public School Headmasters, but was not appointed, and left that same year, going on to become Headmaster of Durham School. He continued to attend Alleyn Club dinners in Gilkes's days.

Wyverns on hammerbeams of Great Hall. (© Len Cross)

PART II

Further travails of Dr Carver – 'The Battle of Dulwich' (1865–82) and the Seven Schemes – The transformation of the Estate – The Gallery and the Almsfolk – Carver and the curriculum – The Common Room – College activities – The Boarding Houses – Careers of early Alleynians – The artists – Joseph and Pharaoh

Further travails of Dr Carver

The Carvers lived in an atmosphere of conspiracies, real and imagined; already in 1859 Eliza Carver was writing letters at the Old College about 'unheard of trickery and intrigue'. [170] Behind the affair at the Croydon Assizes in 1877 lay a really serious threat to the whole College: Rogers and many of the Governors were putting particularly strong pressure on the Foundation to endow new parish schools and reduce the income paid to the College, and this was unsettling the Common Room. In 1868, with the New College under construction, a Governor, Joseph Ingledew of St Botolph's, intervened (unsuccessfully) to thwart Carver's plans for a boarding school at Dulwich and to establish middle-class day schools in three of the parishes. [171] Carver wrote, 'I feel just now very much as a man would feel thrown into the water with hands and feet tied and bid to swim for his life'. He also used the metaphor of himself as a champion bound by petty

adversaries: he was a prostrate Gulliver, trussed by the Lilliputians around him. [172] He perpetually appealed to the Governors for proper salaries for his 'miserably underpaid' and overworked Assistant Masters, and printed in 1877 a pamphlet saying that the College 'practically gains little from the large endowment of the College', and lacked the 'most ordinary necessities of a great public school', namely a fives court, a gymnasium and a swimming bath, and even a covered shed for the boys in bad weather; he was still asking for these amenities in 1881. [173]

Early issues of *The Alleynian* refer to the Governors' refusal to comply with such requests; in 1873 letters ask why there is no Gymnasium, and why the Mill Pond could not be converted into an open swimming bath. [174] In 1881 The Governors claimed that the Charity Commissioners had sat upon Barry's plans for a gymnasium since 1873; they declined to make a decision until a final Scheme for proposed changes in the constitution of the

College made by the Endowed Schools Commission (see below) became law.[175] A fives court was built in 1880 (to be destroyed by a bomb in July 1944). A new cricket pavilion was built in 1881, an improvement on the original thatched open shed with a very small brick wing for the cricket coach (who was also the groundsman) and his stock; the present pavilion was built in 1934. Meanwhile *The Alleynian* commented that it would be hard to find a school 'so highly charged with athleticism'.[176] The masters had to wait until 1879 for a significant increase in salaries. Among Carver's other worries were the lax collection of fees, and the Bailiff and Clerk who disputed Carver's rights to give them orders. A pupil complained about 'infidel and free-thinking' books by Darwin and Voltaire in the boys' Library.

Meanwhile, throughout the early years of the minutes of the Governors' meetings, preoccupied with the business of developing the Estate, the extraordinary progress of Carver's academy seemed to go unnoticed, apart from requests for blackboards, easels and wall-maps, or for an increase of salary for the art teacher John Sparkes. There was no mention at all in the minutes of any discussion of educational policy, although from 1866 onwards the many academic achievements were recorded.[177] Carver habitually made a point of publishing lists of the boys' honours and achievements, including those at London hospitals and the winning of gold and silver medals at the Royal Geographical Society. By 1880 he was able to report to the Governors 160 honours recorded in gold on the panels in the Great Hall, and the fact that for three years running the College had won an Open Scholarship at Corpus Christi College, Cambridge. By 1880 these awards and first class honours, some in Natural Sciences, were commonplace. A 'small and struggling school of less than one hundred boys' had indeed become 'one of the greatest educational institutions of the country', as his staff wrote in the Testimonial on his retirement.[178]

Carver's resentments against the Governors also had to do with major issues about money. He understood, as mentioned above, that offering Scholarships at the College and Exhibitions at Oxford and Cambridge to former pupils was the key to attracting clever boys, and paid in 1861 for two Exhibitions of £40 per annum for four years from his own pocket, the same year that the College moved to limit the expenditure of the Upper and Lower Schools to £1,500 per annum. Edward Everett, recalling this period in an article in *The Alleynian*, wrote that one of the two boys subsidised in this way by Carver, having spent three terms at Cambridge, took his cheque for the next year and disappeared. In 1869 the *City Press* reported that Carver had paid £600 out of his own pocket during the last two or three years.[179] Rogers did

not see the point of the Exhibitions, and his coarse opinion that boys would be better off in a counting house rather than starving as graduate curates echoes the views of the Fellows quoted in the previous chapter.[180]

Carver was originally promised, in addition to his stipend of £400, a 'capitation allowance' that grew with the enrolment. Thus in 1859 his salary amounted to £1,061; in 1872 he was paid £2,300, and in 1882 £2,636. Legally these later figures should have been much larger by this calculation, but in 1868 he had altruistically agreed with the Governors to waive his rights to the full capitation allowance for five years, on condition that there would be in return more provision for Scholarships and Exhibitions and more funds for salary increases and for additional masters;[181] the Board did not honour this promise, claiming that the College could not afford it. Carver in 1875 calculated that over the seven years since he made the 'agreement' he had been paid £15,210 and had lost £14,974 by this clause.[182] Carver made no secret that he frequently contributed to salaries and Scholarships from his own pocket, which of course was swollen by a considerable private income.[183] In 1873 he wrote to the Governors about the 'voluntary surrender of a large portion of emoluments which would legally accrue to me'.[184] With the rise in numbers at the College his entitled income by 1873 would have reached the colossal amount of £6,000 under the Act. In that year a Camberwell resident, in a spiteful pamphlet, complained that Carver not only enjoyed the income of a Prime Minister and a palatial residence, but was labouring to lift the College into the exclusive service of the rich, and was increasing the numbers for his own profit. The writer also prophesied that if Dulwich were allowed to become another Eton, Harrow or Rugby, it could become 'as completely detached from the inhabitants of its locality as if it was a hundred miles away'.[185] All the evidence suggests that Carver's ambitions were disinterested, and exclusively devoted to the educational advancement of the College itself. In this he made some progress: in 1872 the Charity Commissioners agreed to eight more Scholarships in addition to the existing sixteen.[186] In 1879 the Governors gave an extra £800 for salaries, and in 1880 three new Science Scholarships were awarded.[187] In 1883, following the new Scheme, the number of special Scholarships by examination of £20 per annum had risen to 42; boys at the top of the school competed for Exhibitions of £50 per annum, to be held at universities, at institutions for the Fine Arts or for the learned or scientific professions.[188]

In 1875 Carver took the advice of a famous advocate, Sir William Harcourt (1827–1904; Solicitor-General, 1873–4; Home Secretary, 1880), who advised him that

The New College, from the north-east, *c.* 1880. (Dulwich College)

a Petition to the Privy Council, nominally on his own financial rights, would help him defeat the Governors and the Endowed Schools Commission with their proposed Schemes (described in some detail below) that were threatening to spoil the way the College was developing and to strip it of its endowments; it would also gain him good publicity for a change.[189]

The numbers of pupils at the College had risen fast. From 1859 to 1869 there were approximately 130 boys in the Upper School at the Old College.[190] With the opening of the New College the numbers of Upper School pupils rose to 269 in 1870 and to 370 the following year, in spite of the doubled fees. At first the number of boys staying on after the age of sixteen was disappointing. In the three years 1869–71, of a total of 146 leavers only 22 were over sixteen, but in 1872 this figure had 'almost doubled' in the one year, as Carver reported to the Governors.[191] Carver was expecting 600 boys by 1873, and thought that 800 could be accommodated in the New College.[192] In the event it was not until 1891 that the roll reached 625

boys, rising to 803 boys in 1922.[193] The Lower School was not so popular; by 1872 it held 120 pupils.[194]

Carver opposed the first five of the seven Schemes proposed by the government Endowed Schools Commission because they would take away income from the College for other schools. The Governors argued that if they were to continue the school on a suitable scale they could not pay Carver the salary to which he was entitled under the original Act, as they had by then diverted the money to other objects. Harcourt pointed out to the Privy Council the iniquity of Rogers's 'interest' in the Foundation as Chairman of the Governors; £3,000 per annum was being paid to St Botolph's, well over twice the income given to the College.[195] Mackenzie, who had the benefit of conversations with Carver, wrote that 'the Master's resistance was based upon public grounds. It was because it marred and stunted his beloved College that he was resolved to defeat it if he could. There is little doubt that he would have failed, had it not been for the freedom the Scheme took with his vested rights'.[196]

The case was heard by the Judicial Committee of the Privy Council on 27 January 1876; the parishes of Camberwell, St Botolph's, Bishopsgate, and St Luke's, Finsbury, also sent in petitions about their interests.[197] The Council upheld Carver's legal rights to his allowances, and ordered the Governors to pay Carver's costs,[198] but Carver's main victory was that the current Schemes had been overturned by the highest authority on the grounds that they did not provide for his vested interests; he had also managed to reverse much of the bad publicity that arose over the current proposals for the future of the College and its rising wealth. In 1875 Carver was paid his full entitlement of £2,481, but the following year the Governors told him that, with his full emoluments, 'it will be impossible for the Educational Branch to carry on', and asked him therefore what 'modifications' he would accept. Carver refused to acknowledge that this was the real issue; the prosperity of the College, he argued, depended on income to support adequate staff in order to offer the necessary range of subjects. When the New College was opened he had a staff of a mere 16 masters, and the 36 men he now presided over were still not enough; in a year when he had spent £400–500 of his own money on salaries, 'several of our ablest and most experienced masters [were] gone' on account of 'poor salaries and prospects'. There was still the burning need for more Exhibitions to attract bright pupils.[199] Fifty-six pages of minutes of anxious discussion follow; the Governors next appealed to the Charity Commissioners. After some obscure negotiations Carver did make a second 'arrangement' with the Governors, which he described as 'a renewed surrender, voluntarily made in the interests of the College, of a strictly legal claim'.[200] The following year 26 Assistant Masters wrote to the Governors demanding an increase of salary, repeating the claim that good teachers did not stay long.[201]

This, then, was the troubled background to the Hume *versus* Marshall trial; as early as November 1876, the Governors had already passed a resolution that they considered it 'most conducive to the interests of the College and the successful working of any new Scheme that it should be undertaken by a new Headmaster'. Bitter arguments continued until 1879 during the discussion of the proposed Schemes and the radical changes they suggested; Carver meanwhile continued to spend £400–500 per annum on supplementing salaries and paying for Exhibitions from his own pocket.[202] He endowed four prizes for English Literature and Language in 1875.[203] In 1878 Carver agreed to retire after the establishment of the new Scheme, with a pension of £1,200; he did so in 1883, two years after the Act of Parliament was passed.

'The Battle of Dulwich' (1865–82) and the Seven Schemes

It was the best of times, it was the worst of times: even as the foundation stone of Barry's magnificent New College was being laid in June 1866, the very basis of its academic identity was being challenged. The great crisis in the College's history was drawn out over more than 13 bitterly contested years from 1865; it was not until shortly after Carver's victory with the Privy Council that the Fifth Scheme of 1878 at last showed a turn of the tide in his favour. Rogers and his allies continued to threaten to destroy all Carver's aims even after the New College's buildings were asserting that a noble and prosperous academy had stood up in the suburbs, and even while Carver was winning such personal recognition for his pupils' success. Strictly, the close examination of the New College and the questioning of its rationale by external bodies began in 1865, when a report of the Endowed Schools Commission was published which seemed to call into question all Carver's ambitions. Mr D. R. Fearon, an Assistant Commissioner, recommended that at Dulwich there should be just two day schools, one for boys and one for girls. He thought that it made sense of Alleyn's bequest that the distant parishes should be endowed by the Foundation with good day schools. Carver, in his view, had set the Upper School a hopeless and ridiculous task: 'the extent and pretension of the curriculum is ludicrous'. Boys should be taken from humbler backgrounds, Greek should be taken off the syllabus, and the College should sever connections with the universities. The thread of Fearon's argument ran as follows:

> The standard appears to me to be pitched rather too high for the ages and opportunities of the boys.... The school is, as regards the age of its scholars, like what Marlborough or Winchester would be with its two highest forms lopped off.... [The Master and Under Master] are engaged in a task which, from the nature of the case, is hopeless. They are endeavouring to give to middle scholars, chiefly of the second grade, boys who leave school under seventeen, a mainly classical education. In so doing they throw away the substance, the modern languages, modern science, mathematics, and limited Latin scholarship which might really be obtained, to grasp a shadow, classical scholarship in boys of seventeen.... It seems absurd to offer a classical education to the sons of warehousemen, wharfingers [managers of a wharf], solicitors and leather-merchants.[204]

The arguments over the status and future of the College had a great deal to do with social class. A backlash against the case for the best general education for the greatest numbers of the deserving poor came in 1873 from Frederick Hovenden of St Luke's (College Governor 1873–88; Estates Governor, 1882–90, later Deputy Chairman), who was enraged at a proposal for the School Board of London to manage the College:

> Do the Commissioners mean to utilise the property for these gutter children to the exclusion of those who now use the school, or do they mean to engraft these children – too often children of thieves and prostitutes, and always the children of the most degraded – with the respectable pupils now using the College? [205]

Meanwhile the enrolment of boys from the further parishes and the number of them sent as candidates for Scholarships had fallen markedly. The appeal of the New College is reflected in Rogers's statement in his *Recollections* that up to 1870 the largest proportion of boys in the Upper School lived in Camberwell and Dulwich, but by the 1890s they came from all parts of London and indeed the world. [206]

It would be tedious to record the many pamphlets, meetings and articles in the press that made up the 'Battle of Dulwich', but in 1871 the Endowed Schools Commissioners sent their Assistant Commissioner to inspect the College, and a series of preposterous schemes to despoil and dispossess the College were formulated and proposed to the Governors. The overt aim was to close the Lower School at Dulwich, at this point mainly composed of sons of Camberwell tradesmen and others of the lower middle class, [207] to divert the rapidly increasing endowment and 'settle the claims of the parishes' by putting up middle schools for them, and to force the College to dwindle into a 'Second-grade School' by drastically cutting its income, in accordance with Rogers's ambitions and agenda. In this same year, 1871, two of Carver's former pupils were awarded Cambridge Fellowships, at Pembroke and Christ's. Carver's allies were not many, most of them local residents, or parents who naturally resented the threat to the quality of the College and understood that the fees might need to rise dramatically. Opposed to Carver stood the weight of William Rogers and his influence and of the official bodies eager to develop popular education in London, where it was indeed badly needed. Of the parishes, Camberwell stood to gain the most; here schools were badly needed, on account of the extraordinary expansion in population. The main argument in Camberwell against the College, particularly when the fees doubled in 1869 with the New College building in view, was that it was becoming more and more a College for the 'richer portion of the middle class'. [208] On 12 December 1868 the Camberwell Vestry held a furious meeting about the money spent on the New College and the threat of doubled fees. Two adjectives worked hard for the Camberwell representatives in their many attacks on Carver and the College over these years: 'monstrous' and 'rapacious'. [209] One Mr Middlemass declared that to stop the school, now being made a second Harrow, from becoming a second Eton, he 'would go to the House of Commons, to the House of Lords and to the foot of the Throne itself'. [210] By 1873 the College counted 231 day boys from Camberwell on its roll.

Much was made by Carver and the College during the latter half of the century (and indeed by Gilkes after that) of the argument that when Alleyn decreed his final written Statutes in his last years with the provision for 'foreign scholars' or boarders (in the proposed ratio of twelve Poor Scholars to eighty boarders, whose fees were to be fixed by the Master and Warden), he had in mind just such a public school as Eton or Winchester. It was said over and again (marginalising the Poor Scholars) that if Alleyn's wishes had been properly carried out, the College long ago 'would have become one of our most important public schools'. Carver wrote a telling paragraph, somewhat rationalising the issue by shifting the social locus, in a private memorandum:

> The class for whom this Foundation was really 'intended', and by whom it and similar foundations are really needed, is the great 'middle class' of professional men and men of fixed limited incomes who are obliged to maintain the position and appearance of gentlemen, but who without such aid could not fit their children educationally to occupy the same position in life.... The School as organised at present may perhaps be said to be not only the vindication, but the triumph of [Alleyn's] ideas. [211]

Suspicious of an endemic South London philistinism and materialism, it was Carver's understanding that a considerable boarding contingent 'for variety' from a wide area would influence and leaven the day boys. [212] Carver claimed years later that the Governors said to him that if he wanted a first-grade school it must be self-supporting, and that the great buildings comprised a sufficient endowment. [213] It is no surprise to learn that Carver's friend, the Archbishop of Canterbury Archibald Campbell Tait (1811–82; successor of Thomas Arnold as Headmaster of Rugby) offered him a bishopric to escape his troubles; nor any great surprise to know that he turned the offer down. [214] Carver was known as Doctor Carver while he was at the College: he had been appointed Doctor of Divinity 'of Lambeth' in 1861; [215] the sponsor for his doctorate was the same Archbishop John Bird Sumner, the last Visitor of the College, who had made his Injunctions in 1851 (see Chapter Five). The splendid certificate signed by Queen Victoria now belongs to the College. [216] In 1882 he was made an Honorary Canon of Rochester, and was thenceforth referred to as Canon Carver.

The Commissioners had the power to present Acts to Parliament to effect changes at the College, but negotiated with the Governors (and in some notable points deferred to them), putting forward in succession seven separate proposals, or 'Schemes', over ten years. The main elements of the complex Seven Schemes for a new Dulwich College Act are as follows.

SCHEME ONE (1872) proposed that the College should be maintained as a first grade school, with a maximum of 150 boarders. The Headmaster's salary should be £300 with an allowance of £2.10s. for each boy on the roll between the numbers of 200 to 800. The Lower School (formed mostly of Camberwell boys) should be closed. Part of the Trust Estate was to be considered for sale, to raise capital of £100,000 for four parish schools. £30,000 would be assigned for 'second grade' Camberwell schools for boys and girls of 300 pupils, to be called 'Alleyn's Middle Schools', with an income of £2,200 per annum. New schools for girls in St Botolph's were to be endowed; in effect a total of £50,000 would go to Rogers's parish at Bishopsgate and to St Luke's. The College Chapel, containing the Founder's tomb, was to be demolished, and replaced by a new church. The worst insult and threat to Carver was the clause that there was no longer to be a 'Master of Dulwich College', but he and Marshall were to become co-equal Headmasters of the Classical and Modern Departments.

According to SCHEME TWO (1874), capital of £70,000 was to be raised and dispersed roughly as in SCHEME ONE. The College would have its annual income from the Estate halved from £2,588 in 1873 to £1,300. To this proposal – which would mean that the College would either have to reduce radically the scope of its education or else drastically increase its fees – the press responded with such headlines as 'Blunder and Plunder',[217] the *Art Journal* writing of the blow it would represent to the 'numerous and respectable householders' who had settled in the neighbourhood of Dulwich for schooling.[218]

SCHEMES THREE (1874) and FOUR (1875) essentially comprised successive variants of SCHEME TWO, but with a figure of £95,000 in capital to be raised over two years (SCHEME THREE) and a slightly more modest sum in SCHEME FOUR's version, which the majority of Governors found acceptable, subject to minor modifications. In March 1875 William Young explained to the Governors the opposition of Dulwich residents to this scheme,[219] but there is no doubt that had Carver not succeeded in his Privy Council suit in 1876, it is this proposal that the Governors would have sent for Parliamentary approval, and the modern College he had pioneered would have been ruined.

SCHEME FIVE (1878) sought to accommodate Carver's claims for the College by proposing a further endowment of £2,500 and an income of £4,400 per annum. A new Chapel would be built, and Scholarships and Exhibitions were each to be increased. The Lower School would be closed. A figure of £90,000 from Estate funds and resources was earmarked for the building of new schools in Camberwell and for income for schools in the other parishes. A separate board of Estates Governors was to be elected. Carver had nearly won the day. Not to be outdone, however, the Governors convened a special committee meeting in January 1879 to protest at the new Scheme; among their many objections were the change to the constitution of their governing body, the proposed increase of fees at the College, and the closure of the Lower School. They thought that too much money was to be allocated to Scholarships and Exhibitions at Dulwich; they resented the proposal to limit their control of the educational arrangements and discipline at the College; and most of them were opposed to funds going to Wilson's School in Camberwell.[220] Press opinion, however, largely favoured this latest Scheme. The *Standard* remarked on 2 January 1879 that 'within a very few years Dulwich will be one of the richest schools in England, if not the richest, and certainly one of the best administered'; and the *Echo* of 29 January called for a still cleaner sweep of the old Board of Governors, and their tainted legacy of ill feeling.[221]

The next proposal, SCHEME SIX (1881), tabled a reduction in the income to the College from the Estate to £3,900 per annum. The Lower School would be sited elsewhere, with an endowment of £12,000 and an income of £500 per annum. A new James Allen's Girls' School was to be built with a capital endowment of £6,000 and an income of £500 per year; a further grant of £2,000 would follow after ten years. The College was not to expect any increase of endowment when the Estate increased in value. The Master of Dulwich College was to have full authority and powers over the College. A maximum of 100 boarders should pay £50 per annum in a boarding house and £70 in an Assistant Master's house. A School of Art was to be attached to the Picture Gallery.

SCHEME SEVEN (1881) is the basis of the present Dulwich College. It set the sums to be granted at £4,000 for the College, £12,000 for James Allen's Girls' School, and £15,000 for St Saviour's Grammar School. The Lower School was to be reopened as 'Alleyn's School', given a site, £12,000 for its new building and an annual grant of £1,000, to increase to £1,500 after ten years. Eight of nineteen College Governors instead of being chosen by the Court of Chancery were to be the nominees of the Archbishop of Canterbury, the Lord

Chancellor, the Universities of Oxford, Cambridge and London, the Royal Society, the Royal Academy, and the Master and Assistant Masters of Dulwich College. The other eleven were to be co-opted from the present Governors, for life. A parallel body of nineteen Estates Governors was to be formed at the same time. The claims of the College were to take precedence over the parishes. The College was to receive (in addition to the £4,000 in capital) a significantly increased annual income of £4,700. Carver's broad syllabus for the College was endorsed, but Civil Engineering and the application of Drawing to the Industrial and Practical Arts were to be introduced. Thirteen and a half acres were to be added to the grounds, making a total of 42 acres. A Gymnasium and Fives Court were promised.

The Headmaster's salary was fixed at £200 with a capitation allowance of £4 for each boy for the first 200 on the roll, £3 for each boy from 200 to 400, and £2 for each boy above 400, which was estimated to add up to about £2,200 per annum.[222] The College was to lose its orotund and allusive formal title 'Alleyn's College of God's Gift, at Dulwich' and henceforth be known as plain 'Dulwich College' – which had of course been its short name for centuries. James Allen's Girl's School was promised its new building for 1886. After ten years, capital sums were to be paid: £15,000 to St Saviour's, and £50,000 to St Botolph's and St Luke's jointly. Mary Datchelor's School for girls in Camberwell was supposed to receive £10,000. These large grants were not in fact made, since the Estate income did not go up as dramatically as forecast; however, annual payments of £1,500 were made from 1888. It was now agreed that the College and the other two schools at Dulwich were to benefit from the future increase in value of the Estate. The College was to receive an annual sum of £1,000 for Exhibitions at universities, and £1,000 for Open Scholarships at the school. The Picture Gallery was protected; Carver had feared that the parishes would claim a share of the monetary value of the paintings.[223]

In effect, later payments in 'settlement' of the claims of the parishes meant that in 1926, the Tercentenary of Alleyn's death, not just the 900 boys at the College but a total of 4,000 young people could be said to be receiving their education 'under Alleyn's bequest': Dulwich College, James Allen's Girls School, and Alleyn's School; St Olave's and St Saviour's Grammar School in Southwark; and the Central Foundation Schools for Boys and for Girls in the parishes of St Botolph's and St Luke's.[224]

The Act confirming the terms of SCHEME SEVEN received Royal Assent on 18 August 1882. It could be argued that the greatness of the modern College owed more in the end to the Charity and the Endowed Schools Commissioners than to Rogers and the Governors of his day. Rogers might have complained about their bureaucratic delays, but from 1857 they exercised controls and gradually formulated this final and ultimately successful Scheme. Carver and his allies believed that the old set of Governors, while very grudging to the College, mismanaged the Estate by wasting money on it.[225] Carver described the opposition's final capitulation in two speeches he gave at Alleyn Club dinners, in 1891 and 1897. According to this story, he was approached by the Chairman of the Charity Commission at the end of these negotiations, who said to him, "Well, Dr. Carver, you have been very anxious about Dulwich College being a first grade school; and I confess to you it was our intention that there should be no first grade school at Dulwich, but you have been too quick for us; you have forestalled us; Dulwich has already established its reputation in public examinations and at the universities, and we can no longer hold out.... Now that it is a first grade school we do not mean to interfere".[226] 'Too quick for us' scarcely describes the superhuman cunning and patient resolve that Carver had deployed over 16 long years. But his victory indeed established the modern Dulwich College, and paved the way for its 'Golden Age' under Gilkes.

Canon Carver was only 57 when he retired in 1883. The Governors in January of that year recorded, without noticeable warmth, their thanks to him for his 'attention and ability', to which they grudgingly attributed 'the present position which Dulwich College holds amongst the Public Schools of the country'.[227] His pupils and many others were at a loss to understand why he was retiring; there was much comment at the time in the press and much praise for him. Dulwich residents petitioned him to stay, speaking of the College's 'present proud position' with its 'literary, scientific and artistic honours' and mentioning his 'strong moral and religious influence'.[228]

Dr and Mrs Carver settled in a very large detached house with twelve bedrooms on Streatham Common, Lynnhurst, which sold after his death for £5,500 in 1910.[229] It is possible that this was built from the Peek coffers, the 'private fortune' of which Mackenzie speaks.[230] The wealth of the Peek family had grown over these years. Eliza's cousin Francis Peek (1834–82), the multi-millionaire tea merchant and the benefactor of Dulwich Park (opened 1890), lived on Sydenham Hill, and was from 1882 one of the first Estates Governors, and Deputy Chairman of the Estates Governors in 1893.

Carver continued to take a close interest in the College and his former pupils; there was hardly a single Alleyn Club dinner he missed,[231] and, three weeks before his death on 25 July 1909, he returned thanks for a toast. As Chairman of the Governors of James Allen's

Opposite: S. Melton Fisher, *The Revd A. J. Carver* (Royal Academy 1882). (Dulwich College)

Girls' School and Vice-President of the Council of the Royal Naval College at Eltham (now Eltham College), he continued to work for education in South London, although his responsibilities now included writing letters admonishing mothers at James Allen's Girls' School whose daughters persisted in wearing pearls to school. He was very generous with charitable works, and paid half-fees for an orphaned girl. [232] On his retirement, the boys of the College presented him with portraits of himself and his wife, [233] following Francis Peek's presentation to the College of the portrait of Carver by Samuel Melton Fisher (OA), previously exhibited at the Royal Academy, which shows him in his habitual pose with his thumbs in the arm-holes of his waistcoat. [233] Few headmasters have been given the grateful accolade of costly memorials by subscription on the scale of Carver's. There are three: in the Chapel the elaborate mosaic reredos (1911, by W. D. Caröe) and the panelling in the Sanctuary; the elegant Carver Room with its Roman Doric columns (1910, by E. T. Hall and E. S. Hall) attached to the South African Memorial Library (now the Old Library); and the organ in the Great Hall, a project which Welldon was to announce at his first prize-giving. In the event, the funds for this organ were supplemented by Carver himself, which feels somehow appropriate to the various facets of his enigmatic character: the altruistic charm of his demeanour; the 'moral and mental energy' of his culture; and the steely determination of his will. A magnificent oak case for the organ, added in 1907, was also largely paid for by Carver. At its inauguration on Founder's Day in 1908, the Fiftieth Jubilee of the New College and the year before he died, Carver was 'visibly moved'. [234] The great organ, made by Charles Martin of Oxford, survived until Christopher Gilkes took the decision to demolish it after the War in 1945, when it was worn out and hideously dusty and was said to take up too much room on the stage; to restore it would have cost a very difficult £3,000.

The transformation of the Estate

In 1859 the Estate still included thirteen miles of hedges; bridges crossed streams, and stiles let into the fields. [235] The Governors created a pound for those cows that fouled the pathways or were deliberately let loose by their keepers to eat the grass on the boys' playground. Over the next forty years, much of the Estate was eviscerated and built over to increase the density of a dormitory for Londoners. The lucrative railway lines were cut and tunnels were built, with bricks made in temporary kilns from the clay on the site. Stations, embankments, high-level viaducts and cast-iron bridges sprang up; these were overseen by Charles Barry, and many were embellished in

his own 'ornamental' manner and carried the proprietorial initials 'AC' (for 'Alleyn's College'). [236] 28,350 feet of building frontage were added in 1867 alone, and all this involved major works for new roads, drains and sewers. The Knight's Hill section, as recommended by Nesfield (see above), had particularly dense construction from 1860, although in 1869 the Governors, protesting that they were not making 'a glut' of building, said that sixty acres in that area were still to be developed. [237]

Two large churches were put up to house the great increase in congregations, and both were designed by Barry. St Stephen's was consecrated in 1868, [238] and for it in 1872 Sir Edward Poynter (1836–1919; College Governor, 1882–90, and President of the Royal Academy, 1896) painted a masterly fresco of the trial and stoning of St Stephen. The first incumbent, the Revd J. Meek Clark, paid a portion of the cost of the splendid parsonage himself; he called a meeting with Barry on the site to discuss the vibration he suffered from the train tunnel running below the house. St Peter's on Lordship Lane, whose controversial origins are discussed above, followed in 1873–4, with a splendid interior by Barry in the mode of the New College, with polychromatic brick (predominantly red) decorated with angel heads in roundels of buff terracotta. The Infant School was built in 1863, [239] and a temporary 'iron church' was built as a 'chapel of ease' in Croxted Road in 1879 (demolished 1885). [240] Gas lighting was brought to the streets and the telegraph wires were to be set below the ground, so as not to disfigure the meadows. [241]

The Governors thought of the New College as a boon to induce families to settle on the Estate, the new churches performing the same function. [242] The ground rents paid by the brand new small houses were much more lucrative than those paid by the older houses; leases were made at £80 per annum for the new houses, while the older grand houses on Sydenham Hill were still paying £24 per annum on old long leases. In 1868 it was calculated that that if the estate of 1,200 acres was sold in sections year by year over eight years it could realise a million pounds (£64m in today's currency). In theory, the College might retain the Foundation premises and invest the capital to yield £35,000–40,000 per annum. [243] The formula of 'the creation of ground rents in the interest of the charity' was a recurrent phrase used at meetings for proposed developments. [244] As well as the new houses on roads with dense building frontage, Barry designed large villas, such as Brightlands (1863–4) on Dulwich Common for the College Solicitor Charles Druce, a building that derives from the Travellers' Club. Barry had an eye to keeping one particular area of the Estate, on the slopes of Denmark Hill and Herne Hill, with good grounds and timber unspoiled, for the future villas of 'prosperous busy men in the city'. It was here that Sir Henry Bessemer later lived, in a mansion with Pavilion and Observatory all designed by Barry (as described below).[245] Barry also held a number of important leases on the Estate for schemes of his own.[246] In the 1850s Alleyn's Jacobean Manor House belonged to Frederick Doulton, of the Lambeth pottery family and a Member of Parliament for Lambeth. He was also the father of Hubert Victor Doulton, a much respected and long-serving Assistant Master at the College (see below and Chapter Eight). In 1860 he was given permission to develop Alleyn Park (at first called Palace Road) on the east edge of the Manor demesne. In 1880 the Manor House itself was doomed for demolition, and the remainder of its park (including the site of the present Alleyn's Head) for development.[247]

The Governors emulated the Founder by demonstrating great concern for the trees on the Estate, removing many old and unsafe cedars, planting and thinning, introducing avenues of white and scarlet chestnuts, lining roads with limes, elms, willows, scarlet oaks and spring-flowering trees. Nesfield advised them on the trees, as did two of Sir Joseph Paxton's men who were local residents: George Eyles (1815–87), Superintendent of the Crystal Palace Park, and Edward Milner (mentioned above), who planted 5,000 trees at Knight's Hill in 1879. The chestnut avenue at the New College, leading from Dulwich Common, was planted that same year, and the double row of plane trees that mark the boundary of the College (except to Alleyn Park) in 1880, at the same time as the football field was levelled.[248]

The Governors were still preoccupied with the petty details of innumerable leases, squabbles between neighbours about overhanging branches, and with difficult tenants, among which Howard Staunton (1810–74), the chess authority and Shakespearean scholar, seems to have been particularly provoking.[249] Another local celebrity on the Estate was Sir Henry Bessemer (1813–98), the world-famous steel pioneer and engineer, who declined the invitation to be an Estates Governor. Bessemer made the demesne surrounding his mansion below Red Post Hill interesting with deer, prize Alderney cattle, a magnificent pavilion, a stove-house, vineries, and hot houses with orchids and oranges, all minutely described in William Harnett Blanch's *Camberwell* (1875). In 1876 Bessemer proposed giving the College the 'retracting telescope' erected in his grounds, reputedly 'larger than any yet constructed', but the Governors rejected the offer.[250]

One leaseholder of the College, who had lived in two houses on Herne Hill and one on Denmark Hill since his childhood, was the art critic John Ruskin (1819–1900). He recalled the peaceful rural days of the old Estate with its wild roses, buttercups and blackberries, and the early days of the Picture Gallery. Croxted Lane, with its 'slender rivulet', was a favourite haunt: 'there my mother and I used to gather the first buds of the hawthorn; and there, in after years, I used to walk in the summer shadows, as in a place wilder and sweeter than our garden, to think over any passage I wanted to make better than usual in *Modern Painters* [the defence of Turner and the meditation on art and nature he published in 1843–60]'.[251] Ruskin reacted with eloquent outrage to the developments on the Estate, calling the larger villas 'Frankenstein monsters' (from the piecemeal architectural styles they stitched together) and sneering at the 'meagre Gothic' of St Stephen's with Barry's 'useless spire'. He paid the architecture of the New College the insult of not mentioning it at all, but inveighed against the new public houses in the neighbourhood with their gross attempts to imitate the styles and decorative effects of the Stones of Venice. Ruskin devised a plan for a Black Museum in which to display his particular *bêtes noires* in art and architecture, such as the paintings of Claude Lorraine; the works of Charles Barry and his sons were specified for inclusion among the horrors of bad taste.[252]

A notice in *The Times* of the College production of *Much Ado about Nothing* in the School Room at the Old College in 1866 recorded that 'Mr Ruskin' (and also Henry Cole, the famous Director of the South Kensington Museum) attended the 'spirited and successful' occasion, and were also present at the 'splendid supper' at Carver's lodge afterwards. Ruskin wrote to Carver in thanks, praising the performer of Beatrice, in spite of the deep voice.[253] Carver, fearful of Rogers's succession as Chairman to the Board of Governors, had hoped to enlist Ruskin as an ally, persuading him to write to *The Times* in 1865 after Wellington's resignation and the unsettling Report of the Endowed Schools Commissioners. Ruskin replied to Carver that he was 'deeply concerned'. The letter which he sent to *The Times* is lost; according to Ruskin, it was not published as the newspaper was 'in Rogers's pocket'.[254]

Ruskin's paragraphs attacking the ruin of the Estate are trenchant, if occasionally manic. In 1865, in a letter to the editor of the *Daily Telegraph*, he said: 'I would have walked down to hear what Sam Weller had to say; but the high-level railway went through Mr. Pickwick's parlour two months ago'. Railway stations were spoiling the 'once quiet fields'; elsewhere on the Estate he remarked 'a blotch of brick-fields, and then of ghastly houses, washed over with slime into miserable fineries of cornice and portico'.[255] When the Governors ravaged Croxted

The College Pavilion below the Crystal Palace, *c*. 1910. (Dulwich College)

Lane in 1880 to make a building-site for Croxted Road, the loss of his childhood paradise with its stream provoked Ruskin to a nightmare vision:

> The peculiar forces of devastation induced by modern city life have only entered the world lately; and no existing terms of language known to me are enough to describe the forms of filth, and modes of ruin, that varied themselves along the course of Croxted Lane. The fields on each side of it are now mostly dug up for building, or cut through into gaunt corners and nooks of blind ground by the wild crossings and concurrencies of three railroads. Half a dozen handfuls of new cottages, with Doric doors, are dropped about here and there among the gashed ground: the lane itself, now entirely grassless, is a deep-rutted, heavy-hillocked cart-road, diverging gatelessly into various brickfields or pieces of waste; and bordered on each side by heaps of – Hades only knows what! – mixed dust of every unclean thing that can crumble in drought, and mildew of every unclean thing that can rot or rust in damp: ashes and rags, beer-bottles and old shoes, battered pans, smashed crockery, shreds of nameless clothes, doorsweepings, floor-sweepings, kitchen garbage, back-garden sewage, old iron, rotten timber jagged with out-torn nails, cigar-ends, pipe-bowls, cinders, bones and ordure, indescribable; and, variously kneaded into, sticking to, or fluttering foully here and there over all these, remnants, broadcast, of every manner of newspaper, advertisement or big-lettered bill, festering and flaunting out their last publicity in the pits of stinking dust and mortal slime.[256]

The Crystal Palace on Sydenham Hill, seen in a postcard photograph looming vast above the old College cricket pavilion, was regarded by most residents as an amenity to the Estate. When Rogers spoke at the laying of the foundation stone of the New College, he said that, just as Eton College was surveyed by Windsor Castle, so here at Dulwich (perhaps implying a new age) they 'would be cheered by the great Palace of the People, the temple of art and science and cheerful enjoyment, which surveyed them from the heights of Sydenham'.[257] For Ruskin, on the contrary, the Palace, of no more sublimity than a 'cucumber frame between two chimneys', was a blight on the area; plainly enjoying the opportunity of laying a kind of curse of his own on the College, Ruskin asserted that its presence 'would alone neutralize all possible gentlemanly education in the district'. Writing from Denmark Hill in 1875, he blamed the Palace for attracting filthy visitors who trampled the once lovely fields of Dulwich into mud and squalor;[258] and in his *Praeterita* of 1886 he wrote an elegy for the Estate's loss of innocence; for this he directly blamed the Palace, describing the grim evolution of the once-sylvan path to the Palace from Sydenham Hill station:

> Then the Crystal Palace came, for ever spoiling the view through all its compass, and bringing every show-day, from London, a flood of pedestrians down the footpath, who left it filthy with cigar ashes for the rest of the week: then the railroads came, and expatiating roughs by every excursion train,

who knocked the palings about, roared at the cows, and tore down what branches of blossom they could reach over the palings on the enclosed side. Then the residents on the enclosed side built a brick wall to defend themselves. Then the path got to be insufferably hot as well as dirty, and was gradually abandoned to the roughs, with a policeman on watch at the bottom. Finally this year a six foot high close paling has been put down the other side of it, and the processional excursionist has the liberty of obtaining what notion of the country air and prospect he may, between the wall and that, with one bad cigar before him, another behind him, and another in his mouth. [259]

The Picture Gallery and the Almsfolk

The Governors appear to have looked after the Picture Gallery well during this period, and Carver certainly took a great interest. An excellent report on the paintings and their conservation was commissioned from Richard Redgrave RA (1804–88) in 1858, and three further reports followed from 1865 to 1867 by (Sir) John Charles Robinson (1824–1913) of the South Kensington Museum. Robinson saw a danger of the Gallery becoming a 'lounge' for local people. There were, however, some minor developments, and some worries. Charles Barry added a dull and obtrusive entrance porch (later demolished), and the Governors rejected the idea of adding an iron and glass arcade in the manner of the Crystal Palace from it to the road. [260]

The six Almswomen, still housed in the western suite of rooms, caused anxieties about fire. [261] Of the other Almsfolk in this troubled period we learn little. The Chaplain's annual reports to the Governors mention their general good health and spirits, and their 'calm, happy unanxious look'; [262] a minor feud between two Poor Brethren resulted in their summons to the Board and a reprimand. [263]

In the Gallery itself, the pictures were hung very close, and many pictures reached within inches of the floor; a dado was recommended. [264] The Gallery had an income from the Estate of £250 per annum in the 1870s, and was expected to provide lessons in drawing and design in the Upper and Lower Schools. [265] Select pictures were still lent to the Royal Academy for their students to copy. Carver took away and hung the Cartwright collection in his own quarters at the New College, and wrote historical and antiquarian notes on these pictures in the *Catalogue of the Cartwright Collection and other Pictures and Portraits at Dulwich College*, which he and John Sparkes published together in 1884. The pictures were lent to the Bethnal Green Museum in 1876 while the Gallery was refurbished. In 1880 the

Governors noted a newspaper report that the National Gallery might be moved to Dulwich. [266] The Gallery's importance in shaping artists from among the College boys was asserted in the 1890s, when it was claimed as a certainty that 'the study of art has been carried much farther and to higher perfection at Dulwich than at any other public school in the kingdom'. The Sixth Form certainly had the privilege of entry in the days of Michael Glazebrook (1867–72), and consequently were much there, while on the other hand few members of the public were said to visit. Glazebrook and some friends one day burst out laughing when they came upon the Keeper, Hodgkins, touching up Reynolds's 'angel picture' (DPG 102) in one of the public rooms, and the next time he tried to exclude them; he threatened them with a spade in his garden, but fled when the boys taunted him with the subject of Horatius Cocles defending the bridge, the subject of a famous painting in the Gallery by Charles Le Brun (DPG 244).

Little seems to be known about the School of Fine Art that was founded at the Gallery in 1892 following the Dulwich College Scheme of 1881, and did not prosper, despite the keen interest expressed in it by Sir Edward Poynter, the Governor appointed by the Royal Academy. The Governors seemed to have dragged their feet on the project, perhaps deliberately, and the Master of the day, A. H. Gilkes, is not likely to have supported the project and the expense: it was claimed that boys from the College, who were originally to have attended, could not fit the classes into their school timetables. Thirty women students worked in the rooms in the Gallery where the Almswomen formerly lived; then a move was made to rooms in the Old College formerly used by the Lower School boys who left to form Alleyn's School. Leonard Nightingale (1851–1941; see below), an Old Alleynian who returned to the College to join Sparkes as his assistant in 1876, and who was to teach at the College until 1926, acted as the Art School's principal from 1892, with one assistant. It was closed in 1895 for lack of sufficient pupils, after the Governors had voted to continue it for one more year. The competition in South London from the Crystal Palace Art School and the Lambeth School of Art was probably too strong, and the Governors decided that the capital sum of £4,000 in the Scheme should be awarded to the Gallery instead. [267]

According to Carver, when one of the Schemes had proposed transferring the College's collection to the National Gallery, proper objections were raised. Rogers later ruled, however, that Dulwich's College and Gallery were separate institutions, and cancelled the privileges previously enjoyed by the schools in connection with it. [268]

Carver and the curriculum

The Revd Alfred Carver fought for his pupils to be educated by higher ideals than any mere utilitarian preparation for turning the wheels of commerce in 'counting houses'. Naive he may have been, but in the battle to create an ideal modern academy on a Periclean or Renaissance model, Carver proved a noble champion, Milton's Samson or Spenser's Red Cross Knight rather than his own image of himself as Gulliver tied down by Lilliputian Governors and other petty enemies; like these heroes, at important crises he fought alone. In a way Carver resembled John Colet, the liberal, academic idealistic prelate who in 1509 founded (or strictly, revived, as its second Founder) St Paul's School, Carver's own Alma Mater. In 1898, Canon Carver was to present to St Paul's, then at its Hammersmith Road site, a stained-glass window for the Library (destroyed by enemy action, June 1944) which showed Colet presenting his book of Statutes to William Lily, the first High Master;[269] this perhaps gave him private satisfaction as the acknowledged 'Second Founder' of Dulwich College. At the College prize-giving in 1874 he referred to himself and his 'colleagues' as Old Testament heroes, forced to work 'with the trowel in one hand and the sword in the other'.[270] The physical structure and intellectual principles he forged for Dulwich College with these tools remain his greatest testament.

Carver in 1900 referred to his era as 'volcanic'; it is a relief to turn from the forgotten conflicts he withstood to the solid educational achievements he sponsored at Dulwich. The success of his Old Boys in public life, in academic life, in the cause of science, literature, and art, undoubtedly testifies to the quality of enquiry and culture and the ideals of service generated at Dulwich College. Carver's aim was for the boys in the Upper School to maintain 'amongst themselves a high tone of morality, manliness, truth and honour'.[271] Its period evangelical tone aside, the First Founder would surely have approved of what the Second made in real terms, and on such a grand scale, of the Victorian College of God's Gift.

By the time of his retirement in 1883, Carver had energetically stamped the College he had essentially created with his high morality, his zeal and his enthusiasm for knowledge. As previously discussed, the curriculum he devised was broad and adventurous for the day, particularly in the fields of Modern Languages, Science, and Art, and this elastic teaching of subjects was on his considered principle of training boys for 'widely divergent pursuits in life'.[272] In spite of his difficulties with some of his staff, and the fact that so many clever young masters left early, such as Arthur Gray (1852–1940), a Classicist who taught from 1874 until 1877 and was later Master of

Jesus College, Cambridge, there was a core of extraordinarily well-qualified, gifted, and lively teachers who helped to bestow continuity and stability over his era at the College. A variety of sources help us to know something of the nature of what the boys studied. From 1862, for example, Carver published the College internal examination papers in pamphlets, including lists of the prize-winners and of the Upper School in order of merit. The exercises set by the College for examinations include extracts from Shakespeare for translation into Greek iambics and such essay topics as 'the chief points which constitute excellence in a dramatic poem' and 'the proposed memorial to the late Prince Consort'. The Fourth and Fifth Forms were set genuinely abstruse grammatical questions in English and diabolical questions about fractions.[273] The syllabus was printed in detail from 1873, and this remained the tradition until 1947. Examiners from Oxford or Cambridge, commissioned by the College itself, wrote detailed reports on the boys' work in the late 1860s and early 1870s, which were printed in the Governors' minutes; from 1874 these were added to and then replaced by detailed reports made by dons on the boys' performance in the written papers of the Oxford and Cambridge Schools Examination Board, founded in November of the previous year, which were likewise printed in the Minutes. In 1869 the Classical Examiner reported that the Upper School was 'becoming more homogeneous',[274] and the following year he spoke of the 'brilliant future of a great institution', but qualified his praise by warning that there were insufficient masters.[275] Reports in the 1870s did of course make criticisms, for example noting a falling off in Euclid, or 'too little Homer and probably too little Sophocles' in 1872,[276] but Carver must have found the general praise from these outside judges extremely encouraging; in 1873 the Examiner wrote, 'I have never been brought into contact with a school the boys of which showed more careful and excellent teaching', or where such 'a remarkable spirit of uniform industry prevails'; altogether, he summarised, the College was 'in a state of high efficiency'.[277] The examiners also perceived Carver's very own qualities among the boys, praising their spirit of 'alacrity and exertion', their 'tone and gentlemanly bearing', and their 'frank and ready courtesy'.[278]

As Carver's obituarist in *The Alleynian* put it, he detested any 'rigid formula' in education.[279] He took risks, such as would of course be impossible nowadays: boys doing Art, for example, 'may obtain exemption from all subjects except form work and obligatory Mathematics'. The boys worked 32 hours of lessons, and the Sixth Form was officially expected to do two and a half to three hours' preparation daily at home.[280]

Not all parents admired this rigour: an interesting Village resident, the Revd Charles Voysey (1828–1912), founder of the Theistic Church (once an Anglican vicar but defrocked for his heretical denial of the Devil and of everlasting Hell), wrote to Carver in 1877 to complain that his son Arthur was spending three or four hours on prep every night; he went on to attack 'the gigantic evils of a competitive system which leaves the foundations of all good scholarship so terribly incomplete', further asserting that this showed 'the radical fault of our Public School system, substituting quantity for quality'.[281] Not one of his four sons stayed on at the College for the Sixth Form; Charles Voysey, the architect (1857–1941), incidentally, was not one of Carver's successes, or simply did not want the College to take credit for his success. He joined the College in 1872, but left after two years to be articled to John Pollard Seddon; his academic work was undistinguished, and he regarded himself as the dunce of the family. He wrote in later life to McCulloch Christison, the great Secretary of the Alleyn Club (see Chapter Eight), that 'I never felt I had anything to thank Dulwich College for as a school in my day'.[282]

Carver's system perhaps looks better on paper than it actually was. A letter in *The Times* of 13 June 1867 said that the 'greatly extended range of subjects' at Dulwich had 'very important omissions in actual practice up to this date', and in the writer's opinion the College did not work hard enough: 'work is certainly not in the ascendant'. The boys were allegedly granted far too many holidays in term time on various pretexts: 'The Master's cat has got kittens' was a standard joke. Wednesdays and Saturdays were half-days. In 1868 the proper school holidays ran for four and a half weeks at Christmas, six and a half weeks in the summer, and ten days at Easter.[283]

In 1874 Carver reported to the Governors on the Science teaching: the Lecture Theatre was in daily use for the teaching of Chemistry, Physics, and Engineering, and the two large and small laboratories were open to all the boys. He proposed the teaching of Mechanics and Hydrostatics, and asked for a Galvanic Battery, a frictional Electricity Machine, an Air Pump, and both a new Museum and a Botanical Garden.[284] In 1875 an Anatomy classroom and a stink cupboard were added. The Government's *Sixth Report of the Royal Commission on Scientific Instruction and the Advancement of Science (The Devonshire Commission)* in 1875 was full of praise for Dulwich's facilities, and included engravings of the Lecture Theatre and laboratories. A basement laboratory by now held a furnace for metallurgy and there was a separate classroom for Geology. Such innovations yielded swift results: in 1879 the Oxford and Cambridge Schools Joint Board called the examinations in Science 'excellent'.[285] The College was particularly successful in Geography, the boys winning eight gold medals and three silver medals from the Royal Geographical Society between 1876 and 1884, after which the medals were discontinued. The Society praised the academic initiative of the Dulwich boys: one prize essay went 'way beyond knowledge merely from textbooks', and the candidate had read more or less every book recommended by the Society.[286]

By the late 1870s there could be no doubt that Dulwich had become a major academic school; in an equivalent of the modern 'league tables', Dulwich was placed fourth in the Oxford and Cambridge Schools Joint Board in 1877, after Eton, Rugby and Marlborough, and overall second in the whole examination in English. In 1878 the College came third among the schools with 25 'distinctions'.[287] Meanwhile, between 1876 and 1881, former Dulwich pupils gained nine first class degrees at Oxford and Cambridge. The two years 1873 and 1874 were particularly remarkable for the number of boys winning Open Awards: three Scholarships in Classics, one in Mathematics, two in Science, and two Classical Exhibitions. In 1878 there were eleven Old Alleynians at Cambridge and thirteen at Oxford; *The Alleynian* published what was to become a traditional feature, written by one of the undergraduates, describing their own achievements and teasing their contemporaries about their activities.

Each morning in the Great Hall at the College the boys lined up by forms for prayers, facing west to the platform where Carver stood at a lectern, the great panels of the Honours Boards with successful scholars' names in gold to their sides – those on the north dedicated to Oxford and those on the south to Cambridge – and the academic boys among them ready to be pointed towards one of the two poles on which the system turned.

The Common Room

It is to Carver's credit that, despite his continual complaints to the Governors about their poor salaries, he continued to attract a very gifted staff. Eighty masters were employed during his years, the figure in part also a reflection of their frequent desertion for better-paid positions. Their recorded achievements and interests nevertheless demonstrate how stimulating their classes must have been, particularly with the licence given them to teach their forms subjects of their own choice.

Four of these masters were Old Alleynians. Edward Everett (mentioned above), among the first intake of boys in 1858, had been one of the first of the College's Cambridge Scholars; he took part in the first Athletics, Rugby and Cricket matches at the College, and played Dogberry in the production of *Much Ado* attended by Ruskin in 1866 (see above); he served 49 years until retirement at the age of 73, and then continued as Honorary Librarian for another two years. Everett was the producer of the Dulwich Plays, an athlete, a man of culture and wide sympathies, and was promoted Senior Master in 1912. In manner 'somewhat severe' but warm-hearted, it was said that the College would not be there but for his 'fixity of purpose and unrelenting devotion'.[288] The very gifted Charles Lane (1846–84) returned directly from Cambridge to teach at the College in 1870, but (as we have seen) left in 1875 after his mysterious quarrel with Carver. Leonard Nightingale, the artist, was a pupil from 1860 to 1869, when as a sporting Captain of School (Captain of Cricket in 1868 and 1869, and of Football in 1869) he was said by Stanhope Forbes (see below) to be 'adored by all of us youngsters'. Nightingale held a leavers' Scholarship from the College of £50 for four years to study Fine Art, studied under John Sparkes at Lambeth and exhibited at the Royal Academy. He joined the staff at the age of 25, becoming Principal Master in Drawing in 1897; one of his pupils wrote that his magnificent 'preliminary training' was 'the finest any student could have'.[289] Nightingale was to lose one of his four sons, Frank, who taught at the College for eight years, and was killed in action in 1915 near Ypres. Charles Gull (1851–*c*. 1916) was the son of a Governor appointed by St Giles, Camberwell; he set up the Rifle Corps in 1876, becoming its first Captain in 1880.

Modern Languages were taught by native speakers; among them, James Boielle, the principal French master (at Dulwich 1880–1902; d. 1903), was a distinguished translator and lexicographer, who published translations in *The Alleynian*. The memorial book *Gilkes and Dulwich* noted him as a fine reciter, and an excellent and zealous teacher.[290] The Modern Languages were not popular, however; Carver wrote that most Form Masters 'threw cold water' on them and suffered from a typical xenophobia, which probably influenced the boys.[291] A distinguished chemist and physicist, Alfred Tribe (1839–85), who had studied at Heidelberg under R. W. Bunsen and was to become famous in England and in Germany for his experiments 'on the border line between Physics and Chemistry', and also for his inventions, learned articles and lectures, joined the staff in 1874, and in the same year Harry Seeley joined as a Geology master. Tribe taught 'with zeal and energy' at the College until his death in 1885,[292] and Seeley left in 1885 to become Professor of Geography and Geology at King's College, London. Sixteen of the masters published books, some of them on really ambitious historical or theological topics; three were members of the Athenæum or the Reform Clubs. James Brabham, appointed Organist in 1870,[293] composed an 'Edward Alleyn Gavotte';[294] many others were amateur musicians. The Revd George Bell, the Under Master, who was married to a daughter of the landscape gardener Edward Milner, left in 1868 to be Headmaster of Christ's Hospital and later of Marlborough; he made a large contribution to the Marshall Defence Fund. Charles Everard, an Etonian fresh from Cambridge, considered 'brilliant and charming' by the boys, was at Dulwich for three years from 1869, and was said to have improved their manners by example. Not all Carver's appointees were a success, and several he sacked before they could resign, such as Edward Morgan in 1874, the son of a vicar from Bath and a former Scholar of Lincoln College, Oxford, who was over-zealous in caning a boy's hands, and whom Carver described as incompetent and rude; he took up 'viticulture near Florence'.[295]

College activities

The early issues of the College magazines afford some fascinating glimpses of the life of the College. There was first a sixpenny *Dulwich College Magazine for School News, and General Reading* in 1864, with thirteen issues in two years, but apart from showing the intellectual maturity of the schoolboy writers, it did not have much marked individuality, consisting almost entirely of academic articles, interspersed with a little fiction; the brief sections of News concern the Cricket XI and laconic notices of Speech Days, some evening events, and the Cambridge Local Examinations results. The schoolboy editor was the favourite early son of the College, Charles Lane, and the publication folded when he left for St Catharine's College, Cambridge, having won open awards both there and at Magdalen Hall, Oxford. Lane had written in the last issue a description of a fortnight he spent at a lunatic asylum. He shared Carver's ambitions for the College, writing on the last page that by the time

Lunch hour activities.
Esprit de corps.
(Dulwich College)

his magazine came to be resuscitated, the College would surely be counted 'as great as any of England's noblest public schools'. At that time the boys are clumsily referred to as 'Dulwichians' rather than 'Alleynians'.[296] By the time of the first issue of *The Alleynian*, published nine years later in February 1873, Lane's prophecy was coming to prove true. More overtly a chronicle than its predecessor, *The Alleynian*'s first editor was another Captain of the School, Herbert Thirkell White (1855–1931), who was later knighted for his exceptional service as Lieutenant-Governor of Burma (1905–10), and subsequently was President of the Alleyn Club (1912) and Estates Governor. *Esprit de corps* – an ideal of Carver and (after him) of Gilkes – is mentioned on the very first page of the magazine as its rationale; this phrase, and its English equivalent, 'the public school spirit', run through the magazine as frequent motifs. Its first editorial defines its own significance as the 'organ for a great public school as we are fast becoming'. Later editions record the public events at the College, and express contemporary ideals and codes. When the Earl of Carnarvon (1831–90) gave the prizes in the Great Hall in July 1873, he reminded his audience of the great 'principles of the English public schools', chief among them the premise that 'ability and

intellectual strength are great things, but truth, honour, constancy, and above all the conduct of English gentlemen are the greatest of all'.[297]

Carver seems to have acted on these principles, encouraging his boys to grow up fast by developing their initiative with responsibilities; the senior boys themselves ran activities such as the Field Sports, the Debating and Science Societies, as much as was wise to let them do so; this was certainly something they mentioned as valuable in later life. Letters to *The Alleynian* meanwhile clamoured for essential amenities, such as a proper pavilion, a swimming bath and gymnasium, a Fives Court, a workshop. In Carver's time the boys also suggested and founded a Chess Club (proposed 1873), the Debating Society (1874), and a 'Union' (1883) to look after the interests of all their societies.[298] The College's Rifle Corps (see below) was proposed in 1873.[299] The Science Society, Carver told the Governors in 1882, was one of the most valuable and successful of school institutions,[300] and their 'transactions' [lectures and discussions] were printed, carrying a Virgilian slogan: '*Felix qui potuit rerum cognoscere causas*'. Among their many topics of enquiry they analysed patent Hair Restorers and samples of air from tunnels on the Underground. The quality of the

The Masters' Library, *c.* 1870. The archway is a fanciful addition. (© RIBA Drawings Collection)

literary culture of the College is obvious from the translations in *The Alleynian* from Anacreon, Euripides and Horace, and from the Latin versions printed there of Tennyson, then Poet Laureate. Carver's cultivation of the boys' intellects and curiosity is shown there in a series of remarkable pieces of fiction, *belles lettres* and articles; topics include Aristophanes; plants and their food; the current controversy over the study of the Classics; Chemistry; the Armada; travel; and bull-fighting.

The lexical study of Greek and Latin, focusing for so many hours a week on translation, on accuracy and the

mot juste, naturally comprised a major factor in the breeding of the writers for which Dulwich was later to become famous. The same culture as later nurtured the unique style of P. G. Wodehouse or Raymond Chandler evidently sponsored a particular type of metaphysical wit. One example is a brilliant fantasy to be found in *The Alleynian* of 1886, in which the boy writer imagines an Ionian visiting the '*Alleynioi*' at the College, and reporting with stunned incomprehension to his classical Greek contemporaries back home and back in time the transport to the College by horse-drawn chariots and (as if struggling to describe them) the steam trains; arrived at the College, he tells his folk about a snowball fight between the Senior and the Lower School, a Chemistry laboratory, and an Assembly of the tribe with prefects holding open the doors of the Great Hall. [301]

The 'declamations' chosen for Speech Day are also mentioned in the pages of *The Alleynian*, with extracts from Aristophanes, Terence, Shakespeare's *King Lear*, Molière, Goethe and Schiller. The boys write letters protesting against the disgraceful behaviour of the choir, and over the years there were to be many pompous adolescent letters about schoolboy codes of dress and behaviour, such as the following:

> we remark, with disgust, that the habit amongst the Day Boys of swaggering in hats is on the increase. Surely it is the mark of a very small mind to be above wearing the school cap in the field on half holidays. [302]

We also learn from *The Alleynian* that Carver himself found time to take an active part in the boys' organisations outside the classroom, coaching the boys' diction in the Shakespeare plays, and attending debates. [303] The magazine observed the promptness with which he assisted at everything that might tend to promote *esprit de corps*. [304] An obituary mentioned Carver's 'genial courtesy', saying that he was 'exceedingly popular with his boys at school and in their after-life'. His fine scholarship was often recognised by his pupils only after they met lesser teachers at university. Michael Glazebrook wrote that 'his bright friendliness and entire trust did more for my education than much teaching'. Short-sighted as he was, however, he did not appear to notice boys at the back of the class who were reading novels or writing letters while, absorbed in his author, he declaimed passages he liked in his sonorous voice. [305] His admirers wondered how, with all his other cares and activities, he coped with running the school. Carver's many interests included the antiquarian; of all the Masters of the new Foundation that were to follow, he was the one who most recognised the value and interest of the College's great historical possessions. He restored Alleyn's oak Treasury Chest in 1879 and in the same year four 'much worm-eaten' arm-chairs, 'reported to be of the date of the Founder'. [306] He successfully persuaded the Governors not only to have the Henslowe and Alleyn papers catalogued and bound but to publish printed catalogues of both the Manuscripts and the Library. [307] The Museum he planned for the boys was originally housed in 1873 in twelve cases in the Lower Hall, and was for the Science Society; there were exhibits of geology, botany, and entomology. Later it was moved to a former sitting room for the Assistant Masters, high in the Centre

Block above the Board Room, the present Muniments Room, where boys' own collections of natural history specimens were placed alongside gifts to the College. In 1890 a boy presented 'a Thibetan bullet pouch, taken from the corpse of a Thibetan in the Bhulak Pass'; in 1935 there was a penny-farthing bicycle. [308] It was Carver, and not Alleyn, who adopted for the College the motto, *Detur Gloria Soli Deo*, which is first found printed on his writing paper with the College arms by 1867 and on his pamphlet 'Alleyn's College of God's Gift at Dulwich' of 1870. In the past the theory has been that it was vaguely inspired by wording in English in Alleyn's diary or in his will, but it is more likely that Carver neatly subsumed the concepts of God and giving found in Alleyn's phrase 'God's Gift' in the Vulgate version of a saying by St Paul, '*soli Deo honor et gloria*' (1 Timothy 1.17), thus returning bounty from man to God. The College's motto had already been in use by the City livery companies of the Leathersmiths, the Goldsmiths and the Skinners at various times. [309]

A sociable man, Carver gave a large weekly dinner party to introduce the boys to the 'best' people in Dulwich or to show them electrical exhibits for amusement and instruction. Mrs Carver gave 'Cinderella Dances' with hired bands in the large room in the South Block, decorated with greenery, for which the boys wore evening dress: 'swallow-tails', 'pumps' [patent leather shoes] and kid gloves. On his birthday in 1860 Carver was presented with a stereoscope from 'your affectionate boys', and the First Form sent their good wishes in copperplate writing. [310] Once when the boys joining the Sixth Form were waiting for Carver to give his customary address, a 'most impressive talk on duties and example', he was detained, and a young wag meanwhile gave a perfect imitation of the speech, thumbs in waistcoat and swaying backwards and forwards on his toe and heel; Carver burst out laughing when told about it. [311]

Carver was not a strong disciplinarian, and for many years would not allow the prefects to beat boys. However, when Michael Glazebrook, later Canon Glazebrook and a very effective headmaster (see below), was Captain of School in 1872, he 'seized for the prefects the *jus flagelli*' and flogged the leader of the Fifth. [312] Only eleven years later he was selected as one of the eight candidates to succeed Carver as Master. Previously the College Porter, Bidgood, seems to have been responsible for discipline, stopping fights during the breaks with his long stick; known from his uncomely frost-bitten nose and chin as 'Punch', he had accompanied Lieutenant Bedford Pim (the popular 'old tar' who was now a Rear Admiral, a Tory MP, a pioneer in the design of turret war ships, and a College Governor) during the Arctic expedition to

James Collis and the Buttery. (Private collection)

discover Sir John Franklin in 1852–4, when they had sledged for four weeks across the ice to regain touch with their sister vessel; he used to regale the boys with adventurous stories.[313] James Collis, often photographed, who had been in his youth from 1871 to 1880 the head-waiter at the Greyhound, kept the Buttery from 1880 to 1907; it was nicknamed 'the Coliseum' by precocious Dulwich Classicists. Boys would return after they had left the College to talk to him, and when he died in 1914 the Alleyn Club placed a brass tablet to his memory in the Chapel; when Shackleton presented the prizes to the boys after his success on the *Nimrod* expedition and his knighthood, he spoke noticeably more warmly of Collis than of his masters. Collis sold 'three-cornered jam tarts', and these, 'such a feature of life at our mutual school', were later to figure in the hunger fantasies of two famous Alleynians: Shackleton when sledging in an Antarctic blizzard on the *Nimrod* expedition, and P. G. Wodehouse when imprisoned in a Belgian castle during the Second World War.[314]

Carver's boys showed initiative again in 1882: at that time the field of thirteen and a half acres adjoining the College, between the old cricket pavilion and Hunts Slip

Road, land that had been saved from building development by Carver,[315] was still fenced off; here in the lunch hour the boys used to chase cows in rough pasture round the many oak trees, according to the novelist A. E. W. Mason (see below).[316] If we are to believe the story told to Mackenzie, the boys took down the fences one day and marked out pitches and goals;[317] the ground was consequently ceded to the College by the Governors. Sheep were kept on the College playing fields until well into the next century.

Games and the Rifle Corps were highly regarded; at the Speech Day in 1880, as reported in *The Times*, Carver said of the boys that 'the most successful intellectually were also in general the most manly in character and the most robust in health'.[318] Rugby Football was first played in 1865, and Athletics began in 1866. A speaker at the Alleyn Club dinner in 1901 recalled forgotten sporting idols of Carver's time: Arthur Meredith (1856–1915), skilled at Athletics and Field Sports, who later joined the Indian Legislative Council; Ernest Delcomyn (1860–1912), a gifted athlete and rugby footballer, who joined his father's firm; and William Wyld (1859–1900), a member of the First XI for four successive seasons, playing cricket for England from the school, who proceeded from Sandhurst to the Ashanti campaign and to the army in Burma.[319] Official group photographs of school teams were framed and hung up to promote *esprit de corps*, and can be seen in photographs of contemporary College interiors. A letter to *The Alleynian* in 1882 complained that sporting groups were photographed, but not the Sixth Form; it was not until Gilkes's time, in the 1890s, that academic groups were photographed.[320] The College grounds had at first only a rustic wooden fencing around them; an early feature of the College games was the uninvited crowd, some ten to fifteen thousand strong,[321] that used to gather to watch the Rugby football before the grounds were given railings in 1881. In 1872 four thousand spectators attended the athletic sports. In 1880 Sydney Ellis (1859–1937) won an England cap for Rugby, while three others gained 'Blues'. There is no doubt that the appointment of William Shepherd (1841–1919), a well-known bowler in the Surrey team, as Cricket Professional in 1872, and who is to be seen in group photographs wearing a bowler hat, played a key factor in Dulwich's sporting success.[322]

A Drill Master was appointed in 1866.[323] The Rifle Corps, proposed (as mentioned above) in *The Alleynian* in 1873, was founded in 1877. To join the Senior Company, you had to be either 5 foot 4 inches in height or 16 years old. The Dulwich cadets at first were attached to the First Surrey and 60th Rifles, whose uniform they wore; Charles Lane was the first Commanding Officer. Two companies were formed by 1880, under Charles Gull, with a Drum and Fife Band.[324] From this point and over the next decades the College developed a particular skill in Shooting; Alleynian marksmen became famous. On Field Day the Military Band used to accompany the march of the Corps to Tulse Hill station and back. The Gymnastic Class and the Rifle Corps combined to put on what became a great Dulwich tradition and entertainment, the 'Assault at Arms', something which Carver said promoted 'cohesion and public spirit'.[325] The reports in *The Alleynian* mention displays of Foot and Arms Drill, and by the Bayonet Squad; boxing and fencing (including bayonet fencing); and gymnastics with horizontal and parallel bars, the vaulting horse, dumb-bells, and Indian clubs; there was always music. Group photographs of the event show also boys in Cavalier and Roundhead costume.

The cultural life of the College has always benefited from being close to the capital, but at a symbolic remove on the other side of the river Thames; there was also the influence of cultivated parents settled in the locality, and of the artists and the teachers of musical instruments who lived in South London. Carver well understood the importance of the spoken word to give voice to his pupils,[326] and the Dulwich Play, the recitations at the Speech Days, and the Debating Society flourished. The earliest productions at the Old College have been mentioned; the first School Play in a biennial series at the New College was *The Rivals*, produced by Edward Everett in 1875, and its merits were discussed in all the leading papers. Costumes and scenery were hired, and performances were at first given in the large School Room in the South Block; indulgence was asked in the Prologue for the boys playing ladies' roles. In 1879 *Much Ado about Nothing* was the first performance in the Great Hall, followed by a farce; the orchestra played a Rossini overture.[327]

The Debating Society, founded in 1874, was run by the boys. As in its later days, it rose and fell according to the enthusiasm of the boys involved; in earlier years, as well as debates, the Society held many literary 'readings' by the boys from Byron, Tennyson and Dickens, for example, which were attended by Mrs Carver 'and a large number of ladies'.[328] Some of the controversies chosen for debate were Capital Punishment, Cromwell, Cremation, and whether Tennyson was superior to Byron.[329] When A. E. W. Mason was a prominent debater, a skill for which he later became famous at Oxford and in the House of Commons, he and his followers at Dulwich, a 'genial band of *sans culottes*', carried motions both against Monarchy and a Channel Tunnel.[330]

Carver was less interested in Music than he was in Art and Drama, but he believed in the *esprit de corps* of a chorus, and inaugurated special classes for vocal music. The boys met at his house for songs and glees. A report on the Music in the school in 1880 praised both the elementary and advanced classes, saying their work was better than professionals and that their words were properly enunciated, and praised the work of the Music Master, James Brabham.[331] The first Dulwich College concert was held in the newly completed Great Hall in 1871. Mr Brabham's 'male quartette' of boys from the Chapel choir sang, but the most acclaimed performer then was 'the world's finest tenor' and the father of a boy in the school, the tenor Sims Reeves (1818–1900), recalled as being 'but little past his prime', who sang Handel arias and his famous solo, 'The Bay of Biscay', which was received with 'rapture' by the audience in evening dress. The Choir in the Chapel was a disappointment, and Carver assured the Governors in 1866 that he was improving it with a paid choir-master and paid singers.[332] With the arrival of Brabham four years later these singing men were dismissed, and it became part of his job to train the boys.[333]

The boarding houses

Boarding houses for the College were established at the outset in 1858, but to begin with were almost exclusively for Foundation Scholars from the parishes: in 1866, out of a school roll of 120 boys in the Upper School, there were 22 boys from Camberwell, none from Bishopsgate, and only 3 non-parishioners. The leases for two houses in Dulwich Village were taken by Carver himself.[334] For a while the houses were run by 'dames': Mrs Dryland, who had earlier run a preparatory school at Camberwell, at Camden House, 63 Dulwich Village, from 1858 to 1861, and next door to her at number 61, Mrs and Miss Field at Plasgwyn. Mrs Dryland (d. 1889) moved on to Wood-lawn and then to Elm Lawn from 1869 to 1884, which was at the time the largest boarding house, at one point hold-ing 40 boys; she was a strong character, with 'immense energy and commanding spirit', and a great help with the boys' plays.[335] In 1865 the fees for boarding were £35 per annum with a Dame, or £59 with an Assistant Master.[336]

The Revd George Voigt from 1869 until 1885 was the master of Sydenham House at 1 Sydenham Villas, Dul-wich Village, where in 1881 he was looking after seven boys. In 1873 there were 74 boarders in all, and Carver asked the Governors for a licence for one more house.[337] An Assistant Master, John Parish, opened (old) Blew House in 1874; in 1881 there were 18 boys there.[338] (Old) Ivyholme on Dulwich Common (destroyed by enemy action in 1944) was to be run from 1885 to 1916 by the Revd Edward ('Billy') Sweet-Escott, 'cheery and genial', much loved by his pupils, with his 'delightful preju-dices', his dislike of the North Country, and intense affection for Oxford; he kept a cricket stump in his desk in his form-room to throw at inattentive boys, and liked to spend his half-term holidays riding to foxhounds and staghounds in 'glorious Devon'. A boarding ethos was soon established with house choirs and concerts, and the boys were said to be as keen to play for their houses as for the College.

Careers of early Alleynians

Many men succeed notwithstanding their education, but the record of the Alleynians from Carver's days is excep-tional and must reflect credit on the College. Thomas Lane Ormiston's *Dulwich College Register, 1619–1929*, explicitly modelled on *Who's Who*, lists all the boys who enrolled at the College, and records select school achievements and what was known of their later career. We learn from it that the boys who joined in early days came mostly from professional, initially local families. Some rich boys came from the large villas with pleasure grounds on the Estate, such as the Manor House (the Doulton family), Toksawa and Woodvale. In the next

generation after Carver from Kingswood House came George Johnston, the son of the inventor of 'Bovril', and from Belair came the sons of Sir Evan Spicer. Boys such as A. E. W. Mason, whose father was an accountant, came from the prosperous new housing developments, such as Dulwich Wood Park. Among the fathers we find just a very few clerks and warehousemen, and a fishmonger. Local celebrities enrolled their sons: the architectural decorator John Gregory Crace (1818–1900) of Spring-field, and (as already mentioned) Sims Reeves and the landscape gardener Edward Milner. In Carver's early years, in spite of the academic successes of the College, a surprising number of boys left before the Sixth Form to join Marlborough, Harrow, Haileybury, Lancing and other schools.

The careers followed by early Alleynians are, not surprisingly, an anthology of late Victorian middle-class occupations: many joined their father's firm, became stockbrokers or merchants, joined Lloyd's or the Bank of England; a really very large number went into the Church or joined the Army. (Sir) Andrew Stuart (1861–1936) left in 1877; as Major-General Stuart he was Director of Works in the British Expeditionary Force during the Great War. In the same year (Sir) David Mercer (1864–1920) was enrolled, who rose to be the Adjutant-General of the Marines. Two distinguished soldiers joined the College in 1881: Major-General Sir Webb Gillman (1870–1933; see Chapter Seven) and Alexander Lafone (1870–1917), the son of an Estates Governor, who was killed in action, the oldest of the five Dulwich men to be awarded the Victoria Cross in the First World War. Gillman was a College Scholar; although a fine athlete, he was never a member of the First teams for Cricket and Football, but was in the Seconds for both. At his death he was given a most impressive military funeral by his men. Many became teachers, mostly at public schools, including Michael Glazebrook (1853–1926), who has been appeared already in this chronicle, a high-jumper, a brilliant Classical scholar, and author of books on Greek literature and on the Bible, who in turn became a Housemaster at Harrow, High Master of Manchester Grammar School and Head Master of Clifton College. When Captain of School in 1871 he gained an Open Mathematics Scholarship at Balliol College, Oxford, and the Governors congratu-lated Carver on the condition of the school that this showed.[339] Hubert Doulton (1864–1941) was named by Carver to the Governors as the best boy in his year in 1882,[340] and returned to teach at the College immediately after leaving Oxford in 1887. William Martin Leake (1865–1942) also returned to the College to teach from 1889 until 1909, when he became Headmaster of

Dulwich College Preparatory School (which had opened in 1885). Langford Lovell Price (1862–1950), Captain of School in 1880 among other distinctions, became Reader in Economic History at Oxford, and was a College Governor from 1897 to 1921. Edward Horsburgh (1858–1942), who was President of the Union at Oxford in 1881, lectured at the Royal Institution and with the Oxford University Extension scheme; he delivered in all over six thousand lectures, and published books on Savanarola, the Battle of Waterloo and Lorenzo the Magnificent. Arthur Skinner (1861–1911) was Director of the Victoria and Albert Museum for four years from 1905, while the new buildings rose; he was deposed, and 'died of a broken heart' at 50, the victim of an 'official murder'.

The most famous scientist educated in the early days at the College was an all-round Scholar of 1859 who left from the Sixth Form in 1866, Sidney Gilchrist Thomas (1850–85). His practical curiosity and initiative extended beyond the classroom: he used to spend his half-holidays studying the new Dulwich sewer being constructed. He invented a process to eliminate phosphorus from the pig iron used to feed the 'Bessemer converter', making it possible for the first time to use impure materials to manufacture steel. After leaving the College, Thomas took a job as a clerk in a police court and worked at metallurgy in the evenings. Three quarters of a million tons of steel were made by his process; he died early of lung disease at the age of 35.[341] Richard Glazebrook (1854–1935), cousin to Canon Glazebrook, left the College in 1870. He was the first director of the National Physical Laboratory at Teddington from 1899 to 1919, and was knighted in 1917; under him a few huts on a marshy plain developed into a national service. At the time of the Great War he became an expert in munitions and aviation.

Alleynians manned the professions as solicitors, barristers, doctors, civil servants and engineers. Sir A. F. Petersen (1859–1922), a Classical Scholar at Corpus Christi College, Cambridge, in 1879, became a High Court judge and was on the German Crimes Committee in 1918. Horace Marshall (1865–1936), who left in 1881 from the Lower Fourth form, was involved in publishing and in the City, and became Lord Mayor of London in the year of the Armistice and was the first Alleynian to receive a peerage, as Lord Marshall of Chipstead, Chairman of the Star Board of the Eagle Star Company and a very generous public servant; he presented the College with the 'Cock House' Shield for the victorious Athletic House. Frederick Frayling (1846–1920) was the Representative of the Director of Public Prosecutions at the Central Criminal Court. Among other distinguished Alleynians were Professors of Law and of Chemistry, the

editor of the *Academy* magazine, a brewer, and a botanist. Sir George Fiddes (1858–1936), a Scholar of the College promoted from the Lower School, rose to be Permanent Under Secretary for the Colonies. Many Alleynians went overseas, serving in India, Ceylon, the Far East (especially Hong Kong), Burma and Africa; many died young, one when a hippopotamus upset his canoe on the Zambesi, and several were murdered, one by his Cingalese servant for the sake of the public money in his safe. All four who entered the India Civil Service in 1879 were claimed early by the bad climate and the hard life. By 1898 *The Alleynian* estimated that half or more of Alleynians overseas were in India. J. E. Gray (1858–1944) became an expert on wild elephants in the almost unknown upper reaches of Assam and Burma. Sir George Macartney (1867–1945), who left in 1883, was the only Briton in Chinese Turkestan for thirty years. Burma (which would at that time have been included in the statistic for 'India') in particular was a stronghold of Alleynians, inspired perhaps by the great success of Sir Herbert Thirkell White. Appointed Lieutenant-Governor by Curzon, he had run a successful mission to the Yunnan frontier winning over hostile Burmans, and in his book *A Civil Servant in Burma* (1913) showed a profound knowledge and understanding of Burmese customs, beliefs and languages; he gave a dinner in Rangoon to seven Old Alleynians in 1908.[342] Others sought their fortune in Australia, Canada and the USA, including a small number who joined in the Gold Rush. One became a planter in British Honduras, and one member of the large colony of Old Alleynians in Argentina was murdered on a ranch in 1898 by an outlaw, whom he managed to shoot dead, though mortally wounded himself. The account of this outrage, read by P. G. Wodehouse in *The Alleynian*, prompted him to effect a fictional tribal revenge in his novel *Mike* (1909), where the hero has a 'ripping time' in Argentina, among his pleasures being shooting a native Gaucho in the leg.[343] The Old Alleynians in Argentina (who liked to refer to themselves as 'Old Alleynians in the River Plate') recreated their schooldays in Buenos Aires with an annual cricket match (from 1913) against the Old Bedfordians. In Mexico an Alleynian from Gilkes's early days, James Purcell (1876–1923), who had great mining, banking and cotton interests, earned the respect of Francisco 'Pancho' Villa during the Revolution of 1911–20; he would not touch Purcell property, as "that name stood for justice, and at its head was a friend of the poor".[344] Alexander Horsburgh Turnbull (1868–1918) made a fortune as a general merchant in New Zealand and inherited another; a bibliophile who also collected Maori artefacts and accounts of voyages and diaries, he presented to the government his library of 32,000 volumes, now the Turnbull Library, which is rich in Australasian and Antarctic materials, including the diaries of two of Shackleton's men on the *Endurance* expedition.[345] George Ruston became Manager of D'Oyly Carte's Gilbert and Sullivan Opera Company. Frederick Lassam, the son of a Village baker, became the lessee of the Greyhound inn, and also for 15 years was the College caterer, until given the sack by Welldon; he wore a top hat and a frock coat in the Buttery.

Probably the most famous of Carver's Alleynians was A. E. W. Mason (1865–1948), a dashing and complex figure. At school the Governors awarded him a book prize for the way he was praised in an Examiner's Report in 1879.[346] He was an enthusiastic member of the Rifle Corps, and is to be seen as Oliver in photographs of *As You Like It* in 1883, the production remembered years after as the 'greatest glory of the Dulwich play'. After Oxford, where he was Secretary of the Union and a leading member of the Oxford University Dramatic Society, he became for a while an actor with the great Shakespearean company of Frank Benson, touring the provinces for a number of years; he played in the first

production of Shaw's *Arms and the Man*. Mason was also a prolific popular novelist; perhaps the best among his many books are *Clementina* (1901) and *The Four Feathers* (1902). Inspector Hanaud, a Parisian, introduced in *At the Villa Rose* (1910), was to figure in a series of his detective books. Mason was the 'Radical' Liberal Party Member of Parliament for Coventry from 1906 to 1910. Traveller, yachtsman, alpinist and spy in Spain and Mexico during the Great War, he lived and worked long enough to be involved in what seems an anachronistic world, the making of films with Sir Alexander Korda; these included the versions of his own stories, *The Drum* (1938), shown at the Venice Film Festival, and *The Four Feathers* (1939).[347] He was President of the Alleyn Club in 1946, but made a dull speech.

The names and addresses of the parents whose daughters Alleynians married in this era are given in Ormiston's *Register*; if this is a fair indication, there was a marked tendency for Old Boys to improve their social position by marriage; a gentler way of putting this perhaps would be to say that Alleynians proved by their character and prospects particularly eligible and worthy to marry upper and upper-middle-class girls.

As You Like It, 1883. A. E. W. Mason as Oliver, centre. (Dulwich College)

The artists

'A public school is not, as a rule, the place for an embryo painter', declared an article in *Public School Magazine* in 1901; among public school artists, 'Dulwich bears away the palm', providing more incentives than any other of the schools.[348] Carver's Dulwich was indeed marked by the extraordinary success of its artists: they won many Gold Medals at the Royal Academy Schools, and a large number were exhibitors. Three became full Academicians; not a single Old Alleynian was to win this accolade thereafter until Peter Greenham (1909–92; an Oxford History graduate) in 1960. Already in 1879 there were nine pictures at Burlington House by Alleynian artists;[349] the same artists went on to achieve much higher representation, and in 1902 nineteen pictures by seven Old Alleynian artists were on view. 'Pictures by Old Alleynians at the Academy' became a regular feature of the June numbers of *The Alleynian* up until the Second World War. When reminded of the fame of his pupils in art by a speaker at the Alleyn Club dinner in 1896, Carver declared, "I am afraid I was perhaps a little too much of an enthusiast on the subject of art".[350]

This success can of course in part be attributed to Carver's generosity with hours of study for artists, but more perhaps to the recognised brilliance of John Sparkes. Sparkes had many other activities, including designing pottery for Sir Henry Doulton, but with something of a symbolic loyalty, he did not leave the College until the year of Carver's retirement. In a letter to Carver of 1882 he wrote that during their 24 years' association with the 'great work' of the College, Carver's boys 'have done more in Art than those of any other public school in England, thanks to the warm interest and support that you have always given to all propositions made for their advantage'.[351] Sparkes, said Mackenzie, was 'shrewd and humorous', and 'full of the virile principles of Pre-Raphaelitism, a determination to see truly and record faithfully'.[352] The most famous of his pupils was a boy of Irish descent, Alexander Stanhope Forbes (1857–1947; RA 1910), whose elder brother, also an Alleynian, (Sir) William Forbes (1856–1936), a brilliant pianist at school, worked for 51 years for the London, Brighton and South Coast Railway, becoming General Manager.[353] The younger Forbes left the College in 1872 from the Lower Fifth to study at a night school in Kennington, the Lambeth Art Schools, later the City and Guilds School of Art, where John Sparkes was also the Head. Next he was awarded a Studentship at the Royal Academy Schools. He wrote in 1946 to McCulloch Christison, 'I owe my good fortune to Dulwich College and to Mr John Sparkes, my dear master and friend … that admirable art teacher we were

H. H. La Thangue. (Dulwich College)

fortunate in having in those days to guide and encourage us'.[354]

Sparkes's pupils set up their easels out of doors; they were taught to paint strictly truthfully, and to admire Constable and the 'beautiful and natural work of the modern French school' by Corot, Millet and Bastien-Lepage.[355] His most successful pupils went on to study in Paris with the *plein air* school, and their paintings were praised as 'healthy'; others studied and worked in Munich, Antwerp and Italy. Henry La Thangue (1859–1929; RA 1912), from Croydon and the son of a Register Office clerk, left after only one year at the age of twelve, but the *Studio* reported in 1897 that he 'still speaks gratefully' of the 'intelligent manner of study' of Art at Dulwich.[356] According to Stanhope Forbes this was enlightened: in place of mindless copying they were set to draw from casts, and he spent his break times in the cast room in the North Block.[357] Carver reported to the Governors the frequent medals and the showings at the Academy of these artists. In the same year of 1876 Leonard Nightingale, La Thangue and Herbert Bone all won silver medals at the Academy Schools; Bone (1853–1931) was later a designer and teacher at the Crystal Palace School of Art, and was a Master of the Art Workers' Guild. Mouat Loudan (1860–1925) won a Gold Medal for historical painting and prizes for sculpture and figure painting; he studied in Paris and became a painter of portraits and figures out of doors. William Margetson (1861–1940) illustrated the Bible and G. A. Henty's novels, designed costumes and stained glass, and painted altarpieces; he also was later a Master of the Art Workers' Guild. Hugh Glazebrook (1856–1937), brother of the headmaster, Michael Glazebrook, studied in Paris and concentrated on portraits.

Stanhope Forbes and La Thangue both enrolled at the College in May 1869, Forbes being the elder by two years. La Thangue's obituarist in *The Times* wrote that 'each [was] equally inspired by the enthusiasm of their brilliant art master, Mr. Sparks [*sic*]', who 'took his two favourite pupils with him to the Lambeth School of Art';[358] La Thangue enrolled at the same time as Forbes at the Royal Academy Schools, and both became popular Naturalist painters. La Thangue and Forbes next studied in Paris, at the Ecole des Beaux Arts and with Léon Bonnat respectively. La Thangue was perhaps the best of the Dulwich painters; a warm colourist, habitually contrasting bronze with rose, amethyst or violet, he was known as the 'apostle of sun, light and the outdoor life', and the vigour of his peasant-scenes was compared to those of Thomas Hardy.[359] After their Parisian studies he and Forbes spent the summer of 1880 painting together at Cancale in Brittany and on later sojourns in the South of France. La Thangue painted luminous studies of English rural life and orchards in Sussex and Norfolk, and went on to paint scenes in Italian and French villages, often in dappled light and shade. Forbes, who originally intended to paint portraits, became world-famous as the founder of the 'Newlyn School' of painters, near Penzance; his observations of the life of the fishing community began with a more or less photographic exactness but ended with impressionistic light. He also painted two dramatic fire scenes in fresco at the Royal Exchange in 1899 and 1921, the earlier one showing the Fire of London. During the First World War he made a fine study of ammunitions manufacture, *The Steel Workers* (RA, 1915).

Thomas Goodall (1856–1944) was the second of four sons of the Assistant Master at the Grammar School whose articles on the College are quoted above, and he walked as a schoolboy in the formal procession from the Old College to the New. Like Stanhope Forbes he studied at the Academy Schools and won a gold medal. Carver kept a letter from him telling him that on Sparkes's recommendation he and Forbes were 'painting from nature in country near Keston for a month or two'.[360] A really accomplished landscape painter in his youth, he gave up painting 'through ill health and other causes', as his friend Forbes wrote to Christison on his death.[361]

C. F. A. Voysey in later years with a plaster cast of Edward Alleyn's emblematic heart, hand and flames. (Dulwich College)

The three Fisher brothers, all painters, were an example of several families who sent exceptionally gifted brothers to the College, such as the Moores and the de Sélincourts in Gilkes's era. The eldest, Samuel Melton Fisher (1856–1939; RA 1924), followed what was now a traditional pattern on leaving the College in 1881 by joining the Lambeth School of Art. He spent ten years in Venice from 1885. Later, specialising in portraits of rich and titled sitters, he exhibited frequently at the Academy. His are the portraits of four Masters of Dulwich College and of the five VCs (the latter exhibited at the Royal Academy in 1924) that now hang at the College. Horace Fisher (1861–1934), another Gold Medallist of the Academy, painted pleasant rural scenes and lived on Capri, but was not such a worldly success. Harland Fisher (1865–1944) worked in Capri and South Italy and at Etaples in Normandy, before settling to England and portraiture in 1903. Melton Fisher's son, Stef Fisher (1894–1964), was Principal Art Master (or 'Master in Drawing') at the College from 1931 to 1956. The case of the brilliant architect and designer, the ungrateful Charles Voysey (1857–1941), FRIBA and Master of the Art Workers' Guild, has been alluded to above. His idealistic view of architecture, however, is consistent with Carver's noble philosophy of truth and beauty, and a photograph of him in later life shows him standing next to a plaster model of what is distinctly Edward Alleyn's crest, a hand encircled with flames holding up a heart.[362]

Joseph and Pharaoh

Carver's triumph was for him personally a Pyrrhic victory, in that he lost his occupation early and did not fulfil his ambition of becoming a bishop after Dulwich, as the family papers reveal; for the sake of the College (as mentioned above) he had earlier refused the offer of a mitre from Archbishop Tait.[363] By a cruel irony Tait died in 1882, and the new Archbishop of Canterbury was Edward White Benson (1829–96). Both the Carver papers and Mackenzie use the phrase that the reason for the new Primate not making Carver a bishop was that he 'knew not Joseph', alluding to the just man in the Book of Acts who, delivered out of his afflictions and serving God in Egypt, is cheated of his promised reward by the death of Pharaoh and the succession of a new one.[364] The family excuse covers the fact that Archbishop Benson presumably had a long memory and had heard too much in earlier days about Dr Carver. Carver's miserable quarrel with Charles Lane many years earlier had caught up with him: Benson was Head Master of Wellington from 1858, when Carver was appointed to Dulwich, until 1872, three years before Lane joined the staff at Wellington

and, in the close world of the Church and the public schools, must have known about Lane's great success at both schools and the way Carver had treated him. Furthermore the 'Right Rev Dr Benson, Bishop of Truro, formerly Head Master of Wellington College' was conspicuous as the third name printed in the subscription list of the Marshall Defence Fund of 1878, and was on the Committee of the Headmasters' Conference in 1874–5. As many as thirty years after the great battle, Carver was still very bitter about Rogers, who had orchestrated the Fund among his vast network of acquaintance as part of his war with Carver.[365]

At Dulwich it became an axiom that the new College was Carver's 'own creation'. His obituary in *The Alleynian* also showed that it was well understood, in addition to this mighty achievement, just how high his ideal of education was, with his belief that almost every subject could be educational and that education based on one rigid formula was bad. His pupils appreciated the independence and encouragement he gave them outside the classroom and his 'generosity and real kindliness of feeling'.[366]

7

'PUERI ALLEYNIENSES':
THE REVD JAMES WELLDON
1883–5

I am little more than a hyphen between Dr Carver and Mr Gilkes.

– WELLDON at the Alleyn Club Dinner, 1923

The impact of Welldon – Welldon's character and career – Welldon as Master – Music and the School Songs – Founder's Day and other achievements – Welldon's returns to the College – Matthew Arnold's Prize-giving address

The impact of Welldon

James Edward Cowell Welldon (1854–1937) was appointed Master of Dulwich College in 1883 at the age of 29. He stayed for only seven terms, but introduced important features of life at the College that over a hundred years later remain cherished traditions. The immediate impact of his rule was tonic and astringent; during Carver's latter years the discipline of the College was lax, in spite of academic success at Oxford and Cambridge. One of the most loyal Old Alleynians bred at the College in these transitional years was a distinguished public servant and scholar, typical of many well educated and highly principled Alleynians who were successful in public life, Sir Arthur Hirtzel (1870–1937), the Permanent Under Secretary of State at the India Office, who was Chairman of the College Governors from 1925 to 1930; he had been a Fellow of Brasenose College at Oxford early in his career, whose annotated edition of Virgil (1900) was kept in print by the Oxford University Press until the 1960s. Hirtzel joined the College in 1882, and by the time he left in 1889 was the Captain of School; he witnessed three Masters in office. In his opinion, Carver 'had lost his firmness of hand; even a small boy could see things were going wrong'. Hirtzel's terse summary, written in 1919 looking back at the evolution of the New College, was that 'Carver had laid the foundation upon which, after Welldon had removed some rubbish, Gilkes was able to build'. As with many Alleynians, it was above all Gilkes for whose influence Hirtzel was most grateful, and whom he most admired.[1] Welldon pulled the College together as a body in less than two years, and recovered its self-respect. His energetic personality left a persistent legacy: he founded a great and famous musical element in the life of the College; he established the Modern Side, which by the late 1920s was to have twice as many boys as the Classical Side; he made some very shrewd appointments; and he also brought about the building of a Swimming Bath, an essential amenity that had been proposed early in Carver's days. Above all, Welldon impressed the College with the cachet of a Public School: he composed the noble Latin verses for the School Song 'Pueri Alleynienses'; Founder's Day was his idea; the first rule he made on arrival was that the boys should wear uniform. The subfusc jackets of today, carrying the initials 'D C' in white Gothic letters on the breast pocket over the heart, an attempt to brand the boys' loyalty, were the result. An Old Alleynian of Welldon's days, (Sir) Lindsey Smith (1870–1960), later a distinguished judge, recalled this impetuous reform in a speech at an Alleyn Club dinner in 1923 (when Welldon himself was a speaker). Under Carver, he said, boys were used to wearing 'gay tweeds, fancy waistcoats of varied hues, and the latest creations in neckties'. He told how at West Dulwich station the young Smith had encountered the new Master on his first visit to the College; Welldon, looking scornfully at his 'fearful and wonderful check suit' (of which the boy was very proud), enquired whether the boys at Dulwich College were really allowed to wear such clothing.[2]

More substantially, perhaps, Welldon took the bold step of persuading the Governors to allow him to invite Thomas Henry Mason to found an independent Dulwich College Preparatory School, disposing of catering to boys at the College below the age of 13, and thus reducing numbers by about one hundred.[3] For the first few years these boys all joined the College at the age of 13. Welldon possessed a more original and incisive mind than Carver. In the term in which he was appointed, Summer 1883, *The Alleynian* (ingenuously, one must presume) published on opposite pages current photographs of Carver and Welldon, showing a dramatic contrast between the faces of a weary and harassed Carver, and Welldon with his determined jaw. When he left, *The Alleynian* politely described the latter's irresistible will-power as a 'dauntless energy' that had both created a 'noble superstructure' and led the College from its 'trials and troubles of childhood and vigorous youth' into 'glorious manhood';[4] his grateful pupils nicknamed him 'the Butcher' when he used the cane so freely during his first term.[5] (At Harrow he was to be known as 'the Porker').[6] Welldon's claim was that, 'I wished to be unpopular and successful';[7] in 1920 he recalled that it had not been his intention to follow in Alleyn's steps and 'keep a bear garden'. Looking back again in the late 1930s, Welldon wrote a letter to John Ivimey (1868–1961), a colleague from his days at Harrow, who had been Organist at Dulwich for two years from 1908 and was now writing a chapter of his *Boys and Music* (1938) about

J. E. C. Welldon, 1883.
(Dulwich College)

his experiences at the College; in it he gave an interesting summary of how he saw his own part in the history of the College and a prophecy of what would become of it in future years:

> When I became Master of the College, I thought that, partly owing to the rapid increase in the number of boys, and partly owing to the absorption of the Master's time and thought in internal quarrels, which eventually led to a famous action at law, it had never acquired an adequate cohesion, and I tried hard not to increase the number of boys, but to inspire the boys with a sense of unity in their allegiance to the College itself. I instituted what is now the Preparatory School of Dulwich in order to remove the quite young boys from the College.... Looking upon the College, its situation, its history, its wealth, the character of the residents in and near South London, and its spacious playing-fields, I cannot help feeling that Dulwich College is naturally destined to be the leading Day-school in all England. [8]

Robert Noel Douglas (1869–1957), who was at the College from 1878 to 1888 and became Headmaster of Giggleswick School, recalled admiringly that 'his broom swept clean'; Welldon had 'a vigour and a grasp which pulled us up short'. [9]

Welldon's character and career

Carver's roots were a family of landed provincial proprietors, and he was conditioned by evangelical Christianity, by St Paul's School, and by Trinity College, Cambridge. Welldon's tenure at Dulwich brought the College even closer to the centre of the late-Victorian establishment, composed of the Church, the Public Schools, and Oxford and Cambridge. The eldest son of the Revd Edward Ind Welldon (1821–79), Second Master of Tonbridge School, he was a King's Scholar at Eton. A Craven Scholar at King's College, Cambridge, he was a 'brilliant' undergraduate, the Senior Classic in the university Classics Tripos, winning the Chancellor's Medal and the Gold Medal for a Greek Ode; he was President of the Union and one of the 'Apostles', the famous select undergraduate society of liberal-minded and literary intellectuals. His health broke down at Cambridge after the death of his father and sister, and he left for a term to recover at Biarritz. [10] While an undergraduate he became a Freemason. Elected a Fellow and Lecturer in Classics at King's in October 1878, he was promoted to Second Tutor in 1881. Ordained Deacon in 1883, the year he became Master of Dulwich, he was ordained Priest in 1885, the year he left to become Head Master of Harrow.

Six feet five inches tall, Welldon held himself with great confidence, combined with 'robust common sense and untarnished sincerity'. [11] He inclined to arrogance;

his very quick wit, which made him famous for his off-the-cuff puns and bon mots, also made for a sharp tongue. Philip Hope (1869–1943; see Chapter Eight), the great Classics Form Master at the College, thought that Welldon's later disappointments in his Church career, following his resignation as Bishop of Calcutta in 1902, were the consequence of 'his inability to withhold the estranging gibe'. [12]

Welldon published translations of Aristotle: the *Politics* in 1883, *Rhetoric* in 1886 and the *Nicomachean Ethics* in 1892; he had also a wide knowledge of English, French, German and Italian literature. At Eton and King's he had come under the influence of the clever and worldly Oscar Browning (1837–1923), who was sacked from teaching at Eton in 1875 for his fervid friendships with George Curzon (1859–1925; later Viceroy of India and Foreign Secretary) and other boys but was immediately elected a Fellow of King's. 'No man living has had more influence upon me than you have', Welldon later wrote to him, 'and I have not been half grateful enough for so much kindness'. [13] In late adolescence, Welldon accompanied Browning on trips to the Bavarian highlands in 1871, to Norway in 1874, and to the high Alps in 1875. Welldon later travelled with Curzon and another Etonian friend, Edward Lyttelton, to Greece and with Curzon again to North America. [14] In a series of letters preserved at King's from the erstwhile pupil to his master, Welldon at first confides to Browning his greater interest in becoming a Fellow at King's than in 'teaching little boys', but later (having rejected the Law as 'not a beneficent or ennobling profession') writes of his decision to take holy orders and then become a headmaster. To Browning he also reveals that his feelings about taking on the challenge of Dulwich after Carver were not altogether as sanguine as his apparent confidence would lead one to suppose: when Browning wrote to congratulate him on his election, he replied, 'the more I hear of Dulwich, the more difficult and important the work which lies before me seems to have become; and I sometimes doubt whether I was justified in standing for an appointment which would employ the strongest energy of the strongest man'. [15] In July 1883 he wrote of the heavy responsibility he felt; of his teaching Divinity and a good deal of Greek and Latin to the Sixth and some of the other forms, he commented: 'I am sure there is much work to be done here'. [16] By preaching all over the country as Master of Dulwich College, he brought credit to the school. Though he often returned to the College after he left, giving a memorable address when he consecrated the War Memorial on Founder's Day, 1921 (see below), and speaking fondly of his days at the College, he wrote significantly little about it in his two volumes of memoirs;[17] one characteristic remark was that the Board Room in the Centre Block was the best place to interview parents: they were out of breath from climbing the great staircase.[18] It is hard to defend Welldon from the suspicion that he was impatient to move on. In 1884, in his second year at the College, he failed in his application to become Head Master of Eton; the Dulwich boys cheered him in the Great Hall when he announced to them that he had decided to stay on at Dulwich after his Alma Mater had rejected him,[19] but he left them to become Head Master of Harrow the very next year. There seems something disingenuous in a remark he made in his letter of resignation to the Governors that he had hoped to 'serve the College in peace for a number of years', but was denied a fair chance since he was 'so openly suspected of going'.[20] His departure, we are told, 'was viewed with general regret by everyone who had ever had anything to do with him'.[21]

Welldon expressed his hope to Browning that 'the liberal sentiments of Harrow people [would] make reform, so far as it is necessary, comparatively easy',[22] but in the event he seems to have miscalculated. At Harrow he confronted twenty men older and more conservative than himself, and it remained the opinion of Philip Hope that Welldon's move to Harrow was misconceived: the force of tradition there would prove intractable to his progressive ideas, Hope said, while 'Dulwich College, on the other hand, was devoted and plastic, and would have taken his impress'.[23]

Welldon seems in retrospect to have been conditioned by the inbred male world of Eton and King's. Some mild misogyny was certainly at work, as he hardly made a speech without directing droll remarks at the mischief of marriage. His close companion for nearly fifty years was Edward Perkins, the chief footman at Harrow in his day; they travelled the globe together, and on his death in 1932 Welldon retired as Dean of Durham and was said to be inconsolable.[24] In 1895, the year of Oscar Wilde's trial, with his own name and the title 'Head Master of Harrow School' printed on the title-page, Welldon published his only work of fiction, a Public School romance, *Gerald Eversley's Friendship: a study in Real Life*. This novel was loathed and mocked by P. G. Wodehouse for its sentimentality and its precocious hero, who 'spends most of his leisure time forming theories of life and wrestling with spiritual doubts – all this at the age of thirteen'.[25] It expresses with some subtlety the hero-worship and Platonic love felt by a clever and introverted schoolboy, homesick and socially inferior – in effect a bullied swot – for a handsome and uncomplicated athletic boy. 'No being, perchance, is so distinct, none so beautiful', Welldon

asserts, 'as a noble English boy. He is open-hearted, open-handed; there is not a cloud upon his brow; he looks the world in the face; for him all life is, as it were, sunshine without rain'; in the novel Welldon nearly kills off the wholesome athlete, Henry Venniker, with inflammation of the lungs, but he survives to become a tall, manly splendid creature with curly auburn hair, and Eversley meanwhile gains a Balliol scholarship. Gerald now transfers his affections to Venniker's sister Ethel, but she dies shortly after from diphtheria, caught on a charitable visit to a cottage; Gerald is saved from suicide and despair by Venniker, and they grow closer. The novel, with its transparent implications, also tells us something of how Welldon viewed Public School society at the time: 'a world in itself', 'self-centred and self-satisfied', where 'a savage tribe' was to be found, athletic and anti-intellectual, and where 'mediocrity sits on her throne'. The boys 'despise weakness and are wholly unmerciful in taking advantage of it. But they do not resent severity, so long as it is impartial'.[26] Welldon late in life wrote in his *Recollections* that 'it is the clear duty of every master in a Public School to set his face against the worship of athletic games', although he does admit that such sports partly account for the supremacy of the British race in far-off regions.[27]

At Harrow Welldon was again very popular with his pupils, and became a famous schoolmaster. Among his grateful pupils was Winston Churchill, whom he took considerable pains to encourage. Churchill came to his attention by reciting 1,200 lines of Macaulay's *Lays of Ancient Rome* from memory, but later recalled that 'Mr Welldon seemed to be physically pained by a mistake being made.... Mr Asquith used to have just the same look on his face when I sometimes adorned a Cabinet discussion by bringing out one of my few but faithful Latin quotations'. Welldon was forced to 'swish' [cane] the young Winston for breaking window-panes in a disused factory, but the Head Master and his pupil kept up an admiring friendship after the boy left Harrow. Churchill wrote to his brother at the age of 21 in 1896 that while he respected Welldon's judgement on nearly every subject and entertained the highest opinion of Welldon's brains, these had, however, been 'warped by school-mastering and contact with clerics'.

After making some important changes at Harrow, such as introducing full fee scholarships, Welldon left the school in 1898 after 13 years, on appointment as Bishop of Calcutta and Metropolitan of India. He must have hoped for a great career in India, since the Viceroy was now Lord Curzon, his old Eton friend, but he resigned in 1902, having travelled over the sub-continent in an attempt to meet Indian Christians. Poor health and conflict with

Blew House with J. B. Parish, 1883 (detail). (Dulwich College)

Curzon over his attempts to set up Christian Missions, when it was government policy not to interfere with the religious views of Indians, contributed to his return. He proceeded Canon of Westminster (1902–8) and Dean of Manchester (1906–18). He gave the address at Churchill's wedding in September 1908. As Dean of Durham from 1918 to 1933 he was once severely jostled and almost rolled into the river by miners for making a speech criticising the Trade Unions. His relations with his Bishop, the caustic controversialist Herbert Henson (1863–1947), were bad; Henson said that Welldon 'could neither speak with effect nor be silent with dignity'. [28]

Welldon as Master

Welldon once claimed at an Alleyn Club dinner that his brief period at Dulwich had been its 'golden age', [29] and though the phrase was soon afterwards (and with justice) filched to describe the reign of his successor, Arthur Herman Gilkes, [30] the aims Welldon professed from the stage in the Great Hall at his first Prize-giving in 1883 gleamed with noble ambition. To cheers from the audience, he said that his paramount drive was to 'strengthen the moral and intellectual life of the school'. His eminent guest speaker was the famous Anglophile poet and orator, James Russell Lowell (1819–91), then

the American Minister [Ambassador] in London, who recalled Harvard and spoke thoughtfully about the concept of the Alma Mater. [31]

In May 1884 the Sur Master (or 'Under Master') James Marshall, Carver's enemy, left for his headmastership at Durham, and Welldon said of him in *The Alleynian* that he had lost a colleague at once his 'invaluable coadjutor' and 'esteemed friend'. [32] The post thereupon lapsed, and three senior unmarried Assistant Masters moved into the North Block of the Barry Buildings, where Marshall and his family had lived. Welldon did not suffer criticism gladly, and publicly mocked the busybody mothers of Dulwich boys and interfering Village ladies as the 'Dorcas and Tabitha' brigade [after the woman in the book of Acts who was 'full of good works and almsdeeds']. [33] When a boy who copied his prep told the Master his mother refused to allow him to be caned, Welldon had the porter conduct the child off the premises. The mother appealed to the Board, and tried to enrol him at King's College School, but Welldon would not write him a 'character'; the boy returned for a thrashing. [34]

He was equally brisk with the Governors, making fun of his meeting on the playing field a 'little man clearly of immense importance' whom he did not recognise, and who said to him pompously, 'My name is Watchurst. I am the mind of the Governors'. Philip Hope told Mackenzie that Welldon 'habitually browbeat the Governors, and they were afraid of him'.[35]

Although Welldon was to claim, with uncharacteristic modesty, that he was 'little more than a hyphen between Dr Carver and Mr Gilkes',[36] the College owes him a great deal. He put into practice his belief that first and foremost 'the study of language and literature, ancient or modern', was 'the supreme instrument of education'.[37] On arrival he declared to the Governors that he intended 'to develop as circumstances admit, a distinctly modern side of education in the College',[38] and indeed was the founder of the Modern Side, making it possible for boys to begin to specialise in Modern Languages at a younger age by dropping much of their Classics. As Gilkes described the Modern Side to the Governors in his Annual Report for 1908, the boys followed a course consisting of Divinity, English, French, German, Science, Mathematics and Latin. Two-thirds of these boys went into business, and about one-third into their fathers' offices, into banking and insurance, law, accountancy, Lloyd's, the Stock Exchange and lower Civil Service clerkships; the average leaving age was 16.[39] The Oxford and Cambridge Schools Examinations Board in their report for 1884 judged that in general the Classics had declined in Carver's last years, the examiner writing superciliously that, 'I should doubt if the traditions of the School are in favour of Scholarship and classical refinement';[40] under Welldon and A. H. Gilkes this could not possibly be said of the College. The Science and Mathematics were, however, reported as 'excellent'. Arthur Hirtzel (quoted above), though so young, gained maximum marks for his certificates. The Governors in 1885 authorised £390 to be spent on school Scholarships and £282 on Exhibitions for leavers at Oxford and Cambridge.[41]

Welldon appointed three significant teachers, although their heyday was to be achieved in Gilkes's days. The Sixth Form Classics Master, William Lendrum (later Vesey, 1854–1935; see Chapter Eight), was said by Robert Noel Douglas to be 'a joy and an inspiration, … himself working morning, noon and night, he got an amount of work out of the Sixth which would astonish the modern schoolboy'.[42] Frederick William Sanderson (1857–1922), of humble Northumberland origin, taught Science and Engineering; he left to become a very famous Headmaster of Oundle from 1892, transforming it from a small county grammar school into a modern, scientific Public School. H. G. Wells published a complimentary monograph about Sanderson in 1924, the only biography he ever felt stirred to write, called *The Story of*

a Great Schoolmaster, in which he expresses surprise that this man, though no gentleman, no cricketer, no sportsman and no scholar, but possessing an 'exceptionally bold and creative emancipated mind' achieved what he did in the conservative atmosphere of his times, and declared him 'beyond question the greatest man I have ever known with any degree of intimacy';[43] Welldon appointed him in January 1885. Sanderson believed in practical work in the physical sciences, and caused some dismay among the staff by his principle of leaving the laboratories and workshops unlocked for boys to conduct experiments in their own time; greatly admired by Gilkes, he became a key figure in the Dulwich of its 'golden age'. The third signal appointment was Edward Rendall (1858–1920), a truly great Principal Master in Music, who made the serious study of Music the norm at the College.

Music and the School Songs

Welldon himself was musical, and told the Governors roundly on his arrival that the musical instruction was 'very defective', calling for a 'resident Music Master'. He held 'lofty ideas about the value and possibility of the art in education',[44] which far transcended Carver's notion of *esprit de corps* created by the singing of glees. Welldon asked the Governors for eight musical scholarships,[45] but nothing further is to be found on the subject in the Governors' Minutes. Rendall did most of his work under Gilkes, and left in 1901, after 17 years at Dulwich, for Charterhouse (where his cousin was Headmaster) to be their Principal Master in Music. Since he collaborated with Welldon in providing a number of brilliant School Songs, his Dulwich career is treated in this chapter. A Mathematics scholar at King's College, Cambridge, Rendall was part of the musical clique at Cambridge to which Browning and Welldon belonged, and was moreover 'lieutenant' in the world of university music to the great composer and professor Charles Villiers Stanford (1852–1924). He had a particular interest in the revival of Purcell and of seventeenth- and eighteenth-century music. It was a brilliant stroke of Welldon's to persuade him to apply, filling the new post with an intellectual and expressive musician to leaven what was still in some ways a suburban school. Rendall was imbued with the high culture of Cambridge in his day, to which indeed he had been a contributor, with its academic excitements, the productions in College gardens of Greek plays, and its literary and musical culture. Rendall was appointed in January 1884. The son of a country vicar, he was educated at Harrow; his aunt was married to Lord Davey, a Dulwich College Governor from 1893, and Chairman from 1896 until his death in 1907.

Rendall had a good baritone voice, a working acquaintance with most instruments, and had studied for two years in Berlin with Joseph Joachim (1831–1907), famed as the greatest solo violinist in the world. Rendall married the sister of a Dulwich colleague, Frederick Ellis, in 1886, and his wife, 'a frequent exhibitor' at the Royal Academy, designed the new-style black and white cover of *The Alleynian* in 1899, which was in use until December 1937, showing the roofscape of the Barry buildings with a flight of pigeons. Rendall gave himself generously to the College, teaching Mathematics and Astronomy as well as Music, and he was Housemaster of The Orchard from 1895 to 1901. At his death in 1920 he received glowing obituaries from *The Alleynian* and *The Carthusian* and also from *The Harrovian*; we learn that he 'kept the heart of a boy', and had encyclopaedic learning.

Edward Rendall made no compromise with South London taste, introducing boys to real music. At Dulwich he was said to have effected a genuine 'revolution' in music, and great works were heard in the Great Hall: concert reports in *The Alleynian* include performances of Bach, Beethoven, Handel, Haydn, Schubert, Stanford, and Purcell's *Dido and Aeneas*. Rendall published in the magazine *The Nineteenth Century and After* an essay with the title 'A Plea for the Introduction of Music among the Upper Classes', pointing out that schools for the poor, Girls' schools and Sunday schools were better off in musical education than the Public Schools. He stressed that real musical education was not concerned with mere 'finger drudgery' or just 'singing', but in developing the emotional faculties of pupils. He believed in the benefit of 'rhythmical study' and in the value of hearing works of genius for the first time when young. Choral music generated loyalty, sympathy and forgetfulness of self, creating a 'bond of union in community'. In effect he declared war on the philistinism of the 'educated' class and its schools. [46]

The music composed by Rendall for Welldon's words to 'Pueri Alleynienses', wrote *The Alleynian*, was 'full of vigour' and 'a veritable challenge to be up and doing'. [47] Rendall, as we know from the series of Dulwich School Songs, was particularly skilled at setting words to music, and composed a song cycle based on Isaak Walton's *The Compleat Angler*. He also composed much admired witty music for the Greek plays on Founder's Days, such as a solemn march for Aristophanes' *The Frogs*. [48] Rendall also deserves recognition as the founder of the Dulwich Orchestra and Choir, as of its military Brass Band; to the

Manuscript of 'Pueri Alleynienses' by Edward Rendall (detail), rescored 1894. (Dulwich College)

latter Welldon himself presented instruments in 1884. Rendall's was an infectious enthusiasm: he persuaded Assistant Masters to take up less usual instruments.[49]

Of the collaboration between Welldon and Rendall over 'Pueri Alleynienses' we know that the words were written in 1884, and that it was first sung on Founder's Day in 1885, one of Welldon's final days in the College. The glorious song was later given a new orchestral accompaniment by Rendall, performed in 1894.[50] All Welldon's verses of the song are worth studying, expressing gratitude to Alleyn and referring to golden youth, to the pleasures of work, the playing of roles and the rewards of Fame, but asserting that the ultimate glory is to be dedicated to God alone. When 'Pueri Alleynienses' was conducted by Rendall at his own last Concert in the Great Hall it was sung in a revised version, 'given not merely as a chorus, but as originally written, with a very melodious soprano solo, which was well sung by the trebles', and at the singing of the last verse the 'very foundations of the College seemed to shake'.[51] The greatness of the song was early recognised: the Classicist Sir John Sheppard (1881–1968; at the College 1894–1900), Provost of King's College, Cambridge, from 1933 to 1954 (and one of the most famous of all academic Old Alleynians), called it the 'best action' of Welldon and Rendall.[52] The phrase 'quotquot annos, quotquot menses' led to a nickname for Alleynians in the City: 'Quotquots'.

Welldon wrote other good songs for Rendall's music: 'In the Good Days of Old' lightly praises the achievements of his own short tenure, celebrating the College's new superiority in Music and in academic study by comparison with the early days when

> Not a boy in the School
> Knew his scales as a rule;
> But there's now not a fellow
> Who can't play the 'cello....
> 'Tis said that no hammer
> Could drive in Greek grammar;
> But now we can parse
> Better than our mammas,
> Or papas.[53]

Rendall took to writing the words for School Songs as well as the music after Welldon left, but they are inferior: they include a hearty celebration of Rugby football, 'Hair Dishevelled', and a celebration of prep, 'Night-work', which was obviously written to persuade boys that the reason superior Old Alleynians filled the professions such as Law, Medicine and Art, as well as the Forces and Parliament, was the long hours put in eagerly by boys over their homework:

> Do you want for the doctor to give you a pill,
> A soldier or sailor, or what's worse still,
> The Thing that they call an MP, sir?
> For this is the way of a Dulwich boy,
> Although it's a wonderful way, sir;
> Black and blue, it is true,
> But there's stuff in him too,
> As the world will find out in his day, sir.

The tender 'Good-bye Song' of 1889,[54] sung in the Great Hall by the leavers or senior prefects each summer until the 1960s, expresses regrets at leaving the cricket and football fields and the form-rooms. 'Down in the Valley of Dulwich' is a setting by Rendall of words by an Assistant Master, the Revd George Allen (at the College from 1881; Headmaster of Cranleigh School in 1891), Captain of the Rifle Corps, on the subject of *esprit de corps*, celebrating the Great Hall with its Honours Boards and the Ashburton Shield brought to it in triumph, and characterising ideal Dulwich boys in a school 'where no one is sulky or sad or afraid'. Another song they wrote together, 'An Idyll of the King', concerns James I and Edward Alleyn, who is made to say

> Bears I can tackle and freely tame,
> And boys, they tell me, are just the same.

Founder's Day and other achievements

During a short tenure, Welldon managed to get his cherished Swimming Bath built and running, raising £1,700,[55] where Carver had failed. Giving rise to jokes about cleanliness and godliness, Welldon's 'favourite project' was to build a Chapel on the College campus.[56] There is little doubt that if he had stayed he would have achieved this; it was also a devout wish of Gilkes's, and one for which he frequently appealed to the Governors, but Welldon was more wilful and businesslike than his supremely virtuous successor. The Bath was at first open to the skies, and had circular turrets, east and west; Welldon himself paid for a wooden Gallery. The Revd William Rogers turned the first sod when it was constructed, and Welldon declared he would take the first plunge. The temperature was kept at 64 Fahrenheit; Gilkes, characteristically, reduced it to 54 Fahrenheit.[57] Welldon, keen on the Army and the Empire, encouraged the Rifle Corps, in 1885 fitting them out with a Glengarry cap.

According to Mackenzie, it was Welldon who placed the two great plaster casts of Greek statuary in the Lower Hall, the one after the *Fighting Gladiator* of Agasia and the other after the *Standing Discobolos* of Alcamanes, inspiring the boys to fight the good fight.

Given the contemporary cult at Oxford and Cambridge of Grecian Athletic Prizemen, it would make sense if Welldon had been responsible for procuring them. However, a book of 1906 about the artist Stanhope Forbes states that he and other boys had copied these same casts during John Sparkes's time at the College, namely from 1869 to 1872 – so Welldon seems merely to have ordered their relocation to the Lower Hall, where they stood until at least 1912.[58] Since the names and achievements recorded on Carver's Honours Boards in the Great Hall were swiftly in danger of overflowing the plaster panels between the Gothic pilasters, they were painted over in April 1885, and 'only those worthy of permanent record retained';[59] the new lists were prudently painted in smaller lettering, and pentimenti of the old lists can be still seen underneath the new. In 1885 there was a proposal to hang the Cartwright Collection (see Chapter Three) from the Picture Gallery in the Centre Block; at the same time the West Wing of the Gallery was voided of the Poor Sisters, who were housed once again at the Old College.[60]

On All Saints' Day in 1883 Welldon instituted a Midterm Sermon to be delivered by the Master to the whole College, and Gilkes kept up this tradition. It was not compulsory to attend, but Welldon told the readers of his memoirs that of all the boys in the College 'not more than a dozen' were absent.[61] The texts of his Dulwich sermons have not survived, but Welldon was a famous preacher, and when he published a volume of his sermons to Harrow boys in 1891, he gave them what may have been a partly Alleynian title, *The Fire Upon the Altar*, alluding of course to the Fire from Heaven that convinced the people to abandon Baal (1 Kings 18.38), but also perhaps to the emblematical panel of *Piety* in the Masters' Library, which features a flaming altar – or indeed to the perennial flame of the College crest. The Harrow sermons remind the boys that a Public School stands out before men's eyes as a shining light 'that illuminates and enriches the lives of all its members'. The English are 'the elect nation of God', with a 'proud imperial duty and destiny'. The sermons advert to the love of David and Jonathan, and betray a prurient interest in sinful schoolboys, saying that the school is the home of 'culture, piety and virtue', and that they should be as chaste as vestal virgins, warning of the dangers of other boys coming to their rooms with 'foul talk'.[62]

Welldon instituted Founder's Day in 1884 as 'the chief festival of the school year', with an eye to creating *esprit de corps* with traditions to pass on to future years. The date was to be the closest possible Saturday to 21 June, the date on which the royal Letters Patent founding the College were signed in 1619. The Speech Days and Prize Days were now converted into a 'day of the highest order'

with sports and drama. The production of *As You Like It* of the same year was remembered as 'the greatest glory of the Dulwich Play'.[63] The wearing of cornflowers, claimed on no authority whatsoever to be Alleyn's favourite flower and more likely to be consistent with the Oxford blue of the school colours, was said not to have become popular until 'about the last year of the nineteenth century'. The first wreath with cornflowers was laid on Alleyn's tomb in 1907. The school cap with its dark blue ribbons had been introduced as early as 1864; all the boys were said to wear it back to front in Carver's day. A. H. Gilkes added the school arms to it in 1886.[64]

Welldon's returns to the College

Following his departure in 1885, Welldon obviously enjoyed returning to speak at the College or at Alleyn Club dinners. At Prize-giving in 1899, on the eve of his leaving for India, he told the assembled company, 'we should never forget that it was our highest aim as a school to train the men who were to serve England in the Church and the State, in the Army or in business life'.[65] In 1904, in the course of a mordant speech at the Alleyn Club dinner, he used a quaint metaphor that sent a ripple round the room, saying that he used to feel that the relationship of boys to the Master was like that of a husband to his wife. A fictional Welldon appears at an Alleyn Club dinner (referred to as an 'OB dinner') in P. G. Wodehouse's *Big Money* of 1931. Speeches at the Alleyn Club dinners in the early twentieth century were lengthy; they were printed *in extenso* in *The Alleynian* (with interjections of 'laughter', 'applause' and 'Hear, hear!'), occupying twenty or more pages of the magazine. Wodehouse had heard Welldon speak on Alleynian occasions often enough to have taken a dislike to him and his style of oratory. His hero, placed too near to a group of 'boisterous striplings', feels impelled to leave the Banquet-room furtively, 'before the dam of oratory would burst':

> His eye fell on the table at the top of the room, along which, on either side of the President, were seated some twenty of the elect: and it now flashed upon him that of these at least eight must almost certainly be intending to make speeches. And right in the middle of them, with a nasty, vicious look in his eye, sat a Bishop.
>
> Anybody who has ever attended Old Boys' dinners knows that Bishops are tough stuff. They take their time, these prelates. They mouth their words and shape their periods. They roam with frightful deliberation from the grave to the gay, from the manly straightforward to the whimsically jocular. Not one of them but is good for at least twenty-five minutes.[66]

An honoured and famous guest, 'Bishop Welldon, Dean of Durham', as he was styled by *The Alleynian*, consecrated the War Memorial at the College on

Founder's Day, 17 June 1921. The stone cross with the bronze panels listing the appalling numbers of Alleynian dead had been unveiled by the great Old Alleynian soldier, Sir Webb Gillman (1870–1933), who had fought in five 'theatres' of the War and was Chief of General Staff in Mesopotamia. Welldon's rhetoric was eloquent:

> there is not in the College a master who does not feel that the boys who laid down their lives in the War have taught him a nobler lesson then ever in the years of their school life he tried to teach them. … If there is any attribute of the British character which has immortalised itself in the War, it is the Public School spirit: that ennobled and ennobling temper of courage, union, chivalry and self-sacrifice, which is learned in the classrooms and upon the playing fields, and in the chapel of a great Public School.[67]

In 1923 he distributed the prizes, praising the recently dead Shackleton as the possessor of the true spirit of the Elizabethan mariners, and again held aloft the idea of the Public School spirit, as something that could not be turned out with equal success by any other institution in the world. 'God's Gift', he said to cheers, was the most beautiful title ever conferred on a Public School.[68] In 1928 in the course of a brief last speech at the Alleyn Club dinner Welldon recalled how 'an influential newspaper in South London had declared shortly before he left that he 'was becoming more offensive every week', but on his departure said that he was a great loss; he sounded sincere when he said that he wished he had stayed longer.[69]

Matthew Arnold's Prize-giving address

Welldon's first Prize-giving was graced by James Russell Lowell; the speaker at the Prize-giving for his last academic year (following his last Summer term) was the great English poet and critic Matthew Arnold (1822–88), who made it clear that this was the first and only time he would agree to present school prizes. On the platform were Welldon, Gilkes and Rogers, and Carver's memorial organ was in place. Arnold, for 35 years a school inspector who fearlessly pointed out the shortcomings of the British education system, praised Welldon as 'just the strong man when the strong man was most needed', and claimed that thanks to Welldon Dulwich was now an ideal new academy, equal to the way England was evolving at that period; the College, he said,

> is a signal and splendid type of just that description of school which I have long desired, and vainly desired, to see put at the disposal of the professional and trading classes throughout the country. How very seldom the English middle classes else-

where find themselves with advantages of this kind, and how very little they in general seem to care whether they possess them or not! I am filled with admiration for the school.

To cheers, Arnold left the College with a blessing that was also admonitory:

> May you do what a single school can to repair, in so far as in you lies, the intellectual poverty and effacement to which in general those classes have, through their own neglect, condemned themselves.[70]

'Calcutta', Bishop Welldon. *Vanity Fair*, November 1898. (Dulwich College)

8

'THE GOLDEN AGE':
ARTHUR HERMAN GILKES
1885-1914

Canon Carver in his time fought a great fight to save
the body of Dulwich; Gilkes gave it a soul.
– W. D. GIBBON, 1938

PART I
GILKES'S COLLEGE

*Gilkes's career and ideals – The College Mission in Camberwell – The Governors – Buildings – Academic life at the
College, and the Common Room – Science and Engineering under Gilkes*

Arthur Herman Gilkes (1849–1922) was a noble Master of Dulwich College, although some of his qualities are unlikely to impress or to appeal to contemporary readers. His 29 years at the College generated a Golden Age,[1] abruptly ended by the slaughter of young manhood in the Great War. Gilkes was appointed in 1885 at the age of 36; from his twelve years as an Assistant Master at Shrewsbury School he had already gained the reputation of a legendary schoolmaster able to inspire and to form the characters of young men. Gilkes had rectitude, and he lived up to his Platonic ideal of the calling of a teacher. The boys and masters of the day compared the succession at Dulwich of the Athenian Gilkes after the worldly prelate Welldon to the arrival of Aristides ('the Just') after the rule of a Cardinal Wolsey or a Roman dictator; even more momentously, they evoked a transition from the Law to the Gospel, from the Old Testament to the New.[2] Welldon's impact was forceful and he laid firm foundations, but it is Gilkes who must be given the credit for fully transforming a slack school into a keen one. In the larger world Alleynians became admired for their Gilkesian virtues: liberal education, dedication to the public good, trustworthiness, humane moderation, and lack of vanity. They became famous for their Alleynian sense of enterprise; they possessed 'an energy, an enthusiasm, a determination to succeed'; they were called 'the Yankees' of the public schools.[3]

Gilkes's career and ideals

Gilkes's father William (1813–67) was a manufacturer from the Welsh borders of Herefordshire, a chemist, an ink-maker 'and gentleman', who once served as Mayor of Leominster. In his youth he had taken £5 in his pocket and walked across France to the Great St Bernard Monastery. The family was large, and had a reputation for Anglican 'grave living'. The Gilkeses were actually of Quaker stock; when William Gilkes 'contumaciously' married an Anglican he had been expelled from his local Meeting. Quaker forms of speech still featured in the talk of A. H. Gilkes and his mother, Mary, a gentle lady; she kept house for her son in the South Block at Dulwich before his marriage in 1892. Gilkes's staff thought that his family background had conditioned both his metaphysical preoccupation with religion and the meaning of life and his own careful personal discipline of living by rule; it accounted for something monkish and reclusive in his character.[4] Before his marriage, his sister Edith gave the prizes on Sports Days, just as Miss Welldon had done. Schooled at Shrewsbury, after graduating in Classics from Christ Church, Oxford, in 1872, he returned, as Carver had done, to teach at his old school. At Oxford, he is known to have missed the school atmosphere, and to have found the talk of the undergraduates 'rather wild'.[5] As a teacher at Shrewsbury, one of his achievements was to found a Mission for working-class adolescents, directly involving his own pupils; at Gilkes's Dulwich, the school was said to be 'permeated' with the idea of service.[6] The College Mission which Gilkes founded in Camberwell in 1886 (see below) was not a guilt-directed 'charity' of the affluent towards the poor: it was the expression of Christian faith applied to good works and the application of social work, in the spirit of Alleyn, among fatherless boys in a notoriously deprived area of London. This was without doubt a great success, and Gilkes inspired boys and masters at the College to become seriously involved with the project. Although Gilkes was ordained as priest immediately after resigning his post in 1914 as Master, he was not in clerical orders when he was appointed. This was unusual for a Victorian or Edwardian headmaster: of the 55 members of the Headmasters' Conference in 1864 only six were laymen. H. G. Wells wrote in his biography of Frederick Sanderson, Gilkes's Head of Engineering at Dulwich who left to become a famous reforming Headmaster of Oundle (see below), that the English had at the time a fixed belief that only clergymen were capable of maintaining a 'satisfactory moral and religious tone'.[7] Gilkes's tenure challenged that assumption.

Possessing 'features of an Hellenic cast', Gilkes stood six feet seven inches high, and for most of his time at Dulwich wore an impressive grey beard. His habits were healthy, and he was said to display none of the overworked and harassed air characteristic of his contemporary headmasters. His Olympian stature was thought to be symbolic, and boys were said to confuse him with God the Father, Zeus, Thor or Odin.[8] In his early years he wore a top hat and frock coat and would watch the Rugby football clutching his umbrella to him; a grey tweed suit and cap later became his habitual wear. 'Known for his great and generous heart' on his arrival at Dulwich, within three months *The Alleynian* was reporting that Gilkes's kindly interest had made him 'already extremely popular with every class in the school'.[9] Warm tributes to Gilkes by his pupils abound; the great socialist and journalist H. W. Nevinson (1856–1941), a devoted pupil from Shrewsbury, wrote that 'I do not know whether in other great public schools there has been a master who without effort inspired the reverence that he did at Shrewsbury'. He was 'the noblest character I have ever known', he continued, 'my motive and model'. When Nevinson later visited him at Dulwich, Gilkes seemed like 'a mountain pine removed to a suburban garden'.[10]

Gilkes's speech habits were fastidious. His successor George Smith said that he scrupulously avoided words that seemed 'to leave a stain somehow on the spirit of man and to be unworthy of his lips'; he particularly detested all 'slang' and abbreviations such as 'exam' or 'matric'. When reading the part of Lady Macbeth in class, on coming to the phrase 'Out, damned spot!' he is said to have paused and said, "I'm afraid I must say it". The tall bearded headmaster often found in books by P. G. Wodehouse is Gilkes, and in a mischievous early story he is imagined at the breakfast-table correcting his wife as to the proper use of *who* and *whom*.[11] No one, it was said, ever rode so slowly on a bicycle. Although he rarely left the College premises, he rode to suburban villages and to the College Mission on Sunday after-

noons on a specially constructed 'iron steed', said to resemble a giraffe; he took boys on cycling trips to Wiltshire and Hampshire.[12]

Gilkes was so dedicated to his work that even his marriage and family seem an Alleynian enterprise. At eight o'clock one morning before a school day in 1892 he was married to Millicent Mary Clarke, the sister of the current Captain of Rugby, Henry Clarke of Clairville, Sydenham Hill; the courtship was short and an Italian honeymoon was much delayed. Though often sleepless with anxieties over the school, however, he would never confide them to her.[13] The couple had four sons and one daughter (who died at the age of five), and the boys grew up to become, as it were, an extension of their father's devotion to the College. They were all interesting and distinguished Dulwich boys, who, as one may see from *The Alleynian*, contributed greatly to College activities, whether in sporting, military, literary or musical fields. Martin Heming Gilkes (1893–1945), who lost a leg in the War, was a poet and a schoolmaster at his father's Alma Mater, Shrewsbury, and lectured at the Workers' Educational Association in Birmingham; he published *A Key to Modern English Poetry* in 1937, and a timely anthology, *Tribute to England* (1939). Lieutenant Humphrey Gilkes (1895–1945) enlisted on leaving school in 1914, and was conspicuously gallant in the Great War, being awarded the Military Cross with three 'bars'. He went on to take a degree at Oxford and then to study Medicine at Bart's Hospital, and joined the Colonial Medical Service, dying in a flying accident in British Somaliland, where he was Principal Medical Officer, on the eve of his departure for home on leave. A plaque in the Lower Hall records the gratitude of the Protectorate and its people for his kindness and consideration. Christopher Herman Gilkes (1898–1953), Captain of School and a Classical Scholar at Trinity College, Oxford, after teaching at Uppingham until appointed Headmaster of Stockport Grammar School in 1928, was himself to become Master of Dulwich from 1941 until his premature death in 1953. According to Sheila Hodges, the strain of saving the College from extinction after the Second World War 'almost certainly' killed him';[14] he may be seen, perhaps, almost as the Isaac to his father's Abraham, sacrificed for the good of the College of God's Gift. Antony Newcombe Gilkes (1900–77) was born in what is now a classroom in the family quarters in the South Block; he recalled a childhood memory of playing in the Master's large garden (where the Science Block is today), and hearing the cries of the peacocks from Sir Evan Spicer's park at Belair.[15] He was appointed High Master of St Paul's in the year of Christopher's death, and served until 1962; he published *The Impact of the Dead Sea Scrolls* in 1962.

It is hard to think of another headmaster in the history of British schools who was felt to deserve an elaborate book in his memory 16 years after his death, and fully 24 after his retirement. The chronicle and tribute, *Gilkes and Dulwich, 1885–1914: A Study of a Great Headmaster* was published by the Alleyn Club in 1938, its various contributions edited by his admiring and loyal former pupil and colleague W. R. M. Leake (see below). The book quickly sold out. The filial epigraph to the book, taken from Matthew Arnold's tribute to his own father in 'Rugby Chapel', aptly bestows an almost mythic status upon Gilkes, by an implicit comparison of his cheerful zeal and inspiration from beyond the grave with that of Thomas Arnold, perhaps his closest rival in stature in the history of British education, and the founding father of the Christian Public School spirit; the two were like great men of a heroic epoch:

> Yes! I believe that there lived
> Others like *thee* in the past,
> Not like the men of the crowd
> Who all around me to-day
> Bluster or cringe, and make life
> Hideous, and arid, and vile,
> But souls temper'd with fire,
> Fervent, heroic and good
> Helpers and friends of mankind.

The analogy with Arnold is emphasised in the Preface to *Gilkes and Dulwich*: both men believed in the same order of priorities for a public schoolboy: firstly, religious and moral principles; second, gentlemanly conduct; third, intellectual ability.[16] The logic of the code of self-sacrifice and the application of intellect to conduct of course led to the noble part played by the College in the Great War. Most schools have proud stories to tell of extreme gallantry by their servicemen, but there is something distinctively Alleynian in the story of the daring seaborne assault on Zeebrugge on St George's Day, 1918, with the smoke screen devised by Wing-Commander F. A. Brock (1884–1918), in which six Old Boys took part and three, including Brock, lost their lives (see Chapter Nine). Gilkes's didactic emphasis on selflessness undoubtedly played a part in the terrible glory of Dulwich's sacrifice for our freedom. The names of the 510 men who were killed, died of wounds or were lost at sea in the First World War are listed in bronze at the foot of a Cross in front of the College; in a sense they belong to this chapter rather than to the next where chronology places them and where their gallantries are mentioned. Among the 3,052 Alleynians who served, there were five awards of the Victoria Cross, 102 of the Distinguished Service Order and 264 of the Military Cross (see Chapter Nine).

A. H. Gilkes. Carte de visite (detail). (Dulwich College)

Gilkes seldom retired to sleep later than ten o'clock in the evening; he rose early, walked round his garden for an hour, and dealt personally with his school correspondence before school. He taught for three hours a day, including visits to each form in the College in turn; he would appear in the doorway and say, "Mr So and So, may I take your form?" He also regularly supervised both Boarders' Prep in the Great Hall, two evenings a week, and two hours of Detention every Saturday afternoons.[17] In *Gilkes and Dulwich* there are descriptions of his teaching by two Classicist heads of Oxford and Cambridge Colleges (see below), Alic Smith, Warden of New College, and Sir Jack Sheppard, Provost of King's. Smith praised Gilkes's Plato classes in terms which remind one of accounts of Plato's Academy itself, while Sheppard wrote of Gilkes that

> by his touch of genius [he] gave life and made the labour fruit-
> ful. The secret of that genius was the fruit of his character, the
> fruit of his religion; but it was a quality (perhaps the rarest
> quality) of mind that made him a great scholar and a great

teacher, a freshness of imagination, disciplined yet free, unspoilt by any touch of self-aggrandisement or vanity.[18]

Above all he liked to teach Plato, but enjoyed Aristophanes, Virgil, Lucretius and Horace, and also Dryden, Pope, Tennyson and Browning. Being 'extraordinarily susceptible to the pathos of tragedy', he could not bear to read with his class the chorus from Sophocles' *Agamemnon* which describes how the priest demands the sacrifice of the king's daughter, Iphigenia, on her wedding day, in order to obtain fair weather for the Greek ships in their voyage to Troy.[19] He detested the cynical Tacitus and the decadence of late Rome, a judgement reflected in the historical novels he wrote. Although Gilkes was not generally considered a scholar of the first rank, his close questioning of pupils over particular passages from an author's works was designed to reveal what they liked and why, and to make them aware of what they really believed: 'it seemed to us that he was set on leading us to think on many subjects which we had hitherto passed by as being of no concern of ours; that he was guiding us to use our own judgement where we had formerly accepted the prevailing view', wrote R. N. Douglas (see Chapter Seven), in a memorably simple description of the teacher's art. Typical Gilkes digressions might involve the subjects of citizenship, Beau Brummel, or the fads and foibles of Queen Victoria. The Classics master Philip Hope (see below) told how Gilkes had said to him, "The boys take their History paper tomorrow. Can you tell me what is the period?"[20] The aim of his teaching was not to 'cram' set books or historical periods for an examination, but to 'store the boys' minds with noble examples, impressive warnings and all that might fortify and uplift the character'. His faith in the vocation of a teacher is clear:

A master's work is in many respects the best in the world, and the most important. It is the preparation of the young for their lives. … A master should love his work; that is the main point about him: with a love that is not checked by any reverse, and does not know satiety.[21]

Despite Welldon's reforms, discipline at the College was still lax by the time of Gilkes's arrival. Boys were habitually unpunctual, some even presumptuously taking the day off school to watch the Boat Race without asking leave. After Welldon's robust authoritarianism, Gilkes's quietist manner was mistaken for 'grandmotherly' ineffectuality, and at first he struggled to assert his authority. His anger could nevertheless be fearsome; watching a game of Rugby football from the touchlines on one occasion, he was so incensed to hear a forward of the visiting team swear that he strode on to the field, majestic in his top hat

and frock coat, and stopped the game after only fifteen minutes' play. In gentler mode, once when a carter making a delivery was heard to swear at his horse, Gilkes put his head out of the classroom window and said, "Don't say that to your horse; *he doesn't like it*".[22] The rule he gradually effected was not wholly achieved by sweet persuasion, though he seldom caned a boy; at the same time, he confided to his diary in 1896 how earnestly he deplored the 'lawless', noisy indiscipline of certain prominent boys, behaviour that mostly went unchecked by Gilkes's own staff. Matters temporarily improved after some boys were expelled,[23] but incidents of unruly behaviour continued to plague him – boys disrupting concerts by stamping or throwing paper (and even pellets of lead shot), or gathering in packs to snowball a train and its driver. Not that Gilkes's forbearance gained universal support among the boys themselves, as P. G. Wodehouse's stringent account, in a notebook he kept soon after leaving the College, indicates:

Boys respect strength and nothing but strength. They may dislike it, but they respect it. A school is like a child. The mother who alternately spoils and storms at a child makes it unmanageable. Same with a headmaster at a school. Gilkes goes on apologising to everyone, even when he is in the right, and then when things get out of hand he makes them worse by stopping the concert on field day. Or worse, by saying he has stopped it and then giving way at the last moment.[24]

Characterised by his earliest pupils as 'grandmotherly' and later by Wodehouse as an over-indulgent mother, Gilkes's strategic installation of discipline at Dulwich College is perhaps more accurately described as paternal. As the head of the Dulwich family, he believed in replicating the family's hierarchy by developing the loyal unit of the form, or class, with a Form Master acting in the same pastoral way as a housemaster to boarders, infusing them with a group spirit. In 1892 he also appointed a band of Prefects, following Thomas Arnold's model at Rugby; the original number of 24 was increased to 30 in 1900.[25] The Prefect system improved the discipline of a school where the College Porter, Bidgood, had had to stop playground fights at breaks with his stick and where later, under Welldon, Sixth Formers had carried out 'functions of a very vague character'. At the same time the Prefects themselves learned to understand responsibility and to develop their own character. Gilkes was quite extraordinarily unhappy whenever a Prefect let the College down, and he declared that he would rather see one of them dead than hear him swear. As part of the same encouragement, Gilkes continued the policy of boys allowing boys to run school activities; by 1894 there were no longer any masters on the Field Sports Committee.[26]

Gilkes and the Prefects, 1900. P. G. Wodehouse top row, fourth from right, (not facing camera).

Immediately following his appointment in 1885, Gilkes made two significant policy statements to the Governors: first, he declared the salaries of the staff to be grievously inadequate; second, he announced his intention of dividing the Classical and Modern Sides from lower down the school. He inherited an Army Class from Welldon, but soon absorbed it into the Modern Side. Science and Engineering Sides were his additions to the College's structure. Chemistry was taught to large numbers of boys, but only 13 took Physics. He also made a point of talking individually to every boy in the College, and was said to possess their minds like a conscience, in fear of his judgement.[27] This was no small achievement in itself, given the College's roll of 525 boys in his first year as Master.

Gilkes prescribed his boys' routine (up at 7.30 a.m. and to bed no later than 10.30),[28] and even how many hours a day they should work once they moved on to university. He was perhaps fortunate to live in an age when he could be more concerned with boys' characters than with examination successes, believing passionately that knowledge for its own sake was the goal, rather than a means to an end. For Gilkes, education aimed towards the disciplined will in its service of others, and he repeatedly emphasised that 'the end of education is the same as the end of life, and that is the subordination of self to the highest power that can be known'.[29] His calling forth a modern version of the Periclean καλὸς κἀγαθός [Aristotle's ideal of the perfectly educated and virtuous man] from Dulwich boys, and their achievement of a genuine *esprit de corps* at the College, resembled a missionary spirit that led W. D. Gibbon (see below) to pronounce that while Carver fought a great fight to save the body of the College, Gilkes gave it a soul.[30] Gilkes's canons of behaviour and of the qualities to be aimed for in the formation of character were not merely headmasterly truisms, but were observed, meditated and deeply felt; in an article of 1907, 'The Education of Boys', he wrote:

The Cloister, post 1886; a Prefect, left, wears a cap quartered in black and blue. (Dulwich College)

the aim we have is to make the boys who come to us real men. ... The qualities which make a man are truthfulness, cleanness, courage, public spirit, kindness, with an understanding quickened in all directions, and most of all in the direction of that unseen Power which rules us all. ... We should not, for example, scold a willing boy, nor compliment a conceited boy, nor teach a poetical boy nothing but mathematics, nor do nothing but stimulate the imagination of one who loves to deal only with that which admits of accurate measurement.[31]

A second definition Gilkes gave of 'real men' added the virtues of health, self-restraint, patience, judgement, quickness and fullness of intellect.[32] There is much evidence that for many of the boys Gilkes, that bearded patriarch, continued to represent a standard of good behaviour long after they left, as someone to whom they could neither pretend nor lie. He made a point of calling on each Alleynian at Oxford and Cambridge in their lodgings and of attending Old Alleynian dinners at the two universities.[33] Sir Jack Sheppard seems to have kept all the letters that Gilkes wrote to him; among them is one seeking reassurance that he had not participated in some

blasphemous undergraduate mock services at King's that had been reported in the press.[34]

Gilkes cared almost as passionately that boys should not lie as that they should not swear. He also knew that it was important not to trifle with their self-respect, as is shown in the advice he included in a letter to W. R. M. Leake with advice about running a school boarding house and the proper relations he should establish with the boys. He said that a good master should show neither great familiarity with boys nor about them with others, and should avoid personal remarks and jokes about rules and punishments. 'Boys should be treated with the utmost respect and politeness and with everyone's best manner and his company manner – if indeed he has two manners, which perhaps he should not'. He recommends a settled and firm pressure rather than sporadic angry punishment, together with a strict and constant observation of justice. 'Each boy of course needs a different method and tone and treatment to bring out what is good within him', he writes, 'although in our bungling way perhaps ten out of twenty are not much hurt yet the other ten are, and some very badly with wounds that last through life'.[35] At the same time, Gilkes was never particularly supportive of staff who complained of disciplinary problems with boys, saying that they should fight their own battles, or else – which must have felt much worse – that it was the man's own fault and not the boy's: "Your nerves are out of order. Have you not been smoking too much?" 'The boy you dislike most', he also wrote, 'is the one from whom by study you can learn the most. And why does he dislike you?'[36]

It is claimed that Gilkes knew every boy in the College, and stories of his generosity to them are common. Ernest Shackleton, for example – not yet a favourite son of the College – was always in trouble, but was to remember well how Gilkes gave him fielding practice. On another occasion, Gilkes approached the great sportsman and future surgeon W. D. Doherty (1893–1966; Superintendent of Guy's Hospital, 1948–58, and a College Governor). "I saw you play a frightful shot this afternoon," he said, inviting him to his study, where he handed him his umbrella to use as a bat, and bowled him a ball of paper.[37] Another boy, ambitious to become a teacher himself, was coached by Gilkes for three evenings a week to help improve his accent. Once, when he had severely scolded a younger boy in front of the class for neglecting his work, and aware that the boy was obsessed with Egyptology, Gilkes came back into the room to present him with two large volumes of an expensive book on hieroglyphics.[38] Philip Hope thought that Gilkes wasted time with such attentions to the boys, and should mix more with society.[39]

Meanwhile the catchment area and social background of Dulwich boys remained similar to those in Carver's day, but the number of boarders went up; by 1889 they stood at 13.5 per cent.[40] In 1892 Rendall opened a fourth house, The Orchard, on Dulwich Common. At Prize-giving in 1907 the Hon. Alfred Lyttelton (1857–1913), former Colonial Secretary, cricketer and Etonian beau idéal, said he was glad to see boys from Siam and China winning prizes.[41] In 1913 Gilkes mentioned to the Governors more boys from overseas: three Indians, a Turk and two Africans. Many Burmese also attended. In 1914 the Governors limited the number of 'Oriental' boarders to twelve.[42]

At the same time, for all Gilkes's noble idealism, certain blind spots inhibited the College under his tenure. A puritanical suspicion of contemporary art brought an end to the great epoch of Alleynian artists; Gilkes and Dulwich admits that painting got no encouragement. However, Gilkes chose books by Ruskin as prizes, and his unpublished essays show an admiration for Rubens, Turner and Claude. He had a telling dislike of Chopin.[43] His reading habits, beyond Classical texts, he classified as middle-brow, being confined to Scott's

Waverley novels, W. W. Jacobs, and detective stories (a medium in which he wrote himself but never published), together with The Times and the Daily Mail, but he was actually no philistine in literature; P. G. Wodehouse, who told his own biographer that Gilkes always 'scared the pants off me', still recalled 75 years later the 'Old Man' declaiming in his deep musical voice a visionary passage from Carlyle's Sartor Resartus (Book I, chapter iii) describing the panorama of a lurid City of Dreadful Night, the effect of which was 'terrific'.[44] Yet Gilkes also arrested the development of the literary quality of The Alleynian, making it clear that he disapproved of poetry or stories being included 'except as far as these have a direct bearing on school life'.[45] The Alleynian of the period often gives a distinctly philistine sporting impression: of the thirty-six pages of one issue in 1901 twenty-eight were reports of Rugby football. Photographs of the XI and the XV were introduced as frontispieces in 1894, immortalising the College's heroes; it was not until Booth's day in the 1930s that photographs of play productions were given this accolade. Although Gilkes declared on Speech Day in 1889 that the school had achieved 'a happy mean between too much athletics and too little', this was hardly reflected in the magazine.[46]

Gilkes's blind spots were connected with his moral outlook; he did not like individuals drawing too much attention to themselves. "Don't look at that boy," he would say. "He wants to be taken notice of".[47] He notoriously disapproved of Lawn Tennis, as it gave glamour to individuals, and he refused to allow its introduction at the College, in spite of the fact that it was played by almost every other school; a letter to The Alleynian in 1890 claimed that 80 per cent of boys would prefer tennis to cricket.[48] He loathed the swagger of the Henley Regatta and indeed the whole public relations aspect of sporting fixtures, and would not allow the annual match against St Paul's to be played at Lord's Cricket Ground.[49] At a prize-giving in 1913 he gave as his reason for banning tennis that it would harm cricket;[50] cricket, being a team game, had his entire approval. His own appearances as wicket-keeper at the Masters' Matches were famous, as in 1890 when he 'stumped' two boys and caught two others; in 1906, after several years' absence, he scored 13, making 'a fine late cut and two or three nice drives'.[51] His attitude to sports was that they existed for health and courage, to learn the give and take of life, to lose self-consciousness and to learn how to hold your own with your fellows; success was unimportant and selfish, and he would say to boys that he was very glad they had won, but it would probably have been just as good for them if they hadn't.[52] Wodehouse, reading Gilkes and Dulwich in 1938, took great exception to this remark and to Gilkes telling W. D. Gibbon that when he was forty he would be much more pleased to remember that he was in the Sixth Form than in the First XV for Rugby football: 'you rather get the impression of Gilkes as a man who was always trying to damp people, to keep them from getting above themselves', he wrote to Bill Townend, before adding a delicious parody of the 'Old Man': "So you made a century against Tonbridge, did you, my boy? Well, always remember that you will soon be dead, and in any case, the bowling was probably rotten".[53] Gilkes admonished boys who allowed games to usurp the position which work should take in their lives.[54] The conflict between work and sports is a subject of the best of Wodehouse's six school novels and of many short stories based on his Dulwich experiences, including *Mike* of 1909, praised by George Orwell as the best 'light' school story ever written.[55]

One wonders if Gilkes ever thought that the cult of suppressed personality might be dull; he wrote in his diary in the spring of 1904 that he would suppress waistcoats of differing colours among the boys, saying 'the matter is of more importance than appears at first sight to everyone'. Gilkes was, however, something of an actor and must have found a mask convenient: he had a caustic wit and sometimes indulged in merciless chaff; he claimed that Nature intended him for a buffoon, and that he had

Gilkes walking back to the Pavilion after batting at the Masters' match, date unknown. (Dulwich College)

therefore always to be careful to preserve his dignity.[56] All agreed that his Ascension Day addresses to the boys were wonderful; he would begin hesitantly in a low voice, and he spoke simply, but left the congregated boys 'with a sense of solemn things in life and of holiness, and of the worth of human dignity'.[57] On the other hand, some said that his weekly Prefects' Lessons in the Masters' Library were tedious; Wodehouse, moreover, wrote that reading one's essay to him on these occasions was 'akin to suicide'. Gilkes would set essays on the passages he had read aloud, and then comment on the boys' ideas and style; (Sir) William Holdsworth (see below), who became a very famous lawyer, gave Gilkes the absolute credit for teaching him in these classes both how to think and how to express himself on paper.[58] Unlike Welldon and George Smith, Gilkes never published his addresses to boys, but in 1899 he noted in his diary what he said to them about setbacks in the Boer War: it was their duty as Public School men to make themselves 'steady, strong and cheery whatever happens'. One sermon was later printed in *Gilkes and Dulwich*.[59] His rhetorical skill can be seen from many of his speeches to the Alleyn Club reported in *The Alleynian*. However, he made a disappointing farewell speech in 1914, to a record number of 217 diners; even so, as a stratagem 'to cover his distress', which was obvious to his friends,[60] he brought down the house by singing the tribe a School Song, 'Here's to the New Boy of Bashful Thirteen' (with words by his assistant in running the Mission, the Revd George Allen, to Rendall's music):

> Here's to him whose schooldays are done, Sir!
> Here's for the boy who his lessons could say!
> And here's to the boy who forgot 'em!
> Here's to him who right up to the top made his way!
> And here's to the boy at the bottom ...
> Hurrah for Alleynians everywhere!
> Hurrah for the black and the blue, Sir!

Ernest Shackleton spoke after Gilkes's song at this dinner and said it 'was the most human thing he had ever heard'. Alic Smith recalled many years later that Gilkes, with his sense of theatre and of the ridiculous, made his exit through some curtains on a stage in the restaurant where the dinner was held, turning to the company and saying "Good-night".[61]

Gilkes's love of the absurd is seen in his one song, a charmingly ridiculous parlour piece about the Middle Ages, which he would sing in public (for example at the Master's Supper in Great Hall on Founder's Day, or at Cambridge Alleynian dinners): 'Simon the Cellarer' has his six flagons a day and a red nose, while Dame Margery, a beldame with a wicked tongue, keeps a bottle of something to keep out the cold in a cupboard behind the back stair. Simon thinks of taking Margery for a wife, but settles for a tankard instead:

> While ho! Ho! Ho! He will chuckle and crow,
> What, marry old Margery, no, no, no.[62]

Other blind spots that influenced life at the College were his objection to young trebles singing solos and his 'insuperable' objection to boys playing female parts in plays; the latter was the real reason why he stopped the tradition of the highly successful Dulwich Play at Christmas, after the production of *Henry IV* in 1884, although the few female roles had all been excised in the version adapted for the boys. He changed the tribal mode of entertainment from drama to music, and a performance of Handel's *Acis and Galatea* followed, Gilkes claiming that the Play wasted time and that boys became puffed up on reading press notices of it.[63] This was a very unpopular decision. Gilkes wrote that boys playing women's parts was a 'dangerous and unwholesome' practice, and 'open to criticism', by which he meant that it might harm the 'purity' of the boys, leading to adolescent sexual inversion;[64] his staff admired his 'excellent tact in dealing with the purity question', itself the unhealthy preoccupation of many Victorian and Edwardian schoolmasters.[65] Gilkes had no doubts that this ban was for the good of the school.[66] In 1899 he expelled nine boys for 'uncleanness', one of them from the First XV, and the others Fourth Formers, many of them both liked and honoured by him, as he wrote in his diary. His colleagues recalled that for a fortnight he would hardly speak to anyone for grief, and walked with his head bowed.[67] 'Manly' and 'manful' were among his ideals for the boys, as we have seen. In his diary he is accordingly more enthusiastic about the military entertainment called the 'Assault at Arms' (see below), which consisted of gymnastics, boxing, fencing and knockabout silent comedy, than he was about *Henry IV*.[68] The brilliant extracts and scenes from plays presented at Founder's Day, however, provided an opportunity for actors, and here a boy was allowed to play Nerissa in *The Merchant of Venice* in 1888, and another to play Portia in the same play in 1903. One of several similar letters from Old Alleynians printed in *The Alleynian* of 1888 protested that 'no fellow can understand' why the plays are abolished.[69]

Gilkes's own novels and other writings throw light on his beliefs and his mentality. At worst, such as in the short essay *The New Revolution* (1903), about community and religion, about change and the necessity of submission to God's will, his writing tends to vague metaphysical idealism. *A Day at Dulwich* (1905), however, reveals some of the ways in which he saw the school: he thought that the mixture of boarding and day boys was excellent, since in a boarding school boys form their own codes without reference to the opinions of their elders, whereas at Dulwich this was curbed by the more pragmatic day boys.[70] He recalled the prolonged wrangles over the Dulwich Schemes, deploring those men who desired only a school for poorer boys. The boys in *A Day at Dulwich* are obsessed with the Tonbridge match. One boy flaunts a scented handkerchief, a motif that Wodehouse also uses in one of his stories. A Prefect decides to tell a lie and cut school to watch the 'Varsity match. A Socratic younger teacher gives lessons on Cicero with probing questions to extract universal truths and to relate the material to contemporary social, political and ethical questions. In an earlier work, *The Thing That Hath Been; or a Young Man's Mistakes* (1894) another Socratic teacher, an outsider to public schools, comes to appreciate the general development of the average boy as being the most valuable part of a schoolmaster's job rather than the special training of particular faculties, and also comes to understand and to value the sense of honour and the other qualities of 'public school tradition'.[71] *Boys and Masters* (1887) is sharp and penetrating both about bachelor teachers, with their jealousies and favourites, and about boys' pride, vanities and quarrels. A 'crib' [an English translation from the Classics used to save boys from doing homework] is thrown into the river. In both this novel and *A Day at Dulwich* the hero is an honest boy who makes himself unpopular with his peers for a moral cause. The 'steadfast' open boy is contrasted with a snobbish and vain boy whose father loses his fortune and learns from this symbolic punishment.

Gilkes's two novels with classical settings, *Kallistratus* (1897) and *Four Sons* (1916), likewise assert that success and happiness depend not upon wealth and licence, but on morality and faith. In the former, set in the Italy of the fourth century BC, his young Greek hero preserves his integrity in the decadent Empire by a moral stance. As with Gilkes's Classical Sixth, in his novels his thinking men take up arms.

Gilkes was twice moved to take a moral stance himself, offering to resign on principle, in 1909 and in 1914, on both occasions after Reports from Board of Education Inspections (see below) reported that his methods were damagingly conservative. In 1909 the Governors and staff gave him an unanimous vote of confidence and he changed his mind.[72] In 1914 he also gained some notoriety for the distressed letter he wrote to the *Daily Mail* protesting against the outbreak of war: 'could not something be done to stop this miserable nonsense which is making everybody wretched?'[73]

Gilkes is said to have believed that he was more successful with the Mission than with his famous work at the College; when his second offer of resignation was accepted, and he retired in time of war, the current of his feeling and his faith called him in humility to further his work for the poor; in October 1915 he was ordained, and turning to Edward Alleyn's Southwark, he served until 1917 as a curate at St James's, Bermondsey, in a very poor parish near Tower Bridge. A newspaper reports him, characteristically, teaching Greek to the young men in his care, in hope that they would enter the Church. In 1917, at the age of 68, Christ Church, Oxford, appointed him vicar of St Mary Magdalen. At Oxford he transcribed letters received from his three sons, Martin, Humphrey and Christopher, written on service in France and India during the Great War – the youngest, Antony, did not enlist, as he did not leave the College until 1919 – and presented the manuscript to the Library at Christ Church.[74] Because of the War, all his four sons were afterwards contemporary undergraduates at Oxford, at the time that Gilkes and his wife were living there. Here also he wrote a series of short stories on historical, ghost and detective themes, to which he gave the stiff title of *Parerga Scholastica* [incidental school matters]. This included a most remarkable Dulwich story about a boy applying for a London County Council Scholarship at the school (see below). He died of a heart attack on the pavement by his doorstep at 53 Broad Street, Oxford, in 1922.

At one of his beloved Alleyn Club dinners, Gilkes once proposed a Spenserian allegory about the College which shows his absolute devotion to the school and pride in it, and is simultaneously high-minded, touching and faintly ridiculous:

> It is a great College; it is a great School. It is what I may call a great chariot drawn by varied teams of horses: there are the white horses, sacred, spotless – those are the Governors. They are seldom seen in the flesh, except on very exceptional occasions, but they draw. Then there are the black horses – they are the masters; but we are not so black as we are sometimes painted. Then there are the grey horses, the parents; and then the Old Boys; and then the colts, the present boys, whom we all regard with great hope as those to whom we all set a very admirable example of what they should become in due time. Sometimes the horses are taken out of the chariot and they sit down together and chat together and eat heartily and drink pure water from the well. And the lady we draw in the chariot, what a great, beautiful lady she is; her jewels how splendid! How beneficently she comes to us when we are idle and says, "Work! That you may do me honour"; and when we do what we ought not to do she says, "Do not do it, because I should be shamed among my sisters." She is a great lady. I hardly think there is any greater in the land.[75]

The College Mission in Camberwell

Gilkes had hardly settled at the College for a term when, shortly before Christmas 1885, he discussed with the Captain of School his intention of setting up a Mission, along the lines of the great urban Oxford and Cambridge evangelical missions of the late nineteenth century. A letter appeared in *The Alleynian*, and Gilkes held a meeting to inaugurate a Dulwich College Mission.[76] Based on his experience at Shrewsbury, he proposed to involve both masters and boys in subsidising and helping to run a residential Boys' Home for orphans in Camberwell, together with a Club for neighbouring boys from 14 to 17 years old. The motive was to help 'London-born' orphans and the deprived, in the spirit of Edward Alleyn, and at the same time to give College boys a Christian exercise in putting other people first, learning social and moral awareness by experience. Subscriptions were invited, and a house was taken for the first premises at 104 Walworth Road, an area notorious for poverty and ill health, at £45 per annum. The boys who lived at the house paid four shillings weekly out of their wages for their board and lodging, and the Club charged a penny a week for membership. Gilkes began to talk about the Mission at Prize Days, and frequently told the Governors of progress. He wrote in his Annual Report of 1891 that it was flourishing, and was creating 'great pride and interest among the boys of the College'.[77] There is no record of dialogue about the Mission with the Governors, but their attitude seems best described as a polite disdain for a project that swiftly got into debt. The Minutes include no further reference to the Mission after 1893, following Gilkes's slightly plaintive remark that 'I hope the governors will be pleased to hear' some detail of its progress, and his submission to them of a circular about it (which does not survive). Many people said that Gilkes would be better employed talking to his staff.[78] The response from boys, masters and Old Boys, however, was remarkable. The Alleyn Club contributed ten guineas a week until 1909, and then doubled their grant. For many years the amounts collected by the forms at the College and the names of the collector were printed annually in *The Alleynian*; Old Alleynians also contributed: Shackleton's scapegrace brother Frank (see below) sent half a crown for many years, and P. G. Wodehouse sent two pounds in 1905. Stories of extortion by competitive form collectors were current, and boys who would not contribute were thrown out of ground-floor windows.[79] For many decades any coin dropped by a boy had to be donated to the Mission. By February 1888 there were three boys living in the Home and ten members of the Club. *The Alleynian* appealed for board-games, boxing gloves, beds and a Manager. The following year there were four boys and the Club had 32 members.[80] The Mission

The College Mission: the Junior Club, 1924. (Dulwich College)

moved to larger premises at 282 Walworth Road in 1892. There was a Gymnasium, and Edward Everett (see Chapter Six) acted as boxing coach; boxing is still a great strength of the Mission today. It is now called the Hollington Club, after its first premises (originally a donkey-shed) in Hollington Street, and (since 1910) is situated in Comber Grove. An Old Alleynian, Frank Edward King (1877–1945), coached the boys in gymnastics; after the Great War he gave up his career as an analytical chemist to devote himself entirely to the Club. It was a point of honour that the Mission boys learned to swim. An Assistant Master, Norman Graham Brownrigg (1874–1936), gave classes in Mathematics.

Every Sunday afternoon Gilkes would visit the Mission and tell the 'spell-bound' boys stories;[81] often he would be accompanied by a senior boy or two from the College. There followed a service held by the College Chaplain on Sunday at four o'clock, which was well attended. In the evenings a Men's Club, started by Gilkes, discussed moral and religious questions. Some College boys became inspired with a 'missionary spirit'; the movement gathered real strength, and in 1914 some Old Alleynians formed a Guild for Old Alleynians working in missions.[82] Medical examinations and advice were given gratis, and records of these examinations survive, in bound volumes, in the College Archives; for each boy there is a page with an engraving of the thorax, annotated by the doctor, who also wrote comments on the boys'

clothing and cleanliness. In 1908 the Home housed eighteen boys aged from 14 to 18; work was found for them, or help with emigration; and they were clothed by Alleynians. Football and cricket were played. A list of the Mission boys' names and their employments in *The Alleynian* for 1909 is uncannily reminiscent of a list of the Poor Scholars and their apprenticeships from earlier centuries.[83] In 1904 and 1905 W. D. Gibbon, who was both an Old Alleynian and an Assistant Master, was Permanent Resident at the Home and succeeded a paid manager.[84] In 1905 the Old Alleynian Guild took over the management of St John's Institute, a Cambridge mission house. In 1912 an appeal was launched for new premises at 7 Flodden Road, to house twenty boys.[85] Among other surviving records of the Mission are photograph albums of many of the annual camps at Birling Gap in Sussex over more than fifty years, and of holidays on a houseboat at Rye Harbour strung with hammocks, a vivid lost smiling world of cheerful innocence; for many of the Camberwell lads this was their first sight of the sea. The Scout movement was involved and a Mission troop was set up in 1909. Eight Mission Scouts died in a tragic boating accident in 1912, and are commemorated by a monument at Peckham Cemetery.

In 1923 a pleasant article by an anonymous recent Old Alleynian describing a visit to the Hollington Club, which was taken over by the Mission in February of that year, appeared in *The Alleynian*. The writer felt depressed and uneasy on the rough street, he wrote, but on entering the Club was immediately made welcome at the mere sight of his OA tie; he described a cosy room with a fire, a lady cooking porridge, the Mission dog 'Olly [Holly], the pandemonium of 108 boys, games of chess and billiards, boys going out for a run, and taking baths. He also heard about the football team, the Doctor's visits, the camps, and the seventy older boys who belonged to the Club. [86] The highly successful Mission was the direct result of Gilkes's practical social ideals and of his humility.

The Governors

Under Gilkes relations between the Master and the Governors became less volatile, and from the available evidence, they enjoyed each other's confidence and respect after the sorry story of Carver's years. On his retirement Gilkes wrote to them to say that he had always found that they 'easily forgave my faults, and honoured me with kindly feelings and gave wise advice and useful help'. [87] Such public letters are rarely candid, of course, but others have testified to the real sea-change that had come about. The Assistant Master 'Billy' Sweet-Escott (see Chapter Eight) recalled at an Alleyn Club dinner in 1912, 'When I came to Dulwich first more years ago than I care to remember, I thought the Governors were some kind of weird monsters whose only idea was to destroy and upset', but declared that for thirty years now he had been aware of their 'deepest interest' in the welfare of the College. [88] For this Gilkes himself, and a series of excellent experienced Chairmen, were greatly to be thanked.

There was a financial crisis in the Estate in the early years of the new century, which stunted the subsidy to the College. The College Governors were of course no longer responsible for the management of the Estate, although some Governors sat on both the College and the Estate Boards. The College Governors were also a joint Board, responsible for Alleyn's School until 1995. Gilkes was unworldly, and almost always overspent his Budget year after year; he was censured in Governors' Minutes for his accounts, which were called 'unsatisfactory' or 'a little vague'. In particular he habitually dispensed charity to worthy retired people with gratuities, pensions and part-time employment. Gilkes expressed to the Governors his fears that they would think him 'a careless steward exceeding his grants with a light heart', and assured them that this was not the case. He was told sharply to keep expenditure to his estimates in 1907, but in 1913 seriously overspent his allocation again. [89] Through these years Gilkes constantly complained that the staff, 'a most loyal body of men … a source of both wonder and extreme satisfaction', were 'considerably under-paid'. There was a constant stream of 'novices' passing rapidly to better posts, leading, he

said, to inefficiency and mischief, and an 'uneasy and troubled' feeling among the Assistant Masters. [90]

Gilkes demonstrated none of Carver's intransigence, but perhaps applied a touch of moral blackmail, though undoubtedly he meant what he said, in his repeated suggestions to the Governors that they take away as much as they chose from his annual salary – between £2,000 and £2,100 – so that his young masters could be paid more. They would not fall in with this proposal, and he had to wait a good many years for salaries to improve, by which time they were even more unsatisfactory. [91] In 1888 the Governors were at odds over Gilkes's constant appeals for a new Chapel to be built on the New College site, just as Welldon had proposed; one of them suggested that the old building should be made over to a new Ecclesiastical district and a new Chapel should definitely be built, but this was never to happen. [92] Gilkes meanwhile asked for the boys to sit in the chancel at Chapel services, where the Village faithful traditionally sat; it was, he pointed out, 'unseemly' for a great school not to have the main influence on services, and for the boys to occupy the worst seats. The Villagers clung to the Chapel out of habit, although every house was now assigned to one of the new parishes and their large churches in the neighbourhood, St Barnabas (1892–5; paid for by the Estates Governors) and All Saints (1887–91). When Gilkes was refused a new and larger Chapel on the New College site again in 1895, perhaps hoping to shame the Governors, he said that he would raise subscriptions to build a temporary 'iron construction' chapel there for £300. [93] Before Good Friday in 1896 he got his way about the seating in the old Chapel and the Villagers now sat in the south gallery, but he never realised his dream of a new chapel. The Chapel choir in 1906 was formed of boys from the village school and six professional men singers; the services were in the seventeenth-century style, thought to be appropriate to the Foundation. [94]

Given that Alleyn's School in this period was recognised overtly as a school for 'preparation for business or commercial life', [95] just as the Revd William Rogers had once intended the College to become (see Chapter Six), it enjoyed great success under J. H. Smith, the Headmaster from 1888, and under his successors, and bestowed an education well beyond this aim. As time went by, and Alleyn's became filled with London County Council scholars, and accordingly benefited from Board of Education grants, it became less of a financial worry to the Governors; their books balanced better than the College's; moreover, the Annual Reports by the headmasters gave great satisfaction.

By 1905 only one of the 23 Governors, Langford Price (see Chapter Six), was an Old Alleynian. The Alleyn

F. G. Kitton, *The Chapel, Dulwich College*. 1897. (Dulwich College)

Club canvassed 17 schools in an unofficial survey, and discovered that compared with other schools the Old Boys enjoyed very poor representation on the College Board.[96] Later on, between the Wars, Old Alleynians were to give truly remarkable service on the Board, such as Sir Arthur Hirtzel (see Chapter Seven) as an outstanding Chairman, and Gilkes's own pupils Sir Jack Sheppard and Aubrey Attwater (see below) as nominees of the University of Cambridge, and Harold Hartley and Alic Smith of the University of Oxford.

Gilkes inherited the elderly and crippled William Rogers as Permanent Chairman of the Board, and seems to have liked him. Certainly Rogers had mellowed after thirty years on the Board, and appeared by now to be reconciled to the success of the College as a Public School; he was a constant attender at the boys' cricket and football matches.[97] In 1888 he gave the prizes, and said that he wanted the sons of Dulwich College to be gentlemen. Gilkes wrote in his diary that Rogers on this occasion cut a pleasing and genial figure, and admired his dignity. As he hobbled onto the platform with his two sticks, the boys cheered him 'to the echo'.[98] At the time

of Rogers's death at the age of 76 in 1895 he had actually submitted his resignation as Chairman, which had not yet been accepted. The embers of the old feud, however, still burned, and Gilkes recalled that Rogers said to him, "You wish to make Dulwich a public school and I have no wish to enter into a conflict with you: and therefore I shall resign my office"; he added that Rogers held 'too low a view of its mission and its position'.[99]

Rogers was followed as Chairman of the Governors by Horace, Lord Davey (1833–1907), who was at various times an MP, a famous Judge and the Solicitor-General; his obituary in *The Times* praised his 'personal attention' to the College;[100] this was an appointment very suitable for Gilkes's era, as Lord Davey was a Chairman who not only 'spared no pains' in his responsibility, but always wanted to hear about the 'average boy'; D. H. Moore (see below) said that it was Gilkes's ambition 'not to turn out great scholars and athletes, but to turn out numbers of the ordinary boys who would go out into the world better for having been at Dulwich'. On the death of Lord Davey the Governors recorded that 'the personal influence which he exercised was of signal utility and importance'.[101]

Davey was succeeded in 1907 by Sir Alfred Comyn Lyall (1835–1911), who had served in India as Foreign Secretary and hoped in vain to become Viceroy, but who turned down offers to govern the Cape Colony [South Africa] and New Zealand; returning to England, he rose to become Home Secretary in 1873 and Foreign Secretary in 1879. Lyall was a cultivated and an academic man who published poems and books on Tennyson and on the British dominion in India.[102] Lord Cheylesmore (1848–1925) followed Lyall in 1911. He was Chairman of the London County Council for an interesting period when the College and Alleyn's School were involved with scholarship schemes of LCC boys and with financial grants. With an Army background he was very keen to encourage rifle shooting.

In 1893 Gilkes was reported in the Governors' Minutes as deprecating the fact that that 'a large capital sum', which was needed by the College, was belatedly being allocated (according to the Scheme of 1881) to St Saviour's Grammar School in Southwark, which did not need the money.[103] He also told the Governors that they believed that a high standard could be achieved without materially increasing present expenditure. He deplored the fact that a Chapel for a major school would have to be built by voluntary contributions, reminded them that the bath house needed a new boiler, and complained that no money appeared to be forthcoming for new boarding houses or salaries or to improve the playgrounds.[104] In 1898 the Charity Commissioners added £1,000 per annum to the College's endowment to help with repairs, rates and taxes. A plan to build a boarding house at the north-west corner of the College grounds, facing Brightlands, came to nothing.[105] The College was starved financially when Gilkes was Master, despite his tenure coinciding with a broader economic prosperity in the country at large, which of course makes his achievements the more remarkable. Although the Estate was almost bankrupt in 1902, it rallied, and by 1905 it was reserving 25 acres on the Dulwich Common for a College or School of the highest quality for girls, with provision for boarders. The scheme was never achieved, but some of the money proposed for it eventually went to James Allen's Girls' School. The Estate flourished again in the interwar years, and two boarding houses were to be built, just as Gilkes had wanted, on the site of the New College, and a splendid new Pavilion replaced the old one in 1938. In time, even the Great Hall, which smelled of stale food, was considered too small for the College's needs; a projected new Speech Hall between the North Block and Dulwich Common was suggested in 1918. Drawings were prepared as late as 1926, but it was never built. In 1922 Edwin Hall (see below), the architect and the Chairman

of the Estates Governors, computed that in the 40 years ending in 1908 the College Estates had 'contributed to education and other public purposes, whether in buildings or grants of money, in gifts of land etc., and in making roads and sewers for the benefit of the community a sum of nearly £770,000'.[106]

Gilkes, then, managed to maintain Dulwich College's reputation as a great school under conditions of extreme stringency, amidst constant anxiety over money, and in buildings which were ill adapted for modern use. Forced to preside over an endowment that was half the size of that enjoyed by St Paul's School, and to pay 'considerably lower' salaries to his staff, it is no wonder that Gilkes repeatedly complained to the Governors;[107] what is amazing is that he achieved his extraordinary results under such conditions. At every possible point he would raise the issue of staff salaries with the Governors, and from 1891 the question of a pension fund for them, but to little avail. In 1912, however, at long last a significant increase was made to salaries.[108]

A new Scheme of 1913, now under the aegis of the Board of Education rather than the Charity Commissioners, set out an increase in the sums allocated from the Estate to the College, Alleyn's School, the Picture Gallery, James Allen's Girls' School, St Olave's and St Saviour's Grammar Schools and the Central Foundation Schools of London, making provision for further increases when they became available, as they did in 1915.[109]

In 1886 the Governors were approached by the new Dulwich College Preparatory School with a proposal to integrate with the main College; Welldon had encouraged the creation of 'the Prep' as an affiliated, though entirely independent concern, and the Governors accordingly agreed to continue the status quo, but refused to invest any money in the school.[110] Gilkes saw this as a mistake, and when, following the death of its Headmaster, the Revd J. H. Mallinson, in 1910, the College was again offered the opportunity of taking over the premises and boys for £7,500, he was keen to accept, arguing that the merger of the two schools would do away with the needless competition between them. The Governors took a different view, however, declaring that they had already invested so much in recent years on Science that the College could not afford the offer, and moreover that they did not wish to assume the responsibility for boys under ten years of age.[111] The Prep continued to use the College sports grounds, swimming bath and gymnasium, for which a fixed fee was paid.[112]

The first artist to be appointed as Governor by the Royal Academy in Gilkes's era was Sir Edward Poynter (see Chapter Six above) who resigned in 1890, to be followed by Briton Rivière (1840–1920), the son of the Drawing Master at Cheltenham College, a man who was possessed of 'distinction, courtesy and culture', who in 1905 criticised the proposed elevations and embellishments of the New Science Schools (see below);[113] Rivière was succeeded by Philip Hermogenes Calderon (1833–98), the Keeper of the Royal Academy Schools. Throughout this period the biennial Luncheons and annual Garden Party for the Academicians took place at the Gallery, and were to do so even during the Great War and up until 1939. The Royal Academy Governors seem to have played a good part in administering the Picture Gallery, but to have exerted little influence over the teaching of Art at the College. Melton Fisher (see Chapter Six) was never a Governor, but loyally adjudicated the Melton Fisher prizes in Art for the three Foundation schools during this period, speaking quite openly of his disappointment with the College's entries (an early casualty of Gilkes's lack of encouragement) as the Governors' Minutes record.

Sir Raymond West (1832–1912), a local resident, who was a distinguished lawyer and Indian Civil servant, served as a Governor for ten years. His widow presented a pair of two-third-size lions of Pisan marble and a pair of marble vases, seven feet high, which can be seen in photographs of the Lower Hall between the wars. A letter in *The Alleynian* in 1927 asked about their disappearance, to which the editors replied that they were now to be found in the Masters' Garden (between the North Block and Dulwich Common), overgrown with ivy;[114] the lions have departed the College without trace.

One of the Governors to whom the College owes most was the Harrovian merchant banker, philanthropist and famous collector of illuminated manuscripts, Henry Yates Thompson (1838–1929), who served on the Board for 22 years. He was appointed in February 1897, and soon became Chairman of the Picture Gallery Committee. Thompson not only paid for the panelled lobby with double doors that connects the South African Memorial Library and the Carver Room up at the College (see below), but enlarged the Gallery with £1,600 of his own money to create the Annexe on the East side with the Tribune or *Salon carré* (now the entrance) in 1908, donating two more rooms on the east side in 1911.[115] He gave generous gifts of furniture and books, organised the Royal Academy Luncheons, and supervised the intelligent and prosperous management of the Gallery; the substantial Fairfax Murray bequest of paintings to the Gallery in 1911 was undoubtedly owed to his influence.

The College Solicitor, A. D. Druce, died in 1882, whereupon Henry Attlee (1841–1908; father of the Prime Minister, Clement Attlee), the head of the firm of Druce

and Attlee and the Lieutenant of London, was appointed. He served the College well, and in a speech at the Alleyn Club dinner in 1903 said that the Alleynians he met were 'truthful, honest and high-principled' and were also possessed of 'fervent charity and piety'.[116]

It was during this period that the Governors commissioned a history of the College from Robert Jamieson Mackenzie (1857–1912), formerly the Rector of Edinburgh Academy, and the author of a life of a headmaster, *Almond of Loretto* (1905).[117] Canon Carver had originally suggested Mackenzie as the author, and his research included many candid interviews with Carver himself and many of his and Gilkes's staff. Sadly, however, Mackenzie died in November 1912, and the book remained unfinished, though notes on his interviews and the draft typescript survive in the College archives, where they remain fascinating reading both for their close observation of the College of Gilkes's day and for Mackenzie's invaluable insights into the Victorian and Edwardian era. Hopes were expressed in the *Dulwich Year Book* of 1913 to edit and publish the work, along with an account of the recent condition of the school, but the world was soon preoccupied with other concerns.[118]

The main event on the Dulwich Estate in these years was the opening of Dulwich Park in 1890; Gilkes is conspicuous in the photographs made of the stiff formalities. William Rogers in a speech asked Lord Rosebery (1847–1929), who opened the Park as Chairman of the London County Council, to commission a statue of Edward Alleyn, to be paid for by the ratepayers, but was told that the most he could expect was a cheap commemorative stone. A correspondent in *The Alleynian* in 1900 next lamented the lack of a statue of Alleyn,[119] and it was not until 2005 that Louise Simson's animated bronze of the Founder and a Poor Scholar was eventually erected at the Old College by subscription.

The Almsfolk seem to have become increasingly separated from the College, the only reference to them in this period in the College sources being an entry in Gilkes's diary that refers to their attendance at a Prize-giving in 1905;[120] although nominally in the care of the College's Chaplain at this period, the earthly responsibility for the Almshouses and the folk fell to the Estates Governors. Today at Edward Alleyn House, the east wing of the Old College, fourteen flats and two bed-sitting-rooms accommodate the pensioners, cared for by a Warden; they must be over sixty years of age but, while still drawn from the original four parishes, are no longer required to swear on the Bible the statutory 'Oath of the Six Poor Brethren and Sisters'. The Dulwich Almshouse Charity (1995) maintains close links with the Dulwich Estate, which funds it.

Buildings

By the time of Gilkes's arrival in 1885, Charles Barry was less active as Architect and Surveyor, and complained at having his salary and responsibilities cut down. He had been set back, no doubt, by being seriously cheated by a 'rascally contractor' who installed a faulty second-hand boiler for the Baths in 1884. In 1890 he drew up plans (which have not survived) for a Chapel on the New College site, capable of seating nine hundred to a thousand, for which he requested payment from the Governors.[121] On his death in 1900, his son, Charles Edward Barry (1855–1937), the dynastic third Charles Barry to hold the post, was elected Architect and Surveyor, and the following month, after Gilkes opposed a plan to adapt the Cloisters into two storeys of classrooms – they were, he said, an 'indispensable adjunct to the School' – the Governors discussed the need for a new Science Building, which was built to his very pleasing design.[122]

The New Science Building stood approximately where the Shackleton Building and Commissariat stand today; it cost £15,500, and was finished in the New College's Fiftieth Jubilee Year of 1908. The foundation stone had been laid by Lord Rayleigh, the President of the Royal Society, who declared in his speech that the Classics offered too narrow an education nowadays.[123]

Although Barry did not employ the same style as his father's New College, the Science Building harmonised with it in its colours and its relation of the solids to the voids; likewise it flourished a decorative cornice. The construction was of well-toned red brick, and like the New College (originally), it had a red-tiled roof. There were 'beautiful friezes painted in relief'; the doors were of oak, and there were 'artistic' tiles; the College arms were portrayed in stained glass. It housed workshops for Engineering, laboratories for Physics and Chemistry and a photographic dark room. As with his father's work, Barry's architecture for the Science Building was rather more ornamental than practical; noise and fumes were a problem declared to the Governors from the start. The windows had to be equipped with wire-netting against cricket balls from the adjoining pitches. With its 'sumptuous features and costly fittings', Dulwich veterans contrasted it drily with the traditional plain Classics rooms in the South Block with their dusty oak floors and deal dados.[124]

The South African Memorial Library (Old Library) set by the gate onto Dulwich Common, was opened in 1903, following the Boer War; many architectural enthusiasts prefer it to the New College. The Library was designed by Edwin Hall (1851–1923), a local resident and

South African Memorial Library. *The Alleynian*, 1903. (Dulwich College)

Chairman of the Estates Governors from 1908 to 1910. Hall was also the author of an excellent book of local history, *Dulwich History and Romance* (1916 and 1922). His son, Stanley Hall (1881–1940), Captain of School at the College, in turn became a successful architect, being elected President of the Royal Institute of British Architects in 1938. In 1908 Stanley Hall added bronze doors opening onto the garden at the Gallery, and he was employed by the College after Charles Edward Barry's appointment lapsed in 1910.[125] The Library, first proposed in 1901,[126] was paid for by subscriptions from Alleyn Club members, with Gilkes's encouragement; lists of the donors with the amounts they gave were printed in *The Alleynian*. The Library is in a mannered 'English Renaissance' or neo–Baroque style, with conspicuous reversed consoles on the exterior. The materials were red brick and Portland stone, with green slates and copper domes. The great chamber has a barrel vault; the semi-octagonal apsidal room at the end, with a small lantern over it, was for the Prefects. The floor was of polished teak; unlike the New College at the time, it was lit by electricity, and large open fireplaces stood at both ends. The interior was panelled, and here hung a photograph of G. F. Watts's celebrated chivalric painting, *Galahad*; Henry Yates Thompson presented a marble bust of Apollo.[127] An article in *The Builder* for 1902 reveals a magnificent early scheme, which is nowhere mentioned in any Dulwich source: 'it is hoped that parts will be decorated with frescoes by some of the eminent painters who are old Alleynians'.[128] The stone statues on the parapet, originally intended to be metal, were the work of Henry Charles Fehr (who was born at Forest Hill in 1867, and died in 1940) in a style similar to Alfred Gilbert's. *Mars* and *Justice* (the gift of the jurist Lord Davey) are presumably a coded formula signifying British victory in South Africa by divine right. *Minerva* (the gift of Edwin Hall) is an appropriate spirit for a Library. Incidentally, the face given by Fehr to *Justice* reproduces the face of Medusa on the shield of the hero in his sculpture *Perseus Rescuing Andromeda* (1893), now on the east elevation of the entrance to Tate Britain at Millbank. In 1999, thanks to the initiative of the Head of History, Nick Black, the pans missing from the scales of *Justice* were renewed; they were unveiled, using a Union Flag, on Founder's Day. Romantic as the heating of the Library by open fires might seem, in 1933 the Governors were told by the Master, Walter Booth, that the building was very cold and draughty, and that the books were suffering from serious damp.[129] A memorial tablet on the north elevation lists the Alleynian losses in the War. The Halls, father and son, together designed the elegant Carver Room, added to the Library in 1911 with its clerestory windows, Roman Doric pilasters, and a pediment with triglyphs and guttae. Their most famous collaboration was Liberty's department store in Regent Street (1924). Meanwhile the Great Hall, reported as 'dusty' in 1907, was redecorated in 1911, after the President of the Alleyn Club at the dinner the year before referred to it as 'a disgrace to any institution'; this was a poor scheme, since the intricate ornamental panels on the barrel-vault were sophisticated by bland stencil-work on white paint. The worst feature of the scheme was that the wyverns, hammer-beams and upper timbers, originally in a blond-coloured wood, were stained a dark colour (as described in Chapter Six). The Hall now took on an altogether heavier, gloomier effect than it had in its first youth. Oak panelling was also added to the great staircases to the Hall.[130]

Academic life at the College, and the Common Room

Gilkes's ideal at Dulwich was a suburban *academia* bringing to mind Plato's school at Athens; both were set in a pleasant grove. 'Blue books', the College's 'Form and Class Lists', were published twice a year and listed boys' positions relative to their peers. Thus it is possible to trace the progress of old boys for these years by both their general form position and in individual subjects, with some surprising and interesting results for famous Alleynians. Very detailed syllabuses were also printed in this publication, and represent an extraordinary paradigm of academic study at the time; the texts to be read by the Remove and Sixths seem more ambitious than undergraduate courses of today. The subjects Gilkes cared most for were Divinity and Classics. In 1909 he was able to write in his Annual Report that the numbers of boys doing Classics was up, following a dip five years before resulting from unwise attacks made nationally upon the subject in the press.[131] Throughout Gilkes's era the Governors' Minutes print the reports of Inspectors and Examiners, from which to some extent we can observe the vitality of the classrooms. Gilkes always deprecated these reports, even when (as often) they were very positive. He clearly believed that his instinct was a better judge of good educational practice, even when sensible educational reform was proposed in these reports. In 1905 Gilkes spoke at the Alleyn Club dinner making light of Inspectors and Examiners, claiming they missed the point of the excellence that obtained at the College; Inspectors, he said, were 'really something like the people who were sent to examine the peacock and said it was a very unsatisfactory bird because it had an ugly voice'. At the same dinner Arthur Pollard (1854–1934), a former Assistant Master at the College under

Carver, Welldon and Gilkes, and Headmaster of the City of London School for 15 years, called Dulwich 'the premier school of the country'.[132]

Gilkes made Greek compulsory on the Classical Side, where it had formerly been voluntary. The Classics teachers in Gilkes's era were exceptional. He inherited two firebrands appointed by Welldon. William Lendrum (1854–1935) was a 'little, generous, explosive Irishman, one of the most brilliant scholars of his day and an unrivalled teacher';[133] he was also a keen horseman and huntsman who declared that he was never perfectly happy, never perfectly himself, except on horseback. Lendrum left after seven years to take up a Fellowship at Gonville and Caius College, Cambridge, in 1890. His obituary in *The Caian* contained a section written by A. E. Housman, who recognised the 'spiritual value' Lendrum found in the chase and in the friendships he formed in hunting circles. In 1918, on inheriting property in Ireland, he took his mother's surname, Vesey. A valedictory tribute to him in *The Alleynian* said that the Classics had formerly 'found but a barren soil' at the College; that 'we boys were hard blocks to his razor', but that they were inspired to a larger and richer life. In the volume of College *Memories* (1919) his famous pupils recalled 'the perfection of his literary sense, the charm of his manner and the joy of his classes', and noted that he 'got an amount of work out of the Sixth which would astonish the modern schoolboy'. In the obituary in *The Caian*, Sir Arthur Hirtzel described this 'enigmatic and rather romantic figure' at Dulwich:

> You might see him in the morning, a heavy black bag in his hand, trailing a somewhat zig-zag course along the cloisters to the VIth Form room, gazing at the roof, his lips moving silently. As he entered the room the words became audible: it would be a stanza of the Immortality Ode or the Highland Maiden or 'out of the cradle endlessly rocking' or 'Tears, idle Tears', and the day's work did not begin until this rapture was finished. In any one else this would have been regarded as affectation and boys would have laughed at him. Nobody ever laughed at Lendrum – at least not twice.[134]

Gilkes attributed to Lendrum the admirable erudition of the Sixth Form. He was rather cooler about Clement Bryans (1854–1916), who left in 1893, and whose methods were interestingly unorthodox. After Bryans's lessons, a former pupil recalled, 'the world seemed a different place to our chastened eyes'; the boys learned that there was something fascinating about scholarship, and that 'even philology could be romantic'. He would spread a silk handkerchief over his head, and proclaim five minutes' slumber. Philip Hope told Mackenzie a story about Bryans's form, who once, 'seized with the spirit of the Bacchae, went careering round the room playing leap frog over desks and forms as they chanted the mad choruses'. Gilkes heard this raucous enthusiasm and came into the room, but merely remarked, "Oh Mr Bryans, you are here after all".[135] A. C. Pearson (1861–1935), a brilliant scholar who joined the staff in 1893, left in 1900. His obituary in *The Alleynian* described his teaching rather coldly as 'sound', and 'painstaking'; Alic Smith thought that alone among his Classics masters he did not appear to enjoy his teaching.[136] He rose to become Regius Professor of Greek at Cambridge in 1921; he was a College Governor from 1922 to 1926.

The two principal Classics masters whose long service provided both stability and inspiration during this great academic era were Philip Hope and Henry Hose; Gilkes told the Governors the two were 'of extraordinary consequence and extraordinary use to the school'. Philip Hope (1869–1943) was a Scholar of King's College, Cambridge, appointed in 1892 at the age of 23; and Henry ('Teddy') Hose (1876–1967), a Scholar of Corpus Christi College, Oxford, was appointed in 1900.[137] Until 1919 these two masters were in charge of the Classical Sixth and Remove respectively; Hose became head of the Classical side. These were famous teachers, among whose pupils were P. G. Wodehouse and Raymond Chandler.

Hope was acknowledged a worthy successor of Lendrum, and stood 'unreservedly at the disposal of his pupils'. He was congratulated by *The Alleynian* for the three King's Scholarships his pupils gained in 1897;[138] his pupils also won two Balliol Scholarships in as many years. Indeed, he held a long record of such awards, taking special pains with his pupils and freely giving them extra tuition, 'even when they did not seem particularly promising', according to his obituary. The Greek Play on Founder's Day, a development from the Speeches, was his creation, and became a 'merry entertainment' in costume to the music of Rendall and Hubert Doulton.[139] When in 1913 a second 'national debate' questioned the value of the Classics, Hope wrote in *The Alleynian* that the study of Greek uplifted the mind; its contribution to humanism made it part of our birthright. He said that the Classical Sixth Form also devoted five or six hours a week to English literature.[140] Alic Smith (1883–1958), Captain of School, entered the Classical Sixth two years after Wodehouse; at the age of 72, when Vice-Chancellor of Oxford University, he wrote an essay about his own teachers, perfectly recalling for us his master and the Classical Sixth in its heyday:

> To encounter Hope was a new and exhilarating experience. Here was someone who played his part with immense enjoy-

Philip Hope and the Classical Sixth, 1903. (Dulwich College)

ment of his own virtuosity as an artist. He had natural grace of bearing (he was something of an athlete), but his bearing was also studied. With a pile of books (needed or not) under his arm, he entered the form-room dramatically, like an actor who at once takes the stage and is sure of the impression that he makes. We might scoff at this (and often pretended to do so), but we knew that we watched a fine performance. Moreover we could see how hard he worked for us and how carefully he prepared the detail of every lesson; and we never failed to admire the skill of his teaching. Few could have rivalled him in teaching boys to compose in prose and verse, and we were often spellbound by the speed and brilliance with which he gave version after version of the ways in which a sentence or line could be turned in Greek or Latin. [141]

For all his gifts, and in spite of this testimony, Hope was later said to lack 'method'; his health twice broke down for a term or two, and he retired at the premature age of 52. [142]

'Teddy' Hose, the second fiddle to Hope's virtuoso first violin, although he was said to be the finest of the two scholars, had spent most of his years of study at the College, and dedicated his career to it. Under Gilkes's influence for eight years, he had been his 'admirable' Captain of School, President of the Debating Society, and an Editor of *The Alleynian*; Gilkes invited him to return after Oxford, where he had been a Scholar at Corpus, and after one year of teaching at Birkenhead. As his obituary puts it, 'Without any spectacular teaching methods he quietly opened boys' minds to the power and the beauty of language, the importance of sound reasoning and the recognition of great literature'. He took reading parties to Devon and 'Housman country', and to Greece at Easter. As Lieutenant Hose, he was keenly involved in the Rifle Corps; promoted to Captain, he became the Commanding Officer of the Dulwich College Officers Training Corps in 1915. He retired to Devon at the age of 58 in 1934. Knowledgeable in modern languages, he revised the Penguin translation of Goethe's *Faust* when he was over eighty. [143]

Perhaps the most Alleynian of Assistant Masters in all the College's history was another old boy, William Duff 'Scottie' Gibbon (1880–1955), the son of Sir William

Duff Gibbon, a tea-planter in Ceylon. The keenest imaginable schoolboy and teacher, this engaging character, with his strong facial features recognisable in so many sporting and group photographs, was a year ahead of P. G. Wodehouse at school, and passed through the same Classical forms. A truly great sportsman, he was in the First XV for four years running, and its Captain from 1897 until 1899, when he reversed a long series of victories by Bedford over the College. At the end of his first term at Oxford he left to fight for 16 months in the Boer War, returning to take a Modern History degree. Gibbon taught at the College from 1904 until 1922, with an interval for the Great War in which he was mentioned in despatches four times, awarded the DSO and the MC (when he was wounded in Gallipoli). As Major W. D. Gibbon he was Commanding Officer of the OTC from 1919 until he left; he trained the Shooting VIII to win the Ashburton Shield in 1910, and he devised the excellent scheme of the Athletic Houses (see Chapter Nine). In charge of the College's Football, he wrote a standard book, *Rugby Football in Theory and Practice* (1914, 1921), under the characteristic pseudonym 'Alleyniensis', but a later work, *First Steps to Rugby Football* (1922, several times reprinted), appeared under his own name since he had by then taken up the Headmastership of Campbell College in Belfast (1922–43). When George Smith

resigned as Master of Dulwich in 1928, Gibbon applied to succeed him, and qualified as one of three candidates on the short list. It might be regarded as a grievous mistake that this constant and many-sided Gilkesian man, clearly a great headmaster, was in fact rejected by the Governors when they appointed Walter Booth; they thought William Gibbon too old at 49, and they could not but be aware that he was deeply 'steeped' in the Dulwich of the past and its traditions, when change was needed. On his departure for Belfast in 1922, *The Alleynian* called him 'passionate and efficient', qualities he had shown as Captain of the First XV.[144] As a boy, he had climbed the ladder in the Great Hall to place the Lane Shield on Founder's Day, and his Scottish songs ('of pathetic character', and with 'a strange fancy for distressed ladies') at concerts were always encored. Here also he brought down the house by singing 'Rule, Britannia' on the eve of his leaving to fight in the Boer War.[145] On his way from Southampton to Cape Town in March 1900 aboard the ss *Tintagel Castle* he met the Third Officer, Ernest Shackleton: a letter from Gibbon in *The Alleynian* allows us to witness the encounter:

> I went to tea with [Shackleton] in his cabin yesterday, where we talked of Alma Mater; and though ten years had separated our school careers, we found that we had many common friends

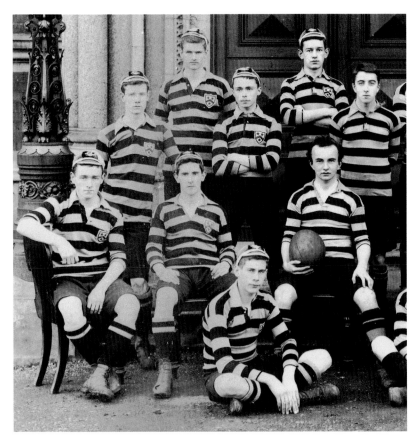

McCulloch Christison, (top row, left) and William Gibbon (Captain), First XV, 1897–8. (Dulwich College)

and memories. His cabin is just about the size of one of the studies in the boarding houses. At one end is his bunk; at one side a writing table, with the wall behind covered with photos of friends, and the other wall a bookcase with the signs of a well-read owner; for in it I saw Shakespeare, Longfellow, Darwin and Dickens, as well as books on navigation. And at the present moment, writing as I do in the fo'c's'le, I can see him on the quarter-deck voluntarily giving a number of officers lessons in semaphore signalling. Bravo, Dulwich![146]

Success at Oxford and Cambridge was recorded on the panels in the Great Hall (see Chapter Six); the President's speech at the annual Alleyn Club dinner and the editorial of *The Alleynian* usually each began by noting the awards made to Alleynians. One aspect of Gilkes's Golden Age was of course its academic achievements: in 1889 there were fourteen awards, and only one school in the country did better; in 1894 seventeen awards set a record for Gilkes's college; in 1895 there were nine awards in Classics, and one in Science, and eleven first class degrees were won; in 1898 there were eleven awards in Classics, one in Science, and two Fellowships. In 1901 among the awards was one in Modern Languages.[147] There were so many Oxford Alleynians in 1892 that a high-minded Literary Society of their own was formed, under Ernest de Sélincourt (see below), soon to become a Lecturer in English Literature at University College, Oxford, and with William Holdsworth as Secretary.[148] In 1906 the record was beaten with nineteen awards, and the Governors recorded in their Minutes that this was how the College was measured. By March 1908 there were eight Old Alleynian dons at Oxford.[149]

The Reports of the Oxford and Cambridge Schools Examination Board, compiled by dons, reveal more about the general quality of the education Gilkes's school provided. In the early years they mentioned individual candidates, and spotted talent, praising P. G. Wodehouse for his work on a Greek text, 'Teddy' Hose and Ernest de Sélincourt, and also two of the talented Moore brothers and the scientist Harold Hartley (see below). 'Brilliant' and 'wonderfully good' are common epithets applied to scripts. With typically combative self-effacement, Gilkes reported to the Governors in 1900 that 'perhaps I should say in justice to the Master of the highest Form that the English subject in which the boys did poorly was not taught by him but by myself'.[150] Two years later a Report on the College by the University of London noted its high position in competition for Open Scholarships at Universities, describing the discipline, 'high public spirit' and 'voluntary activities' on show as 'highly impressive'. In 1903, however, the same Ernest de Sélincourt, returning

to his own school as a distinguished don and scholar for the Oxford and Cambridge Board, found the English papers 'decidedly poor' and the boys ignorant and illiterate in their own language. The following year he noted an improvement, but at the same time expressed surprise at how uncultured and ignorant many boys were. Examiners visited classrooms, and in 1912 declared the oral teaching in French 'weak', a recurring complaint; in the Second Form two boys translated 'my father's room' as *mon père chamber*. However, the spirit and demeanour of the boys 'left nothing to be desired', and the relation between boys and masters was very pleasant. In the Junior School the Examiners said that the work was conducted on old-fashioned Classical lines with 'grammatical repetition and learning of paradigms'. Gilkes responded by defending the old methods and telling the Governors that the examiner wrote as an Oxford don, not a teacher of boys. Later the same year Examiners praised the 'uncrammed' accuracy and thoroughness of the older boys and their alertness and intelligence; they had never seen such work before.[151]

The first full Government inspection was in 1904–5. Inspections of 1908 and 1914 were carried out by the Board of Education, and were unpopular with the staff as a threat to the independence of the College. The reports, however, are convincing, and indict Gilkes with getting out of touch with the current world, to the detriment of the College. Dulwich was characterised as understaffed and overcrowded, and its amenities were out of date, lacking electrical power, blackboards and maps. This they had already been told in 1906 by Mr Stogden of Clare College, Cambridge, who reported that 22 boys were taught in rooms designed for twelve boys, that the deterioration of the air by so many boys and the gas lighting was serious, and, moreover, that the rooms were dreary; he recommended the display of photographs of celebrated cities, buildings and pictures, and of great men.[152]

The Board of Education inspectors reported in June 1908. The annual Endowment had grown from £4,000 in 1882 to £5,370 by 1904. Nineteen boys in the school were on College scholarships. The income was insufficient, as were the salaries. The classrooms and the teaching of Art were described as very defective. The inspectors pointed up many things we would surely notice and condemn if we were to visit the College from our own days of regulated educational reform, record-keeping and and paperwork: there was very little co-ordination; neither Gilkes nor indeed any other masters ever observed others' lessons. The autonomy of the Form Master, a Public School tradition (as the Examiners noted) was to be deplored. Several boys of the age of 15 were kept down in the Lower Second Form because they had been admitted when they were unprepared for entry. A Head of the Junior School was badly needed. Nine hours of Latin a week in the First Form were too many for those going into the Classical Side, and much more so for the others. The English taught in each Side did not include either enough composition or study of literature; the Form Master made the choice of the texts. The History teaching, carried out by Form Masters, was most uneven, and the Geography classes were poor. Although 8 out of 24 boys in the Classical Sixth already held university awards, the Classical Side was selfish, and did not allow for enough specialist teaching in Mathematics. For the older brighter boys, however, the intellectual life was indeed vigorous and the teaching was first rate. In spite of their damning criticisms they considered that the high reputation and overall 'high efficiency' of the College in general was the achievement of Gilkes himself, with his 'kindly severity', his 'long experience and deep insight into character'. (For the 1914 Report, see the end of this chapter, under 'Gilkes's Resignation').

Gilkes responded by saying that Inspectors overvalue uniformity; he admitted that they had about 25 'backward boys' in the Lower School. He insisted that at least eight hours of Latin for the First Form was right, and defended the practice of the Form Master choosing his own books in English. Gilkes said that the university Inspectors did not understand the classes they watched, and were more likely to admire lecturing. The Inspections hindered real work, he complained, and produced theatrical methods of teaching for effect; the business of the teacher was made preposterous by the presence of a stranger in the room. He complained that the College was 'much hampered' in its 'movements towards ideal education' by having to teach for so many external examinations. He thought it telling that the Inspectors made no mention of the Band, Orchestra or Choir. [153]

The 'father of the Mathematical Form' and of the Mathematical Side, founded in 1899, was a recent Old Alleynian, Charles Rumsey (1872–1909), who returned from Cambridge to be the Principal Master in the subject. In 1903 Gilkes reported the success of Rumsey's pupils to the Governors; in 1909 there were five awards in Mathematics. [154] G. B. Doughty (1833–1910), characterised in his obituary as 'simple, thorough and musical', taught Mathematics for 48 years at the College and under three Masters, joining the staff in 1861; at 70 he could sing a song in a clear tenor voice and 'reel off verse after verse from his favourite poets on the least provocation'. [155]

John Baptiste Joerg (1865–1941), a modern linguist, was reported by the Oxford and Cambridge Schools Examination board in 1906 to be 'very enlightened and decidedly competent'. [156] He and his brother, John

Adam Joerg (1865–1949), Head of the Modern Side, who was appointed in 1902 without a university degree, were to be the teachers of the film director Michael Powell (1905–90) in the early 1920s (see Chapter Nine). Powell described the German accent they gave to their French, and called them 'wonderful'. [157] The elder Joerg was Housemaster of Elm Lawn from 1910 to 1915. During the Great War George Smith resisted pressure to sack the two brothers for their German origin (see Chapter Nine).

Arthur Kittermaster (1871–1916), from Rugby School with a Cambridge degree in Classics and Theology, was an inspiring and military young master, taciturn and a strict disciplinarian, who was housemaster of Blew in 1914 after Sweet-Escott; he was killed in action in the War. He served as a splendid Commanding Officer in charge of the school's Rifle Corps from 1903 until 1915 (see below). This was his 'chief hobby', and he 'worked and slaved' at it with extra drills and excursions, constantly explaining to the boys military tactics and how the equipment worked. [158] Kittermaster wrote poems in the manner of Henry Newbolt, expressing his ideal of a schoolboy. 'Portraits' contrasted a mawkish slacker and dandy with the Games and Corps type of boy, 'clear-eyed, clean-souled', and a disciple of Gilkes:

> He marked the towering form of one that stood
> High on the platform in his scarlet hood,
> And on the deep hush of the throng let fall
> Straight, simple words that cleansed the hearts of all!

His best poem, the 'Carmen Alleyniensium', was set to a stirring accompaniment by Doulton, and was a School Song kept current through both wars and the intervening period until the early 1960s, when it was sung at the Summer Miscellany. It asserted the affirming flame of adventurous Alleynian courage and character:

> When Edward Alleyn trod the boards
> In Shakespeare's golden prime,
> And Drake and Raleigh ruffled – lords   [swaggered]
>   Of Ind and Arctic clime,
> A little seed was humbly sown,
> Since then to what huge stature grown!

Chorus:

> Sons of the Mother, forth we go
> To the Tropic Suns, to the Polar Snow.
> Age bows our youth, but still the flame
> Burns inly to the end the same.
> This is our gift at the altar laid,
> Thus shall the vow of our vigil be paid;
> Strong hands, kind eyes, clean hearts and bold,
> By these shall her sons through the world be told.

Other songs showed forth the enthusiasms and pleasures and indifference to fatigue and pain experienced by the boys. 'Bless the Corps' has the refrain 'All the best boys love a rifle'. The 'Football' song was much admired by Gilkes, who said that its doggerel 'catches the young'.[159] Much loved, the song endured until 1964 and was sung at the end of the Christmas concerts of classical music, until the late Alan Morgan, the College's long-serving and much-admired Director of Music (see Chapter Ten), could no longer stand the indignity of conducting its raucous strains.[160] The footballers' Chorus was:

> And it's feet, feet, feet, all the way,
> And it's fall on the ball, till you're black and blue and all,
> And the blue and black I swear shall win the day.

In 1934 a 78 rpm gramophone record of *School Songs* was made by the 'His Master's Voice' company, consisting of 'Pueri Alleynienses', 'Edward Alleyn', and the 'Football' and 'Goodbye' songs. Sold for four shillings, it was subsidised by the Alleyn Club. A. P. W. Gayford (see Chapter Nine) directed the recording, with a School Choir of 75 boys and masters, a large Orchestra and J. A. Westrup (see Chapter Nine) on the piano; S. C. Griffith, a famous Dulwich Rugby player (see Chapter Twelve), was one of the soloists in the Football song.[161] Another recording of these songs on two 78 rpm discs, together with the Cricket songs and 'Requiem Aeternam' from the Fauré *Requiem*, was made in 1944 at the Abbey Road studios; Royden Woodford was the soloist and Stanley Wilson (see Chapter Ten) conducted.

Upon enlisting, Kittermaster composed a kind of farewell poem, 'To those Happy Lads of the Corps'. These were terrible months at the time of Gilkes's resignation; the same issue of *The Alleynian* that included Kittermaster's poem already contained a Roll of Honour, listing seven killed and one missing in the first few months of War.[162]

When Kittermaster was shot dead in Mesopotamia in 1916 at the age of 42, a commemorative volume of his *School Songs &c.* was published with a memorial essay. 'Noble and unselfish', with 'his own love of a clean, manly and strenuous life', he was 'father and friend to all'; he took a great part in the Mission, acting as Treasurer.[163] The Shakespearean critic George Wilson Knight (1897–1984), one of two great literary brothers (see below), left the College in 1914. An introspective boy who disliked the Rugby scrum and the tuck shop, and who was caned by his Form Captain for not attending the First XV game, he nevertheless enjoyed singing 'Pueri Alleynienses' in the Great Hall.[164] He idolised Kittermaster, who had 'a boy's ideal of dignity and friendliness, with an inspiring approach to anything of nobility in literature or action';

Knight sent to *The Alleynian* in May 1916 a memorial poem paying tribute to this quality:

> Thy noble purpose ever was to lift
> The pliant mind to rise more like thine own.[165]

While Art, as mentioned above, was admitted at the time to languish, Music flourished. At the first Concert given by Edward Rendall (see Chapter Seven) under Gilkes in 1885 there were 34 orchestral performers. At his concerts works were performed from the great Classical repertoire, and among his ambitious successes recorded in *The Alleynian* were Beethoven's *Coriolan* overture, *The Messiah* (with the trumpets out of tune and time),[166] Mozart's Requiem, the Bach *St Matthew Passion*, Purcell's *Dido and Aeneas*, Mendelssohn's difficult *Elijah*, and Stanford's *Revenge* (a favourite Dulwich work, which was performed many times, and may have prompted the foundation of Grenville Athletic House).[167] Arnold Dolmetsch (1858–1940), the world-famous performer and reviver of early European music and maker of lutes, clavichords, recorders, viols and violins, lived for a while in Alleyn Crescent; his house with the walls hung with instruments is described in the early chapters of George Moore's novel, *Evelyn Innes* (1898). Dolmetsch led the violins and played solos at the concert in 1885. It was the great musical lexicographer Sir George Grove who persuaded Rendall to appoint Dolmetsch as a part-time teacher; though he only taught at the College during the years 1887–8, in this short time the handful of boy violinists increased to forty. For the concert in the latter year he led eight violins in Handel's *Sarabande*.[168]

Hubert Doulton, the former Scholar at the College in Carver's day who left in 1882 (see Chapter Six), 'came down' from Oxford to teach at the College with a degree in History and Classics. Doulton was a famous Housemaster of Blew House from 1906, succeeding Everett; he was also appointed Choir Master in 1901. He extended the concert repertoire to Beethoven symphonies, to Tchaikowsky and Haydn, and his choir grew to a hundred members.[169] His nickname, 'Spud' [slang for potato], incidentally, had several explanations in addition to that of his appearance: his asking at his first appearance at high table for the 'spuds' to be passed, and the holes in his socks [for which 'spud' was also a slang word]. Nicknames, incidentally, abounded; boys by convention addressed other boys (and even their brothers) by their surname, and first names were taboo. Gibbon told Alleyn Club diners in 1920 that if they were to return, 'your old form will still have its Fatty and Lanky, Bunny and Beetle'.[170]

One of P. G. Wodehouse's Form Masters, admired by him as both a Classicist and an athlete, was William Beach Thomas (1868–1957), who was knighted in 1920

1896 – 99.

J. GIBBONS. H.L.HUTTON. Rev.I.R.COCO. E.D.RENDALL. T.G.TREADGOLD. F.HARRISON. H.G.CHRIST.

T.B.JOERG. W.BEACH-THOMAS. L.HUTCHINGS. H.B.BAKER. G.B.STRETTON. W.R-M-LEAKE. G.H.WADE. F.WILSON. A.N.C.KITTERMASTER. A.C.PEARSON D.J.HUSSEY-FREKE F.J.ELLIS D.L.HOWELL

H.V.DOULTON. J.ROBINSON. Rev.E.H.SWEET-ESCOTT P.HOPE. J.BOIELLE. A.H.GILKES J.B.PARISH. E.M.EVERETT. G.B.DOUGHTY. F.W.MELLOR.

G.R.WOOD W.W.STUBBS Rev.E.G.ASHWIN

Gilkes and the Common Room. (Dulwich College)

for his immensely popular work, read by millions, as War Correspondent for the *Daily Mail*. In 1898 he published an interesting article in *Public School Magazine* about the College, describing its games and organisation, with emphasis on sports and on the government of the school outside the classroom by the boys themselves. Although it was mainly a day school, he commented that there was a feeling of 'corporateness'. The school was playing a part in upward social mobility – 'we are, as yet, *novi homines*, but our sons will be *nobiles*', he wrote.[171] Beach Thomas left teaching soon after for journalism, and Wodehouse himself began to publish stories and articles in the *Public School Magazine*. When Wodehouse notoriously was informed by his father that he could not afford to send him to Oxford even if he got a scholarship, Beach Thomas in 1902 found him work on the 'By the Way' column in *The Globe*, soon after which Wodehouse had the courage to desert his job at the Hongkong and Shanghai Bank; returning to make a speech at an Alleyn Club dinner in 1926, Beach Thomas said,

> I found the first job for that distinguished Alleynian, P. G. Wodehouse. I need hardly say that it was on a comic column in

a now defunct paper, which he and I both helped to kill. In those days I was superior to him and was allowed to tell him his jokes lacked point.[172]

William Martin Leake (1865–1942), an Old Alleynian, was a popular Form Master in the Junior School and Housemaster of Orchard, and was referred to as 'Dulwich personified' in 1903 by *The Captain*, a Public School magazine.[173] In the typical pluralist manner of Assistant Masters of the day he managed the Commissariat, was a conspicuous games player, and founded the 'B' Company of the Rifle Corps, of which he was Captain from 1895 until 1903. He returned to the College in 1889 after Cambridge, yet another example of the willing umbilical attachment of Gilkes's pupils to their Alma Mater. His career is, however, mostly connected with Dulwich College Preparatory School, of which he became a most successful Headmaster in 1909; in the following year he was ordained.

As we have seen, the teaching of Art languished under Gilkes. Painting, as the authors of *Gilkes and Dulwich* wrote, was not receiving encouragement.[174] The Principal Master in Drawing since 1876 was

The Art School, *c.* 1900.
(Dulwich College)

Leonard Nightingale (see Chapter Six), who believed in learning how to draw properly before taking up other media; he taught part time at the College, and held five other teaching positions at various times. Peter Greenham (RA), who left in 1926 and was appointed Keeper of the Royal Academy Schools in 1964, recalled working with Nightingale after school: the gentle and elderly man in the year of his retirement pottered about washing brushes and bottles while the solitary boy in a room with only a dim skylight made a drawing in charcoal powder of the mouth of Michelangelo's *David* from a plaster cast. [175]

Science and Engineering under Gilkes

Gilkes on his appointment in 1885 inherited a division in the College into the conventional Classical Side and Welldon's Modern Side, which was said to be initially more like an Army Class. [176] He set himself to renew the study of Science and Engineering at Dulwich with real commitment, and to that end he introduced important new facilities. Welldon's appointment of Sanderson from Cambridge a few months before he himself left the College (see Chapter Seven) was the significant factor, and Sanderson was the truly brilliant teacher who made it possible. [177] A speaker at the Alleyn Club dinner in 1897 noted this swift change with surprise and admiration; he reminded his audience of the scorn shown to schoolboys interested in Chemistry in the unenlightened days: they were said to 'indulge' in '*stinks*'. [178]

Wodehouse's affectionately satirical portrait of Gilkes in *The White Feather* (1907) corresponds to Gilkes's personal bias, as revealed in his own writings and speeches:

> The headmaster was silent. To him the word 'education' meant Classics. There was a Modern Side at Wrykyn [Dulwich College], and an Engineering Side, and also a Science Side, but in his heart he recognised but one Education – the Classics. [179]

Wodehouse added, however, that the Headmaster knows 'the spirit of the age' and that 'things were not as they used to be'; essentially Gilkes was shrewd enough to realise the College's opportunity to be at the forefront of the age, to serve the new technologies (and the London hospitals), to serve new challenges at home and in the Empire, and of course to serve the boys who had skills and interests other than his own predominantly linguistic and metaphysical culture. From the Governors' Minutes one might conclude that his desire for Engineering workshops and for more laboratories was as devout as his desire for a proper Chapel on the New College site. [180] This did not mean that he intended to create a separate culture within the College or to consign the intellectual and moral development of these boys to others; on the contrary, he believed that the too narrow study of Science was dangerous, and addressed the Science Society in the Lecture Theatre in November 1890 on the portentous subject of 'What is Man?' [181]

Under Sanderson in the Engineering Side the boys studied Mathematics, Mechanics, Physics, Chemistry, and Technical and Engineering Drawing, and also some German and French. Gilkes was said to have paid a sum out of his own pocket towards Sanderson's Steam Engine, needed for classes in Thermodynamics;[182] this is likely, but if it is true he did not make it public, as Carver would have done. Gilkes was extraordinarily proud of this six-horse-power experimental engine and 'Locomotive Multitubular Boiler' with its tanks, gauges and other accoutrements, which cost £250, [roughly £19,145 today] and was one of only six or seven in Great Britain. Gilkes reported to the Governors that Sanderson had said it was hopeless to expect boys to stay in school unless the Engine was bought, and indeed four of his current sixteen pupils did leave before the engine was set up 22 months later in 1888.[183] The Editors of *The Alleynian* at this time betrayed a bias, no doubt typical of many conservative boys and masters, saying that the new studies threatened the liberal education of Classics and Modern Languages for which Dulwich was famous. This view was held in spite of Carver's encouragement of Science and the successes of the College of his day in the subject;

a letter to the magazine complained about the purchase of the Engine, saying it was only for a score of boys, and meanwhile there were no lockers in the gym.[184]

In 1886 the Workshops were constructed to house the Engineering Side and new Science classrooms, adjoining the Swimming Bath. In 1888 the Classics Side was formed of 158 boys, the Modern Side of 117, and the Science and Engineering Sides of 29 boys each. By 1890 there were 59 boys in the Engineering Side;[185] many of them were boys who were formerly likely to have left the College early, and were those boys who might not have prospered in the linguistic ethos of the College. The average leaving age in 1897 was still sixteen years and four months.[186] In 1890 Sanderson was the highest paid teacher at the College; he was only 28 when appointed in 1885, but he knew and was known to all the Engineering and Science men at Cambridge. The *Pall Mall Gazette* of November 1890, in the course of a series of articles celebrating the 'New Era' in Public Schools, 'No II, Dulwich', reported to its readers Gilkes's pride in his large Engineering department of 60 boys, where they

Laboratory in the new Science Building, 1908. (Dulwich College)

were taught the 'scientific groundwork'. Upstairs in the Workshops dissection of frogs by future medical students took place.[187]

Naturally the New Science Building (described above) of 1908 was of great benefit. A very detailed pamphlet of 1911, 'Syllabus of the Science Side and Engineering Side', which names Gilkes as author, explains that the courses were for boys intending to proceed to Universities, hospitals and also into business. There is a description of the facilities including the Steam Engine and dynamo; boys were expected to buy a certain amount of their own apparatus. The range is impressive: Woodwork and Metalwork were taught, along with very advanced Mathematics, Surveying and Applied Mechanics; Biology, on condition that the boys dropped French, could be studied for five and a half hours a week, but Chemistry was allocated between eight and nine and a half hours. Specialisation began in the Upper Fifth Form; for three years previous to this there were general introductory courses, and the boys spent more than half their available time on English, Latin and French, towards their London Matriculation examination. Gilkes reported to the Governors that of the 30 boys who left the Engineering Side in 1890, 90 per cent found jobs in offices or works of firms of high standing.[188] When Sanderson left to become a great educational reformer as Headmaster of Oundle, creating 'an ideal school of the modern scientific type', Gilkes felt his loss very keenly; he admired him as a fiery, but 'shrewd and humorous' man who used no textbooks.[189] It is possible to sense the excitement generated by Sanderson from a dynamic essay he published after the War on the teaching of Science in a book of 1921 called *The Modern Teacher*.[190] This visionary, with his noble view of the extent and value of Science, offers a practical, if costly, plan for schools with laboratories, workshops, an experimental farm and biological gardens, in effect a technological community for teachers and boys, dedicated to regenerate society and England by harnessing the energy and zeal of spirited teachers and enthusiastic pupils; as in his work at Dulwich, Sanderson makes central the idea of entrusting research and experiment to the pupils themselves, but using workshops equipped like those in a progressive university, including ship-model tanks and five-ton testing machines for tension, compression and torsion. Walter Booth, the later Master of Dulwich College and a scientist, declared in 1931 that Sanderson had 'altered the face of English public schools'.[191] After Sanderson F. W. Russell (1871–1943), a fiery and portly bachelor, became Senior Science Master and Head of the Engineering Side.

Herbert Baker (1862–1935) was appointed as a Chemistry Master in 1886 on the death of Alfred Tribe (see Chapter Six), and he also encouraged boys to make their own experiments. Some of his own took place in the Lecture Hall and in the Centre Block cellars, and would presumably have included his own obsession, the properties of gases. Baker immediately founded the Science Side in 1886 with 16 boys,[192] but left in 1902 to be Headmaster of Alleyn's School for just one year before he was elected Reader in Chemistry and Fellow of Christ Church, Oxford. In 1912 he became a famous Professor at Imperial College. The book of Dulwich College *Memories* of 1919 describes Baker as 'of poison gas fame'.[193] According to his obituary in *The Times*, at the outbreak of the Great War Baker was immediately summoned to the War Office, and was the scientist responsible for concocting the ingredients for protection against poison gas in the military gas helmets, the 'PH' (Phenate Hexamine) and the 'Box', used at the Front. The former had two mica eyepieces and an exhaust valve which was held in the mouth. Flannel layers of cloth were dipped in sodium phenolate and glycerine, which protected against chlorine and phosgene; Baker added hexamethylene tetramine, against hydrocyanic acid. The Box Helmet was an unwieldy larger version for officers and men 'requiring unusual exertion', and was claimed to give complete protection. Fourteen million 'PH' masks were made. Baker married the daughter of the prominent and much loved Estates Governor, Harry Powell (d. 1922), who had donated the mosaic panels in the Reredos at the Chapel in memory of Carver in 1911. Baker was helped in his research for the gas-masks by his Dulwich pupil, Captain Bernard Mouat Jones DSO (1882–1953), Assistant Director of the Central Laboratories at the General Headquarters of the Army in France, who had left for Oxford in 1901 with a Balliol Scholarship in Natural Sciences. From only a handful of mud from a shell hole stained by some chemical Mouat Jones hardly ever failed to identify the substance and the gas. In 1921 he became the Principal of the Manchester College of Technology, and later was Vice-Chancellor of Leeds University from 1938–48, during which time, by 1941, he was working for the Government again.[194]

Another pupil and follower of Baker was (Sir) Harold Hartley (1878–1972), who was at the College from 1894 to 1897, and left with a Balliol Scholarship; at an Alleyn Club dinner in 1934 he declared that Baker was the 'greatest of science masters of all time', who conveyed his enthusiasm for investigation. As President of the British Association in 1950 he again paid tribute to Baker, recalling in his Address that from time to time his Dulwich master would invite boys into his private laboratory and talk about his own work, and that within a week of the discovery of X-rays Baker had demonstrated them to his pupils.[195] By 1901 Hartley held a Fellowship in Chemistry and Metallurgy at Balliol, and he married the eldest daughter of the Master of Balliol in 1906. A Major in the Royal Engineers and Chemical Adviser to the Third Army in France, sent to investigate asphyxiating gas at the Front, he was awarded the MC, and was later the 'Controller of the Chemical Weapons Department'.[196] Hartley in later years became an 'industrialist'; after his appointment as Vice President of the London, Midland and Scotland Railways and after running the early British European Airways, he became Chairman of British Overseas Air Corporation from 1947 to 1949. Probably the single most famous and distinguished Old Alleynian scientist, Hartley was a College Governor (first appointed by the University of Oxford, then by the Royal Society and then co-opted) from 1932 until 1970. In 1952 he unveiled a plaque on the first floor of the new Science Block, following the destruction by enemy bombing of (the third) Charles Barry's New Science Building in 1944. He was appointed a Companion of Honour in 1967.

In both the old Workshops and in the New Science Building there were darkrooms. The Photographic Society, founded by Baker with its first exhibition in 1887, was very popular, and for at least two decades its exhibitions and competitions (in which many Old Alleynians

and sometimes boys from other schools took part) were reported in detail in *The Alleynian*.

W. C. Crowther (1885–1962) was appointed as botanist and biologist in 1911, and in the course of a long career at the College until 1945 (see Chapter Ten) he became Head of Biology and commanded the Officers Training Corps. A young Biology master, Lawrence Beesley (1872–1967), a former Scholar of Gonville and Caius, Cambridge, was appointed in 1904 and taught at the College for five years. After Beesley left, he was to become famous: bound for a holiday in the States and to visit his brother in Toronto, he survived the *Titanic* disaster at the age of 40, and wrote an eyewitness account of it, *The Loss of the SS Titanic* (1912), which is still one of the standard books on the subject. *The Alleynian* chronicles the lively part he played as a young master, taking part in debates, giving lectures and judging the Natural Science exhibits displayed by the boys such as rocks, Coleoptera, birds' eggs and botanical specimens. After an inspection in 1905, the Oxford and Cambridge Schools Examination Board praised his Biology lessons on Heat and Practical Electricity.[197] Beesley became a Christian Science healer, and then returned to teaching, as a Headmaster of a preparatory school in Bexhill from 1927 until 1939; he does not appear to have kept up a connection with the College.

*Events – Activities – Gilkes and 'the Public School spirit' – The Army, the Church and the Empire – McCulloch
Christison – Shackleton – Wodehouse – Chandler – Other writers, academics, scientists, doctors, the City, artists, the
stage and music – The London County Council Scholars – The Rifle Corps, the Officers Training Corps and the onset of
the Great War – Gilkes's resignation*

Events

In Gilkes's second year the school hero, Francis Anstie, a
Scholar and the Captain of School, died at 18 years, after
a 'long and painful illness'. For Gilkes and the College his
death and funeral amounted to a tragic event of almost
mythic proportion, resembling the archetypal episodes
in Homer or *Beowulf* where the tribe is unified by loss of
a young hero. Anstie was a notable actor and debater, and
as victor of the Ashburton Shield (wrested from Rugby,
Harrow, Eton, Marlborough, Charterhouse and Clifton)
on the return of the Shooting VIII he had been hoisted
on their shoulders at the College gates. He was interred
at Norwood cemetery, when they sang the boy's favourite
hymn, 'Through the night of doubt and sorrow'. Lendrum wrote an elegy in Greek alcaics, and his mother
presented finely bound volumes of Ruskin to the Library
in his memory.[198]

As the violent twentieth century dawned, Anstie's
loss was joined by others' in the South African [Boer]
War, foreshadowing the slaughter that would twice visit
the College before it was half run. In February 1900 *The
Alleynian* listed 89 Old Alleynians in the Army, and the
March issue began to list deaths in the War. Gibbon's
departure for the Transvaal has been mentioned above.
By the end of the War, in which 146 Old Alleynians
served, seven had been killed in action and four died
of enteric fever [typhoid]. Five DSOs were awarded to
Alleynians. *The Alleynian* published three reports from
soldiers on active duty. Mafeking Day in the spring of
1900 was celebrated with a bonfire and a *feu de joie*,
and the boys carried each other on their shoulders; the
Punishment Book was 'erased'.[199]

That year, Gilkes proposed to the Governors a War
Memorial in the Lower Hall, writing 'I think Memorials of
this kind do good to the School, by making the boys realise
their connection with the great life of their country'. However, in 1901, Frank Rehder (1862–1904), the eldest of
three very loyal and generous Alleynian brothers (and a
cultivator of orchids), instead proposed the construction
of a South African Memorial Library (described above).
A ceremonial chair was made to commemorate Rehder's
death three years later, which is now to be seen at the
entrance to the Wodehouse Library. The construction of
the Library was held up by the Charity Commissioners,

even though it was funded by subscriptions; it was
opened in 1903.[200]

In July 1887 royal visitors had appeared without
warning in the Great Hall: Gilkes was summoned to greet
Queen Victoria's eldest daughter, Victoria, Princess
Royal, then the Crown Princess of Germany, and her
husband, Frederick III ('Fritz'), who was to become
Emperor for a few months in the following year. He was
suffering from a fatal cancer of the throat, and whispered
to Gilkes a request for a half-holiday for the boys. *The
Alleynian* reported 'such cheers being given as have
seldom been heard in Great Hall'; the Prince, with a
melancholy expression, told Gilkes they were cheering
just for the holiday.[201] The visit was in fact absurd, in that
it was founded on the poor memory of the Crown
Princess: she informed Gilkes that her father had been
the first Chairman of the Governors of the College, and
that when it was being built she had come with him and
run about the scaffolding. In fact when work was begun
on the New College she had been 26, and Prince Albert
had died some five years earlier in 1861. The Princess
must therefore have confused Dulwich with Wellington
College, in which the Consort had taken a much closer
interest: it had opened in 1859, when her father, who was
indeed Chairman of the Governors, had presented it
with a small library of books and an annual prize for the
most unselfish boy.[202] Prince Frederick died in Italy a
few months after the visit. During the Diamond Jubilee
year of 1897 five flags were hung, four on the clock tower
and one at the great gates; Gilkes wrote in his diary that
this caused some derision.[203]

In 1893 another foreign dignitary, the Maharajah of
Bhaounagar, paid a visit. He offered a prize of ten
guineas, for which Gilkes devised a competition for a
poem about the College; each form had to submit their
best effort, and the results were printed in a pamphlet,
Dulwich College. Selected Addresses, April 1894.[204] Wodehouse's story 'The Prize Poem' (1901) describes the
panic induced in prosaic cricketing boys by having to
write a poem, and he quotes a specimen stanza which
might at first be thought to be his own parody:

Imposing pile, reared up 'midst pleasant grounds,
The scene of many a battle, lost or won,

At cricket or at football; whose red walls
Full many a sun has kissed ere day is done.

Wodehouse's joke has a further dimension, however: it is a pointed tease directed at his elder brother. The poem in which the lines occur was printed in the *Selected Addresses* anonymously,[205] presumably according to Gilkes's principle of not allowing boys to draw attention to themselves; however, pencilled by a contemporary hand in a copy of this pamphlet held in the College Archives are the names of all the schoolboy poets. Wodehouse's lines turn out to be the first stanza of the competition entry by his fourteen-year-old elder (and rival) brother, Armine (see below).

In 1901 Lord Roberts, the Commander-in-Chief of the British Army, visited the College on his way to the Crystal Palace. With only two and a half hours' notice, a Guard of Honour of 305 boys was mustered from the Rifle Corps, and the Captain of School presented him with Latin alcaics he had written for the occasion; Roberts handed these to Gilkes, and asked for a translation to be sent to the War Office. He was 'surprised and pleased' to be told that the full number of boys in the Corps was 330.[206] This stirring patriotic visit had a dark echo six years later: in 1907 Roberts wrote to *The Alleynian* chiding Old Boys for not joining the Old Alleynian Shooting Club; it was their duty as public schoolboys, he said, to qualify as officers for future 'national emergency' and the 'real danger' already posed to the country.[207]

The Memorial Reredos to Canon Carver in the Chapel was unveiled by the Bishop of Woolwich in 1911. This was the gift, as mentioned above, of Harry Powell, the Vice-Chairman of the Governors. It was perhaps a better idea than the Miniature Rifle Range which Gilkes had proposed to the Governors in memory of Carver. Powell was a partner in the well-known Whitefriars Glassworks, and the glass mosaic panels, designed (or, it was said, 'supervised') by the architect W. D. Caröe (1857–1938), were made by his firm. *The Alleynian* carried an explanation of the meaning of the central panel in which Alleynian symbols are seen to be brought to Bethlehem at Epiphany: one of the Three Kings wears Alleyn's robe from the famous portrait; another King bears Alleyn's 1599 chalice. Two attendants wear the costume of the first Poor Scholars; one carries cornflowers, the other a model of the chapel. The Eastern King symbolises that 'the benefits of Alleyn's College are extended to the sons of the East, and reach to the furthest limits of the Empire'. St Joseph represents the dignity of labour and the honest workman.[208]

In the early hours of Friday 5 September 1913 a Police Constable on duty at Dulwich noticed a fire in a chemical laboratory and lecture hall on the first floor of the New Science Building at the College. Notices reading 'Votes for Women' were discovered to have been affixed to trees with hat-pins; other suffragette literature, and a large can of petrol, were found at the scene. A large platform in the lecture hall was destroyed, and the floor badly burnt; in all, £300 worth of damage was caused. The female arsonists had either clambered over the railings from Alleyn Park road or concealed themselves in the locked grounds.

The College was presumably attacked because of its privileged single-sex education and exclusive laboratories. It is also the case that the former Chairman of the Governors from 1907 to 1911, Sir Alfred (now Lord) Lyall (see above), a 'liberal authoritarian', was a well-known opponent of women being given the vote. This outrage made the Governors worried about protecting the paintings at the Picture Gallery against attack by suffragettes with their slashing knives. The destruction that these women failed to wreak in September 1913 was achieved by Hitler one night in July 1944, when a Flying Bomb ruined the building beyond repair.[209]

Activities

Under Gilkes's Mastership, the quality of *The Alleynian* reached a high point in its history for the quality of its writing, despite his strict notion that it should be a vehicle for *esprit de corps* and not for individual attention-seeking. There is much very interesting writing by schoolboy writers, such as Wodehouse and Raymond Chandler. As one later editor put it, the magazine was developing into a combination of Wisden and *New Verse*. Young Cambridge dons such as Jack Sheppard, G. E. Moore and Aubrey Attwater returned to the College and contributed reviews of the Founder's Day 'Speeches' and Greek plays. Wodehouse and Chandler sent back contributions to the magazine for a good number of years after they had left the College; by no means all of these were minor pieces or as silly as Wodehouse's squib, 'The Secret of Success', a poem about not wearing an Old Alleynian cap, or a tiresome facetious piece about Shakespeare he sent in 1929.[210] Wodehouse was acknowledged as one of the boy editors (when he was in the Classical Remove and the Sixth Form) to have had a powerful impact on the magazine, and indeed wrote a great deal of it himself. He sharpened his wit by satirising other school magazines in a regular feature known as 'Our Contemporaries', for which he was said to be 'far-famed in his time';[211] his eye for the absurd enlivened conventional reports on school activities. From Gilkes's day until after the Second World War a convention persisted that editorials

W. D. Caröe, *Epiphany*. Glass mosaic and oils. Central panel of the Reredos, 1911, Christ's Chapel, Dulwich.
Alleynian allusions: one King wears Alleyn's robe; another bears his 1599 chalice. The Eastern King signifies that 'the benefits of Alleyn's College are extended to the sons of the East, and reach to the furthest limits of the Empire'. (Photograph by John Hammond)

The Prefects' Room. *The Alleynian* cupboard, left, with Editors' names incised. (Dulwich College)

were unsigned and that contributions were anonymous. The use of pseudonyms, however, was allowed, 'Tharn-dec' for example anagrammatically signifying (almost all of) R. T. Chand[l]er (whose second name was Thornton). Wodehouse appears to have been the first writer to print his initials below a poem. Luckily for historians, McCulloch Christison (see below) annotated almost all contributions in his own copies of the magazine with the authors' names. Here are to be found satirical verses by C. D. Broad, the future philosopher (see below), above the signature 'tan theta'.[212] The magazine was in fact fairly outward-looking, extending boys' horizons by including reports from Alleynians overseas. Letters at the end of the magazine allow us to eavesdrop on boys' daily complaints: the food in Hall and Buttery, the lack of amenities, and the apathy of their peers towards the games and activities; there is endless pompous fuss about ties and caps.

Beach Thomas noted the government of the school outside the classroom by the boys themselves.[213] The Debating Society was revived in 1891, by G. E. Moore,

and initially met in Gilkes's garden. In 1889 a letter had complained that it was defunct, and others wrote to say that the earlier society was too frivolous. Masters, such as Beesley and Hose (who had been President when a boy), would speak in the debates, and Wodehouse and other Old Boys return to speak. There was much discussion of rules, and some petty 'private business' at the start of debates, (all reported in the magazine), but such speeches (given verbatim) as those of G. E. Moore, C. D. Broad, and H. F. Hose (as both boy and master) show brilliant rhetoric, dialectic, political awareness and youthful wit. In 1901 Wodehouse made a speech by special invitation, and later in the year there was a dinner, when Alic Smith was President, and 'Mr Wodehouse, one of the guests of the evening, delighted the company with selections from time to time out of his large repertoire of comic songs', after which 'on the dewy grass, under the pale beams of the rising moon', they sang together 'Auld Lang Syne'.[214] After this golden period the Society declined, despite a short-lived revival in 1910.

The annual 'Assault at Arms', originating in the 1890s and continuing into the 1950s, was a much-loved sporting and military entertainment, accompanied by the Band. As mentioned above, it gave particular pleasure to Gilkes. 'Instructor Hawkins', a Gymnast from Aldershot, who taught Wodehouse to box, performed his 'Cavalry sword exercises' with 'whirling, flashing blades' followed by some horizontal bar feats which left the spectators 'all amazed and giddy'. Wodehouse boxed at the Assault in 1898: he and his antagonist entered 'armed with gloves, to show how boxing was done in the best circles. A very warm and even contest followed'.[215] There were also displays of fencing and the aerobic exercises with wooden bats known as Indian clubs, and some comic interludes.

The formula and sequence of events for Founder's Day in Gilkes's era was established in 1890: a communion service in the Chapel at 8 a.m., when a wreath of cornflowers was placed on the tomb of Edward Alleyn; prayers for the School in the Great Hall; three simultaneous cricket matches; a guard of honour for Gilkes from his house in the South Black on his way to announce scholarships and prizes in Great Hall, after all had sung 'Pueri Alleynienses'; a production for the assembled tribe and their guests of Plautus or Terence, and the 'English Speech' performed (as it was until 1893, and again between the Wars) in evening dress; in the evening the Band of the Rifle Corps played and the Choir sang in the Master's Garden. The Latin play was replaced in 1895 by famous performances of Aristophanes. In the course of the *Clouds* in 1899 Socrates was raised in his hammock to 'giddy heights' by 'the sturdy hands of certain Old Alleynians'. The declared aim of the Day was for all who attended to feel part of a great whole.[216]

The Alleyn Club by 1908 numbered 1,225 members, and prosperous dinners were held at grand restaurants such as the Hotel Cecil on the Strand. Gilkes wrote in his diary that it had a tendency to be a dining club, and he was presumably disappointed that it did not develop even more of a social mission. He also thought the subscription was too expensive.[217] Wodehouse, surprisingly for such a loyal alumnus, did not actually join the Club until 1913, but was on the Committee from 1927 into the 1930s; Shackleton was made an Honorary Life Member in 1910.[218]

Gilkes and 'the Public School Spirit'

In *The Longest Journey* (1907), the novelist E. M. Forster (1879–1970), an unhappy day-boy at Tonbridge School from 1893 to 1897, attacked the Public School system by contrasting the misery of school life with the liberation of Cambridge. In this, and in his other novels, the Public School characters he creates are either satirical stereotypes or men, more sympathetically conceived, who have been somehow traumatised or stunted by their adolescent education. In an essay of 1920, 'Notes on the English Character', Forster declared that the products of Public Schools emerge with well-developed bodies, fairly developed minds but undeveloped hearts:

> With its boarding houses, its compulsory games, its system of prefects and fagging, its insistence on good form and on *esprit de corps*, [the Public School] produces a type whose weight is out of all proportion to its numbers. ... [The boys] prolong that time as best they can by joining their Old Boys' Society; indeed some of them remain Old Boys for the rest of their lives. They attribute all good to the school. They worship it.[219]

Some of the speeches at the Alleyn Club dinners of the late 1930s, with their complacent invocation of *esprit de corps*, certainly provide some evidence for this opinion; at the same time, however, many of Gilkes's Alleynians seem to have demonstrated a very well-developed sense of humane altruism. No doubt the College produced examples of the hollow Public School type, but the men inspired by Gilkes became educated men in the best

The Choir in the Master's Garden on Founder's Day. *The Captain*, June 1903. (Jan Piggott)

IN THE CRICKET FIELD

C A WERNER

DICAEOPOLIS
D L DRAKE BROCKMAN

A. MEGARIAN TRADER
H DE SÉLINCOURT

PIPER

A Megarian trader palming off his two daughters disguised as pigs to Dicaeopolis.

INVOCATION

A HERALD

ONE OF THE CHORUS

FOUNDER'S DAY AT DULWICH COLLEGE: CRICKET AND THE GREEK PLAY.

sense. In an (undated) address among his papers, Gilkes described the growth from infancy to manhood, and defined what he called 'the poetry of virtue':

> Boys do not become men, nor do men become old, with a click of the mechanism and a sudden start: children must slowly and watchfully make their own way to manhood if it is to be anything better than a woeful loss of freshness and a hopeless accumulation of impossible duties. …
>
> They readily understand and feel with other minds, are never rude or harsh or rigid; they can work hard without losing their brilliancy and grace. They grow old without making it dreary and hideous, and can speak their minds without restraint or offence.

His ideal is a combination of Christianity and of Greek culture: his disciples should live more in others than in themselves; they will also enjoy the great company of the quiet dead. The study of the Classics, in preference to the 'latest fashion of ephemeral Science' and the 'neat acquirements of colloquial French', develops manhood and broad sympathy:

> Think how dull and brutal we might have been if Athens and Rome had been as barren as England was in their day, or if the Persians had conquered and annihilated the bright cradle of Socrates and Aeschylus? [220]

Gilkes's morality was the fruit of meditation and observation; at Prize-giving in 1886 he exhorted the boys not to believe in rank, riches or privileges, 'but to do their duty manfully wherever they might be, and raise their ideal above routine'. [221] That such ideals germinated virtue in very many Alleynians cannot be doubted, as Hugh de Sélincourt for one recalled:

> Without at all knowing it, while I worked and shirked and played and messed about, I was learning the great lesson of life, not obedience to authority or conformity to custom, but a worship for something that alone animates mankind, something that became manifest to me in that blend in my young heart of the School and of the Old Man: to take later on other forms, no doubt; but never to lose its freshness of appeal; never to become ashes and disillusionment. [222]

The Army, the Church and the Empire

Many schools obviously have successful and interesting alumni to contemplate and to claim credit for, but the fact remains that Dulwich was famous in the first half of the twentieth century for the extraordinary number of successful men in high positions from Carver's and Welldon's College, and more especially from Gilkes's era. In his day *The Alleynian* published useful lists of Old Boys in the Army, the Clergy, Architecture, and Teaching,

LIFE IN OUR SUBURBS.
No. IV.—Dulwich. The Boy—What will he Become?

Cartoon by H. M. Bateman, 1910. (© H. M. Bateman Estate)

at universities and schools. [223] Many joined 'professions', but when the *Dulwich College Register* was published in 1926 (Alleyn's Tercentenary year) it revealed a wonderful range of livelihoods and achievements, including a surprising number of farmers. It is invidious to choose from these highly interesting and admirable men, and what follows is perforce an anthology.

Dulwich became known as a prominent military school; when the most famous Alleynian soldier General Sir Webb Gillman (see Chapter Seven), who left in 1887, was chosen as Chief of General Staff in Mesopotamia in the Great War, both his rival candidates were from Dulwich. The Commandant at Sandhurst declared that the best boys came from Dulwich College. [224] Major-General Sir Herbert Holman (1859–1949), who left in 1888 and 'passed out first' at Sandhurst, was a pupil much admired by Gilkes. Surely Gilkes's true chivalric idealism played a part in the nurture of the high courage and self-sacrifice of his five pupils who were to win the Victoria Cross in the Great War (see Chapter Nine).

Among a group of characterful clergymen was Frank Weston, who left in 1890, devoted to Gilkes, and became a militant high churchman, and a missionary, publishing books in Swahili; as Bishop of Zanzibar, in 1913 he charged the Bishops of Mombasa and Uganda with heresy. [225] J. R. Darbyshire (1880–1948), who left in 1889, was Bishop of Glasgow and Galloway in 1931, and then

Opposite: Founder's Day, 1896. *The Daily Graphic.* (Dulwich College)

Bishop of Cape Town from 1938–48. A. E. J. Rawlinson (1884–1960) who won all the Classical prizes in 1903, the year he left the College, was a tutor at Oxford Colleges until 1926; he served as Bishop of Derby from 1936 until 1959. Reginald Owen (1887–1961), who left in 1906, was a Classicist and sportsman, much influenced by Gilkes; after serving as a most successful Headmaster of Uppingham for 18 years, he became Primate and Archbishop of New Zealand. (Claud) Anselm Rutherford (1886–1952) left in 1905 with an Exhibition in Natural Sciences to King's College, Cambridge; converted to Catholicism at Cambridge by Monsignor R. H. Benson, he joined the Benedictines, becoming the first Prior of Worth Abbey in 1933 and the Head Master of Downside in 1934.

The College continued, of course, to send men overseas in service of Empire, and like the boys' magazines of the era, *The Alleynian* carried many articles they wrote about natives and shooting tigers; 'Elephant Catching in Travancore' is a typical title.[226] In 1902 there were 184 Old Alleynians in India,[227] and in 1910 *The Alleynian* listed Indian Civil Servants (including Burma) with their positions, whether Judges, Collectors, Magistrates or officials of the Public Works Department.[228] Sir John Marshall (1876–1958), who won a Scholarship in Classics at King's, Cambridge, in 1895, was Director General of Archaeology by 1910, responsible for major excavations (in Burma as well as India), and published the *Archaeological Survey of India* (1914–15). T. L. Ormiston (1876–1954) was the loyal compiler of the *Dulwich College Register*, a project (first suggested in 1891) which he took over from McCulloch Christison and on which he worked for five years; he also married a soloist at College concerts, the daughter of his housemaster at Blew House (J. B. Parish). Ormiston studied at Trinity College, Cambridge, and proceeded to Sandhurst, where he 'passed out first'; he served with the Army and the Civil Service in India and Burma, and sent *The Alleynian* an article about the Dalai Lama in 1912.[229] E. Butts Howell (1879–1952) made his career in the maritime customs at Peking; he also published two truly delightful collections of his translations of ironic and subtle Chinese stories of the Ming Dynasty (illustrated by a 'native artist'), *The Inconstancy of Madame Chuang* (1924) and *The Restitution of the Bride* (1926). Sir Clement Hindley (1874–1944) oversaw the addition of four thousand miles of track to Indian railways, returning in 1928 to London, where he filled many important Civil Service positions. Sir J. T. Pratt (1876–1969; elder brother of 'Boris Karloff', who did not attend the College), the author of *China and Britain* (1927), was English Consul in Shanghai; over the Embassy there in 1945 Sir Alwyne Ogden (1889–1981) hoisted the Union Jack. Sir Edward Harding (1880–

1954), who had considerable experience of Africa, rose to be Permanent Under-Secretary of State at the Dominions Office. U Tin Tut (1895–1948), a boarder at Elm Lawn, left in 1914 for Queen's College, Cambridge, where he graduated in Mathematics and Economics; called to the Bar in 1921, he was the first Burman to enter the Indian Civil Service. In 1947 he was the first High Commissioner for Burma in London, but was almost immediately recalled to Rangoon, becoming Foreign Minister. He resigned the post to become Inspector-General of the Auxiliary Forces of the Burmese Army, which he founded when there was widespread revolt. In 1948, nine months after Burma became independent, a Communist threw a hand-grenade at his car and assassinated him; it was well known that Tin Tut still wished to make Burma a Dominion of the British Empire. Phya Srivasar (T. L. Hoon, 1897–1968) who left the College in 1916 and took a First in Law at Oxford, joined the Siamese Diplomatic Service; after the Second World War he had a part in the drawing up of a constitution for the new Siam.

McCulloch Christison

As for McCulloch Christison (1880–1972), he was to be known in the City and at the Stock Exchange by the plain sobriquet 'the Alleynian', which summed him up; his name is deservedly kept in daily use at the College by the Christison Hall (1969; see Chapter Ten). At school he was on the Classical Side (in the year below Wodehouse) and was a keen sportsman, leaving in 1898. In the Great War he was severely wounded at Ypres, mentioned in despatches and awarded the MBE. Undoubtedly the most loyal Alleynian imaginable for over seventy years, this unassuming, conservative gentleman was the longest-serving College and Estates Governor (from 1923 and 1920 respectively), a most famous Secretary of the Alleyn Club from 1906 until he resigned in 1967 at the age of 87, and the Treasurer of the Old Alleynian Football Club for 59 years, an extraordinary feat of devoted endurance; it also fell to him twice to be the tragic compiler of a Dulwich College *War Record*. His ironic nickname for thousands connected with the College was 'Slacker': zealously memorious, he gave his hours to searching the newspapers for references to Alleynians, to annotating record cards, and to filing in his cabinets many thousands of letters and press cuttings; these he kept with questionnaires that had been filled in by a high proportion of Old Alleynians to help compile the printed *Register*, in response to a mass mailing of 1924. He made use of his wide contacts to help countless Alleynians find the right jobs. Although he resented any reference being made to him in speeches, the Alleyn Club contrived to present the College with his portrait painted by Peter

McCulloch Christison. (Dulwich College)

Greenham in 1958. Dulwich College was quite extra-ordinarily lucky to possess in Christison such a Gilkesian man, recognised by the *Windsor Magazine* in 1932 as 'the world's keenest man on his old school'.[230]

Thomas Gray's 'Ode on a Distant Prospect of Eton College' (1747) describes the dreadful Fates gleefully waiting to seize schoolboys, sooner or later, to be victims of 'black Misfortune's baleful train'; anyone who has had long association with schools cannot escape baleful news about former pupils. Particularly sharp, for example, is the report of the two Fearon brothers killed by lightning on the summit of the Wetterhorn in 1902. Among the press cuttings which Christison pasted into his volumes of *The Alleynian* itself, in addition to reports about the famous and successful, are those that reveal the obverse side of Dulwich's prosperity: failures, imprisonments, swindles; the headless corpse of an Alleynian suicide by the railway tracks; the story of a rich young husband who shot first his wife and then himself with a revolver; the case of the country solicitor Harold Greenwood (1874–1929), who after a sensational seven-day trial in 1920 was acquitted of poisoning his first wife with arsenical weed-killer in the wine at Sunday lunch. Stephen Kirby was Captain of School in 1922; he was obsessed with Greek and Latin verse, but his brilliant career as a Balliol

Scholar of a First in Moderations and several Oxford prizes ended with a Fourth in Greats. He committed suicide in 1932 when he was a young schoolmaster.[231]

Other biographies are of course less eventful, and by and large happier. It is instructive to look into the school careers of both Ernest Shackleton and P. G. Wodehouse together with their less famous – and in the case of Shackleton notorious – Alleynian brothers, and also into the Dulwich career of Raymond Chandler.

Shackleton

Ernest Shackleton (1874–1922) was enrolled at the College at the age of twelve in 1887. According to his contemporary Owen Burne, he did little work, and 'if there was a scrap he was usually in it'.[232] He habitually cut school, and spent much time in a dell with a pond in woodland near railway tracks at Sydenham with three friends, all of whom eventually went to sea; the truants had with them objects that uncannily prefigured the experience of being marooned on Elephant Island: a banjo, a model ship, and tobacco.[233] Shackleton appeared from his Form positions to be well below the 'average boy'; he was presumably bored by conventional school-work. However, he twice achieved untypically high results that showed his real ability: he came second out of 18 in his form for English History and Literature at Christmas 1889, his last academic year, and ninth out of 22 for Mathematics in the Lower Third. His attempts at Latin verse, however, were later recalled with mirth by one of his form.[234] Two legends in print grew up about his schooldays, neither of them proven. One was that he lay on the floor during a lesson to observe the Transit of Venus through a piece of smoked glass when he had calculated it would pass over a high skylight;[235] unfortunately the Transit of Venus took place in 1882. He is also said to have climbed on to the roof of the Centre Block up to the lantern (or 'pagoda').[236] A myth also grew up, possibly put about by Shackleton himself, that he ran away from school to sea. Letters in the College archives from his widow Emily (herself the sister of an Old Alleynian) are at pains to insist that he implored his father, a General Practitioner, to grant his consent to the boy's wishes to go to sea; his father eventually agreed in 1890 to his leaving the Lower Fourth Form of the Modern Side for the Mercantile Marine, although he had hoped for the boy to become a doctor. Sweet-Escott claimed the credit for getting him a job with Sir Donald Currie's Castle Line through his influence.[237] Shackleton's first Captain said he had never known such a pig-headed boy. He was saved from drowning, pulled from the sea by his hair, and experienced hurricanes rounding Cape Horn. No wonder that when Shackleton wrote an article for schoolboy readers of *The Captain* in 1910, 'How I Began', he claimed that for all the good points of Dulwich his first year at sea was a better school; he was particularly critical of his English lessons, saying that at the College 'literature consisted in the dissection, the parsing, the analysing of certain passages from our great poets and prose writers.... Teachers should be very careful not to spoil [boys'] taste for poetry for all time by making it a task and an imposition'. On the contrary, he had developed his own appreciation of literature from the long hours of reading in his cabin: 'I seemed to get at the heart of it then, to see its meaning, to understand its message, and in some degree to catch its spirit'.[238] Shackleton's father was a Scholar of Trinity College, Cambridge, in Classics, and the family bandied about literary quotations at the dinner table; he himself was particularly well read in poetry, and could recite literally hundreds of lines of Robert Browning in tents during blizzards to not always receptive listeners. Shackleton

Shackleton at the College to present the prizes, July 1909.
(Dulwich College)

was also a most expressive writer; his account of the *Endurance* expedition, *South* (1919), deserves to be better known. The College kept its eyes on his career, and *The Alleynian*, in the section 'Occasional News', where Old Alleynian achievements were reported, remarked his leaving with Scott on the *Discovery* expedition in 1901, together with his intended work as editor of the expedition paper, *The South Polar Times*, and as an assistant with the scientific research. Eighteen months later it recorded that, chosen as one of Scott's sledging companions, Shackleton attained the farthest south ever achieved (latitude 82 degrees 17 minutes South), after the most arduous sledging of 94 days.[239] As Commander of the *Nimrod* expedition in 1907 to 1909 (as full of interest as the *Endurance* expedition), Shackleton sledged 432 miles further than Scott (just 97 miles short of the Pole), turning back so as not to lose lives. In July 1909, as the man of the hour, he presented the Prizes in the Great Hall; he recalled the many times he left such occasions 'with a chastened spirit', saying "I have never before been so near to the prizes as I have been today". It must have seemed something of a mythical occasion: the Hall was decked out with Union flags to greet him; Gilkes's habitual mild severity relaxed on the dais, according to the young Wilson Knight, and he put his arm round Shackleton. In February 1910 he gave a lecture to the boys with slides and cinematograph on the *Nimrod* expedition, summarised in *The Alleynian*, and he gave the College Museum a collection of Antarctic rocks and minerals (now lost). He moralised about reversals in struggles and praised his men for possessing the 'same spirit as had built up the great British nation'. When he showed the boys a slide of a wilderness of ice and snow with small men and sledges, he fell silent; when they began to shuffle their feet, he said, "You stuck it for 44 seconds: we stuck it for five weeks".[240]

Shackleton attended a good number of Alleyn Club dinners; his exploits were referred to proudly in speeches again and again, speakers giving the credit to the playing fields and the classrooms of Dulwich for his fortitude 'amid the chilly, passionless, monotonous silences of Polar regions'.[241] Shackleton was one of the founders of the Old Alleynian Lodge on 14 December 1920. Alleynian and other Masons always supported him generously throughout his career, particularly in South America.

At the Alleyn Club dinner in 1909 Canon Carver pointed out that Dulwich was greatly interested in Polar investigation long before Shackleton's 'great deed', and that the 'goblin' Bidgood and the 'ideal British tar' Bedford Pim were both part of an earlier Arctic Expedition (see Chapter Six);[242] since we know that Bidgood told the boys his thrilling stories, it is quite possible that

Opposite: Alleyn Club 37th Annual Dinner, Hotel Cecil, 1910. Sir Ernest Shackleton seated midway between the two standing flunkies. (Dulwich College)

Shackleton and Rudmose Brown (see below), an important member of the *Scotia* expedition of 1903, were inspired by them. Belgrave Ninnis (1887–1913) of the Royal Fusiliers was a third Alleynian Antarctic explorer of 'the Heroic Age' (but attended the College too late to know Bidgood). Ninnis died in a tragic fall with his sledge and dogs down a concealed crevasse at the age of 24 in 1913. Turned down by Scott for the *Terra Nova* expedition, Shackleton had persuaded Douglas Mawson to take him on as a member of the scientific staff for his Australasian Expedition.

Edward Everett, ever-loyal Old Boy and Assistant Master, published these lines in *The Alleynian*:

> HAIL! Shackleton, by no mere stroke of luck
> Victor declared in the Antarctic strife.
> Example of the abounding Dulwich pluck
> That lifts Alleynians to the higher life.
> Ennobled by no freak of wealth or birth,
> Knight of the Pole and champion of the earth.[243]

The famous *Endurance* expedition, intended by Shackleton to be 'the greatest Polar journey on record', setting out to 'cross the Antarctic from sea to sea, securing for the British flag the honour of being the first carried across the South Polar Continent', was announced in 1914.[244] Shackleton, just 15 days before he left on what was to be his third Antarctic adventure, declared in his speech at Gilkes's farewell dinner that his days at the College were not days of 'unalloyed happiness', but that for this he had himself to blame. He recited the names of the masters present at the dinner who had taught him; among his 'sacred memories' of Dulwich, Gilkes's influence was crucial: he had spelled out to him 'the things he ought not to do'. He explained that what he hoped to accomplish would be equivalent to pulling a sledge all the way from Dulwich to Constantinople. He hoped that not only his country but also his old school might be proud of his forthcoming exploit. Shackleton ended by declaiming a most stirring verse (modified from James Elroy Flecker's 'God Save the King') about the South Atlantic Ocean – 'the dolphined deep' – and youth conquering 'dim lands where Empires sleep'.[245]

After the *Endurance* expedition *The Alleynian* noted the award of Shackleton's additional 'clasp' to the Polar Medal, and also the publication of his 'thrilling' book, *South*, but it is remarkable that there was no direct reference at that time in the magazine to the actual fate of the *Endurance* and the men on the ice, the astonishing journey of the *James Caird* and the crossing of South Georgia; in other words, the story of the sunk ship and the heroic rescue, now known throughout the world and recognised as Shackleton's greatest achievement, was not mentioned in the College magazine until it published his long obituary in 1922. The Great War preoccupied the College, and there may well have been at Dulwich a feeling that in view of the shortage of officers and men it was bad form to set off exploring three days after war was declared; it was unlikely that anyone at the College knew that Shackleton (as Commander of the expedition) had offered his ship, staff and stores to the Admiralty at their disposal to fight against Germany on the eve of his departure, and had been instructed to 'proceed south'. In 1920, two years before his death on the *Quest* expedition, Shackleton spoke again at an Alleyn Club dinner and referred a second time to his troubled schooldays; he went on to say, "Although my time at Dulwich was short, and I have been a stormy petrel, the love of the College was there when I left, and remained with me during my life". When he died, Shackleton's brother-in-law wrote that he was 'a boy all his life', and was now the 'representative hero' and 'patron saint of millions of Public School boys'.[246]

Although Shackleton was at first charged by Scott with 'scientific research', of an elementary kind, his real interests in Antarctica were romantic, heroic, and imperial. A less famous explorer, Robert Rudmose Brown (1879–1957), was at the College from 1890 to 1896, and served on expeditions at Spitzbergen and at both Poles. He was a botanist, but later, as his obituarist wrote in *The Times*, was to become 'one of the leading agents in Britain for raising the study of geography up to a high academic discipline by freeing it alike from scholasticism and from amateurishness'. His wonderful book *The Voyage of the Scotia* (1906), an account of the Scottish National Antarctic Expedition under William Spiers Bruce to the South Orkneys, was equally eloquent about the transcendent beauty of Antarctica and the forms and colours of the teeming marine contents of the dredge hauled up for their laboratory: sea-spiders, sea-urchins, sea-mice and sea-cucumbers. He gave a slide lecture to the boys in 1905.[247] Brown began his career investigating the pearl oyster fisheries in Lower Burma; he later held a first Lectureship in Geography at the University of Sheffield from 1908, becoming a famous Professor there.

Frank Shackleton (1876–1941) presents an extraordinary and pitiful contrast to his brother Ernest. His Form positions, on the one hand, were high: in the Lower II Form he was top of his class and also top in French, and he came fifth in the Classical V Form in 1893, the year he was to leave at the age of 17. Good looks and dishonesty were his downfall; after a scandalous time in the army with the Royal Irish Fusiliers in South Africa, when it was rumoured that he pilfered Mess funds and was found in bed with a young native boy, he was 'invalided' home, in 1900. Suddenly he was living in a luxurious flat in Park

Lane, without a penny of his own. Involved in swindles and fraudulent shares, often cheating people he knew well in society, he was declared bankrupt shortly after Ernest's knighthood in 1910; he was once followed by a detective to Portuguese West Africa, arrested and brought back to London for trial; at a later date he was sentenced to 15 months' hard labour. He associated with a circle of rich (and even royal) homosexuals, such as a shady group of men connected with the College of Heralds in Dublin, where he was improbably appointed Dublin Herald. Lord Ronald Gower (1845–1916), to whom he had been introduced by Ernest, unwisely brought a law case against him in 1911, involving large amounts he had given to the younger man for bogus investments in Montevideo. Christison, then working for a firm involved in share deals, gave evidence at this trial, and details of the somewhat ridiculous liaison between Lord Ronald and Frank Shackleton circulated in the newspapers. Frank appears to have been completely shameless: Christison sent a printed circular to members of the Alleyn Club warning them that others had been approached by an Old Boy 'with a famous name' begging for loans; and he was the principal suspect in the unsolved theft of the Irish Crown Jewels in 1905, though the case was never proven. Having changed his name to Mellor, the black sheep of the family later lived with two of his sisters in Chichester, making a living as an antiques dealer, with a special interest in jewels.[248]

Wodehouse

Neither Gilkes nor Hose thought much of Wodehouse's writings.[249] However, there is no Dulwich boy about whose schooldays there is a fuller or more interesting account than P. G. Wodehouse (1881–1975). This is partly because he was a conspicuous and original boy, and, as was recognised by *The Alleynian* for 1902, his schooldays were 'singularly full and many-sided',[250] but also because he wrote so much about the College in various ways. After leaving the school he kept up a commentary on Dulwich in the course of over four hundred letters to a close friend from his boarding-house days at Elm Lawn, Bill Townend (1881–1952), who after an abortive career as a black-and-white illustrator was to become a prolific and forgotten novelist, publishing 44 titles.[251] Wodehouse joined the College at the age of twelve in 1894 as a boarder, first in Sweet-Escott's Ivyholme and then from 1896 at T. G. Treadgold's Elm Lawn. For one year in 1895–6 he was a day-boy when his parents took a house at 62 Croxted Road on their return from Hong Kong, and before retiring to Shropshire. It has become a commonplace of Wodehouse biographers that a psychological displacement took place, with Wodehouse, a virtual

orphan of the Empire from the age of two, experiencing a transference from his real mother, of whom he saw little until he was 15, to his Alma Mater Dulwich College. George Orwell, for one, wrote in 1945 that Wodehouse had a 'fixation' on Dulwich. Here instead of the traumas conventionally claimed by writers as productive neuroses of their work, Wodehouse experienced 'just six years of unbroken bliss'.[252] The young Pelham ('Plum', as he was known from his infant attempts to pronounce his name) was awarded a Senior School scholarship at Midsummer 1897, but was eclipsed academically by his elder brother Armine (1879–1936), whose Form positions in the Classical side were higher. Moreover, Armine was the only one of the two to hold the accolade of being invited (on four occasions) to transcribe his Greek or Latin translations (from Milton, Shelley and Tennyson) into a splendid (surviving) manuscript volume, bound in red calf, with a Virgilian title, *Haec Olim Meminisse Juvabit* [this will give pleasure in the future]; this was kept at first in the Classical Sixth form-room, and later was locked in a cupboard in the Prefects' Room. From P. G. Wodehouse's Form positions, based on an average of subjects, printed in the College 'Blue Book', it is seen that he was second in the Lower Fifth out of 27 boys, Sheppard (later of King's) coming eighth; sixth in the Classical Upper Fifth, still two places above Sheppard; and fourth in the Classical Remove of 1898. He was towards the top of his class during the early months of his leaving year in 1900, by his own account springing from his bed at five sharp each morning, eating a couple of *petit beurre* biscuits and working like a beaver at his Homer and Thucydides; seven of the boys won Oxford and Cambridge open awards in Classics, three of them below Wodehouse in Form order.[253] From such figures it seems clear that Wodehouse would normally have followed Armine to Oxford; however (as touched on above), even with the possibility of financial awards from the University and from Dulwich College, Wodehouse's father calculated that since he had retired early (with serious sunstroke) from the Civil Service in Hong Kong and was now living on a pension, and since the value of the rupee in which it was paid had fallen sensationally, he could not afford to maintain two boys at university. As in the equivalent case of Michael Powell a generation later, a highly talented Dulwich boy did not proceed to university for financial reasons, but was found a temporary job in a bank; Wodehouse's father had a friend who worked in the Hongkong and Shanghai Bank. The boy's Form position fell dramatically that year to 19 out of 24. As described above, Wodehouse was rescued after two years from the Hongkong Bank by the ministrations of his former form master, Beach Thomas, who found him a job as a comic journalist.

P. G. Wodehouse, cricketer, 1900. (Dulwich College)

I often wonder if you and I were unusually fortunate in our school-days. To me the years between 1896 and 1900 seem like Heaven. Was the average man really unhappy at school? Or was Dulwich in our day an exceptionally good school? [255]

He recognised that being on the Classical Side was 'the best form of education I could have had as a writer'; the list of texts he would have studied from the Upper Third Form to the Classical Sixth is equivalent to most Classical degree courses now. Gilkes wrote in Wodehouse's report of July 1899 for his Classical Sixth year (if the text was not 'improved' by Wodehouse himself; the original has not survived):

He is a most impractical boy. Continually he does badly in examinations from lack of the proper books; he is often forgetful; he finds difficulties in the most simple things, and asks absurd questions, whereas he can understand the more difficult things. He has the most distorted ideas about wit and humour; he draws over his books and examination papers in the most distressing way and writes foolish rhymes in other people's books. Notwithstanding he has a genuine interest in literature and can often talk with much enthusiasm and good sense about it. He does some things at times astonishingly well, and writes good Latin verses. He is a very useful boy in the school and in the VI Form, and one is obliged to like him in spite of his vagaries.... If he perseveres he will certainly succeed. [256]

Whereas the only records of Raymond Chandler's schooldays are a first-rate series of Form positions and prizes, and the many entries in the Library register of the books he borrowed, Wodehouse participated in an extraordinary range of school life. As a cricketer, he took seven wickets against Tonbridge in the First XI, and a report from *The Alleynian*, very likely written by Wodehouse himself, reads, 'Bowled well against Tonbridge, but did nothing else. Does not use his head at all. A poor bat and very slack field'. As a Rugby footballer, he was 'the weighty Wodehouse', Captain of the Second XV in 1898–9 and then a member of the First XV. He broke the school High Jump record in May 1899; Gilkes described his boxing in his diary. Moreover, he was a journalist, an actor, a songster, a Prefect and a Librarian. [254] He wrote to Townend fifty years after their schooldays:

When Gilkes borrowed Wodehouse's copy of Euripides in class one day he found that Wodehouse had drawn page after page of matchstick human figures (such as are to be seen by his signature in the Alleyn Club book for 6 July 1920) and handed it back saying, "No thank you, this book has got a man in it". As a highly intelligent schoolboy, Wodehouse perhaps defined himself by reaction to the overwhelming, sententious, Olympian figure of Gilkes. With his brilliant satirical eye for the absurd, he figured 'the Old Man' in a final incarnation as the tall, vague, bearded head master of the Grammar School at Market Snodsbury where Bertie Wooster gives the prizes in *Right Ho, Jeeves!* (1934). This scene involves, for all its anarchic brilliance, an understanding of the conventions, taboos and evasions of schoolmasters of the period, and of the formalised language in which they expressed them;

P. G. Wodehouse. Bowled well against Tonbridge but did nothing else. Does not use his head at all. A poor bat & very slack field.
P. G. Wodehouse was 2nd in the 1st bowling averages with 16 wickets at 14 runs apiece.

P. G. Wodehouse's own description of his First XI cricket season for 1899, written by him in his House book, *Mr Treadgold's House*, 1896–1914. (Dulwich College)

P. G. Wodehouse (seated, right) wth mask for *The Frogs*, Founder's Day, 1898. (Private collection)

a review of the earlier *Tales of St. Austin's* in *The Alleynian* said that Wodehouse wrote with 'no tinge of the didactic'. Lost are Wodehouse's Dulwich plays praised by Townend, parodies of Greek tragedies, 'in which he substituted friends or teachers for the citizens of Athens'. [257] Wodehouse was already publishing contributions to Public School and sporting magazines as a Sixth-Former, and his black-clasped notebook, entitled 'Money received for Literary Work' is preserved in the College Archives.

Wodehouse sang three solos in the Great Hall. One was an old College favourite, given at a School Concert in 1900, 'Hybrias the Cretan', with Thomas Campbell's robust lines about the virile archaic Cretan with burly spear and shield, and his joy in drawing his sword to bring down 'hapless heartless drones'; in *Uncle Dynamite* of 1948 Wodehouse, so many years on, imagines Sir Aylmer Bostock singing this song, as an index to his good spirits. [258] He played in the Chorus to Aristophanes' *Frogs* on Founder's Day in 1898, and in W. S. Gilbert's *Rosencranz and Guildenstern* during his last term in 1900, when he added a touch of lunatic fancy in a dance, 'exact species unknown'. [259] As Editor of *The Alleynian* he obviously enjoyed opportunities for mischief, and in response to a letter asking about Christmas customs at the College he wrote back 'a vivid account of the annual snowball fight between masters and the Sixth Form'. [260]

His first publications were in the magazine, including several unsigned pieces of prose (such as the witty 'Dumb-Bells in the Bath') and two poems, one with a ridiculous stanza about builders in the College grounds:

> I raised my eye (which I had fixed
> Upon a book of Coptic),
> And close at hand a dauntless band
> Of diggers met my optic! [261]

When Wodehouse left the College, for seven or eight years afterwards he would bring back guest teams, both 'P. G. Wodehouse's XI' and his 'XV', to play against the College, and was a spectator at countless matches until 1939. He wrote to *The Alleynian* with a proposal for a vigorous and raucous 'Yell' he had devised for use by the College on the touchline, such as he had heard the students use at Penn State College in America, saying, 'This is the right stuff. It would stir a caterpillar'. [262] From 1907 to 1908, and again from 1920 to 1939, he wrote reviews of four First XI and twenty-two First XV matches that sometimes stretched to three pages. In 1932 he wrote to Bill Townend that 'never in [his] life' had he 'experienced such suspense' as during the second half of the Sherborne match, 'culminating in Billy Griffith scoring that superb try'. [263] He would appear clad in grey plus-fours, a grey overcoat and a grey felt cap; sometimes he would take a flight from Le Touquet, where he was living, to see a game, and in 1938 he sent a five pound note, which he could at that date still describe as 'a purse of gold', to Alan Shirreff, the Captain of the unbeaten First XI, which paid for a West End dinner and a show at the Palladium for all his team. Wodehouse lamented the decline, as he saw it, of *The Alleynian* after the Second World War, in particular because detailed reports of the matches had been abandoned; he also told Townend how much he disliked the reports of all the debates and political meetings and poetry societies. He wrote dyspeptically to Christison in 1969 that it was no loss that the magazine was no longer sent to Old Alleynians: 'they have ruined it with all this art photography and bad poetry'. [264]

It is well known that at the same time, living in exiled old age on Long Island, Wodehouse would break open the air-mail edition of *The Times* and at once check the progress of the Dulwich teams. From Paris in November 1946 he wrote to Townend saying, 'Isn't it odd, when one ought to be worrying about the state of the world and one's troubles generally, that the only thing I can think of

nowadays is that Dulwich looks like winning all its school matches and surpassing the 1909 record (because they now play nine schools, and in 1909 it was only five)'. [265]

In *Psmith in the City* (1910), at the point where the cricketer Mike Jackson has recently left the College, there is a piece of elegiac writing, unusual in his work, in which Wodehouse betrays real pangs for his own expulsion from the Eden of his happy days at Dulwich:

> Mike wandered out of the house. A few steps took him to the railings that bounded the College grounds. It was late August, and the evenings had begun to close in. The cricket-field looked very cool and spacious in the dim light, with the school buildings looming vague and shadowy through the slight mist. The little gate by the railway bridge was not locked. He went in, and walked slowly across the turf towards the big clump of trees which marked the division between the cricket and foot-ball fields. … He sat down on a bench beside the second eleven telegraph-board, and looked across the ground at the pavilion. For the first time that day he began to feel really homesick. The cricket-field and the pavilion … brought home to him with a cutting distinctness, the absolute finality of his break with the old order of things. Summers would come and go, matches would be played on this ground with all the glory of big scores and keen finishes; but he was done. 'He was a jolly good bat at school. Top of the Wrykyn averages two years. But didn't do anything after he left. Went into the city or something.' That was what they would say of him, if they didn't quite forget him.
>
> The clock on the tower over the senior block chimed quarter after quarter, but Mike sat on, thinking. It was quite late when he got up, and began to walk back to Acacia Road. He felt cold and stiff and very miserable. [266]

By 1909, when still in his twenties, Wodehouse had published almost fifty short stories and six school novels (almost all serialised in *The Captain* or *Public School Magazine*) based on his years at Dulwich, and a collection, *Tales of St. Austin's* (1903). These show many observed features of the College itself, with the boarding houses on the Common, the neighbouring village and the woods above. The mill-pond at the corner of the crossroads by College Road and Dulwich Common is where a group of Wodehouse's schoolboys duck a policeman. There is also a gallery of teachers, who are variously weak, strong, fussy, sporting, pompous, sarcastic, and other-worldly – rotters and decent sorts. The boys, who play themes from

"ARENT YOU GOING TO DO *any* WORK, BRADSHAW!"

E. F. Skinner, a boarding house scene. Illustration to P. G. Wodehouse, 'Bradshaw's Little Story'. *The Captain*, July 1902. (Jan Piggott)

musical comedies on the banjo, talk robustly, exclaiming 'Rather!' and 'Thanks awfully!', 'By Jove!' and 'Stout fellow!'; their speech is peppered with 'ripping', 'rot', and 'tosh'. 'What's up?' is a characteristic question. There is a ghastly boy who puts eau-de-cologne on his handkerchief and another who could not catch a ball at cricket fielding practice, even 'if you handed it to him on a plate, with watercress round it'. In this way we overhear how Gilkes's boys talked between lessons, and learn about features of College life we might not know otherwise, such as that at the Concert applause was given in relation to the performers' popularity as sportsmen rather than for their musical skill. [267] A great interest is shown in schoolboy codes of behaviour and tribal attitudes; in some ways these are an expression of the 'Public School spirit' with a familiarly Gilkesian emphasis on team work, on unselfish civilised behaviour, on not getting above oneself, and on avoiding affectation or boasting. Mackenzie is presumably echoing the view of Wodehouse's school books in the Dulwich Common Room when he writes, 'with the deeper meaning of school life he does not concern himself, but treats its lighter aspects in the most entertaining fashion'. These are not frivolous books, however: *The Head of Kay's* (1905) concerns a disaffected boarding house, and *The White Feather* (1907) is about the pains of a quiet boy ostracised by his peers, and his perseverance in recovering his reputation by learning how to box. The stories are chivalric 'romances' in the traditional sense, and usually feature the loss of a numinous object whose rediscovery at the end symbolises honour recovered for both the individual and the tribe. The generous and gallant outwit the slack and the bullies. The College rules are treated with some contempt, but to break the boys' own codes is a terrible crime; one boy tells another, "All I can say is that you're not fit to be at a public school". [268] Whether or not deeper meanings of psychology or morality consciously impinged on his school fiction, Wodehouse's schoolboy relish of linguistic play is brilliant, raising nonsense to poetry, as for example when (in parody of John Baptiste Joerg) he gives us the pronouncements of Old Steingruber, a much ragged German teacher:

> As your boet says, of all zad worts of dongue or ben, der zaddest vos dese, it mide haf been…. De condemblation of de Sherman verbs resume let us, my liddle students. I vill a zendence write in idiomatig Sherman, which of these two verbs the pegularities illusdrates. Zo. [269]

In 1939 Wodehouse was awarded the degree of honorary Doctor of Letters (D. Litt.) at Oxford; there was a ceremony in the Sheldonian Theatre where he stood to receive three minutes of acclamation and some Horatian hexameters composed by the Public Orator –

'*Petroniumne dicam an Terentium nostrum?*' ['shall I call him our Petronius or our Terence?']. This glorious accolade from the Hebdomal Council at an Encaenia surely healed any possible injury done to Wodehouse by his earlier forfeit of an Oxford degree and endorsed his reputation as a great comic writer. Wodehouse's later (temporary) fall from grace after he broadcast from Berlin during the War, and its repercussions at Dulwich, are discussed below in connection with his Dulwich contemporary, Sir Eustace Pulbrook.

Armine Wodehouse might have looked set to have a more promising (if more conventional) future than his famous brother, with equal sporting and superior academic achievement; his *Alleynian* obituary in 1936 said that in a 'vintage year' at the College he had great gifts, and also that he held 'renown' for his musical performances, which showed a 'command unusual in a boy'. He returned to play Chopin and Schubert at a concert in 1904. [270] While Wodehouse toiled unhappily in the bank, Armine's Oxford successes were lettered in gold, appearing five times on the Honours Boards in the Great Hall; these were his open award at Corpus Christi College, a First Class in both parts of the Classics degree, and two signal other prizes: he was the only Alleynian ever to win the Newdigate Prize for Poetry, for his narrative poem *Minos* in 1902, with its echoes of his Dulwich reading in Milton, Tennyson and Keats, and which he recited in the Sheldonian Theatre; he also won the Chancellor's Prize for an English Essay in 1903. Armine led an interesting and unusual life, although said in his later years to be overcome with a classic general fatigue and laziness. In 1905 he left England to take up an academic appointment in Bombay. By 1910 he was much engrossed with Annie Besant and other luminaries of oriental wisdom, and became President of her College of Theosophy at Benares. [271] He wrote articles on India and on transcendental matters for the serious London periodicals, and (under the pseudonym 'Senex') light verse for *The Times of India*. Like many Alleynians, he returned to England at the call of the Great War, to fight in the Scots Guards, and as Lieutenant E. A. Wodehouse he returned in 1917 to the Great Hall to play a Beethoven Piano Concerto. [272] A volume of war poems, *On Leave: Poems and Sonnets*, showing intensity of feeling and observation, was published the same year by the prestigious publisher Elkin Matthews, and went into a second edition.

Raymond Chandler

Raymond Chandler (1888–1959), whose five years at Dulwich began in 1900, once claimed in a letter to Hamish Hamilton that it would come as a shock to his critics to know that he studied Classics at Dulwich, though of

Raymond Chandler, Upper Classical Fifth, 1904 (top right), with H. F. Hose. (Dulwich College)

course from his writing this is not truly surprising; he was to call his education at the College 'very good'. Chandler had an alcoholic father, divorced from his mother when the boy was seven, and whom he never saw after that; he came to London from Los Angeles at the age of eleven with his mother and they settled with his snobbish grand-mother in Upper Norwood; his fees at the College were partly paid by his maternal uncle, a wealthy Irish lawyer. He was an introverted boy, and does not appear to have played much, if any, part in activities outside the class-room. He was placed second in the First Form at Christ-mas 1900, and the same in the following year when promoted to the Upper Second Form. In 1903 he came first in the Classical Lower Fifth and won the Form prize. He was quite often absent through ill health, and thus was not placed in the Classical Fourth. Library registers show that he borrowed many books; Thackeray and Charles Lamb were favourite authors. He recalled that he pos-sessed no marked literary ability at school, but that he had 'the qualifications to become a pretty good second-rate poet'.[273] He was withdrawn early, at 16, in April 1905, studied in France and Germany, and then, at his family's insistence, took the Civil Service examination, passing third out of eight hundred candidates, and coming top in the Classics paper. In *The Alleynian* he published his early poems. A recent biography and his entry in the *Oxford*

Dictionary of National Biography assert that Chandler taught for a term at the College, but there is no documen-tary evidence for this; it is quite possible that H. F. Hose, who had been his form-master, arranged for him to take some informal part-time teaching or coaching. He cer-tainly joined the Old Alleynian Football Club, and indeed was 'one of its voluntary ground staff'.[274] In the early 1950s Chandler's thoughts turned from Los Angeles to Dulwich, and he sent 'huge' monthly food parcels (during rationing) in 1951 to Hose, Christison and Bill Townend, and books to Hose. To the latter he wrote on 22 May 1952, 'We are old friends, and a long time ago you did a great deal for me and I have not forgotten it. If there is anything you want, repeat *anything*, and which you cannot afford or which you think you should not afford, I think you should say'.[275] Chandler's obituary in *The Alleynian* says that he hated every minute of his stultifying Civil Service post at the Admiralty. He walked out of it after six months, intend-ing to live on his wits and with his pen; during his unset-tled London years from 1909 to 1912 he again contributed to *The Alleynian* (under his schoolboy pseudonym 'Tharndec') a number of poems and pieces of prose, some slight, all strange, including what he described as a piece of 'satirical burlesque' about an Inferno in which readers, writers, artists and politicians, all of them obsessive types, are punished;[276] one of the poems, 'The Imperfect Poet to his Muse' has the verse

> Though my metre is ungainly
> As a gouty camel's stride;
> Though my language is as shaggy
> As the ourang's blue-faced bride …
> Mayhap in the days of Noah
> I was quite a man of mark.
> Mayhap I thrust my shoulders
> From a window of the Ark,
> And with a muscular emotion
> Hurled a sonnet through the dark.[277]

In the Great War Chandler served as a 'Lance/Corporal' with the Canadian Infantry, Gordon Highlanders, in France, a fact omitted from the *Dulwich College War Record.* Shortly after Chandler's death, Bill Townend wrote to Christison telling him about his alcoholic later visits to expensive London hotels, once his income from his books and films had made him a very rich man, and about his suicide attempt after his wife's death; he recalled how the two men first met and became friends on recognising the Alleyn Club hat-bands on their straw boaters in San Francisco in June 1913, at a time when Chandler was making a very poor income stringing lawn tennis racquets.[278] Chandler may have acknowledged an ambivalence towards the College by coded allusions in his novels. It has been argued that the name of his most famous creation, the detective Philip Marlow, is a tribute to two of the Founder's colleagues, Philip Henslowe and Christopher Marlowe (see Chapter One); [279] at the same time, the decadent Lindsay Marriott, whom Marlow encounters and dislikes in *Farewell, My Lovely* (1940), and who is later bumped off, wears 'a cornflower in the lapel of his white coat'. Critics point out that Chandler asserts 'Kipling ideals'; Marlow confronts Los Angeles like a Gilkesian champion of virtue and truth.

Other writers, academics, scientists, doctors, the City, artists, the stage and music

Gilkes's Golden Age fostered an extraordinary and colourful range of original, talented and successful Alleynians, as the following paragraphs are designed to show. Stanley Portal-Hyatt (1877–1914) used his experiences of sheep farming in New South Wales and of hunting and working among pioneers in the Far East and in Africa to write many novels such as *Biffel, a Trek Ox* (1909) and *The Little Brown Brother* (1911). Claude Houghton (Oldfield) (1889–1961), a permanent Civil Servant at the Admiralty, was a prolific novelist, admired by Wodehouse, interweaving contemporary life with the supernatural and metaphysical. Of his twenty or so novels, some are still popular in translation in France and Spain, and are enjoying a revival; his papers are at the University of Texas. C. P. Hawkes (1877–1951) was political cartoonist for the *Daily Graphic*; among several books he wrote *Heydays* (1933), a genial memoir of worldly people, actors and artists in London at the turn of the century. Major Charles Gilson (1878–1943), after a military career and work in military prisons, published adventure stories in the *Boy's Own Paper*, and many books for boys, including *The Lost Empire: a Tale of Many Lands* (1910), which was often reprinted. Dennis Wheatley (1897–1977), the highly successful writer of thrillers and of occult books, was expelled from Dulwich at 13 after two and a half terms. In his autobiography, *The Time has Come, the Young Man Said* (1977), he gives an elaborate account of how, once he had stolen a brand new cap from another boy (and found it several sizes too large for him) and since he had spent the half-crown his father had given him for a new one, he ran away to Canada, getting as far as Bromley Police Station. His account of his 'rotten school' and of Gilkes, 'tall, grim, unapproachable, … a living symbol in our minds of harshness and punishment', of brutal Rugby scrums and dreary lessons is suitably spiteful. [280]

The four Moore brothers were exceptionally cultivated. G. E. Moore (1873–1958) won prizes and was promoted, as was then possible, to the Lower Sixth at the age of ten. He was Captain of School from 1890 until 1892,

and revived the Debating Society, of which he was President. A typical motion of his days was to abolish the monarchy and divert the revenue to free nationalised railway travel for all; the report in *The Alleynian* referred to the attendance at the debate of members of the 'lowest order of Social-Democrats in our society'. Gilkes noted in his diary that Moore 'was an excellent scholar, very accurate and very learned: and always very attentive to the interests of the school'. [281] Moore was elected Fellow of Trinity College, Cambridge, in 1898, and his career was truly brilliant; an 'Apostle' at Cambridge, he became indeed part of British intellectual history: an early analytic philosopher, the author of *Principia Ethica* (1903). A luminary of the Bloomsbury Group, he was revered for moral and mental purity, and significantly influenced Bertrand Russell and Wittgenstein. To experience his devotion to truth was said to be truly enthralling: 'in argument his whole frame was gripped by a passion to confute error and expose confusion'. [282] He was appointed to a Chair in Mental Philosophy and Logic at Cambridge in 1925. In 1951 he was awarded the Order of Merit, one of the very highest honours in the country. Moore was, incidentally, a good pianist, and played the piano at a Cambridge Old Alleynian dinner in 1901; [283] he remained very loyal to the College for many years, and his name always appeared with generous subscriptions in response to appeals. J. H. 'Bertie' Moore (1876–1955), the youngest, was said in 1903 to be the most distinguished musician Dulwich ever produced; [284] however, after teaching the piano at Charterhouse for two years, he joined the Slade School of Art. Inheriting an income, he settled in Florence, where he painted very slowly, never sold or exhibited his pictures, and never married. [285] The eldest brother, Daniel 'Harry' Moore (1871–1948), was one of Sanderson's best pupils and a prolific winner of prizes, the President of the school's Science Society and of the Photographic Society in 1888–9. A Scholar at Trinity College, Cambridge, he is likely to have had as fine a mind as Harold Hartley; however, he resigned his Trinity fellowship in Natural Sciences to become a Yorkshire vicar in 1899 and later a missionary in Japan, to his family's dismay at his 'sacrificing' a brilliant career. Thomas Sturge Moore (1870–1944) was a poet, artist and wood-engraver, a friend and an important correspondent of W. B. Yeats (who described him unkindly as a 'a sheep in sheep's clothing'). [286]

The de Sélincourt boys, all originally Classicists, were devoted scholarly men of letters. Basil (1876–1966) was appointed Professor of Greek at Sydney University at the age of 23, and published a book on Giotto in 1905. Ernest (1870–1943), Professor of English at Birmingham and Professor of Poetry at Oxford (1928–33), was one of

Greek Play, date unknown. (Private collection)

the greatest authorities on Wordsworth and Keats. Hugh (1878–1951), whose affectionate memoir of Gilkes is quoted above, was a writer and civil servant, Assistant Under-Secretary of State at the War Office in 1926, who became famous for his story 'The Cricket Match' (1924).

In these decades the Oxford and Cambridge 'Letters' in *The Alleynian*, reporting the activities of Old Alleynian undergraduates, convey a lively impression of the pleasures and excitements of the Edwardian 'Varsity. In 1903, a year in which Gilkes's boys won 16 awards at Oxford and Cambridge, the Oxford Letter in *The Alleynian* noted that there were now six Alleynian dons teaching at the University.[287] The great academics of this period have already been mentioned in this chronicle, and they showed their *esprit de corps* by the interest they retained in the College, in several cases (as already mentioned) by becoming the Governors nominated by Oxford or Cambridge.

John Tressider 'Jack' Sheppard (1881–1968), the famous Cambridge Classicist, was asked by his Form Master on his first day at the College whether he wished to take German or Greek as his extra language; impressed by the imposing size of the lexicon on the master's desk, he chose Greek, only to be told by his mother on his return that he had made the wrong choice. Sheppard wrote that he later chose to apply to study at King's at Cambridge because Philip Hope, himself a Scholar of King's, said to him, "if you go to Oxford, they will look at your clothes. At Cambridge they won't".[288] Sheppard preserved all Gilkes's letters to him, including letters of condolence after his mother's death and congratulations on his Tripos. Known at Cambridge as the 'Dullish boy', he was President of the Union, returning that year to review the 'Speeches' at Founder's Day, including the Greek play, for *The Alleynian*.[289] Sheppard was a Fellow of King's College in 1906, and in 1933 he was elected Provost, the first non-Etonian to be so for five centuries.

As well as writing many books, another of his achievements at Cambridge was to direct over a period of 35 years the famous triennial productions of his own translations of Greek plays in the mode of the Founder's Day plays. Genial and a brilliant speaker, Sheppard was a missionary for the Classics; he retained his cherubic lineaments into old age. He also served as a forceful and very active Governor of the College from 1917 until 1922, and again (in some particularly difficult years) from 1935 until 1946 (see Chapters Nine and Ten).

Alic Smith, a Captain of School, who left two years after Sheppard in 1902, gained a Scholarship at New College, Oxford, in 1901. He wrote *The Alleynian* 'Oxford Letter' in 1904. Smith became in turn a Fellow at New College and a very popular Tutor in Philosophy, Warden of the College in 1944, and (at the age of over seventy) Vice-Chancellor of Oxford University from 1954 to 1957. Smith was austere in his features, and was likened by Jean Cocteau to Erasmus; Jacob Epstein sculpted his portrait bust at New College. He was also a Governor of Dulwich College from 1935 until 1947. At his Memorial Service the great Sir Maurice Bowra (1898–1971) praised the way he encouraged and inspired undergraduates in sentences which could have applied equally to Gilkes at Dulwich.[290]

In his biography of J. M. Keynes, Roy Harrod observed that 'Dulwich at this time seems to have been remarkably fertile in the production of men of strongly individual genius.... In type of mind and in mode of self-expression, they were utterly unlike any other human being'; among the 166 new boys enrolled in 1894 listed together in Ormiston's *Register* the names of Sheppard, Wodehouse, Hartley and Smith appear in close succession.[291] Walter Rippmann (1869–1947) was Professor of Modern Languages at Bedford and Queen's College in London, and published works on Dante, Grillparzer and other European writers. Hermann Oelsner (1871–1943), the son of a banker from Forest Hill, left in 1899, and became Taylorian Professor of Romance Languages at Oxford from 1909; Gladstone wrote to him to praise his undergraduate essay on Dante.[292] T. A. Joyce (1878–1942), an anthropologist in the Department of Ethnography at the British Museum, became an authority on the Mayas. Sir Hilary Jenkinson (1882–1961), a Classics Scholar at Cambridge, was Deputy Keeper of the Public Record Office, and after the Second World War he was sent to Italy and Germany where he rescued and preserved immense archives of incalculable value. C. D. 'Charlie' Broad (1887–1971), later a distinguished epistemologist, moral philosopher and philosopher of science, was the son of a prosperous wine merchant and gained a First Class in Natural Sciences at Trinity College, Cambridge, followed by a

First in Moral Sciences in 1910. He then studied in Germany; his first important book was *Perception, Physics and Reality* in 1914, to be followed by many other philosophical works and some writings on psychical research. During the War he both lectured and worked in a chemicals factory. In 1926 Broad was elected Fellow in Philosophy at Trinity College, Cambridge, as G. E. Moore had been earlier, and by the mid-1930s, when Broad had been appointed Knightsbridge Professor of Moral Philosophy in 1933, the two of them were at the forefront of British philosophy. Broad retired in 1953 but continued to live in Trinity, where he much enjoyed entertaining Alleynian undergraduates. In 1946, when Jack Sheppard resigned from the College Governors, he had agreed to follow him as the Cambridge University representative on the Board, but resigned after one meeting, saying it was impossible with his lecture duties; he may also have sensed the miserably contentious issues among the Governors at odds with Christopher Gilkes at the time (see Chapter Ten). The same year he presented the Picture Gallery with four rather good Dutch paintings that had belonged to his family (DPG 614–17); at his death he left capital of £21,844, now worth £300,000, to form a Trust for entrance scholarships at Dulwich, or for grants to Dulwich boys at Trinity College, Cambridge, at other universities and at the College itself. Sir William Holdsworth (1871–1944) was the first of two pupils of Gilkes to be awarded the Order of Merit, in 1943. He left the College in 1890, and became the Vinerian Professor of English Law at Oxford, known as the greatest jurist at Oxford since the eighteenth century, and published in many volumes *A History of English Law* (1903 seq.) on which he spent forty years, as well as specialist works; he served as a College Governor from 1922 to 1932. Aubrey Attwater (1892–1935) was Gilkes's Captain of School in 1909. He became a poet; as an undergraduate he sent a poem for publication in *The Alleynian* in June 1912.[293] At first a Classicist, he joined the new English Faculty at Cambridge, conducting tutorials in the old-fashioned civilised style, as a much loved Fellow of Pembroke College. He too was a College Governor from 1926 until a crippling wound from the time he spent in the War with the Royal Welch Fusiliers caught up with him, causing his death.

George Wilson Knight has already been quoted as a witness to events of his school days. In the Great War he and his brother were both dispatch riders; they were to become highly individual, even eccentric, academics. George won the Form prize for the Classical Upper Third Form in 1911,[294] and kept up high positions in Classical forms, later holding chairs in literature at the Universities of Toronto and Exeter. While his Shakespeare criticism,

such as *The Wheel of Fire* (1930), is deservedly famous, he wrote well on a very wide range of topics, especially on the Romantics and on John Cowper Powys. Knight believed in the theatre, and was himself a performer, making an appearance as Hamlet in 1935 in his own production at the Rudolf Steiner Hall in London.[295] On 3 October 1981 he inaugurated the Edward Alleyn Hall at the College with a solo Shakespearian performance (see Chapter Ten) with a memorable *coup de théâtre* when as Timon of Athens he stripped off all his clothes. His brother W. F. Jackson Knight (1895–1964), Reader in Classics at the University of Exeter, was an authority on Virgil; he published several books on him and translated the *Aeneid* (1956) for the Penguin Classics.

Horace Vernon (1870–1951), a biologist and physiologist, who left in 1888, became a Fellow of Magdalen College, Oxford, and published *Intracellular Enzymes* in 1908, lectures given at University College in London. K. M. Smith (1892–1981), an entomologist at the University of Manchester, was a College Governor from 1944 until 1949. N. D. Riley (1890–1979) was Keeper of the Department of Entomology at the British Museum Natural History Department. Among Alleynians in the medical profession, Sir Hugh Rigby (1870–1944) was Surgeon to the King and Queen's household; he is said to have saved George V's life in 1928. Professor G. E. Gask (1875–1951) served as the first Professor of Surgery appointed by the University of London from 1919 until 1935. Geoffrey Dowling (1891–1976), who left in 1910 for Guy's Hospital, was self-taught as a specialist in dermatology; he raised its status in twenty years to the highest level. Sir Cecil Wakeley (1892–1979), after an exceptionally distinguished career, was President of the Royal College of Surgeons from 1949 until 1954; he was awarded a Baronetcy. Salisbury Woods (1891–1986), a specialist in sports injuries, wrote the autobiographical *Cambridge Doctor* (1962) and was a famous Olympic athlete who represented England in 1924 and 1928.

Sir Eustace Pulbrook (1881–1953), another entrant in 1894, was elected Chairman of Lloyd's of London (the youngest to that date) in 1926, something he achieved altogether a record nine times; he was also awarded their highest honour, the Gold Medal. Pulbrook was President of the Alleyn Club in 1945, at the time of the furore at Dulwich that followed Wodehouse's broadcasts from Berlin during the Second World War. Wodehouse had agreed to speak on the radio after his release from the prison camps and from the castle where he had been interned ever since his arrest at his house in Le Touquet in May 1940; though what he said was witty and innocuous, and few had actually heard the broadcasts, the fact of his broadcasting was seen as collaboration with the enemy. Boys at the College caught with books by Wodehouse in their briefcases at that time were caned by the Prefects; it is said that the sporting group photographs in the Pavilion in which Wodehouse featured were turned to the wall. The BBC banned any lyric by Wodehouse being broadcast for over two years. A statement had been made in the House of Commons threatening prosecution of Wodehouse as a traitor, should he return to England after the War; the spokesman was the Attorney-General, a famous Old Alleynian, Sir Hartley Shawcross (1902–2003; see Chapters Nine and Ten), the leading British prosecutor of Nazi war criminals and British traitors at the Nuremburg War Crimes tribunal of 1945–6.[296] A Judge meanwhile, in the 'Lord Haw-Haw' case, had ruled that it was a crime to have spoken on the German radio in war-time, regardless of what you said on it. It is significant that once Wodehouse was made aware of his dreadful mistake in agreeing to broadcast from Berlin (which was to bring about such miserable consequences for him), his thoughts turned to Dulwich, and early in 1945 he sent the Assistant Master R. T. 'Beaky' Rees (1885–1976) an apologia, in the form of a letter for publication in The Alleynian. Only an extract from his letter to Rees was published, and the original has not been found. He wrote, 'I can see now, of course, how idiotic it was of me to do such a thing, and I naturally regret it very much, but at the time it never struck me that I was doing anything wrong', and he went on to deny the stories that had been invented about his collusion with the Germans and about his living in luxury at their expense in the Adlon Hotel in Berlin. In letters to Townend and Christison he appeared very anxious about how his reputation stood with the College and the Old Alleynians at this time, asking if there was any response to his letter in The Alleynian.[297] The previous year the magazine had printed a letter from a minor Old Alleynian artist, Adrian Hill (1895–1977), who had left in 1911 and had made fine records of Great War scenes of desolation and destruction after being wounded in France in 1917; he was later a teacher of art in Sketch Club on BBC Children's Television. Hill wrote, 'in the light of his past sorry record, am I alone in asking whether it is necessary or desirable to publish the present "activities" of P. G. Wodehouse, or even to retain his name on the register?'[298] The July number printed two angry letters from Old Alleynians in his defence, noting Hill's 'poverty of mind'. At this point Eustace Pulbrook, as Townend reported to Wodehouse, reminded certain members of the Alleyn Club that Wodehouse had not enlisted in the First World War when he was working in the United States; when Christison retorted that Wodehouse had tried to enlist but had been rejected on account of his eyesight, Pulbrook said

that in that case Wodehouse should have returned to England.[299] Wodehouse took a characteristically mild revenge on Pulbrook in a passage in a novel (although he emasculates the man): in The Mating Season (1949) a Miss Eustacia Pulbrook plays an unsuccessful violin solo at a concert in a village hall in Hampshire.[300]

In March 1947 The Alleynian reported that Wodehouse had sent £50, a very considerable amount, to the War Memorial Fund. In April Christison forwarded to Shawcross a letter from Townend asking for reassurance that Wodehouse would not be put on trial if he returned to England after the War. Shawcross was possibly anxious to avert suspicion of an Old Alleynian network behind the scenes, but was also known to have taken a stern view about the broadcasting. In reply he wrote that it would be wrong for him to make any comment on the case, but that there was a risk of prosecution: 'it would be for a Jury of his own country people to decide whether his conduct amounted to being no more than a silly ass; a matter about which two views seem to be held'. Subsequently Evelyn Waugh championed Wodehouse, and the tide of educated opinion in England changed towards him. He was knighted in the New Year honours of 1975, a few weeks before his death on Long Island on Valentine's Day, in what was seen as an official act of forgiveness and reparation for the Berlin broadcasts. Wodehouse was in the Chair at Alleyn Club dinners in New York at least four times in the 1950s, when he enjoyed recalling and discussing the finer points of Rugby and cricket games in the early years of the century with seven or eight companions; the Master, Ronald Groves, lunched with him in New York in 1964.[301] At his death he left to the College a substantial collection of manuscripts, some filed as 'Work in Progress', to inspire Dulwich boys by looking at his methods and his annotations on his own writings in the margins, such as a schoolmasterly 'good' for an idea for a story. Lady Wodehouse gave his desk, typewriter, spectacles, pipe and other contents of his study to the College, and contributed $50,000 towards the construction and fittings of the Wodehouse Library and towards a fund for scholarships. Two P. G. Wodehouse Scholarships were established in 1982 by the Master, David Emms, partly endowed by a group of Alleynians in the United States, the Alleynian Foundation, and are awarded annually to a boy of all-round ability for the Remove and Sixth Form years at the College.

Several Alleynians acquired enormous wealth, for example Sir Edward Mountain, Bart. (1872–1948), who became Chairman of Eagle Star Insurance; (Sir) George Johnston (1873–1943), from the Dulwich mansion of Kingswood, who became the Chairman of Bovril Ltd and owned 3,000 acres in Bedfordshire, was ennobled in 1929 as Lord Luke. These men left the College in 1889 and 1888 respectively; both were generously philanthropic. H. A. Andreae (1876–1965), a Director of Kleinwort's and a notable yachtsman, left a million pounds. Col. W. E. Grey (1895–1986), who left the College in 1914, and whose family firm, Grey and Marten, owned the lead works and Shot Tower (1826; demolished 1951) close to Southwark Bridge on Edward Alleyn's Bankside, was a most touchingly loyal Old Alleynian bachelor and a notable benefactor of the College: in 1948 he presented a row of flowering trees for the Alleyn's Head entrance to the College, and in 1953 trees for the front gardens together with a row of limes (poplars were his first suggestion) to screen the Blew House; he made generous covenants to the College (by the year 2000 worth some £25,000) to establish the bursaries which bear his name. During the few years before his death he made many gifts to the College of valuable books, photographs and other Dulwich memorabilia, including his silver cups and his white blazer, awarded for outstanding performance in a minor sport. Among barristers, Cecil Whiteley, KC (1875–1942), a well-known judge, became a notable College Governor. The Maltese O. F. Golcher (1889–1962) bequeathed the Palazzo Falson ('the Norman House') and its treasures to the island, and his cousin C. M. R. Balbi (1895–1974) published *Talking Pictures and Acoustics* in 1931. Sir E. J. Waddington (1890–1957) was Governor and Commander in Chief of Barbados from 1938 until 1941; B. G. Prytz (1887–1976) was Swedish Minister (Ambassador) in London. Phya Buri Navarasth (1883–1926), who studied at King's College, Cambridge, was Siamese Envoy in London and in Washington.

Among famous Alleynian schoolmasters, Cecil Botting (1870–1930) at St Paul's achieved 'phenomenal' success with university awards gained by his pupils, and was the co-author of the standard Greek textbook, 'Hillard and Botting', used by many thousands of schoolboys. C. M. Wells, Captain of School in 1889–90, was a Rugby 'Blue', a member of the England XV, and a cricketer commemorated in a *Vanity Fair* cartoon in 1907; he taught at Eton from 1893 to 1926, and was its Cricket Master from 1898–1919. On arrival he was presented with a very nicely written ode in Latin, and sent it back in half an hour translated into Greek elegiacs. It was said that Wells, a rich character, had a deeper influence on his Eton pupils than any other teacher in his time. He made a fine and apt gift of the electric clock on the new Pavilion to the College in 1938. Charles Werner (1877–1915), a great Captain of School and an athlete, who was in the XV for three years running, taught Classics at Harrow,

where 'all he did he did with all his might', and 'was as compact as a cannonball'. [302] He died at Aubers Ridge in 1915. Stafford Northcote (1884–1944), the youngest of six Alleynian brothers, a fine sportsman and an editor of *The Alleynian* who left in 1903, returned to the College to teach languages in 1920 and to organise all the sports; he died during a lesson in 1944. F. W. 'Gilbert' King (1891–1971) left in 1909, and returned to teach Mathematics at the College in 1919 for a hundred terms; devoted, courteous and encouraging, and with a lifetime's service to the Mission, he gave his career as if it were in return for his schooling, retiring in 1954 having been President of the Common Room in a very difficult period under C. H. Gilkes (see Chapter Ten).

It is said that the father of the Moore brothers settled close to Dulwich for his boys' sake because of Gilkes's fame. Many celebrated men also chose Gilkes's school for their sons, such as the mordant drama critic and promoter of Ibsen, William Archer (1856–1924), and David Lloyd George (1863–1945), the late Prime Minister, whose son Richard (later Viscount Gwynedd and 2nd. Earl Lloyd George) attended for a year from 1901 to 1902. Archer's son Thomas (1885–1918) was a brilliant prospect, but was a victim of the murderous waste of the Great War. A Scholar, President of the Debating Society, the Captain of School for two years running and Captain of the Shooting VIII, author of satirical verses in *The Alleynian*, he studied Law at Christ Church, Oxford. He returned from New York on the first boat at the outbreak of war to enlist, and died of wounds at Mont Kemmel in April 1918. Sir Ninian Comper (1864–1960) the architect, who lived on Beulah Hill, sent his four sons to the College; two of them were greatly interested in aircraft. Nicholas (1897–1939) left in 1914 and flew in the Great War, after which he was an instructor at Cranwell until 1928; he won air races, and he designed and also flew his own aeroplanes; these included the 'Honeymoon Express' biplane (1924) and the small and exceptionally fast 'Comper Swift', for which he founded a production company. Comper was an inveterate practical joker, and died as a result of his folly in letting off fireworks one night in June 1939 at Hythe. These were mistaken for bombs; he was struck down, injuring his head on the pavement, and died the next day. Wing-Commander T. R. Cave-Brown-Cave (1885–1969), a Royal Naval Engineer Cadet in 1903, researched airship design at the Admiralty, transferring to the Royal Air Force in 1919; he was closely involved with the power plant installations for the doomed airships R 101, R 102 and R 103 up until 1930, and then from 1931 he was Professor of Engineering at the University of Southampton. His brother (Air Vice-Marshal) H. M. Cave-Brown-Cave (1887–1965) DSO DFC,

Schoolboy photographs, *c.* 1900: five boys, five boaters; banjo-player. (Private collection)

was responsible for developments in flying boats and their flights to the Far East. (Air Vice-Marshal) F. C. Halahan (1880–1965) DSO CMG, who left in 1895, was the fourth of six brothers at the College who were exceptionally distinguished for gallantry, two of them dying in the Great War, one at Zeebrugge (see Chapter Nine); he was appointed Officer Commanding RAF Cranwell and Commandant of the RAF College in 1926 for three years.

Some of Gilkes's talented men made their careers in the prosperous showy world of popular music and vaudeville on the far side of the Thames. Frank Boor (1864–1938), actually of Carver's era (leaving in 1879), was for 25 years Manager of the London Hippodrome. Robert Michaelis (1878–1965), who left in 1894, a matinée idol, played in London up to the end of the 1920s, and was particularly associated with Daly's Theatre in Leicester Square, where he starred in famous productions of *The Merry Widow* (1907) and *The Dollar Princess* (1909). He enlisted as a Private in the Royal Army Service Corps during the Great War. Michaelis was the leading man in *The Golden Moth* (1921), a collaboration between Wodehouse and Ivor Novello, and played on Broadway in 1922. Arthur Wimperis (1874–1953), who left in 1892, after fighting in the Boer War, attended the Slade School of Art and joined the staff of the *Daily Graphic* as a black-and-white artist. He later took to the stage, acting in farcical comedies and writing songs; his were the lyrics of the 'smash-hit' show, *The Arcadians* (1909). During the Great War he kept up the

spirits of Londoners by his acting in revues and by his lyrics. The same linguistic culture of Dulwich that produced fastidious scholarship nourished his immortal song of 1914 about a 'knut', [a young man about town], 'Gilbert the Filbert, the Colonel of the Knuts':

> I'm Gilbert, the Filbert,
> The Knut with a K,
> The Pride of Piccadilly,
> A blasé roué.

Wimperis smoked Turkish cigarettes in a bone holder. In later life, he collaborated on scripts for the cinema, including *The Private Life of Henry VIII* (1933) for Alexander Korda, *The Scarlet Pimpernel* (1935), and the splendid Technicolor films of stories by A. E. W. Mason, *The Drum* (1938) and *The Four Feathers* (1939), both directed by Korda's brother Zoltan. In 1940 Wimperis was aboard the ss *City of Benares*, crossing the Atlantic, when it was torpedoed by a German U-boat; he was one of eight in his lifeboat of thirty-two to survive. At Hollywood in 1942 he shared an Oscar for the screenplay of *Mrs Miniver*, a film that portrayed the graceful endurance of an English family at the time of Dunkirk in a way that was said by Churchill to be worth a dozen battleships.

Harold Fraser-Simpson (or Simson; 1872–1944), who was originally intended for a business career, wrote the music for ten West End pieces, including *The Maid of the Mountains* (1917), which was very popular with wartime audiences at Daly's and ran for 1,352 performances, and *Toad of Toad Hall* (1929). He also made some famous settings of A. A. Milne, including 'Christopher Robin is saying his Prayers'. Gerald Kahn (b. 1880; later Carne), an actor, who enlisted as a Corporal in the Tank Corps, wrote popular songs such as 'A Window in Spain', 'I Look into your Heart' and 'Somebody's Rose' (a favourite), which were featured at the Palladium, the Albert Hall and the Pavilion, Torquay. His ballads and marches became increasingly patriotic in subject, and were very popular during the Second World War; he was to publish well over one hundred compositions. The successes of these men were often noted in *The Alleynian*.[303]

Carver's artists continued to win golden opinions at the Royal Academy exhibitions: in 1902 there were 17 paintings by Old Alleynians exhibited, and 20 in 1904. When Herbert Bone wrote a criticism of the Exhibition in 1905 for *The Alleynian*, he introduced some telling quotations from Voysey's theoretical writings, and praised the 'blaze and dazzle' of La Thangue.[304] In spite of Gilkes's lack of encouragement for Art, in his early years Nightingale's pupils achieved some minor successes, although the great days of painting by Sparkes's pupils were never to be equalled. Harry Mileham (1873–1957) won a Gold Medal and a travelling scholarship at the Royal Academy Schools in 1895;[305] he later became interested in Applied Art, particularly church decoration, and over thirty of his works in stained glass and painting are to be seen in Brighton and Hove. Alfred Palmer (1877–1951), who left in 1893, was an exception to the decline in painters in oils to emerge from the College, and had an interesting career as a landscape painter: he attended the Clapham School of Art and the Royal Academy Schools, and later studied in Paris, where John Singer Sargent advised him to copy paintings in Italy, Spain and Holland and Belgium; he divided his time between Paris in the winter, where he exhibited at the Salon, and Germany in the summer.[306] Palmer painted the panels in the Dining Room at the Empire Exhibition at Wembley in 1924; he also painted portraits, and in later life worked in Africa painting Zulu and Bantu tribespeople. Eric 'Jimmy' George (1881–1961), a friend of Wodehouse, studied at the London County Council Art Schools and in Paris, and exhibited elegant, thoughtful and scholarly neo-Classical portraits and scenes with figures at the Academy until the late 1930s; he turned from painting to writing, publishing an excellent *Life and Death of Benjamin Robert Haydon*, (1948) and a neglected narrative poem, a mixture of the mythological and the modern, *Cephalus and Procris, an Episode between Two Wars* (1954), which shows the same elegance and subtlety of mind. Philip Streatfield (1879–1915), who left

in 1895, exhibited at the Academy from 1901 until his death from trench fever. Arthur Watts (1883–1935), a former Slade student who won the DSO and was one of the Dulwich heroes at the Zeebrugge raid, was a black-and-white and poster artist, as was Richard Ogle (1889–1976). Leonard Fuller (1891–1973) left in 1908; after study under his admired master Nightingale at the Clapham School of Art and winning prizes at the Royal Academy Schools, he eventually became the Principal Art Master at the College from 1931 until 1938. He painted the portrait of Walter Booth, the Master, now in the Board Room, and also the copy in the same room of Welldon's portrait at Harrow. On retirement, he became Principal of St Ives School of Painting. In 1914 the Board of Education had reported that the art teaching at Dulwich was 'very defective'; there was no variety in instruction, and the boys just drew simple common objects such as watering-cans, and performed outline pencil work.[307]

The most famous composer to have studied at Dulwich was Gordon Jacob (1894–1984). At school he played the timpani, organised a Concert for the Mission, and performed a piano solo at a Servants' Concert. On leaving school in 1914 at the age of 19 he enlisted, fought and was captured, one of only 800 of his battalion to survive; after the War he studied under Stanford, Boult and Howells at the Royal College of Music; he was appointed Professor there from 1936 to 1966. A composer of great range and variety, accessible, sparse and melodic, he possessed a special gift for composing for wind instruments and groups. He published over 700 pieces. Among his works were an arrangement of the National Anthem with a trumpet Fanfare for the Coronation in 1953, and weekly musical vignettes for the Radio programme *ITMA*. In 1969 he wrote an opening fanfare for the College's 350th Anniversary Commemoration Concert, quoting (with 'contrapuntal curlicues') the opening phrase of Rendall's 'Pueri Alleynienses'; the manuscript is in the College Archives.[308] His four books are also much admired, especially *How to Read A Score* (1944). He was editor of the Penguin series of musical scores.

The London County Council Scholars

Dulwich College is famous in the educational world for the successful pioneering scheme that took place after the Second World War under the Mastership of A. H. Gilkes's son, Christopher, whereby, in the spirit of Edward Alleyn, a great majority of boys at the College were on scholarships from neighbouring Councils, their fees paid from local taxes. This was the forerunner of the national Assisted Places scheme (1980–97), which subsidised pupils at private schools whose parents could not afford the fees. The principal architect of the latter

Gilkes and cricketers at the Pavilion. The Revd E. H. Sweet-Escott to his left; the coach William Shepherd, rear right (in bowler hat). (Dulwich College)

scheme was a great figure in the educational world who was knighted for this work in 1982, Sir James Cobban (1910–99); he was the Classical Sixth Form master at Dulwich from 1936 to 1940 (and again, after war service and administration in occupied Frankfurt, for six months in 1946, just before he was appointed Headmaster of Abingdon School). In the latter half of the twentieth century 'The Dulwich Experiment', as the co-operation of the College with local councils was known, was for several decades to be a major factor in the academic renaissance of the College (see Chapter Ten); it was the famous achievement of C. H. Gilkes. The origins of this scheme date back to an agreement between the Governors and the London County Council in 1903, and in 1906 A. H. Gilkes reported that there were 17 boys whose fees were paid for by the Council; he reported that 'they work well and do well'.[309] In 1914 the Board of Education inspection reported that these Scholars at the College included (as an example) four boys from Brockley County Secondary School. Between the wars the numbers were much increased (see Chapter Nine) and the

issue of the presence of these boys, paid for by the state at a school for gentlemen, became a rather unpleasant matter of controversy among staff, Governors, Old Alleynians and the press.

When Gilkes in his retirement from Dulwich at Oxford wrote his unpublished series of stories *Parerga Scholastica* (see above), he gave them a framework of a schoolmasters' 'story club', also attended by schoolboys, which holds its meetings in a thinly disguised Dulwich College, with its great clock tower and other features; the masters in turn read their stories aloud in their sitting rooms at the top of the North Block at Dulwich or in the Lecture Theatre. Gilkes handles the raillery among these Assistant Masters amusingly, and says of them that they are sometimes idle, sometimes unfair and ill-tempered, 'but as good a body of men as it is possible to find, excepting sailors and soldiers and airmen on duty'.[310] Among this peculiar compilation of ghost and detective stories and short historical romances, together with a poem about Rugby football, is found a moving story about the College, 'A School Scholarship', set during the

Great War. The protagonist in the story is an Assistant Master, Mr James (a teacher also found in Gilkes's novel *A Day at Dulwich*), a rather self-satisfied bachelor and himself an Old Boy of the College, who cares for its reputation as a school for gentlemen's sons. It is easy to underestimate, incidentally, the strength of tribal feeling against the presence of the LCC Scholars at the College, who were known contemptuously as 'brickies', and whose presence was often thought of as a threat to 'the ethos' of the school. This animus can be felt from comments at Alleyn Club speeches, and even in George Smith's measured reports to the Governors. Wodehouse in a letter of 1946 exclaimed to Bill Townend about the 'dire changes' of the 'Dulwich Experiment': 'my Gawd! [C. H.] Gilkes is killing the place. In another year it will be a secondary school!'[311]

In the story Mr James, in common with other masters, is angry because of the 'ill advised' action of the Headmaster and the Governors in admitting ten LCC Scholars. He feels embarrassed for his College, because at a First XI cricket match, one of these Scholars, keeping wicket, betrayed his social origins by his vowels, exclaiming 'aout' instead of 'out'; consequently the other school declined to play any more fixtures with them. One day Mr James is invigilating the scholarship examination in the Great Hall, and is repelled by a young candidate in 'ready-made' clothes and with his hair greased with pomatum; the prep-school boys in the hall evince the same physical repulsion, even drawing away their desks from the boy. At a break in the examination the boy's elder brother and sister bring him his lunch in a basin with a cloth tied over it.

Much later that day, reading the newspaper, Mr James happens on a story about the conspicuous gallantry and death of a soldier in France, an Engineer, and realises from the unusual surname that this hero is the father of the Scholarship candidate. He experiences a complete change of heart, and secretly makes an offer to the College to pay the boy, who turns out to have done conspicuously well in several but not all of his papers, a scholarship from his own pocket. Meanwhile the boy's brother enlists in his father's regiment. This story, written by Gilkes in (perhaps unconscious) prophetic vision, anticipates a change in the social function of Dulwich College in the future, renewing Alleyn's intention of educating fatherless boys (or boys that might in some sense be called fatherless boys) in a comparatively rich academic and educational environment, granting a privilege to these boys rather than perpetuating an exclusive privileged world. Christopher Gilkes's scheme was to save the College financially and at the same time to transfuse it with new blood after the disasters that beset it in the Second

World War. A. H. Gilkes's story suggests that he understood that after the Great War the intellectual prosperity and the general vitality of the College would need to draw on a wider social range for its pupils in order to play its part in a new and more just Britain with its opportunities for real merit and enterprise.

The Rifle Corps, the Officers Training Corps and the onset of the Great War

In 1900 the Rifle Corps numbered 220 boys, but by the next year it had increased to 300 boys, and a hundred attended the Public School Camps at Burley Bottom, Aldershot. The senior boys were issued with Enfield rifles, and the junior boys with light carbines; they paid a subscription of half a crown a term.[312] In 1907 a Dulwich boy won the Sword of Honour at Woolwich and five boys went to Sandhurst.[313] John Baptiste Joerg (see above) was at that time in charge of the Army Class. Gilkes deplored in his diary in 1899 that when the Corps went to Aldershot there was 'always a tendency to regard the whole matter as pure play'.[314] The traditional Aldershot field day was abandoned by the College before the War as it had become too crowded. In 1900 both the Ashburton Shield and the Spencer Cup were brought home in triumph from Bisley by the Shooting VIII. In 1908 the Rifle Corps became known as the Officers Training Corps. In 1910 the Range was doubled in size, and a New Armoury, Store-Room and Orderly Room were constructed, paid for by C. A. Rehder (1866–1943), later a Governor for 25 years (and Deputy Chairman of the Board for eleven) who endowed scholarships. In the spring term a ten-mile route march was practised, and a bugle band was formed; Doulton would lead them on the hottest day playing a trombone.[315] The Corps now wore a uniform of black (called green) with red facings. Drill was practised in the lunch hour.[316] In 1901 the *Public School Magazine* published a letter from Gilkes on the subject of 'the Public schools and National Defence', showing his belief in the Corps, in shooting and drill, and its patriotic function:

> In the interests of the peace of the world it is highly desirable that every boy in England, as well as in all public schools should be given thorough training as a soldier, as complete as it may be.... I should be very glad to see this training considered as the chief matter of the out-door life of the school, thus deposing, to some extent, even such good institutions as cricket and football from the place which they at present hold.[317]

Though aware of the threat from Germany, the Old Alleynian Football Club enjoyed matches held at Easter in Frankfurt from 1903, such as in 1906, 1909, and 1910, all of which were reported in *The Alleynian*.

Three dashing aviators had attended the College. In 1928 George Stainforth (1899–1942), who had enlisted in The Buffs at the age of 15, became the fastest man in the world at 415.2 mph; he was the pilot of the GHS Supermarine 36B (Rolls-Royce) and also one of the best crack rifle and revolver marksmen in the Royal Air Force. He was to die in action in Egypt in 1942. Sidney Sippé (1889–1968) left the Engineering Fifth in 1905. He dropped bombs on Zeppelin sheds at Friedrichshafen (Lake Constance) and at Düsseldorf in late 1914. After the War, when as a Major in the RAF he won the DSO, he was much involved with the construction of flying boats. James Valentine (1887–1917), who left the Engineering Fifth in 1903, was a pioneer of aviation, and in 1911 was the first man to make a circuit of Britain by air, in a Deperdussin monoplane, and was one of the very first to fly over Paris;[318] he was called 'one of the most daring of British airmen', and met his death after many war flights in Russia.

In 1914 *The Alleynian* carried an editorial much changed from the usual mildly flippant comments about how little there was to say apart from the College's sporting and academic successes and the change of the seasons on the grounds. The theme is war against despotism, and the Officers Training Corps occupies of course a prominent position. The first grievous Roll of Honour appears in the same issue, with seven killed, thirteen wounded and one posted missing. The writer records that the new Master, George Smith, has told the boys to do their duty.[319] On 30 November a new and grim form of 'Blue Book' was published, a Roll of roughly eight hundred Old Alleynians already in service.

Gilkes's resignation

In 1909 the Governors' minutes recorded Gilkes's declaration after the Board of Education report that he should retire at the end of the Easter term in 1910, when he would have been just over sixty, and their unanimous request for him to reconsider.[320] Though the Report, described above, spoke in very glowing terms about Gilkes himself and his influence, and of the high efficiency and reputation of the College and the vigorous intellectual life of the older boys, there was enough in it, in spite of Gilkes's rebuttal of the values of the Inspectors, to make him feel that he was not moving with the times. In 1912 he suffered 'serious illness' and an operation. Sweet-Escott was in charge of the College for the summer term while he was in hospital.[321]

The Report of 1914, printed in full in the Governors' minutes, was devastating; it began by complaining that little had been changed in response to the last Inspection in 1908. Though the Inspectors still wrote approvingly of Gilkes's strong personal influence over his boys, and wrote this time that the Band, Orchestra and Choir were splendid, the lower and middle sections of the school, particularly the Lower School (which lacked a Head, called for in 1908), were said to need much improvement. The periods were too long for the younger boys, and a large number of backward older boys were still being kept on there. The ill effects of not keeping up with new methods of teaching were obvious. Though the College had to cope with the 'uncertain and irregular' income from the Estate, the expenditure on scholarships was too little. The Junior LCC scholarships were no longer tenable. Ventilation and lighting were still very bad. The proportion of staff to boys was much too low, and the starting salaries for the masters poor. Gilkes never watched his staff teach; there was no real support or criticism of new teachers, and the masters did not make a serious effort to improve their teaching. English was not taken seriously enough as a new and autonomous subject; one class had spent a whole term on Milton's *Lycidas*; there was a lack of systematic English grammar teaching lower down the school. No Geography was taught on the Classics Side, and the atlases were ludicrously out of date. The History teaching was thin. Only two forms were studying German; French was taught as a dead language. While linguistic skill was highly valued in the culture of the College and 'unusual taste and scholarship' still obtained in the higher Classics forms, the selfishness of the Classics Side was again noted, not releasing those boys with Mathematical interests. A utilitarian bias was apparent in the Inspectors. Mathematics was taught in the old formal way by rote without achieving any proper understanding. Since the last Inspection Science had been introduced into the Third Form, but not into the First and Second Forms.[322]

Thus the great Gilkes, who had written in his diary as early as 1899 that the school had achieved 'the shape and position which when I came I intended it to assume',[323] left the College after 29 years, amid the onset of the Great War. The *Observer* published a piece by an Old Alleynian pointing out, amid the clamourings that Gilkes was old-fashioned, that the Old Man maintained both a reverence for the great traditions of the past and a vision of the future, neither of which prevented his eye from 'twinkling over many dark absurdities' of the present. 'We shall be reading next that the sun has resigned, or the moon has gone elsewhere'. The *Daily Mail* spoke of his deep resonating voice, and of him as the father and friend of all his pupils; his personality 'radiated from the man like the force from a lump of radium'.[324] The Golden Age, however, was at an end, and a tragic scene had already begun.

9

WAR & PEACE – AND WAR

1914-41

A striking capacity for adapting itself to modern conditions.
– Board of Education Report, 1923

PART I

GEORGE SMITH, 1914–28

George Smith – The Great War – The Zeebrugge Raid – Other gallantry and losses – The five Victoria Crosses – The German guns – The literature of the Great War – The Armistice and the War Memorial – The Joerg brothers – The 'James Caird' – Academic life and the Common Room – Events and traditions – Buildings, boarding houses, the Chapel, the Estate, and the Picture Gallery – Alleynians – Smith's resignation

George Smith

Born the son of an Ayrshire coal merchant, George Smith (1867–1957), with his rectitude and culture, was the third Scot to bring distinction to Dulwich College. Trained as a Classicist, and holding a first class degree from Edinburgh, he went on to achieve a double first at Oxford, where he was a Scholar of Trinity College. Kindly, cautious, truthful and quiet, small in stature after the Olympian Gilkes and without his apostolic fervour, he nevertheless possessed the steadfast strength and courage to carry the College through a difficult period of transition.

Smith was 47 years old when appointed as Gilkes's successor, already a veteran of Edwardian education. For 14 years he had been Headmaster of Merchiston Castle School in Edinburgh, a small day and boarding school (with 170 pupils at that date); before that he had taught for one year at Edinburgh Academy, and for six years at Rugby. As well as being the oldest Master of the new College to be appointed, he was also the only man up to this point to arrive with any practical experience of running a school. There were at least four strong arguments, which he must surely have considered, against his undertaking this task: the famous and long-serving Gilkes had just left; the College had fallen drastically behind the times; its financial situation was a cause for anxiety (and in the event did not improve); and a formidable European war was looming – and was indeed declared on 4 August, only a few weeks before he started work.

Smith was elected unanimously by the Governors; it is also probable that Gilkes urged his candidacy. In 1913 Smith had published a book of 24 *School Sermons Preached at Merchiston Castle*, and the values he professed

seemed set to prolong the Gilkesian ethos at the College with their emphasis on the corporate spirit, on cheerfulness, self-discipline, and endurance, and on public service and the responsibility of the educated towards the poorer classes; he held up a code of modern chivalry, of honour, purity and kindness. Nor was he afraid to castigate adolescents from his lectern in the school hall for loafing, or for loud, obtrusive, or coarse behaviour.[1] Gilkes would have approved his axiomatic Christian teaching, his aim 'to vitalize and consecrate our common life by showing its significance in the light of things that are eternal', and his maxim: 'the very noblest and best tradition of life that ever grew up in any public school falls far short of what God would have us be'. Smith declared at an Alleyn Club dinner after the War that, coming from a small school, he was not expecting to find at the College so much *esprit de corps*. He described his first five years, however, as 'one long nightmare' of 'anxiety, strain and sorrow' with everything conspiring to 'throw the work of the school out of stride. It had seemed like a prolonged air raid', while he was trying to uphold the 'old virtue of peace and the old virtue of industry'.[2] Among the many losses he experienced through these grievous years was that of his eldest son, Captain G. A. S. Smith MC, killed in action in the last weeks of the War on 28 September 1918.[3] Yet such were George Smith's qualities that one must struggle to discern the man's inner turmoil from the public pages of *The Alleynian*, the Governors' Minutes, or even from what his contemporaries said of him. When the Cunarder RMS *Lusitania* was torpedoed by a German U-boat on 7 May 1915 with the loss of 1,198 civilians, he addressed the boys simply and nobly, reminding them that the aim of their education was 'to be fit in body, well-equipped in mind, disciplined in character to take our place when the time comes as good citizens of a worthy nation'.[4] Like Gilkes, he was a genuinely modest man, on one occasion pointing out to the Governors that a Classical Sixth he had taught had done badly in their Roman History examination and taking the blame for that failure upon himself.[5] When he retired in 1928, the Chairman of the Governors, Sir Arthur Hirtzel (see Chapter Seven) praised him for piloting the school through the war years and its subsequent period of reorganisation, 'when public and private discipline was loosened everywhere and public spirit at a low ebb'. He had surmounted every obstacle, and now left the school more secure and broadly based than it was before. When George Smith returned to the College at the age of 80 to speak at an Alleyn Club dinner, he said that his first action as Master was to have three inches cut from Gilkes's official chairs so that his feet would not be seen to be left dangling.[6]

Smith was conservative. He often spoke about his job in his speeches at the Alleyn Club dinners, and in 1920 he said that he thought that the tone, tradition and spirit of Dulwich College as he had first found it were excellent, 'and if by any means I can keep them up, I shall feel that at least I have not failed'.[7] The boys gave Smith the peculiar sobriquet 'Gunboat', after his namesake, the famous heavyweight American boxer Edward Smith (1887–1974), who at the time of Smith's arrival fought matches at the Albert Hall (and whose fame was at its height in the years 1912–15); the nickname was ironic, in allusion to Smith's pacific manner. He was self-deprecating about the way he ran the College, telling the Club diners that 'I mainly corrected Latin proses and adjusted time-tables', or again that he could not take credit for any Dulwich achievements in scholarship or games, nor indeed 'that most essential thing, keeping up the tone and tradition of the College'; all he did, he claimed, was to collect fortnightly reports and interview those boys who had received a 'C' grade two weeks running; he was fond of repeating that delegating was the secret of success.[8] Smith is also said to have maintained two separate note-books for masters' suggestions: one to remember – and one to forget.[9] Smith had an endearing way of complaining about the poor facilities and constriction at the College, as for example his beguiling assertion that

> Few places look finer than Dulwich College, at least in the moonlight. On the other hand there are some of the internal arrangements which look best in total darkness, and some of them can be modified without aesthetic loss, and with great practical gain.[10]

The press meanwhile reported Smith as saying that the cultivation of the scholar's brain was more important than his efficiency in games;[11] however, the College under his regime flourished in both spheres. He spoke out against the bad influence of day boys and the mischief of their spending evenings away from home in visits, theatres and amusements in term time, and would send out circulars beginning 'The Master desires to draw the attention of parents …' on such disobliging subjects.[12] Smith kept up Gilkes's traditional afternoon Monday afternoon lessons with the prefects on general literary and moral topics, and they were remembered with gratitude by Sir George Pickering (see below) in 1968 at an Alleyn Club dinner; he personally conducted 22 hours of teaching a week, and the Board of Education inspection had decreed that he must regularly visit all classes.

Smith meanwhile addressed himself to the 'fundamental reforms' called for in organisation and administration, particularly the case of the Junior School and its obvious defects.[13] A characteristic story shows him to have been both an understated wit and a mild, but stubborn, reactionary: when asked to allow dancing in the Library he assented, so long as no women were present.[14] Mrs Carver's genteel dances for the Sixth Form of sixty years earlier (see Chapter Six) seem by comparison with this ban a pleasant Victorian way for boys and girls to meet and learn manners.

The new Master obviously cared very much for his teaching and his subject, and for literature in general, and when he left and prizes were to be awarded in his name, he asked that they should be for the study of Horace.[15] Smith's Gilkesian quality is likewise shown in his advice to the young Eric Handscomb (1901–85), an Old Alleynian who left in 1919 and taught French from 1927 until 1961: "Don't let teaching interfere with your work".[16] His wisdom in understanding the value of appointing recent graduates to the staff is shown in a passage from his Report on the Teaching Staff of 1919:

> It is always advisable that there should be on the staff a fair number of quite young men, not too far removed from the adventurous spirit of youth, finding it easy to sympathise with the natural interests of boys, and not yet content to accept things as they are. Such young masters will, of course, make the mistakes that are natural to their age. But they provide on the staff a useful form of stimulus and freshness, which, speaking broadly, older men lack.[17]

He also said that in his view the young men did not have enough training, and on retirement from Dulwich he was to turn his attention to the training of teachers – an innovative approach at the time. Smith thought the ratio of staff to boys should be somewhere between one master to twenty and one master to seventeen boys. Masters should automatically retire, he said, at 60.[18] In general, he carried on Gilkes's moral leadership, without the passion, but nevertheless teaching the value of service, honour and generosity by his own example as well as by his sermons; the great Professor Guthrie, Master of Downing College (see below), recalled how deeply he admired the 'genuine humanity' of his Master and mentor.[19] As the Great War progressed, fatherless boys became a common phenomenon, and this melancholy fact meant that numbers at the Mission increased considerably. Smith took an active part in its administration, if again not such an apostolic part as Gilkes, and maintained the involvement of College boys and masters; he proclaimed it an 'integral part of education for citizenship'.[20]

The Great War

A total of 510 Alleynians were killed in the Great War, just over one-sixth of the 3,052 who are recorded as having fought. On Smith's arrival in 1914 two teachers enlisted, and two retired masters returned to teach: Gilbert Stretton (1861–1948), who was an early appointee of Gilkes in 1886, a Form Master on the Modern Side and School Secretary from 1894 and who had retired in 1912; and Edward Sweet-Escott (see Chapters Six and Eight).[21] Stretton, something of a bachelor dandy and a literary man admired by Alic Smith (see Chapter Eight), was to leave the College a considerable legacy of £15,000 for scholarships.[22] By August 1915 seven of the older and better boys from the Sixth Form had been withdrawn for service in the War; six masters joined up that same year, by which time there were seven substitute masters. The Captain of Football, Paul Jones (see below) who was the editor of *The Alleynian* wrote, 'Nothing – not work nor games – must be allowed to stand before the Corps till the War is over. We call on everyone in the school to join the Corps at once'.[23] The Officers Training Corps held Camps in the holidays, and in term time Captain Hose, the brilliant Classics teacher and Old Boy (see Chapter Eight), as Commanding Officer from 1915 until 1919 directed fortnightly exercises, for example a night operation guarding a bridge. The membership rose from 262 to 353 boys, and by 1917 there were 425 members. No public functions were held in 1915 because of 'the claims of national duties', although there was a Speech Day the following year when George Smith had persuaded the very distinguished Oxford Professor Gilbert Murray (1866–1957), campaigner for the League of Nations and for women's rights, to attend.[24] With so many men on active service, the Old Alleynians could only raise one sports team on Founder's Day in 1917.

While *The Alleynian* commented in Michaelmas 1914 that at home the College was very successful at its work and play, by February 1915 the tone of the magazine had changed, with letters reporting the death of Old Alleynians in the trenches with the grisly detail of their getting their heads blown off, and the poems in the literary section turning abruptly to the themes of dying and dead soldiers, and graves.[25] Even the pieces the boys selected for the Anstie Reading Prize deserted Tennyson for harrowing war pieces. The announcements in *The Alleynian* of the publication of Wodehouse's new novels from New York, or his musicals such as *Kissing Time*, seem among the other material more like a frivolous lack of tact than an escapist boost to morale. 'Letters from the Front' became a regular feature. In general the quality of the magazine was at its lowest, with paper expensive and poor and the boys' contributions either dreary or heartily facetious. George Smith appears to have had no influence on the magazine. In May 1915 the editorial expressed what must have been on every mind connected with schools, namely that the War was 'seizing more and more ruthlessly on the best and healthiest of British manhood'.[26] The 'glorious sacrifice' of Dulwich men gave a new tragic meaning to both *esprit de corps* and *Detur gloria soli Deo* .

The *War Record* of 1923 was compiled by McCulloch Christison (see Chapter Eight), and to it he gave an epigraph offering the book to count and assess Dulwich's contribution to the spirit of duty and self-sacrifice, at the call of King and Country. When Gilkes returned to speak in the Chapel in 1915 at a memorial service for the dead, he recalled how he had admitted the men, and wished them goodbye and all happiness; the relation between the College and its soldiers was umbilical:

> I know that they would have wished to be loved and remembered here. In times of danger and trouble the thoughts of these boys turned, I know it, to their school, and welcome always to them was the knowledge that the thoughts of their school turned in love and admiration to them.[27]

The College published the first Roll of the 1,500 serving Alleynians, and it carried a dreadful litany of martial classifications: 'Honours, Mentioned in Despatches, Killed in Action, Died of Wounds, Lost at Sea, Reported Missing, Prisoner of War, Wounded'. Christison began his memorious task of sticking into interleaved pages of his bound copies of *The Alleynian* photographs of the dead the size of postage-stamps.

Ten Old Alleynians were Major-Generals, and five were knighted. By the end of 1916 there were 2,150 Old Alleynians on service, with 1,558 officers; the death toll amounted to 264 Old Boys and three masters; three

VCs had already been won (see below). By early 1918 there were a reported 2,500 in the forces, with 360 dead, and awards of 4 VCs, 59 DSOs, 5 DSCs and 120 MCs. Three masters were killed in action: G. W. Beachcroft (1880–1917), a linguist, Master of the Band and Orchestra and a sportsman; T. O. Garside (1886–1917), who taught for a few months in 1915; and the much loved A. N. C. Kittermaster (see Chapter Eight). Several masters, as well as George Smith, lost their sons, including the long-serving Drawing Master Leonard Nightingale (see Chapter Six), whose son Frank Nightingale (1881–1915), a good scholar and cricketer and himself an Assistant Master at the College from 1906 until 1915, was killed on the Menin Road near Ypres a few months after joining up. The War Office was taking boys at seventeen and a half, and by 1916 all Dulwich boys from the age of fifteen had ten hours a week of military training. This involved map-reading, signalling, field telephones, and bayonet practice, with lectures on chemistry and explosives. All this took place, as Smith said, partly in 'play hours': 'leisure has practically ceased to exist at school'. Munitions were made in the workshops. For six weeks of the holidays in 1917 fifty boys attended harvesting camps near Hexham in Northumberland. The National Service Department had requested this activity, but, once arrived, Captain Hose had to find work on the farms for the boys, cutting wood, harvesting corn, and lifting potatoes. [28]

Potatoes and vegetables were grown on the College fields, in allotments. When the U-boats made supplies of food scarce and meat was rationed, tripe and vegetarian luncheons with nut cutlets were served in the Great Hall; there was little for sale in the Buttery apart from teas, ginger beer and buns. In 1917 the government Food Controller took out a full-page advertisement in *The Alleynian* reading in heavy type, 'EAT LESS BREAD'. Smith suggested the abandonment of prizes for War purposes. [29] Zeppelin raids the same year hit the covered courts, and windows were blown out of the North Block; the Lower Hall was decided on as the largest shelter from blast or bombs. A Motor Ambulance for Russia was subscribed for by the boys and Old Alleynians, and was photographed on the gravel. [30] Bombs were noted in the Governors' Minutes as having fallen near the Gallery, but it was not hit. The twelve most valuable pictures were despatched in December 1914 to the basement of the Royal Academy in Piccadilly where they were placed under an eighteen-inch layer of sand, but by February 1917 they had been returned. [31]

*

The Zeebrugge Raid

On St George's Day, 23 April 1918, the very great Alleynian naval enterprise of Zeebrugge was carried out, although with tragic loss of life. The daring and brilliantly conceived raid aimed to cripple the German submarine fleet at Bruges by blocking the canal outlet used by the U-boats at Zeebrugge, sinking three old British Apollo Class light cruisers (HMS *Thetis*, HMS *Iphigenia* and HMS *Intrepid*, all built in the early 1890s) laden with cement in the harbour. The Raid did not in fact succeed in blocking the canal, but it was nonetheless seen as a very heroic effort, and it both raised morale at a time of gloom (during the German spring offensive) and restored the prestige of the Royal Navy at a time when the Army seemed to be bearing most of the brunt. The eldest of the six sons at the College of a great local family, Wing-Commander Frank Brock OBE (1884–1918) was both genius and hero in planning and carrying out the Raid. The Brocks were in an eighth generation as manufacturers of fireworks with large factories, first in Lower Norwood and then in Sutton. They were also famous the world over for weekly firework displays of patriotic and artistic tableaux, on an enormous scale, on the terraces of the Crystal Palace which included pyrotechnic moving pictures and acrobats wearing asbestos suits covered in fireworks. Frank Brock had left the College in 1901, and eventually became a Director of his father's firm, for which many of his brothers also worked. One of them was Alan Brock (1886–1956), at one time an architect, who also published 14 books, including novels, a life of William Blake, works on crime and a wonderful *History of Fireworks* (1949).

Frank Brock joined up at the start of the War in the Royal Artillery, and was seconded to the Royal Naval Air Service, swiftly becoming an expert pilot, for the raid on Friedrichshafen. The whole English Channel next became an arena for Brock's fireworks: his invention of the Dover Flares, one million candle-power each, proved an effective barrage against submarines. A true pupil of Herbert Baker (see Chapter Eight), he carried out some very dangerous experiments with Prussic acid for a Poison Gas. The Brock Bullet, which he also invented, destroyed Zeppelins by bursting into flames on striking the fabric of the air-ship and blowing a hole a foot wide in the fabric, and so rapidly deflating the air-ships. This device brought down the first three or four Zeppelins, and he was given a £12,000 reward by the government.

At Zeebrugge Brock's smoke-screen covered the approach of the raiding forces with a night-smoke resembling fog (without flame); his buoy with lights, his incendiary bombs and flame projectors were all used in the attack. Brock himself led the storming party onto the harbour wall, or Mole. His death was in character (and indeed in the spirit of a Dulwich scientist taught by Baker): he had heard of a German range-finder which was superior to its British counterpart, and was determined to learn more about it; while examining it on the Mole he was killed by a sniper.[32] Also at Zeebrugge fought Captain H. C. Halahan DSO (1883–1918), who was killed at the head of the landing party of blue-jackets (marines), and Major A. A. Cordner (1880–1918), who died from a shell explosion alongside the Mole before the order could be given for the assault; four other Old Alleynians took part in the Raid, from the Royal Navy, the Royal Naval Volunteer Reserve and the Royal Naval Reserve (a Lieutenant, a Sub-Lieutenant, a Midshipman and a Leading Mechanic chemist), and of them only two survived. The Sub-Lieutenant, Cecil Darley (1889–1919), blew up the Lock Gates during the raid. In 1919 on a flight to Cairo with his younger brother Squadron Leader Charles Darley (1890–1962), his plane crashed near Rome and he was killed; Charles was awarded the Albert Medal for his attempt to save his brother's life. He left the College in 1908 from the Army Class, having been Captain of Boxing, Fencing and Athletics in Gilkes's days.

Other gallantry and losses

The College numbered its men at the end of November 1917 as approximately 3,000 serving, and 315 dead.[33] The final tally was 3,052 sent to War, and 510 dead. Stories of gallantry are legion, such as Captain C. H. Collet (1888–1915) of the Royal Naval Air Service and their first officer to 'loop the loop', who was the hero of one of the earliest aerial exploits of the War, for which he was awarded the DSO: gliding down from 6,000 feet, the last 1,500 in mist, he dropped three bombs from just 400 feet onto the Zeppelin sheds at Düsseldorf. After a number of further heroic adventures and exploits he died in an accident in the Dardanelles when an unfamiliar plane he was taking to another aerodrome crashed and burst into flames. When Captain Francis Townend (1885–1915) of the Royal Engineers, the younger brother of Wodehouse's friend Bill Townend (see Chapter Eight), had his legs blown off by a shell when laying telephone cables, standing on their stumps, he told his rescuer to attend to his men first as he was all right; he then told the dressers (who found another terrible wound in his arm) that he thought he would give up Rugby football next year; he died shortly afterwards. The full list of awards and honours is given in the *Dulwich College War Record, 1914–19*; British awards for gallantry were 5 Victoria Crosses, 102 Distinguished Service Orders, 10 Distinguished Service Crosses (for the Royal Navy), 264 Military Crosses, 14 Distinguished Flying Crosses, 1 Distinguished Conduct Medal (for civilians), 1 Distinguished Service Medal, 10 Military Medals and 1 Distinguished Flying Medal.

The five Victoria Crosses

The five Dulwich College holders of the Victoria Cross from the Great War showed in great measure the traditional, most conspicuous valour. Major Alexander Lafone (1870–1917) fought an entire brigade of Turkish cavalry in Palestine, vastly outnumbered, for seven hours under shell-fire, driving back the cavalry charge with heavy losses; all his men but three were killed and the trench was so full of wounded that it was difficult to move and fire, but he ordered these men to move to a trench to the rear; as he stepped into the open he was wounded, but fought until he was dead.

Major Stewart Walter Loudon-Shand (1879–1916) leapt onto a parapet while attacking the enemy trenches on the Somme; meeting with very fierce gun-fire, he helped and encouraged his men over the parapet, until he was hit; fatally wounded, he insisted on being propped up in the trench, and cheered on the men until he died.

Lieutenant Richard Brandram Jones (1897–1916), at the age of 19, with his platoon was holding a crater at Vimy Ridge recently captured from the enemy when a mine explosion and a heavy barrage of fire isolated them. He kept his men together, steadying them by his fine example, and managed to shoot 15 of the enemy. Jones had been a member of the College Shooting VIII and had twice represented the school at Bisley; he counted off the Germans as he shot them, which much encouraged his men. When his ammunition was exhausted he picked up a bomb, but was shot through the head while getting up to throw it. The men were so inspired that they threw stones and empty ammunition boxes at the enemy until only nine of them were left; they were able to retreat finally under cover of darkness.[34]

Lieutenant Cecil Harold Sewell (1895–1918), who had intended to become a solicitor, was killed in action on the Somme in charge of a Mark A 'Whippet' light tank. Within full sight and short range of heavy shell and machine-gun fire, he saved the lives of the crew of another tank that had slipped into a shell-hole, overturned and caught fire, digging away an entrance to the door, which had been jammed against the side. Returning to his own tank to help his wounded driver on the ground, he was hit, but managed to reach him, and was dressing his comrade's wound when he was hit again, this time fatally.

Captain (later Vice-Admiral) Gordon Campbell DSO, RN (1886–1953), one of eight brothers at the College, was the only VC to survive his gallant feat. Campbell came to the College in 1928 to talk to the boys about the inventively disguised vessels known as 'Q' or 'Mystery' ships, of which he published a popular account in the same year, *My Mystery Ships*. At that time he also presented to the College the binnacle of his ship HMS *Q5* (originally SS *Loderer*, and later HMS *Farnborough*), on which he had won the VC in 1917, and which now stands in the Lower Hall. George Smith said at Speech Day that the episode was 'a reminder to the present and future generations of Alleynians of the high deeds of Alleynians, and of the responsibility that lay upon them not to be unworthy of their heritage'.[35] Campbell's 'Q' ships were decoy ships, pretending to be coasters or colliers, that successfully managed to lure a good number of enemy submarines to surface in order to use their deck guns (and thus to save their torpedoes); the 'Q' ships did this by subterfuge involving canvas painted to show railway wagons on deck or loads of hay concealing guns, and they managed to sink the U-boats when they surfaced and came within range of the artillery and depth charges. The crews even deployed acting skills in this theatre of war when a panic party appeared to be abandoning ship, leaving another crew on board, whereupon the sides of the ship opened to reveal guns.[36] Campbell received his VC for a 'supreme test of naval discipline': on 17 February 1917, at the age of 31, he was in command of HMS *Q5* when it was struck by a torpedo, severely wounding some of his men and flooding the engine room; he saved the crew by engaging the enemy when the ship was lying very low in the water, sinking the submarine with 45 shells as it drew alongside. Campbell served as an MP, from 1931 until 1935, as did his brother Sir Edward Campbell, 1st Bart (1879–1945), from 1924 until his death. Their nephew Lorne Campbell (1902–1991) was to win a VC in the Second World War. The College was presented with the original VC medals of Lafone and Jones (the latter on loan), and that of Gordon Campbell together with the clasp holding all his other medals; Melton Fisher painted the splendid series of portraits ('at a much reduced rate') of the Great War VCs now in the Lower Hall.[37]

The German guns

A war relic, in the form of a collection of German artillery, was presented in 1919 by the War Office in recognition of the work of the Dulwich College Officers Training Corps before and during the War, and was placed in the chestnut avenue to the west of the North Block, on a concrete platform next to the seventy-foot flagstaff presented by the Alleyn Club in 1910. The three field guns, or cannons, became a focus for debate in the mid 1930s about the current European situation, provoking a lively correspondence on what they meant in terms of the Great War and the German nation, and whether they constituted an embarrassment as boastful emblems.[38] Two Old Alleynians who became Assistant Masters wrote to *The Alleynian* about them. 'Scottie' Gibbon (see Chapter Eight), in reply to an earlier letter suggesting that they should be removed, declared robustly in 1934 that 'the present generation at the College and any German friends visiting the College should have a visible reminder that Britain, being bound by the Locarno Treaties to take common action against any disturber of the peace of Western Europe, intends, as she did in 1914, to keep her pledged word, if called upon to do so';[39] on the other hand, George Grange (1896–1975; see Chapter Ten), an Oxford Classicist who returned to teach at the College from 1924 until 1956, wrote in 1937 that they were 'an insult to a great nation', and should be removed.[40] McCulloch Christison moved the Governors to give them to the Ministry of Supply to be melted down in May 1940; they left the College after the Blitz later in the year.[41] No photograph of them has been found.

The literature of the Great War

Many Alleynians contributed to the literature of the Great War. Robin Rees (see Chapter Eight), an Assistant Master who arrived at the College in 1914 to teach English and History, joined up the following year, and was wounded; returning to the College after the War, he published *A Schoolmaster at War* (1935), in which he described the effect of leaving the classroom for the training camp and the Front. Wodehouse's brother Armine's strong volume of war poems has been mentioned (see Chapter Eight); H. R. 'Rex' Freston (1891–1916) was up at Oxford when war broke out, and was killed after only ten days in the trenches in 1916. A brief 'soldier-poet', his poems appeared in *Oxford Poetry*, *The Times* and the *Daily Mirror*. He published *The Quest of Beauty* in 1915, and *The Quest of Truth* appeared posthumously in 1916. Paul Jones, whose parents published *War Letters of a Public-School Boy* in 1918, was on the Modern Side and the Captain of the College XV; he was a philosophical Balliol Scholar who venerated Gilkes.[42] As well as his anguished and gallant letters from the Front, the book included tributes to him from George Smith, Philip Hope, John Adam Joerg, and Gilkes himself.

The Armistice and the War Memorial

The effect on the staff of the losses sustained in the War can be imagined. T. G. Treadgold (1853–1949) retired in 1928, a Mathematics teacher with a sharp edge to his tongue, having served from 1876 for 52 years under Carver, Welldon and Gilkes (whose Head of Lower

Major-General Sir Webb Gillman unveiling
the War Memorial, Founder's Day, 1921.
(Dulwich College)

School he became in 1910); he told the *Evening Stan-dard* and the *Evening News* on his retirement that his room was 'full of shadows before the end'.[43] When the Armistice dawned, in November 1918, an editorial in *The Alleynian* was suitably elegaic, but expressed two hopes for the College: more leisure, and more build-ings. The first priority, however, was to memorialise the dead. In 1918 the Old Alleynian architect Stanley Hall (see Chapter Eight) argued that the best memorial would be free places for fatherless sons of Old Alleyn-ians, for 'boys, good, bad or indifferent'; others thought a Speech Hall to replace the Great Hall was the best idea.[44] Half-fees for sons who had lost Old Alleynian fathers in the War were an early concession, increased in 1917 to all fees and exemption from the entrance fee.[45] The War Memorial, a 29-foot Latin cross, was unveiled by Webb Gillman (see Chapters Six and Seven) and dedicated (see Chapter Seven) by Bishop Welldon in 1921. The design was by the Old Alleynian W. H. Atkin Berry FRIBA (1869–1932). The first proposal called for red granite, but the Governors (disappointingly) asked for the conventional Portland stone.[46] At first a new Chapel or Speech Hall was hoped for, and in 1919, the tercentenary year of the College Foundation, the Alleyn Club voted as follows for the means of memorial: 277 for a Chapel, 170 for a monument, and 45 for a Hall. In the event, too few contributions were forthcoming, and a Memorial monument was decided on; by 1920, £7,000 had been raised. The Alleyn Club determined on pro-vision for dependants, a Memorial and three School scholarships.[47] At the Chapel a cross of Hopton Wood stone to commemorate the losses of the whole Foun-dation was dedicated, designed by the architect W. D. Caröe, who had designed the Reredos in memory of Carver (see Chapter Eight); the Governors rejected a proposal for bronze figures of a soldier and a sailor.[48]

The Joerg brothers

The amiable Joerg brothers (see Chapter Eight) were on the staff throughout the War, making the College vulner-able to criticism both in the Village and the press on account of their German origin. John Baptiste resigned on the outbreak of War as House Master and as Master of the Army Class; he and John Adam later both sent George Smith letters of resignation from their teaching; these he declined to accept, but was told by the Govern-ors to keep the letters,[49] although no action was taken. Smith's rectitude in the case is perhaps compromised by a minuted exchange with the Governors in 1919: the Col-lege was much embarrassed, he said, but the brothers had served the school for 17 and 23 years respectively; John Adam had been naturalised twenty or thirty years before, and John Baptiste at the beginning of the War. 'We were able to retain these masters on the staff, and I think we were right', he wrote, but added that he would in future prefer not to have masters of foreign origin or education on the staff.[50]

Slowly activities and traditions revived, such as the Greek Play. The sporting superiority of Dulwich under-graduates was dramatically highlighted in 1919 when the two opposing Rugby captains for the 'Varsity Match, J. E. Greenwood and E. G. Loudon-Shand (the youngest brother of the VC), were both Old Alleynians, and were photographed with the King at the start of the match.

The 'Varsity Match, 1919.
King George V with the two
Old Alleynian Captains at the
Queen's Club: J. E. Greenwood
(Cambridge), shaking hands, and
E. G. Loudon-Shand (Oxford).
(Dulwich College)

The 'James Caird'

Shackleton's whaler, the *James Caird*, from the *Endurance* expedition (see Chapter Eight), was offered to the College as a gift in March 1922. In this small boat, after the loss of the *Endurance*, crushed and sunk by the ice of the Weddell Sea, Shackleton (with five cramped companions) made what is probably the world's most famous open boat journey. Setting out to South Georgia on 24 April 1916 to save the lives of his men marooned on Elephant Island, the explorer endured 16 days in the South Atlantic in winter, the most dangerous waters in the world. The *James Caird* was named after a generous sponsor of the expedition, the Dundee jute merchant and philanthropist Sir James Key Caird (1837–1916). The boat was accepted by George Smith in public on Speech Day in August, but was said by *The Times* not yet to have been installed at the College. Twenty-two feet and six inches long, it was designed by the navigator Frank Worsley and built in London.[51] A rich Old Alleynian, John Quiller Rowett (1876–1924), gave it to the College, together with its oars and sails, and a sledge; the mizzen lug sail survives, the other is lost. Rowett, two and a half years younger than Shackleton, is said to have walked to school over Sydenham Hill with him. He gave Shackleton a particularly generous contribution of £70,000 for the *Quest* expedition, strictly the 'Shackleton–Rowett Expedition', of 1921–2. Rowett's fortune came from what amounted to a monopoly to supply rum to the Royal Navy. He was a man of

many interests and charitable concerns: he endowed facilities for agricultural research at the University of Aberdeen, for dentistry at the Middlesex Hospital, and elsewhere for medicine and for chemistry.[52] The RYS *Quest* was fitted out with advanced technology: an Avro 'Baby' sea-plane, and a crow's nest and set of overalls for the watch fitted with electric heating. Shackleton in gratitude had apparently given Rowett the *James Caird*, which was kept at first in the open air in the grounds of his mansion at Ely Place, Frant, in Sussex. Shackleton's widow, Emily, wrote privately on 7 August 1922,

> I saw that J. R. had presented the 'James Caird' to Dulwich
> College, and it cut me to the quick. I did not know it was his.
> I thought he was only harbouring it in a granery [sic]. The boat
> is a living sacred thing to me, and I think it is nice for it to go to
> the old school, failing a museum, if they will take *care* of it? but
> I should have liked our name associated with the gift.[53]

Rowett was deeply depressed after Shackleton's premature death from a heart attack off the shore of Grytviken in South Georgia before he even arrived in Antarctica on this expedition; soon after this his business collapsed, and he took his own life.

In 1925 the painting *An Epic of the Sea* by Norman Wilkinson (1878–1971), shown the same year at the Royal Academy, was given anonymously to the College. It shows the *Caird* with its three sails like 'handkerchiefs' amidst the waves of the South Atlantic, just as in

Worsley's description, during the 16 days of 'supreme strife amid heaving waters'.[54] The painting is very skilled, but gives no adequate idea of the sixty-feet waves. The *James Caird* is now world-famous, and has become an emblem of Dulwich College's 'spirit of adventure', as the *Daily Telegraph* put it in the course of an article on the College of 1932, praising Shackleton and the College's military, naval and aeronautical achievements. The journalist listed the living Major-Generals Sir Webb Gillman DSO of the Royal Field Artillery, Sir A. M. Stuart of the Royal Engineers (1861–1936), and Sir H. C. Holman DSO of the Fourth Army (British Expeditionary Force) (1869–1949), along with George Stainforth (see Chapter Eight).[55]

The Shackleton Fund, in response to an appeal to Old Alleynians after his death, brought in a disappointing £220, perhaps for the suspicion that Shackleton had evaded military service in the War. In fact, following his return to England after the *Endurance* expedition in 1916, and after recruiting for the Army in Australia, he was appointed Director of Equipment and Transport to the North Russian Expeditionary Force in Murmansk.[56] The Governors in any case made up the difference to build a 'shelter' for the *Caird*; it was decided to place the 'Shackleton Memorial' up against a wall of the Baths, between the turret and the Engineering Workshop, after considering a setting by itself among a clump of trees to

the west of the Baths.[57] The brick and wrought-iron shelter, open on one side to the elements, and resembling a cage, was designed by F. Danby Smith FRIBA (1876–1936), an Old Alleynian, after a sketch by Stanley Hall.[58] Along with the Baths the shelter was destroyed by the V1 bomb in July 1944 (see Chapter Ten) but the boat was unscathed. It was then moved to the Boiler House and then to the east end of the Baths, where it became the site for thousands of roll calls to be taken. Meanwhile a letter to *The Alleynian* in 1925 had declared that the boat should be painted or treated with preservative; the editor replied that 'everyone is agreed that to paint the boat would alter its character entirely'.[59] Antarctic whalers were actually painted white, but the *James Caird* had lost its paint; also, parts of the topsides of the boat had been burnt in King Haakon Bay on South Georgia by Vincent, Macnish and McCarthy while Shackleton, Worsley and Crean crossed the uncharted mountains and glaciers for help. The boat at Dulwich at this time resembled more a heroic Viking boat, with the ribs of its interior structure visible. It was painted white in 1959, and again when it was 'restored' by the National Maritime Museum in 1968 with two extra strakes, decking and new mast, rigging and sails.[60] The boat was intended after this restoration to rest in the Cloisters to the new Dining Hall, but with its mast it was found to be too tall, and it was returned on loan to the Museum. There it stood on display (in the

The *James Caird* (before restoration) and a *Nimrod* sledge. The Shackleton Memorial, post 1922. (Dulwich College)

Neptune Hall and the 'Half Deck') for another two years, but was then placed in storage from 1970 until 1974. In 1986 the Master, David Emms, the Librarian, Margaret Slythe, and the Old Alleynian and enthusiast Harding Dunnett (1909–2000), founder in 1994 of the James Caird Society, negotiated its return. Dunnett accompanied the boat round the South Circular Road, blowing his motor horn. For three years it lay on the margin of the playing field until installed in the North Cloister in 1989, when Shackleton's son Edward, Lord Shackleton (1911–94) opened the Shackleton Building; it now lies on a bed of shingle bagged by Duncan Carse at the head of 'Caird Inlet' in South Georgia (where the boat landed), supplemented with a lorry-load of similar rocks from Aberystwyth, supplied by the local council.

Following its first arrival at the College in 1920s, the boat was lent to the Polar Exhibition in Central Hall at Westminster in July 1930.[61] Two members of the *Endurance* expedition gave lectures to the boys at the College, Frank Worsley in 1929 and Lionel Greenstreet in 1936.[62] In 1924 Messrs J. and T. Bailey, who fitted out Shackleton's *Nimrod* expedition, presented a sledge 'used in the dash towards the South', now in the North Cloister, but it appears possibly to be in too good a condition to justify the claim.[63]

Academic life and the Common Room

When Smith arrived at the College and was shown the Board of Education Report of 1914, he responded by saying, like Gilkes, that Inspectors looked on boys as standardised creatures; he nevertheless vowed to remedy their main complaints: too many masters were teaching subjects they did not know; there was too much freedom of choice as to subjects, books and methods; and the teaching of English in the College was generally poor.[64] Not until 1929, however, did Smith's successor Walter Booth report to the Governors that while he was retaining the Form Masters' lessons as a good Public School tradition, French and Mathematics were now all taught in sets by specialists. Smith reported to his Governors in October 1918 that he was having difficulties in finding staff; the views of his teachers, especially the Scientists, were too 'specialistic'.[65] The following year Smith gave statistics to show how the boys studied: 120 were on the Classics Side, 273 were on the Modern Side (studying Languages and History); 95 boys were studying Science and Mathematics, and 156 Engineering; 195 boys were in the Junior School.[66] When the War ended, the College's results for Oxford and Cambridge entrance and scholarships quickly improved. Of the great Classics teachers, Philip Hope retired in poor health in 1919,[67] and 'Teddy' Hose in 1934, after practically a lifetime at the College.

Hose had published in 1924 a brilliant textbook, *Dulwich Latin Exercises for Middle Forms*; it included passages of Malory and Defoe for translation. In 1919 there were six Alleynian dons at Oxford and one at Cambridge.[68] In Michaelmas Term 1922 there were 822 boys, rising to 924 in 1926. In 1922 five scholarships at Oxford, and one at Cambridge, were awarded, and in 1923 a total of ten awards were achieved, a record for the College. At the Alleyn Club dinner that year Bishop Welldon said that the College today was 'perhaps the most distinguished of all Public Schools in regard to the honours it takes'.[69] In 1930 the College was still awarding £1,000 annually for exhibitions up to £75 for its boys at Oxford and Cambridge. In 1920 there were five scholarships at Oxford and two at Cambridge; in 1933, Walter Booth's fifth year, there were six open scholarships and thirteen firsts at Oxford and Cambridge. That the characters and minds of the undergraduates from Dulwich at this period were thought more of at Oxford than conventional Public School boys is shown by a letter of 1923 written at Magdalen College by the famous don and writer C. S. Lewis (1898–1963), who had himself spent a very unhappy year at Malvern College:

> I sometimes wonder if this country will kill the public schools before they kill it. My experience goes on confirming the ideas about them which were first suggested to me by Malvern long ago. The best scholars, the best men, and (properly understood) the best gentlemen, seem now to come from places like Dulwich, or to be wafted up on county scholarships from secondary schools. Except for pure Classics (and that only at Winchester, and only a few boys even there) I don't really know what gifts the public schools bestow on their nurslings, beyond the mere surface of good manners: unless contempt of things of the intellect, extravagance, insolence, self-sufficiency, and sexual perversion are to be called gifts.[70]

After the War the Board of Education began to have a greater say in the affairs of the College because of their Inspections and because of the increase in the numbers of the London County Council scholars. In 1919 they stopped the College putting up tuition fees, which were to be kept at the lowest possible rate of £28 10s per annum, but allowed the boarding fees to go up to £74 per annum.[71] The College needed to find additional income from the Board of Education, since further endowment from the Estate seemed unlikely, but once on the Register of 'grant-earning' schools, the Board could demand to elect Governors from the Local Educational Authorities, and in general reduce the independence of the College. Alleyn's School had adopted this course, taking up to 25 per cent of its pupils from the London County Council. In effect the Board of Education agreed to pay its grant to the College with a reduced requirement of an intake of 10 per cent, as it did in the case of Manchester Grammar School, Bedford School, and King Edward VI School, Birmingham, saying that they were all in various ways special, and their character should be preserved.[72] The Minutes of November 1919 report ponderously that 'the Governors have consulted with the London County Council as to the way in which Dulwich College can best co-operate in the public system of education. In accordance with the suggestions made to them, the Governors propose to inform the London County Council that Dulwich College may be placed on the list of Schools to which Junior Scholars are admitted'. They were also prepared to admit 'pupils nominated by the Governing bodies of Schools in receipt of grants from the Board, set in 1920 at £7,000 per annum, in order that they may receive advanced or special education'. Before the War LCC 'Intermediate scholars' had applied to the College, and the College had been able to admit 'practically all'.[73]

Severe anxiety about the College's finances bedevilled Smith's years. 1918 was hardly the time to consider once again taking over Dulwich College Preparatory School, but the offer was made, discussed, and rejected for a second time in June. In July of 1920 the College was overdrawn by £5,270. George Smith carried on, but the deficiencies of equipment and the condition of the classrooms and the Art rooms were deplorable, and the salaries were still poor by comparison with the state schools. The Governors meanwhile acknowledged in 1920 Smith's services 'in years of great difficulty during and since the War'.[74] Privilege was under siege, to the dismay of conservative elements: the College's finances were in 'a very serious state' early in 1920, while on the other hand the accounts at Alleyn's School were balancing, and the College applied to the Board of Education for 'grant-aided status', awarded on 1 August, which obtained from 1921 until 1928; at the same time the Borough Council was proposing 'seizure' of part of the Estate for housing. The College was awarded £6,000 in 1922 and 1923 by the Board, in addition to the grants from the London County Council. The total number of Governors was increased from 20 to 21, the co-opted Governors at the same time being reduced by half from eight to four; the London County Council governors were increased to seven.[75]

The masters' salaries were still considerably below the new 'Burnham Scale' for teachers drawn up by the Government. Given the expense of living near a select London dormitory suburb, the dedication of many staff who stayed at the College was strong, although of course they valued the compensation of teaching a good number of very bright pupils. George Smith nobly declared that his aim was that no qualified boy should be debarred

from attending the College for lack of means, while the College was struggling with dwindled funds. There was no sign of falling applications. When in 1921 the tuition fees were actually increased by £17 to £45 per annum, and the grants were applied, the situation slowly improved. George Smith thanked the Governors for their patience with the financial situation, which, given the general quiescence of his character, probably meant that he was having an intolerable time making ends meet. In spite of the financial situation, the College was becoming 'more definite, more stable and more uniform'. Smith reported that the Junior Scholars were 'assimilated' satisfactorily.[76]

In 1923 the Board of Education again inspected the College and reported, giving some useful statistics and insights. The catchment of the boys was now 78 per cent from London, 19 per cent from other districts in England, and 3 per cent from abroad. The College received £5,370 per annum from the Estates Governors and up to £2,000 of surplus. £300 of the grant from the Estates was dedicated to the Picture Gallery. George Smith, we read, was 'a man of great tact' who got on exceedingly well with both staff and boys, a very able teacher 'who does not hastily make up his mind'. At the same time, Form Masters were still teaching subjects in which they were not specially qualified, such as Latin, French, English and History, and sometimes Geography and Mathematics. Indeed, throughout the 1920s the teaching of English was left to 30 out of 44 masters without specific qualifications in the subject, and the teaching of History and French to twenty or so such masters.[77] In 1923 Eric Parsley, a much loved figure, was appointed, an exceptionally cultivated and witty French master (see Chapter Ten) who was to become Head of the Modern Side in 1933.

The division into the Classical and Modern Sides was deemed to be mischievous, particularly since the Classical Side sustained its long tradition of regarding itself as the premier Side of the School. The general conclusion, however, was strong and complimentary:

> the way [the College] has dealt with the Free Place pupils in the last couple of years shows that it has, under the present Master, a striking capacity for adapting itself to modern conditions, and this is an indication of real strength. There is probably no Public School in the country better able to reconsider the system it has inherited from the past, and without surrendering the most valuable features of that tradition.[78]

Things were not quite so well on the ground, however, and by 1925 Smith was voicing reservations to the Governors about the presence of the London County Council boys, an issue recorded several times in his reports to the Governors. Forming one-eighth of the admissions of the previous years, he reckoned that the LCC Junior Scholars would eventually form between 20 and 25 per cent of the whole school; they were good workers, 'but there was sometimes a little difficulty in winning them from a purely selfish view of education'. The following year he was more outspoken about the resistance of the LCC boys to the Public School ethos of the College. There were now 896 boys in Dulwich College of which 166 were free-place holders from elementary schools; this was expected to rise in the following year to 180. 'I am inclined to think that that number is rather too large', wrote Smith. 'They are, generally speaking, and with a certain number of exceptions, good pupils. But when they come they have, again generally speaking, much to learn in the way of corporate spirit and they are unfamiliar with the idea of subordinating their individual interests (often selfish) to the interest of the School and the tradition of school discipline'. In a telling phrase, he said that 'they may dilute the spirit too much'. The Governors should have the power to limit their numbers, he argued, but obviously could not if the College continued to be grant-earning. [79] In the same year, 1925, the Governors symbolically rejected an offer by the London County Council for them to meet (without paying for the hire of the room) at their headquarters in County Hall, and they approached the Estates Governors with a request for additional endowment. In 1927 at a Governors' Meeting it was said that Edward Alleyn intended 45 per cent of the income from the Estate to go to the College, but that they now received only 6.6 per cent; since 1913 the Estate had a large and increasing surplus. [80] By 1926 the fringes of the Estate had undergone development; the Central Foundation School for Boys in Cooper Street, Finsbury, and for Girls in Skinner Street, Bishopsgate, as well as James Allen's Girls' School and Alleyn's, still received income from the Estate. The *Morning Post* reported a scheme of the College Governors to open a Girls' School of the highest class, on the lines of Cheltenham College; they had reserved a site between the Golf Course and Dulwich Common with room for boarding houses (where there are now sports grounds) but the project was not realised for lack of adequate funds, and because the scheme would mean that the College's share of the surplus would diminish. The Estates Governors proposed to grant £7,370 to the College, £1,600 to Alleyn's School and £1,200 to James Allen's Girls' School, and £1,000 to St Saviour's and St Olave's. George Smith meanwhile wanted the hundred boarders increased to 160. [81] It was proposed to discontinue the special scholarship for boys to transfer from Alleyn's to the Upper School at the College, on the recommendation of the Headmaster of Alleyn's. This was resisted by the Governors, but was accepted in 1926, when it was proven that the boys themselves generally wished to stay on at Alleyn's. [82]

By 1926 the Governors were reporting a 'strong and unanimous feeling' to dispense with the Board of Education grant altogether and be 'relieved' of the 'freeplacers'. A new Governor who joined the Board in the same year and served until 1934 was (Sir) Harold Webbe (1885–1965), the Chairman of the Educational Committee of the London County Council. The College now had a roll of 909 boys; the Governors resolved to reduce the entry of the 'free-placers' from 27 to 11. Returning to the subject in 1928 the Board of Education and the LCC declared that the Governors had initiated the grants voluntarily before 1920, when they were in financial difficulties, and together they intended to continue with the scheme. George Smith offered his opinion that the College could absorb eighty to a hundred boys without detriment to its general educational efficiency or alteration of its traditional character. With 157 LCC scholars at the College, the Governors determined to limit the number to 50, and put out a New Scheme Draft to discuss with the Board of Education. Sir Arthur Hirtzel, Chairman of the College Governors, presented a statement at a Whitehall meeting with representatives of the Board of Education and the LCC on 15 February 1928:

> The Governors realised fully their duty towards education and society in general. They felt that their first duty was to the College, which, since its virtual foundation in 1857, had directed its ambitions towards being a Public School, and had progressed so far in its ambitions that it was now one of the foremost Public schools. The Governors felt bound to hand on to posterity the College with its claims to be a first-class Public School undiminished. On the other hand, they realised that every institution must take its share in the burden of the whole; they had recognised this as far back as 1903, when Junior County Scholars were first admitted to the College. Dulwich had been the first Public School to admit such scholars voluntarily, and no other Public School had, or was at the present time prepared to admit them in the same way. Whether other Public Schools would in the future, follow their example, depended, in a large measure, on the way in which critics of the present scheme conducted their case.

The financial and educational arguments were of course interwoven; much was made of the 'character of the school'. Reading between the lines, the Governors seem to have believed that too many Junior Scholars were entering at 11-plus, and by their majority were creating a discrete culture in the Junior School (where the boys were mostly aged eleven to thirteen) perhaps inimical to that of the fee-payers who mostly entered at 13, a division that of course made it harder to unify the School. Thus the Council scholarship holders might expect to stay at the College for six or seven years, and the fee-payers an

CRYSTAL PALACE

UPPER NORWOOD

WEST NORWOOD   STREATHAM

WEST DULWICH
ALLEYNS HEAD

SANATORIUM

FOOTBALL AND CRICKET GROUND

ALLEYNS

PAVILION

SCIENCE BUILDINGS

MUSIC ROOMS

FOOTBALL AND CRICKET GROUND

SWIMMING BATH

FIVES COURTS

SHOOTING RANGE

HEAD MASTERS GARDEN

HEAD MASTERS HOUSE

HALL
AND CLASS RMS

WAR MEMORIAL

TO SYDENHAM

CARVER MEMORIAL

ENTRANCE FROM COLLEGE ROAD

TO DULWICH VILL
AND LONDON

THE MILL POND

ALLEYNS HEAD

DULWICH COMMON

DETUR · GLORIA · SOLI · DEO

THE OLD COLLEGE IN DULWICH VILLAGE

G.G. WOODWARD

Drawn by G. G. Woodward.

DULWICH COLLEGE AT A GLANCE

Alleyn's College of God's Gift was founded in 1619 by Edward Alleyn, the celebrated actor. In 1857 and 1882 the College was reconstituted, and now comprises Dulwich College and Alleyn's School. The original buildings are in Dulwich Village, but in 1870 the Prince of Wales, afterwards King Edward, opened the buildings here shown, designed by Bank and Barry. Mr. George Smith is the Master of the College. There are about 850 pupils.

average of just four years. George Smith said that the Junior Scholars tended to group together and were less 'malleable' in later stages of school life. The London County Council said at the meeting that they were grateful for the facilities offered to their boys, but further declared that they did not want a diminution in numbers.

Lord Eustace Percy (1887–1958), President of the Board of Education (and a Conservative), now said that, were Dulwich to refuse to yield on the matter, its willing co-operation might be sacrificed, and its hand forced. It was at this point that the Master declared openly that the current arrangements were 'endangering' the character of the College.[83] Hirtzel had written to *The Times* to assert that the College should have 50, not 150, of these boys; the Board of Education replied, repeating publicly its hope that the London County Council scholars would not drop below one hundred; the College resolved to withdraw from the grant-aided status at the end of the academic year. George Smith now suddenly chose to tender his resignation, in June 1928, a few days before his sixty-first birthday; he had been appointed Director of the Teacher Training at Oxford University – a measure of how highly he was regarded in the educational world. Under Booth's Mastership in the years before the Second World War, and under pressure from the Alleyn Club (whose spokesmen deplored the loss of autonomy by the presence of the LCC scholars) and perhaps also from the Staff, the numbers of the Junior and Intermediate Scholars were eventually reduced, though not without high-level meetings between the College and the Board of Education (see below) and much comment in the press.

When Smith wrote on the teaching of Classics in a book of essays on educational aims and methods, *The Modern Teacher* (1921), he stated his views in a modest but rather dull way, particularly by comparison with the visionary essay on Science and Engineering in the same volume by Sanderson (see Chapter Eight). Even so, he was persuasive, saying that the predominant position held by Classics in the conservative curriculum of liberal education was actually a handicap, as it led to complacency. Smith pointed out the way that the subject-matter of classical literature gave rise to discussion of political philosophy (just as it had done in Gilkes's classes), and he praised the intellectual exercise of translation for its scrupulous attention to semantic range and accuracy, a factor that has been noted in Chapter Six as a catalyst to the minds and diction of those Alleynian writers who had studied Classics while at the College. He reported that the teachers of Natural Sciences said those of their pupils who were trained in the Classics generally did better.[84]

Howard Rubie (1894–1970), a Science master in plus-fours who was on the staff from 1925 until 1955, brought the College some attention for his pioneering work as Careers Master by inventing aptitude tests for Fourth- and Fifth-Formers; these involved the reassembly of door locks from their constituent parts, an early version of the Rubik's Cube, and the slipping of balls of varying diameters through holes – from which exercises he deduced the candidates' ideal career. He published *Round Pegs* (1935), an early book on vocational guidance. Rubie was an important figure in the Public Schools Employment Bureau (and its Bursar for ten years), established in 1939.[85]

A disappointing feature of the College between the wars was the teaching of Art, particularly by comparison with the illustrious early days under John Sparkes (see Chapter Six). In 1916 Mr W. E. Hine of Harrow had written scornful reports to the Governors, in particular deprecating how little use was made of the special advantage of the Gallery for inspiration; George Smith had replied that Art was an 'additional' subject and, since there was a war on, the Officers Training Corps preoccupied the boys after school. He added that it was tempting to think of the Gallery 'as a natural focus from which inspiration ought to radiate', but this was mainly a sentimental value. The masterpieces were 'not of the kind from which a young and unlearned student would naturally learn'; he went on to assert that 'to use it directly or much with boys as an instrument of aesthetic education would be like setting boys of twelve to read Spenser and Milton'.[86] In 1919 the Governor Henry Yates Thompson (see Chapter Eight) proposed an Art School at Dulwich (such as those at Charterhouse – and at Harrow, which he had himself presented to the School in 1895 at a cost of £3,000); his idea was that it should be sited symmetrically to the (Old) Library, on the other side of the drive by the gate onto Dulwich Common, and plans (not known to survive) were drawn up by E. S. Hall.[87] The fact is, however, that the College at this time hardly deserved such a highly desirable suggested amenity and architectural flourish proclaiming the value of Art to education at its gates, and little appeared to improve in the teaching of the subject. Melton Fisher in 1927 called the entries he was judging for the Foundation prize in his name 'a little depressing'.[88] The Royal Academy nominee on the Governing body from 1908 until his death was the portrait painter Walter Ouless (1848–1933), who while not himself an Old Alleynian was nevertheless a pupil of John Sparkes. An old-fashioned gentleman with great charm, he undertook a new 'hang' of the pictures in the Gallery,[89] but seems to have had no interest in (or impact upon) the teaching of Art at the College. By 1932, when Stef Fisher (see Chapter Six) was Principal Art Master, the Art lessons were taken by part-time artists with their own studios, an arrangement that seems to have sponsored mixed results.[90] Meanwhile throughout the 1920s the annual RA exhibitions were a reminder of John Sparkes's glorious years (see Chapter Six), with predictable subjects by Old Alleynian Academicians on view, no doubt seriously out of fashion, such as Stanhope Forbes (with West Country titles such as *A Village Rendezvous with ducks and horses*) and La Thangue (*A Provençal Flock* or *An Old Italian Garden*); Forbes painted stirring frescoes at the Royal Exchange of *The Great Fire of London* and *Destruction by Fire of the Second Royal Exchange* in 1921.[91]

In spite of the efforts of certain teachers the College must have seemed more than a little philistine between the wars: a letter to *The Alleynian* in 1929 complained that boys, whether individually or in classes, were never seen at the Picture Gallery, nor given talks there. In the same year Jack Westrup (see below), who had brought in string players to play the Ravel Quartet, said that audiences were merely 'adequate'; he protested that 'it is a delusion to suppose that these concerts are a highbrow entertainment for the unathletic'.[92] In 1933, however, the May issue of *The Alleynian* was an 'all-literature' number, with remarkable pastiches of the Classics and Icelandic sagas by W. B. Fagg (1914–92), who left that year from a brilliant Classical Sixth under H. J. Dixon (1895–1971; Form Master of the Classical Sixth, 1921–1934, Commanding Officer of the CCF for a year in 1933, appointed Head Master of King's College School, Wimbledon in 1934, where he remained until 1960). Fagg was to become the Keeper of Ethnography at the British Museum from 1969 until his death. A fascinating eccentric and polymath, he was an authority on African sculpture, and a friend of the sculptors Jacob Epstein and Henry Moore; he published *The Nature of African Art* (1953). In February 1938 Stef Fisher designed a plain but dull heraldic cover for *The Alleynian*, printed on cornflower blue paper, replacing Mrs Rendall's long-serving silhouette of the New College roofs and flight of pigeons (see Chapter Seven).

Events and traditions

Perhaps the most important post-war innovation of Smith's day was the introduction of the Athletic House system, a change to the internal organisation of the College announced in *The Alleynian* for March 1920.[93] This was to have far-reaching beneficial effects in encouraging and organising competitive sporting aspects of life at the College, and in more recent years also cultural activities, such as music and drama. 'Scottie' Gibbon is usually given the credit for initiating this reform, but George Smith told the Alleyn Club diners in

1922 that it was his own idea, while Gibbon had implemented its detailed planning.[94] A good summary of the system, giving the reasons why it was necessary, later appeared in a supplement to the *Daily Telegraph* for 14 November 1932; it will be remembered that the importance of the loyalty of the boy to his Form in work and play was one of Gilkes's tenets:

> By an admirable scheme originated during the recent Mastership of Mr. George Smith, the whole school, day boys and boarders alike, was divided into six houses, known as Grenville, Marlowe, Spenser, Sidney, Drake and Raleigh. About a hundred boys belong to each, the remainder forming the Junior School, and this system of dividing up the school has been found extremely practical for purposes of games.
>
> The six houses meet one another not only at football and cricket, but in athletics, gymnastics, fives, boxing, shooting, and all the other recreations in which the boys take part. At the end of each year the Cock House shield or cup is awarded to the house which leads in results. Each house has a master in charge, with another as his assistant, while boys act as house captain, vice-captain, and football and cricket captains.
>
> Before this arrangement was in force games at Dulwich were organised on a basis of forms, and scholastic rather than athletic ability was the ground on which sides were composed. Obviously this could not last long. A league of three divisions was arranged from the Senior forms, and this was employed both for purposes of cricket and football. In addition, there were games between the occupants of the various boarding houses and between boys on the four sides of the school [Classical, Modern, Science, Engineering]. But the whole system was at fault, for it imposed too much strain upon individual form masters, as so much depended upon their enthusiasm. Boys were constantly changing from one form to the next and consequently, having to move from one games division to another. The extreme popularity of the matches between the boarding houses indicated the best way for reform to be carried out, and in a very short space of time the scheme has been most fully justified.

In March 1932 the *Windsor Magazine* explained that, appropriately to the origins of the foundation, 'the six Houses were named after famous Elizabethans; Shakespeare's name being omitted, as being considered preeminent'. 'Grenville' included the boys of the Blew House; 'Marlowe', The Orchard; 'Spenser', Elm Lawn; 'Sidney', Ivyholme. There were two houses entirely for the day-boys, 'Drake' and 'Raleigh'. The magazine listed the sports named above as the basis of matches between the houses, but also mentioned platoon and other competitions for the Officers Training Corps (OTC).[95] Two houses were to be added in 1982, 'Howard' and 'Jonson', after Alleyn's associates (see Chapter One).

In June 1921 the whole College sat for a group photograph against the backdrop of the South Cloister, the first to be taken by a 'panoramic' camera that rotated from one side to the other; the Head Porter, Harry Smith, appears at both ends, having run round the back to be photographed twice.[96] Smith, a veteran of the Boer War and at first a gym instructor at the College, retired in 1936 after 42 years, a familiar figure with his row of medals, waxed moustache and cap with the College arms.

At the time of the General Strike from 3 May to 12 May 1926 (in support of miners' wages), when almost the entire British work force and all public transport was at a halt, Sir Edward Campbell (OA; see above), the Conservative Member of Parliament for North West Camberwell and the brother of the VC holder Gordon, visited the Old Alleynian Football Club and offered £1 to the Club for every member who would enrol as a Special Constable. Led by McCulloch Christison as a 'very, very fierce' Inspector, a role he was to play for ten years, 85 men joined up, and Campbell paid up £100. A Flying Squad of 'Specials' was the result, using private cars and motor-cycles. Eventually 147 Old Alleynians were enrolled, including twenty Assistant Masters. Christison plainly relished his role in the organisation, just as he was to enjoy organising the Air Raid Wardens at the College during the Second World War.[97]

In 1926 further Tercentenary celebrations, this time to mark Edward Alleyn's death, were reported in *The Times*, reminding its readers of the 4,000 children who were benefiting from his bequests (see Chapter Six); the eminent Renaissance theatre scholar Sir Walter Greg (1875–1959), who had published works on Alleyn and Henslowe, spoke in Great Hall about the Founder.[98]

Hubert Doulton (see Chapter Eight) continued the College concerts with ambitious pieces through the difficult circumstances of the Great War. In 1923 Arthur 'Guts' Gayford (1889–1960), an Oxford Historian, a passionate teacher, a hospitable and a highly cultivated man who had joined the staff in 1914 (later to be Head of History, and in 1934 of English also), was appointed Principal Master in Music. Gayford was to teach at the College during both wars; incidentally, he was also was the author of an excellent pamphlet on the history of the College (1936, revised 1950). Gayford's musical era was greatly admired by his pupil Professor A. G. Lehmann (1922–2006), who left in 1939. Lehmann (while at school the Junior Fencing Champion for England) was to become Professor of French at the University of Reading, an expert on Sainte-Beuve, and on the Romantic and Symbolist movements in France; he said that the music of Gayford's era was the work of a great and true spirit, 'who lived and played without hype or vanity, and set a noble standard'.[99] The Orchestra at his Christmas Concert in 1925 consisted of 60 members, and the choir of 140, and they played among other pieces the first movement of Beethoven's Fifth Symphony. In 1937 an early performance of Fauré's *Requiem* was given. According to Jack Westrup, Gayford 'would work himself to breaking point to get the best results out of choir and orchestra'.[100] Gayford, with his amazing energy, also would lead the Military Band on Field Days, marching in the street with the cadets from the College to Tulse Hill station, and amidst all his other commitments would mount ambitious productions of plays. *Esprit de corps* was still strong, if not fervent; the 'Good-bye Song' (according to *The Alleynian* in 1939) was parodied with mock sentimentality during the 'disillusioned 'Twenties'.[101] Founder's Day flourished again soon after the War, and in 1923 the Agincourt speech from *Henry V*, extracts from Molière and Aristophanes' *Frogs* were performed. The Assault at Arms was still performed in 1929 with boxing, fencing, a Farcical Drill, a Grand Tableau and 'God save the King'.[102] The 'Corps Shout', begun in 1924, became a traditional annual entertainment expressing 'animal spirits', for which Bob Monkhouse, the future famous comedian, designed programmes in 1945; according to A. R. Taylor of the OTC, this was intended to be 'unfettered' and 'a spontaneous burst of jollity'; Taylor (1882–1964) was an Assistant Master from 1905 until 1943 (and Housemaster of Elm Lawn, who 'dressed' in a dinner jacket nightly for the meal, whatever the menu). One of the first actions of the new Master, Christopher Gilkes, in 1942 was to walk out of the Corps Shout in disgust, and publicly to deprive the prefects who were involved in it of their office.[103]

At the Alleyn Club Jubilee dinner in 1923 twelve members of 1873 were present.[104] The Club inaugurated the Old Alleynian Cricket Club in 1927. In the same year a Dramatic and Operatic Society was formed, open to former pupils and College masters and ladies connected with them; before the Second World War, with two productions a year at the Cripplegate Institute (conscious that it was practically on the site of Alleyn's Fortune Theatre in Golden Lane), they had put on 26 shows of new plays and of operettas. These were mostly middlebrow, and included a production of Wodehouse's *Psmith* with Eric Parsley as the scintillating *flâneur*. The Club was revived after the Second War in 1947 and carried on until 1966; as the members aged, the plays they chose were almost all revivals of familiar interwar favourites, such as Sheridan, Shaw and Wilde.[105] An Old Alleynian City Lunch club was founded in 1920, meeting at first near Chancery Lane tube station.[106] The Old Alleynian Lodge was founded on 14 December

1920, with Shackleton a Founder Member. The Lodge has an excellent reputation for generosity to the College for the Bursary Appeals and in (undisclosed) support to individual boys, and meets currently at the College.

The 25th Camberwell (First Dulwich College) Scout Group was established by the Mathematics Master, H. V. Styler (1900–89), in February 1929, two years after he joined the College. George Smith suggested this to him, and gave him a disused classroom and some funds. Walter Booth was very enthusiastic, and visited a Surrey summer camp in 1930, when a Second Troop was founded, bathing in the cold waters of the Shere millpond. By 1931 there were 55 boys in the Scouts; the boys learned pioneering, canoeing, rock-climbing, abseiling and forestry, and wrote lively and witty accounts of their camps in log books. In the 1930s local weekend camps were taken in the fields of Shortlands, with the Scouts pulling their equipment from the College on trek carts (which the Scouts still own). Eric Parsley played the piano at their entertainments. Scout displays on Founder's Day became a regular feature from 1931. Together with the OTC, of course, their service and training was appreciated as a very significant factor in preparation of the boys for (another) war. In 1966 the Venture Scout Unit was launched (taking over from the Senior Scout Troop) and, under the inspiring leadership of Stephen Howard (see Chapter Ten) was a great success; Barry Evans, John Cottle (who retired in 1985), Garth Davidson and Christopher Field (see Chapter Ten), helped out. The longest serving Old Alleynian to help with the Scouts was Ivor Gipson (1916–95), who left in 1934. Since 1953 over one hundred of the boys have won the Queen's Scout Award. [107]

Buildings, boarding houses, the Chapel, the Estate, and the Picture Gallery

At the New College a copper vane was added to the Clock Tower in 1922, designed by Edwin Hall (see Chapter Eight), and Charles Barry's large red roof-tiles (in deliberate colour harmony with the brick and terracotta) were replaced with Westmoreland slates in 1923. The patterned tiled floor of the Lower Hall had been relaid in 1915. [108] Accommodation gave way to more classrooms: Gibbon, Hose and F. J. Ellis lost their living quarters in the North Block in 1920, and the 'poky little attics' (intended originally as dormitories for the Foundation Scholars) at the top of the North Block in 1925 were turned into so-called 'lofty form rooms'; thus by 1926–7 the whole of the North Block was given over to classrooms. [109] In 1935 the Great Hall was redecorated. [110]

The Governors came to agree that the Master's quarters in the South Block, unchanged since Canon Carver and his family had occupied them, were woefully inadequate for the 1920s. George Smith told the Governors in 1919 that his house was 'particularly unsuitable for domestic habitation', and there were a hundred steps from the kitchen to the servants' bedrooms. A new house for the Master in the College grounds was contemplated at the cost of £10,000, and classrooms were to be made from much of the previous accommodation, but in the same month the Governors took a lease of the historic and architecturally very fine Bell House (1767) on College Road for Smith and his family. The Master reported finding the garden of four acres (as it was then) 'a little overpowering'. [111]

In 1917 the Governors bought Elm Lawn on Dulwich Common, since 1869 in use as a boarding house, followed by The Orchard in 1919. [112] In 1926 a new Hall was first discussed by the Governors, at a cost of £1,200. By 1929 it was said to be impossible to serve lunch in one sitting to 400 in the Great Hall, and the tables and benches made Assembly distinctly uncomfortable. Walter Booth asked the Governors for an entirely new Hall, for the College needed a 'corporate identity'. When the admirable Old Alleynian Sir Arthur Hirtzel (a Governor since 1914 and Chairman of the Board since 1925) made his farewell speech on retirement in 1930 he championed this cause. A new Great Hall was to be sited on the Masters' Garden (as it was known) at the north-east corner of the campus, but the scheme came to nothing. [113]

In spite of the Depression (1928–33) the increased prosperity of the Dulwich Estate meant that the College could afford three new important buildings in the 1930s. The new Chairman after Sir Arthur Hirtzel was Major-General Lord Loch (1873–1942), a most distinguished soldier and a generous public servant after the Great War. [114] In 1931 the Governors reviewed specifications for new boarding houses; they aimed to close the houses on Dulwich Common and (as Gilkes had wanted) to have boarding houses on the campus. A design submitted by the 70-year-old Professor Arthur Beresford Pite (1861–1934) of Beckenham (in his youth the inspired architect of Christ Church, Brixton Road, 1897–1903) was accepted, and that of Francis Danby Smith, an Old Alleynian and Estates Governor (at one time the Chairman; see above), rejected. Two houses were in mind, but one only was to be built at the present. In 1932 the Earl of Harewood gave the prizes and opened (new) Ivyholme, built on part of the former Master's Garden. Boarders were back to their pre-1914 numbers this year, and it was particularly hoped that boys would be attracted from the Dominions. [115] The boarding fees relative to other schools were not expensive: in 1931 a Dulwich boarder paid £135 per annum, while an Eton boarder paid £230; St Paul's

Assembly in the Great Hall. (Dulwich College)

charged £150, and Westminster £165.[116] Plans for a second new Boarding House and a new Cricket Pavilion were discussed by the Governors in 1933.[117] The Cricket Pavilion of July 1934, designed by Danby Smith, cost £8,000; it was paid for, as the Fives and Squash courts had been, by the Commissariat, which had been brilliantly reorganised to make large profits by the Old Alleynian and Governor, C. A. Rehder (see Chapter Eight). When air raids caused alarm in late 1939, the Pavilion made a convenient First Aid Post with gas decontamination sheds, and drawings in *The Alleynian* show its sand-bagged entrances and signs.[118] At the time of discussion of the new House, there were 108 boarders: 32 in the new Ivyholme, 25 at Elm Lawn, 27 at (Old) Blew, and 24 at The Orchard. By 1934 the (new) Blew House was commissioned from Beresford Pite, to be slightly larger than Ivyholme. In 1937 in fact the number of boarders was reported to be falling, as was indeed the total College roll of 857; Elm Lawn was closed. The two new boarding houses were never full before the Second War;[119] a figure of 84 current boarders was given in October 1938, during a crisis of imagined air raids, when parents would not

consider London an ideal place for their boys on the flight path of German bombers to the City, and the possible closure of The Orchard was also discussed.[120] It was indeed closed the following year, when the figures were given of 32 boys at the Blew House (with provision for 40); 30 at Ivyholme (out of 40) and 16 at The Orchard (out of 28). Ivyholme was closed in 1941, when the RAF Air Training Corps used part of it (see below). The new Master, Christopher Gilkes, when he arrived in November 1941, took up residence there.[121] Planned in 1939,[122] the new Boiler House, with its stark modernist chimney, was opened in 1940, supplying central heating and marking a dismal change in the architectural style of the College. The Commissariat in these years, managed before the Great War by an Assistant Master, but now set up with a Manager, was an ambitious commercial operation, much resented by the local Chambers of Commerce who sent a formal complaint to the Governors; it offered a 26-page catalogue, with items such as bicycles, radios, gramophones, and tailor-made suits, sold to boys and Old Boys all over the country.[123] The considerable profits contributed to building schemes.

At the Chapel the Founder's Tomb was lowered in 1923. Five bells were recast in the same year, one a new bell in memory of J. M. M. Marshall, the son of a Governor, killed in the Great War.[124] Lorraine Wilson (1865–1924), who left the College in 1883, a local resident, and commemorated still in Prizes at the College, was a very active member of the Chapel Committee from its commencement until this era.

The Dulwich College Estate and its residents successfully resisted proposed tramways and various omnibus routes between the Wars;[125] servants were expected to walk to the boundaries of the Village. A scheme was proposed for a new South London Arterial Road, by which the widened road would turn right at the crossroads of College Road and Dulwich Common, go up College Road passing close to the main elevation of the New College, and then continue up the Toll Road to Crystal Palace. Eventually the houses on Dulwich Common lost some of their drives and carriage-sweeps and front gardens when the modern South Circular Road was extended to its present width, though not without protest.[126] In 1938 the popular local magnate Sir Evan Spicer (b. 1849) of the paper-making family and Vice-President of the Equitable Life Assurance Society died, a College and Estates Governor. At Belair on his farm there were Guernsey cows and pigs; on his hospitable lake hundreds of Dulwich boys learned to skate, including P. G. Wodehouse, who in a letter to Bill Townend of 1956 recalled the heavy winter of 1895, when they skated there every day. The College in February 1929 gave a half-holiday for boys to take up Spicer's offer of an afternoon's skating.[127]

The Picture Gallery, lacking Henry Yates Thompson's direction, was not quite so prosperous; a mere 12,000 visitors attended per annum. In 1924 their Committee actually discussed the possible sale of 69 paintings, including Edward Alleyn's Kings and Sibyls, but mercifully this was not carried out.[128] The last Royal Academy lunch was held in 1937. In 1938 (during the College's temporary evacuation to the Forest of Dean described below) the Gallery also sought asylum in the west, and Messrs Evan Cook's van full of the best paintings spent a night in the car park at Aberystwyth, guarded by the British Legion. The international situation appeared to have improved overnight after the Munich agreement, and the next morning they were ordered back to Dulwich. However, the following year 79 paintings were sent for safe keeping to the National Library of Wales at Aberystwyth, and in October, following the declaration of War, the Gallery was closed for the duration.[129]

*

Alleynians

Alleynians, as mentioned above, were recognised between the Wars for their 'spirit of adventure'; such energies as fired the men of Smith's era were mostly sporting, particularly in the case of cricket: of the famous Gilligan brothers, Arthur was Captain of the England XI after the Great War; H. T. Bartlett, Captain of the Cambridge team, and S. C. Griffith, who kept wicket for England, were household names in the second part of the 1930s (see Chapter Twelve). Three men highly distinguished in medicine educated at Dulwich between the wars were Sir George Pickering (1904–80), an authority on arterial circulation, Regius Professor of Medicine from 1956 until 1968 and Warden of Pembroke College at Oxford thereafter until 1974, who played a vital part in medical education at the university; Geoffrey Harris (1913–1971), Dr. Lee's Professor of Anatomy at Oxford in 1962; and Sir Reginald Murley (1916–97), the Hunterian Professor of Surgery and President of the Royal College of Surgeons from 1977 until 1980, who was a well-known critic of the National Health Service. Professor Ian McCallum (left 1938) studied at Guy's Hospital, and became a medical Professor at Newcastle.

The achievements of Smith's men in general were generally in a lower key and a narrower range than those of the men of the Golden Age; there were, however, two very original Old Alleynians in the Arts who both spent a relatively short time at the College: C. S. Forester (1899–1966), creator of Hornblower, a 'best-selling' author much admired by Churchill, with over eight million copies of his books bought before his death, and Michael Powell (1905–90), who is at last being recognised by many as Britain's greatest film director.

C. L. T. Smith (C. S. Forester was a *nom de plume*) entered the Science Remove at the College at the age of nearly 16 in September 1915, an unhappy time of 'casualty lists', as he recalled; he came from Alleyn's School, which he had joined in the Fourth Form. He left after a single academic year, to become a medical student at Guy's Hospital. As well as the world-famous series of a dozen Hornblower books, Forester wrote other adventure novels, such as the nautical *Brown on Resolution* (1929), set in the First World War, the Napoleonic *The Gun* (1933; filmed as *The Pride and the Passion*, 1957), and *The African Queen* (1935; filmed 1952), well known to lovers of the cinema. He declined, like A. E. W. Mason before him, the offer of Honours. His view of Dulwich in his (posthumously published) autobiography, *Long Before Forty* (1967), is jaundiced: he found the boys snobbish and feared the 'bloods' (the prefects who beat smaller boys); he described boys bullied into semi-idiocy; the first month after his arrival some local girls were found to be pregnant, and there were enquiries and expulsions. The teaching, he said, was slovenly, and faulty historical, political and economic facts were taught; indeed his experience amounted to 'a long list in fact of things which cried out for reform'. It is only fair to say that, on the other hand, many of his contemporaries reading this account say that they do not recognise the College from Forester's version. [130]

Michael Powell was obviously an engaging, unusual, romantic and literary boy, who responded (for the most part) enthusiastically to the College, as is evident from surviving letters and his autobiography. He wrote home to his mother from Hubert Doulton's boarding house, the Blew House, describing the dedication of the War Memorial and echoing George Smith's Christian Public School ideal in his touching vow to her: 'I will always try to be your true and pure knight'. [131] The fascination with the Armed Forces which informs so many of his films began before Dulwich, but he was, like his brother John, an enthusiastic member of the Corps. He enjoyed being a boarder, and his letters home describe the pleasures of a midnight feast and of telling the other boys ghost stories after dark in the dormitory. He writes with excitement about his reading, in particular 'Alexander's Feast' by Dryden and 'an orgy of Kipling' from the School Library. Founder's Day, he reported, 'went with a whiz'.

Powell had arrived at Dulwich at the age of 14 in January 1920, rather unsettled for a number of reasons, to follow his adored elder brother, John Miles Powell; he came from King's School, Canterbury, where he had been a King's Scholar. Two severely traumatic blows blighted his schooldays: the sudden death of his brother John at 15 from a ruptured appendix in September 1918, for which the family blamed the slow response of Doulton, who had also been the elder boy's Housemaster; and his totally unexpected suspension, when his fees were not paid once his father settled with a French mistress at a hotel he had bought in the south of France. Powell was hoping to stay at Dulwich to get a scholarship to read History at Oxford or Cambridge, which it is very likely he would have done; [132] he wrote plaintive uncomprehending letters to his mother, saying how much he wanted to stay on to the Sixth Form and to become 'that shadowy personage, "a blood"'. [133] In his autobiography, A Life in Movies (1986), Powell praises the Joerg brothers, so 'passionately French' and 'passionately good', to whom he owed his love of French prose and his ability to think in French. [134] He claims that he spent most of the time at the College up a tree, reading a book; trees certainly figure in his letters to his mother. [135] He recalls a glimpse of Queen Mary on her annual drive to Dulwich Park when the rhododendrons were in bloom,

'her back straight as a poker, her toque firmly nailed to her head with formidable hatpins, her face covered by a veil with such large purple spots that she looked as if she might be contagious, bowing graciously to the occasional curtsey and the frequently doffed hats'. [136] Thanks to Christison, and his carefully annotated copies of The Alleynian, we know that a poem, 'One Non-athlete to Another', poking fun at Rugby football – a rather surprising item in the magazine for its advice, 'Don't wallow in mud like a pig in the mire' – and an anonymous prose satire, 'Tarzan the Unquenchable', were both written by Powell. [137] A very bright boy, he was second in form order in the Classical Upper Fifth at Midsummer 1922; [138] he set himself to win the John Miles Powell prize which had been endowed by his aunt in memory of his brother for prowess in Greek and English, and which offered books (to include a Greek Testament and a copy of Keats's poems), and did so during the same months. Powell left in July 1922, to take up a job perforce in the National Provincial Bank at Ringwood in Hampshire; soon afterwards, however, staying with his father, he took a holiday job at the Studio Victorine near Nice where the American film director Rex Ingram (1895–1950) was working, an encounter that was to define his future. In 1946 The Alleynian was to report that the first Royal Command film to be chosen was Powell and Pressburger's A Matter of Life and Death.

It is tempting to discern a connection between Shackleton's heroic voyage aboard the James Caird and the Dulwich spirit of adventure immortalised by these two very different Dulwich contemporaries, as if having entered their psyche: Forester's African Queen (1935) and Powell's I Know Where I'm Going (1945) both entail an ordeal in a small boat.

The Shakespeare scholar C. Walter Hodges (1909–2004), another boarder at the Blew House, published a poem in The Alleynian for December 1924, 'The School Bell'. [139] Hodges quitted Dulwich from the Upper Fourth in 1925 for Goldsmiths' College. A gentle boy, he later described his time at the College as a wretched imprisonment, breeding in him an enduring fear and distrust of his teachers. At the age of ten he wrote a story in an exercise book, 'Walks in Our Museums', which imagined going to sleep in various favourite museums and then finding himself transported to the past. [140]

Hodges was a perfectionist, a respected writer and a brilliant illustrator and stage designer, who became a world authority on Elizabethan and Jacobean playhouses. He once wrote in a letter that Dulwich College had seemed only to respect Edward Alleyn for his royal connections as Keeper of the King's Bears; 'in my time nothing, but truly nothing, was made of the great bond the College has with the Elizabethan theatres'. [141] Hodges was more of an artistic and practical enthusiast for Elizabethan and Jacobean drama than a dry academic, teaching the world, through his drawings and books, such as *The Globe Restored* (1953), how the theatres worked and how they looked; a companion volume, *Shakespeare's Second Globe* (1973), was a successful plea to rebuild the Globe and included a detailed projected reconstruction. A splendid early book (perhaps more for his illustrations than his text) was *Columbus Sails* (1939). He made illustrations for novelists, such as Ian Serraillier with *The Silver Sword* (1956). He himself wrote and illustrated *The Namesake*, about King Alfred (1964), and *The Marsh King* (1967). *The Overland Launch* (1969) involves an epic cross-country journey dragging a lifeboat, thought to be impossible, that is again strongly reminiscent of Shackleton's exploits. *Enter the Whole Army* (1999), published when he was almost ninety, was a summary of his research and insights into the stage of Edward Alleyn's day. R. G. G. Price (b. 1910), who left in 1929, was a favourite pupil of Eric Parsley's and a light of the Literary and Debating Societies; he became a teacher and a regular contributor to *Punch*, publishing a much admired *History of 'Punch'* in 1957, and a famous essay *How to Become Headmaster* in 1960.

Peter Greenham (1909–92), a scholarly boy, wrote editorials and a poem for *The Alleynian* in 1926, his final year. Melton Fisher awarded him the Henry Yates Thompson Prize at the age of 14 for his drawings and designs, commenting that 'he should have an artistic future'. [142] Greenham studied History at Oxford, and then indeed became a well-known portrait painter; his *Ronald Groves* (the Master), and his *Lorne Campbell* and *Philip Gardner* (the two Old Alleynians to win the VC in the Second World War) were commissioned from him by the College. He was also a painter of landscapes and other subjects, with a particular fondness for shore scenes with beach, sea and figures. He was also a long-serving Keeper of the Royal Academy Schools (see Chapters Six and Eight) from 1964, and was to join the College Governors in 1982.

An extraordinarily gifted musical boy of Smith's era was (Sir) Jack Westrup (1904–75), who rose to become Heather Professor of Music at Oxford (1947–71) after an earlier six-year spell on Dulwich's teaching staff; he had come from Alleyn's School in 1917 and left in 1922. He gave very generously to the cultural life of the College, both as a boy, when his 'Suite for Orchestra' was performed at the College on 18 December 1920, and again (after studying Classics at Balliol College, Oxford, where he was a Music Scholar and took a first in 'Mods') from 1928 when he joined the staff as a Classics master. Among

his accomplishments were productions of *Macbeth* in 1933 and *Twelfth Night* in 1934 with his own settings of the songs. [143] He played the euphonium in the Military Band on their marches to the railway stations. Appointed Assistant Director of Music in 1934, he left later that year to pursue 'a musical career' of writing and composition; he sent a long account to *The Alleynian* describing his pleasure at working in solitude in the country the following year. His composition *A Motet* was noted in *The Alleynian* in March 1940. [144] At Oxford Westrup became famous for his musical analysis, for conducting choirs and orchestras, for popularising medieval song, and from 1947 for his much-admired productions of operas with the Oxford University Opera Club, very few of which were familiar to audiences of his day but many which are familiar now because of his pioneering work, particularly operas by the then under-regarded Monteverdi. His many publications were mostly lively introductions, such as his *Purcell* (1937), *Bach Cantatas* (1966), and *Musical Interpretation* (1971) for the BBC, but included specialist works; he also made recordings for the HMV *History of Music in Sound*. Westrup found the time to continue to serve the College as a Governor from 1947 to 1972. William Reed (1910–2002) read Classics at Oxford, and was next a Scholar in composition at the Royal College of Music; he composed piano, organ, chamber, orchestral and choral works, and his *Scherzo* was performed at a Promenade Concert in 1942. The pianist John Vallier (1920–91) composed a *Toccatina* and *Cornish Sketches*. Donald Mitchell (left 1941), a distinguished musicologist, after a successful career in music publishing was the founding Professor of Music at the University of Sussex, and among his many books are works on Mahler and on Benjamin Britten; he is Life President and Director of the Britten estate.

W. K. C. Guthrie (1906–81), who acknowledged the influence on him of the Classics teaching of Hose and of H. J. Dixon, left in 1925. As a pupil of Hose, who in turn had been a pupil of Gilkes, Guthrie was heir to the great tradition of Dulwich Classics teaching. A young antiquarian, he investigated inscriptions in Asia Minor, and was fascinated by early cosmology. Later an expert on Greek religion and Philosophy, he published a six-volume *History of Greek Philosophy* from 1962 to 1981, which was a brilliant scholarly and publishing success, lucid without flamboyance. During the Second World War he was in the Intelligence Corps, working at Bletchley Park and in Istanbul. A Fellow of Peterhouse College, Cambridge by 1930, Guthrie later served, from 1957 to 1972, as Master of Downing College, where his Presbyterian upbringing made him particularly impatient with student restlessness and demonstrations. He was a

Governor of Dulwich College from 1946 until 1961. An obituarist wrote of him as 'a giant among scholars, a veritable prodigy for the range of his learning, the authority of his views and the clarity of his mind'.[145] Another academic, Bruce McFarlane (1903–66), later a famously diffident but celebrated History don at Magdalen College, Oxford from 1927, an expert on late medieval England, was conspicuously clever at school. A memoir by Karl Leyser claims that McFarlane held Gayford in affectionate respect at Dulwich, but that the master did not know what to make of him, and that McFarlane's debt to him was never profound; when the Gayford Memorial Prize at the College was set up by his Oxford pupils, McFarlane certainly supported it generously.[146] A perfectionist, he was reluctant to publish, but wrote a brilliant series of articles, and monographs on *John Wycliffe* (1952) and (posthumously) on the painter *Hans Memling* (1971), which are now acknowledged classics.[147] W. B. Fagg's contribution to the study of African sculpture and to the Department of Ethnography at the British Museum has been noted above. Ian Fletcher (1920–88), who published a poem in *The Alleynian* in October 1935,[148] was an academic of an unusual type who did not attend university but left the College for financial reasons at the age of fifteen, taking a job at Lewisham Public Library. The College owns a book of manuscript poems of his, compiled in 1935. He spent the Second War in the Middle East, mostly in Cairo, where he was a member of a coterie of interesting British poets. By his extraordinary reading and book collecting, Fletcher became the world authority on the literature of the 1890s, and (without a degree) was appointed to a lectureship at the University of Reading in 1953, later becoming an internationally admired Professor. As well as academic books and articles, he published two collections of his poems, *Orisons, Picaresque and Metaphysical* (1948) and *Motets* (1962).[149] The first book is sensuous and passionate, with slightly precious aureate vocabulary, but contains a marvellous sequence of poems about Héloïse and Abelard.

G. E. 'Tony' Fogg (1919–2005), who left in 1937, at school an artist as well as a scientist, after teaching at University College, London, became Professor of Marine Biology at the University of Wales at Bangor, with a special interest in the biology of polar habitats; he made important discoveries about the medical use of kelp and algae. Among the leavers of 1939 are found three distinguished men. R. F. McNab Jones became a Consultant Otolaryngologist at St Bart's Hospital. J. A. Crook (d. 2007), the son of an orchestral musician from Balham, was an LCC Scholar (later giving generously to the Bursary Fund), who after a first class in his Part I at Cambridge enlisted as a Private; a Prisoner of War in

Silesia, he survived the death march to Berlin. Crook rose to become Professor of Ancient History at Cambridge, an old-fashioned bachelor don at St John's College, expert in Roman Law and social history, who served as the University of Cambridge representative Governor of Dulwich College. A. F. 'Pat' Thompson became an influential History don at Wadham College, Oxford, and served as the University of Oxford representative Governor; he was the recipient of *Politics and Social Change in Modern Britain* (1987), a tributary book of essays. R. R. Tilleard-Cole (left 1940), also an LCC Scholar who has contributed very generously towards the Bursary Fund at the College, became Professor of Psychiatry at Oxford, an Honorary Fellow of Worcester College; as Her Majesty the Queen's Representative Colonel of the Oxford University OTC, he wore a uniform of his own design. Tilleard-Cole has published several specialist books, including *Medical Knowledge for Fun* (1995), under the pseudonym 'Richard Worcester'. A. F. Kersting (b. 1916) is a distinguished photographer of historical architecture and landscape; while his subjects have been mostly British, he has done work on the continent (including a remarkable series of views of crusader castles) and some further afield, such as in Thailand. His schoolboy photographs in 1934 were thought remarkable enough to call them the 'backbone' of the Photographic Exhibition at the College and to reproduce as a frontispiece to an issue of *The Alleynian* his infra-red view of London from the tower of Westminster Cathedral.[150] At school Kersting had a precocious interest in Wren's City churches. The Principal Mathematics master F. C. Boon (1875–1939) was a great enthusiast for photography and encouraged Kersting and other schoolboy photographers.

Ray Noble, the band-leader and singer (1903–78), left the College in 1921 from the Upper Modern Fifth; he won prizes in the Hobbies Competition in his last year for his piano sketches, 'Fairies in the Moonlight' and 'Garden at Twilight'.[151] He first worked in a bank at Streatham while leading a local band, and later recruited 'the New Mayfair Dance Orchestra', and then 'Ray Noble and his Orchestra' (which featured Al Bowlly as vocalist) in 1930–36. He appears as a tall, rather vapid, urbane young Englishman (who has nothing to do with music) in the Fred Astaire film of Wodehouse's *Damsel in Distress* (1937), where he accompanies the addle-brained Gracie Allen in a gondola in a Tunnel of Love at a fairground – a curious fate for an Old Alleynian. The *Oxford Dictionary of National Biography* praises his 'polished sound, rich ensembles, firm beat and tasteful arrangements'. One of Noble's contemporaries was the horticultural writer Arthur Hellyer (1902–93), who left the College in 1918.

Suffering from tuberculosis, he was advised to take a job in the open air, and this led to his success and fame. Alan Howland (1899–1946), who left in 1917, first an actor, was a very popular BBC News announcer from 1940–42. Peter Dimmock (left 1937) was in charge of the cameras at Westminster Abbey for the Coronation in 1953, and later became Director of Outside Broadcasting at the BBC. Trevor Bowen (left 1939) an actor, with a special gift for playing judges, has also published novels.

The poet Hamish Henderson (1919–2002) was one of the most brilliant and original Dulwich writers since Raymond Chandler; he contributed many editorials, essays and poems to *The Alleynian* from April 1938, almost single-handedly for several issues bringing the magazine to one of its high points. Henderson saw at first hand the evil of Hitler's regime during a school trip to Germany in 1937. A student of Modern Languages at Cambridge, he was attacked by Conservative rioters at Cambridge for his communism. He next worked as a courier for a Quaker organisation helping Jews to escape from Germany, leaving at the outbreak of war, whereupon he served in the Intelligence Corps alongside the famous 51st Highland Division in North Africa and in Italy; in the latter campaign he worked closely with the Italian Communist partisans (who quoted Dante to him). This led to his lif-long commitment to socialism and to a translation of some of the prison letters of the revolutionary Antonio Gramsci (1891–1937); it was while working on these that he was asked to leave Italy, following the capitulation. Henderson played a part in the history of the War: it was at his order that the Fascist War Minister, Rodolfo Graziani, made his broadcast appeal to the Axis troops in Italy to lay down their arms. He returned to his native Scotland where he made a notable contribution, as a member of Edinburgh University's School of Scottish Studies, to the folk song and story revival of the 1950s and 1960s. His *Elegies for the Dead in Cyrenaica* (1948) is a very moving sequence of poems, meditating on the war in the Libyan desert, on death, and on individual soldiers, particularly the Scots and the Germans – 'the sacrificed of history's great rains'. Henderson wrote fondly and gratefully of Dulwich, particularly on account of two masters, 'Guts' Gayford (see above) and Arthur Macpherson, (at the College 1927–56, d. 1965; a Quaker, and one of the best-known German teachers in Britain, the author of the most widely used German textbook of his day, *Deutsches Leben*, incidentally also used by the Germans for the schools in Jersey during the occupation). Gayford encouraged him to read the poems of Hugh MacDiarmid (1892–1978), a minority taste at the time, and Henderson gave a talk in his Sixth Form year about his long poem 'On A Raised Beach'. He recalled

reading MacDiarmid, alone, in the Picture Gallery at the age of 16. Gayford also told him about Gavin Greig (1856–1914) and his folk-song collecting in the North East of Scotland, perhaps initiating his life-work. [152]

Dulwich College is not particularly well known for its politicians, but Lord Shawcross (see Chapter Eight) who left in 1919 from the Modern Side, was elected as a Labour MP in 1945 with a 'landslide vote', at the same time as his brother Christopher (1905–73). Atlee immediately appointed him Attorney General. Shawcross was unquestionably the finest advocate of the twentieth century, acting for the Crown in a number of *causes célèbres*, and with an international reputation for his work as Chief Prosecutor at Nuremburg in 1945–6; here he delivered his noble speeches in summing up, saying, for example, that the international trials of war criminals are not about revenge, but about justice. He was certainly the most famous public figure from Dulwich of the second half of the century; as well as being the Attorney General, his many posts included a Cabinet position as President of the Board of Trade. His obituary in *The Times* when he died in 2003 (at the age of 101), described him as 'a man of commanding intellectual stature, whose brilliance led him nearly to the top of a number of different professions – legal, political, administrative and commercial'. Though Dulwich figures hardly at all in his autobiography *Life Sentence* (1995), Shawcross served the College loyally, as President of the Alleyn Club in 1947, supporting Christopher Gilkes's unpopular reforms, and found time among his extraordinarily active public duties and practice at the Bar to become a College Governor in 1953 and indeed Chairman of the Governors for twelve years from 1959 until 1971. In 1972 Sir Walter Annenberg (1908–2002), the billionaire philanthropist, who was American ambassador in London at that time, gave the College $2,500 for a scholarship in the name of Shawcross; at the same time he gave an equivalent amount to the Picture Gallery. In 1964 two Old Alleynians were elected to parliament for the Conservatives, and two for Labour; the idealistic Sam Silkin (Lord Silkin; 1918–88) who left in 1930, a barrister, was the Labour MP for Camberwell from 1964–74, and became Attorney General from 1974–9; his brother John (1923–87) was also a Labour MP, in turn the Government Chief Whip, Minister for Planning and Local Government, and the Deputy Leader of the House of Commons, and they both became members of the Privy Council. Their father, Lewis Silkin, was a College Governor from 1934 until 1946. Sir Melford Stevenson, PC (1902–87), who left from the Modern Side in 1921, was a colourful and outspoken High Court judge. A group of eminent lawyers left the College between 1932 and 1936: Sir Dennis

S. Melton Fisher,
George Smith,
(Royal Academy, 1928).
(© Dulwich College)

Marshall, a solicitor, was elected President of the Law Society; Sir John Boynton became Chief Executive of the Cheshire County Council; R. E. T. Birch became Director General of the Federation against Copyright Theft. Over the years several Alleynians became distinguished members of the Roman Church: Julius G. Caesar (left 1914) was elected Superior of the Benedictine Fathers of St Anne's in Liverpool in 1941; Monsignor Cyril Conrad Cowderoy (1905–1976), who left the College in 1922, was the Roman Catholic Bishop of Southwark in 1949, and in 1965 the first Archbishop, a prelate well liked for his diffidence and whimsical humour.

Smith's resignation

After fourteen years at the College, and after the disputes detailed above, Smith retired to take up his post at Oxford, which he held for nine years. The Governors thanked him for his 'cordial and happy' relations with them; he had certainly served the College generously and calmly in very trying conditions. [153] At the Alleyn Club dinner he referred to his portrait by Melton Fisher, then on view (as a preview before exhibition at the Royal Academy), and, in joking about his persona, revealed aspects of his real character: he said that he had tried when sitting for it to look 'at once wise and just a little witty, philosophic but withal humane', but prayed that his real thoughts could not be read. He said he realised it was time to leave when he found that his hand was too rheumatic to cane a boy; instead he had just apologised for his failure and shaken the boy's hand.[154] Lorne Campbell vc (see Chapter Ten), a Captain of School while he was Master, wrote of Smith that he 'never sought popularity or played to the gallery', and that 'even when angry he was quiet and restrained, and only the blaze in his eyes and the tenseness of his voice showed his annoyance'.[155] This good and quietly great Master, probably prescient of the future of the College in the next half-century and aware of possible disagreements about it, in his same farewell speech reminded the members of the Alleyn Club of the free places for the London County Council boys which the College had accommodated because of their financial constraints, saying further that the College should never be glad to be rid of its responsibilities for public service. During the Second World War he came out of retirement to teach English and Classics at Glenalmond College in Perthshire, where his son, C. P. C. Smith (1902–84) was Warden. Christopher Smith

had been a boy at the College in his father's years, leaving in 1921 to take a First in Classics at Oxford and to become a Rugby 'Blue'; his school career was distinguished, and he was just that sort of well balanced and full member of the College his father would wish for: a Scholar, a member of the First XV and the First XI (for two years), the Captain of Athletics and an Editor of *The Alleynian*. He was to leave Glenalmond to become Master of Haileybury from 1948 until 1963.

George Smith's 1957 obituary in *The Times*, while recording the 14-year span of his years at Dulwich, oddly neglects to detail any of his achievements at the College, choosing instead to praise features of his earlier career and the 'men of sound character' he produced during his eighteen years at Merchiston Castle: they became 'persons of trust and influence'. Unfair though the piece's emphasis undoubtedly was – the result, perhaps, of lazy journalism – Smith himself might not entirely have disapproved. Ever a modest man, Smith kept the great school, and its reputation, afloat through rough waters with wise and careful guidance, and earned much genuine affection among both boys and masters.[156]

PART II

WALTER BOOTH, 1928–41

Walter Booth – Academic changes – Boarding and the London County Council Scholars – The approach of war – The evacuations – The first years of the Second World War – The Battle of Britain – Booth's resignation

Walter Booth

While the College waited for its new Master, following Smith's resignation, the sterling Hubert Doulton was appointed Acting Master. The Governors showed that they were determined on change by rejecting an obviously and admirably Alleynian candidate for the new Mastership, 'Scottie' Gibbon, now Headmaster of Campbell College, Belfast, as being not only too old but too much 'steeped' in the Dulwich of the past (see Chapter Eight); when Gibbon was awarded an Hon. Doctorate of Law at the University of Belfast in 1947 after running Campbell College for 21 years, he was praised for his discipline and service to others, for his principles without sophistry and for his ability to inspire diligence. The new man the Governors eventually chose was an Old Boy of Bradford Grammar School and a scientist. Walter Reynolds Booth (1891–1963) was 37 at the time of his appointment in 1928, when he was Headmaster of Wolverhampton Grammar School; a Scholar of Corpus Christi College, Cambridge, in 1910, he graduated in

Natural Sciences and History, and thus was the first modern Master of Dulwich College who was not a Classicist. He had served with the Royal Artillery in France in the Great War, where he spent over a year in one of the most notorious German Officer prison camps; he then taught at Wellington College for eight years, where he had been a Housemaster for two years. He thus bestrode the division between the public and grammar schools comfortably enough to preside over Dulwich, a school that successfully combined the best of both these elements; with his appointment the College might perhaps now incline more towards the city day-school.

The *Evening News* reported him as 'a man without fads', and keenly interested in drama.[157] His first initiative was to place boys on their honour not to go to the cinema in term time, and the press soon showed an interest in his introduction of such rules to civilise his charges: they were not to wear their coat collar turned up, nor to have their hands in their pockets when passing a master or speaking to him. Booth's speeches at

Walter Booth.
(Dulwich College)

Alleyn Club dinners were poor by comparison with his predecessors'; in one of them he displayed annoyance at the press reporting his rules. In 1931 he attracted publicity again by banning boys from wearing gloves to and from school, which their mothers thought unreasonable. [158] Booth was to marry in 1934 at the age of 42; he lived at Bell House while he was Master, until air raids made this dangerous. The characteristic of Booth most remembered by boys seems to be his love of riding; he would leave Bell House to watch school games fixtures astride his mount or to canter round the pitches on a Monday, and was often seen in riding breeches at the College. He wore a morning suit on Founder's Day, and liked to host lavish alfresco parties beside a swimming-pool at Bell House; his guests, it is said, were served from a silver salver by a black page-boy. [159]

Academic changes

A remarkable, but unsurprising, eclipse of the Classical by the Modern Side was evident from Booth's statistics in 1929, compared with the clear lead of Classics in 1914. In 1929 there was a record number of 936 boys: of these, 334 boys were on the Modern Side and 190 on the Classical Side; the number of boys studying Science, Engineering and Mathematics was 239, and there were 173 boys in the Junior School. The number of boys studying Science, Engineering and Mathematics was in fact proportionately lower than in 1914.[160] A Board of Education report in July 1934 called for an overhaul of the organisation of the teaching at the College and pointed out the low number of thirty scholarships on offer (by comparison with the other London Public Schools). Booth wrote to the Governors in response, showing satisfaction at outside bodies calling for reforms. He was puzzled why 'two very competent Headmasters, Mr Gilkes and Mr Smith, did not feel inclined to change things radically. Was it just conservatism, or was it the feeling that something vital might have been lost in the process? Or that the moment for changes was not yet arrived?' Booth said that he thought the answer was a mixture of the second and third. He said that most of the changes called for by the Board had recently been put into operation quietly without upsetting any of the College's great traditions. The curriculum of each Side in particular was much more liberal. The next year he announced that the traditional division of the College into Sides (which connoted rivalry, and led to the boys committing themselves too young by choosing career-defining courses) had been replaced by various combinations of Subjects. In fact the term 'Sides' was to be used for at least three more decades, although options became more flexible. By 1938 a 'New Form' was introduced in the Fifths and Sixths, in which the boys studied a combination of History, Economics, Company Law, Book-keeping, French and Spanish.[161]

The quite extraordinary academic successes of Gilkes's days were thought to be over, although in 1938 the College had more scholarships at Cambridge than any other school in the country and in 1940, under very trying conditions, six awards were gained at Oxford and Cambridge.[162]

Boarding and the London County Council Scholars

Booth made few interesting statements about his job or his College, but in one particular Report to the Governors something of his quality is to be seen, showing that he understood the school and its unique advantages. Booth, in spite of his background, seemed particularly keen on developing Dulwich as a boarding school, probably for the same reasons as Carver, in order to leaven the suburban day boys; of the 600 boys in the College before the Second War, 112 were boarders; Booth wanted the number to rise to 160. He gave reasons why a parent should send a boy to Dulwich as a boarder: apart from it being the 'most liberal of schools I have seen' for the education it offered, there were

the advantages of being actually in the centre of the Empire where all the art and learning of different civilizations of all parts of the world have their witness; where all classes of

Science lesson,
W. C. Crowther at rear.
(Dulwich College)

society come together with understanding and good will; where the conditions of daily life, despite all the advantages of a great city, yet resemble that of the country; and where the advantages of both the day boy and the boarding systems are brought together.[163]

Incidentally, one advantage for the boys of witnessing different civilisations in London was going to the cinema, in spite of Booth's edict, and a study of public school slang in 1940 reported that Dulwich boys, unlike boys at country boarding schools, relished using many Americanisms learned from the movies.[164]

As the 1930s progressed and the Estate income improved, the Governors appear to have turned more to developing its boarding side than to offering free places. In 1927 there were 170 such boys. The following year, with a £20,000 surplus, the Governors asked the Board of Education to reduce the numbers of scholars on 'free places'. This reopened old wounds: Mr G. C. Ammon, MP for North Camberwell, protested in the House of Commons that this move, debarring large numbers of lads from the London County Council elementary schools from places at the College, had 'robbed the poor of this Foundation', just as had happened to the poor in the case of 'many other educational institutions in this country'.[165] At the time the Council would pay full fees at Dulwich for one of their Scholars from a family with only the one child and an income of £450, and full fees for boys from a family of eight children with £800 per annum. It was argued in Parliament, on the one hand, that it was a waste of national resources to deprive the country of the very best brains it could get by not sending more South London boys to Dulwich, but Lord Eustace Percy, who was still (until 1929) the President of the Board of Education, presumably recalling Smith's words three years earlier, insisted that 'you have to maintain the character of the school'. The Governors declared that they would like to cut the entry to fifteen Junior Scholars a year.[166]

G. C. Whiteley (see Chapter Eight), who left the College in 1894, and was a College Governor from 1924 until 1933, said in a Presidential speech at the Alleyn Club dinner in 1929 that he was grateful that the Estates Governors had increased their grant, 'so we can get rid of the government grant, and again be masters in our own house'.[167] By 1934 the College's intake was modified along these lines; it was formed of 157 boys from preparatory schools from the age of eleven to fourteen, 18 from elementary schools at the age of eleven, and 27 from other public schools and secondary schools from fourteen to sixteen years.[168] The view of the staff seemed to differ from that of the Old Alleynians; when the College was in

dire straits in 1940, unsettled by air raids and evacuation and in grave financial trouble, the Assistant Masters sent a 'Memorial' to the Governors, saying that in fact ever since the College regained its independence from the Board of Education in 1928 (as had been much desired at the time), without the financial support of their grant this had proved a liability, not an asset. It had brought 'no improvement in efficiency; and no added prestige, whether social or educational, has accrued to us as part of our independent status'. They were eager to have the London County Council scholars at the College, saying that 'interference from the Board of Education' was 'quite unnoticeable last time'; they added, plainly hinting their dissatisfaction with Walter Booth, who could not cope by this time, that 'in any case it might be beneficial'. However, the reply came from the Board of Education that they were 'not entertaining applications'.[169]

The approach of war

In the 1930s very cordial relations and exchange visits existed between the Old Alleynian Football Club and a Frankfurt Rugby club; in 1931, for example, the visiting German team played a match, and were taken to dinner at the Criterion and to a show at the Palladium.[170] A German boy attended Scout Camp the same year. In 1933 a Dulwich boy wrote for *The Alleynian* an account of a visit from a German pen-friend who posted him a book about Herr Hitler on his return. The following year a party of 14 German boys from a school in Bad Godesberg (which Dulwich boys had visited to play Rugby three years earlier) expressed their 'extreme dislike' of the ginger beer they were given in the Great Hall.[171] In 1937 a boy mounted a production, on his own initiative, of R. C. Sherriff's *Journey's End* (1928), the play about the trenches in the Great War.[172] In early 1938 the Dulwich College Officers Training Corps introduced a searchlight section.[173]

The evacuations

The most testing years in the College's history, in particular an extended nightmare for Walter Booth, began in earnest in 1938, when the College became something of a displaced institution or one under actual physical siege, in danger of death and destruction. Booth's obituary in *The Alleynian* says that his Mastership had two phases: after the first, which was a success, he lost his grip in this year.[174] In October, as the international situation deteriorated and following widespread fears of air raids over London, an elaborate evacuation took place: 400 boys and 30 masters left for Cinderford in the Forest of Dean. Parents were given three choices: their boys could stay at the College with a very much reduced staff; they could be evacuated privately; or the boys could come to Cinderford, bringing light hand-luggage and £3. Six dozen boys set off on bicycles; six coaches and cars with mattresses on the roofs set off down crammed roads.[175] 250 stayed at a disused fever hospital. This evacuation was said to be a success, 'of great value to the College', as Booth reported to the Governors; others said that it rained all the time, was bitterly cold, and the sporadic lessons were not a success. It was organised by the brilliant young Classics master, James Cobban (see Chapter Eight), who in 1936 had published the famous textbook *Civis Romanus*, which sold half a million copies. 400 boys and 40 masters were actually accommodated, and masters' wives cooked for 250 boys.[176] The boys returned to the College after less than a week, during the false sense of security after Chamberlain's return from Berlin declaring 'Peace with Honour' at Heston airport with Hitler's phoney document in his hand.

Booth's anxieties were also complicated by difficulties with finding staff to replace masters who joined up, and by sudden acute financial distress. Within a year, by September 1939, the wartime reduction of the Estates subsidy by £1,000 per annum, the charge of £2,000 for air-raid shelters at Tonbridge (see below) and the loss of fees from withdrawn boys put the College £12,000 into the red.[177] He was naturally worried about numbers at the College; parents would obviously prefer a country boarding school in war-time. He seemed to imagine the College buildings as actually under siege; he put to the Governors a scheme for the boys to dig trenches all round the school grounds against attack, which the Board did not accept. The College playing fields were ideally placed for Balloon Barrage, and a plan for the RAF to take over the Pavilion and the fields was mooted in April 1939, but postponed.[178]

On 19 May 1939 arrangements were made for a full evacuation of the College to Tonbridge School, and Christison, now Vice-Chairman of the Governors, was made Chairman of the Air Raid Precautions Committee, which was also responsible for the evacuation.[179] Booth had to enter King's College Hospital for an operation at this time, and was hardly recovered by the time the evacuation began. Meanwhile the Barrage Balloon unit, 903 Squadron RAF Balloon Barrage, booked the College fields and premises for June to October of the year while the school was away; they would take over the Barry buildings as their headquarters and the boarding houses for billets. In the event they found the College's charge of £100 per week too high, and by November declared they would leave.[180] No photographs of the Squadron's tenure seem to survive.

Around 600 boys were to be billeted at Tonbridge. On arrival they did not seem to be expected by the School, and billets for all of them had to be found. James Cobban, as Billeting Officer, heroically found the boys better places to sleep than the floor of the Tonbridge Gymnasium, taking over a large empty house and finding folk in the town willing to put up the boys. He was helped by a young Assistant Master who had joined the staff in 1937, S. C. 'Billy' Griffith (1914–93), the brilliant cricketer and Captain of School in 1932–3; a few months later Griffith joined the Second Glider Pilot Regiment of the Army Air Corps and was to win the Distinguished Flying Cross. The Tonbridge landladies complained about the low rate of the government allowance, which was six shillings and sixpence a week for small boys and ten and sixpence for those over 16. Cobban found billets for 25 boys at a seventeenth-century mansion, Somerhill, amid six hundred acres, the seat of Sir Osmond d'Avigdor-Goldsmid (1877–1940). When Cobban telephoned Goldsmid to ask for this favour, the elderly baronet said that he would be happy to put the boys up; however, he was frightfully sorry, but they would have to do their own valeting, making their own beds and cleaning their shoes.[181] The boys dug excavations for air-raid shelters; the College had to pay £2,000 for these structures. Boys of this epoch were, incidentally, good at 'mucking in'; an appeal from the groundsmen for volunteers to weed the sports fields in 1936 had brought out the entire school with dining forks, and the job was done in an hour.[182] A proper financial agreement had not been worked out with the Skinners' Company (the Governors and benefactors of Tonbridge) in advance, and the bill they presented for the evacuation, which was not (in general) a success, was too large, leading to jokes about the Skinners' name. A total of 71 pupils had been withdrawn by their parents, rather than sending them on the evacuation (four out of five parents continuing to entrust their boys to the school); 615 boys and 47 masters, including Booth, eventually took part in the evacuation. Tonbridge and Dulwich performed a somewhat ridiculous 'Box and Cox' circus, taking turns in the classrooms, the laboratories, the fives court and the armoury. Sir James Cobban's memoir of the evacuations, *Dulwich goes to War – and from it* (1995) and an article in *The Alleynian* for December 1939 give details of the surreal schoolboy day endured by Dulwich: in the morning the boys played rugger and did their prep; lessons were held in the early afternoon, from lunch until 3.40, and again in the evenings. They were split into groups of twenty to thirty boys under 'House tutors'. The parents objected to their boys being taught at night-time and having to 'blunder and grope' their way to evening school through a blacked-out Tonbridge from their lodgings.

W. S. Wright and his class at Tonbridge. (Dulwich College).

One parent withdrew his son, complaining of 'inadequate tuition', and that his time was being wasted. Dulwich lost its Rugby match with Tonbridge. Stories that the staff and boys of the two schools were at odds are said not to be true, but James Cobban said that with the utmost goodwill of the two schools the system could not last, and it would have been suicide for the College to stay. Tonbridge asked for £1,000 for the term's rent, while Dulwich argued that £480 would be a fairer fee. In the event only £272 was paid. [183] After a few months a circular and a postcard ballot was sent to parents: 515 were willing for their boys to return to London, and 61 unwilling; the rest did not reply. The financial strain on many parents of the day-boys had of course been difficult. In a few months the RAF would be vacating the College, and the Governors would then have to pay maintenance, rates and taxes on the empty buildings. Booth declared that the boys had learned 'adaptability', which was one way of putting it; when they left Tonbridge, *The Times* report mentioned that the Governors admitted to 'serious handicaps' there. [184]

From July 29 until 25 August the Dulwich College OTC carried out a highly successful Camp at Southwold in Suffolk; a special issue 'Esprit de Corps' of *The Alleynian* celebrated its excellent morale, and indeed its high spirits. September 1939, the month when War was finally declared and when Booth recommended a return from Tonbridge after just one term, must have seemed both to him and to the Governors a nadir for the College. Booth hoped for one thing: that if they came home, an increase in pupils would bring in £3,000. The Governors noted that Booth had been instructed to make reductions of £5,000 per annum, but had so far made no proposals, and the staff must be reduced.

By February 1940 seven masters had left for war service. The playing fields witnessed some unusual scenes: the boys played cricket below the barrage balloons; in late May and early June Dulwich boys playing cricket broke off their games to cheer each passing train carrying weary men returning from Dunkirk. Boys arrived at school carrying briefcases and gas masks. Cobban recalled how 'a boy would come to school late and explain that their house had been blitzed and he had to clear up broken glass. But he would somehow have done his homework'. Cobban was in charge of the Home Guard with another master and half a dozen boys on duty as Air Raid Wardens all night, each of them ready with rifles and three rounds of ammunition should parachutists or (we are told) even aeroplanes (more probably, gliders) land on the College fields, which were thought to be a possible landing ground in an invasion, while the boarders and eleven masters slept in the unheated cellar of the North Block; in the event one aeroplane landed in Brockwell Park, and only one enemy pilot baled out by parachute, landing by day in a garden near the Toll Gate. It is said that an Old Alleynian airman made a 'forced' landing on the College grounds to visit his parents in Thurlow Park Road, after which rugger posts were propped up in unusual places. [185] A fire brigade of 25 was on call day and night, and a team of four masters and eight boys put out at least 19 incendiary bombs. During the summer holidays Booth arranged for two hundred boys to farm in Buckinghamshire and Worcestershire. [186] Dulwich was the only Public School to remain in London; Alleyn's went first to Maidstone and then to Rossall School in Lancashire, where they experienced a most happy and successful partnership; they returned in the summer of 1944. During the Autumn Term of 1940 London was attacked for 91 consecutive days and nights, and the number on the roll dropped from 675 to 450 boys in two weeks. The demoralising effect of the war on Booth and his masters attempting to carry on with normal life and education can be imagined: the drone of bombers at night, the winter of air raids, fire bombs, shrapnel on all the Rugby pitches, a bomb crater on the First XV pitch, the loss of the ten Fives courts, and shattered windows at the College. Walter Booth had moved into the study in the South Block when Bell House was quite badly damaged from bombs falling in the garden. The great Entrance Gates to the College were bombed on the night of 28 August 1940, destroying for ever the terracotta heraldic beasts and the iron lanterns that crowned them. The iron railings of the Cloisters and the perimeter at the College and at the Picture Gallery had by this time been sent off to be melted down for munitions for the 'War Effort', but Charles Barry's actual magnificent iron gates themselves had earlier been removed so as not to be lost for ever by the College, and were hidden under tarpaulins and coalite by the College Architect and Surveyor, Austin Vernon (1882–1972; at the College 1896–99; appointed 1937). A bomb that fell on the playing fields on the night of 15 September shattered windows and dislodged plaster ceilings. The windows of the Lower Hall were bricked up, and an eighteen-inch 'baffle wall' was built in front of the main elevation. [187] Four basements in the Barry Buildings were reinforced with steel and brick as air-raid shelters, to hold 636 people; the steps of the entrances that were made to give speedy access from outdoors to the cellars of both North and South Blocks on the west elevation are still in place, although the porches are gone. Two sand-bagged forts with field-telephones were set up at the ends of the grounds, Fort Alleyn and Fort Edward. The latter was actually named after Edward Lax (1903–68), a Mathematics Master from 1929 until 1963 and an outstanding Commanding Officer of the Corps from 1936 until 1946; Lax, a courteous, cheerful and enthusiastic man with many interests, including working at a printing press with the boys, was a tower of strength during the War and had been left in charge of the College during the evacuation to Tonbridge. Three brick look-out posts were proposed, but were not built. [188] When the sirens went off, at their peak seven or eight times a day, the Classical Sixth dived under their desks; the corridors led to a better chance of safety in the cellars. A boy wrote, 'when the banshee howls, we double to and fro in apparent chaos between dusty underground shelters, equipped with benches made by experts in the art of torture, and classrooms, whose boarded windows shed only a dim religious light'. A Roll of Honour of fallen Old Alleynians was placed in the Lower Hall. In the same Lower Hall the windows were bricked up, and here Boarders' Prep and Holy Communion on Sundays took place. [189]

The Battle of Britain

From 8 August until 31 October 1940, while boys were sitting at their desks in classrooms at the College, 'very often literally over our heads' as *The Alleynian* reported, Old Boys in their twenties helped fight the Battle of Britain, risking and giving their lives to save London from the devastating bombing that had befallen Warsaw and Rotterdam. In the skies above the College from time to time could be seen white vapour trails left by the tiny specks of Spitfires that caught the sunlight like diamonds; the occasional chatter of fire could be heard against the duller sounds of the planes, indicating mortal skirmish. In Goering's first phase of air attack these encounters were at their most intense over and on the borders of the catchment area of the College itself: above Croydon, Kenley, and Biggin Hill; in September, at the climax of the attack, the full force of the Luftwaffe would be launched against London. [190]

Thirteen Old Alleynian airmen fought, their ages from 20 to 28; this was a very high number of the glorious 'Few' for a single institution. Two DFC awards were made to Alleynians for 'gallantry under intense fire' in the Battle. Eight of the thirteen died in the Battle or soon after in the War; mostly in Spitfires, matched by day and night against raiders in Messerschmitts and other German planes, they fell from the skies in Kent, over the Channel, at Flushing in Holland, among trees in York-shire, into the sea off the Shetlands, and one of them in the thirty-foot crater made when he crashed in a sub-urban road at Hildenburgh.

Noel Le Chevalier Agazarian (1916–41) was an out-standing sportsman and athlete at school, playing 'with great gusto' in the First XV for two years, and then study-ing Law at Wadham College, Oxford, where he was a Boxing 'Blue'. His father was Armenian and his mother French; if his friend Richard Hillary, the author of the famous Battle of Britain reminiscences, *The Last Enemy* (1942), can be believed, he applied to Trinity College at Oxford, but the President wrote to Booth that the College could not accept him, giving as a reason that when the last coloured gentleman at Trinity was admit-ted in 1911 'it had really proved most unfortunate'. His family, famous for courage, is commemorated at the College by the Agazarian Sword, which was presented by his brother Levon (at Dulwich 1927–31), a replica of the one installed at St Clement Dane's Church. His brothers, his sisters Monique and Yvonne, and his sister-in-law Francine, all lived gallant lives well out of the ordinary – including Jack (1915–45), who left the College in 1932, and joined the secret Special Operations Executive; on a visit to a double agent in Paris he was trapped by the Gestapo, and then tortured, murdered, and cremated two weeks before the Americans liberated his concentra-tion camp, Flossenbürg. Moments before his execution he tapped in Morse to a neighbouring cell, "Looks like my turn now, chaps. Cheerio, and love to my wife". Noel Agazarian was described by Richard Hillary as 'by nature cosmopolitan, intelligent and a brilliant linguist'.[191] This dashing airman with an individual style shot down or damaged no fewer than thirteen enemy planes during the Battle of Britain. After the Battle was over he asked to be posted to the Middle East, saying that he felt 'things were getting too quiet for his liking in this country'; he was shot down and died in Libya after three months. Noel Agazarian's Supermarine Spitfire Mark 1A of 1940, *R 6915*, in which he made most of his sorties, hangs proudly in the Atrium at the Imperial War Museum. G. A. Denby (1915–42) won the DFC for his extraordin-arily dangerous night flights during the Battle. The son of a 'colonial produce merchant' of Burbage Road in Dulwich Village, he wrote letters to Christison from Cambridge describing parties and Rugby matches; from RAF Prestwich he wrote thanking him for his congratu-lations on his DFC, saying, 'It is rather pleasing that the only OAs in the squadron have got the only DFCs'.

Denby was reported missing over the North Sea; he had ditched his plane at sea in a terrific storm when he devel-oped engine trouble after giving chase for two hundred miles. E. B. King (1911–40), in command of a Hurricane squadron, died when he was shot down over Rochester against heavy odds falling in a terrific power crash at full throttle in a street at Strood. His brother wrote letters about him to Christison, and his mother in 1946 endowed a Memorial Prize for the Air Training Corps at the College in his memory. Norman Hayes (b. 1912), who had been in Denby's squadron, was awarded his DFC for performing a truly amazing sequence on 10 May 1940, when he flew one of six Blenheims which attacked an airfield at Rotterdam in daylight. Climbing away, they were attacked by twelve Messerschmitts, which he was unable to see, but from which, guided by his gunner, he skilfully manoeuvred his escape. Shortly afterwards he saw a Junkers; hard pressed by superior numbers and with his own aircraft damaged, he sent down the Junkers with its port engine on fire. He evaded his attackers and, heading for home, running into three Heinkels, he used his remaining ammunition to break up their formation, and got safely back to base, the only one of the six Blenheims to do so.[192] In 2002 Norman Hayes, at the age of ninety, attended a ceremonious unveiling of a plaque in the Lower Hall naming these heroes, which was given to the College by the Battle of Britain Historical Society.

The first years of the Second World War

In July 1941 *Old Alleynians in the Forces*, the second such pamphlet to be published, listed some 2,000 names. Captain Leslie Barefoot (1887–1958) of Gilkes's day, an architect who designed many buildings in East Anglia, won his George Cross, at the age of 53, for bomb disposal; at the start of the War new and ever deadlier types of bombs were constantly being found, and he discovered much valuable information about them in the course of his work. In September 1940, supported by his men, within twelve hours he defused six live bombs of a delayed-action type that were blocking the London and North Eastern Railway line, work that would have normally taken a week, and in defiance of the prudent safety regulation of leaving bombs alone for four days after they fell.

Christison once again began to paste into his copies of *The Alleynian* the postage-stamp-sized photographs of the dead, young and old, who were to appear in his second *War Record*. In December 1940, after three months of bombardment, there was more discussion of evacuation, and Booth himself made melancholy fruit-less excursions to various places, such as Leicester, where there had been recent bombings, looking for premises; the Royal Agricultural College at Cirencester seemed to fit the bill, but it was snapped up by a government department. It was also thought that the College might be taken over by the government. In his same Report to the governors Booth was able to report that in spite of the evacuation and the shortened school hours (9.50 a.m. to 3.35 p.m.) the exam results were successful, and (as mentioned above) there were six awards at Oxford and Cambridge. *The Alleynian* reported that boys were responding well to difficulties. [193]

At this point Sir Jack Sheppard (see Chapter Eight) for the Governors asked the Assistant Masters if they would take a reduction in salary, but their cost of living in war-time had gone up, and they rejected the idea. Rugby matches were briefly suspended, and while the staff accepted the need for drastic economy, they deeply resented the cuts in music, games and the OTC. Six members of the Common Room had left, and at the same time the number of boys had increased from 615 to 640. In early 1941 the Governors noted a deficit of £4,000 on the College account and loans of £16,000 to repay; the heating of the swimming bath was cut off in July 1941. The cricket season, however, was a great success in spite of the Blitz, and the rise of the young Trevor Bailey (b. 1923), who was in the College XI for five years, was noted in the Governors' Minutes. [194]

There were positive signs of life and spirit in adversity: in 1941 the schoolboy Colin Cole (1922–2001), Captain of School, later in his career to be appointed Garter Principal King of Arms and knighted, and who was moreover the Chairman of the College Governors from 1989 until 1997, wrote in an *Alleynian* editorial, 'Dulwich is as quick as ever'. At the Prisoner of War Camp, Oflag VII C/H in the Bavarian Alps, in Germany, ten Old Alleynians celebrated Founder's Day. [195]

Booth's resignation

Meanwhile, however, the kindly Walter Booth seemed to be done for, and could not cope, although every evening he visited the shelters under the Barry buildings during the air raids to see that the Boarders were safe; the last months would no doubt have broken a stronger man. Booth from 1931 had told the Governors practically every year that there were too many boys in the school; by now he was drinking heavily. Boys recalled that his breath smelled strongly of whisky in the mornings, and there was a notorious service in the Chapel when he stumbled badly descending the precipitous steps from the pulpit after delivering a sermon of one line, and (according to legend) was escorted out of the side door by the Captain of School. Many people regarded Booth with affection; Billy Griffith thought that Booth genuinely understood what the College represented, and was desperately anxious to retain this spirit, but in his heart of hearts was never convinced that he was up to the job. The Governors had heard grievances about his condition from individual masters, and senior staff delivered a 'private and confidential' document, but Booth suddenly resigned on 25 April 1941, suggesting that the College should be closed. Lewis Silkin, the Governor, asked at the Board if Booth had been coerced, but was told that he resigned on his own initiative. *The Alleynian* announced that he was leaving 'to take up work of national importance'; [196] a joke of the day was that his portrait by Leonard Fuller (see Chapter Eight) shows him 'under a cloud'. Ralph Allison of Alleyn's (Headmaster 1940–45) was a strong candidate among the four short-listed to succeed Booth, and he had been approached to return from his evacuated school at Rossall to be Acting Master; the LCC would not allow him to be in charge of both schools, and he wrote that he would not accept the post unless it was to be permanent. In the event it was the steady Mathematics master and housemaster of both the old and the new Blew House, the gently assertive Revd H. H. 'Dickie' Dixon (1887–1968; at the College 1909–71), brother of the Classics master H. J. Dixon, who saw the school over the interregnum of the Summer Term and the first part of the Autumn Term. After one year Booth recovered his equanimity, and was appointed Headmaster of Cockermouth Grammar School in Cumbria, a post which he held until 1956. He died in 1963. In time of war, Christopher, third son of Arthur Herman Gilkes, was about to return to the South Block at Dulwich, where he had been brought up, to occupy the Master's Study, a champion to save and to transform the College.

'THE DULWICH RENAISSANCE'
& THE SECOND ELIZABETHANS
1941 TO THE PRESENT DAY

The most significant and exciting school in the country today.
– ERIC PARSLEY, 1960

PART I
CHRISTOPHER GILKES AND
'THE DULWICH RENAISSANCE', 1941–53

Gilkes's life and achievements – The Oriental Course – Life during the war – Alleynians at war – The Victoria Crosses – The 'Gilkes Experiment' – Gilkes and Dulwich College Preparatory School – The Governors – Education and the Common Room – Music, drama and the societies; 'The Alleynian' – Sports, Scouts and the Mission – The boarding houses – Buildings and the Estate – The Chapel and the Picture Gallery

Gilkes's life and achievements

When a boy at the College, Christopher Herman Gilkes (1898–1953) was known for his 'determination and obstinacy' as Captain of Boxing (1915–17);[1] he was George Smith's Captain of School in 1916, played in the Rugby XV for two years running, and was an editor of *The Alleynian* whose opinions came across with a marked voice. Gilkes joined the College in 1909, at the point when his father was offering to resign but was persuaded by the Governors to remain. In effect he was very much a product of his father's establishment, taking full advantage of its opportunities, and, like all his brothers, it is clear from the pages of *The Alleynian* that he struck a conspicuous figure; he showed himself to be his father's son by his idealism and his culture, but it was also clear that he was an independent boy, unafraid to speak out with criticisms and suggestions.

After serving on the North West Frontier in India during the last year of the Great War (attached to the 109th Infantry, the Indian Army Reserve) he took up his Classics Scholarship at Trinity College, Oxford. He next taught at Uppingham School under R. H. Owen (see Chapter Eight), who was very much his father's disciple; there followed twelve years as Headmaster of Stockport Grammar School before he was appointed to Dulwich in 1941. Inheriting his father's imposing height, he wore a gold-rimmed monocle.

As his Chairman of the Governors, Lord Gorell (see below), remarked, Gilkes was by no means content to keep things as they were in his father's time.[2] Certain features he retained: just like his father, he held weekly

lessons for the Prefects in the Masters' Library which were rather more like Oxford or Cambridge tutorials, during which he would read and discuss passages from Plato and other Classical texts, and the boys would read out their essays on such topics as Discipline, Responsibility, and the Family, before he turned abruptly from ethics to administrative matters. By most accounts he was an admired and respected figure among the boys. In moral and physical courage he was truly in his father's heroic mould: as mentioned in Chapter Eight, in a sense he was to lay down his life to save and transform the College after its own near death in the early days of the Second World War; it was generally believed that it was these trials that killed him prematurely. Reflecting on Christopher Gilkes's twelve years as Master in 1967, Sir James Cobban declared that it was the 'vigour, often the ruthless vigour of Gilkes that saved Dulwich'.[3]

The condition of the College was desperate when Gilkes arrived, and he set himself to achieve three things: a broadening of the social intake of the College; the full restoration of its academic pre-eminence, in part by stemming the tide of boys leaving school before the age of 18; and the construction of proper facilities for a great post-war Public School. Famous for his vitality, he made of the College just what he set out to do, making possible the scholastic era of national fame under Groves. Gilkes was a scholar and an athlete, and was also highly cultivated, particularly on the subject of music, of which he was said to have an encyclopaedic knowledge. He played the violin and viola, and also the euphonium; indeed he was said to be among the top ten amateur viola players in the country. The quartet he formed was very important to him, and he liked to play Haydn. Greeting a newly appointed master one day, he asked him how his flute-playing was coming along. When the man looked blank, Gilkes said to him, "Oh bother, I must have appointed the wrong man".[4] He vigorously encouraged music, drama and the boys' societies, and they flourished conspicuously.

Gilkes was unpopular with many of his staff, however; just like his father, his dealings with them lacked sympathy, tact and understanding. A boy of his day recalled that 'within a few months of his appointment most of the masters who taught us had indicated unmistakably that they had serious misgivings about him'.[5] He was also unpopular with many (or indeed most) of the Old Alleynians, and found himself repeatedly at odds with the Governors. Against these groups he instituted and defended the reforming scheme that became famous in his name, the 'Gilkes Experiment', whereby at the time of his death in 1953 the fees of as many as 80 per cent of the boys were paid for by the London County Council and other southeastern educational authorities out of the rates taxed on householders. Gilkes did not always manage to persuade his critics that the College of his day was the highly significant venture that it truly was, something unique in England which would later be imitated; in a telling phrase he called the changes at Dulwich 'the reaction of a living organism to the great changes which have taken place in its environment'.[6] Gilkes's father had of course wholeheartedly approved of the very modest London County Council scholarship initiative at Dulwich in the early part of the century (see Chapter Eight). Retiring in 1917 to Oxford, then also home to his undergraduate sons, the table-talk of this bearded patriarch can only be speculation. Nevertheless it is tempting to imagine a discussion among them of Plato's *Republic*, and the possible models it provided for the class systems of contemporary England, by which the social status of lowly but worthy men might be advanced through learning. Plato was concerned with the education of a select class of ruling Guardians, or 'lovers of wisdom'; this was the ideal that Christopher Gilkes now intended to promote at Dulwich.

On Gilkes's arrival in 1941, the College was demoralised by Booth's collapse, in fear of physical bombardment and destruction, and close to bankruptcy; the numbers on the roll, already declined from 934 to 800 in the years 1928–38, had fallen by half since then; the cultural life outside the classroom was greatly impoverished by the War; one boarding house on the Common was a bombed ruin. Under his leadership morale was restored. "It was our duty," he later declared, "if we claimed to be a great school, to give a lead to London in resisting the attempts of the

Christopher Gilkes. (Dulwich College)

enemy to paralyse the normal life of the City, and I am proud to be able to say that we were the only school in London to continue to work above ground, in spite of the dangers and difficulties that beset us".[7] Numbers increased dramatically: from 450 in 1941 to roughly 600 in 1943; to 700 in 1944; to 1,000 in 1946, and to 1,100 in 1949. Gilkes was at pains to point out in 1951 that this increase was a 'lengthening' in the ages of the boys in the College, and not a 'broadening' in the numbers of boys admitted at the same age; the College held exactly the same number of boys at 13 plus as it did during the last five years before the War.[8] The danger and disturbance of war was actually worse for Gilkes and the College than it had been in Booth's time, and later, in 1950, when there was a war scare after the first atomic bomb test by Russia and the onset of the Korean War, Gilkes, not surprisingly, told the Governors this time round that plans for full evacuation should be made in plenty of time; he proposed a search for a large country house.[9]

Gilkes declared to the Alleyn Club in 1947 that 'a school which neglects its scholarship has one foot in the dustbin'. He often declared that the cleverest boys were the ones that gave the most to the life of the school, a debatable point of view, and he was at pains to 'prove' this by statistics. He had a great faith in the power of intelligence tests in selecting boys, demanding a very high 'intelligence quotient' from boys at entry, and it is clear that some of the most admirable and famous sons of Dulwich from previous eras would have been refused entry in his time. In the same speech, Gilkes said that the Junior School now presented a cross-section of the whole of South London; it was a 'noble ideal' to educate the cleverest boys regardless of their parents' income. His vision was to create 'the very best education' to prepare Dulwich boys to serve the 'new England' with prominent roles. "Intellectually we have the cream", he declared; this was to be a College slogan (with ironic variations) for many years. [10] Unrecorded in *The Alleynian*, but reported by the *Evening News*, he said also that "the new blood is a great deal better than the old", which cannot have improved his relations with the Alleyn Club. [11]

Gilkes, from long and affectionate observation, understood how Dulwich College was evolving: in Carver's day, he told the Alleyn Club, its backbone was formed by the sons of the large affluent families in the villas on College Road leading up to Sydenham Hill; his father's prosperous era was the equivalent of the Roman Empire at its Augustan height with the boarders and day-boys from local families. Then, between the wars, there came a change: more than half the boys were coming to school through the Penge railway tunnel from (in general) rather less affluent London dormitory suburbs further south down the line than the Village; before the Great War, the neighbouring day-boys and the boarders had looked down on 'train boys'. [12] In Gilkes's day there was a conspicuous increase in the national birth rate, popularly known as 'the Bulge'. Social change after the Second War meant that with the Gilkes Experiment the College could draw on a catchment area of the brightest boys from South London, and beyond.

The Oriental Course

When Gilkes arrived, the College accounts were £8,684 in debt, and a loan of £15,250 from the Estates Governors at the time of the evacuation in 1940 was outstanding. The College was, moreover, running at a loss of £5,500 per annum. Gilkes said it must be looked on as a bankrupt concern. When the staff were asked to accept a reduction in their salaries of 5 per cent, they refused, and suggested the alternatives of a rise in the fees, a grant from the Board of Education, or further loans from the reserves of the Estate. [13] In the event, however, the College was able to start repaying the loan to the Estates Governors as early as 1943. This surprising situation was the result of Gilkes's opportunism: he accepted a proposal to accommodate a

War Office scheme (in conjunction with the School of Oriental and African Studies in London) to teach Oriental Languages to a select group of boys from secondary and public schools; they were to be qualified to serve as Intelligence Officers, behind enemy lines in the Near and Far East. 'The Course', as it was known, made the College a substantial profit. By 1943 there was a credit balance of £4,949. [14] Very bright boys of 17 and over, seventy in number, on government scholarships of £200 per annum, were boarded at the College and given some general tuition in the afternoons as well as facilities for games and for the Corps (including the recently founded Air Training Corps). They would travel up to Westminster in the mornings to be taught in government premises on Broadway, returning to Dulwich for lunch. Gilkes himself sat on the selection committee, and he re-opened two boarding houses: in (new) Ivyholme he himself looked after the boys studying Chinese and Japanese (an 18-month course); the boys studying Turkish and Persian (for one year) were boarded with Arthur Gayford (see Chapter Nine) in The Orchard. [15] The (new) Blew House was, meanwhile, the only boarding house open to the College boys during the War. The income from the Course meanwhile accounted for half the fees received by the College during this period. The 'Course Boys' included some who later achieved distinction in the diplomatic service or in universities, and also Sandy Wilson (b. 1924), the composer of musicals, and (Sir) Peter Parker (1924–2002), Chairman of British Rail. They were given their own section in *The Alleynian*, and formed a Rugby team, 'London Orient'. A Revue in the Great Hall with 'song-hits' and 'good-natured satire' was reported in *The Alleynian* as written, composed and produced by A. G. 'Sandy' Wilson with Peter Parker as 'a brawny red-faced cook'. [16] The Course ended in 1943 when the age of call-up was lowered. [17]

Life during the war

At the height of the Blitz in 1940 there were five or six raids on London a day, and boys at the College carried gas masks and identity cards; a bomb fell on the First XI outfield. When two boys who had thrown themselves to the ground in the 'Clump' when the bomb fell ran to the edge of the crater to look for souvenir metal, they were caned by Trevor Bailey, according to legend – for breaking the College rules by walking on the sacred pitch. The young Colin Cole (see Chapter Nine) remarked in an editorial in *The Alleynian* the keenness of 'the boy in the Butt' [the Buttery] to carry on. By March 1941 *The Alleynian* reported that there were fewer air raids, and in 1943 the bricks over the windows in the Lower Hall that protected the boarders at their prep were removed. [18]

Clearing up after the doodle-bug damaged the Science Building, 10 July 1944. On the rope: Brian Capon (left, striped shirt), Alex Hemming (right, white shirt). Other legible faces, left to right: Dick Mumford, Pat Leigh, Joe Jennings, David Cornell, David Wright, William Whowall (in CCF uniform). (Dulwich College)

However, the fury of aerial bombardment returned the next year. The College lay on a main flight path of the enemy bombers, and was part of the suburban area where bombs intended for Westminster and the City were ditched on return flights. A German newspaper reported a belief that the College had been evacuated and was now given over to army or government use, close to a convenient golf course for the officers. [19] In 1944 the dreaded sound of the engine of the 'doodle-bug', the v1 rocket bomb, and its silently sinister 'cutting out' just before striking, became well known to the schoolboys, who would take shelter under their desks in lessons or under the tables at luncheon in the Great Hall. Out of doors, interrupted at their games or at Physical Training exercises, boys and masters lay prone on the ground in cricket flannels or shirt-sleeves. [20] Of the 2,400 houses on the Estate, over 2,000 were partly damaged or destroyed during the War; on Dulwich Common (old) Ivyholme (also known as Tiverton) and The Orchard were badly damaged; the former, still ruinous in 1953, was demolished after Gilkes, living in Elm Lawn, complained that undesirable squatters had taken up residence next door. [21]

The College was prepared to open its doors to the wider stricken community: in December 1943 the Great Hall was at first thought secure enough for billeting of local people during air raids, but the idea was rejected in favour of the ground floor of the North Block; [22] in the event this offer of sanctuary was not taken up. Conditions in the College kitchens deteriorated, and an outbreak of dysentery in March 1943 added to Gilkes's problems. [23] That year the London County Council erected an emergency static water tank on one of the College fields (still known as 'the tank field'); this was removed in 1948. [24] A near-miss raid early on 4 February 1944 left the majority of the school's windows shattered; the boys were pictured in *The Times* manfully (and cheerfully) clearing wood and plaster from a ground-floor window of the Centre Block. The paper concealed the identity of the College, but gave the photograph a caption designed for maximum effect: 'Bombs in Grounds of a Public School'. [25]

The strain was relentless, and Gilkes later recalled wondering how long they could keep going; the roll of boys had dipped down to 450. [26] Then, despite a heroic recovery from the Blitz, on the night of 10 July 1944,

The Science Building after
the v1 bomb explosion,
10 July 1944.
W. C. Crowther standing.
(Dulwich College)

disaster struck. Ten minutes after the eighty boarders had crossed the grounds to sleep in the shelters in the main building, a flying v1 bomb fell on the gravel between the Science Building and the Armoury, Squash and Fives Courts, roughly at the back of the present Edward Alleyn Theatre, destroying half the old Science Building, the Armoury, several Fives and all four Squash courts, collapsing the roof of the Gym and the Baths, and badly damaging the Engineering Block, the new Boiler house, and the roofs of the new Ivyholme and Blew boarding houses; in the Barry Buildings every room was damaged in some way, and hardly a single pane of glass was left intact. Miraculously, no one was hurt. H. I. Alexander (1908–2006), the teacher of languages and the enthusiast for Chess, Swimming and Fencing, retired after 25 years at Dulwich in 1968; after this bomb, he recalled, the College, just like Milton's Samson, was 'eyeless in Gaza'; his desk in a South Block form-room was blown to the far end of the room and stood on end. In the Master's study the lenses of a pair of Gilkes's glasses were found to have sprung out of their frame from the impact. At the Alleyn Club Dinner in 1951 Gilkes told how, when he had arrived in the morning at the school to view the wreckage, there was 'not a single room in which we could safely sit'. Less than two weeks later, on 21 July 1944, another bomb caused 'severe and extensive' damage both to the Chapel and the Picture Gallery, rendering them unusable. The College was resilient, of course, and boys were soon taking their Science lessons in temporary wooden huts near the old Science Building and at the laboratories at James Allen's Girls' School. [27]

Daily life at the College during the Blitz is hard to imagine; some details of the conditions can be found in *The Alleynian*. School ended at 3.15 p.m. because of the black-out, in time for the boys to reach home. The hands of the clock on the Campanile were removed, on the strange pretext that invaders should not be able to tell the time. Beetroot and carrots were grown on the front lawns, a part of the 'Dig for Victory' campaign, and there were allotments adjacent to the site of the present PE Centre. Until the glass was replaced (for the first time) in the summer of 1942, flimsy celluloid and boards covered windows; boys would gaze at the RAF balloon during double French periods. A play-reading of *The Merchant of Venice* took place behind black-out blinds, with M. T. V. Hart, who left school in 1944 and was later to join the staff as a brilliant Physics teacher (see below), taking the part of Launcelot Gobbo. Fencing took place in the Memorial Library (Old Library) by the gates. In the Spring Term of 1944 Arthur Gayford mounted a production of *Twelfth Night* (with Mike Hart as Feste) and wrote the music for it, in spite of his house being bombed earlier in the term. [28]

Of the 450 boys at the College in 1941, 212 were members of the Corps. On a Field Day at Knole Park drums and buglers marched them to Tulse Hill station and again up the High Street at Sevenoaks. [29] An Air Training Corps was founded in 1941. [30] In the holidays boys went on Farming Camps in Warwickshire and Dorset. Getting in the harvest proved an excellent lesson for some, and indeed one boy wrote lyrically about it in *The Alleynian*; a group of these boys sang 'Pueri Alleynienses' in the streets of Coventry. [31] The boys debated the motion 'Don't be beastly to the Germans' (after Noël Coward's 1943 song), which was narrowly defeated. The proposers claimed that the German people were to be treated as a sick mental patient might be; the opposition replied that the German people supported Hitler and despised kindness, and that only punishment could overcome them. [32]

Christopher Gilkes told the Alleyn Club in 1945 that the previous two years had been the most dangerous and anxious time in the College's entire history: another direct hit and the school would have 'gone under'. [33] Victory, when at last it came, does not seem to have been celebrated with much excitement at the weary College; the school lined Dulwich Common on both sides in May 1945 to cheer the King and Queen on their visit to South London. Shortly after VE Day blast walls in front of the main building were demolished. [34] It was a long time before the damage caused by the War was totally eradicated: piles of rubble still surrounded the Boiler House, where Shackleton's boat (sand-bagged, and unharmed by the bomb) was exposed to the elements once again, until it was given a new boat-house in 1953; [35] the main gates remained in ruins (see Chapter Nine and below). A National Service 'call-up' of a minimum of two years in the forces intervened in the boys' careers after leaving school from 1946 until 1957; in 1956, according to *The Alleynian*, the boys debated the motion that it was a waste of time for all, but the result of the voting went unrecorded. [36]

Alleynians at war

As already mentioned in Chapter Nine, in July 1941 *Old Alleynians at War* was published, an echo of the title issued during the Great War, listing two thousand men. Alleynian gallantry was again the theme, so few years after the Great War, and exploits such as the night flights of D. F. W. Darling DFC (1918–43) to intercept raiders were mentioned in *The Alleynian*; Darling was to meet his death in a raid over Berlin. [37] The extreme heroism of the Battle of Britain pilots has been commemorated in Chapter Nine; other RAF heroes included Sub Lieutenant C. M. 'Pat' Kingsmill DSO (1920–2003), who piloted one of six elderly Swordfish biplanes in the famous 'Channel Dash' to halt the largest German fleet of the War, moving from Brest to Cuxhaven in the straits of Dover, on 21 February 1940, accompanied by the largest Luftwaffe escort ever seen. This was something of a suicide mission; the biplanes, each carrying a single torpedo, were forced to make their approach at low speed. Although the attack was unsuccessful, many of the ships were damaged, and Kingsmill was one of only five men to survive in a desperate sortie above a wall of fire surrounding the ships. His torpedo missed its target. Wounded, with the engine and one wing on fire and the petrol tank penetrated by a shell, he ditched into the sea; climbing from the cockpit with serious burns, he crawled along the fuselage to the tailplane, helped his two fellow crew-members to escape, and slipped into the icy sea. The three men were picked up by a British motor torpedo boat. [38]

Honours and Decorations began to be recorded back at Dulwich. Lieutenant-General Sir W. H. Stratton DSO

(1903–89) left in 1920; as Brigadier General Staff of the 8th Army in Italy in 1944, after forcing enemy lines near Rimini, he found himself for a few days 'acting unpaid Doge of Venice'; after the War he was Chief of Staff, Army of the Rhine, from 1947 to 1949 and Commander of the British Forces in Hong Kong from 1955 to 1957. He was a College Governor from 1960 until 1964. Vice-Admiral Sir Peter Cazalet DSO, DSC (1899–1982), who left in 1917, commanded many ships with great courage between the wars and saw action up until 1949. Victoria Crosses (see below) were won by Lorne Campbell, and by 'Pip' Gardner, and a George Cross by Leslie Barefoot (see Chapter Nine). Stoker 1st Class J. H. Capes (b. 1910; at the College 1924–7) was awarded the British Empire Medal: presumed killed in the sinking of HM Submarine *Perseus*, he reached shore after swimming for eight hours, and managed to live for two years in enemy territory before escaping and reaching home in August 1943.[39] Sub-Lieutenant R. G. Dove (1921–2005; left 1938), awarded the DSO, formed part of a 'human torpedo' in a night attack on an enemy base at Palermo; one of two men straddling a miniature submarine in diving suits, steering with head above water or using a periscope, he attached a mine to the underside of a cruiser and sank it. By June 1944 *The Alleynian* reported that 2,910 were serving in the Forces, 224 had died, and 90 were held as prisoners of war.[40] When the true account was known, of a total of 3,320 Alleynians who served, 330 died of wounds or were lost at sea, and 115 were interned in prison camps. Awards for gallantry were as follows: 2 Victoria Crosses, 1 George Cross, 33 Distinguished Service Orders (three with bar), 16 Distinguished Service Crosses (one each with bar and two bars), 56 MCs (four with bar), 58 Distinguished Flying Crosses (7 with bar and 1 with two bars), 1 Distinguished Conduct Medal, and 2 Military Medals. There were two awards of the George Medal, the second highest award for civilian gallantry: W. G. Adam (1886–1969) of the Gas, Light and Coke Company, during a heavy attack on a large gas works with high explosive and incendiary bombs, three times entered blazing retort houses to shut off valves amid steam and dense sulphurous fumes; John Beeston (b. 1916), a doctor who left in 1935, saved the life of a woman trapped in the wreckage of a house in Willesden after a flying bomb attack by giving her a blood plasma transfusion for ninety minutes while she lay beneath a very dangerous load of debris and close to a gas escape.

Christison's second *Dulwich War Record (1939–1945)* of 1949 is a harrowing book, with its photographs of the fallen, many of the young faces resembling Dulwich College pupils of the present. It records their daring, courage and endurance across theatres of war in Europe, the Mediterranean, the Middle East, in North Africa, Rhodesia, the Balkans; in Burma, Singapore and Japan; in air raids and air accidents; torpedoed in the Persian Gulf, the North Atlantic and the North Sea; at Dunkirk, at landings in Normandy and Sicily; in prison camps. As well as their wartime exploits and heroism, the book mentions the education and careers of the dead and also the surviving widows and families.

Eric Parsley, a famous master at the College (see Chapter Nine and below), raised money from Alleynians to carry out a highly successful ambitious scheme to encourage Old Alleynian prisoners of war, dispatching Red Cross parcels of books, gramophone records and tins with 300 cigarettes to their camps, each with 'cheering' individual letters; it was reported that most of the parcels got through.[41] F. W. King (see Chapter Eight) raised money for two light ambulances with the Dulwich College arms painted on them.

The Victoria Crosses

On 11 November 1952, Armistice Day, Lorne Campbell and Pip Gardner unveiled their own portraits in the Lower Hall painted by the Old Alleynian, Peter Greenham RA (see Chapter Nine), following their display at the Royal Academy. Brigadier Lorne Campbell VC, DSO, OBE, (1902–91), who left in 1921, came from a family (father, brother, seven uncles and a cousin) greatly represented at the College; one uncle, Vice-Admiral Gordon Campbell, had won the VC in the Great War (see Chapter Nine). Lorne Campbell, Captain of School in 1920–21, was also the first Captain of Marlowe when the athletic houses were introduced. After Oxford, where he held a Postmastership at Merton College in Classics, he joined the Argyll and Sutherland Highlanders; it was said that the Argylls would follow him anywhere. At the bridgehead of Wadi Akarit in Tunisia Campbell led his men through the enemy minefield and an anti-tank ditch, and in the midst of determined enemy counter-attacks he showed 'valour and utter disregard for personal safety, which could not have been excelled', rallying and encouraging his men in the forefront where the fighting was heaviest, standing in the open under close-range fire although painfully wounded in the neck.[42] After the War Campbell worked in his father's business as a wine merchant. At the College Memorial Service at the Chapel in 1947 for the Alleynians killed in the War, he gave a very moving address, paying proud tribute not only to the Old Alleynian dead, but to his fellow infantrymen; he said that doing your duty is the one thing worth doing in life, and that the heroic story of the war amounted to one great cry of '*detur soli Deo gloria*'.[43]

Captain Philip Gardner VC, MC (1914–2003) left the College in 1932, and first worked for the family firm that made air-conditioning equipment. He joined the Territorial Army (Westminster Dragoons) in 1938, telling a friend, "I must do my duty, but I'm no soldier". Commissioned into the Royal Tank Regiment in 1940, he was posted to North Africa in April 1941. He was awarded both his MC and his VC for leaving his tank in the desert and attending to the safety of others under fire. He won his VC at Tobruk, when he led two tanks in an effort to rescue two armoured cars that had broken down and become easy targets for enemy gunfire. He tied a tow-rope to one of the cars, which broke; returning to the car, despite wounds to his own arm and leg, he managed to carry a man who had had his legs blown off back to his tank, and eventually to safety, all the time under heavy shell fire. Gardner wrote simply to his parents, 'I went back again and got the poor chap out of the car and on to the tank and set off again'. Talking to some Alleynians late one night years later, he said of this exploit, "Anyone would have done the same". [44] Captured at the surrender of Tobruk, he was imprisoned in Italy, where he was caught digging an escape tunnel and moved to another camp, from which he escaped. Walking and cycling through Central Italy, he reached Rome, where he went to a performance of *La Traviata* surrounded by German and Italian officers. Betrayed and recaptured in 1944, he was imprisoned in Rome and then at Oflag 79 near Brunswick in Germany. On release, with other former prisoners he helped to found the Brunswick Boys' Club in Fulham, which they had planned in an attic at the camp. His experiences are the subject of *One Man's Desert* (1986) by Rex Woods. At the age of 71 he caught a robber in a suburban street, and held him on the pavement until police arrived. Pip Gardner served as a College Governor from 1973 until 1980, and as President of the Alleyn Club in 1970.

The 'Gilkes Experiment'

In 1947 Gilkes told both his Governors and the Alleyn Club that the scheme by which the London County Council and other local authorities paid the fees for 90 per cent of the boys at the College was a 'noble ideal', and that in future no boy would be debarred by social position or poverty from entering Dulwich College. 'To fashion material completely in the rough' in this way, he said, would depend on his prefects and masters. He had 33 new masters, and the atmosphere was 'invigorating'. The free places paid full fees without 'means tests'; only 18 places a year by this date were kept for fee-payers. Gilkes told the Old Alleynians that their sons must now either apply for places through the entrance examinations of the Local Education Authorities and the College admissions system – or apply for admission as boarders. [45]

The Scheme was a function of Gilkes's idealism, but was also a strategy of survival; Gilkes spoke of 'the dead weight of war damage like a millstone' round the College's neck. [46] The Estate had also of course been badly hit by the war, and its annual endowment had declined from its figure ten years earlier, amounting in 1945 to £11,543. Gilkes's achievement in managing the Scheme was both to keep the independence of the College, and to retain control of selection. As already chronicled in the last chapter, the staff in 1940 were suggesting that the Board of Education should bale out the school; they must have realised that this would risk subjecting Dulwich College's independent status to control by the London County Council, as in fact was soon to be the case with Alleyn's School for more than thirty years. In 1943 Gilkes paid a visit to Sir Graham Savage, the Education Officer to the London County Council, to discuss terms. By now there were just 27 boys with LCC awards in the school, but the Council were asking to send 20 per cent of all the entrants and to pay their fees. In Governors' meetings in 1944 the Scheme took direction. Gilkes declared that he did not wish to risk the College developing into bankruptcy or becoming second-rate. The College needed to secure an additional £10,000 per annum; he reminded them that St Paul's received an enviable endowment of £30,000 per annum (from the Mercers' Company) on top of its revenue from fees, and that two-thirds of that endowment was spent on staff salaries. He presented the case in November that the College was now faced with three options: to stay independent, and seek large-scale aid from the Estates Governors; to become a Class 'A' Scheme 'aided' or 'controlled' school; or to sever all connection with the Estates and turn to the London County Council as the 'first great experimental school of the multi-lateral type'. Unanimously the Governors decided to stay independent. Gilkes was clearly sending signals to the Estates Governors, repeating the following month that unless their large-scale aid was forthcoming the College should end its association with them. City companies were mentioned as possible alternative sources of revenue, and vague plans were expressed to approach Old Alleynians or Americans. In December Gilkes had a further interview with the LCC to discuss whether as an experiment the College could become a 'comprehensive high school', and was told that in that case fees would have to be abolished. [47] Returning to the issue at the Board in January 1945, Gilkes suggested three options: boldly moving the College to a new site in the Orpington area and keeping its independence; becoming an LCC 'multi-lateral school'; or (his real hopes were always

Examination in Great Hall. (Dulwich College)

offered as his last suggestion) becoming an establishment 'parallel to Manchester Grammar School to serve South East London'. The fee income could be increased by raising the numbers, by 100 boys, to a total of 800; Gilkes also said that to continue independent the College would need an annual income of £20,000 from the Estate. [48]

Alleyn's School had meanwhile returned to Dulwich from Rossall (see Chapter Nine) in summer 1944; their premises had been used for an improvised 'South London Emergency Secondary School for Boys', catering for local boys who had not been evacuated. The Chairman of the joint Board, Lord Soulbury (see below), suggested that the College and Alleyn's should be reunited as a single institution, which was actually agreed; in consequence a resolution was passed, in effect seeking to sell off Alleyn's to the LCC. A row among the Governors resulted, which may well have been the reason that the Board lost (through their resignation soon after this) two significant and eminent Old Alleynian Governors from

Gilkes senior's era, Provost Sheppard from Cambridge and Warden Smith from Oxford (see Chapter Eight). Sir Jack Sheppard, who had been closely involved with Alleyn's for many years, was plainly outraged at the proposal to obliterate Alleyn's from the Foundation and betray its character; he eloquently described the 'really noble life and work of Alleyn's School', and said that it was 'every bit as good and great a school as Dulwich College'. Alic Smith agreed with him that the strong tradition it had built up should not be abandoned to the London County Council. At a meeting when neither man was present, with Christison in the chair, a resolution was passed, notwithstanding, to transfer the Governors' interest in Alleyn's School and for it to become a state County Secondary School. A figure of £200,000 was mentioned as the price for the establishment and its grounds. What the Governors would gain in having no longer to pay the annual endowment to Alleyn's would be used for more scholarships at the

College, and initially two hundred Alleyn's boys would be taken at the College as fee-payers at Alleyn's rates. Alleyn's was actually offered in this way to the London County Council,[49] and was saved only because the offer was refused; by that time the Council had plans for a new County Secondary School to be built 'as a complement to Alleyn's' to offer 'education of a technical and modern type'. This school was put up below Champion Hill on Estate land,[50] first the Strand Complementary School, then the William Penn School and now the Charter School. The Council also put the Governors in their place morally, writing that the College Governors were legally bound to carry on the school.[51] Gilkes did not reveal his views on this issue; 'ruthless' was the word applied to him by Cobban. Smith and Sheppard had unsuccessfully moved to rescind the decision;[52] when Smith protested that the resolution to abandon and sell Alleyn's had been made without full discussion by the Governors, he was told that it had constituted a Board decision. Sheppard resigned the following year, and Smith in October 1947; although these two liberal and loyal academics had served the College long and were now fairly elderly, the row over Alleyn's appears to have led to their resignation, as indeed it did with another Governor who resigned over the resolution. A letter to the *Times Educational Supplement* from 'An Alleyn Old Boy' argued, very properly, that the proposal was monstrous, as the School was part of the original Foundation and of the new Foundation of 1857.[53] Alleyn's became a 'voluntary aided' school. The Chairman, still responsible for the School, proposed a separate governing body for Alleyn's, composed half of College Governors and half of LCC Governors; he still hoped to sell off the School with ten acres to the LCC. In 1948 the Governors seriously discussed its demolition.[54]

By 1945 at the College there were just 150 LCC 'free-placers' out of a roll of 650 boys, with 20 places for boys from overseas. The Scholars took the state 'Eleven Plus' examination, the College's entrance examination papers in English and Mathematics and the fashionable 'intelligence tests'. One manuscript volume containing 'the Master's Remarks' on the Councils' candidates survives: Gilkes's comments (in 1947) include such quick judgements as 'I don't care for him' or 'awful hair' (in both cases for a boy actually accepted by the College), and comments such as 'overpushed', 'bad father, no ideas', 'mother's darling'; 'nice manners', 'funny little rat', 'cheerful little sparrow'; 'v. refined', or 'slummy'. He contrasts those who are 'sulky, bad type', 'flabby and spoilt', 'stodgy', and 'goes to pictures' with another he notes who 'writes poetry', or with one who is assigned the numinous word 'violin'. He records in many cases the father's employ-

ment and next to that the boys' replies to his questions about their own ambitions; 'football pro' was a common reply. Though this book is doubtless partly just an *aide-mémoire* for later discussion about admissions with his colleagues, it is fascinating not only to recognise how little South London boys applying for places at the College have changed, but also to see Gilkes's mind at work in selection according to his ideal of transformation.[55]

In 1944 the College admitted 89 boys with LCC awards, 44 from Kent and 40 from other areas. All of these boys were day-boys, but shortly afterwards Surrey, Southend, Croydon and East Sussex also sent a small number of boarders. Gilkes agreed that 50 per cent of the places at the College would be kept for the LCC; he was careful to insist on his control of admissions, saying that of these, 25 per cent were dependent on suitable candidates applying. In February 1946 Gilkes was able to report extraordinary progress from the dire situation he had inherited. In 1942 the College had a roll of 450 boys, a debt of £15,000 and an annual loss of £7,000; recovery would take ten years, Gilkes had said. Now, however, it had 800 boys and was making a satisfactory profit, apart from 'the terrible question of capital expenditure'. From the days when there was no proper entrance examination and very few candidates he had been able to raise the standard of entry considerably. He admitted to problems: the examination did not eliminate heavily 'crammed' boys, for example; and, in an echo of George Smith, Gilkes described the 'question of manners and tone' that complicated the College's efforts 'to absorb and mould [the LCC boys] to our standards', in buildings that were dilapidated and overcrowded. In 1946 the LCC also took some boarding places. Kent was promised 20 per cent of the intake; Croydon took 5 to 10 places, Surrey 27 day places and four boarders. Southend, enterprisingly, took up to six boarders' places.[56] Southend sent no more boys in 1952, and Surrey reduced their places by four each, day and boarding, in 1952. Bromley became a separate council (formerly Kent) in 1964 with the break-up of the London County Council and the creation of the Greater London Council, and undertook to send about thirty boys a year.

In 1951 Gilkes told the Governors that it was now the free-place boys rather than the prep-school boys who formed the backbone of the College and its sports; he also claimed that the profile of Dulwich parents was of much 'the same sort' as before the War, now so heavily taxed that they could not afford to pay the fees.[57] Gilkes told the press that one of the glories of the previous quarter-century had been the rise of the grammar and secondary schools, and that there had been a levelling up; while the church schools and public schools had been the leaders of the British Empire and the Army in the First World War, the officers in World War Two had been from the grammar schools. The hard-working Clerk to the Governors and College Bursar, W. S. 'Stan' Connop (1905–63), who also coached Rugby football, shared Gilkes's principles and was equally unpopular with many of the staff; he commented that Dulwich was 'the first public school to return to the object set out in its charter and become a public school for poor boys'.[58] The government Fleming Report of 1944 had recommended the gap be closed between the public schools and the rest, and in a long article in the *Times Educational Supplement* of 17 June 1949, 'After Fleming: New Policy at Dulwich College', Gilkes wrote that a mixture of social classes in a school was positively valuable provided that the boys were all of the same intellectual level. At the College, he said, the boys of below average intelligence gained and gave little. He believed in intelligence tests, and that there was a correlation between citizenship and intelligence quotient. The boys with LCC awards did more for the school than the average boy, formed the higher percentage of prefects (and at times all the prefects); they took the lead or fully held their own in games. Former boys of that era recall that Gilkes frequently asked the prefects or members of teams to put their hands up if they held LCC places, and he would count them. It was his stated view that boys still in the school who were below the Grammar School entrant level were neither prominent in the Corps, nor in the Choir, nor in the Orchestra; Gilkes in fact by 1947 had created what was called a 'Special Side' for the less academic boys.[59] By now he could depend on the 'assured supply' of 'quite first rate all round boys' from Greater London south of the river. Given the ratio of the boys at this date, what he said was hardly surprising; a local headmaster wrote to the *Times Educational Supplement* in response to Gilkes's article on 1 July 1949 complaining that Gilkes's 'intellectual aristocracy' was impoverishing the neighbouring schools, since Dulwich had skimmed off the cream.

In 1951 an interesting article in the *Evening News* reported that Gilkes called himself 'a heretic', that many in the Common Room were not convinced by the Scheme, that there was 'a great deal of internal criticism' by Governors and Old Alleynians, and that Gilkes had been greeted by ironic cheers at an Alleyn Club Dinner. The newspaper reported that the accents of some of the boys 'which might pain the ears of fastidious Old Alleynians' were subject to 'speech training'. Seventy per cent of the boys from Dulwich were now proceeding to university or technical and advanced study, but on the other hand it was regretted by some that the more backward

'good type' was no longer being admitted; no second Shackleton would ever attend.[60] By the mid-1950s the College was rejecting two out of three candidates.

Before this era the day-boys at the College joined at the age of thirteen; now the majority joined at eleven plus. In 1945 Gilkes had also created fee-paying classes for boys of ten and eleven, and in 1952 he initiated two classes for nine year olds and one for eight year olds, which Groves was to abolish in his first year. The boys in these junior forms applied by examination for free places at eleven plus. Gilkes deplored boys entering the College at thirteen rather than eleven, and deprecated the 'artificial and undesirable class barrier' within the College recognised by Smith (see Chapter Nine) whereby the LCC boys came at eleven and prep school boys at thirteen. He told the Alleyn Club that the preparatory and primary schools were now on a level, and repeating to them that Old Alleynians might now only have to pay the boarding fees for their sons; the snag of course was that many sons of Old Alleynian fathers might fail to get in, and Gilkes advised their fathers to give them a good education earlier, which might have been taken as a hint to 'cram' them for the College entrance. W. C. 'Butcher' Thomas, his Deputy Master (see below), said after Gilkes's death that in practice, when faced with two boys of 'equal merit' at entrance Gilkes used to give the place to the son of an Old Alleynian.[61] It became the norm for boys to stay on at the College for the duration of the Sixth Form, and many stayed on after that to study further for university scholarships, before having to join up for National Service at the age of eighteen; before the War many boys actually used to leave before taking their School Certificate examination at fifteen or sixteen. By 1951 most boys were spending at least seven years at the College.

Gilkes was determined for the College once again to be the best school in London, reminding the Governors how it had 'slipped slowly backwards' since his father's day.[62] When the Old Alleynian Hartley Shawcross, the socialist Attorney-General, first a knight, and then a peer (see Chapter Nine), became President of the Alleyn Club in 1947, he voiced his approval for all that Gilkes was doing, telling the annual diners of the Club that the Local Education Authorities did not want the boys whose fees they paid to become men who just wear an old school tie and do nothing for society.[63] The more conservative alumni among his audience must have abandoned hope for their College. Certainly some of the 4,500 members found it difficult to understand the justice of Gilkes's vision of the school at that period. Wodehouse's letter to Bill Townend of 20 January 1946 (quoted in Chapter Eight), containing his outburst that

Gilkes was ruining the College and turning it into a secondary school, was followed by replies from Townend reporting conversations with 'Slacker' Christison about Gilkes. Townend described in particular a miserable return to a grey and cold Founder's Day in 1952 when Christison told him that he had been responsible for Gilkes's appointment, and that he had 'pulled various strings' with the other Governors to get them to approve, but that once he was appointed, and when Slacker had suggested reforms, Gilkes paid not the slightest attention. Slacker told Townend that he wished Gilkes would become an Anglican vicar (it was an open secret that Gilkes intended to do this) [64] and leave the College; he lacked tact, trod roughshod on people, took no advice, and would not delegate authority or allow others to make decisions. [65]

Christison wrote to Gilkes himself in 1951 saying that, as Master, he had come to the end of his five-year term on the committee of the Alleyn Club, and was not eligible for re-election; as Gilkes said in his speech at the Dinner that year, no one had ever informed him that he was actually a member of the committee. In the same speech Gilkes criticised the Club: for almost ten years, he said, they had neither offered advice nor requested information; as far as he could see, they had been of no practical assistance to the College at all. Moreover, their organisation meant very little to the boys themselves; he suggested the Club give a Dinner for his prefects. His remark at the same Dinner that local authority housing was 'going to sweep across the green part of Dulwich' seems almost spitefully designed to inflame his audience. [66]

Gilkes and Dulwich College Preparatory School

It was to take Gilkes's successor, Ronald Groves, several years to undo the harm done by Gilkes to relations with Dulwich College Preparatory School, 'the Prep', which suffered a decline in fortunes and certainly in academic standards during and after the Second World War. Gilkes told his Governors that there had in fact been a signal decline over the previous 25 years before he became Master of Dulwich College. The Prep offered itself for sale again to the Governors in 1942, and at one of Gilkes's first appearances at their Meetings he opposed this, saying the school was in a poor state, and that the College should open its own preparatory department; this cannot have been the whole story, as four months later at a Governors' Meeting an aggrieved letter from its Headmaster, John Leakey, was read out, protesting that Gilkes had made him an offer to take over the school 'on ridiculous terms'. [67] Meanwhile Gilkes complained to the Governors about the low standard of work and behaviour and the general 'poor quality' of the

boys from the Prep at the College. He spoke habitually now of their 'marked inferiority', and in 1944 he seemed delighted to report that in the Sixth Form they were twice over outnumbered by the LCC boys. [68] The following year Leakey once again offered to sell the school. When this was again rejected, he wrote to the Governors about the 'hardship' experienced by his boys – presumably in reaching the standard of entry, when his school had been used to an easy transfer – and the deterioration of relations with the College. [69]

These relations reached such a low ebb that in 1950 the College approached the Prep to request that they drop the words 'Dulwich College' from the title of their school. Leakey wrote a plaintive letter in reply, expressing his hopes of reducing the friction between their neighbouring institutions, indeed of strengthening their shared bonds, but it fell on deaf ears, Gilkes repeating the request the following year, and reminding his counterpart of the findings of a recent government report: the Prep was privately owned and completely independent of the College, to which it now sent increasingly fewer boys; its name was therefore seriously misleading. [70] Gilkes now chose to renew his proposal to the Governors for the opening of a 'real' Dulwich College Preparatory School in the following year, 1952, but by that time he already had the two nine-year-old forms at the College itself. Leakey's next letter rather bitterly recalled the days before 1939, when up to 80 per cent of his boys graduated to the College, and bemoaned the passing of that period of happy relationships; since the present Master was appointed, he wrote, there had been neither advice nor co-operation. [71]

The acrimonious dispute was halted a few months later, when Gilkes was advised by his doctor to take three months' rest; he had a 'heart condition', compounded with a 'congenital malignant hypertension' that rendered him isolated and highly irritable; it was said openly in his obituary in *The Alleynian* in October of that year that a possible foreknowledge of 'something of the physical condition which brought about his sudden, tragic death … disturbed his judgements'. [72] The poor relationship with the Prep School in these years, no doubt not altogether of his own making, is another example of Gilkes's single-minded will.

The Governors

Major-General Lord Loch, Chairman of the Governors since 1930 (see Chapter Nine), died in 1942, and was succeeded for the next five critical years by Herwald Ramsbotham, Lord Soulbury, GCMG, PC, OBE, MC (1887–1971), a distinguished soldier and politician, who had been a reforming President of the Board of Education from 1940 until he was succeeded by R. A. Butler in July 1941; he was Chairman of the Burnham Committee on teachers' salaries until 1949. As well as being a champion of state education (as might be deduced from his proposals for Alleyn's School recorded above), Soulbury, though shrewd and with a reputation for hard work and common sense, does not appear to have shown all that much interest in the College; moreover, when pressing his successor as Chairman to take up the post upon his own appointment as Governor-General of Ceylon in 1949, he told him that it would never be necessary for him to go to the College. By contrast, others warned his successor that his would be the most difficult Chair in the country.[73]

In 1942 the Governors included the famous Camberwell Labour politician Lord Ammon (1873–1960), Sir Gerald Kelly, the Royal Academician (see below), and an excellent anthology of three enlightened Old Alleynians: Sir Harold Hartley, Sir Jack Sheppard, and Alic Smith. Other Old Alleynians on the Board were Sir Edward Campbell (see Chapter Nine) and Ralph Everett (1879–1954), who served from 1936 until 1951 and was also an Estates Governor. Everett was the son of the famous original pupil of the New College and subsequent Assistant Master, Edward Everett (see Chapter Six); a wealthy man, he devoted himself to the College Mission. Professor Jack Westrup (see Chapter Nine), the eminent Old Alleynian musician from Oxford, was appointed in 1947.

Soulbury's successor, Ronald Gorell Barnes, Lord Gorell, CBE, MC (1884–1963), was a truly great Chairman, regarded with much and wide affection; a prominent member and chairman of many committees in London, he was a minor poet and prolific man of letters (the author of a study of John Keats published in 1948), and earlier in his career had been a journalist and editor. According to Ronald Groves, he was 'kind and friendly', making constant visits to the College – despite Soulbury's earlier advice – and had a real knowledge of the staff.[74] In 1952 Harold Hartley summarised the differences between the College Governors and the Estates Governors succinctly: the former desperately needed to reconstruct the College buildings for modern needs; the Estates Governors needed to safeguard the income and resources of the Estate. After some years of opposition to the proposal, in 1972 the Foundation attempted to terminate by law their connection with St Olave's, St Saviour's and the Central Foundation Schools and the annual benefits they paid to them, with a capital grant of £250,000 each. In 1979, however, the Estate was still paying St Olave's an annual sum of £11,494 and the Central Foundation Schools £38,822.[75]

Education and the Common Room

Gilkes's tenure was notable for the appointment of a large number of young members of staff, though many of these soon left on account of the price of housing and the inadequacy of their salaries; these problems were not addressed until Groves's day. Meanwhile, some steady and magnificent teachers provided such intellectual stimulus that the young Michael Rich QC, writing an *Alleynian* editorial in 1952, before leaving the College that year with an award in History to Wadham College, Oxford, doubted if he would need the 'illumination' of a university career to follow his Dulwich education.[76] Gilkes zealously fostered the College's many Societies and its Music and Drama (see below): "What goes on after school is a real measure of success or failure", he told the Alleyn Club.[77] The rapid success he achieved for the College in its prestigious Oxford and Cambridge awards was matched by the rich cultural context he supervised, and which endures today, of debates, outside speakers, visits and Society meetings. Art alone did not flourish; Stef Fisher (see Chapter Nine) was in poor health, and once again the Governors were told by the Royal Academician adjudicating the Foundation art prizes in 1950 that the College's work was not up to standard. The complaint was repeated in 1955 by Sir Gerald Kelly (see below), who described the prizes as a futile waste of Academicians' time. Nor had the deplorable standard of entries improved by 1958, when the Governors were informed that all supervised instruction in Art customarily ceased after the age of twelve, but that plans were being made for its introduction as an optional subject thereafter.[78] This dreadful situation was to be remedied by the appointments made by Groves and his successors.

Among the members of the Common Room there were some men of quite extraordinary character, culture and intellect. Prominent among these was a great wit, Eric Parsley (1900–71), who was Head of the Modern Side until 1946, and was also Housemaster of a particularly happy Blew House from 1942 until 1952; from 1954 until 1960 he also served as a most popular President of the Common Room. Many stories are told of this immaculately dressed apostle of French culture, and his inspiringly catholic literary tastes. Perhaps the most famous is the story behind the ribbon he proudly wore as an Officier de l'Académie des Arts. This honour he held as a reward for presenting to the Château of Versailles a priceless copy of Racine's *Phèdre*, which he had heard was for sale in a second-hand bookshop in Dulwich Village. Abandoning his class, he had set off on his bicycle, casually inspected the book – and immediately realised that its title-page in fact contained a scrawled inscription by Louis XIV to his mistress Mme de Maintenon. The *ancien régime* was a particular area of Parsley's expertise – he would explain to his class with relish the various scandals of Louis's court, when not using a classroom ruler as a telephone during his imaginary conversations with Charles de Gaulle – and he pedalled home in triumph with his purchase. He was also musical (which alone must have recommended him to Gilkes): a pianist, he had a good enough baritone voice to sing a solo role in *Elijah* at a school concert in 1943, and he habitually contributed sketches for the Corps 'Shout'. In 1949 his only son David was killed in a flying accident with the RAF in the Middle East at the age of 22.[79] On his retirement ten years later, Parsley spoke at an Alleyn Club Dinner, praising the high tone and unvarying good nature of the Common Room in what was 'the most significant and exciting school in the country today'; no doubt thinking back to Gilkes's years, he said of the masters that they could be 'an awkward lot, very awkward, but they are all right if you treat them right. You can drive them, but they cannot be led'.[80]

Philip Vellacott (1907–97) was another inspired appointment by Gilkes, who had encountered him in 1942 at Stockport Grammar School, where he was serving as a temporary teacher.[81] An enormously influential master, of exceptional culture and intellect, Vellacott was Head of Classics from 1960 until his retirement in 1967. He possessed a lofty character; early in his career he had worked in East End missions and had thought of entering the Church, before losing his faith.[82] His reputation as a Classical scholar and translator of Greek tragedies (in the Penguin Classics series) was international, and he gave himself most generously to the College, giving talks to Societies on such topics as 'Justice and the Gods', and reviving the College's enviable reputation for its drama, of which he was placed in charge. This involved (including minor productions) the annual School Play, which at first he produced himself, and there followed 24 productions of Shakespeare. His own translation of Euripides' *Ion*, performed in the Master's Garden on Founder's Day in 1945, was regarded as a significant return to pre-war standards – though the suburban parents might have preferred a spot of Gilbert and Sullivan. In addition he founded and directed the Attic Players, who put on productions of his translations of Euripides and other classical plays in a hall in the Village; the members came from outside the College. Vellacott also performed a movement of a Mozart piano concerto at a College concert that year. His first full theatrical production, also in 1945, was *Henry IV, Part One*, with Derek Barton-Chapple (see below) as Prince Hal, followed by a *Macbeth* in 1946 with Barton-Chapple as Lady Macbeth. Under Vellacott Dulwich became famous for its 'unusual'

Shakespeare productions, civilising in the midst of barbarity, as Peter Coveney, a History master from 1945–50, wrote in *The Alleynian* in 1948.[83] *Julius Caesar* (1957) with Ian MacKillop, Barry Boys and Colin Niven (see below), was a great success. Vellacott's most famous production was probably *The Tempest* of 1949, with songs composed by the music master Stanley Wilson (see below), which was said to be 'inspired' – 'the most finished and polished yet'.[84] In 1955 he received an Arts Council bursary for a sabbatical year to write a new book. Although a scholar of real refinement, he was by no means a narrow academic, for example teaching boys Aristophanic chants to use while supporting the Rugby teams from the touchline; on his retirement he was described by Stephen Howard (see below) as 'a devoted servant of the College Mission'; when a case of 'flu robbed a production of the boy playing Shakespeare's mad Queen Margaret, Vellacott took over the part at a few hours' notice.[85] Before Vellacott's day the longest-serving member of the Common Room automatically became its President; when Eric Heeley (see below) chose not to serve, Vellacott was elected President, serving from 1963 until 1967.

There were characters among the staff Gilkes inherited, too. Frank Bamford (1904–54), Vellacott's predecessor as Head of Classics, had been appointed in 1937. He would thunder at his class, "Don't sit there like so many buckets waiting to be filled".[86] C. S. 'Doggie' or 'Father' Marriott (1895–1966), who taught Modern Languages from 1921 until 1953, was a brilliant cricket coach. While at the College he played for England; his fielding was said to be bad and his batting worse, but he was a famous leg-spin bowler, among whose Dulwich charges were some famous cricketers indeed: Hugh Bartlett, Trevor Bailey, 'Billy' Griffith, Denys Wilcox – a dozen cricket 'Blues' in all (see Chapter Twelve). Marriott was also an accomplished trombonist, very well read and an enthusiast for English poetry; he wrote in an article in *The Alleynian* in 1956 that modern English poets were nowadays 'batting in bad light on a crumbling wicket'. He was famous for turning up at the Oval on his motor-bike wearing goggles and carrying a shabby cricket bag.[87] G. G. (thus 'Horsey') Grange (see Chapter Nine), an Old Alleynian who left in 1915, had joined the staff in 1924 after fighting in the Great War and studying History at Oxford. He carried on the elder Gilkes's torch; restless, exuberantly humorous, his subjects were English, Classics and History. With his massive frame, he rode his bicycle with panniers full of books, wearing his Army-issue steel helmet from the First World War for years after the Second War was over. The comedian Bob Monkhouse (see below) obviously admired him greatly, describing him as a 'shambling unmade bed of a fellow with a thatch of unruly hair and tweedy jacket pockets that sagged as if once used to smuggle turnips'. [88]

Two other shrewd appointments to the staff were Gilkes's own. William Darby (1915–68) joined the school in 1946 to teach Classics and Modern Languages, eleven years after leaving its Sixth Form, and in the immediate wake of a hazardous war service. An excellent local historian, the author of *Dulwich Discovered* (1966) and *Dulwich: A Place in History* (1967), Darby had also drafted a history of the College by the time of his sudden death at the age of 52. The English specialist James Gibson (1919–2005) was appointed in 1949, having impressed Gilkes during an earlier stint of teaching practice at the College. He was put in charge of English in 1950,[89] and served until 1962.

Jim Gibson persuaded Gilkes to build up a department of English specialists, to replace the mass of thirty or so masters without special qualifications who had previously taken turns at teaching the subject. In the space of just three years the boys were to achieve 15 English awards at Cambridge, while the next ten schools in the 'league tables' won only nine between them.[90] Gibson later became the foremost authority on Thomas Hardy. He was followed by another outstanding teacher, Raymond Wilson (1925–95), who joined the staff in 1957 and was Head of English from 1962 to 1965, a scholar with particular interests in Jane Austen, in Coleridge and in the history of literary criticism, and a most inspiring and generous teacher, profoundly absorbed by the composition of poetry and how it is taught to children. He put together several anthologies, one with Jim Gibson, the most famous being the result of his Dulwich days, *Poems to Compare* (1966). Wilson left to teach at the University of Southampton and became a famous Professor of Education at the University of Reading for 21 years. He was succeeded in the English department by the legendary Laurie Jagger (1925–2007; see below).

W. S. Wright (1900–98), a great scholar, was appointed in 1924 and became Head of Classics in 1955; when he retired in 1960 he devoted himself to the Archives and the Fellows' Library, transcribing thousands of manuscripts in the College's care.[91] C. A. 'Alick' Hamilton (1903–85) devoted a career to the College from 1925 until 1963, a civilised teacher of History who was Housemaster of a happy Ivyholme and of Spenser, and in charge of all the College games. Ernest Heard (1911–95), who was Head of Modern Languages for 22 years until 1971, was a cultivated teacher who produced outstanding scholars. Eric Heeley (1912–2002), appointed in 1935, Head of Physics in 1961 and Head of Science in 1970 until he retired in 1973, was also in charge of the Combined Cadet

Force from 1946 until 1949. Another excellent Commanding Officer of the CCF from 1955 until 1962 was Wing-Commander Ronald Turner (1912–89), who taught general subjects from 1945 until 1962; he was the father of the Ven. Canon (Air Vice-Marshal) Robin Turner (left 1961), Chaplain-in-Chief of the Royal Air Force, who later returned to the College as a very popular and active Chaplain from 1998 to 2002. Michael Langley-Webb (1916–73), a most stimulating Historian and a gifted artist, who was also in charge of boxing, was appointed in 1946, leaving in 1971. A rare failure was Gilkes's unsuccessful attempt in 1950 to appoint to the staff Alan Shirreff (1919–2006), a first-rate athlete and cricketer and a loyal Old Alleynian who had left in 1938.[92]

The academic performance of the Sixth Form responded to Gilkes's schemes and initiatives, and to the zeal of the teachers. In 1944 the College won seven awards at Oxford and Cambridge; in 1948 and 1949 they won ten, and in 1952 twelve. The same year the boys were awarded fifteen of the coveted State Scholarships, that covered both full fees and maintenance at universities; this represented a thirtieth portion of the 450 scholarships available to all the schools in the country.

When Gilkes heard how public school boys joining the Army were judged to be physically unfit, he inaugurated compulsory daily Physical Training sessions for the whole school at morning break, in which he would sometimes take part himself; the boys would remove their stiff collars and afterwards sat sweating in class. In 1945 the whole Senior School performed these exercises at the Assault at Arms.[93]

From 1951 Gilkes relied too heavily on the man he had appointed in 1944 and now appointed his Deputy, W. C. 'Butcher' Thomas (1900–65; at Dulwich 1944–55), who was a good organiser, but was unpopular with most of the Common Room. Thomas, as frightening a disciplinarian to young boys as his nickname, was Head of the Lower School, and was Acting Master for a year after Gilkes's sudden death. Derek Akers, a very energetic Alleynian who was in the First XV in 1942 and left in 1944, had been encouraged by Gilkes to return to teach at the College. He was appointed in 1951, and left to become Headmaster of Purley High School in 1968. Ralph Starr (1903–59), an athlete who ran the 5,000 metres in the Paris Olympics in 1924 and the 800 metres in the Amsterdam Olympics just before the War, Housemaster of Carver House from 1948 until 1955 and of The Orchard from 1955 until 1958, was Head of the Lower School from 1955 until 1959. He was succeeded in turn by John Gwilliam (appointed 1956), the Welsh Rugby Captain, from 1960 until 1963, when he left to become Principal of Birkenhead School. Derek Akers, next appointed Head of the Lower School, was followed by Terry Walsh (see below), who was Head from 1969 until 1978. The twelve-year-old boys were taught in the South Block until the 1956–7 Extension was opened. The Lower School is now comprised of the eleven- and twelve-year-old boys, and Junior School is now for the seven- to ten-year-old boys, under a separate Head.

Music, drama and the societies; 'The Alleynian'

Gilkes, as has been mentioned above, was a passionate musical enthusiast and performer, and Music flourished in his era. In 1945 he appointed a very able Head of Music, Stanley Wilson (1899–1953), who enjoyed a celebrity beyond the College for his compositions, the possessor of a 'sensitive mind and a powerful technique'.[94] Wilson had won an open scholarship for composition at the age of 15 to the Royal College of Music, where he studied with Stanford. At his first Christmas concert Beethoven's Eighth Symphony and Bach's *Christmas Oratorio* were performed. A first performance of his first Piano Concerto, conducted by himself, was given at a Promenade Concert in 1938; it was played again at a College concert by Terence Beckles (1912–95), a 'peripatetic' piano teacher for many years in the Music Department, whose fame (for his piano performances) also extended beyond the College. The Cello Concerto was broadcast over the BBC Home Service. Other works by Wilson, such as the Piano Trio, a Coronation Anthem, and the *Skye Symphony* (1927), were performed in the College's concerts. It also became a tradition to include a piece by a British composer each time.[95] At the Memorial Service in 1947 for the Alleynians killed in the war Wilson's *Requiem Aeternam* was sung in the College chapel.[96] *The Messiah* was sung in Southwark Cathedral in 1951, the whole school travelling from North Dulwich station by special trains to attend. In 1951 at the time of the Festival of Britain a choir of sixty trebles from the College sang at the Festival Hall from a very difficult score in one of the earliest performances of Benjamin Britten's *Spring Symphony*, conducted by the composer; Britten earlier came to the College for a rehearsal in the School Music Room.[97] Gilkes liked to involve the whole school in tribal occasions, such as a mass Physical Training event involving (practically) the whole school; this took place as the climax of Founder's Day in 1949 and again at Parents' Day, a new institution, in 1952.[98] Thus, encouraged no doubt by the *Spring Symphony* event, the whole school joined in singing the choruses in *The Messiah* at the Royal Festival Hall in 1952, occupying the choir seats and the front stalls. The 'mammoth' Concert in the Festival Hall now became an annual tradition for many

years, and was followed by a Grand Coronation Ball in 1953 with 1,300 people attending; they danced to Victor Sylvester's band until 4 a.m. A profit of £597 was recorded.[99] One-third of the boys in the College in 1951 belonged to the choir. The Madrigal Choir flourished, 'splendid, enthusiastic' according to *The Alleynian*,[100] founded by Alan Morgan (see below) and conducted by a most admirable Captain of School, Hector McLean (left 1953). Wilson died suddenly of a heart attack in 1953, within months of Gilkes himself, a double blow to music at the College.

The College owes to the inspiration of Christopher Gilkes two further momentous benefits to activities outside the classroom: the founding of House Music and House Drama in 1948. This went some way to ending the century-long supremacy of sports as the basis for competitive rivalry among boys, and encouraged them to develop expressive skills. His great belief in the value of the Societies resulted in their proliferation; ever since his days these have prospered and declined according to boys' and masters' enthusiasms and initiatives. Some of the Societies were bold and some eccentric; of the latter, the 'Cabbage Club' of the late 1950s and early 1960s was a witty exclusive society for Prefects, election dependent on declarations of failures of various kinds which were posted on a notice board and assessed by the committee. There existed Societies for all the main cultural categories, except that no religions other than the Christian Union were represented at that time. Many happy careers have been defined for some of those who belonged to such groups at a formative time. P. G. Wodehouse, incidentally, wrote a letter (of 31 August 1969) to the editor of *The Alleynian*, in which he wistfully reflected on 'All those societies. In my time all we had to do after school was stroll down to the station and read the weeklies and magazines at the bookstall. A boy going to Dulwich now must have a wonderful time'. In a private letter to Townend, on the other hand, he says that he had just received *The Alleynian* and felt his 'usual disapproval for all these darned societies they have now'; he frequently complained that the three-page reports for single big cricket and Rugby matches were no longer a feature of the magazine.[101] In House Music and Drama competitions the boys to this day choose and direct the performances quite independently of adults. The young Christopher Field (see below) sang folk songs and an Elgar solo. In judging the House Drama in 1957 Philip Vellacott paid homage to Gilkes for founding it, and said that (just as today) the results were erratic, with some brilliance and some bathos.[102]

In 1946 *The Alleynian* wrote proudly in an editorial about 'the Dulwich Renaissance', emphasising the part played by Societies.[103] By 1948 there were 21 such groups. Meetings took place at the most dangerous times of the Blitz, when the Gramophone Society listened to records in the History Room. The standard of debating (as usual) varied, but was brilliant at its best. Architecture, Travel and Film societies were formed, and the Mermaid Society heard papers on literary and academic topics by the boys. Later the Twentieth-Century Play Society was very popular, and here a prominent part was played by Ian Mac-Killop (1939–2004), who was later a lively lecturer in the English Department at the University of Sheffield who published studies of F. R. Leavis and of François Truffaut. The Natural History Society involved the biologist Colin Tudge (left 1961), who is now an eminent philosopher of science, with expertise in agriculture and food, genetics, human and animal evolution, and the fate of species. In 1949 there was a small furore over the Modern Rhythm Society, founded in the Lower School for the study of dance music, swing, and jazz;[104] older boys made strong protests, and the cause rumbled through several issues of *The Alleynian* with pompous letters written on both sides. The great Alleynian alto saxophone and clarinet player Bruce Turner (1922–93), of the Freddy Randall band and his own Jump Band, the Humphrey Lyttelton and Acker Bilk bands, wrote to the magazine that at Blew House in 1939, the year that he left the College, he and his friend Nevil Shrimshire, of the Humphrey Lyttelton Band, had a collection of 300 jazz records, which served them better for their future career than their Latin Grammar Primer.[105] Bruce Turner published an autobiography, *Hot Air, Cool Music* (1984), which tells us that at the College he was obsessed with jazz and played the clarinet. He had greatly disliked the fagging and corporal punishment at Blew House, but had managed to play truant to the cinema once a week; he refused to come back for a final year. The Gallery Club visited the theatres, during what was a golden period for the London stage. The Radio Society was experimenting with television in 1952.

Not surprisingly, with the rise of the Societies, *The Alleynian* also once again became a serious magazine rather than a chronicle. As the magazine itself commented, the school was changed and pupils were 'more interested in life than some of their more immediate predecessors'.[106] The editorials, which for many years sometimes lamely described the premises and the progress of the seasons, the Dulwich mud on the playing fields and the chances of beating Bedford at Rugby, became longer and more discursive, and began to touch on social and intellectual upheavals, questions of freedom, leisure, and diversity; one Editor rejoiced that uncritical reverence for the past and for authority was gone.[107] By 1949 the Contributions section of poetry

and prose, which had been suspended during the War to save paper, became once again something of which any school might be proud. Serious articles by boys on art and on writers such as T. S. Eliot featured, with reviews of books new to the Library; the overt aim was to create a proper magazine.[108] Precocious and fascinating contributions from writers well known today (see below) are to be found. The editors pointed out that the original *Dulwich College Magazine* of Canon Carver's great academic era was hardly parochial: in 1864–5 the ratio of 'serious' discursive contributions compared with reports of school activities had been twenty to one.[109] The boys (sadly) proposed to split the magazine from its Alleyn Club section, and indeed published an Old Alleynian section (once only) in 1951. The Alleyn Club Newsletter took over function of a record. In 1953 the editors had the confidence to persuade the school to publish a separate *Alleynian Literary Supplement* with poetry, prose, essays, drama and book reviews, and a contribution successfully solicited from P. G. Wodehouse, 'To the Editor, Sir'.[110]

Sports, Scouts and the Mission

During Gilkes's era the sporting prowess of the College reached significantly greater heights than the years between the Wars, particularly with the career of Trevor Bailey, a household name for his performances in Test Cricket, who first played for England in 1949, against New Zealand; in 1944 the College XI was unbeaten (see Chapter Twelve), to Gilkes's great pride. The photograph of the smiling Bailey and his team, dressed without swagger blazers but with silk squares at their neck, up against the Centre Block with its windows bricked against bombardment, shows the spirit of the boys and the College in these times. Press coverage of Dulwich cricketers such as Wilcox, Griffith and Bartlett gave great satisfaction. The Rugby team in 1946–7 won all its matches. Three athletic records of the great C. N. Lowe were beaten in 1950.[111] On 18 November 1950 Geoffry Higgs, the Captain of the Cricket XI in 1950 and also the Captain of Athletics and of Marlowe House, broke his neck with a flying tackle while playing for the First XV in the Bedford match and, paralysed, died five months later; Gilkes went to visit him in Dulwich Hospital and appointed him Captain of School, at which he smiled. Prefects discussed their policy round his hospital bed.[112] A Memorial Bat was given annually to the Captain of the School XI in his name for some years. In 1952 and again the following year Brian Howes (left 1953), who later taught at the College for five years from 1963 and enjoyed a successful career as Headmaster of St George's English School in Rome and in the Schools Inspectorate, won

The First XI of 1941, photographed against the bricked-up windows of the Lower Hall.
D. W. Walton, O. F. Jackson, D. E. Tunnadine, A. R. Langston, J. M. Hitchen, H. R. Woolmer.
H. P. H. Kiddle, A. W. H. Mallett, T. E. Bailey (Capt.), R. G. Hulbert, A. F. Harlow. (Dulwich College)

the Sabre of the Public Schools Fencing championships. Frank Turner (b. 1922), a splendid Gym Instructor, was appointed by Gilkes in 1948; in spite of serious injury at the Sicily landings during the War he was twice a member of the Olympics team, at London in 1948 and at Helsinki in 1952. [113] Hockey was introduced in 1953, the particular enthusiasm of P. R. Thomas (see below), a Cambridge 'Blue'. C. B. Howland (left 1955), of a prolific Dulwich College family, was Captain of Cricket, Rugby and Hockey.

The Scout movement (see Chapter Nine) was specially prosperous and popular in Gilkes's days; in 1953 there were a total of 200 Scouts. From the three patrols in 1929 the boys now formed five, including Troop III, 'Lorne Campbell's Own', run by Old Alleynians. In 1949, when Campbell opened the new Scout Headquarters, H. V. Styler (see Chapter Nine) wrote, 'in liveliness, enterprise and comradeship our troops would be hard to beat'. [114]

In 1951 Gilkes reported to the Governors that his prefects had told him that the College's part in the Mission, including the boys' subscriptions, should be discontinued, because the state now ran social services; moreover, the boys felt that the housing estates nearer the College would now be more deserving of their attention. [115] However, the following year the Mission took over another local youth club in Camberwell, the Hollington Club; this became very active and prosperous under the energetic leadership of Bryan Thwaites (left 1940) as Chairman and Treasurer; this well-known mathematician and inventor later taught at Winchester College, and is now Professor Sir Bryan Thwaites, Principal of Westfield College from 1966 until 1983, recently a great benefactor of Dulwich College, at which he has founded an annual Bach Festival, and to which he has presented a magnificent pipe-organ. The great Classics master Stephen Howard (see below) was to take a great deal of interest in the Mission in later decades.

The boarding houses

Gilkes, with his visionary notion of the College as the intellectual power-house and catalyst for social improvement for the boys of South London, was also remarkably keen to develop the boarding side of the College. When the War Office Course finished, the two boarding houses, Ivyholme and Blew House reopened their doors in 1943 to College boys; Elm Lawn and The Orchard on Dulwich Common served as two junior houses. In 1942 the Governors took over the finances of boarding from the Housemaster, a very sensible reform. 'Weekly boarding', whereby boys went home for the weekend, was said to be popular in 1943. In 1944 Gilkes was very angry when the Estates Governors leased Brightlands to Dulwich College Preparatory School, when it would have made an ideal boarding house for the College.[116] By 1947 three houses were full, and Gilkes reported to the Alleyn Club at their Dinner that the Governors were contemplating a maximum of eight Houses over the next five or six years, to take up to three hundred boarders;[117] this project was intended to attract sons of Old Alleynians from the provinces and boys from overseas, but the proposal also came at a time when it looked as if there would be a greater demand for boarding places from Local Authorities. When all four boarding houses were full to capacity in 1945 and accommodation was needed for 28 new boys, the Cricket Pavilion, now that the Borough of Camberwell were no longer tenants with the First Aid Post, was converted into a junior boarding house, called Carver House, with accommodation for the Housemaster, W. C. Thomas, his family and a matron; it was not to be restored to cricketers until 1956. Christopher Gilkes claimed of this ten years' arrangement that all that was lost was an amenity for the visiting football and cricket teams, who had now to use the boys' changing rooms.[118] In 1948 the junior boys of Carver House moved, confusing their identity, from the Pavilion to Bell House; in 1955 they moved back to the Pavilion briefly. By 1949 there were 204 boarders, of which 155 were 'fee-payers', 13 were from the LCC, 18 from Southend, 5 from Croydon, and 13 from Surrey.[119] The following year Croydon announced it would take no more boarding places, and Southend followed suit in 1952; Surrey reduced its numbers to 6 day-boys and 4 boarders in 1952.[120] Gilkes announced to the Governors that he recognised (against his personal wishes) the need for 'a certain degree of modest splendour' for a Master's residence in the eyes of the world; he had been living uncomfortably in The Chestnuts. An eighty-year lease of Elm Lawn had been bought from the Estate for £2,750, and this was presented (anonymously) to serve as a residence for the Master by the devoted Ralph Everett in 1949.[121]

Buildings and the Estate

The decorative Science Building designed by the third Charles Barry was half destroyed by the V1 bomb, as described above; some temporary repairs were carried out early in 1945, and it was not demolished until 1950. For eight years laboratory work took place at James Allen's Girls' School and in the huts (bought from a farmer by Gilkes) erected by the side of the ruined Block; two science lessons were taking place in the same room, Gilkes reported to the Governors in 1949.[122] Gilkes saw that in any case the old Building would have been quite inadequate after the War; the College needed appropriate and progressive facilities to play its part in the New Britain that he constantly reminded the Old Alleynians the College was to shape. Planned from 1946, and designed by the Old Alleynian architect Austin Vernon (see Chapter Nine), with the foundation stone laid on the site of what was once the Master's garden in 1950 by the Chairman of the Estates Governors, L. J. Styles, the Science Block opened in 1952. *The Alleynian* commented that it had 'unusual architectural features, yet nobody seems either to like or dislike it'. The Estates Governors gave £50,000, and the final cost was £106,000; for the sake of economy the Mechanics Laboratory and a lecture hall for 300 included in the original plans were not built.[123] Eric Parsley published a facetious poem in *The Alleynian* about the smell of flowers and of illicit cigarettes being replaced by that of chlorine.[124]

The new Junior School was opened in 1948. Frank Dixon, Chairman of the Estates Governors, opened the building, a 'gift'.[125] The building, two floors with ten classrooms, was paid for from the proceeds of compulsory purchase by the London County Council of four large houses for the Denmark Hill council housing estate, as was sanctioned after long negotiations by an Estates 'Altering Scheme' of 1948; the Second Form extension was added in 1957.[126] By 1950 the Governors' relations with Austin Vernon, the College Architect and Surveyor since 1937, a first-rate architect who had been on hand during the War with repairs and 'first aid' for the damaged buildings, deteriorated badly with the discovery of very poor work to the running track and tennis courts which he should have supervised and other complaints expressed by the Governors, and in 1951 he was willing to resign; his nephew and partner, Russell Vernon, took over and wound up the works in hand, including the Science Block which was now under construction.[127] In the neighbourhood meanwhile a 'comprehensive high school' for 2,000 boys and girls on Alleyn Park, later named 'Kingsdale School', for which eight large red-brick villas were to be demolished, was proposed in 1950 by the London County Council.

At first the Governors considered opposing the plans 'as it might seriously endanger recruitment at the College', but they changed their minds at their next meeting. [128] In 1951 there was friction between the College and Estates Governors. The issue is mysterious, but it appears that they had covertly approached the Ministry of Education, hoping for an assurance that the state would from now on subsidise the College; why else should the College Governors at that time have needed to assert that the College was 'the prime charge on the property of the Estate foundation'? Indeed the Estate Governors sent a warning that they were unlikely to afford further capital grants to the College, now that the local education authorities were supporting it. At the same time the College Governors heard of plans for 'further and serious encroachment' on the Estate from the London County Council. [129] In 1953 another 80 acres were taken by the Council for housing.

Meanwhile it was daily evident with the increased numbers that a new Hall, kitchens and dining rooms were desperately needed; by 1949 the Great Hall was 'up to its limit and beyond' for both prayers and meals. It was also inadequate for the ambitious concerts that evolved; Gilkes told the Alleyn Club at the Dinner of 1952 that to perform *The Messiah* there would only leave room for an audience of 25, and consequently he had no alternative but to hire the Royal Festival Hall. A War Memorial Hall was desirable, and this is what Gilkes proposed to the Alleyn Club at the Dinner of 1946; funds were solicited for this hall, specifically as a Memorial, to seat the whole school. [130] The South African War Memorial Library was also by now 'most unsatisfactory and unsuitable for school purposes', and could not hold the books, Gilkes told the Governors in 1950. [131] There seems something symbolic of the burden of past eras in the once great, now obsolete Carver organ with its many pipes occupying (on both sides) so much of the stage in the Great Hall; the instrument was now described by the top firm of organ builders, Henry Willis of Liverpool, invited to tender an estimate for its refurbishment, as 'junk'; another firm, the John Compton Organ Company, offered to rebuild it for £3,000; however, they were commissioned in 1951 to install an 'electronic' Organ (as it was called in those days, but having nothing to do with computers) in its place; this was paid for from the F. C. Cooper Will Trust (administered by an Old Alleynian, L. C. McMurdie, b. 1919). [132] In 1949 Gilkes characteristically suggested that a permanent Elizabethan stage at the west end of the Great Hall could be constructed from the splendid old oak casing from the Carver Organ, with the help of the boys and the woodwork staff. [133]

The Chapel and the Picture Gallery

The damaged Chapel was closed for repairs in October 1942; as already mentioned, 'severe and extensive' bombing both to the Gallery and to the Chapel took place on 20 July 1944, ten days after the serious damage wrought by the V1 on the College itself. [134] Dramatic photographs show the ruined Chapel and the Chaplain's house; the tower was reported insecure after bombing. After repairs and a long closure Bertram Simpson, the much admired Bishop of Southwark (1883–1971), rededicated the restored Chapel in 1952. [135] In 1954 a new east window was installed, paid for by the War Damage Commission; the design by Russell Vernon shows St Nicholas of Myra (Santa Claus, the saint who once saved the lives of three poor schoolboys), Edward Alleyn at prayer with the almsfolk, and an emblematical pair, Charity and Faith. Discussions about what were difficult issues for many decades – the position of the Chapel, which was still serving both the College and the Village, and the role of the College chaplain – revealed that the wealthier and more influential people in the Village still preferred to use the Chapel rather than their parish church, St Barnabas. [136]

Although a few rooms and walls of the Gallery were left standing, the bomb that hit the Chapel destroyed the Mausoleum. The stone coffins of Bourgeois and Desenfans were broken, and the wooden coffins inside them badly damaged; a Funeral Director in Peckham sealed these in sheet copper coffins. [137] A venerable catalpa tree in the Garden, two hundred years old, fell in 1944 from the blast of the bomb, and a Judas tree up against the Chapel, said to be three hundred years old, blew over in 1946; large oaks were taken down in the garden in 1949.

Because of the efforts of the former Clerk to the Governors, S. W. Bickell (who took up his job from Wales in 1907, and died in 1947), the most important pictures had been given sanctuary during the War at Aberystwyth, where he was retired. [138] Six pictures left at the Gallery were destroyed by the bomb, including Reynolds's *Death of Cardinal Beaufort* (DPG 483); the remainder were stored in the shelter in the cellars of the North Block. In 1947, while the pictures were homeless, a selection were shown on loan at Welsh galleries and country houses, and 59 were selected for exhibition at the National Gallery and at Temple Newsam, near Leeds. The National Gallery display was arranged by Sir Gerald Kelly RA (1879–1972), the ebullient Governor appointed by the Academy to succeed Francis Dodd RA (1874–1949) in 1944, who was to have a great deal of influence on the recovery of the Gallery after the war. Kelly went to Wales to examine the pictures, and reported that of the Gallery's 367 paintings at least 334 required urgent attention; for sixty years they had been treated with linseed oil and were blistered. His friend, the expert Dr Johann Hell, undertook an extensive programme of cleaning over many years, and luckily eschewed the over-cleaning fashionable at the time. Kelly brought back 74 pictures from Aberystwyth and they were stored in the vaults at the Royal Academy in 1946.[139] Bell House was to be occupied as a store and a temporary Gallery for display of the paintings; letters in the press by now were complaining that the pictures were not on view, despite Soane's charming Gallery being a war casualty. Bell House was at the time leased as a furniture repository for Messrs Evan Cook; their furniture was moved to the five rooms at the back of the Gallery which were still fairly sound in order to evacuate the house. Kelly in the event decided that Bell House was not suitable as a store, and it never displayed the pictures, and thus Bell House was freed in autumn 1947 to act as a temporary boarding house. The Governors appointed Kelly the Honorary Surveyor of the Picture Gallery in 1945, and (although there was a Picture Gallery Committee) he seems to have been given a free hand. Kelly, brilliant as he was, appears

to have come to regard the Gallery as his own province; he was angry when the Governors arranged a lunch in the Gallery for the opening of the new extension to the Science Block in 1957 without asking him first. He was also generous; for example he would himself occasionally pay for a new frame.[140] Kelly had been brought up in Camberwell, where his father was vicar of St Giles's, and knew the Gallery well as a boy. The *Dictionary of National Biography* describes him as charming, but indomitable, petulant and tactless. At the age of 70 in 1949 he was elected President of the Royal Academy.

Austin Vernon had made measured drawings before the war of important details of the Gallery. He told the Governors in 1945 that it would cost £20,000 to £30,000 to rebuild it.[141] The great architects, Giles Gilbert Scott, Herbert Baker and other Academicians, fearing the economies and simplifications of a 'restoration', wrote letters to Kelly urging him to reinstate the Picture Gallery 'in every particular'; and the great Sir John Summerson (1904–92) of the Soane Museum also wrote, suggesting the demolition of Charles Barry's Victorian entrance and

HM the Queen Mother after the reopening of Dulwich College Picture Gallery, 27 April 1953. Juliet Gilkes, Christopher Gilkes, Lord Gorell, Hector McLean (Captain of School); Alick Hamilton and David Knight in group to right. (Dulwich College)

saying that Soane's original sketch plans showed the entrance of the Gallery at the rear. [142] A friend of Kelly's was brought in over Austin Vernon to act as Honorary Consultant Architect; this was Arthur Davis (1878–1951) of Mewès and Davis, architects of splendour at the Ritz, Luton Hoo and Polesden Lacy. Davis in turn condemned Barry's 'expensive and meretricious' additions and other changes made to Soane's original plan. The Government, however, refused a grant to rebuild the Gallery; other urgent works were 'essential in the national interest'. Kelly thereupon persuaded the Pilgrim Trust to give a grant of £20,000, and the Governors agreed to restoration of the Gallery 'as near as possible in its original form', including the demolition of the Barry porch. [143] Austin Vernon told the Governors he was quite prepared to take responsibility for the rebuilding of the Gallery unaided, [144] something which (with his sophisticated historical architectural knowledge and eye) he was well qualified to do, and in the event he did much of the work. In 1951, however, there was an 'incident' at the site, when Vernon encountered Kelly and the wheelchair-bound Davis, which was reported to the Governors; they said that Vernon should resign. A few months later Davis died, and another Academician, Sir Edward Maufe (1883–1974), was appointed to take his place. [145]

The meticulously restored and rebuilt Gallery was reopened on 27 April 1953 by Queen Elizabeth, the Queen Mother, who visited the College afterwards for tea in the Great Hall; the school lined both sides of the front drive. She did not inspect the new Science Block, as originally suggested. Her Lady-in-waiting wrote in advance that she was keen to meet the teachers and others who actually did the work at the College as well as the Governors. Returning to a Garden Party at the Gallery in 1969 for the Foundation's 350th anniversary, she asked to see the Chapel. [146]

The pictures were described at the re-opening, fallaciously, as 'cleaned for the first time'. All the pictures from Aberystwyth were now returned; they were hung on bare grey plastered walls with fine lines in gold leaf, although Kelly had asked for brocade as background. [147] Scotland Yard suggested a burglar alarm for the most valuable paintings, to be directly connected to the Yard, but despite this precaution, a series of well-publicised thefts was to occur over the next decades. In 1962 an attempted theft of a Rembrandt was foiled by an attendant and the would-be thieves escaped to the Park; the Gallery, reported *The Times*, was visited by 'surprisingly' few people. [148]

In these years valuable work was done for the Gallery by Sir Harold Hartley, who was Chairman of the Picture Gallery Committee until 1970, and by K. S. Carpmael (1885–1975), one of four Old Alleynian brothers concerned with law and the City. In 1964, although the Picture Gallery was running at a serious loss, the Governors rightly expressed their appreciation of the great services and generosity of Sir Gerald Kelly. [149] Many now thought and said that it was ridiculous for amateurs like the College Governors and an Academician in his spare time to attempt to run the Picture Gallery in the modern world. A separation between the Gallery and the College (rather than a divorce) seemed in the air, and in 1955 the new Master, Ronald Groves, wrote to the press to complain of the Gallery being referred to as 'Dulwich Picture Gallery' rather than as 'Dulwich College Picture Gallery'. [150] The same year the Royal Academy Garden Party was resumed.

It was Kelly who first caused the Gallery to close on Mondays to rest the attendants. A 'Friends of the Gallery League', now a flourishing organisation, was first proposed in 1953. Scholarship began to be taken more seriously; in 1959 Michael Jaffé of the Fitzwilliam Museum identified two pictures as the work of Rubens. [151]

RONALD GROVES, 1954–66 – The Local Educational Authorities and the Awards at Oxford and Cambridge – Buildings – The curriculum and the College culture – The Common Room – The Combined Cadet Force – The Hollington Club and the 'Teen Canteen' – Alleynians – Chaplains

Ronald Groves, 1954–66

After a decade of dedicated, often inspired work, Christopher Gilkes's prematurely white head was bludgeoned but unbowed; now his health collapsed. There had been warning signs when he was away from his work for several weeks in 1948; five years later, in June 1953, his doctor ordered him to take three months' rest. [152] While on leave, he died of a heart attack at the wheel of his car at Nolton Haven, near Haverfordwest, on 2 September 1953; he was 54. W. C. Thomas, to whom the weary Gilkes had delegated much, was appointed Acting Master, and made efforts to be appointed Master. Luckily his shortcomings, obvious to the Common Room but apparently not to Gilkes, were detected, and a great Master of Dulwich College, Ronald Groves (1908–91), succeeded to the post in March 1954.

Groves was born and bred in Yorkshire, and possessed its characteristic pragmatic approach to life, as well as a certain Puritanism, shown in his wariness about school play productions. He was a less controversial Master than Gilkes, well known for his 'unremitting hard work', and he stabilised a jangled College. Short and kindly, he was very popular among his staff, got on well with his Governors, established an affectionate respect from the boys, and healed relations with both the Alleyn Club and the Preparatory School. It was necessary to create good will for the new Dulwich amongst old boys, but also the local grammar schools and other critics, including some Assistant Masters, whose hostility to the Scheme for places paid by the LCC and other councils had rumbled on for eight years; the system for selecting these free-place boys in any case needed humanising. After Groves had been in office for only one year, in April 1955, Bill Townend wrote to Wodehouse in Long Island quoting a letter he had received from McCulloch Christison. 'As regards the school', Christison had written, 'things are going all right and what is more important the Common Room is a happy family which it hadn't been for years under Gilkes. The latter did not hit it off with me or the other Governors with whom he came into contact, so all round things are running smoothly.

Gilkes would never take advice from anyone and if anyone made a suggestion he would do just the opposite. Groves has made a very good impression and I really think Dulwich will do well under him'. [153]

Lord Gorell, a first-rate Chairman of the Governors from 1949, was also a factor in the newly trustful and confident atmosphere of government at the College. Reflecting well, probably, on both men, the Governors' *Minutes* read more smoothly and happily than at any period in the College's history. Building on Gilkes's work, the 'Experiment' grew into a confident and prosperous venture under Groves, and with the free-place boys the College created its own rich culture and the most brilliant academic era in its history: insofar as a school's success can be measured by the number of awards at Oxford and Cambridge (a figure that more than doubled in Groves's day), Dulwich was acknowledged to be one of the two 'best' schools in the country, and a national model for the future. Groves was able to tell his Governors truthfully in 1959 that 'the pace and intensity of the Sixth Form teaching are as exacting as any school in the country'. [154] In addition, Gilkes's nurture of the College's Societies significantly enriched the boys' education. The boys themselves were proud of the national significance of their school: in 1958 an editorial in *The Alleynian* confidently announced that the College was 'expansive' and the 'school of the future'. At the Alleyn Club Dinner in 1960 the speakers referred proudly to a recent *Sunday Times* headline, 'Dulwich College goes to the top'. [155]

Groves's appointment was a very shrewd one: his career had proved him a mature schoolmaster, and quite apart from his remarkable qualities of character, his experience seemed ideally placed to fit the various needs of the College at this point in its history. He also already had two links with the Dulwich community, the strongest of which was his marriage to Hilary, the younger daughter of the earlier Master George Smith, whom she matched in good sense, 'calm, serene and gracious'. [156] At the time of his appointment, furthermore, Groves was Headmaster of Campbell College in Belfast (a boarding school of about 350 boys), where he had succeeded Dulwich's influential Assistant Master William Gibbon (see Chapter Eight). An old boy of Bradford Grammar School, Groves had attended one of the more worldly Oxford Colleges, Christ Church, where he took a First in Chemistry. He first taught at Bradfield College for a year, from 1931, and then at Worksop College, the Woodard school in Nottinghamshire; the Headmaster at Worksop, the

Peter Greenham RA,
Ronald Groves.
Dulwich College.
(© Estate of Peter Greenham /
Bridgeman Art Library)

formidable Canon 'Fred' Shirley (1890–1967), a dynamic figure with great financial skill, took Groves with him to King's School, Canterbury, where he was appointed as a very young Senior Science Master and a Housemaster from 1935 until 1943, the year in which he moved to Belfast. Groves's additional post as Bursar at King's, Canterbury, including responsibilities for new buildings, comprised a further and impressive set of credentials for the College Governors to consider – and Groves's tenure at Dulwich indeed coincided with the planning of a major phase of new building works. Such a range and variety in a schoolmaster's duties is unthinkable today, but Groves's disparate responsibilities proved his energetic dedication. His early experience in the family building industry comprised an excellent qualification for a headmaster or a bursar. [157]

Groves's policy may best be described as cautiously progressive; he spent some sabbatical months in the United States to study Science teaching in 1963, for example, and his was the first appointment of a teacher of Economics. Although the College rose to the very top of the country's academic schools, he told the Alleyn Club that he cared more 'to turn out the right kind of schoolboy of character and guts who is prepared to give a lead in this shattered world of ours than that he should break records at all times'. [158] He took bold decisions, such as consigning the College catering (but keeping the same staff) to the LCC Catering Division in 1960. [159] On a national level, Groves's integrity and equanimity made him a desirable Chairman of government committees, and in 1959 he accepted the post of Chairman of the Food Standards Committee for the Ministry of Agriculture and Fisheries, concerned with the composition, description, labelling and advertising of food. He was a member of the King's College Dental School Committee and later of the Medical Council and its Appeal Committee. In the event it was a committee that claimed him from the College; he retired to chair the Joint Committee of the Governing Bodies Association for Independent Schools and of the Headmasters' Conference to put the case of the public schools to the government Newsome Committee, which was set up to discuss the relation between the public and state schools.

Groves recalled that when he first arrived at Dulwich College he had no idea of the magnitude of the task awaiting him.[160] When he left, it was typical of him to describe his conscientious overworked tenure as being 'extraordinarily exciting', at 'one of the fastest moving' schools in the country.[161] In his Memorial Address at Groves's death, the Revd Nick Earle (see below) praised him as a builder of relationships. His eye to the modern age and to his charges, and the accustomed moderation and balance with which he carried out his job, are typified perhaps by his statement to parents about haircuts, an apparently minor matter which within a decade was to become a symbolic struggle between schoolmasters wielding shears, and their young flock with sleek fleeces: 'it is difficult to define a hair style for men, but many of the modern innovations I do not like, and ask therefore that boys have their hair parted and kept reasonably short'.[162] History repeated itself from the week of George Smith's arrival in the Great Hall exactly forty years earlier, for, succeeding the second Gilkes as Master, Groves once again had six inches sawn off the lectern in the Great Hall; small in stature he was, but, as one of his Governors remarked, he was large in understanding. He also retained an excellent sense of humour. Groves took great pains with his staff and boys; it mattered enormously to him what boys were in his school and who taught them. Trivial offenders sent to him were the subject of his special encouragement. He also discussed individually two hundred university applications a year with his Sixth-Formers. He would play cricket with junior boarders on a Saturday evening. A mark of his good nature was his filial piety: on his first teaching appointment he sent his parents his first salary cheque.[163] He chose over a hundred assistant masters during his twelve years; twenty of the men who served under him became headmasters. The boys resented their best teachers being 'poached', and said so in *The Alleynian*.[164]

Groves told the Governors that he did not want W. C. Thomas, the former Acting Master, to act as his Deputy any longer, nor indeed did he want a Deputy Master at all, preferring to run the College with a committee of his

academic Heads of Sides; the Governors received a 'private and confidential' report from the staff on 'Butcher' Thomas, who left abruptly in 1955, appointed Headmaster of the LCC Strand Complement School at Tulse Hill. In fact Groves was to appoint Eric Handscomb (see Chapter Nine) as Deputy Master in 1960, which was Handscomb's own last year at the College; he had started the Air Training Corps in 1941 and organised the timetable. He was succeeded in 1961 by George Way, (1910–88; Head of Chemistry 1937, Housemaster of Blew House, Head of Science 1945) a former Boxing 'Blue', who was said to be 'firm but fair, unselfish in the extreme', and who was to be Acting Master for a term when Groves resigned, retiring in 1970.[165]

In 1959 Lord Gorell resigned as Chairman after an operation, saying he was making way for a younger man,[166] and was succeeded by the very busy national figure, Lord Shawcross. Groves presided with great satisfaction over a highly successful era in sports (see Chapter Twelve). The Rugby field, however, was once again the site of a tragic event, seven years after the death of Geoffry Higgs: Hamish Park died in 1957, after being unconscious for eight days. Ronald Groves told the Governors in 1964 that boxing was likely to be suspended for ever, as it was now thought too dangerous. One boy swam for England in 1965.[167]

The Local Educational Authorities and the Awards at Oxford and Cambridge

By 1957 ninety per cent of the boys at the College at entry held full-fee awards from local authorities, who also paid the boys' fares to and from school.[168] That the boys valued the Scheme can be shown from a letter from one of them written to *The Alleynian* in 1961, reflecting that the College 'united many good qualities of both the public schools and the grammar schools'. He claimed that the school produced 'well educated and progressive men' rather than 'smooth gentlemen'.[169] In 1968 Ronald Groves, returning to speak at an Alleyn Club Dinner, declared that although it was independent, the College had 'the closest of ties' with the LEAs, and could be 'the model for the future'. The number of 'free places' was eventually to decline after about 35 years since Gilkes's first major annual intake, and all such state subsidies were to disappear within fifty years. Charles Lloyd, Groves's successor as Master, forecast in 1968 that free places would be replaced by 'assisted places'.[170] The new scheme of Assisted Places, which ran from 1980 until 1997, was in the form of a grant from central government rather than the local Council, and was based on a statement of family income, rather than an award paying for full fees. This scheme was undoubtedly the consequence of the success of the 'Gilkes Experiment', and the architect of the Scheme was the highly successful schoolmaster and headmaster Sir James Cobban, who earlier contributed to the College so generously as an Assistant Master (see Chapter Nine).

Groves judged the College Roll too high on his arrival: there were 1,391 boys in 1955, and he thought that 1,200 would be an ideal figure. He managed to reduce the numbers to 1,309 by the following year, but remained unhappy with the size of classes, which now held as many as thirty boys. [171] By 1962 the number of LCC boys entering the College showed a slight fall; the Council ascribed this to a decline in population. Groves in 1964 resisted LCC approaches to send 'non-Grammar-School types' as boarders, presumably difficult boys from broken homes. [172]

The fees rose from £105 per annum in 1955 to £168 in 1962. In 1959 twenty-seven State Scholarships were won by the College, consequent on the same number of Oxford and Cambridge awards; again only 450 were awarded for the whole country, and this meant that Dulwich was now awarded a seventeenth part of all the grants for that year. [173] Awards at Oxford and Cambridge became in this era a matter of great competition and satisfaction, reflecting of course real and great credit on the Sixth Form teaching and culture at Dulwich, and they became a matter of perhaps more competitive interest to the College and indeed to the public in general than the kudos attached in former times to success in the annual Rugby football fixture against Bedford School. Also, as Groves pointed out to the Governors in 1958, the awards were gained in a wider spread of subjects than any other school. [174] As all understood, they supplied an index to the College's standing. The main competitor for the highest number of annual awards in both Groves's and Lloyd's era was Manchester Grammar School, a formidable rival; Winchester and St Paul's were naturally also challengers in the arena. In 1955–6 Manchester won 43 awards at Oxford and Cambridge, and Dulwich came ninth in the 'league tables' with 15. Dulwich at this time was roughly equal to Winchester College. The very next year the College was second with 27 awards, and for at least a decade it rarely fell below third. In 1958 *The Alleynian* quoted a phrase jeering at the College as 'a scholarship factory' current at this time, and which remained in common usage for several decades; undoubtedly success generated spite and envy. Groves told the Alleyn Club at their Dinner the same year that the 72 awards made to the boys in the last three years amounted to as many as they had won in the previous ten. [175] In 1959–60 the College headed the national 'table' of awards, but in 1964 Manchester gained 33 and Dulwich 28. It is further worth noting that, in addition to the award-winners, 26 boys gained places as 'commoners' in 1964 for entry at Oxford and Cambridge. Since Dulwich had one of the four largest Sixth Forms in the country, and the 'best' boys from one side of a river dividing a great metropolis, its achievement is perhaps unsurprising: by now it was the second largest independent school in the country, second only to Manchester Grammar School. The quality of mind of the Dulwich candidates was of course stimulated by the questioning habit of mind of the free-place boys, many of whom took very little on trust, and was quickened by the wide variety of opinion and the general dialectic among the teachers – a stimulating circumstance denied to most of their potential rivals, particularly in more old-fashioned country boarding-school sanctuaries favoured by many middle-class parents. Doubtless competition and ambition was also a spur in animating the specialist lessons with small groups for Oxford and Cambridge applicants. The boys were used to constant competition, for Groves insisted on form positions and a grading of effort from 'A' to 'C' (known as 'the ABCs') to monitor boys every two weeks, [176] which was soon amended to four weeks; before the War the custom had been established for the boy who was at the bottom of a weekly list of 'form order' to report to the Master with the list in his hand. Of the 28 awards made in 1964, History gained 9, English 7, and Science 6.

Buildings

Under a new Scheme of 1956 the Estate, rather than extricating itself from subsidising the College as its Governors had attempted to do, agreed to pay half of its annual grants to the College; the allocation to Alleyn's School was reduced, presumably since it was receiving a government 'direct grant', its portion computed in a manner reminiscent of the College in Stuart days and of Alleyn's prescriptions: sixteen of eighty parts of a quarter. In 1962 the grant was revised again, this time upwards, and both the College and Alleyn's received rather more funds. [177]

When Groves arrived to take up his post, piles of rubble from the bombings still disfigured the College. Although ten years had passed since VE Day in 1945, it was only now that the Front Gates were to be rebuilt. Russell Vernon argued for a complete restoration including the terracotta wyverns and other flourishes on the pediment, a costly option, but one in keeping with the 'highly decorative' style of the Barry Buildings. The War Damage Commission (which was paying for the work), however, insisted on a 'simpler reinstatement' in brick and Portland stone. [178] Gravel was replaced by tarmac in 1955; Dulwich still refers conservatively to the North and the South 'Gravel'. Under Groves the College's second

Swimming Bath (on the same site as the first) and the changing rooms were constructed in 1955. While the builders were at work the boys were taken by bus to swim at the new Crystal Palace Sports Centre. The pool was emptied in the winter months and covered with a wooden floor: this vast space – 'the Baths Hall' – was used for Physical Training, boxing, plays and concerts. Shackleton's boat was moved from the obscurity of the Boiler House to the east end of the Bath in 1957.[179] In the same year, Sir Cyril Hinshelwood, the President of the Royal Society, opened a suite of laboratories in an additional building to the rear of the Science Block, called 'the Science Wing'. The Wing, which was entirely paid for by the Industrial Scientific Fund for Public Schools, was badly needed, and included a room for lectures or films; for all its advanced design, the original Science Block had only eight teaching rooms. *The Alleynian* in 1962 called for the Honours Boards in the Great Hall to be cleaned and brought up to date, although for the time being nothing was done.[180]

Although the Christison Hall, with the kitchens, courtyard and surrounding studios and workshops, was not officially opened until 1969 during Charles Lloyd's Mastership when Prince Philip came to the College for its 350th anniversary, the project was mostly the result of Groves's planning. In 1954 the Alleyn Club voted War Memorial funds to go towards new buildings, and in 1958, when many Old Alleynians were saying that it was a poor show that 13 years after the War no names were commemorated, the Governors proposed a War Memorial Hall. In 1960 an appeal for £100,000 for a new Hall was launched. An impractical early idea had been to extend the Great Hall. A campaign for a Development Fund in 1966 made use of architect's designs for a Computer Centre, dining halls, a new assembly hall, and a bizarre plan to convert the Great Hall into a Library, with carrels and stairway to a gallery.[181] Stephen Hadjucki (left 1968), now an Edinburgh architect and urban designer, made a wonderful drawing, reproduced in *The Alleynian*, showing a fantasy conversion of the Great Hall into a Gothic Revival railway station.[182] The prosaic Commissariat, Music Block and Squash Courts (1963) were the work of Leslie Preston FRIBA (1903–94), an Old Alleynian architect who designed much of the new University of Reading. At first it was proposed to site a Dining Hall and kitchens between the North Block and Dulwich Common.[183] Sir William (later Baron) Holford (1907–75), a recent President of the RIBA, responsible for planning and design of buildings at Whitehall and in Cambridge, advised the Governors to glaze the Cloisters, which was carried out in 1965; this was an idea which Groves had first proposed in 1957. Holford also brutally

urged them to demolish the Memorial Library and replace it with kitchens and a dining hall, traducing this fine building with the comment, 'I have seldom seen so much architecture used to enclose so little space'. The Governors voted unanimously to follow this advice, but mercifully the Old Alleynians successfully opposed the plan.[184] The new Assembly Hall, an enormous concrete box for which designs survive, was to have stood west of Barry's Great Hall, replacing the Buttery, at right angles to the axis of the Barry Buildings; as the young Gavin Stamp (left 1967), soon to become the brightest architectural polemicist in the country, pointed out in an article on the College buildings in *The Alleynian*, this nasty project would ruin the view of the College from the railway.[185] Eventually the Christison Hall, representative of the period's 'brutalist' architectural style, was sited at the far end of the campus, rather like a garden shed.

The curriculum and the College culture

In 1966 a letter to *The Alleynian* complained about the lack of Music, Art and Drama in the curriculum, but the same issue shows that outside the classroom an extraordinarily active culture prevailed.[186] Criticism and protest from 'students' were of course in the air in these stirring times of change; there were some self-lacerating editorials about the identity of the College, and letters in the magazine attacking the school organisation and activities became frequent. In about 1960 two very large white hammer-and-sickle motifs appeared painted on the western outside wall of the top floor of the North Block, the result of some very dangerous witty mischief by boys; though painted out with brick paint by the authorities, the pentimenti of these signs stubbornly resisted suppression for the next 25 years, harbingers and then relics of the political activism of the Sixties that were to make daily life at the College uneasy for the Establishment in Lloyd's era; Groves's only recorded comment at the time, looking up at the North Block, was characteristically humane: "Thank God nobody was killed".

Music at the College, we are told, sometimes might seem to amount to the Football song accompanied by the stamping of feet of dozens of Middle School boys, but there was also fine work in hand, and Professor Westrup returned from Oxford to adjudicate House Music in 1956.[187] In 1957 the chorus at the Royal Festival Hall involved 800 boys and an orchestra of seventy instrumentalists. When the popular Cecil Johnson, who succeeded Stanley Wilson as Director of Music from 1953 until 1957, died suddenly, and after an unsuccessful stay of one year by Laurence Crosthwaite, the brilliant Alan Morgan (1925–2006) was appointed to the post. His utter devotion to music, his energetic performances and his conducting all 'inspired enthusiasm', according to Philip Vellacott. A fine pianist, and a lover of the English choral tradition, the first of his famous Royal Festival Hall Concerts, often with Christopher Field (left 1959) as baritone soloist, took place in 1958, and included a composition, *Petite Suite*, by Peter Fall (left 1959). In 1961 the entire audience at the Festival Hall rose to their feet and applauded his conducting of the dances from Borodin's *Prince Igor*.[188] In 1964 he recorded a 'Long Playing' gramophone record of twelve items with the Madrigal Group. He continued as Director of Music until his retirement in 1986, making Dulwich College music prosperous, and conducting the great traditional choral, orchestral and stage works; many of his pupils made careers in music, and very many Old Alleynians testify that they owe to him their joy in making and listening to music. His farewell concert at the Royal Festival Hall in 1986, including Walton's *Belshazzar's Feast* and Vaughan Williams's *Serenade to Music* (a choral and orchestral setting of Shakespeare's lines from *The Merchant of Venice*, which had special meaning for him) was a truly joyful occasion, attended by many past and present pupils. Alan Morgan, generous to the College with his worldly goods as with his life-spirit, left a legacy for an Alan Morgan Bursary for a talented musician and bequeathed his house to the College.

The record of dramatic performances of the era includes many performances that were manifestly remarkable. Christopher Field played the Duchess of Malfi in 1955; Ian MacKillop played T. S. Eliot's Becket in 1956, in a production by a Sixth-Former, Barry Boys (left 1957), who was himself an exceptionally gifted actor, playing Falstaff and other parts, and was also an excellent critic, writing on Anouilh in *The Alleynian*. Drake won the House Drama Competition twice under his direction, with excerpts from Anouilh's *Antigone*, and Sartre's *Les Mains Sales*. Barry Boys turned down an Exhibition offered by Pembroke College, Cambridge, to study at RADA, and after a while left for the United States for a career as an actor and director, where he has performed a remarkable series of great classical and modern roles and directed serious drama in theatres all over the continent. Simon Brett (left 1964) played Richard II in 1963, later achieving fame as a clever and very popular writer: he is a novelist and script-writer, author, for example, of the television series *After Henry* (starring Prunella Scales). Geoffrey Reeves (left 1958) later became Artistic Director of the Northcott Theatre, Exeter. For a production of *Henry IV, Part I* boys and masters joined forces to transform the entire west window of the Great Hall into a facsimile of stained glass;[189] Alan Morgan composed

music for Vellacott's *Julius Caesar* in 1957. In 1960 Tony Palmer (1916–2005), a cultured Modern Languages teacher at the College from 1950 until 1977, produced Simon Brett and others in *A Midsummer Night's Dream*. The cast list contains many names mentioned in this chronicle for their distinguished later careers, almost all in the Arts. Giles Block (left 1960) is now the textual authority and Master of Verse at Shakespeare's Globe Theatre on Bankside, and directs plays. Andrew Wilton (left 1960), who also designed the forest scenery for the production,[190] is now the world authority on J. M. W. Turner, and was appointed the first Director of the Clore Gallery at Tate Britain. Wilton contributed to *The Alleynian* four sonnets and some striking drawings of a crucifixion and a priest at prayer in 1959 and 1960. *Hamlet*, with music by John Heath (see below), was produced in 1963.

The Revd J. N. F. 'Nick' Earle (b. 1926), in possession of a lively intellect and vocal delivery, and of a Double First in Mathematics and Theology from Cambridge, arrived in 1961. The same year he published a popular Penguin book, *What's Wrong with the Church?* In ten years, before leaving to become Headmaster of Bromsgrove School, he made a strong impact on the College, setting up the earliest computers (with a gift of the first computer from BP),[191] and devising a programme of Liberal Studies, in which teachers offered courses not for examination on one afternoon a week: boys could choose from subjects such as the Queen's Courts, Man and Machines, Philosophy, and Psychology. These courses were informed by Assistant Masters' interests and special knowledge; the intention was in part to bridge the gap between the Arts and Science cultures, then a thriving debate.[192]

E. N. Williams (1917–93), 'Ernie' to the boys and 'Taffy' to the staff, was appointed in 1957 and retired in 1977; with his depth of scholarship and his inspired and disciplined teaching he must count as one of the outstanding History schoolmasters of all time. The famous Sir John Plumb (1911–2001) of Christ's College, Cambridge (with whom Williams had been at school) said that he was 'perhaps the best teacher of his generation', and that 'Oxford and Cambridge colleges competed for the historians he produced at Dulwich, year in and year out'.[193] Master of six languages, while at the College he managed to research, write and publish important books on English and European History, such as *The Eighteenth-Century Constitution* (1960), *Life in Georgian England* (1962), and *The Ancien Régime* (1972), and in retirement he was the author of the *Dictionary of English and European History*, (1980, many times reprinted). Ernie Williams also organised the Sixth-Form Talks; no wonder the boys of this era were so sharp, as in addition to their Sixth-Form classes they heard speakers who included luminaries of the age in many disciplines, among them A. J. Ayer (who visited twice), Richard Crossman, Niklaus Pevsner, Isaiah Berlin, Ernst Gombrich, Gordon Russell, and Cleanth Brooks. *The Alleynian* published an interview between Ayer and two boys after one of his talks. [194]

This was a time when both *The Alleynian* and the boys' societies reached perhaps the zenith of their prosperity. The latter were combined in 1964 into a 'Union' to administer them, as Michael Rich had proposed as early as 1956 (four years after he actually left the College) in a letter to *The Alleynian*. [195] The 'Union' had been in fact a feature of Carver's day (see Chapter Six), but it now was revived as a powerful force and with its own committee and a popular master as President, and it held amusing open meetings. The society meetings and excursions in which the boys of this generation took part were extraordinarily rich, particularly when one thinks of the time they and their masters devoted to their academic work: the Mermaid Society (see above) prospered, and at the History Society both masters and boys would deliver papers for discussion, for example when Ernie Williams spoke about his research into the eighteenth-century middle classes. At one point there were five separate societies for literature and drama, including the influential Twentieth-Century Play Society (see above). A boys' Film Unit in 1956 made a documentary about the Hollington Club, *Somewhere to Go*, which contrasted a boy's life before and after joining the Club. [196] In 1955 it was feared that the Societies would perpetuate the split in English education and life between 'the two cultures' of the Arts and Science; four years later in 1959 when C. P. Snow (1905–80), the celebrated writer and scientist who famously diagnosed the problem, addressed the boys, the magazine referred to this as a 'dangerous' schism within the College. [197] In 1958 *The Alleynian* reported a decline in the Societies; at the same time a decline in the quality of contributions to the magazine was noted by a correspondent. [198] At the Debating Society boys made speeches who later made a living with their tongues and pens, such as Alastair Niven OBE (left 1963; see below) and P. A. J. Woods (left 1963), a solicitor and the author (as 'Anthony Paul') of *Wolf on the Mountain* (2007); [199] Eddie George (see below) made a patriotic speech. The Gallery Club visited *Beyond the Fringe* and the best of West End productions of drama, and wrote reviews of them in *The Alleynian*. The satiric magazine *Private Eye*, founded in 1961 by a group of clever young men from Shrewsbury School, was plainly a cult periodical among the boys, stimulating mockery and rebellion, and the Library subscription to it was to become an occasion of friction for Charles Lloyd in the challenging days of the Sixth Form Forum (see below).

The Alleynian in the 1960s was a serious magazine, including boys' editorials on co-education or the threat of nuclear armament; there was also an article on McCarthyism. Eddie George reported on Rugby matches and Scout troops, and reviewed *The Messiah*. [200] Among the literary contributions to *The Alleynian* of this period are to be found poems by Simon Brett written from his early days at the College and throughout his school career, and the sardonic stories he wrote in the Upper School; there is also a fine poem by Graham Swift (left 1966; see below), 'A Fish out of Water', that might not be out of place in his masterpiece *Waterland* (1983). [201] In the issues of the magazine in its heyday are also the first publications of David Thomson (left 1959), the brilliant film critic and historian, author of the *Biographical Dictionary of Film* (1970 &c.), who wrote on James Dean and Ingmar Bergman in 1959, and on Hitchcock in 1960. [202] John Newman (left 1955), active in the Classics Society, and who became a noted architectural writer and the Deputy Director of the Courtauld Institute, wrote on City churches and other buildings. Gavin Stamp contributed memorable articles on the architecture of the Dulwich Estate and of the railways crossing it, illustrated with his own drawings. [203]

As with the literary contributions of all school magazines, one can too often tell the famous poems that writers have been studying that month, but there is still much power and originality. An Old Alleynian wrote in to say how 'dismal and obscure' the writing was, which surely delighted the writers. Two years later a correspondent remarked the magazine's 'dangerously esoteric intellectualism'. [204] In 1959 the magazine was given an improved heraldic cover, white lines against cornflower blue, by the art master, Michael Preston (at the College 1955–64).

The literary culture of those days, inspired by the new style of English teaching under Jim Gibson and Raymond Wilson, by the literary societies, and by the professional standards expected of contributors to *The Alleynian*, placed an emulative value on individual composition; although outsiders might be irritated by the young Hamlets of the North Block, the real sophistication of many of the 'English' boys was equal, perhaps, to the days of clever young courtiers and lawyers in Renaissance London; from this era the successful novelists from the College are well known (see below), but the fine poets are less famous. No other school in Britain can claim to have produced three of the names that dominated the Cambridge school of poetry in the 1960s and 1970s.

In the early 1950s Jon Silkin (1930–97), cousin of the more famous political Sam and John (see Chapter Nine), and of the third generation of a Jewish immigrant family, was making a name for himself as a poet and editor of

Stand poetry magazine (declaring a stand against the social, moral and artistic apathy of his day), which he founded in 1952. Left-wing, and never at ease at the College, he was eventually expelled for his truancies, which he spent reading and writing poetry; after serving in the Army Education Corps for his National Service, he lived on London streets, tending graveyards and lavatories for a living. His subjects and his style were both traditional and political, concerned with suffering and growth, with outrage at cruelty; his inspirations included Wilfred Owen, Isaac Rosenberg, D. H. Lawrence, the Bible and Jewish history. His most famous poem is 'Death of a Son' from *The Peaceable Kingdom* (1954). Later Silkin studied at the University of Leeds and was awarded the Gregory Fellowship in Poetry, in a particularly fertile poetic decade; in the few years before his death he twice returned to Dulwich College, invited by Jonathan Ward, the Head of English (and himself a poet and an inspired teacher of creative writing), to give readings of his poems and to talk to English classes. Anthony Barnett (left 1958), poet, translator of poems, and editor, published the new Cambridge poets; a collection of his own poems, *The Resting Bell*, was published in 1987. Andrew Crozier (left 1961), a major figure in the avant-garde Cambridge poetry movement, founded the Ferry Press and the influential journal *The English Intelligencer*. He taught at both the University of Keele and at the University of Sussex, where he became Professor of Literature. Impressed and influenced by contemporary verse in the United States, particularly the Black Mountain College group, he brought their work to the attention of other young poets who found contemporary British poetry pusillanimous; his own collection, *All Where Each Is*, was published by Anthony Barnett's press in 1985. In 1987 Crozier's anthology, *A Various Art*, included poems by Nick Totton (left 1965), whose talent was early recognised by his teachers: from the age of 14 he had nine poems published in *The Alleynian*. Now a psychotherapist by profession, he has published *Press when Illuminated: New and Selected Poems, 1958–2003*. Invited by Ian Brinton, at one time Head of English at the College, to return to the school, he gave the first reading he had allowed himself for ten years. John Freeman (left 1964), whose career might be said to have been inspired and defined by Norman Howlings reading Keats's 'Ode to Autumn' to his class, is another Cambridge English graduate of this era, who now teaches English and Creative Writing at the University of Cardiff, and since 1975 has published a number of collections of his disciplined, meditative free verse, including *A Vase of Honesty* (1976), *The Light is of Love, I Think* (1997) and *Landscape with Portraits* (1999); he gave readings of his poems in recent years at a Dulwich College Literary Festival (see below).

Two Alleynian novelists from this period have won the Booker Prize: Michael Ondaatje (left 1962) and Graham Swift. Nobody seems to have realised the potential as a writer of Michael Ondaatje, from Sri Lanka; the *Alleynian* report for the Third XI in 1962, on the other hand, mentions him as 'a wicket keeper who scored a six each match and contributed most to funds'. [205] Ondaatje studied in Canada, settling in Toronto, where he became a lecturer, an editor of literary magazines and a poet, as well as a novelist; he is best known for *The English Patient* (1992), the film version of which won nine Oscars. Swift, on the other hand, was marked for a writer in his schooldays, his teacher Laurie Jagger, to whose inspiration he has freely paid tribute, writing on his final report card in 1966 of the 'most unusual maturity in his written work', and commending his economical style. Graham Swift won an Exhibition at Queen's College, Cambridge, in English in 1967; *Last Orders* won the Booker Prize in 1996.

The Common Room

When G. W. R. Treadgold, the fearsome 'Treadie' (1893–1981), retired in 1954 (the year that Ronald Groves was appointed) 78 years of a Treadgold teaching at Dulwich College – father (see Chapter Nine) and son – came to an end. His departure marked, perhaps, the end of an outmoded view of education: the boys were later grateful to him for their well-drilled Latin, but his method was fear and punishment. A Classics scholar at Keble College, Oxford, he joined the staff after three years at St Paul's in 1922, and quickly established a reputation for harsh discipline and tantrums. If you made three mistakes in his School Certificate tests, you had to attend his celebrated 'Tea Party': a detention after school for the boys (without refreshments), while he sat being served with tea and cakes. On the last day of his career he kept in his entire form in this way. It is also recorded that he visited a pupil in hospital daily to read to him.

C. D. A. Baggley (1923–99), who left in 1957, was a formidable and meticulous Head of History, whose forms consistently gained an extraordinary number of awards; he left to become Headmaster of King Edward VI Grammar School at Louth, and then of Bolton Grammar School, elected Chairman of the Headmasters' Conference in 1959; he later had a hand in developing the Assisted Places scheme. Alan Cooper, Head of Mathematics from 1956 until 1966, and (himself an Oxford 'Blue') Master in charge of Rugby from 1963, left to become Headmaster of the King's School in Macclesfield. S.A. 'Sam' Cole served from 1945 until 1976 as

Head of Biology and Master in charge of the First XV; he was President of the Common Room from 1970 until 1973. Michael Hart, as noted above, had been a conspicuous schoolboy at the College, when he had been Captain of Spenser, an actor, and President of the Literary and Debating Societies, and was also officially dubbed 'Head of the Science Side'; he was already known for his 'caustic wit'.[206] Returning in 1955 to teach Physics at the College for 31 years, to take charge of Athletics and to serve as Housemaster of Sidney for many years, this forceful intellect and eloquent provoker of debate was a formidable influence on boys and masters, and was much respected by both; the corridors of the Science Block would echo to Hart's diatribes, including such widely repeated sayings as "I am not paid to be kind", or "If you are the cream, God help the milk!"

In 1956 Peter Rees was appointed, from the Instructor Branch of the Royal Navy, to serve 35 years as a schoolmaster of naval rectitude, a man as honourable as a schoolmaster might aim to be, who, after serving as Head of Chemistry and Head of Science in turn, was promoted to Deputy Master in 1989. Rees commanded the Naval Section of the CCF, and was also Commanding Officer of the Royal Naval Reserve, London Division, ADC to Her Majesty the Queen for a year in 1978, and Deputy Lieutenant for London.

Also appointed in 1956 was the Oxonian Classics master John Heath, whose contribution to the musical and cultural life of the College was exceptional, and who retired in 1988. A pianist of genuine distinction, a composer of songs from the English poets and of choral works, with his fine ear he was also master of the spoken and written word. His recitals in Assembly, performances of three or four Scarlatti sonatas, for example, would quell and still even the most restless of boys, and his spoken introductions to the pieces inspired awe among the Assistant Masters for their originality and subtlety. Whether teaching his habitual form in the Lower School, 2B, or upper Classical forms, he communicated his pleasure in exactness and in metaphor and his sharp metaphysical wit; he was also generous in his relations with many in the Common Room. The encyclopaedic (and, some might say, eccentric) History teacher Mark Whittaker was appointed in 1960 and retired in 1991, a quiet inspiration to several generations of meticulous historians with his methods and habits of mind. A veteran pedestrian and cyclist, familiar with the neglected byways of England's landscape, he also counts music as among his passions.

David Knight (1920–99), a splendid sportsman at school (left 1939), was another Alleynian who returned to teach at the College after Cambridge. When he volunteered to join the Army on leaving school, a medical examination revealed to his total surprise that he was diabetic. Spotted attending a cricket match, he was invited by Christopher Gilkes to come 'for a term or so', and stayed to serve his Alma Mater from 1942 until 1980. Housemaster of Drake for 25 years and a happy Housemaster of Bell House for twelve, he was also a very good Head of the Middle School – never an easy post – for five years after Stephen Howard was promoted to Second Master (see below). The College published a memoir of his days as boy and master, DVK, Dulwich Man (1987). His son Roger (left 1966), was also to teach at the College from 1978 until 1983 (for the two terms of the year when he was not fully occupied as Captain of the Surrey XI), and was appointed by David Emms to be in charge of Rugby. He left to become a Housemaster at Cranleigh and subsequently Headmaster of Worksop College, later serving as Secretary and Chief Executive of the MCC (until 2006); he is now a College Governor. Two men who were to become Housemasters were appointed in 1952: Brian Jones, the biologist, teacher of many now in the medical profession; and John Llewellyn, the mathematician, who followed him at Blew House. Basil Cridland, appointed in 1957, taught Chemistry; a superb administrator, he was Examinations Officer for many years. He was also a highly conscientious and kindly President of the Common Room from 1973 until 1976; on retirement in 1983 he bought a nursery garden and brought flowers and other produce for sale at the Masters' Coffee Room for many years. John Dewes, appointed in 1963 and leaving in 1987, taught Geography and was Careers Master; he was a formidable sportsman, an excellent player of Hockey and especially of cricket: the opening batsman for the Cambridge XI, he went on to play for Middlesex and then for England, taking part in five test matches. T. J. Walsh was appointed in 1954 to teach Latin and History, a modest start to a famous and distinguished Dulwich career. Housemaster of The Orchard from 1968 until 1978, he was appointed Head of the Lower School in 1969, and as Major and then Lieutenant-Colonel T. J. Walsh was also a long-serving Commanding Officer of the CCF from 1964–78. On the death of Stephen Howard he took up the post of Deputy Master from 1978 until his retirement in 1989. Supremely possessed of what Tony Verity (see below) described as the 'Alleynian cast of mind',[207] and holding aloft the flame of tradition at the College for over fifty years, Terry Walsh was Secretary of the Alleyn Club from 1989 until 2002, and from 1989 until 2003 was the Director of the Bursary Appeal, raising £2.6 million. With his phenomenal memory and his utter devotion to the College, its staff and its sons, he continues a worthy Christison of our day.

W. C. Crowther.
(Dulwich College)

The Combined Cadet Force

Groves told parents that it was the 'public duty' of boys to belong either to the Scouts or the Combined Cadet Force,[208] and both institutions flourished under him; Groves disapproved of the 300-odd boys who still took no part. Major W. C. 'Wilf' Crowther (1885–1962) had been from 1922 until 1930 the Commanding Officer of the Officers Training Corps, a very popular and individual teacher of Biology and Botany, with a menagerie of pet snakes and alligators; he was Head of Biology for 35 years, retiring from teaching in 1945. Major H. M. Morris took over the command from Crowther in 1930, and was followed by Major H. J. Dixon (see Chapter Nine) in 1933, Major C. R. W. Jenkins in 1934, Major E. Lax (see Chapter Nine) in 1936, Major E. G. R. Heeley (see above) in 1946, and Lieutenant-Colonel P. R. Thomas in 1949. The Junior Training Corps (established in 1942), was combined with the Air Training Corps and the Sea Cadets to form the Combined Cadet Force in 1950. A. M. 'Paul' Pennington (1906–98), who taught English

and History from 1929 until 1950, had been in command of the Sea Cadets. A victim of polio in his youth, he nonetheless founded, with Alick Hamilton, both the wartime Farming Camps and the Sea Cadets, for the first time introducing sailing as a recreation. Voluntary Service was fostered by the excellent Douglas Hillier (1917–2003), who followed Crowther as Head of Biology and built up a strong medical and biological tradition, developing trial Nuffield courses in Biology at the College; he was also an excellent sportsman and preacher, and left to train Science teachers at the University of Cardiff. E. W. Tapper (1905–83) – 'Bill' to his colleagues, 'Ernie' to boys – who joined the College in 1930, expanded the Physics and Engineering Department, teaching the boys the very latest developments in radar, and designing the extension to the Science Block described above. He became Head of Science and was Housemaster of Bell House from 1947 to 1957. On retirement he became the first paid Secretary of the Science Masters' Association, for which duties he was awarded the OBE.

The Hollington Club and 'The Teen Canteen'

In 1954 the College Mission attracted articles in the Press for its admirable venture of opening 'The Teen Canteen', twenty yards away from the Elephant and Castle. This was a 'milk bar', open to 15- to 20-year-old local 'Teddy boys' and girls, who had to be members to be allowed in. The Canteen's aim was to keep its clientele away from boredom, drunkenness and trouble; it attracted from thirty to forty local young people a night. It was open from 6 to 10 p.m.; not oppressively 'respectable', it was furnished with a neon sign and – that emblem of the age – a jukebox, and decorated in a 'Festival of Britain' style, with murals, bright colours, low-hanging lanterns and a front window full of indoor plants; in the basement was a dance-floor. It was run by a boxing champion and ex-naval Physical Training Instructor, and continued, highly successfully, until 1959, when it was sold to the Red Cross. [209]

Alleynians

A number of Alleynians of this era have already been mentioned. Khun Anand Panyarachun (b. 1932) who was at the College from 1948 to 1951, studied Law at Trinity College, Cambridge, and was then for 23 years in the Thai Foreign Service, appointed Ambassador to the United Nations; he was twice Prime Minister of Thailand, once in 1991–2 after a military coup, and again in 1992. He drafted a constitution for his country, and instituted admirable economic and democratic reforms. He was later Chairman of the Saha-Union Corporation until 2002, and Chairman of the United Nations Ethics Committee. He is an Honorary International Adviser to the College Governors. Peter Lilley (left 1961) rose to become a prominent and influential member of the Conservative Party: Secretary of State for Trade and Industry in 1990, Secretary of State for Social Security in 1992, Shadow Chancellor 1997–8, and Deputy Leader of the Conservative Party in 1998–9. An earlier distinguished Alleynian politician was Sir John Hunt (left 1948), at one time Conservative MP for Bromley, who represented the United Kingdom at the Council of Europe and the Western European Union from 1973 until 1997. Lord Norman Warner (left 1958), Director of Social Services for Kent and Chairman of the Youth Justice Board served as a junior Health Minister under Tony Blair, and John Spellar MP (left 1965) as a junior Defence Minister.

E. A. J. George, 'Steady Eddie', Lord George of St Tudy PC (left 1957), gave generously to the College in his schooldays as a sportsman and as Patrol Leader of the Senior Scout Troop. After studying Economics at Cambridge, he worked for the Bank of England, and was to become a household name as the greatly admired and respected Governor of the Bank for ten years from 1993.

He became a Governor of the College in 1998, and since 2003 has been Chairman of the Board. Roy Amlot QC (left 1960), reported as a schoolboy to have been driven by a sense of fairness and truth, rose early in his career to be the leading Treasury Counsel, and in 1987 was appointed First Senior Prosecuting Counsel at the Central Criminal Court, with some famous causes and inquiries to his credit. He was Chairman of the Bar Council in 2001, and from 1990 was a College Governor. Sir Robert Clarke (left 1947) played in the famously undefeated First XV of 1946 and studied at Pembroke College, Oxford, of which he is now a Fellow; in turn Chairman of United Biscuits and of Thames Water, he served with brio as Chairman of the Dulwich College Bursary Appeal. Ian Hay Davison CBE (left 1949) is a famous financial watchdog, commissioned at one point to police Lloyd's of London, which resulted in sixty convictions. He is the author of *Lloyd's: A View of the Room: Change and Disclosure* (1987). Sir John Ritblat (left 1952) founded Conrad Ritblat & Co., the property firm, and from 1971 until 2006 served as Chairman and Managing Director of British Land; he is a well-known benefactor and member of committees for the Arts, especially honoured at the British Library, the Wallace Collection and the Tate Gallery. He is also Chairman of the British Ski Foundation, and in 2003 he became a College Governor. Alan Brookes (left 1959), who was chosen to be a member of the College First XV at a young age, has interests in property, and is a major benefactor of the College Bursary Appeal. Stewart Till (left 1969) was Chief Executive and Chairman of United Artists International Pictures and Chairman of the United Kingdom Film Council; he is currently Chairman of Millwall Football Club and a College Governor. Lord Iain Vallance of Tummel (left 1958) was Chairman and Chief Executive of British Telecom. Tim Franey (left 1964) is a very successful industrialist, and a most generous benefactor of the College. John Lovering (left 1968) is the Chairman of Debenhams and of Somerfield Ltd., and a Vice-chairman of Barclays Capital. Mark Coombs, who played in the First XV and left for Cambridge with an award to read Geography in 1978, is Chairman and Chief Executive Officer of Ashmore Securities. Edward Dolman, who left in 1979, was a splendid Rugby player at the College, a member of the First XV in 1977 and Captain in 1978, and played in teams after he left the College (see Chapter Twelve); he is now the Chief Executive of Christie's International plc.

Law was a natural choice of career for quick-witted boys from Upper School classrooms. The Walton brothers both became QCs: Sir Raymond, a High Court Judge, had been elected President of the Oxford University Union in 1939; Anthony Michael Walton had achieved the same accolade in 1944. Sir Colin Rimer (left 1962) and Sir Nicholas Wall PC (left 1963) are Lord Justices of Appeal; Michael Rich (left 1952), Timothy Ellison-Nash (left 1957), Anthony Ansell (left 1964), and Andrew Goymer (left 1965) are Circuit Judges; and Sir Gavin Lightman (left 1958) is a High Court Judge. Roy Amlot QC is mentioned above. James Lingard (left 1953) is a solicitor pre-eminent in Banking Law and Insolvency; C. S. Porteous (left 1954) is Solicitor to the Commissioner of the Metropolitan Police; Richard Plender (left 1964), a barrister, has many publications.

Of the many Old Alleynians in Her Majesty's Armed Forces, two deserve special mention for their particular loyalty to the College, and both are well known to the Alleyn Club as eminent Presidents. Air Commodore Owen Truelove (1937–2006; left 1956), a proud 'Gilkes boy' as he used to say, won the Sword of Honour as a cadet at the RAF Technical College at Henlow, and became Director of Air Engineering at the Ministry of Defence. In 2005, at the age of 68, he flew his glider from his home in Cornwall to New Zealand for charities, including the College Bursary Appeal. Truelove and his son died in a tragic gliding accident during a race in New Zealand the following year. In 1961 Lieutenant-General Sir Peter Duffell KCB, CBE, MC (left 1956), then a young Lieutenant training in Borneo with ten men from the First Battalion of the Second King Edward VII Own Gurkha Rifles, broke the record for the ascent of Mount Kinabalu, one of the very highest mountains in South East Asia, by 53 minutes. Among many other eminent servicemen must be counted Colonel A. 'Tony' Hunter-Choat (left 1952) OBE, famous as a distinguished member of the British Section of the French Foreign Legion; and Air Chief Marshal Sir John Willis (left 1954), who was Vice-Chief of the Defence Staff from 1995 until 1997.

No less distinguished was Dulwich College's contribution to the academic professions in these years. A veteran of Gilkes's days, Peter Branscomb (left 1948) is Emeritus Professor of Austrian Studies at the University of St Andrews, and is also a notable authority on Music. Ewan Anderson (left 1956), the holder of three doctorates and the author of books on Geography and Education, was Professor of Geopolitics at Durham (1995–2001); he is also a specialist adviser to independent schools. Two remarkable mathematicians were Cambridge Wranglers (i.e., First-Class graduates of the Maths Tripos) and went on to undertake significant research and to gain teaching posts at universities: Professor Christopher Lance (left 1959) at Leeds, and George Reid (left 1959), who became a Governor of Dulwich College, at St John's College, Cambridge. John Mason (left 1959) is Emeritus Professor of Mathematics at the University of Huddersfield, and

Nigel Kalton (left 1964), a world leader in the field of the geometry of Banach Spaces, is Professor of Mathematics at the University of Columbia. Two boys from the Mathematics forms who left in 1961 are D. R. J. Chillingworth, who is Senior Lecturer at the University of Southampton, and Joe Stoy, originally a physicist and a Fellow of Balliol College, Oxford, who is now a computer scientist.

Professor Brian Gibbons (left 1956) taught at York where he devised and taught a Shakespeare course with drama workshops, subsequently holding Chairs in English at Leeds, Zürich, and Münster. An authority on Renaissance drama (who dedicated his first publication to Laurie Jagger), he has written two lively, original books on the period; a brilliant editor, he was largely responsible for The New Mermaid Drama series and The New Cambridge Shakespeare, writing a magnificent introduction in his Arden edition of Romeo and Juliet (1980). The first publications of John Barrell (left 1961) were a poem, and an essay on Turgenev, in The Alleynian; [210] with a discursive mind ranging over the literature, painting, sociology and politics of the turn of the eighteenth and nineteenth centuries, and a special interest in John Clare and De Quincey, his books have included The Idea of Landscape (1972) and The Dark Side of the Landscape (1980). Barrell was to become an admired don at King's College, Cambridge, and is now Emeritus Professor at the University of York. Jeremy Tambling (left 1966), Professor of Comparative Literature at the University of Hong Kong (1988–2006), now Professor of Literature at Manchester, has wide interests, particularly in Victorian literature, Dante and critical theory, Opera and Film, and has published on Blake, Dickens, and Henry James.

The three Niven brothers, sons of a City of London Police Officer, all achieved entries in Who's Who. Peter (left 1956) is a Consultant Obstetrician and Gynaecologist at the United Bristol Hospitals. Colin (left 1960), the Captain of School, paid the College the ultimate compliment in his final term by announcing that he wanted to teach; after joining the staff at Fettes and serving as Head of Modern Languages at Sherborne, he was first appointed Headmaster of the Island School, Hong Kong, and then of St George's English School in Rome, returning, a loyal Foundation man, to become Headmaster of Alleyn's School from 1992 until 2002, when he was appointed Headmaster of Dulwich International College in Shanghai (see Chapter Twelve) and Master of Dulwich International Colleges in China. Alastair (left 1963), a formidable debater at school, became Director of Literature at the British Council and at the Arts Council, expert in Commonwealth Literature; he is now Principal of the King George VI and Queen Elizabeth Foundation of St Catharine's, Cumberland Lodge. Gavin Armstrong (left 1960), Colin Niven's Vice-Captain of School, became Headmaster of Hutton Church of England Grammar School, Preston.

Christopher Field JP, ARAM, a musician of legendary ability at school as well as an accomplished actor, won a Choral exhibition to Trinity College, Cambridge, in 1959. Another loyal Foundation man, he returned to the College to teach Music and Chemistry in 1969, and was by turns Head of the Lower School from 1978, Deputy Master from 1991 until 2000, and Acting Master for 14 months in November 1995. He was also President of the Common Room from 1976 until 1979, and a very committed Group Scout Leader (taking over from John Cottle: see below) from 1982 until 2000. Arriving at the Edward Alleyn Theatre one evening to take part in a staff revue, fresh from presiding over a Magistrate's Court, he stripped off his formal suit, shirt and tie to reveal the tattoos he had drawn in make-up on his torso and arms in preparation for his performance as one of Noël Coward's 'Three Juvenile Delinquents'; his final theatrical flourish, in his last term as Deputy Master at the College in Graham Able's era, was to play the Pirate King in Gilbert and Sullivan's *Pirates of Penzance*.

Dulwich College's long musical tradition – as old as the Founder himself – has been variously honoured. Professor Alan Hacker (left 1955) of the Royal Academy of Music is a distinguished clarinettist; Anthony Payne (left 1955), a prolific composer and musicologist, put together Elgar's posthumous Third Symphony from the composer's notes, which was then performed by the BBC Symphony Orchestra under Andrew Davis to great acclaim in 1998. David Greer (left 1955) studied under Jack Westrup at Oxford, and became Professor of Music and Head of the Department at the University of Durham from 1986 until 2001. Clifford Hughes (left 1956), a sensitive light tenor, sang professionally in Scotland and entered the Church. Phil Manzanera of Roxy Music (left 1969; Targett-Adams at school, later adopting his Colombian mother's surname), who was Captain of Blew House and of swimming and in general a fine sportsman at school, is now a world-famous guitarist; his brother Eugene (left 1962) was Captain of School. Later prominent musicians include Andrew Watkinson (left 1970) the violinist and Leader of the Endellion Quartet (founded 1979); Graeme Jenkins (left 1977), Musical Director of the Dallas Opera, who has an international reputation for conducting operas in several continents; and Paul Brough (left 1981) who is conductor of the Hanover Band.

Of churchmen, two belong strictly to the previous Chapter: Kenneth Evans (1915–2007, left 1934) was Bishop of Dorking from 1968 until 1985 and a College Governor from 1971; Peter Baelz (1923–2000, left 1941),

a tennis 'Blue' at Cambridge, was a conscientious objector during the War while his two elder brothers (of whom Robert was Captain of School in 1937) served in the RAF; he became Regius Professor of Moral and Pastoral Theology at Oxford and Dean of Durham (1980–88); Alan Warren (left 1950) is Provost Emeritus of Leicester, and his brother Norman Warren (left 1953) was Archdeacon of Rochester; both compose choral music. Wesley Carr (left 1960), first Dean of Bristol and then Dean of Westminster until 2006, was a College Governor until recently.

Alleynians have achieved distinction in a wide variety of fields. Raymond Keene OBE (left 1966) was obsessed with Chess as a schoolboy and was the first schoolboy player with the Under-21 team for England. He went on to defeat Botvinnik in 1967 and to become British Chess Champion in 1971, playing Board One for England in Olympiads; he has the great distinction of being a Grand Master since 1976. The author of over a hundred books on the game, he writes Chess columns in the *Spectator*, *The Times* and the *International Herald Tribune*. Each Founder's Day since 1990 he has returned to play forty boards of simultaneous Chess against the boys. Peter Oosterhuis (left 1967), at 18 was the Captain of the England boys' golf team and was selected for the Walker Cup team while still at the College. Later a professional Golf player, he was for ten years from 1971 a member of the Ryder Cup team.

Derek Waring (1927–2007; at school called Barton-Chapple) joined a repertory company and recorded commentaries for documentary films; later, acting heroic roles at the Shakespeare Theatre at Stratford-upon-Avon (and appearing in *Z-Cars*), he married the actress Dorothy Tutin; together they performed as Victoria and Albert in *Portrait of a Queen* (1965). Derek's brother Richard Waring (1925–1994), also an actor, joined the BBC and wrote lyrics and sketches for cabaret. Bob Monkhouse (1928–2003), a national figure in the world of entertainment, was an accomplished cartoonist at the College, winning the Melton Fisher Art Prize; he left in 1945 to begin his career by working at first as a stand-up comedian and a cartoon animator. In 1952 he and his friend from the boarding house, Dennis Goodwin (1929–1975), became the script-writers for *Calling All Forces*, a BBC 'top variety show', as *The Alleynian* reported to its readers.[211] David Drummond left in 1946, and after studying at RADA acted in the Granada TV *Biggles* series and toured in many plays; taking a stall in Camden Passage in 1961, he later became a prominent and expert dealer in theatrical memorabilia. His brother William (left 1947), a dealer with a fine eye for watercolours, for many years ran the prestigious annual Watercolours and Drawings Fair in London.

Robert Smith (left 1953) as well as his work as Executive Director for the United Kingdom Committee of UNESCO, for which he was awarded the CMG, is a man of the theatre. Derek Goldby (left 1958) directed the original production of *Rosencrantz and Guildenstern Are Dead* for the National Theatre, as well as on Broadway. He has worked as a director in the United States, Canada and throughout Europe. Paul Mayersberg (left 1959), the Film Critic for *New Society*, wrote *Hollywood: The Haunted House* (1967) and was the co-writer of the script for *The Man who Fell to Earth* (1976). Colin Everard (left 1948), an authority on airports and flight safety, worked for 40 years in Africa and other developing countries; also a writer, he has published *The Guardian Angel* (1996) and a novel set in Bhutan, *Safe Skies* (2005). David Wilson (left 1955) is a prolific writer of novels and plays for children. Nigel Hinton (left 1960) is the author of many popular children's books, including the Beaver Towers series. Tony Sloman (left 1963) is a film director, and was Governor of the British Film Institute. Paul Joyce (left 1959), a photographer and freelance writer, has made film biographies and documentaries. Brian Curtois (left 1954), a boarder sent by Southend-on-Sea, was the BBC Westminster Correspondent. Peter Riddell (left 1966) is the much respected Political Correspondent of *The Times*.

Bob Monkhouse, programme cover for the 'Corps Shout', 1945. (Dulwich College)

Among scientists and mathematicians, Bruce Smith CBE (left 1958), a Physicist, worked with NASA to put a man on the moon, before returning to this country to become Chairman of the Smith Institute for Industrial Mechanics and System Engineering. Dr John Ockendon FRS (left 1958) of St Catherine's College, Oxford, teaches at the Mathematical Institute. The many distinguished medical Old Alleynians include John Pendower (left 1944), the former Dean of the Charing Cross and Westminster Medical School; Cedric Prys-Roberts (left 1953), Professor of Anaesthesia at Bristol University; and David Harvey (left 1955), Professor of Pediatrics and Neonatal Medicine at Imperial College. Professor Hugh Tunstall-Pedoe (left 1958), at Dundee University, for many years, researched cardiac illness; his twin brother Dan, another cardiac specialist, was adviser to the London Marathon from its beginning. George Brownlee (left 1960) is Abraham Professor of Chemical Pathology at Oxford and a Fellow of Lincoln College; Christopher Stephens (left 1960) is Professor of Child Dental Health at the University of Bristol; Professor Andrew Tomkins (left 1961) is Director of the Centre for International Child Health, University of London; Surgeon Rear Admiral Ralph Curr (left 1962) is the Medical Director General (Naval) at the Ministry of Defence; Professor M. W. Eysenck (left 1962) is Professor of Psychology at Royal Holloway, University of London; John Price (left 1963) is Consultant Pediatrician at King's College Hospital. Professor Robert Michell (left 1958), a veterinarian, is Emeritus Professor of Biochemistry at the University of Birmingham; Professor Karol Sikora (left 1965), the oncologist, is Dean of the Medical School at the University of Buckingham.

Chaplains

Chaplains officiate at services and assemblies and exercise their pastoral duties; at Dulwich, in a school of predominantly day-boys, they also contribute much to the classroom teaching. Canon Roy McKay, who served from 1937 until 1942 became Head of Religious Broadcasting at the BBC. The Revd T. H. Ward-Hill, author of Mathematics textbooks, appointed in 1951, was succeeded by Revd John Boxley in 1962 and by the Revd Tom Farrell in 1974; the latter, an evangelical sportsman, was popular with the boys partly because he had been Captain of the British Athletics Team. The Revd Linford Smith served from 1981, and was followed by the Revd Tony Edwards in 1991. The Revd Jonathan Winter was appointed in 1995, followed by the Ven. Canon Robin Turner OA (see above) in 1998, and by the Revd Dr Stephen Young in 2002.

*

CHARLES LLOYD, 1967–75 – The end of the Free Places – The Governors – The curriculum; Awards at Oxford and Cambridge – Buildings; the Chapel – The Common Room – The Union, music, the CCF, Voluntary Service and the Scouts – The Picture Gallery – Alleynians

Charles Lloyd, 1967–75

When Ronald Groves resigned, the steady and amiable George Way was appointed Acting Master, as has been mentioned above; his Acting Deputy Master was Philip Thomas (1916–99), Head of Geography and House-master of Ivyholme, appointed in 1946. Thomas was to serve as Deputy Master from 1970 until his retirement in 1976.

The Master chosen by the Governors to succeed Groves was Charles Lloyd JP (1915–1999). The Head Boy of St Olave's School, and thus a beneficiary of Edward Alleyn, Lloyd was to requite the Founder by serving as Headmaster of Alleyn's School and the Master of Dulwich College. A graduate in History and Geography from Emmanuel College, Cambridge, he served with the Royal Artillery during the War. From 1944–5 he was on the staff of Supreme Headquarters Allied Expeditionary Force in Europe, involved in operations using captured German V1 and V2 rockets that advanced rocket technology and eventually propelled the spaceship programme in the United States; for this work he was Mentioned in Despatches. After teaching History at Gresham's School, Holt, from 1946 until 1951, he was Headmaster of Hutton Church of England Grammar School at Preston for twelve years, increasing the roll from 350 to 500 boys and raising its academic standing to the first rate, before returning to his native South-East London as Headmaster of Alleyn's School for three years in 1963. Shawcross gave him 24 hours to make up his mind whether to accept the post of Master of Dulwich College. Charles Lloyd's promotion to the College was said to be much resented by his staff at Alleyn's, a healthy sign.[212] He announced to the Alleyn Club at the Dinner of 1967 that he was interested in the ordinary boy as well as the outstanding boy.[213]

The main physical event of Charles Lloyd's nine years at the College was the opening of the Christison Hall.

John Ward RA, *Charles Lloyd*, 1975. Dulwich College. (© Estate of John Ward)

The academic life of the school was to be affected by the end of the Local Education Authorities awards and the introduction of the Assisted Places Scheme, changing the College in his day from a school of two-thirds 'free-placers' to a school where two-thirds of the boys had their fees paid by their parents. The curriculum became more broad and liberal. In the 1950s until the mid-1960s an 'accelerated course' was successfully introduced again, allowing bright boys to take their Ordinary Level examinations a year early; in some cases they took the examinations two years early if they had been 'accelerated' at primary school, and had entered the College at ten rather than eleven years old.

With dignity and a fairly light touch Charles Lloyd took the brunt of the 'student movement' of the day. Partly through the discussions in the Sixth Form Forum, founded in Lloyd's day and chaired by a lively young Philosophy teacher, Peter Collins (at the College 1966–71), some reforms which improved the daily life of the boys took place; Sixth-Formers expected to have more of a say in their schooling. The boys on Council free places possessed questioning, challenging minds which made them very rewarding to teach. The obverse of their intellectual brilliance was that some could be prickly and rude, while others hid behind an 'I defy-you-to-teach-me' persona. Clamour for change and, in particular, for 'school democracy' was in the air, and on Monday break-times Lloyd and Philip Thomas would visit the Sixth Form Centre to face boys demanding the end of roll-calls and of Christian assemblies, an end to compulsory sports, the abolition of rules about uniform and haircuts, and an end to vetoes (or censorship) of play productions and of articles in *The Alleynian*; they demanded to smoke. [214] Student iconoclasm, malaise, and disillusionment spawned spiteful (if witty) subversive magazines: *Voice*, the 'anarchic' censored *Worm*, and *Paper Tyger*, hand-produced on duplicating machines, were circulated along with materials from the Schools Action Union and the National Union of Socialist Students. [215] The Governors promised Lloyd that they could obtain an injunction to stop these Unions giving the boys 'offensive' literature to distribute. [216] In a very interesting report to the Governors the year before he left, Lloyd said how much he had relied on his Chairman, since 'the exercise of authority was questioned at every turn', and the headmaster's job was one of isolation. [217] Boys who were at the College under Groves and Lloyd say that while Groves knew their names, and themselves up to a point, Charles Lloyd appeared somewhat austere and aloof; his bright sense of humour was not always in evidence, and his clothing and manner might appear a touch grey; it was a commonplace to compare him to a

bank manager – though of course, by this was meant a wonderfully respected bank manager.

Under Groves traditional Public School hierarchies had still obtained after the War; still in 1960 these involved rituals of respect for the masters, such as touching one's cap to them, and also involved rituals of precedence among the boys themselves: Prefects used a separate door to the Buttery, and did not have to wait their turn with the other boys to place their orders from Mrs Crisp at her counter; prominent sportsmen in their striped jackets had the right to proceed first through the narrow doors of the Centre Block. There were also conventions of dress: boys with their Rugby colours wore special caps (pie-shaped 'porkers' with tassels); prefects wore caps quartered on the peak in blue and black, and were the only boys allowed to unbutton their jackets or to keep their hands in their trouser pockets. Blazers and boaters gave summer a pleasantly Edwardian look on the fields and gravels, and 'pin-stripe' trousers were worn by the boarders to Chapel every Sunday and by some day-boys. While traditional stiff detached shirt-collars and studs were still worn by many boys, the wearing of shirts with attached collars became optional at some stage around 1967; in Lloyd's day there was a general loosening around the neck while many irksome College rules were abolished. Corporal punishment was abolished among the Heads of School under David Emms in 1984, when it would have been against the law to cane an Assisted Place pupil. In Groves's day, the Captain of School and the Captains of the boarding houses still caned boys; the Edwardian drama of a boy caught breaking the rules bending over to be beaten by the Captain of School, the other prefects standing witness against the walls, was regularly played out in the Prefects' Room in the South Block at the College until 1960. The Prefects themselves stopped caning boys for trivial offences that year, but they reserved the right to cane for severe cases.

Lloyd was aware that he was inheriting what he told the Governors was 'probably the biggest and fastest moving day school in the country'. 'Anything I did could only be for the worse', he wrote some years after he left:

> The staff were absolutely united, and the academic standards so high that it was rather like driving a spirited coach-and-four; I felt that I was there to keep it running as smoothly as possible in every department. It would have been fatal to say 'Here's a place to try out my ideas', or to make changes which would have harmed the traditions of the school. The school has so much driving force of its own that it rolls on regardless. [218]

Charles Lloyd was a superb administrator; he could also be magnificent in rebuking boys from the platform at an assembly for rudeness to the groundsmen. He was acknowledged by those he over-ruled, both masters and boys, to be fair and courteous. He had a wise respect for the knowledge and experience of teaching of his Heads of Department, and would not interfere with their methods, saying that his job was to create the circumstances in which they could get the very best out of the boys. Even when he made unpopular decisions, the Common Room was felt afterwards to be a hundred per cent behind him. Lloyd was a devoted family man, and his wife Doris was a very considerable support to him.

On Parents' Day 1968 there was a demonstration by the National Union of Socialist Students in College Road; according to legend they asked for the great gates of the College to be closed so that they could be filmed climbing over them by the BBC television crew. When Charles Lloyd saw the banner 'Down with Public Schools. Lloyd is obsolete', he said, "I would worry more if my name was not there".[219]

The 350th Anniversary of the College was celebrated in 1969 with style: the Archbishop of Canterbury, Michael Ramsey, preached at Commemoration in the Chapel; the Queen Mother attended a Garden Party at the Picture Gallery; Prince Philip officially opened the Christison Hall on 12 June; at a Commemoration Dinner the guests were served with a lavish menu of antiquarian dishes imitating Edward Alleyn's Foundation Dinner of 1619 (see Chapter Two); there were special productions of drama and a Festival Hall concert that included the 'Sanctus' from the *B Minor Mass* of Bach, movements from Britten's *Spring Symphony* and the specially composed Gordon Jacob Fanfare (see Chapter Eight); an 'Edward Alleyn Ball' was to follow at the Festival Hall, and thus the audience for the Concert sat wearing black tie and evening dress.[220]

The end of the Free Places

When Lloyd took over the College in 1967, over the past three years the ILEA had dropped its number of annual entrants at the College from 85 to 50, as was the case at Alleyn's School. Bromley, who were pressing the College continually to 'select from a wider range of ability' from 1967 until 1969, were sending 31 new boys; Croydon meanwhile (the second of the two larger southern boroughs) sent 20.[221] In 1968 the College received £39,021 from the Estates Governors as their annual grant; Alleyn's was still benefiting from its Direct Grant status, and received almost £8,000.[222] In 1970 the College admitted the last quota of the ILEA boys; Bexley also sent 2, Bromley 31, Croydon 20, Surrey 3 and Sutton 2. The fee-payers now entering the College amounted to 110 boys, roughly balancing the number of Council 'free-placers'. By 1976, however, the number of free places at entry had fallen to nil when the other boroughs dropped

out of the scheme, a decline over eleven years since the era when they had formed 85 per cent of the total College roll. The era when Christopher Gilkes could boast of an assured supply of the brightest boys of South London was over and done with. In 1974 Lloyd was able to tell the Governors, however, that the College had made good the loss of the ILEA places, without a decline of standards.[223] Charles Lloyd was aware, as mentioned above, that the Assisted Places scheme, funded by the central government, could be expected soon. The ILEA, incidentally, was still under contract to the College for catering until 1976, when the arrangement was abandoned, on the grounds that it was expensive for what it offered.

The Governors

Meanwhile Lloyd had taken part in discussions with the Board of Governors about the possibility of radical changes in the constitutions of the three Foundation schools; it was said that the endowments from the Estate were now insufficient for them to preserve their separate identities. Lloyd suggested that since from now on the College would be encountering a wider range of ability, the Sixth Forms at the College and at James Allen's Girls' School might be amalgamated. However, the Heads of the two other schools preferred to keep their identity, and in fact the Board thought it would make more sense to combine the Sixth Forms of James Allen's and Alleyn's.[224]

The loss of the ILEA places resulted in a change to the constitution of the Governing Body. In 1974 Lloyd told the Governors he was dissatisfied: a long overdue change to the Board was imperative, and a joint body for the College and Alleyn's now involved conflicting interests among the Governors. He pointed out that some Governors only visited the College every two years. The seats held by the eight Governors from the ILEA and Bromley on the Board had strictly never been necessary, as the independent College did not receive a 'direct grant' from the government. However, he paid homage to two excellent Governors nominated by the ILEA, the local residents Charles Pearce (d. 1982) a Governor from 1945 until 1973, and A. W. Scott JP, a Governor from 1949 until 1973 and Deputy Chairman of the LCC from 1950 until 1951. To retain Governors from the Councils now, he said, might well mean that some members of the Board would not believe in independent education.[225] A separate Board was founded, retaining one Governor each from the ILEA and from Bromley Council, and retaining members nominated by the Archbishop of Canterbury, the Lord Chancellor, the Universities of Oxford, Cambridge and London, the Royal Society and the Royal Academy; two were to be nominated by the Estates Governors, and four were to be co-opted, two from the vicinity.

When McCulloch Christison retired from the Board through ill health in 1968 the Governors in valediction remarked on his long service, 'almost impossible to exaggerate'. [226] The great benefactor sat humbly at the back of the Hall named after him while Prince Philip spoke in tribute to him at its official opening in 1969. Christison died in 1972, as did Sir Harold Hartley, marking the end of an epoch.

Shawcross, Chairman of the Board, presided over planning and developments at both Dulwich and Alleyn's worth well over a million pounds, until he resigned in 1972. He was succeeded for a few months only by Frederick ('Eric'), tenth Earl of Bessborough (1913–93), the blue-blooded diplomat and politician. In 1974 the Board approved a scheme for separate Governors for Alleyn's School but retaining a Foundation Board, and this was effected in 1976. Meanwhile, in 1975, the year of Lloyd's retirement from the College, Alleyn's became co-educational. This was a decision taken to preserve its independence; the Labour government at this time ended the Direct Grants to numerous schools, forcing them to make a choice between full independence; to come under the ILEA control; or to close, like Mary Datchelor's School in Camberwell. It was not until 1995 that entirely separate Boards were created for the College, Alleyn's School, the Picture Gallery and the Chapel.

Lord Bessborough resigned; he had been appointed Deputy Leader of the Conservative UK delegation to the European parliament. He was succeeded in October 1972 by the remarkable Jack Wolfenden (1906–85), already a famous public servant and chairman. Wolfenden had played Hockey for England, and had been Headmaster of Uppingham School (at the early age of 27) and subsequently of Shrewsbury School. Chairman of the Headmasters' Conference for four years, he was now Vice-Chancellor of Reading University, where during his thirteen years there was extensive building ('the House that Jack Built'), and the numbers rose by 50 per cent; later Wolfenden was Director and Principal Librarian of the British Museum. An earlier achievement of his had been the Wolfenden Report on homosexual behaviour of 1957, which significantly influenced both the law and public attitudes. Wolfenden had an exceptionally sharp mind and was diligent, firm, wise and unassuming. Sir Leonard ('Joe') Hooper, a College Governor originally appointed to the Board by Alleyn's in 1975, and a former director of GCHQ, followed Wolfenden as Chairman from 1985 until 1988. The energetic and lively-witted Old Alleynian Sir Robert Lawrence (1915–84), from the Science VI of Walter Booth's era, was elected as a Governor from 1970, proposed as his successor by Sir

Harold Hartley, and became Vice-Chairman of the Governors from 1983. He used to declare that he learned all he knew about how to manage men from his days as a prefect at the College. A railwayman all his career, apart from distinguished war service, he joined the London and North Eastern Railway from school, and rose to be the Chairman and General Manager of the London Midland Region from 1968–71, Chairman of the British Railways Property Board in 1972, and Vice-Chairman of the BR Board in 1975. He quickly made his mark on the Board at Dulwich with his affable, brisk and worldly manner, and was in the chair for many meetings.

The curriculum; Awards at Oxford and Cambridge

Under Lloyd the curriculum was extended, in particular in the Sixth Form, where thirty combinations of Advanced Level subjects were available to boys by 1974, opening up more choices of study at university. [227] Nine-tenths of the boys wanted to go on to universities. The revival of the 'accelerated' course, mentioned above, reaching the Ordinary Level examinations in four rather than five years, was an intensive and exciting venture that undoubtedly helped to produce more awards at Oxford and Cambridge by stimulating and 'stretching' select boys at a younger age than some people thought right. [228]

At the time when Lloyd inherited Groves's Sixth Form, the competitive statistics relating to Oxford and Cambridge awards showed that from 1960 until 1965 the College gained 140 awards, second only to Manchester Grammar School; no other school gained more than 113. In 1968 the College gained 25 awards, while St Paul's (with a smaller Sixth Form) gained 24, Eton 23 and Winchester 20. In 1970 there were 32 awards. In 1969 the College led the field by seven. [229]

The College led the field also in Computing, and in 1968 Sir Harold Hartley, in his ninetieth year, opened the Mathematics and Computer Centre in the Science Block named after him; Sir Harold greeted the Duke of Edinburgh at the Centre after His Royal Highness opened the Christison Hall in the following year. In 1972 *The Alleynian* reported that the Computer Centre offered the best facilities of any public school, supplied without charge to the College by an outside commercial provider, but added that the College had no proper theatre. [230] The signal improvement in the status and teaching of Art at the College, noted by the Governors in 1966, [231] had much to do with the presence from 1966 on the Board until his death of the lively painter James Fitton (1899–1982) as the Governor nominated by the Royal Academy; living at Pond Cottages, he took an active interest in the Art Department and its prizes. He was succeeded by Peter Greenham OA.

Buildings; the Chapel

The lease of The Orchard ran out in 1967; that of Bell House in 1968, and again in 1982. New leases were taken out until 1988.[232] The Physical Education Centre had been opened, sited across College Road and beyond Pond Cottages, by the great A. E. R. Gilligan (see Chapter Twelve) in September 1966, while George Way was Acting Master. The Hall now called after Christison was at first to go under the suitably 'brutalist' name the 'Composite Block',[233] as part of a development including a courtyard, workshops and the Art School. The Estates Governors agreed to pay £15,000 for a Dining Hall and Kitchens; the estimate for the whole Block was £57,000.[234] Shawcross laid the foundation stone on Founder's Day 1967. In 1967 plans for a Memorial Hall that could seat the entire College and possessing 'modern facilities for drama and music productions', first proposed in 1958, were abandoned. Charles Lloyd pressed for a small theatre, aware that staff and old boys wanted better facilities for drama and music, and that two ambitious productions a year could not properly be housed in the Baths Hall.[235] The Christison Hall was combined with a War Memorial consisting of an unlovely open-air screen with ceramic plaques naming each of the dead of the Second World War. The Governors had debated awkwardly how the Dining Hall could constitute a War Memorial, at first proposing a 'Book of Honour' in the foyer and no bronze plaques.

The Governors rejected the proposal of Professor Philip Rhodes (Dean of Medicine at St Thomas' Hospital, who was on the College Board from 1966 until 1974) to give the *James Caird* to the National Maritime Museum on permanent loan; a West Cloister to the Composite Block was planned to receive the restored boat behind glass, but since the restoration unexpectedly included the addition of a mast and sails, it was not practical to show her there; she stayed at the Museum until David Emms's day (see Chapter Nine).[236]

The Great Hall was now freed to be used for drama, the Governors said.[237] The same year it was decided to cover the Honours Boards with wallpaper, as they had deteriorated so badly and some called them 'elitist'; this offence against the historic achievements of pupils at the College was carried out in 1970. In 1993 (in Tony Verity's day) they were uncovered again and the names were expertly restored. One panel revealed a broad gash of white plaster where the wall had cracked and crumbled; thanks to the professional photographs taken just before they were papered over and to the extraordinary skills of the conservatrix, Jane Rutherfoord, it was possible to repair the panel so that it passes now for the original.[238] The Sixth Form Centre was opened by Pip Gardner in

1969 in the Centre Block, and in 1971 it was also decided to move the Boys' Library next to it; at one point the Lower Hall had been proposed for a Lecture Theatre.[239] The Chapel was 'reordered', following the fashion of the day, in 1974; the result was a small loss of character to its pleasing Collegiate character by the lowering of the Chancel Screen. In Graham Able's day the Chapel received a full redecoration from the Estates Governors, reopened by Wesley Carr (see above) in 2000, when he preached at the Commemoration Service.

Changes in the Scheme of Government of the Estate in 1974 allowed for the sale of Dulwich freeholds following the Leasehold Reform Act of 1967. The same year the College was offered £95,000 by the Estate for the surrender of the leases on the Common of Elm Lawn, The Orchard and The Chestnuts, and the Governors voted to sell Elm Lawn. With Russell Vernon they planned a new boarding house with a medical wing on the site of the Sanatorium and a new house for the Master on the tennis courts to the east of the PE Centre. In the event, however, Elm Lawn, The Orchard and The Chestnuts were saved for the College.[240]

The Common Room

S. F. A. Howard (1928–78), a remarkable Wykehamist and a graduate in Classics from Christ's College, Cambridge, joined the staff after two years in the RAF in 1952; for 26 years he exerted a powerful influence for integrity and good behaviour in the College. Appointed Head of Classics in 1960, he was promoted to a new post in 1972 as Head of the Middle School, in recognition that improvements could be made in the teaching and in pastoral care. Stephen Howard, a noble figure, inspired such feelings of affectionate respect among the boys and the Assistant Masters (perhaps particularly the younger ones) as did A. H. Gilkes at the beginning of the century; he was a true Christian gentleman, a self-disciplinary schoolmaster of the old school, a great supporter of the Hollington Club, and an extraordinarily civilised and humane man who possessed a profound intuition into the minds of boys and masters. Howard was a bachelor, and although obviously he had many academic and literary interests beyond the College, such as Hannibal's routes over the Alps and the novels of the obscure George Birmingham [Revd J. O. Hannay], he appeared to devote his entire being to the College (together with his work as a Samaritan), and was an inspiring Venture Scout Leader [for older boys] from the early 1950s until his death. He became a wise and just Deputy Master to David Emms in 1976.

Ray Payne was appointed Head of Mathematics in 1964, and was appointed Third Master in 1976. He was an admirably watchful Director of Studies, controlling a desperately complex timetable before the use of computers, until his retirement in 1988. With his encouragement the large number of boys who studied Double Mathematics and Physics earned the College a formidable reputation for success in these subjects.

Intramural politics in Lloyd's era were largely driven by the Upper School boys responsible for the 'English' culture in the College and a group of influential teachers. While it may have seemed to masters and boys in other departments that this had more to do with adolescent protests about rules, a real rebellion against philistinism and prejudice was at work. Laurie Jagger (1925–2007), appointed in 1953, served as Head of English from 1965 to 1980, and was a keen cricketer and a versatile sportsman; comments about his dedication and enthusiasm as a teacher recur in *The Alleynian*. This bearded apostle of the literary imagination championed the individual against the school mould: opposing charm, worldly success, complacency, insincerity, examinations, and the parroting of sub-urban parents' mealtime opinions by their sons, he guided his pupils to understanding and to integrity. The boys learned to think and to use their own voice; reading and discussion brought compassion. Jagger was a pioneer of creative writing (including parody or 'imitation') and of internal assessment. He introduced boys as young as fourteen to the great writers, and would stride up the stone staircases of the Blocks with thirty copies of his beloved eighteenth-century writers tucked under his chin. He seemed quite unaware of the profound influence he exerted, not only on his 'star' pupils who became famous in the arts, but on his colleagues and on countless 'ordinary' boys. Other members of the Department in his day are also spoken of with much affection and gratitude by their pupils, such as Norman Howlings with his fine sensibility, and the witty and elegant Michael Fitch (d. 1999), appointed in 1950 and 1955 respectively. Jagger, who appointed for diversity and dialectic, was supported by remarkable English Department colleagues, such as the follower of F. R. Leavis, Brian Worthington, learned and witty, a Socratic gadfly with a touch of cynicism, who taught from 1962 until 1970; by Tony O'Sullivan and Bradley Winterton, appointed in 1965; and by the gentle and courteous Giles Jackson, with his passion for William Blake, appointed in 1967. Jackson was President of the Common Room from 1991 until 1994, and retired after 28 years' service. Chris Owens, who taught English from 1969 until 1974 was an exuberant and very popular figure, encouraging the more lazy or unconfident boys in their work, mounting daring productions of plays and presiding over the boys' Union. Jan Piggott, appointed in 1972, followed Laurie Jagger as Head of English in 1980.

Alan Cowling, a sparkling heterodox teacher appointed in 1972, had a gift for firing others with his own enthusiasms, such as Hollywood, Wordsworth, Al Bowlly, D. H. Lawrence, Elvis Presley, Thomas Hardy, and Fred Astaire; he also taught History of Art (a new A Level course) and staged a Dada Exhibition in the Art School with Dada 'happenings', such as a performance of *Swan Lake* on the South Gravel in the lunch hour. Neil Fairlamb, likewise an eloquent enthusiast but with a reactionary intellect, counterpoised Cowling with his passion for the Church of England and its parish churches, and for seventeenth-century poetry and with his admiration for Enoch Powell. Provoked by schoolmaster's frustrations, he was to be heard exclaiming "Merciful powers!" A real connoisseur of opera and wine, a Visitor at Brixton prison and a covert encourager of less happy boys, once he had been ordained in Southwark Cathedral, the Revd Neil Fairlamb left for parishes in Wales in 1994 after 22 years at the College.

Among the very many successes in Drama of Lloyd's era were *The Alchemist* (1967) and *The Jew of Malta* (1969), *Hamlet* with Simon Bailey (left 1972), now Keeper of Archives at Oxford University, and productions of Harold Pinter. The operetta *Orpheus in the Underworld* brought together staff and boys as performers (1971), including Fergus Jamieson (see below) as Icarus. Also very impressive were the productions by the boys themselves after their Oxford and Cambridge examinations, such as *Long Day's Journey into Night* (1978), Yeats's *At the Hawk's Well* (1973), and plays by Pinter and Beckett. The performers of *Long Day's Journey* made a vow at the time to revive their performance in the Fencing Salle (the long upper chamber of the Pavilion) 25 years on, and the entire cast returned, some from far places, to do so in 2003.

During this era the Art Department achieved a remarkable height, headed by the quiet-spoken genius of Barry Viney, a meticulous and subtle draughtsman, who was appointed to succeed Michael Preston in 1964, retiring in 1994. Barry Adalian, appointed in 1967 and working for 27 years, made a flamboyant contrast to the perfectionist Barry Viney, opposing the avant-garde and experimental to the traditional, and created some spectacular sets and original productions in the Baths Hall. Viney, expert in printing and book design, transformed *The Alleynian*, with sans-serif text and imaginative use of photographs and boys' drawings; with 47 issues over 25 years, it was surely the most wonderful and inventive school magazine of its day. Viney mounted an exhibition at the South London Art Gallery about Dulwich College artists past and present, *A School and its Art*, in 1981. With his stage designs, such as for *Forty Years On*, and a masterpiece, *Guys and Dolls* (1979), paying poetic

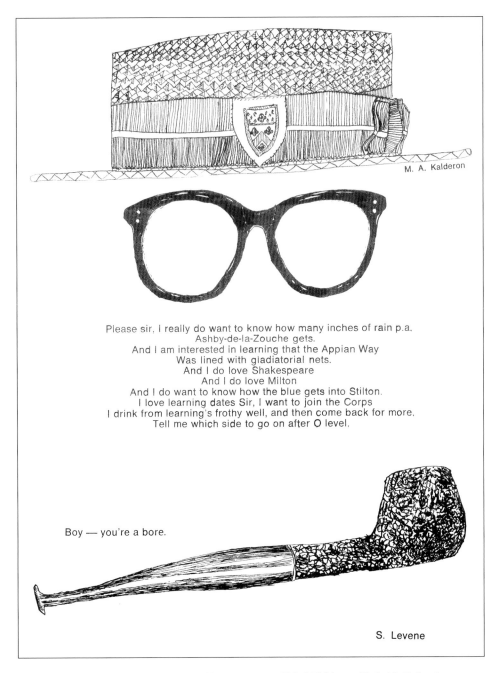

M. A. Kalderon

Please sir, I really do want to know how many inches of rain p.a.
Ashby-de-la-Zouche gets.
And I am interested in learning that the Appian Way
Was lined with gladiatorial nets.
And I do love Shakespeare
And I do love Milton
And I do want to know how the blue gets into Stilton.
I love learning dates Sir, I want to join the Corps
I drink from learning's frothy well, and then come back for more.
Tell me which side to go on after O level.

Boy — you're a bore.

S. Levene

The Alleynian, 617, Winter 1969. Simon Levene and Mark Kalderon. (Dulwich College)

homage to Hollywood and the 1950s, it was hard for the audience to remember that they were not watching a National Theatre production but an amateur adolescent company on a temporary stage over a covered swimming pool. Indeed, the National Theatre mounted its own, very successful production of the musical three years later. The Art School, with a nationwide reputation for excellence, produced again after a long interval several fine painters, and introduced a pioneering graphic course, 'Visual Communication', for the Third Forms in the Middle School.

John Cottle (1924–92), the Classics teacher, was appointed in 1949 and retired in 1985; his achievements were outside the classroom: he was a famous House-master of Grenville. He put a great deal of energy and time into the Scouting movement as Group Scout Master and Leader at the College and also in the neighbourhood, for which forty years' service he gained the highest award, the Silver Wolf. His stout Edwardian figure, stylised (from time immemorial) in an affectionate caricature known as the 'Cottloid', showing a triangular man in baggy Scouting shorts with short moustache and broad-brimmed hat, was chalked thousands of times on blackboards (and was once spotted in graffito in Hong Kong), a sort of Masonic sign recognised by Alleynians of many years. Cottle coached many boys in life-saving; he once put up a notice, 'Boys who wish to learn Life-saving should see me in the Bath'. The Union profited from his many interests, such as archaeology, and he founded the important Society for International Affairs. Another splendid teacher who retired in 1983 after 26 years of teaching, mostly in the Lower School, and who seemed to have come from an earlier and more character-ful era of British schoolmasters, was Barry Evans (1922–88), a polymath (especially an astronomer) who possessed great wit and humanity, and was also was a notable Scout Troop Leader. The school published *Dulwich Collage*, a collection of his satiric pieces and drawings, in 1983; his subjects included the Scouts and John Cottle, the daily life of schools, and a wicked parody of the Practical Criticism exercise beloved by English masters. Barry Evans' assemblies to the Upper School were always hugely applauded, and he liked to introduce boys of eleven to the pleasures of translating Horace. Austin Hall, the first full-time qualified Librarian at the College, was appointed in 1969, and organised the new Library. Many boys owe much to the encouragement of the highly popular no-nonsense Economics teacher, Philip Keith-Roach, who taught at the College for 23 years from 1973; a marvellous Rugby coach, he left to work at Rosslyn Park and as scrummaging expert for the England and for the Cambridge University forwards.

The Union, music, the CCF, Voluntary Service and the Scouts

The boys' Union comprised 35 societies in 1969. John Cottle's Society for International Affairs conducted some memorable meetings with talks from distinguished travellers and politicians. The birthday party of 'Muse', a society for performing arts, in 1973, was celebrated with popular music groups and sketches.[241] Music at the College under Alan Morgan continued to produce performers and concerts of quite extraordinary excellence, with the 'exciting sound' (noted by Lloyd in his report to the Governors) of the full Dulwich choir and orchestra in great and ambitious classical works.[242]

In 1967 the CCF numbered 186 boys and the Scouts 166.[243] The following year Lloyd told the Governors that the numbers were falling in these two organisations, but that Voluntary Service, where the boys made visits to the local community and carried out gardening and decorating, now numbered two hundred.[244] During this period it was John Charnley (see below) who meticulously planned and oversaw these operations.

Scout camps abroad became a frequent venture. In 1972, however, three boys, Christopher Burn, John Twyford and Michael Wickes, fell to their death on Snowdon on 20 February; this terrible event for the families of the boys and for the College preyed gravely on the mind of the great Stephen Howard who was leading them, although the consequent report declared that he had not been negligent. Charles Lloyd drove from Dulwich through the night to take charge of the situation.

The Picture Gallery

While the College was at an apogee of its fortunes, in about 1969, the Gallery, at a nadir in its history, nearly closed for lack of funds. It had become clear that the Gallery really needed professional management and fund-raising, and that with the best will the Governors could not cope. In 1947 they had decided against selling paintings as a short-term solution, but in 1960 another move to sell 'surplus pictures' from the store was mooted. By 1966 the Gallery was running at a very serious loss of £3,000 per annum. The Governors discussed alternatives: to sell an important picture, to make a new Foundation scheme for the Gallery, or to seek support from the Arts Council or from the local Councils of Lambeth and Southwark. Sir Anthony Blunt was asked for advice, and was strongly against selling a picture. At this point the second of a series of startling thefts must have undermined even further the morale of those who cared for the Gallery, both locally and nationally. Six of the choicest paintings were taken on 30 December 1966: three Rembrandts, a Rubens, the Gerard Dou *Lady at the Clavichord* (DPG 56), and the *Susannah and the Elders* (DPG 22; thought at the time to be by Elsheimer). They were recovered unharmed a week later, three in a bed-sitting room and three under a bush on Streatham Common, carefully wrapped in newspaper. In 1970 a collection of miniatures bequeathed in 1963 was auctioned,[245] and once again desperate measures were discussed: to sell lesser paintings; to sell one or two major paintings; to consign the Gallery to the nation or to the GLC; to make the Gallery an 'outstation' of the National Gallery; or to send the pictures on elaborate money-making tours of Japan or the United States. Domenichino's *Adoration of the Shepherds* (DPG 283) was put up for auction, and made £100,000; the government, having previously refused to help the Gallery, paid £30,000 towards it, and the painting ended up in the National Gallery of Scotland. Questions in the House of Commons made the transactions look farcical, and bad publicity followed. An admission charge was imposed.[246]

*

Alleynians

Some distinguished Alleynians of this era have been mentioned above. Many others of Lloyd's era achieved fame and fortune, such as Peter Bazalgette (left 1971), the television producer and magnate; he had published a poem in *The Alleynian* in 1970 and he won the mock election the same year. [247] Bazalgette was President of the Cambridge Union, and went on to found Bazal Productions and to become Chairman of Endemol UK. Robert Gildea (left 1970) is Professor of Modern History at Oxford and a Fellow of Worcester College, and has published much admired books on French history such as *Marianne in Chains* (2002). Miles Hewstone (left 1974) is Professor of Psychology at Oxford, Fellow of New College, and Director of the Oxford Centre for the Study of Intergroup Conflict. Lionel Barber (left 1973) is the Editor of *The Financial Times*. Mick Imlah (left 1975), a cricketer, actor and writer at school, and himself a poet, is now Poetry Editor of *The Times Literary Supplement*. Jerry Howe (left 1975) is BBC Radio 4's Commissioning Editor for Drama. Stephen Deuchar (left 1975) is Director of Tate Britain. David Lambert (left 1977) is an authoritative and subtle writer on historic gardens, parks and cemeteries; he has published *Indignation* (2000) on the subject of conservation, and articles in the *New Arcadian Journal*. Many others live by their pens, such as Peter de Bolla (left 1975), Director of Studies in English at King's College, Cambridge, who was editor of *Granta* in a very interesting period; he is an expert on the Sublime and the author of several acclaimed books of theory, such as *Art Matters* (2001). Ian Thomson (left 1979) is a critic and an authority on modern Italian literature, the author of a highly successful biography, *Primo Levi* (2003).

Professor Anthony Pople (1955–2003) of Nottingham, at Dulwich the leader of the School Orchestra, left in 1973 to study Mathematics at Oxford, and died prematurely and highly regarded, a brilliant young musicologist, an expert on twentieth-century music with important works on Alban Berg and others to his credit. Of tragic early deaths of Alleynians others occurred more recently: that of Justin Howes (1963–2005), an English Scholar at Oxford in 1981, from boyhood a most original character (the son of Brian Howes; see above) famous early in his career as a typographer; and that of Mike Hearn (1972–2005) in Africa, where he had had been doing remarkable work for the Save the Rhino Trust in Namibia. Flt Lieutenant Jonathan Tapper (1965–94), the pilot of a Chinook helicopter with twenty top security men on board, died in an accident on the cliffs of the Mull of Kintyre flying from Northern Ireland to Scotland.

*

DAVID EMMS, 1975–86 – The academic scene – The Alleyn Club – The streets of South London – Drama, music and the Union – The Wodehouse Library – Computing – The Field Centre – The War Memorials – The Common Room – Alleynians – The Picture Gallery

David Emms, 1975–86

David Emms (b. 1925) was at Tonbridge School when Dulwich College shared their quarters during the evacuation. He served as a paratrooper in 1943; after the War he studied Modern Languages at Brasenose College, Oxford, and was a Rugby 'blue'. Early in his career appointed Head of Modern Languages at Uppingham, where he was also master in charge of Rugby and the Commanding Officer of the CCF, he served as Headmaster of Cranleigh School in Surrey from 1960 and then of Sherborne School in Dorset from 1970. David Emms brought to the purlieus of the South Circular Road something of the pleasant open air and space of the pre-war country boarding school (and something of its idiom) after more tense and grey eras. In the demanding and difficult job of running Dulwich College, it was obvious how greatly he valued the support of his wife Pam, the model of a gracious headmaster's wife but a genuine person of great warmth. Energetic, affable, at times applying a 'scrum down and heel it' Rugby dynamic to management and ruffling the more staid of his staff, he also possessed a more subtle cultured side; resilient and enthusiastic, he accentuated the positive and declared war on apathy. Rugby and the Prefects can hardly ever have received such encouragement from a Master as from David Emms, but he also fostered Drama and Art. Mothers and fathers, on his initiative, were now involved more than before in the process of their sons' education. Before David Emms became Master, Parents' Day, held on a Saturday once a year, was a business day, and appointments would be made for a brief discussion with the Form Master; only one Parents' Evening was held annually, and that for the Second Forms alone, to discuss what their options were for their main subjects on entering the Middle School. David Emms introduced the present system of Parents' Evenings. This was not a popular move with the old guard who would have preferred to communicate an Olympian written report posted to the home, sometimes a trenchant exercise of wit and irony, though often containing wonderful insightful prose. David Emms, bringing parents and families onto the College campus with a bold welcome, founded the Friends of Dulwich College, with mutual benefits, in 1980. Gregarious by nature, he liked to speak of 'the Family of Dulwich'. The idea came from the very successful Fête organised to raise funds for the ambitious

David and Pam Emms. (Private collection)

Cricket, Hockey and Rugby Tour of Sri Lanka and Thailand in 1978, led by Tim Francis, an enlightened Head of Physical Education (at the College 1970 to 1980). Within the first year over a thousand families were in membership; their Fêtes and Dances and a newsletter raised considerable funds, culminating in a very large grant for the purchase of the Field Centre (see below) in 1984. The first Chairman was Brian Capon (left 1945), who had been in the First XV in 1944 and was the President of the Alleyn Club in 1992. The Master's wife is traditionally the President. Already socially diverse, the College became richer culturally by diversity of racial origin as well: one form included a Christlieb and a Sivalingam. By the early 1990s there were more Patels than Smiths in the school, and in one year 43 Patels were listed on the roll; regular charity football matches between Hindu and Muslim teams became a feature under Tony Verity.

In the course of 1981, a year described by David Emms to the Governors as an *annus mirabilis*,[248] the Edward Alleyn Hall was opened, where superb music and drama was to be performed (see below). In the same year the Assisted Places scheme was successfully introduced at the same time as there was a large-scale revival of parents

paying full fees for their sons. Prep School Headmasters were entertained at dinners at the College and successfully persuaded to send their pupils at 13, reassured by David Emms that the College would not seek to entice their boys away at an earlier age. Among David Emms's many achievements were a further broadening of the curriculum, the new Library and Theatre, and the encouragement of Art and of links with the Picture Gallery. In 1979 Ivyholme was changed to a house for middle forms, and Blew House for senior forms. The War Memorials were at last honourably combined in a pleasing form. In 1983 David Emms enjoyed a most prosperous year as Chairman of the Headmasters' Conference; he had previously published a pamphlet *HMC Schools and British Industry* (1981). In 1985 Robert Runcie, who as Archbishop of Canterbury was 'Visitor' to the College after more than three and a half centuries of unbroken tradition since Alleyn's Foundation, accepted his invitation to preach in the Chapel at Commemoration. In response to a suggestion from a spirited and persuasive Sixth Former, Richard Cross, who left in 1986 and is now a barrister, the College put up a flag post between the College Gates and the Main Elevation.

Whereas Shawcross and Bessborough were too busy elsewhere to be fully involved and effective Chairmen of the Governors, Jack Wolfenden (from 1976 Lord Wolfenden), made the time to take an interest in many aspects of the College, and his partnership with David Emms was an obvious factor in the general prosperity of this era. Among many eminent Governors generous with their time and interest the Board had lost three local men, the Royal Academician Jim Fitton (see above), Charles Pearce, who served from 1945 until 1973, and Sir Noel Hutton QC, who served from 1966 until 1982, and was Chairman of the Picture Gallery from 1971 until 1977. Harry Peace OA (1916–2000), for twenty years a Governor and an exceptionally loyal Old Alleynian, President of the Alleyn Club in 1986, was at one time both Chairman of the Estates Governors and Chairman of the College Finance Committee; late in the War he had won the MC and Bar with the Wiltshires in the space of 24 hours at Mt Pincon.

The Bursar and Clerk to the Governors, David Banwell, was also an important factor in the success of the College in these years, working quietly as he did for over 25 years and retiring in 1986, giving the utmost support successively to Groves, Lloyd and Emms, with always the best interests of the College at heart. Banwell filled a superhuman position involving acting as Clerk to the Governors and Bursar not only to the College, but also to Alleyn's School, James Allen's Girls' School, the Picture Gallery and the Chapel. It was reckoned to be necessary to divide the work of this formidable and distinguished administrator when he retired, and he was replaced by four men.

After several years of lobbying to end the (mostly unpopular) feature of College life, lessons on Saturday mornings, a reform rejected in his last year by Charles Lloyd after heated discussion, it was abolished from September 1981. The final argument for the change was that it was given as the main deciding factor in replies to a questionnaire sent to parents who had rejected a place at the College for their sons, apart from offers of scholarships at other schools. The damage to school sporting fixtures on Saturday afternoons that was predicted did not in fact occur. In fact there are today more representative sports teams (and also from younger boys) playing on Saturday mornings than ever played before.

The academic scene

The staff were aware that the general 'intelligence quotient' of the boys, as was to be expected when the free-place boys no longer attended, was slightly in decline; however, the College held its position well at the final stage of the Oxford and Cambridge system of Awards to school pupils, made after written examination papers and interviews at the time of their application to the Colleges. This came to an end in 1985, and Awards are now only given to undergraduates once they have proved themselves. In 1979 the Dulwich College Committee were told some interesting statistics: at the height of 'the Dulwich Experiment' the College had chosen its entrants from the ratio of six applicants for one place; in 1977–8 this had declined to 'two and a half' for one place, and in the current year the ratio was three for one. In September 1975, for the last time, 62 boys with places paid for by the Local Authorities had entered the College, half of them from Bromley, and the others from Bexley, Croydon, Sutton and Surrey.[249] The Eleven Plus intake that year was remarkable; the six Old Alleynian undergraduates who gained First Class degrees in PPE at Oxford in 1986 were of this vintage. After a period of 15 years of decline from the point when 85 per cent of the boys had their fees paid from Council rates, the College in 1976 was admitting only boys (apart from those who won College Scholarships) whose parents could afford the fees. The Estates Governors' grant to the College in 1979 was £172,935, while Alleyn's received £21,366.[250] In September 1981, when the roll had settled at about 1,400 boys, the first Assisted Place boys arrived, composing a quarter of the intake at the ages of eleven, thirteen and sixteen, and amounting to 46 boys.[251] It was said that many parents in Bromley were dissatisfied with the Council schools. David Emms assured potential parents that persistent local myths about the College were untrue; the teachers were not only interested in boys of very high academic ability, and boys did not feel lost in such a large school. He told the Governors that pastoral care needed to be taken more seriously.[252]

The decline in the birth rate and the increases in costs and fees were unsettling. An issue much discussed by Emms and his Governors and by the Common Room, resulting from the changes in the College's intake, was a proposal to turn the College into a co-educational school, as was the course adopted by many famous former boys' schools at this time. David Emms favoured a 'controlled number' of girls joining the Sixth Form only.[253] The staff, some of whom had experienced the success of small specialist teaching groups including a few girls who joined the College for one term after their A Level examinations to prepare for Oxford or Cambridge entrance, were almost unanimously in favour of the proposal; they declared that it would improve both the numbers and the quality of their A Level groups, and that the College's 'results' would be higher, raising the standard of entrance to the Sixth Form. They sent the Governors in 1978 a resolution to this effect.[254]

Their arguments for co-education were essentially pragmatic – to improve the academic standing of the College – rather than ideological. The Governors, some of whom sat on the Board of James Allen's Girls' School, rejected David Emms's proposal, but promised to reopen discussion in three years' time. The rapid success of Alleyn's as a co-educational establishment from 1975 pre-empted this change at Dulwich, and the liberal options for local families within the Foundation to place boys and girls at two single-sex schools or at Alleyn's School now obtain.

The Alleyn Club

David Emms enjoyed the company of Old Alleynians, and he brought the Alleyn Club, the College and its Master closer than at any time before. He would travel any distance for a Reunion lunch or dinner, where he was a popular guest; he was the first man who had not been a pupil at the College to be elected President of the Alleyn Club, in 1985. Since then the same honour has been awarded to Terry Walsh and Graham Able. He persuaded the Dulwich College Committee to award life membership of the Club to all boys leaving the College over the age of sixteen. The Club helps the College and individual boys in many ways, and in 2007 they bought for the Fellows' Library a rare volume of Dekker's *Magnificent Entertainment* (1604), recording Alleyn's welcome to King James I (see Chapter One). A complete list of the Presidents of the Alleyn Club is published on the Old Alleynian website.

The streets of South London

Dulwich College, in spite of its iron railings, cannot isolate itself from surrounding social problems; attacks and thefts carried out by rough youths on uniformed boys on their way home from the College have occurred intermittently ever since the War. The boys from Kingsdale School on Alleyn Park grabbed caps from the Dulwich boys; the Sixth Form from 1965 no longer were obliged to wear caps, and shortly afterwards they ceased to be part of the uniform for all boys.[255] Later attacks and thefts were worrying enough for David Emms to report them to the Governors, with complaints about insufficient support from the Police.

During the Brixton riots of 1981, the Metropolitan Police were welcomed by the College to use the premises as a depot for a week, when a number of other institutions had refused for fear of recriminations; on one Sunday as many as two and a half thousand officers were on the premises at the same time.

*

Drama, music and the Union

David Emms's energy animated many successful projects, in particular the building of the Edward Alleyn Hall. This 'multi-purpose' hall contained a properly equipped theatre; it was fitted with tiers of 'bleachers' for the audience, designed to retract and to reveal a large floor for an examination hall or other purposes. It was made clear that the Hall was on no account to be referred to as the Edward Alleyn Theatre. First planned in 1979, when it was hoped that Lady Wodehouse would sponsor it, it was hard to raise the money: David Emms reported that the parents wanted a theatre, but that a joint Appeal to the Old Alleynians showed that they were more interested in the option of endowing bursaries. The Hall was designed by Tim Foster and Theatre Projects in 1980; seating an audience of only 290, and with other economies, it cost £400,000, just half of what was originally in mind. The actress Virginia McKenna formally opened the Hall on 3 October 1981, and this was followed by some scenes about Edward Alleyn devised by Robert MacDowell, the Head of Drama from 1975 (who joined the English Department in 1969 and left in 1988). The world-famous Old Alleynian Professor of English Literature, George Wilson Knight (see Chapter Eight) inaugurated the theatre the next evening, at the age of 84, with his one-man show *Shakespeare's Dramatic Challenge*: he went on all fours as Caliban, and for the finale he cast off his loincloth, standing naked as Timon of Athens.

The great dramatic event of this era, mentioned above in connection with its sets, was the production of *Guys and Dolls* in 1979 in the Baths Hall by Alan Cowling, with the music under the direction of Peter Buckroyd (appointed in 1974); both of these brilliantly talented members of the English Department left in 1980. *Guys and Dolls* achieved astonishing intensity and excitement; the audience were overwhelmed by this school production, fresher and livelier than the professional stage, which brought out such incomparable singing, acting and dancing from the College guys and their dolls, who were sourced at JAGS and other local schools. The rapturous success was the result of two hundred hours of rehearsal. Among Robert MacDowell's most accomplished productions was a marvellous *Forty Years On* in 1975; Alan Cowling directed a bold and original *Macbeth* in 1977. A memorable production of Andrew Lloyd Webber's *Jeeves* by MacDowell and Barry Adalian enlivened the Edward Alleyn Hall in 1982. Here also, from 1981, a regular entertainment called *Mufti*, a successor to the Corps Shout and to the Summer Miscellany, took place; this mostly featured bands and singers, and was enormously popular until its demise in 1989. It was organised by the debonair English and Physical Education teacher,

Andy Archibald, who was at the College from 1979 until 1991 and was the producer of several plays; he had been in the British Modern Pentathlon team at the Montreal Olympics in 1976, winning a gold medal. Richard Vanstone, who left in 1985 after 15 years' lively teaching of English, inaugurated many original excursions and ventures; he took boys on visits to Highgate Cemetery and to Covent Garden market at dawn, and he offered classes in Cookery and in Modern Dance. One evening in Great Hall his dancers took only a few seconds to win over a potentially hostile philistine audience. He produced versions of the Stravinsky ballets *The Rite of Spring* and *Petrushka* in 1974 and 1975.

Alan Morgan's direction of Music kept up the College's reputation for first-rate performances and improved on it. The department continued to benefit from the many outstanding visiting instrumental London musicians who have taught over the years, and the chamber music was greatly enhanced by the teaching of David Price, the Head of Strings (who left in 1984). One lunch hour he conducted a deeply moving performance of Richard Strauss's *Metamorphosen* in the Lower Hall.

The boys' Societies flourished within their Union, and fifty were meeting in 1977. Clive Bull (left 1977), now of LBC, founded College Radio, whose programmes were distributed on cassette tapes, and the work was continued by Alex Nelson (left 1980). A suggestion from Ben Mingay (left 1983) that boys should be eligible to receive College colours for other achievements as well as sport was taken up, and this undoubtedly went some way to reducing some residual philistinism. Admirable continental school trips to France and Germany in the holidays had occurred in the 1950s, and now teachers habitually took groups of boys to Russia, to the War cemeteries in France and Belgium, and to the galleries in Paris and to Italy; such opportunities are now even more frequent and the destinations even more ambitious and further afield, such as to South America, to the lower slopes of Mount Everest and to China.

The Wodehouse Library

David Emms was determined to create a Library for the College to be proud of, and in this project Margaret Slythe, appointed as Head of Libraries in 1981 and retiring in 1992, played a crucial part; she furnished superior facilities and took note of the boys and their interests. The development of the Archives in 1981, with proper security and conservation standards, air-conditioned stacks for the Fellows' Library, a display area and study room, was also her achievement. She popularised the Shackleton and Wodehouse collections at the College both to boys and to the many scholars and visitors who came singly or in groups to study the Theatre Papers and the treasures of the Fellows' Library; the access of the boys in general to their heritage at the College was much improved. The Wodehouse Library was opened by Sir Edward Cazalet QC (of the Wodehouse family, who had contributed generously to its furnishings) in 1982. A bequest of Wodehouse's desk, typewriter, pipe and other relics from his study at Remsenburg, Long Island, was housed in a glazed shrine. The Lower Hall was refurbished the same year, controversially, with a chandelier, a carpet and leather sofas; the intention was that the boys would be influenced by this new environment to behave like gentlemen. A fire on the night of Whit Monday, 30 May 1983, did serious damage to the Masters' Library; the Masters' Common Room, at that time housed on the ground floor below the Library, was totally destroyed. The magnificent Library, which would have been ruined along with all its books from an explosion of heat had the Fire Brigade arrived ten minutes later, was carefully restored, and many books were rebound; many still smell of smoke. A devoted group of ladies from the North Kent NADFAS cleaned these books; they stayed on to clean and catalogue the Fellows' Library during weekly visits for many years afterwards. Margaret Slythe was succeeded by Hugh Eveleigh from 1992 until 1999; with his intellect and culture, his restless impatience and his success in getting things done (and his expertise with new computer technologies) he developed the Library into perhaps the most advanced of any school in the country. Marianne Bradnock who succeeded him as Head of Libraries until 2006, with her patience and dedication, her concern for the boys' interests and welfare, also kept well abreast of the advances of library technology; the ratio of boys using the Library to the total roll of the boys increased significantly.

Computing

In the Computer Centre, carrying on the great pioneering work of Nick Earle (see above), the boys were benefiting from the most sophisticated new equipment and expertise. John Charnley (see below), who was to become Director of Studies and Third Master, and who had already given himself generously in many ways to the life of the College and had been an excellent President of the Common Room from 1979 until 1985, now enabled the College to take advantage of the most advanced computer systems, thanks to his own pioneering 'programs'.

The Field Centre

David Emms's habitual tenacity in getting things done was also shown by a successful initiative in 1984 to buy and to adapt for the College a 'Venture Centre' for study and outdoor activities, now called the Field Centre.

This was a disused two-classroom primary school in a magnificent setting at Glyntawe, 20 miles north of Swansea in the Brecon Beacons. A very loyal Old Alleynian working in Cardiff, Bill Ricketts (1940–99), sifted through 150 possible properties to find the best one for the College. The refurbished Centre took its first series of form visits and reading parties in 1985. The Friends raised £35,000 and the property cost £25,000.

The War Memorials

Honourable amends were made at last in 1984 to the dead of the Second World War, through the efforts of David Emms and others, by the demolition of the memorial screen next to the Christison Hall and the addition of two 'monoliths', or *stelae*, with the names inscribed on brass tablets. These standing stones were sensitively designed by John Wells-Thorpe, Vice-President of the RIBA, and were placed to flank the Great War Memorial on the front lawns.

The Common Room

When Philip Thomas retired in 1976, Stephen Howard and Ray Payne were appointed as Second and Third Master. In 1978 The College was shaken by the tragic death of Stephen Howard who, with a cruel symmetry of fate after the loss of the Scouts on Snowdon, tripped on a rope, fell onto rocks and was killed while hill-walking with the Venture Scouts, on a comparatively safe hill-path in the Cévennes. Many tributes were paid to this unassuming king of men and of schoolmasters, such as John Heath's obituary in *The Alleynian* (possibly the single best piece of writing ever to appear in the magazine);[256] it was for a while as if something of the honour and the moral core of the College had been lost, and the accident seemed to bode badly. When two more Athletic Houses were created in 1982, namely Jonson and Howard, the latter, while specifically commemorating Charles Howard, the Lord High Admiral and Alleyn's theatrical patron, among so many famous Howards in British history (see Chapter One), also alluded covertly to Stephen Howard.

As has always been the case at the College, the boys benefited from two broad types of teachers: continuity was provided by the very committed masters who served at Dulwich for most of their careers, but the boys also enjoyed the lively youthful stimulus of teachers who left after a few years through restlessness, ambition or the cost of living near Dulwich. It is impossible to do them all the justice they deserve individually in this chronicle. J. R. Hughes, appointed in 1953, the Head of Geography, as (Lieutenant-Colonel) commanded the CCF from 1962 until 1964, and retired in 1978. Six women teachers were

appointed by David Emms to the staff; the first to teach full-time at the College, in 1976, was Michele Conway whose subject was Mathematics, and who left in 1981. In the very early days these women were amused to be addressed as 'Sir' by the younger boys. A. C. V. Evans was appointed from Winchester College to run the Modern Languages Department in 1977; with his high academic principles and his organising skill, he was appointed to a post that David Emms created for him, the Head of Humanities. Tony Evans, an inspiring teacher and (like three other members of staff and a boy at that time) a runner in the London Marathon, left in 1983 to be Headmaster of Portsmouth Grammar School and later of King's College School, Wimbledon, and to win renown in his year as Chairman of the Headmasters' Conference. In 1982 David Emms dissolved Groves's Heads of Side Committee, with its large membership, and divided it into two: his Cabinet, composed of five senior men, and a large Academic Policy Committee ('Capcom').

Among outstanding History teachers who followed Ernie Williams was the exceptionally civilised and humorous Peter Southern, appointed 1973, who left in 1978 to teach at Westminster, and was later appointed Headmaster of Bancroft's School and soon after of Christ's Hospital. Ian Galbraith, an Old Alleynian (left 1966), a starred First in Geography at Cambridge, an excellent musician and a friend of Stephen Howard, shared some of Howard's qualities; from Head of Geography, he was promoted to follow Tony Evans as Head of Humanities, and he then became the first Head of the Upper School of the modern Dulwich College, but left in 1993, appointed Head of Ipswich School. Galbraith did much to encourage expeditions, and several boys carried out scientific work in Greenland, Norway and the tropical forests of Australia with the British Schools Exploration Society. In 1982 Frank Loveder, a Chemistry teacher from 1974 until 1988, took a group of Venture Scouts to walk the entire length of the Pyrenees from the Atlantic to the Mediterranean in seven weeks. Several other members of the Common Room became headmasters: Tristram Jones-Parry at Westminster; Simon Dawkins at Merchant Taylor's School, Crosby; David Gray at Pocklington School and then at Stewart's Melville School, Edinburgh; Ian Walker at King's School, Rochester; Stephen Meek at Hurstpierpoint College and at Geelong Grammar School, Australia; David Lamper at Kent College.

At David Emms's final assembly in the Great Hall the boys of the Upper School secretly arranged for a visitor, a pretty girl from an agency in fishnet tights who bussed him on both cheeks, sang (badly) a song written by the boys in his praise, and proceeded to sit in his lap on stage; this was a 'Kissogram' (the latest fashion that year, an improvement on 'saying it with flowers'), and the Master received the accolade with great aplomb.

Alleynians

Those who benefited from the College of God's Gift have richly responded with their own gifts to the world, bringing to mind the profusion of the Horn of Plenty in Edward Alleyn's painted panel of *Liberalitas* in the Masters' Library. A number of select Alleynians from Emms's day onwards who have distinguished themselves in particular fields have been mentioned already; together with those that follow here these names make up, with regret, a brief unjust anthology of the talents and success that deserve to be recorded in a full chronicle. Gabriele Finaldi (left 1984) is Deputy Director of the Prado Museum in Madrid. Jeremy Deller (who also left in 1984) won the Turner Prize in 2004 for a multi-media installation, *Memory Bucket*, documenting his travels in the state of Texas. Robert Smith (left 1983), a Prize Fellow at All Souls College, Oxford, published among other works *Derrida and Autobiography* (1995). Tom Scholar (left 1986), after serving in the Treasury and as British representative at the World Bank in Washington, has recently been appointed Chief of Staff and Principal Private Secretary to the Prime Minister. Dominic Shellard (left 1984), English Professor at the University of Sheffield, is an authority on British Drama since the War and has published a life of Kenneth Tynan (2003). Nicholas de Somogyi (who left in 1981, the youngest of three Alleynian brothers, each of whom went on to study English with distinction at Pembroke College, Cambridge) is the editor of the Nick Hern Books Folio Shakespeare series, author of *Shakespeare's Theatre of War* (1998) and other books. Tom McCarthy, who left in 1986, has published two novels, *Remainder* (2005) and *Men in Space* (2007), and an original piece of criticism, *Tintin and the Secret of Literature* (2006); also leaving in 1986 were Matthew Parker, a playwright, the author of *Celaine* (1999), and Ed Simons, one of the Chemical Brothers popular music band, who spent the Sixth Form at Alleyn's School. Vin de Silva (left 1990) is Associate Professor of Mathematics at Pomona College, California, and has published many articles in specialist periodicals. Henry Nicholls (left 1991) is the author of *Lonesome George* (2006), about a Galapagos tortoise. Four bookish school-leavers of 1992 have recently achieved distinction. Richard Scholar, the Captain of School (and the brother of Tom), is a Fellow of Oriel College at Oxford, and a Tutor in Modern Languages with expertise in the literature and thought of early modern Europe, who has published *The Je-Ne-Sais-Quoi in Early Modern Europe* (2005); Nicholas

Saunders, now a barrister, published *Divine Action and Modern Science* (2003); James McConnachie, a travel writer, journalist and broadcaster has published *The Book of Love* (2007) about the *Kamasutra*, and Robin Tudge *The Bradt Guide to North Korea* (2003), the first western travel guide to the country. Ian Phillips (left 1999) is a Prize Fellow of All Souls College, Oxford, and an authority on Logic and Language and the Philosophy of Mind.

The Picture Gallery

Matters at the Gallery reached another crisis in David Emms's day. After renewed proposals to hand over its administration to the National Gallery or to the National Maritime Museum in 1976, or to limp along by selling pictures from the store, the Gallery was £25,000 in debt the following year, and its annual deficit steadily increasing.[257] In 1978 the Charity Commissioners opposed the sale of more paintings. The Board devised a scheme whereby each of the three schools would contribute a per capita grant, in return for educational advantages at the Gallery. The association of Dulwich College with its Gallery was betrayed in the process, at least in the eyes of the world and of visitors to the Gallery: it was now agreed to filch and discard the word 'College' from the title 'Dulwich College Picture Gallery', alluding to its historic foundation, and to orphan it as 'Dulwich Picture Gallery', a bald indicator of its location; although 'Dulwich College' had for centuries been a generic name for the whole Foundation of Alleyn's College of God's Gift (but admittedly was now not even a truly ambiguous name), the Headmistress of James Allen's Girls' School objected to the title 'Dulwich College Picture Gallery' since, now her own school was contributing funds, the Gallery's name might be taken as implying that it was the preserve of school-children of the male gender.[258]

Basil Greenhill (1920–2003), a famously successful Director of the National Maritime Museum and the father of two boys at the College, was a dedicated and resourceful Chairman of the Picture Gallery Committee. With the appointment at last of a proper professional Director of the Gallery, the young and most charming Giles Waterfield, in 1979, a stirring new era began, marked by scholarship, elegance, initiatives, special exhibitions at the Gallery, ambitious fund-raising and major exhibitions of the Gallery's pictures overseas (at Washington and Los Angeles in 1985, and in Japan in 1996), making the Gallery well known all over the world and dramatically increasing its attendance, in spite of its distance from Central London. One journalist wrote that Waterfield's boldest stroke was to rescue the Gallery from Dulwich College.[259]

In 1981 the Gallery was re-hung and re-decorated.

£25,000 had just been spent on security when on 14 August of the same year Rembrandt's portrait *Jacob de Gheyn* (DPG 99) was stolen again. Thieves entered the Gallery through a roof-light and got away in the three minutes it took before the alarm brought the police to the Gallery; the picture was recovered from a taxi in Holland on 2 September, during an extraordinary criminal investigation involving members of the Dulwich police station disguised as waiters in a Dutch restaurant. In 1983 permanent closure of the Gallery again looked imminent, but a very substantial benefactor, Lord Sainsbury of Preston Candover, and major fund-raising elsewhere saved the Gallery. Gillian Wolfe, appointed Head of Education in 1984, has made the Gallery famous for imaginative and highly successful programmes that are so obviously popular with local schools and communities; in 2005 she was awarded the CBE for 'social action through art education'.

PART III
THE TURN OF THE CENTURY, 1986–2007
ANTHONY VERITY, CHRISTOPHER FIELD & GRAHAM ABLE

ANTHONY VERITY, 1986–95 – The Governors – Buildings and other initiatives – Drama – Music – Founder's Day – 'The Alleynian' – The James Caird Society – The Common Room

Anthony Verity, 1986–95

Anthony Verity, appointed to succeed David Emms, attended Queen Elizabeth's Hospital School for Boys in Bristol, and brought with him outstanding academic qualifications in Classics and Oriental Studies from Pembroke College, Cambridge. Tony Verity's scholastic and administrative career was already distinguished, as a classroom teacher, as Head of a large Classics Department and then of a large civic school; he knew the Dulwich College of Groves's era well, as a member of the Classics Department from 1962 until 1965. He had left the College to teach the Classical VI Form at Manchester Grammar School, from which he was appointed Head of the Classics Department at Bristol Grammar School. He was chosen as Headmaster of Leeds Grammar School in 1976, a boys' school whose history resembles Dulwich College and Alleyn's School in its origin, its Victorian Gothic premises (since abandoned) designed by a son of Sir Charles Barry, and in its twentieth-century fortunes.

A man of wide culture and intellectual interests, Tony Verity has published translations of Theocritus (2002) and of Pindar (2007). He is a keen cricketer with a particular love of music, and likes to walk in the high places of the world. As Master of Dulwich College he showed himself to be genuinely interested in educational theory, in the curriculum, and in classroom transaction. Ataraxic by nature, however, he disliked the fast pace of Dulwich, questioned whether the many administrative meetings in the lunch hours were really necessary, and was disappointed that the over-worked members of the Common Room spent less time sharing intellectual interests than during the era when he was a member as a young man; the staff on the other hand were amused when he declared at his first staff meeting that there was not enough time to look out of the window at Dulwich College. [260]

The College now developed a more cosmopolitan view. Tony Verity played a central part in the foundation of the new Dulwich College in Thailand and the signing of its Licence Agreement, launching what has become the very significant venture of the Dulwich International Schools (see Chapter Eleven). Another of his achievements was to promote at the College a Headmasters' Conference scheme to bring East European scholars to study at British schools; this admirable programme, partly the initiative of Roger Wicks, a former Assistant Master at the College and at that time Head Master of Kent College, has now lapsed. The United World Colleges and the Polish Children's Fund sent some exceptionally interesting boys to the Upper School at Dulwich from Poland, Hungary and the Czech Republic who went on to achieve great success at, for example, Cambridge and Harvard; Pawel Nowak, who left in 1997, became a notable teacher of Linguistics in the United States. Dulwich boys in A Level groups benefited meanwhile from a sharp encounter with the European intellectual tradition. New languages were added to the curriculum in Tony Verity's days: Spanish had been introduced in the 1980s; Tony Verity now introduced the teaching of Arabic, and Ian Brinton, who was at that time Head of the Upper School, introduced after-school classes in Japanese in 1994.

Susannah Fiennes, *Anthony Verity*, 1997.
Dulwich College. (© Susannah Fiennes)

The Governors

The traditionalist Old Alleynian, Sir Colin Cole, Garter King of Arms (see Chapter Nine), was Chairman of the Governors from 1988 until 1997. Sir James Swaffield, Clerk to the Greater London Council for many years, was the Chairman of the Dulwich College sub-Committee of the Governors until 1995; his son Stephen Swaffield had been Captain of School in 1980. Roy Amlot (see above) was Staff Representative. Cole's Deputy Chairman was Professor C. D. 'Jeremy' Cowan, former Director of the School of Oriental and African Studies and Pro Vice-Chancellor of the University of London, and a local resident; Mrs Jean Gooder, Fellow in English Literature of Newnham College, Cambridge, who was on the Board from 1995 until 2002, took a real interest in the academic side of the College.

Buildings and other initiatives

Developments in Tony Verity's years included the construction of the pleasing Shackleton Building, of which the foundation stone was laid by Sir Colin Cole, and which was opened by Lord Shackleton, the son of the explorer, in 1989; housing the Third Forms, the new building eased the heavy pressure on classroom space in the North and South Blocks. It was designed by John Wells-Thorpe, its red and buff brick livery harmonising with the Barry buildings. The post-modern quarters of the Junior School, for seven- to ten-year-olds and with a separate Head, Mrs Penny Horsman (appointed soon afterwards), sited at the south-east verge of the College, were opened by Sir Peter Duffell in 1993. The Medical Centre (see below) was put onto the building timetable by Tony Verity, although work did not begin until 1996.

The Dulwich College Kindergarten School, acronymically 'DUCKS', developed from a staff crèche started in 1992 in rooms at the Old Sanatorium and then settled at Eller Bank, across College Road; a new Infants' Building was opened in 1998. The Head Teachers were in turn Ann Christine Andersen, Fiona Johnstone (who left to open a new 'DUCKS' in Shanghai; see Chapter Eleven), and Heather Friell.

Tony Verity launched the Bursary Appeal, with Terry Walsh as Director, in 1990. On his initiative very successful reunion Dinners were inaugurated for Old Alleynians in the various professions. In 1994 Tony Verity made in good faith a move to improve the pastoral system by assigning boys to Tutor Groups, with teachers as counsellors who would not get to know them in the classroom; a committee, set up to review the scheme, condemned it, and it was dissolved by the Acting Master, Christopher Field, when Tony Verity retired. Horse-riding flourished, organised with much enthusiasm by the German teacher, Ursula Player (left 1998; died 2003); Rowing was founded in 1991 by Trevor Charlton with ten members and an ancient boat called *Jock*; within a decade a Boat House on the Embankment at Putney was in use and then was bought for the Dulwich College Boat Club.

Tony Verity will be remembered for the great encouragement he gave to the intellectual life of the College, and to its culture; he was deeply interested in Art, Drama, and (most of all) in Music, and they flourished accordingly. The Art Department under Barry Viney prolonged its heyday from David Emms's era, properly recognised as a serious and adult institution (regardless of contemporary fashions).

Drama

We know that Edward Alleyn's Poor Scholars at the College 'played a play', presumably under his direction (see Chapter One). Peter Jolly, an Old Alleynian (left 1980), was appointed Director of Drama in 1991. In 1996 Tim Foster was commissioned to enlarge the Theatre foyer and to build a rehearsal room at the back of the stage. On completion in 1997, the Edward Alleyn Hall became at last the Edward Alleyn Theatre, and was opened by the actress Jane Asher. This event marked a fundamental change: Drama was now to be thought of as an integral part of the College and of the education it offered to all. Curriculum Drama had been introduced into Lower and Middle School forms in 1987, taught by (mostly unqualified, but enthusiastic) English teachers, and A Level Theatre Studies was offered as an option from 2000. The range and number of plays produced was extended, and younger boys had more opportunities to appear on stage; productions also took place involving both staff and boys. House Drama over the years has been the origin of many careers on the stage and in television: the playwright Michael Punter (left 1987), author of *The Wolves* (1997), wrote a play for House Drama. Two winners of the Best Actor award at House Drama, who also played leading roles in College productions, are now well known: Rupert Penry-Jones (left 1989), who played Caliban and Faustus at school in 1985 and 1989, went on to win awards for his title role in *Don Carlos* with the Royal Shakespeare Company, and is a household name for his performances on television as Adam Carter in the serial *Spooks* and as the romantic lead in *Persuasion* (2007); Chiwetel Ejiofor (left 1995) won the Olivier 'best actor' award in 2008 for his Othello; his screen performances, such as in *Dirty Pretty Things* (2002), are much admired. He first appeared on the Dulwich stage at 13, undertook Angelo in *Measure for Measure* in 1993 (while in the Fifth Form) and in his last two years at the College played Ernest in Wilde's comedy and a main part in Jez Butterworth's *Huge* (with Ian Bartram, now also an actor), going on to act with the National Youth Theatre. A particular highlight of House Drama was the winning play in 1991, *Arctic Willy*, written by Damian Mole; it was selected for performance on the National Theatre's Olivier stage as part of the Lloyds Bank Challenge.

Productions of Elizabethan and Jacobean plays have been central to the recent repertoire, including Jonathan Ward and Kim Eyre's production of *Dr Faustus*; Stephen Jacobi's *Massacre at Paris*; Tony Binns's *The Changeling*; Peter Jolly's *Measure for Measure*; and Matthew Edwards's *The Magnificent Entertainment*, performed on Founder's Day 2003, and repeated at Shakespeare's Globe Theatre. In the latter the boys recreated Edward Alleyn's welcome to King James I on behalf of London (see Chapter One). Michael Ashcroft (see below) and Peter Jolly collaborated on operas, including Benjamin Britten's *Paul Bunyan* and a sequence of lively and highly popular Gilbert and Sullivan operettas. A series of musicals was jointly directed by Peter Jolly and by Andrew Storey, Head of ICT, teacher of Mathematics, computing and music, and included *Calamity Jane* and *Kiss Me Kate*.

There have been many overseas tours of College productions, to Poland and to Chicago, for example, and more recently to 'Shakespeare and Company' in Massachusetts. The successful collaboration in recent years with James Allen's Girls' School has been important for the Drama Department; and indeed a couple of actual marriages of youthful Foundation actors and actresses have ensued. Dulwich staff have directed plays at the Prissian Theatre at JAGS, and JAGS drama teachers have directed at the College. Maggie Jarman costumed thousands of actors over the years and directed many polychromatic productions with younger boys. The annual Junior School musical is always sold out. 'DUCKS' perform at the Edward Alleyn Hall three times a year.

Music

When Alan Morgan retired, Michael Ashcroft was appointed, retiring in 2004 after 18 years; an outstanding and vigorous conductor of choir and orchestra, he possessed a special flair for the choral. Encouraged by Graham Able, in 1998 he was to revive Edward Alleyn's Chapel Choir (intended by the Founder to equal the Chapel Royal). This was achieved with great acclaim, and raised the performance of his 16 choristers to a very high level, with some remarkable treble soloists; the Chapel Choir in fact now comprises 26 boys, including up to six probationers, two tenors and two basses. It became used to being called upon to substitute for the resident choir at Westminster Abbey. Ashcroft added to the musical calendar smaller, more specialist concerts at the Royal Naval College Chapel, Greenwich and St John's, Smith Square, in addition to the grand musical statements made at the Fairfield Hall at Croydon. Inheriting the famous high standards of the College, and creating more opportunities for performance with new ensembles, the Junior Strings, the Big Band and groups of unaccompanied singers (the 'Alleynian Blues'), and giving more prominence to the Second Orchestra and the Wind Band, he extended both the concept of music and its living presence on the platform at Dulwich concerts well beyond the tradition of the Classical. There was already a Head of Wind and a Head of Strings; to these Tony Verity appointed a new position, the Head of Keyboard in 1992. A Head of Singing was to be added in 1998. A new extension to the Music Block was opened on Founder's Day in 1995 by Mrs Margaret Jacob Hyatt, widow of Gordon Jacob OA (see Chapter Eight). There were now frequent recitals of boy pianists, instrumentalists and singers in the Recital Room, and frequent lunch-time promenade concerts in the Lower Hall. The open-air Fireworks Concert on Founder's Day has become an institution. Ashcroft also introduced difficult and contemporary works to the repertoire, such as *The Children's Crusade* by Pierné. It is invidious to select names of the many professional musicians who graduated after studying at the College in Ashcroft's era, but Rodney Clarke (left 1996), also a superb actor, is a most gifted and successful baritone opera singer and soloist on stage and has performed in a great many concerts. The magnificent Barbara Lake, Head of Wind and conductor of the

Wind Band, conducted the Wind Quintet in the Throne Room at St James's Palace in 1996, as part of an RSCM charity reception, arranged by Christopher Field, and Her Majesty the Queen afterwards chatted with the participants.

Founder's Day

By 1990 Founder's Day was in serious decline and looked likely to be abolished through waning conviction, not least since it came at the end of a wearied summer term at the end of an academic year. It was revived in 1995 by Jan Piggott and John Bardell (see below), with tireless and cheerful support from a committee including Mette Turner (the nonpareil Music Co-ordinator), Joan and Esmond Rand (see below) and Nick Black, among others; attendance on the Day was made compulsory both for the boys and staff. Founder's Day is the sole occasion in the year when an Alleynian tribe of past and present boys, staff, Governors and parents gather together. After the traditional Communion service, wreath-laying, and prize-givings for the Upper and Lower Schools, a brass Fanfare from the parapet of the Science Block and the singing of 'Pueri Alleynienses' heralded once again a full afternoon's programme of cricket, music and drama, with appearances by boys on stilts and by jugglers. The motive was to entertain, in the enduring spirit of Edward Alleyn, and to celebrate out-of-class activities such as the boys' Societies with lively displays in the Cloisters. On a glowing evening of the last Saturday in the Summer Term, after the shadows fall on families encircling picnic suppers and wine bottles on the front lawns and the sun sets on the red brick and terracotta of Barry's great front elevation of the College, a triumphant firework display, accompanying the last item in an alfresco concert from orchestra, choirs, swing and wind bands, affirms that a Dulwich year does not end with a whimper.

'The Alleynian'

From 1991 to 1996 *The Alleynian* was edited by Tony Binns, who transformed the magazine into a hardbacked Annual; in general the contents became more accessible, and the look of it more contemporary. Binns was followed as editor by Stephen Pugh. Since Michaelmas 2004 *The Alleynian* has been edited by Dorothy Wright. Appearing each term, it is also now sent to all Old Alleynians who have registered their addresses.

The James Caird Society

The James Caird Society was founded in 1994 by the genial enthusiast Harding Dunnett OA (1909–2000), the twin brother of the artist Val Dunnett OA (d. 1988), who was a boy at the College in the year when the *James Caird* was installed. The intention is to promote the study of Sir Ernest Shackleton and of the Antarctic in general. The explorer's granddaughter, the Hon. Alexandra Shackleton, a great friend to the College, is Life President. The Society meets twice a year for lectures, dining by the *Caird* in the North Cloister; they publish a Newsletter and a Journal.

The Common Room

Many long-serving and dedicated members of staff retired in the course of Tony Verity and Graham Able's tenure. The eupeptic English teacher Gerry Thornton (1926–2007) completed 31 years in 1986; he had also served as Master in Charge of Cricket and as Housemaster of Ivyholme. Brian Jones, Head of Biology and a Housemaster of Blew House, left the same year. The benign Geoff Tomlinson (1928–2003), who succeeded Stephen Howard as Head of Classics, left the College in 1988. Learned, decent and dispassionate, a player of the French horn and a pipe-smoker, early each morning in the Common Room he would preside at the centre of a circle of five or so masters who completed *The Times* crossword in fifteen minutes before morning school; he then might write turn to writing mischievous comments in the current copy of *Country Life*. Garth Davidson, an Old Alleynian who had taught in Nigeria for eleven years, retired in 1994 after 25 years; a teacher of Classics, he also contributed greatly outside the classroom: to sports and to the Scouts, to the Lower School as its Deputy Head and as junior Housemaster of Grenville, and to the Christian Union. In 1995 Malcolm Ewens, a great teacher of Lower School boys and a cricketer, unassuming in the old style of the totally committed bachelor schoolmaster, retired after 37 years, but died from cancer a few months afterwards; a Memorial Garden at The Orchard keeps his name in mind.

The great Peter Rees (see above), the Deputy Master, retired in 1991. Christopher Rowe, a much-admired Head of the Middle School, appointed in 1980 from St Paul's School, and a mathematician, left in 1993. John Charnley, the remarkable hard-working teacher and administrator, who served the College for 36 years, as Head of Physics, and from 1988 as Director of Studies and Third Master, left in 2001. Tim Price, who taught Classics and (as Squadron Leader T. F. Price) was Commanding Officer of the CCF from 1983 until 1991, was Head of the Lower School from 1991 and the Registrar from 1998; he left in 2003 after 33 years at the College. He was succeeded as Commanding Officer of the CCF by Major (now Lieutenant-Colonel) G. E. Rutter. The same year two excellent men left the Science

Block: Esmond Rand, a cheerful Head of Chemistry and of Science, after 35 years, and John Johnston, Head of Physics and of Careers, after 38 years. Joan Rand, teacher of Physics and Head of Lower School Science, left in 2004. David Cartwright, Head of Classics from 1988 and the author of *A Historical Commentary on Thucydides* (1997), a Housemaster of Ivyholme, left in 2007. His successor as Head of Classics, Neil Croally, an Old Alleynian who had left in 1980, published *Euripidean Polemic: The Trojan Women and the function of Tragedy* (1994).

Intellectual stimulus during this period was conveyed with keen pleasure in their own subjects and in others by Nigel Wood, appointed in 1968, who was Head of Physics and then Head of Science from 1989 until 1995, and served for 32 years; and also by Paul Keyte, philosopher and teacher of Religious Studies and a sparkling conversationalist among boys and masters, appointed in 1986 and leaving in 1994, who was in charge of Liberal, Optional and General Studies. Two very pleasant and gifted teachers of this epoch left to become Headmasters of preparatory schools: Mark Adams, whose exceptional range of gifts included celebrated productions in the Theatre (such as *Cabaret* in 1983 and a wonderful *Toad of Toad Hall* in 1981) and a knack of interesting young boys in Science, left in 1984 to become Headmaster of Clifton Hall Preparatory School near Edinburgh; Philip Evitt, an outstanding History teacher from 1985 until 1999, became Headmaster of Highfield School, Liphook. Ted Bowen-Jones, a remarkable and unconventional Biology teacher for 39 years who fostered many medical pupils and gave generously of his time to the Scouts and to Photography, left in 1998. Nick Tumber, teacher of Physics and Electronics, left in 1997 after 28 years, and Hugh Bain, athlete, Physicist and Examinations Officer, after 38 years in 2002. F. R. F. 'Rick' Wilson taught French from 1970 until 2000, and was housemaster of The Orchard; it was generally agreed to be a great advantage that Wilson, a member of the teaching staff, also had responsibility for the entire Games system at the College; this he carried out with conspicuous success, and was himself an outstanding coach of both cricket and Rugby. Terry Kent, Head of a prosperous Department of Design and Technology, retired after 31 years in 2003. The College was shaken when Tony Salter, of the same department, a popular contributor to the CCF and (as Major A. J. D. Salter) its Commanding Officer (from 1979 to 1983 and again – as Lieutenant-Colonel Salter – from 2003), died suddenly in 2006, while still at work. Of two long-serving Geographers, David Smart, the founder of idealistic and ecological Societies, retired in 1987, and David Rose in 2003 after 36 years. Jim Reddaway, Head of Biology and (like Nigel Wood) a polymath, retired in 2005 after 24 years' service. In 2005 and 2006 retired Steve Burton and Chris Wall, excellent Mathematicians, cricket and Rugby coaches, after 37 and 38 years. The flamboyant and reactionary Nick Hulme, a linguist, left after a short stay in 1996, having brought colour and sheen into some relatively common-place classrooms, teaching the Lower School boys in Form Period how to set a table for a dinner party and how to reply to invitations in the third person singular. Fergus Jamieson, a cultivated teacher of French, an inspired Form Master, a musician and an accomplished actor, retired in 2002; he had also been a first-rate Secretary of the Common Room for twenty years from 1978. Allan Ronald, an erudite and self-effacing Deputy Head of the English Department, whose twenty years of teaching included some Latin and History to lower forms, and who gave stirring traditional assembly addresses, left in 2003. Professor Stuart Malin, the former Director of the Royal Greenwich Observatory, brought a further dimension of intellectual distinction to the Common Room from 1987 until 1994 (with one year away). The notably efficient Bursar of 18 years' service, Will Skinner, retired in 2005. In 1994 a greatly loved Sister at the Sanatorium, Abbie (Sister Dorothy Simmonds-Abbott), left the College after eight years to return to South Africa. Alistair Slabczynski, the Head of Spanish, leaving in 2002, for 22 years had shown devotion to his pupils, his subject and to his work in the boarding house. Chris Gold, appointed in 1973, an outstanding linguist, modest and cultured, became Head of French in 1991 and also taught Arabic, retiring in 2007. The same year David Burns, at one time Head of Economics, left after twenty years. Jonathan Brownridge, appointed in 1987, a teacher of Physics, as Major J. P. Brownridge was Commanding Officer of the CCF from 1996 until he left in 2003; he served as President of the Common Room from 1999 until 2002. The retirement of the lively Physicist John Bardell in 2004 (although he returned part-time to help with his former department, Audio-Visual Aids) marked 29 years of tireless service to the College, engaging the boys' interests in how things work and what they mean in the classroom and explaining the universe in his assembly addresses; he inspired affection by his cheerful and apparently effortless kindness to all. Terry Walsh, retired but now a member of the staff in the College Archives where his memory of all Alleynian matters is a major resource, celebrated Fifty Golden Years at the College in 2004 with speeches and lunch in a marquee with his loyal admirers.

*

CHRISTOPHER FIELD, ACTING MASTER 1995–6

When Tony Verity took early retirement in November 1995, Christopher Field was appointed Acting Master, and served until January 1997. In a very interesting Report to the Governors, recalling his own schooldays and based on his long observation and deeply committed service at the College, he mentioned the features that had improved at the College since 1959 when he left it as a schoolboy. These included staff appraisal and the improved monitoring of teachers and lessons, the aims and practice that had led to maintaining excellence, and the broader spectrum of syllabus available to boys. He wrote that the pastoral care at the College was nowadays more compassionate, and made the important observation about the culture of the College that boys recognised more diverse talents among themselves than in earlier days. He welcomed the involvement of parents that David Emms brought about. Much more than a safe pair of hands, Christopher Field, transmitter of the best of Dulwich values, also coped in these months with a full-scale Inspection. He was strongly supported in his tenure by R. A. 'Bob' Alexander, the Clerk to the Governors, and by the members of the Senior Staff Discussion group: John Charnley, Gardner Thompson (see below), Ian Brinton (Head of the Upper School), Ralph Mainard (Head of the Middle School), Tim Price (Head of the Lower School), and Esmond Rand.

GRAHAM ABLE, 1997 – The Governors – The pupils – The World Wide Franchise – The Sheppey Academy – Exhibitions – Debating and the Literary Festivals – Buildings

Graham Able, 1997

Graham Able, the current Master of Dulwich College, attended Worksop College (where Simon Northcote-Green's father was his Headmaster) and studied Natural Sciences at Trinity College, Cambridge. At the age of 16 he felt a calling to teach;[261] his career began at Sutton Valence where he served for 14 years, seven as a boarding Housemaster. He was appointed as a Deputy Headmaster young in his career, serving for five years at Barnard Castle School, the co-educational day and boarding school, and then as Headmaster at Hampton School, the boys' school in south-west London, recently independent, for a further nine. His subject is Chemistry, and Cricket is a special enthusiasm. Among his many achievements at the College are the founding of the College's licence schools in China (see Chapter Eleven) and the planning behind the opening of more Dulwich Colleges in India and the Middle East (see below).

Graham Able appointed two outstanding Deputy Masters: Gardner Thompson to the Academic position, and Simon Northcote-Green to the Pastoral – a new system of divided care. Gardner Thompson, who retired in 2007, was a powerful and influential teacher and a good sporting master in charge of boys' teams, and had served as Head of History; with a special interest in Russia and expertise in African Colonialism, he is the author of *Governing Uganda* (2003). The English teacher Simon Northcote-Green, also a notable creative writer, was earlier Housemaster of Blew House and Master in Charge of Cricket and of Hockey; he had proved himself a sterling, compassionate and generous President of the Common Room from 1994 until 1999, and was an admirable Acting Master while Graham Able was on sabbatical.

Graham Able's bold and highly successful revival of Edward Alleyn's Chapel Choir in 1998, with Michael Ashcroft as their choir-master, has been mentioned above. In the same way, looking to the early days of the Foundation to animate the present and the future, he revived the appointment of Fellowships at the College, a title now awarded to contemporary benefactors to reward very significant contributions, whether of wealth, wisdom or work. Terry Walsh was, most appropriately, created the first Senior Fellow of Dulwich College in 2003, in recognition of his years of selfless devotion to its cause.

The Governors

In 1995 the Board of Governors had been reconstituted, with a smaller body and altogether lacking the traditional institutional appointments, whether academic or national; eminent parents, Old Alleynians and local residents were well represented. A great debt is owed by the College to Lord Butler of Brockwell KG, GCB, CVO, the genial and nationally respected former Cabinet Secretary and Head of the Home Civil Service and until recently the Master of University College, Oxford, whose Chairmanship lasted for six years from 1997. Lord Butler displayed his noted integrity and also a genuine interest in and encouragement of life at the College, at the same time working tirelessly behind the scenes to resolve a complex set of negotiations with the Estate. He reformed the constitution of the Governing body and introduced term limits for Governors, thus ensuring that the College would never henceforward suffer from the stagnation which has adversely affected the governance of many schools in recent times. Lord Butler was succeeded as Chairman in 2003 by Lord George of St Tudy (see above); his Deputy is Lord Turnbull, a successor to Lord Butler as Cabinet Secretary and Head of the Home Civil Service.

The pupils

Graham Able is a great internationalist and traveller, neither allowing the College to suffer from introversion nor to feed off its reputation. He introduced the study of Mandarin as an option for the boys in 2004. Speaking at Dublin as Chairman of the Headmasters' Conference in 2003, he drew attention to educational practice overseas, referring to initiatives in the USA, Australia and New Zealand. It is his belief that the habitual traditional syllabuses should be tempered by the greater imperative of equipping pupils nowadays with qualifications that fit the current purpose, and that such an outlook might serve as an influence in reducing the burdens of examinations and coursework, and to prevent internet abuse; press coverage has often been given to his opinions.

Graham Able believes that the majority of boys do better academically in single-sex classrooms.[262] Confidently facing the loss of the Assisted Place boys, arriving in the very year that they ceased, and in an increasingly competitive environment, he set out to attract boys from the top 20 per cent to 25 per cent of the academic spectrum and was remarkably successful both in doing so and also in ensuring that all boys admitted to the College were challenged academically. The College Roll from 1990 until 2000 varied only from 1,398 to 1,419 boys, including the Junior School, but not 'DUCKS'. In September 2006 the numbers were 1,438. Recent academic achievement is hard to highlight without serious injustice, but striking success was achieved at A Level by the Mathematics Department under its Head of over eight years, Jeremy Lord, and including the dedicated Helen Johnson, who for many years has encouraged, guided, and expedited thousands of applications to university; the boys won very many prizes in the Mathematics Olympiads. Astringent and broadening courses were introduced in Critical Thinking and in General Studies (the latter – unlike the courses with the same title formerly taught in the first year of the Upper School – towards an A Level examination taken in the Removes on just four periods a week).

Extra-curricular activities continue to be a great strength of the College, and remarkable service was given (until his recent retirement as President) in encouragement and in organisation of the boys' Union by Robert Weaver, the Head of Religious Studies. In 1997 the First XV was unbeaten and two of its members went on to play for England (see Chapter Twelve). In 2000 five boys were playing in the National Youth Orchestra.

*

The World Wide Franchise

A proactive entrepreneur on behalf of the College, for Graham Able the franchises he negotiated in China and elsewhere (see Chapter Eleven) are aimed at funding 'needs-blind' bursaries at the College in the future, by which is meant that no boy who is worthy to join the College would lack a Bursary if his family could not afford the fees. As Able himself writes,

> Following protracted negotiations between a Dulwich team and Fraser White, the holder of our franchise contract for the People's Republic of China, a world-wide franchise agreement was signed on 7 November 2007 between Dulwich College Enterprises (Overseas) Ltd – a new company set up for this particular purpose – and Educational Index Ltd, Fraser White's holding company, to form a new company, Dulwich College Management International, which will finance and develop Dulwich branded schools worldwide. The College, through its commercial subsidiary, will be given a 5% shareholding in the new company and so will share in any future prosperity as well as deriving an index-linked income from each school. It is envisaged that the income from the overseas schools, together with the ongoing commitment of Old Alleynians to the Bursary Appeal, will take the College to a 'needs blind' entrance situation within 15 years. Throughout the necessarily long and complex negotiations for this agreement, the Master was supported throughout by the diligence of Ralph Mainard, the Deputy Master for External Relations (formerly Head of the Middle School), and the exceptional voluntary contributions of Nick Tatman (OA), Chairman of the Governors' Finance Committee, and Andrew Seth, former Vice-chairman of Governors and a Director of Dulwich College Enterprises (Overseas) Ltd. Both Andrew and Nick will serve as non-executive Directors of Dulwich Management International from its foundation, thus ensuring that the College's best interests are well protected.

The Sheppey Academy

The College has recently been involved with the Government in discussions about setting up City Academies, and it hopes to play a significant part in their progress. Graham Able writes:

> The College responded positively to a direct Government request to take the educational lead in setting up a new, state-funded academy for secondary education. After a false dawn with a local authority in the eastern approaches to London, the Isle of Sheppey was identified as the location for this project. Ralph Mainard, as Deputy Master for External Relations, is leading the Dulwich input into the setting up of this academy and Lord Turnbull, as Vice-chairman of Governors, is also closely involved in support of both Ralph and the Master.

Although contributing no financial sponsorship, the College has been designated 'lead sponsor' in this project and hopes that the experience gained overseas in quality control at a distance will make a noticeable impact on the education available to the young people of Sheppey. The Academy opens in 2008, although it will not have the benefit of all its new facilities for at least another year after that.

Exhibitions

Jan Piggott (see above) became Keeper of Archives in 1995. *Shackleton, the Antarctic and Endurance*, an exhibition he organized in the Old Library in 2000, was opened by Alexandra Shackleton. For the first time a large display of pictures, photographs and artefacts borrowed from museums and collectors across the world and from the families of Shackleton and his men was to be seen; among the exhibits was the Union Flag presented by Queen Alexandra to the *Endurance* expedition, intended for Shackleton to carry across the entire continent of Antarctica, which was returned from Elephant Island to Sandringham by the explorer in 1917 and was now graciously lent by HM the Queen. The exhibition attracted over 10,000 visitors. The actor Kenneth Branagh (who was at that time playing Shackleton himself in a film) was among them, and the exhibition made a profit of £20,000. In 2001 Sir Colin Cole bequeathed his very significant heraldic library of some six hundred volumes to the College; from this an exhibition was put on, and heraldry for a while was included in the Lower School History syllabus. Of the many exhibitions in the Archive, *Edward Alleyn and the Theatre* (2000), including a selection of the Alleyn and Henslowe papers, aroused a great deal of interest outside the College as well as within, and was curated by Nicholas de Somogyi (see above) who was later the guiding force behind some excellent exhibitions at Shakespeare's Globe Theatre. Other exhibitions were specially popular with visitors: a Founder's Day display commemorating the Old Alleynian gallantries at Zeebrugge (see Chapter Nine), mounted by Nick Black, the Head of History, and his pupils; Allan Ronald's learned displays of rare books from the Fellows' Library; and an ambitious centenary exhibition about the Old Alleynian film director Michael Powell (2006). Mrs Calista Lucy, who succeeded as Keeper of Archives in 2006, has organised exhibitions on the College's Athletic Houses and on the Dulwich Victoria Crosses (on the occasion of the 150th Anniversary of the Award); the latter was opened by Sir Peter Duffell.

*

Debating and the Literary Festivals

Two initiatives came from the English Department. Dulwich boys have usually written well, but placing more emphasis on oral work the Debating Society, run by the Head of English, Stephen Farrow (first appointed as a teacher in 1986 and leaving in 2007), achieved heights in national and international competitions; this reflected very well on the new GCSE syllabuses which encouraged oral fluency of boys in the classroom – a development of which the Founder, with his 'well-tun'd audible voice', would surely approve. In 1994, when Tony Verity was Master, a Media Festival was devised for the boys by an English teacher, Stephen Jacobi (at the College from 1988 until 1995), himself a published novelist. The Dulwich College Literary Festivals were founded by Jan Piggott and Jonathan Ward in 1998. The Festivals were held for a further two years (directed by Jonathan Ward), and were popular with the College boys and with local people. Lectures and readings were given by speakers and writers from the College, and by well-known academics and writers, Old Alleynian and others; the poet Barry MacSweeney (1948–2000) was a particularly welcome and fascinating regular visitor.

Buildings

Graham Able, who wrote a thesis for one of his MA degrees on the relation of the physical environment of schools to their pupils, improved several areas of the College significantly. The Dr Richard Penny Medical Centre, named for a much-loved Old Alleynian (1937–96) who was the College Medical Officer, was opened by Professor Karol Sikora OA in 1997. A superb new Swimming Pool, grafted onto the PE Centre and costing £2.5 million, was opened by Lord Butler in 2002. Ivyholme and Blew now offer luxurious accommodation with individual en-suite facilities, renewed at great expense in 2000, popularly known as 'The Dulwich Hilton'; these were acknowledged at the time to offer the best facilities of any boarding school in the kingdom, for pupils who are now almost entirely from overseas. These facilities, taken together with the College's annual list of university destinations, are naturally very persuasive factors when parents overseas elect to send their boys to board at Dulwich. The Libraries and computing facilities are also at the forefront of educational resources. The College offers improved pastoral care, and the range of courses and of the universities taken up by leavers is now much wider; a good number of leavers join Ivy League universities in the United States. On Founder's Day 2007 the Master in a yellow 'hard hat' removed the first brick from the old Swimming Bath site, for an ambitious new development. This will house an Economics and Business Studies Centre, a Careers Suite, an Upper School Centre for study and recreation, a Café, an improved Commissariat and Changing Rooms, and for the Music Department an auditorium to seat 250, new practice rooms and classrooms. As the young century develops, should the 'needs-blind' bursaries result from Graham Able's enterprise and the generosity of Old Alleynians, the modern College will draw ever closer to the ideal of Edward Alleyn, the old player, munificently transforming Poor Scholars into the future Platonic 'Guardians' of London and the nation.

Vivit Fundatoris nomen

'FORTH WE GO'

THE DULWICH COLLEGE INTERNATIONAL SCHOOLS

by Graham Able, MA, MA, FRSA,
Master of Dulwich College

with assistance from Colin Niven, D de l'U,
Palmes Académiques, FRSA (OA)

A little seed was humbly sown,
Since then to what huge stature grown!

Sons of the Mother, forth we go,
'Neath tropic suns, to the Polar snow.

– A. N. C. KITTERMASTER
'The Edward Alleyn Song', 1911

D I C Phuket – Dulwich College Shanghai – Dulwich College Beijing – Dulwich College Suzhou and the future –
Governance and the Management Company

Edward Alleyn planted an acorn which has now become a sizeable Dulwich wood. There is, as yet, no Dulwich College on the equator or in Antarctica, but we have gained valuable experience with one in Thailand, have started a bold and successful project in the two major Chinese cities of Shanghai and Beijing, and are looking carefully at potential expansions elsewhere, including India.

A famous school with nearly four hundred years of history and tradition does not embark lightly on such an undertaking. One major motivation is that of Alleyn's original foundation to support 'twelve poor scholars'[1] – very much akin to the motivation for the Dulwich Experiment negotiated by Christopher Gilkes. All the income from the franchise schools is passed by Dulwich College Enterprises Limited (DCEL) to the College and used for additional bursaries for boys needing help with their fees at the mother school. The overseas schools also provide exchange opportunities for all students in the Dulwich family, and raise the profile of the College in areas of the world from which our international boarders are traditionally recruited. Through the franchise schools an excellent Dulwich-style education is being offered to boys and girls whose parents otherwise would be faced with difficult schooling decisions. China, for example, urgently required foreign expertise to maintain its economic growth, and unless expatriates

wish to send their children to boarding schools, they need a high quality English-medium school within commuting distance. Moreover, with their eventual return home in mind, ideally they need a school which follows a relevant academic system, in this case the enhanced Dulwich version of the English National Curriculum. The Deputy Governor of Pudong identified Dulwich College Shanghai as integral to his planning in the Jin Qiao district, and the price of residential properties in the area rose by 25 per cent in the weeks following the announcement that the school would open.

The Dulwich international schools foster relationships between students of many nationalities. This has always been a strong feature of our College in London, and our franchise schools have students from a very wide range of cultural and ethnic backgrounds. These young people learn another language in a new cultural environment and make friends with their local counterparts. The new Dulwich Colleges are required to adhere to the spirit of our Foundation, ensuring that the ethos of the schools is based on mutual respect and encouragement; educational values are always the highest priority, and this should enable many more young people to benefit from this latest Dulwich project. Nor does the Dulwich connection end on leaving school: the Alleyn Club has extended reciprocal membership facilities to the alumni organisations of all Dulwich Schools worldwide.

DIC Phuket

The first overseas Dulwich venture was in Thailand on the beautiful island of Phuket. The regular alumni dinners in Bangkok are a popular tribute to the warm links between our Thai Old Alleynians and their Alma Mater, so the combination of Dulwich and Thailand was highly appropriate. Thai boys have excelled at the College for over seventy years, and the Guest of Honour at Founder's Day 2005 was that most distinguished Alleynian, Anand Panyarachun, twice Prime Minister of Thailand and Chairman of the Committee on the Future of the United Nations. Khun Anand spoke movingly of his debt to Dulwich.

The idea started from a discussion of the huge strain placed on children's education by the Bangkok traffic: many had to leave home at six o'clock in the morning and return late after a two-hour journey. Several OAs in Thailand felt that a boarding school outside the capital could be the answer. Khun Praoranuj Chandrasomboon recognised this need, and the then Master, Anthony Verity, wrote to her on 20 June 1994, 'It was your vision and energy which brought the project into being'.[2] Tony Verity should, however, take most credit for the foundation of the new school: he worked hard as a

consultant to assist the growing number of supporters of a new Dulwich College in Thailand, and negotiated the Licence Agreement.

After some local wrangling, Khun Praoranuj faded from the negotiations, and an agreement was reached between the Master and Dr Arthit Ourairat, a businessman and government minister. This was drawn up by Abbott, King and Troen as legal advisers to the College in collaboration with Tilleke and Gibbons in Bangkok. Tony Verity had consulted widely with Thai OAs and College Governors before announcing the signing of the Licence Agreement on 28 November, 1994.[3] He travelled to Bangkok for a dinner in December 1994 hosted by Arsa Sarasin, OA and a former Foreign Minister, at the Siam City Hotel. Khun Anand was present, as was Dr Arthit. The British ambassador, Christian Adams, and other interested parties also attended.

Tony Verity recommended a former Dulwich teacher, Michael Haywood, as the first Master of Dulwich International College. He had been Headmaster of Sutton Valence School and was appointed to Phuket from 1 January 1995, eighteen months before the school opened.

The main school building recalls Barry's Dulwich College, its red brick offset by the vertical white frame-

Dulwich International College, Phuket, 2005. (Dulwich College)

work of the windows whilst its Thai features give its own unique charm. Surrounded by the tree-covered arena of the nearby hills, the campus is stunningly located, and the combination of flower-beds, playing fields, swimming pools, boarding houses and specialist facilities created a school of rare beauty. As the 2004 prospectus states, 'established in 1996, Dulwich International College is a co-educational day and boarding school set in an extensive safe and beautifully landscaped campus in the heart of the picturesque island of Phuket in southern Thailand. Here western and eastern philosophy, culture and wisdom blend in a stimulating environment conducive to intellectual, social and physical development. The school delivers a British international curriculum to children of all nationalities from 18 months to 18 years of age, with external examinations being offered in the IGCSE and the IB (International Baccalaureate)'.[4]

Michael Haywood did not find it easy to match the aspirations of Dulwich with the need to attract pupils to a new school in the middle of a Thai financial crisis. He made a presentation to Dulwich College Governors in London shortly after Graham Able arrived as Master in January 1997.[5] After some discussion, the Governors decided that the new Master and his wife, an experienced teacher and school governor, should inspect the school in January 1998. Michael Haywood had suffered heart problems at this stage and had retired, leaving his deputy, Nick Rugg, as acting Head. At Dr Arthit's request, the College advertised and interviewed for Mr Haywood's replacement: the selection committee comprised the Master, Andrew Seth – then Vice-Chairman of the College Governors – and Nicholas Tatman (OA), the newly elected Finance Committee Chairman who had previous business connections with Thailand. As the licence agreement stipulated, the committee submitted two names to Dr Arthit, and he chose Christopher Charleson, the Head of Secondary at St George's School, Buenos Aires. Chris arrived in January 1998 as Headmaster (the term 'Master' was not well understood locally) and immediately had to host an inspection from Graham and Mary Able. He coped admirably, and quickly realised the need to start a primary and kindergarten section. He rapidly gained the confidence of both the DIC Board and the College in London. The terms of the licence agreement were financially difficult, and the Master negotiated a new deal with Dr Arthit which related to pupil numbers and was judged fair to both sides.[6] Neil Smith was recruited as Head of Primary, and the next four and a half years were spectacularly successful with numbers growing from 150 to over 800. The school staged its official Royal opening graced by HRH Princess Mahachakri Sirindhorn; Nick Tatman and

Ralph Mainard (then Head of the Middle School at Dulwich and deputising for the Master) attended, as did Tony Verity. Despite this success, the DIC Board of Directors decided that they could no longer work with Chris Charleson for various reasons which neither he nor Graham Able could determine. This led to a crisis meeting in Bangkok between Dr Arthit and the Master, accompanied by Andrew Seth and Nicholas Tatman. Eventually it was decided to allow DIC to part company with Mr Charleson – on suitably generous terms – but also to tighten the licence agreement [8] to ensure that any future difficulties would be referred to the College in London before any precipitate local action. Dulwich College also agreed, in return, to remove any requirement for the DIC Board to consult with the local OA consultative committee appointed by Lord Butler (then Chairman of the College Governors) and chaired by Khun Anand. This committee had been very supportive of both the school and Chris Charleson, but Dr Arthit was very wary of it. DIC's loss was to be the gain of those seeking a British International education on the Costa del Sol – as can be seen from the growing numbers and reputation of Sotogrande International School under Chris Charleson's headship.

Nick Rugg took over as acting Head for a term. Much to the amazement of the Master and Governors back in London, Dr Arthit requested a search for a new Head despite Mr Rugg's evident qualifications for this role. As before DCEL, acting for the College with the same selection committee as previously, put forward two names, Nick Rugg and David Cook, an experienced and successful head. Dr Arthit chose Mr Cook who had previously run Quatar Academy and Lewes Old Grammar School. Nick Rugg was shortly thereafter appointed to the Headship of Redlands School in Santiago, Chile, and Tim Creber became Deputy Headmaster.

David Cook was proud of what his predecessor and the staff had achieved: improved sports and drama facilities, expansion of the boarding houses and other developments all boded well for the future, and he continued the good work. There were 850 students in the school at the end of the franchise agreement in June 2005. In their distinctive blue and white uniforms, the mix of nationalities gave a true international flavour to the campus, and all enjoyed the wide range of opportunities for sport, culture and study essential to a Dulwich ethos. DIC hosted successful primary and secondary sports meetings for the Federation of British International Schools in South East Asia, involving children from many countries, and the Dulwich pupils performed very well. An English Academy was opened for those needing extra help with language. The boarding houses, named after local beaches (Yon, Surin, Kata, Kamala, Nai Harn, Rawai and Karon) fostered a cheerful social mix. Public examination results improved regularly over the years and compared very favourably with those of other international schools. The end came with sad irony: shortly before the Thai owners decided to go their own way with the school, a tsunami struck Phuket and hundreds perished. Safely inland, DIC immediately opened its facilities and acted as the primary site of refuge. Staff and local students volunteered their various talents as divers, translators, drivers and statisticians to give help and comfort in any way possible. David Cook and his colleagues were rightly regarded as heroes, and Dulwich International College knew its finest hour.

Like Christopher Charleson before him, David Cook was rapidly appointed to another headship and is now to lead Repton's new venture in Dubai. Tim Creber, Neil Smith and Paul Friend, formerly Head of Boarding at DIC, have also moved on to headships, so the senior management team which served the Phuket School so well continues to contribute greatly to international education.

So why did the relationship go wrong? Certainly the discovery by David Cook and Tim Creber that the Thai Manager (equivalent to a bursar but also a director) had been dishonest with school finances may have put Dr Arthit into a difficult position. The manager duly resigned but his relationship by marriage to the Arthit family may have caused ongoing problems. The DIC Board had previously been given permission by DCEL to open a 'feeder' nursery and primary school on Koh Samui. Graham and Mary Able visited this offshoot in January 2005 and commented favourably on it;[8] it was thus invidious for DCEL to be told one month later that this project was to be abandoned. A DCEL offer to find an alternative investor was under discussion when Dr Arthit issued an ultimatum to Dulwich: either confine your advice to academic matters only and agree to the immediate removal of the Headmaster and the imposition of a Thai-style management structure, or the franchise ends.[9] This ultimatum was accompanied by the unacceptable harassment of David Cook and his family, and – with much sadness – the very successful ten-year relationship with Phuket had to end. There is something of 'unfinished business' about it, however, and who knows what the future may bring?

From its opening in 1996 until the withdrawal of the franchise on 24 June 2005, Dulwich International College gave a fine education to many children. Dulwich College, through the efforts of the Master, Andrew Seth, Nicholas Tatman and especially Ralph Mainard, with his shuttle diplomacy at and beyond the eleventh hour, laboured long and hard for the sake of the teachers, pupils and parents to keep the concept alive. Sadly, in the end, the Master and the DCEL Board acting with the Governors' approval took the only realistic decision available.

DCEL arranges annual inspections by the Master or senior Dulwich colleagues of all our franchise schools. The College, through DCEL, approves the appointment of teachers, checks on curriculum matters and liaises with local managers. A key part of the Dulwich franchise is the College's right to approve and take part in the appointment of the Head. This was eventually unacceptable to Dr Arthit who wrote to the parents that 'the selection of the Headmaster will be the exclusive right of the DIC Board'.[10] Despite many hours of discussion between DCEL and Dr Arthit, it was impossible to find a way forward to continue the franchise: the DIC Board were determined to manage the school in a way which would marginalise the Head's role and compromise the essential Dulwich ethos. As Deputy Master for External Relations, Ralph Mainard spent many days in Bangkok and Phuket pursuing every option and briefing the Master on all issues as they unfolded. Dulwich did not give up on Phuket lightly, and, as mentioned above, there may yet be another chapter in this story at some future stage.

Dulwich College Shanghai

How did Dulwich College become involved in China? As Chinese writers might observe, the stars were aligned in a most harmonious way, for the right people happened to be in the right place at the right time. Paul Sizeland (OA) had been Deputy to the British Ambassador in Thailand; he had forged strong links with Dulwich International College and had got to know Graham Able well on the Master's annual visits to the school. When he was appointed Consul General in Shanghai, he quickly appreciated that there was a need for a school similar to DIC in this city, and he invited the Master to meet various potential partners. In a three-day visit the Master held separate meetings with ten different groups while his wife took copious notes. The first meeting was a lunch hosted by Karen White, then the chief executive of the local British Chamber of Trade and Commerce; the last was with her husband, Fraser White, and his co-investor, Eric Li. It became immediately apparent that the Master and Fraser White shared a common vision of high quality education, and links were further strengthened when the Whites, Eric Li and his then fiancée came to Founder's Day at the College two months later. Negotiations followed in the November with Andrew Seth and Nicholas Tatman supporting the Master, and a franchise contract, carefully drawn up by Stephen Sidkin and Jane Elliott of

Dulwich College Shanghai, Jin Qiao, main campus, 2006. (Dulwich College)

Fox Williams, was signed on 21 May 2003.[11] DCEL, which holds the right to market the intellectual property of the College, awarded GEICC (a company set up by Fraser White and Eric Li to manage the franchise schools) the right to open up to four schools in China, the first to be located in Shanghai. The Master subsequently introduced GEICC to SAHA Union, a Thai public company with major business interests in China and with links to Dulwich through its former Chairman, Anand Panyarachun. Saha Union became co-investors in the project and allowed a more rapid programme to be developed.

The investors were very keen to establish strong links with the College, and this was achieved through the appointment of Colin Niven as the inaugural Master of Dulwich College Shanghai. Dr Niven was Captain of School at Dulwich in 1959, and had just retired as Head of Alleyn's School. He also had considerable international experience as Head of St George's British International School in Rome and Principal of the Island School in Hong Kong.

Dominating the leafy residential area of Jin Qiao from its central position stands Dulwich College Shanghai. John Cahill, the architect who also designed the new swimming pool for the College in London, has captured the spirit of Barry's building, and a bell tower rises above the dignified red-brick school. Tony Blair, the Prime Minister, came out to China on an official visit on 22 July 2003, and spent four hours in Shanghai. Colin Niven had taught him French and German at Fettes, and they had kept in touch. He offered to inaugurate the school. In the top suite of the Westin Hotel, just below its famous lotus-leaf roof, a photograph was taken of Mr Blair and Dr Niven holding a picture of a model of the main building.

The Kindergarten opened on 26 August 2003, sharing a building recently vacated by the Song Qing Ling Infants' school with the Chinese 'Golden Key' Kindergarten. The main building opened a year later just 200 yards from the Kindergarten which has since occupied the whole of its building as a fully fledged 'DUCKS'. Graham Able unveiled the Dulwich crest on the DUCKS building in a joint ceremony with the Headmistress of 'Golden Key' in October 2003, which featured a countdown in Chinese by Colin Niven. He suggested, because the school is in Jin Qiao (Golden Bridge), the very appropriate motto – *Detur Pons Mundo* – let there be a bridge to the world. Rowena Arney had moved from DUCKS in London to give an authentic Dulwich teaching input, and Fiona Johnstone joined Dulwich Shanghai a year later to lead both DUCKS and the Junior School; she had successively been Deputy Head of Junior School and then Head of DUCKS in London, and worked hard to ensure that a genuine replica was created in Shanghai. By the time she left for Australia in December 2005 she had established high standards and the essential Dulwich ethos.

Colin Niven presided over a rapid expansion during his two years in Shanghai, and was greatly helped by Karen White who gave up her role with the Chamber of Trade and Commerce to become successively Admissions and Development Director at DCS. Fritz Libby, an American who joined the GEICC Board, had considerable experience of 'start-up' schools, and made a major contribution to Shanghai before moving up to Beijing.

The initial target of 97 children for August 2003 was soon surpassed, and by the time the main campus opened a year later the school roll was 550; in August 2005, as the oldest students reached Year 10, numbers had grown to over 700 with 400 on a waiting list. A second phase creating a larger adjoining building opened in the autumn of 2006. The school is expected to grow to 1150 students when Year 13 commences in 2008.

Colin Niven had also been appointed in 2003 to the wider role of Master of Dulwich Schools in China. John Taylor, previously the Head of the British School in Ankara, was appointed in August 2004 to the Headship in Shanghai. This did not work out as anticipated, however, so Colin returned to spend the remaining two terms of his contract at Dulwich Shanghai. It was John Taylor who officiated at the formal opening of the main school building on 23 October 2004. Jo Brooke, then Director of Music and now Director of Educational Administration, created impressive choral and instrumental entertainment after only a few weeks in her post, and the students looked immaculate in their dark blue blazers with the College badge and their blue and red striped ties. Sue Bishop, Paul Sizeland's successor as British Consul-General, and Zhang En Di, the Deputy Governor of Pudong, spoke warmly of the new school and cut a ceremonial ribbon. Graham Able brought messages of congratulations from London, and welcomed all staff and students into the Dulwich fold. A Founders' board was unveiled in tribute to Fraser and Karen White, Eric Li and Fritz Libby. Mary and Graham Able had their contribution to this new Dulwich recognised in the naming of the library after them. Next day there was a party at which a thousand parents, pupils, teachers and friends of the school enjoyed a memorable picnic on the soccer field. Sack races, football competitions, balloons and dragon dances helped to celebrate the official birth of Dulwich College Shanghai.

Other early distinguished visitors included Lord Butler, Chairman of the Dulwich College Board when DCS first opened and thus its first President, Lord George, his successor in both roles, and Khun Anand, after whom one House at DCS is named.

On Colin Niven's retirement, he handed over the Mastership of DCS to Edward Groughan, an Australian who had recently joined the school as Head of Secondary. Unfortunately, Dr Groughan announced after only half a term in post that he wished to return to his native country for family reasons. This could have produced a crisis of leadership, but support came from the Master, contacted via his mobile phone whilst holidaying in Spain, and Governors in London. At their request, Ralph Mainard, Deputy Master for External Relations, agreed to go to

Shanghai for two terms as acting Master. He already knew the school well, and had enjoyed regular contact work with both senior staff and the management company through his responsibility for giving support and advice to the franchise schools. Ralph spent two terms commuting (four weeks in Shanghai and one in London), and DCS will always owe him a great debt of gratitude for his wise leadership and strong team-building during what would otherwise have been a difficult period. He left an excellent legacy for Stuart Bryan, previously Senior Vice-Principal and Head of Secondary at the British School of Brussels, to develop.

Dulwich College Beijing

Encouraged by the immediate success of the Shanghai school, Fraser White looked for a suitable site and the necessary authorisation from both the Chinese Education Department and DCEL to open a Dulwich College in Beijing. Dulwich College, through the established if unofficial 'committee' of the Master, Nicholas Tatman and Andrew Seth, were enthusiastic and the Beijing Government indicated that a licence would be possible.

Caroline Chen had founded the International Montessori School of Beijing (MSB) some 13 years earlier. She was ready to pass responsibility for its future on to a suitable purchaser and heard that Dulwich were considering an expansion into Beijing. The idea of linking MSB to a well-known British independent school appealed strongly, as this would guarantee the educational future of her pupils. As the discussions between the interested parties progressed, it became evident that considerable tact would be required if two respected but rather different approaches to education were to co-exist. The famous aphorism enunciated at the handover of Hong Kong, 'one country, two systems', had its parallel in what Dulwich and MSB sought to achieve.

The challenge was very different from that in Shanghai, as Dulwich would be taking on over 400 children being educated in a different system, but, after successful meetings between the Master, Caroline Chen, some representative parents and Fraser White, it was decided to proceed. On 24 October 2004, a dinner was held in the Capital Club to toast the amalgamation at which the Master spoke of Dulwich hopes for Beijing. Initially Sharon Keenan ran the School as Academic Principal of MSB: at this stage few changes were made to the curriculum, but a 'Dulwich Year 7' was introduced as a precursor for the following year when Brian McDouall arrived as the inaugural Master of Dulwich College Beijing (DCB) in August 2005. Brian had been Deputy Principal of King George V School in Hong Kong and had been initially appointed to start Dulwich College Suzhou.

Dulwich College Beijing, Legend Garden, 2007. (Dulwich College)

It was decided to postpone this project, however, and invite Brian to develop Beijing instead. Fritz Libby was posted to Beijing as GEICC's Development Director for the school and his partnership with Brian McDouall has been key to the project's success.

MSB had four sites – the main Riviera campus 'Little Riviera' close by and two satellite Kindergartens at Sanlitun and River Gardens. Initially the two satellites continued under MSB management whilst Brian Mc-Douall and his team grasped the thorny problems involved in introducing a Dulwich-style English National curriculum to a pupil and parent body firmly wedded to the rather different Montessori traditions. There was also the additional problem of where to accommodate the necessary specialist facilities for secondary pupils, and this was solved by leasing a building just the other side of a golf driving-range from the main Riviera campus.

This was only a temporary solution, and Fraser White conducted delicate negotiations to secure both a freehold site and the right to develop it. Legend Garden is well situated, fifteen minutes by car from the Riviera campus. It was built as a shopping mall and sports complex, but the mall was never occupied; with its adjacent grounds it was an ideal school site, and the American architects Perkins and Will were commissioned to trans-form it into Dulwich College Beijing. They have created a most impressive school.

The complex was owned by the China Poly Group, the commercial and social arm of the People's Liberation Army. The official handover ceremony was a splendid occasion at their headquarters in Beijing: a tour of the excellent China Poly Group museum and a grand dinner with speeches from Graham Able, Fraser White and Chinese dignitaries before the signing of protocols at a table bearing the flags of China and the United Kingdom. With DCB moving towards 900 pupils in August 2006, Brian McDouall was able to strengthen his leadership team by appointing Heads of both Junior and Secondary sections. He worked hard throughout his first year to ensure that parents, staff and pupils realised the benefit of a Dulwich-style education, and the ties to MSB have finally been severed. DCB has come a long way very quickly – as befits an institution in twenty-first century China.

Dulwich College Suzhou and the future

As this book goes to press, Dulwich College Suzhou has recently opened as a Year 3 to Year 8 School. It will probably send its senior students on to Shanghai (90 minutes by road). The school occupies part of the new out-of-town campus of Suzhou Middle School, one of the oldest and most respected high schools of China. Nicholas Magnus, previously Head of Braeburn School, Nairobi in Kenya, is the inaugural Head, and the school opened in August 2007 with over 200 students. Other schools will doubtless follow, but all will need to work hard to establish and preserve the ethos which characterises Dulwich and makes all our schools very special places.

Governance and the Management Company

The Management company GEICC was renamed Dulwich Management Shanghai Limited in July 2006, and Andrew Seth, retired as a College Governor but still a director of DCEL and a Dulwich China Governor, joined their board as a non-executive director. The company from its foundation had benefited from the wisdom of its vice-president, Li Jung – Eric Li's father and formerly general secretary of the PRC Education Committee. Patrick Hoey had previously taken on the role of Chief Operating Officer for the company and allowed Fraser White more time for strategic development. Richard Barnard, an Old Alleynian who decided to spend a post-university gap year learning Chinese, had joined GEICC at an early stage, and became Company Secretary. David Yung, Karen White's brother, left his accountancy career to take up the post of Finance

Director. The team was further strengthened in August 2006 by the appointment of Ian Strickland as GEO. He had formerly headed B&Q's successful expansion into China. Although Patrick and Ian have since moved on, there is now a growing management team planning further expansion.

The Dulwich Schools in China have a single Governing Body which represents the College in London, DCEL and the investors. It has an independent Chairman, currently Lance Brown, a long-time Shanghai resident and former GEO of Standard Chartered in China. All DC China Governors are formally invited to serve by the Chairman of the Dulwich London Board. This arrangement has proved successful in providing the necessary checks and balances between educational and financial perspectives, but the increasing links between Dulwich Management Shanghai and DCEL may encourage further streamlining.

The real success of the Dulwich franchise schools has been the export of the essential Dulwich ethos where good teachers enthuse their students both inside the classroom and in a wide range of co-curricular activities. Also, as in London, students from a great variety of cultural backgrounds learn from each other in a supportive and tolerant environment.

GAMES & SPORTS

by Terry Walsh, BA
Senior Fellow, Dulwich College

The new boy, donning the Dulwich cap for the first time, may well deem himself a potential hero – if not, indeed, a hero *ipso facto* – for he stands dazzled in the descended glory of past years which scintillate with innumerable grand deeds and grander men. Prick the lists of sports where you will, and you will prick a famous Alleynian. Whether it be King Cricket, Rugby football, hockey, athletics, Badminton, shooting or even the games of maturer life, Dulwich has made for itself a glorious place that many schools might enjoy.

– *The Westminster Gazette,* 1922

Introduction – Cricket – Rugby football – Hockey – Association football – Athletics – Boxing – Fencing – Golf – Rowing – Sailing – Shooting – Squash – Swimming – Badminton, basketball &c. – Bridge and chess – Fives – Lawn tennis

Introduction

Although Dulwich College was founded in 1619, some 250 years were to elapse before there was any real development of organised games. The change of attitude was largely the work of Thomas Arnold of Rugby and Edward Thring of Uppingham. They were the first to institute the idea of developing the whole boy – *mens sana in corpore sano*.[1] The emphasis was always to be on the team rather than on the individual. Team matches were to develop an *esprit de corps*. This was to be strengthened by the compulsory watching of matches by the other boys. Clearly the system was also designed to develop boys as leaders and who were thus to take their place in Britain's imperial role. The teaching staff who were involved in games did so in a purely advisory capacity. From the beginning at Dulwich, the Field Sports Board, consisting of senior boys, was the controlling body in terms of the appointment of captains. Today the Assistant Masters in charge of Games act much more as coaches and are expected to produce successful teams. Almost certainly this has led to a higher standard of performance, although perhaps something has been lost in the educational process so far as the boys are concerned. This reduction in boy control is also due to legislation which has meant that inevitably boys cannot take as much responsibility as formerly. For example, junior Rugby house matches were normally refereed by senior boys. Dulwich has always been fortunate to have over the years great and dedicated Assistant Masters who have been prepared to pass on their expertise to boys and give up vast amounts of their own time.

The introduction of day houses in 1922 (see Chapter Nine) greatly fostered team spirit, and those who were not good enough to get into their House teams were sent to 'the Dump'. These boys were looked after by a games master, and in later years were proud to announce that they had been members of this illustrious group. A few

"Both you chaps play cricket, I suppose?"

Psmith, Mike Jackson and Adair (left to right)
Illustration by T. M. R. Whitwell to 'The Lost Lambs'
by P. G. Wodehouse, *The Captain*, XIX, 1908. (Jan Piggott)

Informal group of cricketers, 1893, including members of the First XI. (Dulwich College)

years ago, the widow of one of these generously offered to donate a bench seat to those who watched 'the Dump'. Not only was there great rivalry between the day houses but the boarding houses also held their own fiercely contested competition for the Gordon Bowl.

Today there is a vast variety of sports from which boys can choose because it is hoped that many boys will continue with those sports after they leave Dulwich. There are many more representative teams at all ages than ever before, and this of course gives more boys the opportunity to play for their school.

None of this would be possible without the right facilities. Dulwich has without doubt some of the best playing grounds in the country which are in superb condition. Often independent schools in large cities are criticised for keeping their facilities to themselves and not sharing with other schools, but these facilities are fully in use throughout the term, including weekends.

Cricket

The first proper cricket fixtures began in 1873 when Dulwich played Christ's Hospital, Epsom College and St Paul's School. This was followed in 1874 with Tonbridge School, in 1882 with Bedford School and in 1883

with Brighton College. It is interesting that of these six fixtures five are still being played today, sometimes with a break of several years during their history. The names of members of the First XI are displayed on the recently refurbished team boards in the pavilion. From 1860 to 1870 records give only the names of the First XI Captains, but after 1871 all members of the teams are named. It is interesting that from 1871 to 1873 the name of *Mr.* C. H. Lane appears, a very distinguished Old Alleynian who had become a member of staff (see Chapter Six).

Seventy-nine Alleynians have played first-class cricket from that time until the present day. Seven have played Test cricket. It is clearly impossible to name them all, but detailed research of this subject has been carried out by Charles (C. H.) Fellows-Smith (OA). In the years before the First World War a number of names are prominent. One of the most illustrious is 'Monty' (M. P.) Bowden. He was a member of the First XI of 1881–3 and was described as the best schoolboy wicket-keeping batsman in England. In 1883 he played for Surrey, and in 1888 captained England against South Africa. This was the second game of a two-match series in South Africa. In the first game England had been captained by Sir C. Aubrey Smith; Aubrey Smith was taken ill after the first Test, and Bowden became England's youngest-ever test cricket captain at the age of 23 years and 144 days. He stayed in South Africa and led Transvaal to victory in the first Currie Cup competition. Being short of money, he immediately pawned the cup. After several unsuccessful business ventures, he went north in one of Cecil Rhodes's pioneer columns, fell off his ox-cart and was trampled to death by oxen. A coffin was hastily made from whisky cases and was guarded overnight by two armed sentries to keep off marauding lions. He was buried the following day at Umtali. Thus died England's only totally successful cricket captain. He was just 26. A fine memorial was later erected over his grave, but this has been totally vandalised and destroyed by President Mugabe's 'veterans'. [2]

James Douglas was in the XI from 1885 until 1889, and was the most famous of three brothers. He played for Cambridge and Middlesex, and scored 9,099 first-class runs. He returned to teach at Dulwich. Cyril (C. M.) Wells 1886–90 played for Cambridge, Surrey and Middlesex, and took 465 first-class wickets. [3] A famous family were the Gillinghams. John (J. R.) was in the XI in 1891–2 and Arthur (A. H.) in 1895. The best known of these brothers is Frank (F. H., 'Parson') Gillingham who scored over 10,000 runs for Essex. It was said that he packed them into the county grounds and also into the pews, and was reputed to be the most amusing after-dinner speaker in London at the time. Frank (F. P.) Knox, in the First XI 1895–7, played for Oxford, and Neville (N. A.) Knox, 1900–03, played for Surrey and England and took 411 first-class wickets. In 1907 he was named one of *Wisden*'s five cricketers of the year, the first OA to be so honoured. Sir Jack Hobbs described him as 'probably the best fast bowler I ever saw'. P. G. Wodehouse was in the XI 1899–1900, and never lost his love for the game. As described in Chapter Eight, Wodehouse wrote very many detailed and amusing accounts of cricket and Rugby matches that were published in *The Alleynian* for many years after he left the College. John (J. H.) Lockton was in the Surrey side for many years. Karl (R. K.) Nunes, 1910–12, played for Jamaica and the West Indies and captained the West Indies in 1928, the year in which they obtained Test match status.

It was in 1911 that the name of Gilligan first appears as a member of the First XI. Arthur (A. E. R.) Gilligan was to be part of the Dulwich team for a total of four years and Captain in his last two. In 1914 he took 78 wickets at less than 9 each and scored over 500 runs. He went on to captain Cambridge, Sussex and England. In all he took 868 first-class wickets and scored 9,140 runs. In 1967 he was President of MCC when S. C. ('Billy') Griffith was

Arthur Gilligan, Captain of the England XI, with H. L. Collins, Captain of Australia, tossing up at the start of the Test Match of 1924–5. (Dulwich College)

Secretary. This was the first time in the history of MCC when the President and Secretary had come from the same school. At the end of the previous year he had returned to Dulwich to open the new PE Centre. It was raining heavily, and the water was coming through the flat roof. In the middle of his speech he said to the assembled audience, "I hope you will forgive me if I put on my hat. I am getting rather wet". He was a fine golfer, and in 1959 became President of the English Golf Union.

Frank (F. W.) Gilligan was in the XI of 1912–13 and later captained Oxford and played for Essex. He became a distinguished headmaster of Wanganui School in New Zealand. The youngest brother, A. H. H. (Harold) Gilligan, was in the XI of 1913–15 and also went on to captain Sussex and England. In 1914 he scored 190 against Bedford, which was the highest score by a Dulwich player until then. He scored 8,873 first-class runs. In 1913, all three Gilligans were in the Dulwich XI. *The Times* reported, 'The Gilligans of Dulwich seem destined to become as famous in sports as the Fords of Repton, the Lytteltons of Eton, the Fosters of Malvern and the Ashtons of Winchester'.

From 1916–19 it was the turn of Anthony (A. N.) Gilkes, son of A. H. and brother of C. H. and, later, a distinguished High Master of St Paul's (see Chapter Eight). Max Joubert, a fine all-round games player, was in the team for four years from 1918 until 1921. Geoffrey (G. A.) Rimbault, of 1924–6, played for the Public Schools XVI against a full Australian side in 1926. Sadly, this game was ruined by rain. In the war, he was to be awarded the DSO to follow an MC won earlier. In retirement, he became President of the Army Sports Board.

One of Dulwich's best cricketers of the period was Denys (D. R.) Wilcox. In the XI from 1926 until 1929 and Captain for his last two years, he scored 1,025 runs at an average of 54.06 in his last year. He went on to captain Cambridge and Essex, having first played for Essex in 1928 while still at school. In the 1932 University Match he made 157, the highest innings of his career. Altogether he was to make 8,392 first-class runs.

Frank King, of the 1927–9 XI, gained a Cambridge Blue as a medium-fast bowler and a good batsman. He spent the whole of his teaching life at Sherborne where he was much loved, and for many years played for Dorset.

Hugh (H. T.) Bartlett was five seasons in the Dulwich XI, and (uniquely) three as Captain. In his final season at school in 1933 Bartlett's reputation as a destructive left-hand bat was confirmed with two double centuries. He went up to Pembroke College, Cambridge, the following year and was a Blue in all three seasons, making a career best of 183 against Nottinghamshire in 1935, and captaining the University in 1936. Bartlett made his debut for Sussex in 1937, and by the following season had confirmed his reputation as one of the leading batsmen in the country. Two innings in particular from the season stand out: 175 not out in a crushing victory for the Gentlemen against the Players at Lord's and 157 against the touring Australians at Hove. This latter performance won Bartlett the Walter Lawrence Trophy for the season's fastest century, three figures coming up in just 57 minutes. He toured South Africa with MCC. Like many others the War took what might have been the best six years of his cricketing career. Bartlett served in the Airborne Division, and reached the rank of Lieutenant Colonel and was awarded the DFC as a glider pilot at Arnhem. He died in 1988 at the County Ground at Hove, virtually fifty years to the day of his devastating 157 against the Australians, the innings for which he will always be remembered.

First XI, 1914. M. Z. Ariffin, C. F. Brown, H. A. Gilkes, L. F. Jenkin, L. D. Chidson. R. T. Lloyd, A. H. H. Gilligan, A. E. R. Gilligan (Capt.), I. O. B. Shirley, R. L. Paton. J. K. Rowbotham. (Dulwich College)

First XI, 1933. L. Beaumont, R. I. S. Booty, P. H. McA. Fielding, J. G. Chiverall, J. G. Haycock, M. F. S. Thornton.
C. A. Holliman, S. C. Griffith, H. T. Bartlett (Capt.), G. V. Blaine, K. G. C. Campbell. (Dulwich College)

Billy Griffith holds the unique distinction of being the only England player to score his maiden first-class hundred in his first Test. Following four years in the Dulwich XI with his Cambridge and Sussex contemporary Hugh Bartlett, he took up wicket-keeping in his penultimate summer at school. He won a Blue at Cambridge during his second season there in 1935. That winter he toured Australia and New Zealand with the MCC before returning to Cambridge. He then qualified for Sussex, and made his debut at Hove in 1937 against the touring New Zealanders, keeping wicket throughout an innings of 546 without conceding a bye. During the war, he reached the rank of Lieutenant Colonel as a glider pilot in the Airborne Division and, like Bartlett, won a DFC at Arnhem. He played in all five 'Victory' Tests against the Australians in 1945, and eventually won his first Test cap in Trinidad on the West Indies tour of 1947–8. During the second test, Griffith batted for 354 minutes whilst making 140. He continued with Sussex until 1954 during which time he served as both Captain

in 1946 and Secretary of the County, before moving on to the MCC as an able and devoted administrator. He later served as MCC President during 1979–80.

An interesting member of the 1932 XI was Bill (W. G. R.) Wightman who after leaving Dulwich became a successful racehorse trainer. He called his autobiography *Months of Misery – Moments of Bliss*. Sam (S. C.) Silkin, 1934–6, was a good wicket-keeper who later became Attorney General in a Labour government (see Chapter Nine). Records suggest that he is the only Labour MP ever to have played first-class cricket, which he did for Glamorgan.

Alan (A. C.) Shirreff was in the XI of 1935–8, and was Captain in his last two years. In 1938, under his captaincy, the XI won all its matches. After the war, he played for Somerset, Hampshire and Kent and captained the Royal Air Force and Combined Services teams for ten years. F. S. Truman often described Alan Shirreff as the best captain he ever played under; Truman had this experience while doing his National Service with the

First XI, 1938. T. E. Bailey, P. C. B. Ashbrooke, H. L. Hammond, G. R. Turner, D. V. Knight, J. L. Nainby.
W. O. Thomas, J. C. Bartlett, A. C. Shirreff (Capt.), B. E. Collingwood, J. A. Barnett. (Dulwich College)

Royal Air Force. In the 1938 XI was David (D. V.) Knight (see Chapter Ten) and Bill (W. O.) Thomas, always known as 'Spongy' because as a slow left-arm bowler he was successful in a school match, and *The Alleynian* reported that the spongy conditions suited Thomas. After the war, he returned briefly to Dulwich but soon left to teach at Gresham's School, Holt, where he spent the rest of his career. Also in the 1938 successful XI was a young 14-year-old named Trevor Bailey.

Trevor (T. E.) Bailey, the greatest Old Alleynian cricketer, was spotted as a precocious seven-year-old at prep school in Westcliff-on-Sea by Denys Wilcox (OA). The school appropriately was Alleyn Court, founded by Wilcox's father and named after the founder of Dulwich College. It was only logical that Bailey himself would move on to Dulwich from Alleyn Court at the age of 13. He was selected at fourteen for the First XI by Alan Shirreff. Bailey's bowling partner at school for the next four summers was Tony (A. W. H.) Mallett, future Oxford Blue and Kent cricketer, and later headmaster of Diocesan College (Bishops), Cape Town, South Africa. While the war-time bombs dropped around Dulwich, these two cut a swathe through the opposition. Bailey's

66 wickets at 6.17 in his final year constituted a school record. He wrote his own excellent description of his years at the College in *Wickets, Catches and the Odd Run* (1986). After the war, Bailey finally made his Essex debut in 1946 before proceeding to St John's College, Cambridge, that autumn on a two-year degree course. At Cambridge he won a Blue for football as well as cricket, prowess he was later to display in winning an FA Amateur Cup Winner's medal with Walthamstow Avenue. He resolved to sacrifice pace for accuracy, grafting a natural outswing on to line and length at fast-medium. By combining this with a high action and the ability to cut the ball, Bailey developed a technique that enabled him to garner over two thousand first-class wickets over a twenty-year career, taking one hundred or more wickets in a season on nine occasions. His first full season with the county in 1949 was one of huge success: he scored nearly 1,400 runs, took 130 wickets and was the first man to the 'double' on 1 August. He made his England debut at Leeds against New Zealand, taking a wicket with his eighth ball in Test cricket and six wickets in the innings. That first Test series was highly successful for Bailey, as he followed this performance

with 93 at Lord's, and 6/84 and 72 not out at Old Trafford. He scored 1,000 runs in a season on 17 occasions, and performed the all-rounder's 'double' no less than eight times in all. Bailey's best bowling figures in Tests, however, were against the West Indians, his 7/34 in Jamaica at the end of the 1953–4 series being the best English analysis at that time against those opponents. Bailey also took 7/44 at Lord's during the 1957 series during his fiftieth Test, the best figures returned in a home series against the West Indies, and followed it up with 4/54 in the second innings. By this time Bailey had already completed the test match 'double' of a thousand runs and one hundred wickets, a feat achieved at Johannesburg earlier in the year. This made him only the third Englishman to do so following Wilfred Rhodes and Maurice Tate. In 1959 he completed the 'double' of 2,000 runs and one hundred wickets in the season, the only post-war instance of this remarkable feat. On retiring from first-class cricket, Trevor Bailey became an active writer and commentator on the game, well known as a member of the BBC's *Test Match Special* team. He also wrote Sir Garfield Sobers' biography. He has also remained true to his Dulwich roots, as a fifty-year-old being part of the Old Alleynian side that got to the final of the Cricketer Cup in 1974. On Founder's Day 2006

"Substitutes", he pointed out, "were allowed only to field, not to bowl."

Illustration by T. M. R. Whitwell to 'Shields' and the Cricket Cup', by P. G. Wodehouse, *The Captain*, XIII, 1905. (Jan Piggott)

he 'unveiled' the newly restored honours boards in the Pavilion; he then renamed the Honor Oak ground on the Common, recently acquired by the College, 'The Trevor Bailey Sports Ground'. Travellers along the South Circular will always be reminded of Dulwich's greatest cricketer.

In 1940–41 a member of Trevor Bailey's XI was Horace (H. P. H.) Kiddle. He was described by Bailey as 'the best bowler of the three of us'. In 1941 he took 50 wickets at 7.8 each. This included some remarkable analyses. Against St Paul's he took 4 for 5, against King's College School 8 for 3, against University College School 7 for 5 and against Merchant Taylor's 5 for 13. He was killed at the end of the war in a night-flying exercise.

In the 40s the name of Evans appears prominently both in cricket and Rugby. This was yet another Dulwich sporting dynasty. Glyn (G. D.) Evans was in the XI 1942–4 and Captain in his last two years; John (J. B.) was in the XI of 1946–7, and Alan (A. H.) in 1948.

Also in the 1940s was Oliver (O. J.) Wait in the XI 1942–4, who afterwards bowled quickly for Cambridge and Surrey when the regular Surrey bowlers were on Test duty. He took a total of 125 first-class wickets but died young of cancer after a distinguished teaching career at Mill Hill. Ian (I. D. F.) Coutts 1943–6 and Captain in his last two years was a Double Blue at Oxford, and later played Rugby for Scotland. Tony (J. A. C.) Bentall, a remarkably fine wicket-keeper played for the First XI for 5 years from 1943 until 1947. Bill (W. M.) Mitchell, of the 1945–8 XI, was an Oxford Blue and one of a long line of good Dulwich leg-spinners. Mike (M. H.) Bushby 1947–9 was later to captain Cambridge and to spend his teaching career at Tonbridge where he ran the cricket for many years and was a much respected and much loved housemaster.

In 1951 the name of Howland first appears. Chris (C. B.) was in the XI of 1951–5 and Captain in his last two years. He went up to Cambridge where he also captained the XI. The Howlands are another sporting dynasty: C. B.'s younger brother Peter (P. C.) was in the XI of 1964–6, his older son Simon (S. B.) in 1977–80, and his younger son James (J. P.) in 1987–8.

Another remarkably good cricketer of that period was Geoff (G. W.) Cook, of the 1951–5 XI, who, like Chris Howland, also obtained a Cambridge Blue. In 1957 he shared a partnership of 289 for the seventh wicket against Oxford with G. Goonesena, and in the same year shared a partnership of 200 for the ninth wicket for Cambridge against Lancashire with C. S. Smith (Sir Colin Stansfield Smith).

Also in the 1950s were a very good batsman, Mike (M. A.) Shirley, and a bowler, Euan (E. W.) Anderson

First XI, 1963. R. C. W. Wood, R. D. V. Knight, N. P. R. Wall, N. J. Cosh, J. Destefano, M. J. Ross.
J. Dobson, J. S. Bottle, H. J. George (Capt.), C. A. Jones, N. B. Bennett. (Dulwich College)

1954–6. At the end of the decade Mike Kirkman, 1957–60, another very good leg-spinner, obtained a Blue.

In the 1960s some names stand in considerable prominence. Nick (N. J.) Cosh 1962–4 obtained a double Blue for cricket and Rugby at Cambridge and scored 100 in the 1967 University match. He would undoubtedly have gone on to great things but for an illness which much restricted his activities. Roger (R. D. V.) Knight, son of D. V. K., was in the XI of 1963–6 and Captain in his last two years. A tall left-hander who reminded some people of Frank Woolley, he was a fine player of fast bowling. He also obtained a Cambridge Blue and went on to captain Surrey. In his first-class career, he made 19,558 runs and took 369 wickets. His other achievements figure in Chapter Ten.

Simon Dyson 1964–7 was probably one of the best Dulwich cricketers never to have played first-class cricket. He was a leg-spinner who bowled at medium pace with unerring accuracy. In the Cricketer Cup, a competition for 32 Old Boys' Teams from the leading cricketing schools, he tops the bowling averages, having taken 96 wickets at 11.48 each with an economy rate of 2.28. In the history of the competition, which began in 1967, only two bowlers have taken 100 wickets.

Barry (B. A.) O'Connor 1969–72 was a prolific run scorer. Jim (A. R.) Dewes 1972–5 obtained a Cambridge Blue in 1978. He was the son of John (J. G.) Dewes, of Middlesex and England, who taught at the school for many years (see Chapter Ten). Vikram (V. H.) Kumar 1996–9 is the most recent Blue.

In the first decade of the twenty-first century the names of Ruel (R. M. R.) Brathwaite 2003–5 and Chris (C. R. J.) Jordan 2006–7 have added considerable pace to the Dulwich attack. Brathwaite, since leaving school, has played in a one-day match for the West Indies and Jordan, who has just left the College, played regularly for Surrey at the end of the 2007 season with considerable success. He is only the third Dulwich cricketer to have played first-class cricket while still at school, the other two being Monty Bowden and Denys Wilcox.

Tours have developed considerably in the last 30 years. The first major tour, which involved Rugby and hockey as well as cricket, went to Sri Lanka and Thailand in 1978. In the introduction to the tour brochure the late E.W. Swanton wrote, 'There are not many public schools who since the dawn of the century have contributed more to English cricket than Dulwich'. The touring party consisted of 63 boys and 10 staff, and was certainly the most ambitious tour ever undertaken. Since that time, tours have been predominantly one-sport only, and there have been several successful cricket tours. These are not limited only to senior boys because in 2007, although the First XI went to the West Indies, the under-16s went to Goa.

Over the years, Dulwich cricket has been extremely fortunate in having a succession of cricket masters who have devoted many years of their teaching career at Dulwich to running the First XI. The most distinguished of these was 'Father' Marriott who ran the cricket at Dulwich from 1922 until 1948. Charles Stowell Marriott (see Chapter Ten) was one of the best leg-break and googly bowlers of his era. He gained a Blue at Cambridge in 1920 and 1921. In all first-class cricket he took 724 wickets at an average cost of 20.04 runs, and his bowling skill so far outreached his ability as a batsman that his victims exceeded his aggregate of runs by 169. He was an extremely poor fielder of whom it was said that like the Ancient Mariner, 'He stoppeth one of three'. Cunning flighting, allied to the ability to turn the ball sharply, made him a menace to batsmen even on good pitches, and when the turf gave him help he could be well-nigh unplayable. His action was high with a free, loose arm which he swung behind his back before delivery. He met with great success on the occasion of his one appearance in a Test match for England. That was at the Oval in 1933, when he so bewildered the batsmen that he took five wickets for 37 runs in the first innings, and, with second innings figures of six for 59, hurried the West Indies to defeat by an innings and 17 runs – a feat described by *Wisden* as one of the best accomplished by a bowler when playing for England for the first time. Marriott contributed a lively chapter on Dulwich to *Public Schools Cricket 1901–1950*, (1951) edited by W. N. Roe. It is not surprising that Dulwich has produced so many good leg-break bowlers not only during his time at Dulwich but also in the years that have followed.

The late Gerald (G. N.) Thornton ran the cricket from 1956 until 1976 with great success and produced many fine sides. He was a shrewd Yorkshireman with a deep appreciation and understanding of the game. For the last ten years, John Cooper has continued with great success.

Again, Dulwich has been fortunate in the professional cricketers who have come to Dulwich to coach. The early days of Lance and Shepherd were followed by those of Bill Brown. Tall of stature, easy of action and gentle of manner, he gave guidance to generations of Dulwich cricketers and was much loved. Bill Smith and the Australian Alex Ranson gave great service, and today the College is extremely fortunate to have Bill Athey of Yorkshire, Gloucestershire, Sussex and England who scored 25,000 runs in first-class cricket and was a member of Mike Gatting's team in Australia 1986–7 which won the Ashes. The main difference now is that the cricket professional is employed for the whole year and not just for the summer term. This clearly gives much greater opportunity for coaching and is extremely beneficial.

Old Alleynian CC v. Mr C. S. Marriott's XII, 23 April 1950.
G. J. Whittaker, G. Cox, J. Laker, A. W. H. Mallett, O. J. Wait, F. King, C. Oakes, A. E. R. Gilligan.
W. Brown, L. A. W. Simmons, R. J. Christiani, A. C. L. Bennett, T. E. Bailey, J. H. Lockton, A. C. Shirreff, W. J. Edrich, J. Parks, W. M. Collinson.
J. Young, D. R. Wilcox, G. E. Gomez, G. A. Rimbault, C. S. Marriott, E. R. T. Holmes, J. D. Goddard, H. T. Bartlett, K. V. Seale, S. C. Griffith.
Result: OACC, 108; Mr Marriott's XII, 179 for 8. (Dulwich College)

Rugby football

The first recorded Rugby match played by Dulwich against another school was in 1859, when Dulwich defeated the City of London School 1–0; this probably means that Dulwich made the only score of the game. This was twelve years before the Rugby Football Union was founded, and so Dulwich can claim to be one of the first schools in the country to have played Rugby football. In the 1870s, Michael (M. G.) Glazebrook claimed to be 'the radical' who got soccer disestablished in favour of Rugby football, and introduced the wearing of football jerseys.[4] 'The first were 'thick, scrubby jerseys of a pinkish grey with blue trimmings with a heraldic rose (from the College Arms) on the front'.[5] By 1873 the First XV were wearing jerseys in blue and black. The new playing fields were opened that year.

As with cricket, the years 1862–72 record only the names of the Captains, but since 1873 there is a record of all members of all teams. In 1873–4 Mr C. H. Lane (OA) is recorded as playing for the school. He was a member of staff and, as has been mentioned with cricket, it was not uncommon for him and his colleagues to play for the school.

The earliest regular fixtures are recorded in 1872 when Dulwich played Christ's Hospital, Epsom, King's College School, Merchant Taylor's and St Paul's. In 1874 Tonbridge was added to the list, and in 1881 Bedford appeared. The fixture against Bedford is traditionally the most important, certainly in the minds of Old Alleynians. It is the fourth oldest continuing school fixture in this country. 1929 was the only year between the two World Wars when Dulwich actually beat Bedford. An interesting comment on this fixture was that for years at the end-of-term Rugby supper if Dulwich had beaten Bedford turkey was the main course, but if Dulwich had lost it was only roast beef. The first fixture against Haileybury was in 1891.

Today tours abroad occur regularly, but in 1903 Dulwich travelled to Paris to play the Ecole Albert le Grand. This must have been one of the earliest tours ever undertaken by a school.

It is clearly not possible to mention every distinguished player by name but, on the international scene, 14 Old Alleynians have played for England, seven for Scotland and one for Ireland. Some twelve have played for other countries. In all, Old Alleynians have represented ten countries. In 1922 the match between Uruguay and Argentina featured five Old Alleynians.

Among the names which appear before the turn of the century is William (W. R. M.) Leake who was in the XV for three years 1882–4 and was Captain in his last two years. He was a Cambridge Blue from 1885 until 1887,

and in 1891 obtained three English caps. He was later to return to teach at Dulwich and then become Headmaster of Dulwich College Preparatory School. 'Scotty' (W. D.) Gibbon was in the XV for four years 1895–8 and was Captain in his last two years. He also returned to teach at Dulwich (see Chapter Eight). 'Slacker' (McC.) Christison, 'the Alleynian' (see Chapter Eight), was in the team 1897–8 and Thomas (T. G.) Treadgold was also in the XV at the same time. He was to return to Dulwich, and become largely responsible for the development of the playing fields. P. G. Wodehouse was in the 1899 side. Before the turn of the century Sidney Ellis and Cyril Wells played for England, and Henry (H. T. S.) Gedge and Nelson (N. F.) Henderson for Scotland.

The 1909 XV won all its matches. This was the period of the 'Famous Five' who all played in the University Match of 1913. *The Times* reported, 'Yesterday five Old Alleynians kindly invited 25 other Rugby players to join them in the University Match'. In 1919 John (J. E.) Greenwood was the Captain of Cambridge and Eric (E. G.) Loudoun-Shand of Oxford. The first of the 'Five' was the Irishman William (W. D.) Doherty, a member of the First XV for four years from 1909, captaining the team in his last year at school. Doherty left Dulwich to study medicine at Cambridge, later becoming a consultant surgeon and a College governor for eleven years. He represented Cambridge in that famous 1913 game. Like many of the other players World War One stifled his playing career, but in 1920 he fought his way into the Ireland team, winning a total of seven caps, captaining his country in the 1921 season.

Graham Donald was an all-round sportsman, winning school caps at both cricket and Rugby. He was a regular member of the First XV for three years, and on entering Oxford to study Natural Sciences, was immediately picked for the 'Varsity team, which he represented for a further three years. In 1914 he was awarded two caps for Scotland. Graham Donald entered the services during the war – winning the DFC, AFC and Greek Military Cross – and later became an Air Marshal. He was knighted in 1944.

The Captain of the Oxford University XV in 1913, as mentioned above, was Eric Loudon-Shand who, like Doherty, played in the First XV for four years. A centre three-quarter, he also represented Scotland in 1913 and the university again in the 1919 game. He fought in the Army in both wars. Tragedy hit the family in 1916 when one of his younger brothers, Major S. W. Loudon-Shand, was killed on the Somme in an action for which he was awarded the Victoria Cross (see Chapter Nine).

The other Captain in the 1913 'Varsity Match was John Greenwood, a member of the First XV from 1908–10.

While studying Mathematics at Cambridge, he played five times against Oxford, also captaining the team in 1919. John Greenwood won 13 international caps for England from 1912–14 and in 1920. He also represented Cambridge on the Rugby Football Union, and from 1935–7 was President of the RFU, the first Old Alleynian to achieve this distinction.

The most illustrious of the Famous Five was undoubtedly Cyril (C. N.) Lowe, a First XV member between 1908 and 1911, when he was Captain. A winger (who did not play Rugby until he was 16), he was immediately selected for the Cambridge team when he arrived at the university to read Mathematics. He played in the 'Varsity Match for three consecutive years, and in 1913 was rewarded with his first England cap. Lowe's exploits then were quite amazing, considering claims that at just five feet six inches tall and weighing only eight stone seven pounds he was regarded by many as too slight for international Rugby. Lowe proved them wrong; in the 25 consecutive games he played for England in 1913–14 and between 1920 and 1923 he scored a record 18 tries. This record stood for 68 years. In his earlier internationals he had received little of the ball, which prompted P. G. Wodehouse to write his doggerel poem 'The Great Day' (which appeared in *London Opinion* and also in *The Alleynian* for March 1913). Taking as epigraph sporting journalists' frequent comments that 'Lowe has yet to receive a pass in International football', and noting his famous prowess at tackling, Wodehouse recounts how just at the moment when he was lighting his briar on the touch-line in a high wind, Lowe was actually passed the ball:

> His astonishment was utter.
> He was heard to gulp, and mutter,
>> "What on earth has happened now, I'd like to know?"
> And incredulous reporters
> Shouted out to the three-quarters,
>> "Do we dream? Or did you really pass to Lowe?"
>
> There was sweat upon his forehead,
> And his stare was simply horrid:
>> He stood and goggled feebly at the ball.
> It was plain he suffered badly,
> For the crowd, now cheering madly,
>> Saw him shudder, start to run, then limply fall.

Off the pitch, Lowe was flamboyant, becoming a Group Captain in the RAF and, between 1934–8, a member of the Rugby Union Selection Committee. It is also said that the author W. E. Johns based the character of the fictional flying hero Biggles on Lowe and his exploits, perhaps because during the War he had been awarded the MC while serving with the 1st Reserve Horse Transport, and then the DFC after transferring to the Royal Flying Corps.

Between 1912 and 1914 the name of Gilligan appears, perhaps not so prominently as in the realms of cricket, but Arthur Gilligan was in the XV 1912–13 and Harold 1913–14. Christopher (C.H.) Gilkes, later to become Master of Dulwich College, was a member 1914–16, and Alan (A. M.) David 1915–16 obtained his Blue at Oxford for the two years 1921–2. Christopher (C. P. C.) Smith 1919–20 was in the side and was the son of George Smith, Master of the College; he was himself to become Master of Haileybury (see Chapter Ten). Also in the 1920 side was Lorne (L. M.) Campbell who was to win the Victoria Cross in the Second World War. Max Joubert was in the XV for four years 1917–20 and Captain in his last year. Arthur (A. F.) Heppenstall 1921–3 obtained two Oxford Blues in 1926–7, and Arthur (A. M.) Dixon 1922–4 also gained an Oxford Blue in 1928. One of the outstanding games players of the period was Denis (D. H.) Frankford. He was remarkably skilled at all games and would undoubtedly have achieved great things but for a crippling illness which left his spine literally at right angles. He retained his great love of games despite his disability, and was a much loved President of the Alleyn Club. He was for many years the snooker champion of the London clubs but always maintained that he cheated because he could get lower over the table than anybody else. Scott (J. S.) Young 1929–31 gained a Cambridge Blue in 1935. After the war he returned to teach at Dulwich, and ran the First XV for a few years. Hugh Bartlett and Billy Griffith were both in the XV for three years from 1930 until 1932. Noel (N. Le C.) Agazarian was in the XV 1933–4. He fought with distinction in the Battle of Britain, and was later shot down and killed in North Africa (see Chapter Nine). B. J. ('Tim') Brennan played in 1935 and later became a Barbarian. Alan Shirreff, as well as being a fine cricketer, was in the Rugby team 1935–7. David (D. V.) Knight, who later returned to Dulwich for many years, obtained an unofficial Cambridge Blue in 1941. A. C. Cole, later Sir Colin Cole, Garter Principal King of Arms and Chairman of the Dulwich College Governors, obtained an Oxford unofficial Blue in 1941 while his brother Bruce (B. W.) Cole achieved the same distinction 1943–4. The Evans brothers were as distinguished in Rugby as in cricket. Glyn (G. D.) 1942–3, John (J. B.) 1945–7, and Alan (A.H.) 1948, were all members of successful Rugby teams. Alex (A.C.) Hemming 1943–5 became an England triallist, and was the English reserve scrum-half in Paris in 1952. He was a popular liaison officer for 15 international touring teams visiting the British Isles. During these war years, the First XV pitch often had to be cleared of shrapnel before play could begin. Robin (R. D.) Gill obtained an Oxford Blue in

First XV, 1946. J. A. C. Bentall, J. L. Jealous, B. M. Cox, R. L. Meyrick, R. G. Jones, J. J. R. Goldsmith, D. L. Ogilvy, R. C. Clarke, G. L. White.
J. B. Evans, P. J. R. Byford, J. F. Mockford (Capt.), R. R. Maddison, J. R. Aldhous.
M. Godfrey, E. H. S. Woodward. (Dulwich College)

1947 and Ian (I. D. F.) Coutts, having obtained an Oxford Blue in 1950, was capped by Scotland in 1954. He spent the whole of his teaching career at Oundle. In 1946, John (J. F.) Mockford captained an unbeaten XV, the first time that this had happened since 1909. The members of this XV have held very successful reunions in 1996 and 2006, fifty and sixty years respectively, after their wonderful season.

The 1950s saw a great tragedy when Geoffry Higgs died at the age of 18 following an injury received while playing for the First XV. For over five months he lay paralysed in hospital and throughout his illness he set a magnificent example of courage. Christopher Gilkes, the Master of the day, made Higgs School Captain while he was in hospital (see Chapter Ten).

Ieuan (I. J.) Thomas 1951–3 captained an unbeaten XV in his last year. As usual the crucial match was against Bedford, and some twenty coach-loads of Dulwich supporters travelled to Bedford to watch the game. There were more Dulwich supporters at Bedford than there were for Bedford. Chris (C. B.) Howland, as with cricket the senior member of the Howland dynasty, was in the XV 1952–4 and Captain in his last year. His brother Peter (P. C.) was a member in 1963–5, his elder son Simon (S. B.) in 1978–9 and his younger son James (J. P.) in

1987. In 1953 Ted (T. E.) Priest refereed Ireland v. France in Belfast, and became the first Old Alleynian to referee an international match.

The 1950s saw a number of remarkably good players. Geoff (G. W.) Cook 1952–4 was a very powerful wing three-quarter, and Ewan (E .W.) Anderson 1954–5 a very versatile scrum-half. In 1956 there appears the name of Eddie (E. A. J.) George, scrum-half and wing-forward, who was later to become the Governor of the Bank of England and is now, as Lord George of St Tudy, Chairman of the Dulwich College Governors (see Chapter Ten). Dick (R. M.) Trembath 1956–7 played as an extra outside because John Gwilliam, the Master in charge of Rugby, decided that the Dulwich forwards were sufficiently strong that only seven were necessary. This also meant that the ball came back from the set scrums more quickly. This ploy received considerable attention in the national press because it enabled Trembath to play either as an extra full-back or, what in New Zealand is often known as a five-eighth. Two outstanding wing three-quarters of the period were Peter (P. G. R.) Lyon 1958–9 and Peter (P. W.) Cook 1959–61, who in 1964 was to gain two caps for England.

In the 1960s Nick (N. J.) Cosh 1962–4, Captain in his last two years, gained a Cambridge Blue in 1966. Roger

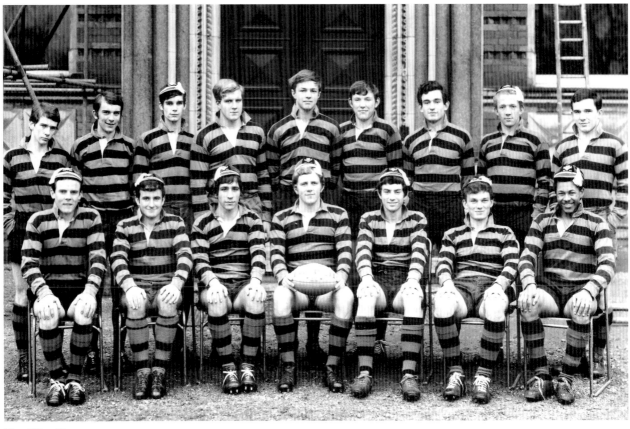

First XV, 1968.
J.J. Phillips, J. Dunbar, M. R. B. Telford, R. F. Looker, G. N. C. Ward, B. A. Bowers, P. A. J. Martin, M. R. Stapleton, J. I. W. McMullan.
T. H. Roff, D. T. M. Jones, G. M. Cryer, R. J. Kendall (Capt.), B. B. Henfrey-Smith, J. J. Saville, R. H. Brewer. (Dulwich College)

(R. D. V.) Knight 1964–5 was to captain Sussex and Simon Dyson 1965–6 was to play scrum half for several years for Rosslyn Park. Robin (R. J. D.) Linnecar 1964–8 was to captain an unbeaten side in 1967 when Dulwich played and won eleven matches. The XV scored 187 points and conceded only 18. In 1968 Dick (R. J.) Kendall who hooked for the First XV for four years and was Captain in 1968, led an unbeaten XV, which also played and won eleven matches, scoring 173 points against 40. Roger (R. F.) Looker 1968–70 was later to play for Harlequins and become the club's Chairman. Another good scrum-half of the period was Barry (B. A.) O'Connor 1969–71.

In the 70s James (J. F.) Thornton 1973–5 obtained a Cambridge Blue in 1976, 1978 and 1979. There is no doubt that but for injury he would have gone on to greater things. Stephen (S. E.) Killick 1971–2 also obtained a Cambridge Blue in 1978. Simon (S. J.) Newth 1976 on leaving school was to play 487 first team matches for the Old Alleynians between 1977 and 2000. This is a club record and is likely to remain so. Ed (E. J.) Dolman 1977–8 was to play for Kent and the Combined London Old Boys. Despite his position as Chief Executive of Christie's he has retained

his interest in Dulwich Rugby. Ruaidhri (R. R. W.) Maclean 1977–9 represented Scotland.

In the 1980s Andy (A. R.) Mullins 1981–3 and Captain in his last two years was to obtain one English cap against Fiji and made just over 100 appearances as a prop-forward for Harlequins. Justyn (J. P. S.) Cassell 1983–4 was a member of the victorious England 7s in the 1993 World Tournament at Murrayfield. Two powerful forwards of the period were Jim (J. A.) Overall and Rupert (R. W.) Penry-Jones 1987–8, now a well-known actor of stage and television particularly for his role in *Spooks*.

In the 1990s Sam (S. D.) Howard, Captain in 1991, was to play for the Barbarians and later in 2001 gain a Cambridge Blue. He has returned to Dulwich and will be coaching the First XV from 2008. The period 1995–7 produced a number of very distinguished names. Nick (N. J.) Easter 1995 was to play for England in the 2007 World Cup, as was Andrew (A. J.) Sheridan 1995–7. Stephen Jones, not particularly noted for his praise, wrote of Sheridan's performance against France in *The Sunday Times* of 7 October, 'It was surely one of the greatest ever individual displays by a forward'. In the World Cup Final Sheridan gained his nineteenth English cap and Easter his eleventh cap. Also in Dulwich's 1997 First XV was David (D. L.) Flatman 1996–7 who was also to play for England, and Jon (J. J. R.) Dawson who was to obtain a Cambridge Blue in 2006 and was awarded Man of the Match. This team, containing seven schoolboy internationals, was superbly captained by Tim (T. A.) Dux whose quiet authority and the respect with which he was regarded by other members of the team played a major part in their success. They played and won 15 matches, scoring 826 points against 47. Sheridan scored 22 tries at number 8. It must be remembered that, by mutual agreement, some of the matches were ended early because of the overwhelming superiority of the Dulwich team. Since 1997 not surprisingly no team has matched this performance, but in the December 2004 issue of *Rugby World* Dulwich College was 'Team of the Month' under the captaincy of Tom (T. F.) Mercey.

Dulwich Rugby over the years has been very fortunate in the members of staff who have been responsible not only for the First XV but for the organisation of Rugby throughout the school. The earliest recorded master was H. V. Doulton who took charge in 1887 to be followed by W. R. M. Leake in 1889 and J. Douglas in 1894. These were all Old Alleynians, to be followed in 1904 by another OA, W. D. Gibbon. He ran the Rugby until 1927, and was followed by R. T. Rees. Even after his retirement 'Beaky'

Rees followed the First XV to all its away matches. In 1936 G. W. Parker, a Cambridge Double Blue for cricket and Rugby, was a member of staff, and during that period played for England. He is the kicker in one of the first Rugby Football Union instructional films which was seen by thousands of players. After World War Two, J. S. Young (OA) was in charge followed by E. C. C. Wynter, assisted by S. A. Cole. David Knight (OA) was responsible for a few years until succeeded by the legendary J. A. Gwilliam, a Cambridge Blue and Welsh international. He made 23 appearances for Wales, 13 as Captain and led his country to two Triple Crowns. David Parry-Jones in his three-volume history of Welsh Rugby has called the second volume *The Gwilliam Seasons – John Gwilliam and the Second Golden Era of Welsh Rugby*. Not only was he an outstanding coach but insisted that masters in charge of all teams coached to his methods. Clearly this was a great source of strength to Dulwich Rugby because all boys played in the same way. Gwilliam became a very distinguished headmaster of Birkenhead School. He had been assisted by A. H. Cooper, an Oxford Blue who took over from him. There followed T. B. Richards, also a Cambridge Blue and Welsh international. T. D. Francis and R. D. V. Knight (OA) followed to be succeeded by I. M. Gibson who was also the coach of the English 18 group. P. d'A. Keith-Roach was on the

First XV, 1997. A. J. E. Thompson, N. S. West, F. S. N-A. White, J. D. Nurse.
F. E. Reynolds, M. D. Woolsey, N. O. Andersen, H. J. Stewart, J. R. St. L. Franklin, J. J. R. Dawson, D. L. Flatman.
P. R. Szewczyk, N. A. Martin, A. J. Sheridan, T. A. Dux (Capt.), C. J. King, M. R. A. Graham, U. Makhanya. (Dulwich College)

staff at this time, and his experience of coaching the English forwards was a great asset. In recent years P. A. Allen and I. R. Martin have coached the XV with equal success. Of course, over the years Dulwich Rugby owes a vast debt of gratitude to the very many members of staff who have given thousands of hours to coaching with great dedication and enthusiasm. The name of Rick (F. R. F.) Wilson will always stand very high on this list.

The importance of Rugby at Dulwich is well illustrated by this notice posted by the Master, Anthony Verity, in 1992:

> Mrs Thatcher will be visiting the College at 12.00 noon on Saturday 21 March. She will probably join a rugby practice on the First XV pitch, and then visit the Wodehouse shrine and the Archive.

Hockey

Although hockey was not officially recognised as a school sport until 1953, a few Old Alleynians had already distinguished themselves in the game. Frank de la Solbé played for England between 1887 and 1899, and Edgar (E. G. S.) Hose played for England between 1897 and 1899. In 1899 Solbé scored once against Ireland and twice against Wales. Percy (P. M.) Rees gained international honours for England in 1905, and in 1908 played for England in the Olympic Games.

In 1953 it was agreed that the last four weeks of the Lent Term could be used for hockey. The time allowed was short and the pitches appalling, but it was a beginning. In the first year one game was played against an invitation team of international and county players. It is not surprising that Dulwich lost. Next season, 1954, saw the first school match, against Whitgift School, under the able captaining of Chris Howland. Dulwich won by 4 goals to 1, Howland scoring all four.

In the early years, the only pitches were grass ones on either side of the old Covered Courts. Over the latter years of the 1950s and in the early 1960s Dulwich had some very successful sides and one or two unbeaten seasons. In 1960 Dulwich took part in the Oxford Public Schools Festival. In 1963 the school took part in their first overseas festival, in Brussels, where much to their embarrassment they were billed as 'Londres'. A member of this team was Ian (I. S.) McIntosh, Captain of Kent and later Captain of the England Indoor team. Glen (G. E.) Wisher was also to play for England indoors. During these early years hockey had been run with great determination and skill by P. R. Thomas of Cambridge and Middlesex (see Chapter Ten).

In 1965 John Dewes took over. Under his guidance the side became a regular visitor to the Dutch school tournament at The Hague, where in 1974 Dulwich was the first British team to win the tournament against Dutch, German and other continental opposition. In 1971, Norman Porter, the Scottish International, became master-in-charge, and it was during his time that the Redgra pitch was laid. It was in this period that the status of hockey was confirmed, when it became the third major sport. Next came Tony Forbes, followed in 1977 by Steven Long, a distinguished international player who had won 56 caps for England and 22 caps for Great Britain and scored 68 goals. After Long's departure to Bryanston, Peter Callender was in charge of hockey for many years. At one time it was a great fillip to Dulwich hockey that Martyn Grimley, who won gold with Great Britain in Seoul in 1988, was on the staff.

Association football

Soccer had been played for many years by day-boys unofficially in the Sunday morning leagues on Clapham Common. In the 1960s it became an option in the Lent Term, although at a very low key. In 2000 a decision was made to give soccer equal status to hockey. To some extent this decision was influenced by the impression that some bright boys were choosing other schools rather than Dulwich because those schools played soccer. To upgrade soccer was almost certainly a correct decision, because it is important that boys have as much choice over the games they play as they do in the choice of academic subjects for A Level. Since 2000 Dulwich has won the London Schools Soccer Cup twice.

In earlier days John (J. H.) Lockton had refereed regularly in Football League matches, and Trevor Bailey had been a distinguished amateur footballer both at Cambridge where he obtained a Blue, and also for Walthamstow for whom he obtained a Football Association Amateur Cup Winner's Medal in 1953.

Athletics

The first record of an athletics sports meeting at the College is in the Lent Term 1866. *The Alleynian* reported that 'the visitors could not have numbered less than four or five thousand'. In 1884 the first meet of the College Hare and Hounds is recorded when the course was via Sydenham Hill, Lordship Lane, Court Road (Lane) and home by the village.

In 1914 Reginald Salisbury Woods (see Chapter Eight) was 'putting the weight (shot)' for England against Scotland and Ireland, and after the war he represented England from 1920 to 1929 including the Olympics in 1924. In 1927 Vivian (V. P.) Brown ran the eight hundred metres for England against France. Since the Second World War the most outstanding athlete produced by Dulwich is Trevor Llewelyn, currently the Head of

Assault at arms, 1927. (Dulwich College)

Geography at the College, who represented Wales and Great Britain in the high jump and broke the Welsh national record in 1978 with a high jump of seven feet one and a half inches. He is an athletics coach of national repute. In 1986 Simeon (S. B. C.) Robbie represented Great Britain in the pentathlon.

Emeka (C. V.) Udechuku (1990–97) has won national recognition in both discus and shot. He represented Great Britain in the Athens Olympics and came seventh in the final of the discus at the Commonwealth Games in Melbourne in 2006. In the shot he was the first man ever to win AAA titles at U–15, U–17, U–20, U–21 and Senior levels.

During this period for most of the time athletic sports were held in the Lent Term in order not to conflict with Rugby or cricket. The number of events was steadily increased, and in 1965 the running track was relaid. The annual sports for the Lower School (under-13) were now held as a separate event and records were established for these year groups. For a number of years the starter on this day was Alan Pascoe, who had won a gold medal in the hurdles at the Olympics in Mexico City and was a member of the Physical Education department. On one occasion, as the sports were about to begin, a violent storm occurred and Alan Pascoe asked the Head of the Lower School whether the sports should continue. The Head of Lower School replied in the negative. This decision may have been partly influenced by the fact that his umbrella had just been struck by lightning.

Boxing

Boxing classes at the College were started by the Corps in 1879, almost certainly as part of military training. In 1921 boxing was an integral part of the Quadrangular Tournament which involved Bedford, Dulwich, Eton and Haileybury. This competition also included fencing. The semi-finals took place in the morning and the finals in the afternoon. In the 1960s boxing was abandoned by many schools as a sport because of medical and public opinion. This marked the end of the Quadrangular Tournament, although fencing did continue for about five years. In some ways Martial Arts have taken the place of boxing.

Dulwich produced a number of very good boxers. Probably the two most distinguished were Terry (T. A. A.) Adams, a remarkably fine sportsman who was also in the First XV, put the shot and was a very good swimmer. He captained the Oxford University boxing team and later pursued a career in the Regular Army. Adrian (A. H.) Hobart captained Cambridge University and won the Canadian Golden Gloves Championship at the age of 35. He is now a surgeon in Toronto. Graham (G. N. C.) Ward also gained a boxing blue. The success of Dulwich boxing in the post-War period was largely due to Wally Cromey who was a former Army boxing champion and was a physical training instructor at the College for many years. He was a very good referee who in house competitions stopped fights early once he was sure who would be the winner. This encouraged boys to compete for their houses because they had total confidence in him.

Boxing 1953.   A. H. Taylor, T. F. Howe, R. J. O. Smith, J. W. V. Wright, L. G. J. Edwards, P. Bunyapana, A. Sarasin, M. J. C. Wiggins.
M. D. Wright, T. A. A. Adams (Capt.), W. F. Cromey, MBE, J. M. D. Morris, J. S. Burton. (Dulwich College)

John (J. M. D.) Morris (OA; left 1953) was a very efficient and well-liked secretary of The British Boxing Board of Control over a long period.

Fencing

In 1939 George (A. G.) Lehmann (see Chapter Nine) fenced sabre for England against Scotland and Ireland, and in the same year Gordon (G. F.) Wright also fenced the same weapon for England. In 1947 Kenneth (K. G. C.) Campbell fenced for England and in 1957 Brian (B. W.) Howes represented Great Britain in the World Student Games in Paris in all three weapons and went on to represent Great Britain in sabre in the World Fencing Championships. In 1960 Donald (D. D.) Stringer represented Great Britain in the Olympic Games and was appointed captain of the sabre team. In 1962 John (J. F.) Anderson fenced épée for England in the International Quadrangular in Dublin. In the same year he had won the Public Schools Championship.

The success of Dulwich fencing owed a great deal to Ted Day, a former Army fencing champion and, like Wally Cromey, a former Army physical training instructor. Fencing is still flourishing at Dulwich but, as in many schools, perhaps not to the same standard as was once achieved.

Golf

Sidney (S. H.) Fry played golf regularly for England between 1901 and 1909. In 1902 he lost in the final of the Amateur Golf Championship by one hole. Incidentally, in 1921 he won the Amateur Billiards Championship for the seventh time which was a record, particularly as he had first won the Championship in 1893. William Brander played for England in 1905.

Since the Second World War the name which looms largest is that of Peter (P.A.) Oosterhuis. He played for the Walker Cup team as a schoolboy in 1968 and was later, as a professional, to win the Canadian Open.

The main competition for Old Boys is the Halford Hewitt which is fiercely contested each year. Although the Old Alleynians have never won this competition they have come very close. Bob (R. C.) Deakin has made over fifty appearances in this competition strictly on merit, a remarkable performance.

Rowing

In 1936 Thomas (T. R. M.) Bristow rowed for Great Britain in the Olympic Games in Berlin, having gained a Cambridge Blue in 1935. In the 50s Roger (R. T.) Weston coxed in the University Boat Race. In 1962 Bill (W. L.) Barry won the Diamond Sculls at Henley Regatta, and in

1964 was a member of the Great Britain Coxless Fours at the Tokyo Olympics.

The Dulwich Boat Club itself was not started until the Lent Term 1991 by Dr Trevor Charlton. Despite an initial membership of only ten boys, within a decade it had its own boathouse and a national reputation. It has won gold medals in the Schools' Head of the River, the National Schools' Regatta and the Belgian International Regatta at Ghent, as well as having shown fine performances in the National Championships and the Henley Royal Regatta.

In 1992 Damian (D. R.) West gained a Cambridge Blue and, at the 2000 Sydney Olympics, his brother, Kieran (K. M.) West, Cambridge University Boat Club President, became Dulwich's first ever Olympic gold medallist when the Great Britain eight powered their way to victory over Australia in the final on Penrith Lake. Since then he has had further success in the Great Britain coxed four, winning gold at the world championships.

To the present day Dulwich maintains a strong rowing squad with members competing both nationally and internationally as well as at domestic regattas. Levels of commitment, enthusiasm and competition have risen and remain high at all ages.

Sailing

In 1961 Alan (A. H.) Emus, sailing *Shrike II*, won the New York International Challenge Cup over a triangular three-mile course inside Chichester Harbour.

Sailing is an option for boys at Dulwich, but a tremendous contribution has been made by the Alleynian Sailing Society which each summer takes a group of boys sailing in the Solent as a sort of master class. In 2006 the Old Alleynians won the Arrow Trophy which is competed for annually by 16 independent schools. In 2007 they won the Belvedere Cup which is organised by the Royal Thames Yacht Club in London's Dockland. This cup was first competed for in 1845. Sadly, in 2006 two Old Alleynian sailors and their friend who had been with them at DCPS were drowned when their yacht *Ouzo* was in collision with a large car ferry.

Shooting

In the early years shooting played a very prominent part in the sporting life of the College, largely because it was part of the Corps training. In 1878 Dulwich entered the Ashburton Competition and won it in 1886 and again in 1900. The Lane Shield named after C. H. Lane (OA) who had taught at Dulwich and then at Wellington where he died at a young age (see Chapter Six) was first competed for against Wellington in 1884. In the years when Dulwich won this shield it was hung over the south door

inside the Great Hall. A number of prints of the Great Hall show the shield in position.

In 1905 Stanley (S. F.) Thöl shot for England and also won many prizes in the years that followed. Robert (R. T. D.) Alexander shot for India at Bisley in 1910 and also again in 1926-7. Years later he was to shoot in the Old Boys Veterans Competition at Bisley with 'Scotty' (W. D.) Gibbon. In 1912 Hugh (H. M.) Leake shot for India, and in 1920 Henry (H. P. T.) Lattey shot for Ireland as he did regularly until 1949. Other internationals of the period were Alan (A. F.) Marchment for England 1927-30, Charles (C. W.) Simpson for Scotland in 1923 and John (J. B.) Martin for Scotland in 1928. In 1931 the name of Frederick (F. C.) Halahan appears in small-bore for Ireland. He was later as an Air Vice-Marshal to become Chairman of the Royal Air Force Rifle Association.

After the Second World War, Donald (D. F.) Boadella shot for Great Britain in 1967, and in 1977 Frank (F. O.) Harriss won the Queen's Prize at Bisley, the most distinguished of shooting prizes. In 1985 Faisal (F. M.) Al-Harden shot for England, as did David (D. E. R.) Holmes.

There are more cups and prizes for shooting at Dulwich than for any other sport which illustrates the importance that was attached to it. Sadly, increasing safety regulations and the loss of the .22 range have made it very difficult for boys to shoot. Fortunately the Old Alleynians continue to shoot regularly at Bisley.

Squash

Squash has always been a prominent part of Dulwich life, although the destruction of the courts by enemy action during World War Two restricted the amount of squash that boys could play.

In 1949 Glyn (G. D.) Evans represented Wales against Scotland, as did his brother John (J. B.) Evans, an Oxford Blue, in 1953 and again in 1957. In the same year Soli (S. J.) Lam and Adi (A. F.) Gazdar represented India.

Swimming

Dulwich was one of the first schools to construct a swimming pool as opposed to using local ponds and rivers (see Chapter Seven). This pool was open air and was refurbished on a number of occasions. In 2002 a new pool was constructed next to the Physical Education Centre (see Chapter Ten). In 1924 Edouard (E. G.) Vanzeveren represented England in the 100 metres in the Olympics in France. He also represented England in 1926 and 1927. George (G. H.) Purchon represented Great Britain in Copenhagen. In 1965-6 Andrew (A. F.) Wilson swam for England in a number of international matches and also in the Commonwealth Games in Jamaica.

⇒✠ THE ✠⇐

WIMBLEDON ⁂ EIGHT,

⇒✠ 1886 ✠⇐

H. Carpmael,   F. C. Christmas,   C. J. Paton,   F. B. Hannen,   E. Lovegrove,

J. R. F. Frazer,   H. L. Martley,   F. W. Anstie (Captain),   Sergt. Morgan.

THE ALLEN SHIELD.   THE ASHBURTON SHIELD.

Badminton, basketball, croquet, curling and powerboating

At badminton in 1921 Archibald (A. F.) Engelbach played for England against Ireland, and in 1927 Percy (P. D.) Macfarlane also played against Scotland and the following year against Ireland; in 1930 Kenneth (K. G.) Livingstone played for England. After the Second World War, John (J. R.) Best gained international honours for England against Denmark and Sweden, and toured South Africa. Badminton is now a largely recreational game, although some matches are played.

Although basketball had been a recreational sport for many years, it was not until the early 1990s that Paul Toney, who had represented British Universities, was appointed to the Physical Education staff and gave the sport very real drive. At the same time the London Independent Schools Basketball League (LISBA) was formed, and Dulwich has been regular finalists in their competitions. In 1992 the Dulwich basketball teams won 51 of their 54 games and the senior team travelled to play in Florida; in 1995 the Under-16 team journeyed to North Carolina to play eight games. In 2003 Andrew (A. A.) Milne took over the basketball and gave this sport even greater impetus. Among the leading players in the last twenty years have been boarders, especially those from China and Hong Kong.

At croquet David (D. W.) Curtis in 1962 played for England against Australia and New Zealand in the triangular test match in New Zealand. Over the years he played a large part in rewriting the laws of the game. Today at the College croquet is extremely popular, and in the summer during most lunchtimes boys can be seen playing on the front lawns.

As for curling, in 1934 Clarence (C. B.) Krabbé and Charles (C. F.) Krabbé played for England against Scotland and Switzerland.

At powerboating in 1926 Edward Johnston-Noad represented England, and again in the following two years. In the 1970s Edward (E. J. N.) Chater held the record for the fastest run from the Pool of London to Monte Carlo.

Chess and bridge

At chess in 1947 Robert (R. H.) Newman played for Great Britain against Russia and Australia and in 1948 against Australia by radio. In 1950 he was fourth in the International Chess Tournament. Probably the most distinguished chess player ever produced at the College is Raymond (R. D.) Keene (see Chapter Ten) who became a Grand Master and writes the column 'Keene on Chess' regularly in *The Times*.

Over the years bridge at the College was actively encouraged by the late H. I. Alexander (see Chapter Ten) and S. W. Burton. In 1968 Anthony (A. J.) Walkden and Howard (H. J.) Oken both played bridge for England.

Fives

The earliest recorded fixture is in 1894 when Dulwich played St Paul's. Fives continued to flourish with ten courts available until the Second World War when they were destroyed by enemy action. Despite much campaigning over the years they have never been rebuilt, although Alleyn's School has kindly made their courts available to the College from time to time.

Lawn tennis

A. H. Gilkes disapproved of tennis, and would not allow boys to play the game (see Chapter Eight). In 1925 Cyril (C. G.) Eames played doubles for England and again in the following two years. In 1929 he was Captain of his country. As a game at the College it continues to flourish, and this has been greatly helped by the construction of more all-weather surfaces.

Games at Dulwich are in a very healthy state, despite the increasing pressure of examinations. In the school year 2006–7 there were 35 Rugby teams, 26 cricket teams, 14 hockey teams, and 39 football teams, as well as teams for basketball, badminton, athletics, cross-country, swimming, tennis and rowing in each year group. In addition boys represented the College at golf, fencing, squash, skiing, water polo, table-tennis and rugby fives, which has been recently re-introduced.

The Arms of Dulwich College
granted in 1936 by the College of Arms:

Argent a Chevron between three pierced Cinquefoils Gules
(the Arms of Edward Alleyn) with the augmentation
On a Chief Ermine a pierced Cinquefoil Gules

Edward Alleyn's Crest, 1619
*A dexter Cubit Arm couped holding a human Heart
issuant from Flames of fire all proper*

ABBREVIATIONS
NOTES & INDEX

ABBREVIATIONS

Note: the printed Governors' Minutes are sometimes confusingly paginated or not at all; minutes of the various committees (abbreviated below) are to be found in bound volumes of the annual *College Governors' Minutes*, Dulwich College Archives. References to *The Alleynian* in recent decades are complicated by the lack of figures for volumes and by confused issue and month definitions.

A	*The Alleynian*	*Interviews*	*Interviews, Anecdotes, collected by RJM, June and July 1910*, ms, R. J. Mackenzie (see Mck), DC Box 376
Alleyn's Diary	DC MS IX: from transcript in Young (see below)		
BL	British Library (formerly British Museum)	M	Muniment, Dulwich College (see Warner, under MS below)
BM	Board Meeting, Governors' Minutes, Dulwich College	Mck	R. J. Mackenzie, unpublished typescript, History of Dulwich College (1912), DC Box 28
Cerasano	S. Cerasano et al., *Edward Alleyn. Elizabethan Actor, Jacobean Gentleman*, Dulwich Picture Gallery, 1994	*Memories*	*Memories of Dulwich College in the 'Sixties and 'Seventies by Old Alleynians*, tercentenary publication, Dulwich College, 1919
CC	Charity Commissioners' Report of 1854 (manuscript): DC Box 285	MRG	Master's Report to the Governors, Governors' Minutes, Dulwich College
Darby	*History of Dulwich College*, ts., DC Box 370	MS	Manuscript, Dulwich College. See George F. Warner, *Catalogue of the Manuscripts and Muniments of Alleyn's College of God's Gift at Dulwich* (1881). The theatrical documents in the Alleyn and Henslowe papers, including Henslowe's and Alleyn's Diary, digitally photographed by Dr Grace Ioppolo and Dr David Cooper in 2006 and 2007 (with support from The Pilgrim Trust, The Leverhulme Trust, The British Academy, and the Thriplow Charitable Trust), may be viewed at **www.henslowe-alleyn.org**
Diary	A. H. Gilkes, Ms. Diary, Dulwich College		
DC	Dulwich College		
DC Box	Dulwich College Archives		
DPG	Dulwich Picture Gallery: R. Beresford, *Complete Illustrated Catalogue*, 1998		
DPL	Boxed Letters Series, Dulwich College Archives		
DVK	D. V. Knight, *DVK, Dulwich Man*, Dulwich College, 1987		
EC	Education Committee, Governors' Minutes, Dulwich College	MSS(2)	F. B. Bickley, *Catalogue of Manuscripts and Muniments of Alleyn's College of God's Gift*, second series, Dulwich College (1903)
EFC	Education and Finance Committee, Governors' Minutes, Dulwich College	NPG	National Portrait Gallery
		OCSEB	Oxford and Cambridge Schools and Examination Board, Governors' Minutes, Dulwich College
Ex Com	Executive Committee, Governors' Minutes, Dulwich College	ODNB	Oxford Dictionary of National Biography (2004–); **http:www.oxforddnb.com**
FC	Finance Committee, Governors' Minutes, Dulwich College	Ormiston	T. L. Ormiston, *Dulwich College Register, 1619–1926* (1926)
FGP	Finance and General Purposes Committee, Governors' Minutes, Dulwich College	PGC	Picture Gallery Committee, Governors' Minutes, Dulwich College
G & D	W. R. M. Leake, ed., *Gilkes and Dulwich*, Dulwich College, 1938	PRO	Public Record Office (now the National Archives)
GM	Governors' Minutes, Dulwich College (printed)	PS	Private Sittings
		RA	Royal Academy
GPC	General Purposes Committee, Governors' Minutes, Dulwich College	RIBA	Royal Institute of British Architects
		S&C	School and Chapel Committee, Governors' Minutes, Dulwich College
Henslowe's Diary	DC MS VII: *Henslowe's Diary*, ed. R. A. Foakes and R. T. Rickert (1961; second edition, 2002)	Sp C	Special Committee, Governors' Minutes, Dulwich College
Hodges	S. Hodges, *God's Gift*, 1981	Young	W. Young, *The History of Dulwich College*, 2 vols. (1889)

NOTES

Chapter One

Approximate equivalents (2006) for the value of £1 sterling in the seventeenth century, to help calculate the sums mentioned in Chapter One, are given below, reckoned according to the Retail Price Index. These figures are taken from the calculators available at:

www.measuringworth.com/calculators/ppoweruk

but have been rounded up and down without a decimal figure. 1590, £153; 1600, £135; 1610, £141; 1620, £146; 1640, £130; 1660, £103.

1. Warner, p. xv.
2. Joseph Hunter (1783–1861) doubts rather snobbishly if Alleyn's claim of kinship with the great eponymous landowners of Townley in Lancashire can possibly be true. *Chorus Vatum Anglicanorum*, BL. Add. Mss 24487, f. 167.
3. J. Freeman ed., T. Fuller, *Worthies of England* [1633], 1952, p. 368. Street names in that quarter still commemorate Cavendish and Devonshire; Devonshire House was the town house of the Cavendish family before they moved to Piccadilly. See contemporary engraved map of Moorfields and Bishopsgate in 1559, F. Barker and P. Jackson, *London*, 1974, p. 92.
4. MS IV, 4.
5. J. Andrews et al., *The History of Bethlem*, 1997, pp. 61, 131, 133; P. Allderidge, 'Management and mismanagement at Bedlam, 1547–1633', in C. Webster, *Health, medicine and mortality in the sixteenth century*, 1979, pp. 147–8.
6. E. G. O'Donoghue, *The Story of Bethlehem Hospital*, 1914, p. 141; Andrews, op. cit., p. 724. Repertories of the Court of Aldermen 12/2/483v, Corporation of London Record Office; Journal of Common Council 6, f. 342; 7, f. 187v.
7. O'Donoghue, p. 131.
8. MSS(2), 100, 143 (Lease of 1701: 'where it 'lately stood').
9. MSS(2), 14, *Weekly Accounts*, 25 May 1678, f. 22v.
10. MSS (2), 15, *Weekly Accounts*, 4 October 1681.
11. MS IV, 21.
12. E. K. Chambers, *The Elizabethan Stage*, 1923, II, pp. 298–9.
13. Cerasano, p. 12.
14. J. P. Collier, *Memoirs of Edward Alleyn*, 1841, p. 3, muddles two Brownes, John and the actor Robert.
15. A. Highmore, *Pietas Londinensis*, 1814, p. 458.
16. (Begun by) John Stow, (continued and augmented by) Edmund Howes, *Annales of England or a General Chronicle of England*, 1631, p. 1004; Stow says fourteen playhouses were built in sixty years.
17. Information from Susan Cerasano.
18. MS III, 56; see n. 12.; information on John Alleyn from Susan Cerasano.
19. *Sotheby's Book Sale*, 1939, n. 21.
20. MS I, 2.
21. MS I, 2.
22. MS I, 4.
23. See n. 3.
24. Chambers, II, pp. 220–4.
25. A. J. Gurr, *The Shakespearean Stage*, 3rd ed., 1992, pp. 36–8; Gurr, *The Shakespeare Company, 1594–1642*, 2004, pp. 27, 222; P. Honan, *Christopher Marlowe*, 2005, p. 250; for Lord Admiral's Company, see Chambers, II, pp. 134–92.
26. MS VII, 2r.
27. MS V, 22.
28. M 496; Henslowe's Diary (MS VII).
29. *Encyclopaedia Britannica*, 1929, XI, p. 450.
30. S. Cerasano, 'Going down the drain in 1616: Widow Henslowe and the Sewers Commission', *Shakespeare Studies* 32, 2004, pp. 83–98.
31. Op. cit., section 4, p. 120. Baker mentions Alleyn's charitable Foundation, conferring 'a kind of reputation to the Society of Players', section 4, p. 151.
32. Gurr, 2004, p. 13.
33. MS I, 27.
34. MS I, 29. See also Privy Council Order, 22 June 1600. Gurr, 2004, p. 252.
35. *Henslowe's Diary*, p. 172. See also G. L. Hosking, *The Life and Times of Edward Alleyn*, 1952, pp. 55–66.
36. MS I, 6.
37. *Henslowe's Diary*, p. 85; DC MS X, f. 5v, Alleyn sold the Bear Garden 'to my father Hinchloe' for £580.
38. MS VII, p. 43r.
39. M 106 (26 April 1595).
40. MS III, 17.
41. Young, II, p. 159.
42. Samuel Rowlands, the low-life satirist, in a character sketch, 'A Gull': 'The Gull gets on a surplis / With a crosse vpon his brest / Like *Allen* playing Faustus, / In that manner was he drest / To make a Deuill rise', *Knave of Clubbs*, 1611 edition, sig. D 2v; Prynne, op. cit., f. 556.
43. O.L. Dick, ed., *Aubrey's Brief Lives*, Penguin, 1972, p. 107.
44. Honan, p. 292. *Edward II* is not recorded with Henslowe's company, ibid., p. 308.
45. T. Nash, *Four Letters*, 1592: R. B. McKerrow, ed., *Works*, 1904, I, p. 296.
46. 1594 Quarto: see W. W. Greg, *Two Elizabethan Abridgements: 'The Battle of Alcazar' and 'Orlando Furioso'*, 1923, p. 195; cf. MS I, 138 ('pugnant'); Gurr, 2004, p. 81.
47. See n. 3.
48. *Biographia Britannica*, 1723–44, p. 115.
49. *Henry IV, Part Two*, II, iv; *Hamlet*, III, ii; *fustian* = a metaphor from a cheap imported cotton cloth: Elizabethan *denim*, as it were.
50. *Timber* (1632), Temple Classics, 1951, p. 41; E. Gayton, *Pleasant Notes upon Don Quixot*, 1654, I, vii, p. 24. Tucca, a strutting captain, in Ben Jonson's *Poetaster*, 1602, jeers at Histrio, an actor, as 'a twopenny teare-mouth', III, iv, 126 (W. F. McNeir, 'Gayton on Elizabethan Acting', *PMLA*, 56, 1941, p. 581).

51. *Henslowe's Diary*, p. 137 (f. 70v). S. Cerasano, 'Edward Alleyn's "Retirement" 1597–1600', *Medieval and Renaissance Drama in England* 10, 1998, pp. 98–112.

52. J. P. Collier, *Memoirs of Edward Alleyn*, 1841, p. 97.

53. Weever, 'Epig. 23, In Ed: Allen', *Epigrammes in the oldest cut, and newest fashion*, London, 1599, sig. E 6v; see also Thomas Nashe, *Pierce Pennilesse, his Supplication to the Devil*, 1592, sig. H 3, the 'due commendation of Ned Allen': 'Not *Roscius* nor *Æsope*, those Tragedians admired before Christ was borne, could ever performe more in action than famous *Ned Allen*'; Jonson, *Epigrammes I Booke*, lxxxix, 'To E. Allen', *Workes*, 1616, p. 793. Dekker's 'Eulogium' of Alleyn is lost; its enclosing letter to Alleyn is MS I, 108.

54. On the platt of *Battle*, see W. W. Greg, *Two Elizabethan Stage Abridgements*, 1923, pp. 7–93; on *Cutlack*, see *Henslowe's Diary*, June–Sept. 1594, pp. 21–4.

55. C. F. Tucker Brooke, ed., *The Works of Christopher Marlowe*, 1910, p. 239.

56. Anon. (Everard Guilpin), *Skialetheia, or, a Shadowe of Truth*, 1598, sig. B 2v; A. Gurr, 'Intertextuality at Windsor', *Shakespeare Quarterly* 38, 1987, p. 193.

57. Third edition, as *The Actor's Vindication* [1658] 'printed by G. E. for W.C. (William Cartwright)', pp. 14–15; M. C. Bradbrook, *The Rise of the Common Player*, 1962, pp. 130–2; W. A. Armstrong, 'Shakespeare and the acting of Edward Alleyn, *Shakespeare Survey* 7, 1954, pp. 82–9; A. J. Gurr, 'Who strutted and bellowed?' *Shakespeare Survey* 16, 1963, pp. 95–102; B. L. Joseph, *Elizabethan Acting*, 1951, pp. 1–112.

58. Young, II, pp. 199, 229.

59. MS II, 19; Chambers, II, p. 186.

60. MS III, 93.

61. R. Dutton, *Jacobean Civic Pageants*, 1995, pp. 21, 36; complete text, pp. 27–115.

62. *Workes*, 1616, p. 848.

63. J. Burke, *A General Armory of England, Scotland and Ireland*, 1842, n.p.

64. In 1608 Alleyn performed again in front of King James at Salisbury House; Alleyn, Inigo Jones and Ben Jonson were paid £20 each. See G. Ioppolo, *Dramatists and their Manuscripts in the Age of Shakespeare, Jonson, Middleton and Heywood*, 2006, p. 59.

65. *Henslowe's Diary*, pp. 12, 262; M 86–7.

66. E.g., *Henslowe's Diary*, 1594, p. 234: 'layd owt for my Lorde Admeralle seruantes as foloweth'.

67. M 163; MS XI, f. 30.

68. MS V, 21.

69. MS I, 38.

70. PRO, LC2/4/4, quoted in S. Cerasano, 'The Geography of Henslowe's Diary', *Shakespeare Quarterly* 56, 2005, pp. 337–8.

71. M 16; M 22.

72. MS I, 38.

73. MS XX. *The Tell Tale* was produced at Alleyn's School in 1994 by Eileen Chivers.

74. See Chapter Three, and G. A. Waterfield et al., *Mr Cartwright's Pictures*, Dulwich Picture Gallery, 1987.

75. MS XIX. Three other 'plats' belonging to Alleyn: E. Malone, *Plays and Poems of William Shakespeare*, ed. Boswell, 1821, III, p. 357; David Kathman, 'Reconsidering The Seven Deadly Sins', *Early Theatre* 7, 2004, pp. 13–44. Andrew Gurr, 'The Work of Elizabethan Plotters and *2 The Seven Deadly Sins*', *Early Theatre* 10 (2007), pp. 67–87, however, questions Kathman's re-dating.

76. D. Lysons, *The Environs of London*, 1792, I, p. 112.

77. Three of the cue-scripts were bought by the British Museum from the sale of Richard Heber in 1836: *Dead Man's Fortune, Frederick and Basilea, Battle of Alcazar*, BL Add. Mss 10449. For *Tamar Cam*, see Young, II, p. 331. T Heywood, *Apology for Actors*, Shakespeare Society, 1841, p. xiii.

78. BL Add. Mss 10306. *Mr. Cartwright's Pictures*, p. 83 (1.25, n. 3) wrongly says it was sold by the College in 1823.

79. MS I, 30; Warner, p. 21. Collier nonsensically added Shakespearean characters (Lord Chamberlain's Company) to the genuine Marlowe characters (Lord Admiral's Company).

80. Some papers remained with Malone from *c.* 1790 to his death in 1812, and were not returned by his executor, the younger Boswell; Warner, p. x; Edmond Malone, *Plays and Poems of William Shakespeare*, ed. Boswell, 1821, XXI, pp. 311–13; A. and J. I. Freeman, *John Payne Collier*, 2004, p. 352; *Henslowe's Diary*, pp. 319–21. *The Platt* and *The Telltale* (MSS XIX and XX) were in the sale-catalogue of James Boswell's library in 1825, but were claimed by the College and given up before the sale; Warner, p. 343.

81. BL Add. Mss 30262, f. 66. Collier stole a loose folio page with a costume and property inventory and valuation of *c.* 1589, in John Alleyn's hand, including a wig and a beard, now at Harvard, MS Thr, f. 276 G. B. Evans, 'An Elizabethan Theatrical Stock List', *Harvard Library Bulletin* 21, 1973, p. 254 ff.

82. Over 325 plays: Grace Ioppolo, *Dramatists and their Manuscripts in the Age of Shakespeare, Jonson, Middleton and Heywood*, 2006, p. 14.

83. MS I, 73; MS I, 79.

84. *Henslowe's Diary*, p. 73.

85. MS I, 135-6; MS I, 24.

86. Chambers, 1923, II, p. 341; ODNB.

87. *Henslowe's Diary*, p. 264; information from Susan Cerasano.

88. Ibid., p. 139.

89. MS I, 12.

90. *Henslowe's Diary*, pp. 180–1, 184, 187, 204–5, 217.

91. Ibid., pp. 6–7.

92. Ibid., p. 186.

93. MS I, 21.

94. MS I, 69; see M 52; James Wright, *Historia Histrionica*, 1699, p. vii.

95. MS 95 v.

96. MS I, 104; MS I, 106.

97. MS IV, 21.

98. J. Stow, *A Survey of the Cities of London and Westminster and the Borough of Southwark* [1598], 1755, p. 9.

99. *In the Clink*, 1977, p. 9; *Bawds and Lodgings, a History of the London Bankside Brothels*, 1976, p. 154; cf. p. 162, n. 23, which describes a tavern belonging to the Alleyn brothers as 'this brothel'. For the *Bell*, the *Barge* and the *Cock* and Southwark brothels, see H. S. Kelly, 'Bishop, Prioress, and Bawd in the Stews of Southwark', *Speculum*, Massachusetts, Vol. 75, 2, 2000, pp. 358–9, 379.

100. W. Rendle, 'The Stews on Bankside', *Antiquarian Magazine*, II, 8, July 1882, p. 76.

101. See n. 98.

102. M 16.

103. MS I, 18.

104. MS I, 16; MS I, 17.

105. MS I, 39.

106. PC Order, 26 June 1600. Gurr, *The Shakespeare Company*, 2004, pp. 252–3; E. K. Chambers, *The Elizabethan Stage*, II, 1923, pp. 435–43.

107. MS I, 28.

108. MS I, 27; MS I, 29.

109. MS I, 28.

110. M 56. These leases were drafts, and not necessarily executed.

111. Young, II, p. 104.

112. Quoted in Cerasano, p. 20; N. E. McClure, ed., *Letters of John Chamberlain*, Philadelphia, 1939. See MS VIII, f. 6v, 'What the Fortune cost me', 1599: £240 for the lease, £520 for the building. Ben Jonson's poem 'An Execration upon Vulcan', mentions the fire at the Fortune.

113. Young, II, p. 225.

114. Wright, *Historia Histrionica*, 1699, p. x.

115. Young, II, p. 225.

116. MSS, 2nd Series, 22 &c.

117. MS I, 125.

118. MS I, 113.

119. G. A. Hosking, *The Life and Times of Edward Alleyn*, 1952, p. 183; Mck, pp. 109–10.

120. MS I, 124–6.

121. M 126.

122. MS I, 131.

123. *Londina Illustrata*, 1819, vol. II, p. 141.

124. Day 5, p. 213. DC Box 285.

125. GM, 1 June, 1860, p. 336; BM, 11 April, 1871; EC, 27 Oct., 1864, p. 52; GM, 16 Jan., 1866 p. 21; EC, 1 March, 1866 pp. 16–17, 126; EC, 1871, p. 14.

126. M 16; MSS I, 10,11, and 14.

127. MS II, 7.

128. M 22.

129. *Henslowe's Diary*, pp. 232–4.

130. 'Howse, wharfe and Docke for his Ma^te Barges': petition from 'Mr Allen M^r of the Beare Garden' for annual rent to Lord Cranfield, Lord High Treasurer, October 1622, Sackville-Knole MSS I, old number, 5200; see J. Briley,

131. Horace Walpole (trans.), *Paul Hentzner's Travels in England*, 1797, p. 29.

132. Young, II, pp. 116, 143. Mck, p. 488.

133. Cerasano, p. 38; E. Croft-Murray, *Decorative Painting in England, 1537–1836*, 1962, pp. 181, 194, names William Heron as the painter of Queen Elizabeth's panelled barge, 1574, with 'five stories of poetry'; 'the unusual construction of the panels, with their rough hewn horizontal (rather than vertical) members, may indicate that they were taken from a larger structure' (information from John Ingamells, forthcoming Dulwich Picture Gallery Catalogue, British School).

134. ODNB. See n. 130.

135. M 49.

136. Briley, p. 106; *Bartholemew Fair*, Induction. N. Robins, 'A Player for Posterity', *TLS*, 6 January, 1995, p. 16.

137. MS I, 107.

138. See n. 32.

139. MSS II, 1–3, 5.

140. PRO LC 2/6; S. Cerasano, 'The Master of the Bears in Art and Enterprise', *Medieval and Renaissance Drama in England*, 5, 1991, pp. 195–209.

141. MS II, 15. MSS II and (passim) III relate to animal enterprises.

142. Stow, 1631, pp. 835-6.

143. Briley, p. 108; B. Ravelhofer, '"Beasts of Recreacion": Henslowe's White Bears,' *English Literary Renaissance* 32, 2002, pp. 287–323; Cerasano, cited in n. 140 above.

144. MS II, 10 and 13; I am grateful to Dr Nick de Somogyi for information about the names of the bears.

145. T. Birch, ed., *Court and Times of James I*, 1846, II, p. 410; Young, II, p. 235 and n.

146. MS II, 9.

147. MS II, 36; Young, II, pp. 85, 178, 207, and 238.

148. MS XI: accounts for the 'keeper' of the queen's bears and mastiffs.

149. Robert Crowley, 'Of Bearbaiting', 1550; see C. L. Kingsford, *Paris Garden and the Bear-Baiting*, 1920, p. 161.

150. Cerasano, p. 21; Warrant Book II, 198; II, 32; John Taylor, *Bull, Beare, and Horse, Cut, Curtaile, and Longtaile*, 1638.

151. MS II, 38, n.d.

152. MS II, 41.

153. Stow, *Survey*, p. 8.

154. Walpole, *Hentzner's Travels*, p. 30.

155. E. K. Chambers, *Elizabethan Stage*, 1923, II, p. 455; H. B. Wheatley, ed., *The Diary of Samuel Pepys*, 1893-9: August 1666, V, p. 375; cf. ibid., September 1667, VII, p. 100; 'Seuen of Mr. Godfries Beares, by the command of Thomas Pride, then hie Sheriefe of Surry, were then shot to death, On Saterday the 9 day of February 1655 [= 1656], by a Company of Souldiers'. Quoted in J. Leslie Hotson, 'Bear Gardens and Bear-Baiting during the Commonwealth', *PMLA*. 40, 1925, pp. 276–88 (p. 286).

156. M 584.

157. ODNB.

158. Young, II, p. 81.

159. J.M. Robinson, *The Dukes of Norfolk*, 1982, p. 111.

160. 28 May 1621, Young, II, p. 208; Prince Charles reconciled the peers.

161. ODNB.

162. MS V, 22–3; Cerasano, pp. 25–6. PRO C24/431/48. Cerasano, 'Going Down the Drain,' *Shakespeare Studies*, 32, 2004, pp. 83–98.

163. MS X, 1 July 1623.

164. MS I, 42 (letter draft on verso).

165. MS I, 38.

166. MS I, 9. A play called *The Wisdome of Doctor Doddypoll* (a French doctor), as acted by the Children of St Paul's, was published in 1600.

167. MS I, 13.

168. MS I, 15; Pyk signs as witness on MS IV, 30.

169. MSS I, 11, 13, 12, and 38.

170. DPG 444.

171. Young, II, p. 161.

172. Funeral certificate, certified by John Gifford, 'Senior Fellow and Preacher', and Martyn Symonds, 'Fellow, Minister and Schoolmaster', both of the College.

173. College of Arms, Painters' Work Book, 1619–34, 1 July 1623.

174. *Biographia Britannica*, p. 119; O. Manning and W. Bray, *The History and Antiquities of the County of Surrey*, 1804, III, p. 434.

175. I, iii, 92.

176. J. B. Leishman, ed. *The Three Parnassus Plays*, pp. 350–1.

177. Alleyn in fact claimed the early sixteenth-century arms of John Allen of Essex, which he persuaded Augustine Vincent to accept as his in the 1619 Visitation of Surrey, when they first appear as his (information from Thomas Woodcock, Norroy and Ulster King of Arms). In 1936 the College of Arms gave a separate grant to the College derived from Alleyn's arms, adding 'a chief ermine, thereon a cinquefoil of the second'. See G.L. Hosking, *The Life and Times of Edward Alleyn*, 1952, p. 228.

Chapter Two

Approximate value of £1 sterling [see Notes to Chapter One]: 1600, £135; 1605, £143; 1606, £134; 1611, £153; 1640, £130; 1843, £77.

1. William Hone, *The Table Book*, 1827, p. 335.

2. M Butlin, ed., *Samuel Palmer: The Sketchbook of 1824*, 2005, p. 81.

3. *The Pickwick Papers* (1837), Chapter LVII, 1948, p. 796; Wodehouse, op. cit., pp 102–3.

4. Cerasano, pp. 26–7.

5. James Wright, *Historia Histrionica*, 1699, p. vii.

6. John Stow, *A Survey of the Cities of London and Westminster and the Borough of Southwark* (1598), sixth edition, ed. John Strype, 1755, pp. 5–7.

7. MS III, 71.

8. Stow, p. 9.

9. MS I, 108.

10. Stow, p. 9.

11. MS I, 47. Collier inserted a forged list of Southwark inhabitants including 'Mr Shaksper' among the Alleyn and Henslowe papers (MS 1, 20, f. 29).

12. Highmore, *Pietas Londinensis*, 1814, p. 458; Cerasano, p. 23; MSS(2), 57, *Private Sittings*, p. 91.

13. ODNB (Henslowe); Stow, p. 17.

14. Mck, pp. 210, 552; Day 6, Charity Commissioners, Thomas Hare, inspector, DC Box 285; *Dulwich College; a Model for Free Grammar School Reformation in a Letter to Lord Cranworth*, third edition, c.1854.

15. Young, I, p. 29; ibid., II, pp. 87, 95, 96, 110.

16. MS I, 47 and (with list of names, 1608–9) 48.

17. MS I, 49.

18. MS V, 16.

19. MS I, 51.

20. MS IV, 72.

21. MS IV, 63; possibly the bargeman Kellock (see Chapter One, n. 138).

22. MS III, 19.

23. MS IV, 73.

24. MS IV, 72.

25. MS III, 42.

26. MS I, 149.

27. MS I, 137.

28. MS III, 100.

29. MS VIII, ff. 22–30v, 34–42.

30. Young, I, p. 453; E. T. Hall, *Dulwich History and Romance*, 1922, p. 6.

31. M 456; MS V, 19; MSS(2), 94, 13.

32. MS III, 15.

33. M 471.

34. M 156.

35. MS III, 93.

36. MS III, 59.

37. Young, I, p. 94.

38. MS IV, 75 and 78; Alleyn gained the missing documents: see M 344 and 345.

39. MS III, 93.

40. MS VIII (Memorandum Book), ff. 8v–18v, 19v–21v, 22, 33v, 34–35, 36v–38.

41. MS III, 73 and 123. Hall, 1922, p. 5.

42. BL Cotton Mss., A.8, f. 110.

43. MS III, 93.

44. M 471.

45. MS IV, 9.

46. O. Manning and W. Bray, *The History and Antiquities of the County of Surrey*, 1804, III, p. 432.

47. MSS(2), 40. The house was demolished in 1888 after the lapse of a lease; the grounds were split up into 51 building plots (including 13 shops); for map, advertisement,

and list of demolition materials, see grangerised copy of Blanch's *Camberwell* in the Minet Library, Lambeth.

48. M 471.
49. Highmore, p. 448.
50. M 558.
51. D. Wilkins, *Concilia Magnae Britanniae et Hiberniae*, 1737, IV, p. 455.
52. M 572.
53. Young, I, p. 36; Lymer kept up both appointments, but had left Dulwich by September 1617.
54. Wilkins, 1737, IV, pp. 455–8.
55. ODNB.
56. 29 September 1618.
57. MS X, f. 19; ODNB (Henslowe).
58. Manning and Bray, Surrey, III, p. 435.
59. B. Montagu, *Life of Francis Bacon*, 1834, p. 152.
60. E. Howes (contin. and augment.) in J. Stow, *Annales*, 1631, p. 1017; Young, I, pp. 34–5; Ormiston, pp. 15–18.
61. Young, II, p. 99.
62. B. Montagu, ed., *Works of Bacon*, 1830, p. 259; first printed in R. Stephens, *Letters of Sir Francis Bacon*, 1702; original letter missing.
63. J. Freeman, ed., Thomas Fuller, *The Worthies of England* (1633), 1952, pp. 368–9.
64. £8,504.04s.8½d. spent over five years.
65. *Alleyn's College of God's Gift*, pamphlet of 1870 by Dr Carver: motto engraved surrounding College arms in roundel on cover, and quoted in gothic type on final page before his initials.
66. MS V, 45v; 'Dictionarie of 11 languages' (still in Fellows' Library), and bought in 1619. Young, II, pp. 123 and 137.
67. MS VIII, f. 1. 'Yet art thou still but *Faustus*, and a man … I [aye], we must die an euerlasting death', lines 51–74; for the Deadly Sins, see lines 720–91.
68. MS III, 96 and 97.
69. W. S. Lewis, ed., *Horace Walpole's Correspondence*, XXXVIII, 1974, p. 367 (to Lord Hertford, 12 April 1764).
70. MS II, 66.
71. ODNB ; see also W. Urry, *Christopher Marlowe and Canterbury* (1988).
72. T. Heywood, *The Actor's Vindication* [1658], 'printed by G. E. for W.C. (William Cartwright)', p. 29; portrait of William Sly from Cartwright's bequest at Dulwich Picture Gallery (DPG 391).
73. Young, II, p. 144.
74. Ibid., p. 95 (13 July 1618).
75. M 581.
76. MS V, 48; see illustration in Young, I, facing p. 461, from J. I. Pontanus, *History of Amsterdam*, 1611 (not in Fellows' Library).
77. Young, II, p. 138.
78. Young, II, p. 41.
79. Statute 77.
80. MS V, 46 and 47.
81. Young, II, p. 51.
82. ODNB.

83. C. W. Scott-Giles, *The History of Emanuel School*, 1948.
84. Willliam Oldys, op. cit., p. 119; Warner, p. vii.
85. M 584.
86. Op. cit., p. 1032.
87. Young, II, pp. 146 and 149.
88. Ibid., pp. 149–50.
89. See also Grymes to Alleyn, 25 August 1618; MS III, 81; Stow, *Annales*, contin. Howes, 1631, p. 1033.
90. B. Lib., Harl. Ms. 389, f. 337; Chambers, II, pp. 190–2, 285; Young, II, p. 174. Joan Alleyn paid £3 for the relief of the Queen of Bohemia in 1620: Young, II, p. 187; BL Harl. Ms. 389, f. 337.
91. Built in 1732 to commemorate Marlborough's victories; the church of St Giles, Cripplegate, is visible from the terrace of the Barbican Arts Centre.
92. Fuller, (1952), p. 369.
93. Folger, MS X d 255; Young, II, p. 39; S. Cerasano, 'The Geography of Henslowe's Diary', *Shakespeare Quarterly*, 56, 2005, p. 352.
94. Op.cit., p. 119.
95. M 558; on Benson's offer of glazing, see MS III, 61.
96. MSS(2), 29, *Register Book III*, 4 March 1712; Young, II, 157.
97. MS IV, 7 (16 October 1612); payments for Chapel were made 19 June 1613 to April 1614.
98. J. Summerson, *Inigo Jones*, 1966, p. 102; Gordon Higgott, letter to author, 2005.
99. GM, 26 July 1890, p. 49a.
100. Young, II, p. 82; anon. 'D.C.', *Musical Times*, 1 July 1907, pp. 439–40.
101. A. Galer, *Christ's Chapel*, 1905, p. 14; MSS(2), 12, *Weekly Accounts* (15 March 1670).
102. *Biographia Britannica*, p. 118; on gilding organ pipes, see Young, II, p. 143.
103. MS VI, 9.
104. *European Magazine* XX, 2, August 1791, p. 88.
105. Young, II, p. 143.
106. Op. cit., p. 107. New floor in 1662, MSS(2), 9, *Weekly Accounts*, 11 June 1662.
107. W. S. Lewis, ed., *Horace Walpole's Correspondence*, Vol. XI, 1944, pp. 288–9.
108. Young, II, p. 193. See S. Foister in Cerasano, pp. 33–61. For Calvin, Luther &c., see DPG 368, 370, 419, and 421.
109. E. W. Brayley, *A Topographical History of Surrey*, III, 1842, p. 234.
110. Lysons, *Environs of London*, 1792, I, p. 112.
111. Young, II, p. 162.
112. MSS(2), 3 (22 February 1635).
113. MS V, 45v (n.d.): Robert Greene (d. 1592) was author of *Orlando Furioso*, the part-script from which Alleyn owned (see Chapter One); Alleyn also bought a book of witches for 3d, June 1619 (Young II, p. 137).
114. MS X, 171v; Cerasano, pp. 63–5.
115. MS II, 12. The entry's authenticity has, however, been disputed; see K. Duncan-Jones's 1998 Arden edition of the Sonnets, pp. 7–8.

116. Young II, pp. 64,114.
117. ODNB.
118. MS II, 26.
119. Young II, p. 251.
120. Young, II, pp. 116, 143 (twice), 148.
121. Mck, p. 61.
122. E.g., Young, I, p. 278.
123. Statute 12.
124. *Illustrated London News*, II, 54 (May 1843), pp. 315–16.
125. Young, I, pp. 169, 178, 180.
126. MS III, 85, 86; Young, I, p. 59.
127. Warner, p. 109, n. 3.
128. Young, I, pp. 175–7; ibid., pp. 300, 349.
129. MS III, 73.
130. *In the matter of Dulwich College …*, Charity Commissioners pamphlet, 1854, p. 6.
131. MSS(2), 9–22, *Weekly Accounts*.
132. Young, II, pp. 75, 116, 119, 170.
133. Statute 43.
134. MS X.
135. MS II, p. 68.
136. Young, II, p. 192.
137. Young, II, pp. 178, 188.
138. Op. cit., III, 14, April 1875, p. 24; 1883 pamphlet, *Dulwich College, Notes, Historical and Statistical*, p. 4.
139. Statute 77.
140. Young, II, p. 206.
141. Young, II, pp. 199, 229.
142. E.g. MSS(2), 12, *Weekly Accounts* (23 October 1669), 2s.4d.
143. Young, II, pp. 185, 206.
144. See n. 14.
145. MSS(2), 56, *Private Sittings*, III, pp. 91–2.
146. MSS(2), 22, *Weekly Accounts* (15 October 1728).
147. MS III, 70.
148. Young, II, p. 174.
149. Ibid., I, p. 104; MSS(2), 27, *Register Book I* (5 March 1632).
150. Statute 109.
151. MS I, 101.
152. Young, II, p. 147.
153. Ibid., p. 217.
154. MS II, 239.
155. Young, II, pp. 137, 171.
156. MS III, p. 56.
157. Young, II, pp. 137, 171.
158. MS III, 56.
159. MS II, 171.
160. MS X, f. 19.
161. Lysons, I, p. 89.
162. Young, II, pp. 120, 187, 244, 249.
163. *Calendar of State Papers*, 1623–25, p. 132; E. Thomson, ed., *The Chamberlain Letters*, 1966, p. 297.
164. E. Gosse, *Life and Letters of John Donne*, 1899, II, pp. 110, 144, 171.
165. MS III, 81; full text in Young, II, p. 38; MS III, 103.
166. Gosse, II, p. 362.
167. MSS, III, 102. See J. Stubbs, *John Donne*, 2006, Chapter 21, pp. 407–32.
168. Gosse, II, pp. 192–3.
169. MS III, 102. Printed in full in Young, II, pp. 36–8.
170. Gosse, II, p. 217.
171. Op. cit., line 33, 'Bajazet encag'd, the shepherds scoff'.
172. Young, II, p. 37.
173. R. C. Bald, *John Donne, a Life*, 1970, p. 232.
174. J. Hunter, *Chorus Vatum Anglicanorum*, BL Add. Mss. 24487, f. 292; ODNB (Donne); College of Arms, Donne's Funeral certificate, I, 23/39v.
175. Young, II, p. 51.
176. Ibid., p. 104.
177. Ibid., p. 64; Lady Clarke, see ibid., p. 50.
178. Ibid., p. 255.
179. Ibid., pp. 82, 126.
180. MS III, 108.
181. M 135–143; MS III, 107.
182. MS III, 108.
183. MS X, *Register*, ff. 4r, 171v.
184. Young, I, pp. 92–5. PRO, PROB 10/443 6312; for tapestries, see Young, II, p. 162 (22 November 1619).
185. Cerasano, p. 67.
186. *Biographia Britannica*, p. 119.
187. MS X, f. 25.

Chapter Three

Approximate value of £1 sterling [see Notes to Chapter One]: 1616, £126; 1618, £135; 1632, £122; 1637, £114; 1642, £127; 1644, £133; 1649, £86; 1667, £123; 1668, £118; 1680, £121; 1696, £103.

1. A phrase from the Dulwich College 'Founder's Prayer', which gratefully refers to Alleyn by name. There is no documentary evidence that the prayer was written by Alleyn, but it may have been; on the other hand members of the Society in the eighteenth and nineteenth century could have composed the prayer in antiquarian style (with seventeenth-century formulae such as 'humble and hearty thanks').
2. Op. cit., p. 188.
3. Young, I, p. 96.
4. Ibid., p. 101.
5. MSS(2), 35, 'the ffortune Rentes' etc., 1626–31; MSS(2), 27, 1649; MS I, 114.
6. Young, I, p. 147.
7. MSS(2), 100, 111.
8. Mck, p. 112.
9. Young, I, pp. 105–8.
10. Ibid., I, p. 112. It was specified that the letter was to be copied into the College Register, but it is not to be found there.
11. Ibid., I, p. 111. MSS(2), 27, *Register I*, 11 April 1636 and (n.d.) 1639.
12. MS VI, 1.
13. MSS(2), 27, *Register Book I*, 1644; Young, I, pp. 125–6.

14. MSS(2), 28, *Register Book II*, 5 April 1669, 1 March 1669/70.

15. MS VI, 31.

16. MSS(2), 28, *Register Book II*, 11 February 1667/8, August 1682; Young, I, pp. 159–61.

17. Ibid., p. 164.

18. Ibid.; Mck, p. 90.

19. Young, I, pp. 172–3.

20. Ibid., pp. 179–80.

21. Ibid., p. 169.

22. MSS(2), 2, *Weekly Accounts II*, 24 October 1635.

23. Lambeth Palace MSS, *Petitions to Abp. Laud*, V, 6, 1640.

24. Ibid., p. 114.

25. MSS(2), 4, *Weekly Accounts IV*; MSS(2), 27, *Register Book I*, 4 September 1638.

26. Mck, p. 23.

27. House of Commons, *Plundered Ministers Committee*, 3 May 1644, Young I, p. 128.

28. MSS(2), 5, *Weekly Accounts V*, 28 March 1646, etc. See also MSS(2), 84, assessments levied on Camberwell and Dulwich College, 1636–49.

29. Lysons, *Environs of London*, I, p. 128.

30. MSS(2), 5, *Weekly Accounts*, 15 July, 28 August 1647; MSS(2), 27, *Register*, August 1647.

31. Young, I, p. 128.

32. Op. cit., I, p. 103; source, 'the politeness of the present members', Lysons, I, p. 87. MSS(2), 27, *Register Book I*, September 1646 – February 1646/7.

33. Young, I, p. 132.

34. MS VI, 21.

35. Young, pp. 136–42.

36. Ibid., p. 146.

37. MSS(2), 6, *Weekly Accounts VI*, 1 May 1652.

38. Young, I, pp. 130, 442.

39. Young, I, p. 139.

40. MS VI, 16; MSS(2), 7, *Weekly Accounts*, 10 March 1656.

41. MSS(2), 28, *Register Book II*, 26 August 1661.

42. MS X, *Register*, f. 2b, 28 May 1703.

43. Ibid., ff. 65–7.

44. MSS(2), 17, *Weekly Accounts*, 6 September 1690.

45. MS VI, 37, Bynes's university accounts.

46. MSS(2), 17, June 1689; MSS(2), 29, *Register Book III*, 4 March 1690; Young, I, p. 188: the reason was his objecting to Sheldon's injunctions as illegal.

47. Young, I, p. 190.

48. Mck, pp. 189–90; Young, I, p. 167; Young's transcript, DC Box 46; a relative left books to the College in 1704, MS VI, 44.

49. Young, I, 198.

50. Ibid., p. 195.

51. Ibid., p. 204.

52. J Carnelley, 'The John Reading Manuscripts of Dulwich College', M.Mus. dissertation, University of London, 1997. Ormiston, p. 14, has misread Reading's dates at Dulwich. Neither father nor son wrote the carol 'Adeste Fideles' as was thought in the nineteenth century.

53. MSS(2), 86–92 etc. Reading was also the author of *A Book of New Anthems*, c. 1715.

54. Prince's Servants and the Private House in Salisbury Court, see J. Wright, *Historia Histrionica*, 1699, p. vi.

55. M 56.

56. J. Downes (the Drury Lane prompter), *Roscius Anglicanus, or an Historical Review of the Stage*, 1708, pp. 2, 4, 6, 7, 39; T. Heywood, *An Apology for Actors,* Shakespeare Society, 1841, p. viii; H. B. Wheatley, ed., *The Diary of Samuel Pepys*, 1893–9, VII, p. 172 and n., 2 November 1667: Pepys praises Cartwright's Falstaff, especially his 'What is honour' speech; however, earlier, see I, p. 278 and n., 5 December 1660, his Falstaff in *Merry Wives* was 'very poorly'.

57. Cartwright's Will or 'Resolucion', G. A. Waterfield, et al., *Mr. Cartwright's Pictures*, Dulwich Picture Gallery, 1987, pp. 10, 87; see annot. to Picture Gallery Catalogue, DC Box 574.

58. MS XIV.

59. MS XV; 'View of London, taken by Mr John Norden in 1603 with the Representation of the City Cavalcade on the *Lord-Mayor's* day', engraving admired by Aubrey: R. Rawlinson, *Natural History of the Antiquities of the County of Surrey*, 1719, p. 195, long since lost through damp (information from John Ingamells).

60. *Gentleman's Magazine*, LX, July 1790, p. 587. A section of a list of books, apparently in Cartwright's hand (as in the catalogue of paintings, MS XIV), including both these titles was found on an end-paper stuck to a board removed by the College bookbinder in 2002; both this list and MS XIV, however, were possibly written by the Warden, who was paid £1.10s. on 18 April 1696 to catalogue Cartwright's books, MSS(2), 18, *Weekly Accounts*. On the College's incomplete First Folio, see A. J. West, *The Shakespeare First Folio: The History of the Book. Volume II: A New Worldwide Census*, 2003, pp. 95–6.

61. MS VI, 39; MSS(2), 74, 26 June 1689.

62. MSS(2), 29, *Register Book III*, 1686.

63. *Mr Cartwright's Pictures*, pp. 7–8.

64. Ibid., p. 9.

65. W. Bray and H. B. Wheatley, ed., *Diary of John Evelyn*, 1906, II, p. 314 (2 September 1675).

66. MSS(2), 2, *Weekly Accounts II*, 18 October 1630.

67. MSS(2), 29, *Register Book III*.

68. Ibid., *Weekly Accounts*; Bickley, pp. 27, 32, 35 etc.; accounts missing for 1642–5.

69. Ibid., *Weekly Accounts*; Bickley, e.g. pp. 6, 33, 40, 44.

70. MSS(2), 13, *Weekly Accounts*; MSS(2), 28, *Register Book II*, 4 March 1674.

71. MSS(2), 28, *Register Book II*, 5 March 1666; MSS(2), 10, *Weekly Accounts*, 16 July 1666.

72. MSS(2), 17, *Weekly Accounts XVII*, 29 March 1690; MS VI, 33: list (1626–77) of 'all ye boyes y^t haue gon to ye vniversity since ye founders death'.

73. Ormiston, pp. 16, 18.

74. Mck, p. 192.

75. Ormiston, pp. 15–18.

76. MS VI, 42 (list of indentures and apprenticeships).

77. *London Gazette*, 2288, 22–26 September 1687. Though Goulding does not appear in Ormiston's *Register*, Sherborne Lane is not far from Cripplegate.

78. Ormiston, p. 17.

79. MSS(2), 54, *Private Sittings I*, 16 August 1759. James Fossets (at Dulwich 1753–60) later apprenticed to gingerbread baker, Ormiston, p. 42.

80. MSS(2), 18, *Register Book II*, 4 September 1655; Young I, pp. 135-6.

81. W.H. Blanch, *The Parish of Camberwell*, 1875, p. 385.

82. MSS(2), 1–26.

83. MSS(2), 2, *Weekly Accounts*, 4 February 1634.

84. MSS(2), 8, *Weekly Accounts*, 1636; MSS(2), 7, 28 January 1662; MS VI, 5.

85. MSS(2), 17, *Weekly Accounts*, 8 February 1690.

86. MS VI, 21–32; 323 deeds and lawsuits 1604–1788, MSS(2), 100.

87. MSS(2), 27, *Register I*, 4 September 1630; Young, I, p. 103.

88. MSS(2), 11, *Weekly Accounts*, 31 March; Mck, p. 112.

89. MSS(2), 114; MSS(2), 28, *Register II*; MS VI, 28.

90. Quoted by Darby, 'A Dulwich Digress', typescript, p. 83 (DC Box 370) from documents about the dispute with Sir Edmond Bowyer (the younger) over tithes. These are referred to in Young, II, p. 339, but I have been unable to identify them. See also Young, I, p. 148; MSS(2), 100, 157, 1712.

91. Mck, pp. 188-9.

92. Ibid., pp. 86-8; MS VI, 25.

93. MS VI, 29 (mutilated).

94. W. H. Stocks, (Organist and Master in Music, 1887–1906), *A Short History of the Organ, Organists and Services of the Chapel of God's Gift at Dulwich College*, 1891, pp. 7, 10, 12–13; MSS(2), 11, *Weekly Accounts*.

95. Young, I, pp. 148-55.

96. Young, I, p. 167: Tanner Mss., Bodleian Library.

97. Darby, p. 25.

98. MSS(2), 29, *Register Book III*, 4 March 1695.

99. Young, I, p. 197.

100. Young, I, pp. 174-5.

Chapter Four

Approximate value of £1 sterling [see Notes to Chapter One]: 1706, £78; 1715, £80; 1726, £86; 1730, £87; 1737, £87; 1740, £87; 1752, £86; 1759, £76; 1760, £76; 1778, £63; 1790, £56; 1796, £69; 1805, £38.

1. Young, I, pp. 216, 270.

2. For Hume's parentage we have to rely on circumstantial evidence: the Revd James Hume was minister of Kirkmahoe until 1689 (*Fasti Ecclesiae Scoticanae*); on arriving in London Hume wrote to a Mr Malcolm in Scotland to tell him that he had been helped by the former minister of Kirkmichael (BL Add. Mss. 29,477, hereafter Hume MS, f. 78r). The minister of Kirkmichael was James Ferguson, who signed the testimonial for Hume's ordination in 1705, and the minister of Holywood was the Revd John Malcolm (*Fasti* for Dumfries, 1688). Both parishes were contiguous with Kirkmahoe, and this seems convincing proof of Hume's identity as the son of its minister. In the letter which he wrote to Malcolm, Hume mentions that he is continuing to 'roll the grammarian's stone' [labour in the classroom] in London, suggesting that he had done so before.

3. Guildhall Library, MS 9535/3, *Ordinations in the Diocese of London*.

4. Lambeth Palace Library MS V, *Act Books*, p. 230; (Dulwich) MS X, *Register 1616–1757*.

5. Hume MS, f. 59r.

6. Hume MS, f. 3.

7. Lambeth Palace Library, MS VV 11/2, f. 48.

8. Hume MS, f. 3r.

9. Hume MS, f. 5r.

10. Young, I, p. 436.

11. Ibid., I, p. 226 and MS XXIX and XXX, *Register Books of Accounts*.

12. Hume MS, f. 13v.

13. MS XXIX, XXX.

14. Young, I, p. 230.

15. Wake MSS, Christ Church, Oxford: *Epistles 27*, pp. 218–20.

16. DCL III, A 1. Richard Grinsel [1714] and James Bennett [1718]; both were awarded Exhibitions at Cambridge by God's Gift College.

17. Hume MS, f. 35v.

18. A school run by an aged woman who offered only the most rudimentary form of education to very young children.

19. Hume MS, f. 59r.

20. He was sixty-eight in 1725 and suffered from colic, rheumatism and kidney stones. In September 1720 he had passed a stone 'half an inch long and three quarters round' (Lambeth Palace MS 1770, *Wake's Diary*).

21. MS XXII, *Weekly Accounts*, 24 January 1729.

22. Hume MS, f. 94r.

23. D. Duncan, *Thomas Ruddiman: A Study in Scottish Scholarship of the Early Eighteenth Century*, Edinburgh, 1965, gives a good account of the last generation of this Scoto-Latin culture.

24. B. Green, *To Read and Sew: James Allen's Girls' School, 1741–1991*, 1991.

25. GM, 3 December 1859, 2 March 1861; A. M. Galer, *Christ's Chapel*, 1905, p. 12; J. Armstrong, MD, *Poetical Works*, Edinburgh, 1781, p. 11, lines 121–2.

26. A useful, if partial and tendentious, overview of his life is to be found in M. A. Wren and P. Hackett, *James Allen: A Portrait Enlarged*, London, 1968. The authors use selective misquotation from the Hume MS in the British Library.

27. Lambeth Palace Library, MS 1118.

28. Young, I, p. 276.

29. He used College money to purchase provisions for his own family: Young, I, pp. 271–2.

30. Young, I, p. 274.

31. A. and H. Taylor, *1715: The Story of the Rising*, pp. 276–83; Pitsligo was no backwoods laird.

32. *Gentleman's Magazine*, XV, August 1745, pp. 426–7.

33. Young, I, p. 293. William Swanne matric. Oxford, 1747, Schoolmaster at Dulwich, 1752; Edward Bayly matric. Trinity College, Oxford, 1748, but 'expelled' (Ormiston, p. 42).

34. Young, I, pp. 294–5.

35. At this time England had only two universities, as had Aberdeen.

36. Ormiston, pp. 41–4.

37. CL XXXIII, 189, 1784.

38. Ormiston, p. 44.

39. *Statutes of Merchant Taylors' School*, XXV.

40. A. Quick, *Charterhouse*, 1990, pp. 7, 14.

41. F. M. G. Higham, *Southwark Story*, 1955, pp. 331 ff.

42. ODNB.

43. Young, I, p. 286.

44. Ibid., pp. 286–7.

45. Lambeth Palace Library, MS 1118, no. 34.

46. Ibid., nos. 37 and 38.

47. Young, I, p. 297; GM, 14 May 1915, p. 69; P. H. Highfill et al., *A Biographical Dictionary of Actors, Actresses, Musicians, Dancers and other Stage Personnel in London, 1660–1800*, vol 12, 1987, p. 256.

48. 'This holy state [matrimony] was deemed by the Founder incompatible with the duty of this magisterial chair' (*Gentleman's Magazine*, LXVI, 1796, p. 85).

49. Young, I, p. 317.

50. J. W. Ivimey, *Boys and Music*, 1936, p. 47.

51. Young, I, p. 304.

52. Darby, *Dulwich*, p. 52.

53. Young, I, p. 307.

54. Ibid., p. 311.

55. Ibid., p. 313.

56. W. S. Lewis, ed., *Horace Walpole's Correspondence*, Vol. 11, 1944, pp. 288–9. The divine was the Revd Thomas Jenyns Smith, Usher, 1783 and Preacher, 1785–1830.

57. Young, I, p. 316.

58. MSS(2), 54, *Private Sittings I*, 3 August 1759.

59. Young, I, p. 490. DCL XXVII, 91, 27 July 1799; C. Howes, ms. note to extract from Highmore, *Pietas Londinensis*, 1820, p. 454, DC Archives A0436.

60. BM, 1878; Galer, *Christ's Chapel*, 1905, p. 16.

Chapter Five

Approximate value of £1 sterling [see Notes to Chapter One]: 1738, £139; 1775, £94; 1805, £58; 1808, £57; 1810, £52; 1813, £46; 1818, £55; 1821, 1824, £67; 1827, £70; 1829, £68; 1832, £72; 1841, £67; 1842, £71; 1843, £77; 1856, £62; 1857, £64; 1870, £66; 1873, £61.

1. *A Day at Dulwich*, 1905, p. 2. Carver judged that they were 'cultured men, receiving much good society, but not over-burdened with a sense of duty to their fellow-creatures; leading, no doubt, an easy self-indulgent life' (Alleyn Club dinner, 1904): *A*, XXII, 237 (October 1904), p. 346.

2. PRO, HO 107/1051/4.

3. CC, Day 3, p. 180.

4. Op. cit., by 'a candidate for the Charity Trust Commission', p. 7.

5. Op. cit., 1884 ed., p. 73.

6. 'The Dulwich Gallery', in G. Keynes, ed., *Selected Essays*, 1930, p. 666.

7. *Pietas Londinensis, the History, Design, and present state of the various Public Charities in and near London*, 1814, p. 488.

8. J. Goodall, 'Dulwich College, the Story of a Foundation', *Macmillan's Magazine*, November 1867, p. 63.

9. 'A Walk from Dulwich to Brockham', *The Indicator and the Companion*, 1834, II, p. 319. The Greyhound was on the west side of road until demolished in 1898, when the present Crown and Greyhound was built on the east side of the road. It was popular with famous Londoners and for public dinners; Ruskin took his sketching working-men there for tea.

10. Quoted in an anonymous typescript, 'Dulwich', DC Box 246.

11. Op. cit., XX, 2, August 1791, p. 88.

12. MSS(2), 58, *Private Sittings V*, p. 25.

13. *Literary Reminiscences and Memoirs of Thomas Campbell*, 1860, II, p. 198.

14. Op. cit., p. 213.

15. Highmore, 1814, p. 490.

16. *Reminiscences*, 1888, p. 189.

17. CC, Day 1, pp. 124–5; MSS(2), 58, *Private Sittings V*, 1854, p. 38; Ormiston, pp. 41–7.

18. *In the matter of Dulwich College ...*' p. 9. DC Box 285.

19. Ormiston, p. 16; *A*, XXV, 189 (October 1897), p. 251.

20. CC, Day 1, p. 280.

21. Young, I, p. 387; C. Howes, ms. note to extract from Highmore, *Pietas Londinensis*, 1820, p. 453, DC Archives, A 0436. Hereafter 'annotated Highmore'.

22. Young, I, pp. 391, 406.

23. Op. cit., II, 54 (May 1843), pp. 315–16.

24. ODNB (John Allen); Sir J. G. Craig to Fox, quoted in J. Allen, *Inquiry into the Rise and Growth of the Royal Prerogative in England*, second edition, 1849, p. 24.

25. ODNB (J. P. Kemble).

26. *Annual Register*, 1853, p. 248.

27. ODNB (3rd Lord Holland).

28. G. O. Trevelyan, ed., *Life and Letters of Lord Macaulay*, 1876, I, p. 256.

29. C. R. Fox in Allen, *Inquiry*, 1849, pp. xxii–xxiii.

30. The miniature is mentioned in his will (Young, II, p. 417); the bust was by Edward Pierce (C. F. Bell, annotation to G. S. H. Fox-Strangways, *Chronicles of Holland House*, 1937, p. 164, NPG Library).

31. Fox in Allen, *Inquiry*, p. xxviii.

32. Op. cit., pp. 61–2.

33. H. Reeves, ed., *Greville Memoirs: a Journal of the Reign of Queen Victoria*, 1885, II, p. 155.

34. Young, I, p. 364.

35. Trevelyan, 1876, I, p. 248.

36. Reeves, 1885, II, p. 155; cf. Allen, *Inquiry*, p. xxiv.

37. L. Marchand, ed., *Byron's Letters and Journals*, 1974, III, p. 239.

38. A bronze bust of the Emperor was displayed with an epigraph from Homer protesting his exile to St Helena, 'the captive of a foeman base'. H. (Lord) Brougham, *Historical Sketches of Statesmen who flourished in the time of George III*, third series, 1845, II, p. 178.

39. Memorial tablet to John Allen, St Michael's Church, Millbrook, Bedfordshire.

40. Brougham, *Historical Sketches of Statesmen*, (1894 ed.), pp. 342, 348.

41. Reeves, 1885, II, p. 154.

42. H. Reeves, ed., *Greville Memoirs: a Journal of the Reigns of George IV and William IV*, 1874, III, p. 135.

43. Ibid., II, p. 154; K. Cave, ed., *The Diary of Joseph Farington*, XII, 1983, p. 4167.

44. F. M. Redgrave, *Richard Redgrave RA, a Memoir*, 1891, p. 269.

45. Highmore, pp. 454–5; Darby, p. 144.

46. M. Liechtenstein, *Holland House*, 1874, I, p. 268.

47. *Edinburgh Review*, LIV (December 1816), pp. 459–92.

48. Reeves, 1885, II, pp. 153–4.

49. L. C. Sanders, *Holland House Circle*, 1908, p. 83.

50. See n. 28.

51. Liechtenstein, I, p. 270.

52. Fox, in Allen, *Inquiry*, 1849, pp. xix–xxiv.

53. John Allen to Professor John Thomson, Young, II, p. 401. The Master and Warden had an allowance of six weeks' absence in a year.

54. Allen, *Inquiry*, p. xxii.

55. Young, II, p. 410.

56. Young, I, pp. 438–9.

57. MSS(2), 55, *Private Sittings II*, p. 121 (15 April 1831).

58. MSS(2), 57, *Private Sittings IV*, p. 1.

59. Young, I, pp. 357, 365.

60. MSS(2), 23, *Register Book VII*.

61. MSS(2), 57, *Private Sittings IV*, pp. 20–4, 56.

62. Ibid., p. 99.

63. Young, II, p. 416.

64. *Annual Register*, 1843, p. 248.

65. Corry, *Gentleman's Magazine*, n.s. IX, March 1838, p. 328; Linley, *Illustrated London News*, II, 54 (May 1843), p. 316.

66. J. Sinclair, *Old Times and Distant Places*, 1875, p. 150–9.

67. Information about Vane's father from John Gowar, see **www.wringtonsomerset.org.uk/history/johnvane.html**; MSS(2), 56, *Private Sittings III*, p. 130.

68. CC, Day 2, p. 203.

69. Ibid., pp. 166, 177–8, 203, 211–12. *A*, XXXIII, 243 (June 1905), pp. 157–9.

70. The gift of relatives of the New Zealand bibliophile and philanthropist, Alexander Horsley Turnbull OA, 1920.

71. *Alleyn's College of God's Gift*, 1870, p. 10, DC Box 91.

72. *A*, XXXII, 237 (October 1904), p. 346 (Alleyn Club dinner).

73. *The Times*, 27 June 1866; J. C. Horsley, *Recollections of a Royal Academician*, 1903, pp. 294–6.

74. MSS(2), 57, *Private Sittings IV*, p. 9.

75. Young, I, p. 467.

76. Ormiston, p. 14, mistakenly gives Stratford-on-Avon.

77. Marten and Carnaby, *A Guide to Residential Dulwich and Vicinity*, DC Box 574.

78. Highmore, p. 487.

79. CC, Day 3, pp. 163 ff.

80. Portrait by H. P. Briggs, DPG 499.

81. Young, I, p. 358, n.

82. A. Barry, *Memoir of the Life and Works of the late Sir Charles Barry*, second edition, 1870, p. 67; in 1841 he designed a house for John Allen's close friend C. R. Fox (of Holland House) in Addison Road.

83. O. Manning and W. Bray, *History and Antiquities of the County of Surrey*, 1814, III, p. 436.

84. E. T. Hall, *Dulwich History and Romance*, 1922, p. 4; BM, 1869, p. 93.

85. MSS(2), 56, *Private Sittings III*, p. 73.

86. Darby, p. 67.

87. Young, I, p. 347. For drawings by Prout and Cox of the mill, see P. Darby, *The Houses-In-Between*, 2000, pp. 131 and 225.

88. W. H. Blanch, *The Parish of Camberwell*, 1875, p. 386; Lysons, op. cit., I, p. 86.

89. Blanch, pp. 389–90; A. M. Galer, *Norwood and Dulwich Past and Present*, 1890, p. 54; CC, Day 2, pp. 119, 122.

90. Op. cit., ed. 1850, p. 326.

91. CC, Day 2, pp. 52–3, 116.

92. Young, I, p. 356.

93. In 1823 £8 per seat.

94. Highmore, p. 492.

95. Young, I, p. 333. The map currently hangs in the ground-floor corridor, South Block, Dulwich College.

96. MSS(2), 56, *Private Sittings III*, p. 32.

97. Young, I, p. 322.

98. Mck, p. 120.

99. MSS(2), 56, *Private Sittings III*, pp. 34 (14 April 1809) and 86 (27 April 1814).

100. CC, Day 2, p. 117.

101. MSS(2), 56–7, *Private Sittings III and IV*, passim; CC, Day 2, p. 79.

102. Op. cit., III, p. 431.

103. Op. cit., III, p. 229.

104. MSS(2), 57, *Private Sittings IV*, p. 92.

105. Date on pediment, Highmore, p. 453.

106. MSS(2), 56, *Private Sittings III*, p. 98.

107. Highmore, p. 454.

108. F. Nevola, *Soane's Favourite Subject*, 2000, p. 14.

109. H. J. Hartley, *A*, XXXIII, 244 (July 1905), p. 264; CC, Day 2, p. 183.

110. MSS(2), 56, *Private Sittings III*, p. 128.

111. Manning and Bray, III, p. 444.

112. Young, I, p. 252; Highmore, p. 453.

113. MSS(2), 56, *Private Sittings III*, p. 145; Nevola, p. 197.

114. DCL 28 (19 March 1821).

115. MSS(2), 57, *Private Sittings IV*, p. 9 (May 1831), where £3,586 was sanctioned; annotated Highmore, 1814, p. 458.

116. DC, architectural drawings, P 147, 165.

117. Palace of Westminster built 1835 seq.; Barry would have preferred an Italianate style, but Parliament's prescription of Gothic was political and nationalist.

118. MSS(2), 57, *Private Sittings IV*, p. 68.

119. Manning and Bray, III, p. 432.

120. *European Magazine*, XX, 2 (August 1791), p. 89.

121. E. W. Brayley, *A Topographical History of Surrey*, 1841, III, pp. 236–7.

122. Darby, p. 46 (1841 population: 1,904. 1871: 4,041, in 294 houses).

123. MSS(2), 56, *Private Sittings III* (31 May 1816), p.107; DC MSS (not in Bickley) *Weekly Accounts 1813–17*, 1 Feb 1817: 'Pd Westmacott black marble slab £40'.

124. *A*, XXVI, 189 (October 1898), p. 243.

125. *Builder*, XXIV, 1227 (11 August 1866), p. 604.

126. Annotated Highmore, p. 456.

127. Invoice and correspondence, DCL 26 (1847), DCL 24 (1850). Clarke was the author of *Schools and Schoolhouses*, 1852; see also M. Seaborne, *The English School*, 1971, II, p. 214.

128. Galer, 1905, p. 16.

129. Anon., *Sydenham, Dulwich and Norwood*, 1881, p. 49; cf. Hartley, *A*, XXXIII, 244 (July 1905), p. 264: robes, surplices and the metrical version of the 90th Psalm.

130. G. A. Waterfield, '"That White-faced Man": Sir Francis Bourgeois', *Turner Studies* 9, no. 2, 1989, pp. 36–48; 'J. T.', *Memoirs of the Late Noel Desenfans, Esq.*, 1810, p. 22; Waterfield, *Collection for a King*, 1985, pp. 9–17.

131. Appendix to Manning and Bray, III, p. cxxxiii.

132. Four of his fake signatures are to be seen in the Dulwich collection: see R. Beresford, *Dulwich Picture Gallery*, 1998, p. 16, n. 4.

133. *Gentleman's Magazine*, LXIV, pt. 1, no. 4 (April 1794), p. 390.

134. *Memoirs of the Late Noel Desenfans, Esq.*, 1810, pp. 3, 18, 25, 27–9, 73ff., 106.

135. *Library of the Fine Arts*, III, 16 (May 1832), p. 425.

136. Op. cit., XV (17 January 1824), p. 232.

137. *Library of the Fine Arts*, III, 16 (May 1832), pp. 425–6.

138. Waterfield, *Collection for a King*, p. 12.

139. Brayley, III, p. 240.

140. Soane Museum, Private Correspondence IX/D/D/2; G. A. Waterfield, *Soane and Death*, 1996, pp. 123–5.

141. Portrait by William Beechey, DPG 111.

142. G. A. Waterfield, *Soane and After*, 1987, p. 5.

143. *Annals of the Fine Arts*, II, 1818, pp. 43, 47; Manning and Bray, III, appendix cxxxiv.

144. *Memoir*, pp. 73ff.

145. Farington, *Diary*, X, p. 3822.

146. *The Indicator and Companion*, II, 1834, p. 320.

147. Illustrated in colour in Nevola.

148. MSS(2), 56, *Private Sittings III*, p. 70.

149. Nevola, pp. 26, 72.

150. Waterfield, *Collection for a King*, p. 27; Waterfield, *Soane and After*, p. 8.

151. MSS(2), 56, *Private Sittings III*, (11 August 1811).

152. Nevola, p. 34.

153. A. T. Bolton, *The Portrait of Sir John Soane, RA*, 1927, p. 174.

154. Manning and Bray, III, Appendix, p. cxxxiv.

155. *Memoirs of the Professional Life of an Architect*, privately printed, 1835, p. 39.

156. MSS(2), 56, *Private Sittings III*, p. 63.

157. J. Summerson, *Sir John Soane*, 1952, p. 39.

158. Manning and Bray, III, Appendix, p. cxxxv.

159. B. Cherry and N. Pevsner, *London 2: South*, 1983, p. 623.

160. Farington, *Diary*, XI, p. 3863, mistakenly gives the sum as £2,000 each.

161. Manning and Bray, III, Appendix, pp. cxxxiv–cxxxv; MSS(2), 82, *Bourgeois Book of Records* (hereafter *Bourgeois Book*).

162. Soane Museum, SM P 265, centre left; MSS(2), 56, *Private Sittings III*, p. 76; Farington, *Diary*, XIII, p. 4577.

163. Desenfans, *Memoirs*, p. 8.

164. Manning and Bray, III, Appendix, p. cxxxvi.

165. *Bourgeois Book of Regulations*, n. p.

166. *Bourgeois Book*, n.p. (Van Dyck, 19 Feb 1825; Du Paggi, October 1825; Poussin, no. 300, 11 March 1828).

167. MS(2), 56, *Private Sittings III*, p. 90.

168. *Bourgeois Book*, 6 June 1817.

169. Ibid., 26 January 1821

170. MSS(2), 57, *Private Sittings IV*, pp. 25–6.

171. Farington, *Diary*, XVI, p. 5697.

172. Robert Brown, detailed ledger with Dulwich accounts for cleaning, National Art Library, MSL/1993/3/1, 1810–17; Brown's invoices to 'Mr Allen', 1813–15, DC Box 29; Farington, *Diary*, XIII, pp. 4581–3, mentions Cockburn as responsible for the cleaning.

173. *Bourgeois Book*, 1825, n.p.

174. Farington, *Diary*, XVI, p. 5530.

175. Nevola, p. 14.

176. Farington, XIV, p. 5042; XVI, p. 5529.

177. Ibid., XVI, p. 5697.

178. *Bourgeois Book*, 1824.

179. *William Wetmore Story and his Friends*, 1903, pp. 277–8; four-in-hand carriages: *Interviews*, p. 25.

180. Farington, XVI, p. 5529.

181. Sir Thomas Lawrence was involved when a distinguished academician, John Jackson, was found to have made a full-size copy of a painting by Richard Wilson (DPG 171) which was then engraved, and the engraving

then placed in the window of W. B. Cooke's shop: see *Bourgeois Book*, 31 July 1823.

182. *Library of the Fine Arts*, III, 16 (May 1832), p. 425.

183. Reprinted in 'Criticisms upon the Picture Galleries of England', *Criticisms on Art*, 1843, I, pp. 19–39.

184. MSS(2), 56, *Private Sittings III*, p. 59.

185. Op. cit., pp. 120–21.

186. October 1782: DC Box 504.

187. A. and J. Freeman, *John Payne Collier: Scholarship and Forgery in the Nineteenth Century*, 2004, I, p. 352.

188. Young, II, pp. 326n., 330n., 331.

189. See Chapter One, n. 77.

190. British Library, MSS, hand-written inventory by Edward Capell.

191. MSS(2), 56, *Private Sittings III*, p. 137.

192. Op. cit., I, p. 112; cf. Manning and Bray, III, p. 434.

193. *Beauties of England, Surrey*, 1813, p. 234.

194. Freeman, I, p. 356, n. 12.

195. Young, II, p. 329.

196. DC Box 504.

197. The forgeries are noted in Warner's 1881 *Catalogue*, pp. 170 and 175.

198. MSS(2), 57, *Private Sittings IV*, p. 21; Freeman, I, pp. 345, 366.

199. MS I, 20; Freeman, I, p. 206.

200. MSS(2), 94 ('Literary Papers'), piece 10 is identified as Collier's in Bickley's *Catalogue* (second series), p. 107.

201. Hodges, p. 35.

202. 'Dulwich College', *European Magazine*, 2 (August 1791), p. 89.

203. DC Box 29.

204. CC, Day 2, pp. 38, 43; Day 6, p. 58; MSS(2), 57, *Private Sittings IV*, 1854, January 1857, p. 122. The hotel schemes were abandoned as the Palace needed to profit from its own catering.

205. CC, Day 2, p. 63; Young, I, p. 412.

206. CC, Day 2, p. 107.

207. Ibid., pp. 43, 56, 69, 167.

208. Ibid., p 108.

209. Ibid., p. 38.

210. Ibid., pp. 27, 109.

211. *In the matter of Dulwich College ...*, p. 10, DC Box 285; CC, Day 2, p. 27; MSS(2), 57, *Private Sittings IV*, 1852, pp. 14–15.

212. CC, Day 2, pp. 41, 113; GM, 18 July 1858.

213. CC, Day 2, pp. 116, 73, 43; MSS(2), 57, *Private Sittings IV*, p. 134.

214. Ibid., pp. 137, 139.

215. *Times*, 8 July 1913, p. 10; *Times*, 1 August 1913, p. 6.

216. *Memories of Dulwich College*, 1919, p. 48; *Macmillan's Magazine*, 104 (June 1868), p. 136.

217. GM, *Abstract of Accounts*, 1860, p. i.

218. CC, Day 2, p. 79; a contemporary architectural painting of *High Level Station* at Dulwich College is illustrated in J. R. Piggott, *Palace of the People*, 2004, p. 147.

219. CC, Day 2, pp. 108–9.

220. GM, 10 January 1860.

221. MSS(2), 57, *Private Sittings IV*, 1855, p. 80.

222. The College received major payments from railway companies, recounted in the text of Chapter Six.

223. Chapter XV, Penguin edition, 1994, p. 143.

224. Anon. article in untitled magazine cutting, 'n.s., VII, xxxvii, January 1873', p. 111, DC Box 5.

225. Young, I, p. 371.

226. MSS(2), 56 and 57, *Private Sittings III* and *IV*, passim.

227. [S. Bannister], *Dulwich College, or the Orphan and the poor defended from the errors of the Charity Trusts Board*, 1856, p. 10.

228. Young, I, p. 380.

229. Young, I, p. 408.

230. MSS(2), 57, *Private Sittings IV*, pp. 80, 91.

231. Op. cit., p. 498.

232. Young, I, pp. 365–5.

233. MSS(2), 57, *Private Sittings IV*, pp. 25, 66.

234. H. Bickersteth, Lord Langdale, *The Attorney General against Dulwich College, Judgment*, 29 July 1841, pp. 1, 11, 12.

235. MSS(2), 57, *Private Sittings IV*, pp. 66–7.

236. Attorney-General, *Judgment*, 29 July 1841, pp. 14, 15.

237. *Times*, 13 April 1850, p. 8; *Times*, 15 April 1850, p. 8; MSS(2), 57, *Private Sittings IV*, p. 134.

238. *Times*, 21 August 1851, p. 6.

239. CC, Day 3, p. 26; Day 4, pp. 127, 149, 150, 151 (evidence of Martin Maylard, silk draper, Assistant 1851-3, and later a College Governor); Day 5, p. 43.

240. Young, I, p. 386.

241. Statute 70.

242. Manning and Bray, III, p. 446.

243. CC, Day 5, p. 91; B. Green, *To Read and Sew*, 1991, pp. 18–21.

244. Ormiston, pp. 5–6.

245. MSS(2), 57, *Private Sittings IV*, p. 101.

246. CC, Day 2, pp. 26, 33.

247. MSS(2), 56, *Private Sittings III*, pp. 102, 124.

248. Charity Commission, *Further Report*, 1833, p. 898, quoted Brayley, III, p. 224.

249. MSS(2), 56, *Private Sittings III*, pp. 91–2.

250. CC, Day 5, p. 22.

251. Howes, Annotated Highmore, p. 453; cf. anon., *Sydenham, Dulwich and Norwood*, Fisher Unwin, 1881, p. 49.

252. MSS(2), 57, *Private Sittings IV*, pp. 66, 136.

253. MSS(2), 57, *Private Sittings IV*, 1856.

254. *The Petition of H. J. H., one of the poor scholars of Dulwich College to the Archbishop of Canterbury*, 1844: DC Box 91, pp. 10–11.

255. CC, Day 2, pp. 5, 163 ff..

256. Hartley: *A*, XXXIII, 242 (May 1905), p. 102; ibid., 244 (July 1905), pp. 262–5; ibid., 243 (June 1905), p. 156. Davies: *A*, XXVI, 189 (October 1898), p. 242. Cf. J. Goodall, 'Dulwich College: the Story of a Foundation', *Macmillan's Magazine*, 104 (June 1868), p. 135.

257. *A*, LIV, 396 (October 1926), p. 725.

258. MSS(2), 57, *Private Sittings IV*, p. 71; CC, Day 5, p. 206; Ormiston, p. 47.

259. MSS(2), 57, *Private Sittings IV*, p. 13.

260. Mck, p. 197.

261. MSS(2), 57, *Private Sittings IV*, p. 64.

262. CC, Day 4, p. 220.

263. Ibid., p. 57.

264. *Dulwich College School Association, established 6 April 1841*, pamphlet, p. 11: DC Box 171.

265. Young, I, p. 410.

266. *Dulwich College, or a Model for Free Grammar School Reformation in a letter to Lord Cranworth*, 1884 ed., p. 13.

267. Young, I, pp. 394, 405.

268. *In the Matter of Dulwich College …*, p. 8.

269. *Times*, 2 April 1851, p. 8.

270. *The Queen vs. the Master and Fellows of Dulwich College*, 8 May 1851, ms., first day of proceedings. DC Box 207.

271. Young, I, pp. 396–402.

272. ODNB.

273. CC, Day 3, p. 207; Day 1, p. 131; Day 4, pp. 37, 71, 16; Day 3, pp. 46, 60; Day 4, p. 37; Day 5, pp. 170, 15, 49. Not all of this material seems to have been used by William Young in 1889; Mackenzie's typescript history of the College made use of a missing volume.

274. CC, Day 1, p. 99; Day 4, p. 16; Day 3, pp. 46, 60; Day 4, p. 37; Day 5, pp. 170, 15, 49.

275. CC, Day 1, pp. 65–6, 114–15.

276. Young, I, p. 418; BM, 14 September 1880, p. 143.

277. 'Dulwich College or the Orphan …', p. 9.

278. Mck, p. 324.

279. CC, Day 6, pp. 7, 8; Day 5, pp. 238–45.

280. CC, Day 1 (printed version), p. 3; see also evidence from Webb, CC, Day 3, p. 81; Day 2, pp. 127, 129, 150.

281. Young, I, pp. 420–2.

282. CC, Day 1, pp. 88–9.

283. Anon., *An Account of the Charity of 'God's Gift'*, Dulwich, 1853, pp. 4, 7.

284. *Dulwich College, or a Model …*, p. 11.

285. CC, Day 1, p. 30; Day 5, pp. 22, 61, 38, 39, 89.

286. A. W. P. Gayford, *History of Dulwich College*, second edition, 1967, p. 23.

287. 'Dulwich College, the Orphan …', p. 11.

288. CC, Day 6, p. 42; cf. Day 5, pp. 105–8; Day 5, p. 223.

289. Op. cit., pp. 15, 5, 16.

290. *Illustrated London News*, XXVIII, 790 (22 March 1856), pp. 301–2.

291. MSS(2), 57, *Private Sittings IV*, p. 80.

292. DC Box 855.

293. *The Dulwich College Act, 1857* is printed in full in Young, I, pp. 496–511; for rejected clauses, see Mck, p. 211.

294. J. R. Adams, *Dulwich College and the Endowed Schools Commissioners, a Tract for the Times*, 1873, p. 14.

295. *A*, XI, 73 (November 1883), p. 152.

296. BM, 22 January 1858, 27 February 1858.

297. Gayford, p. 22; *Book of Schoolmasters' notes of Lessons*

298. BM, 13 May 1873, p. 137.

299. Annotated Highmore, quoted by Young, I, p. 503.

Chapter Six

Approximate value of £1 (see Notes to Chapter One): 1855, £63; 1857, £64; 1858, £71; 1859, £70; 1860, £65; 1861, £64; 1863, 1865, £67; 1866, £63; 1867, £60; 1868, £62; 1869, £66; 1870, £60; 1872, 1873, £61; 1874, £64; 1875, 1876, 1877, £65; 1878, £67; 1879, £70 ; 1881, 1882, £69; 1883, £69; 1888, £77; 1895, £79; 1908, £72; 1910, £70; 1945, £30.

1. 'Second Founder', see e.g. Carver ms. DC Box 574; Smith at the Alleyn Club, see *A*, XLVII, 354 (October 1919), p. 224.

2. DC Box 191.

3. RIBA *Transactions*, 1867–8, pp. 268–9; 'Literature of Queen Elizabeth' (first draft), 1848: DC Box 574; on theatrical suppers, see Gilkes, ms. Diary, p. 7.

4. Obituary, *A*, LIII, 387 (March 1925), pp. 65–6.

5. Printed testimonial, p. 8, DC Box 92.

6. Ibid., pp. 2, 6.

7. 1870 pamphlet, *Alleyn's College of God's Gift*, DC Box 92.

8. 'Dulwich College: the Story of a Foundation', *Macmillan's Magazine*, June 1868, pp. 137–8.

9. Op. cit., February 1891, p 63.

10. *A*, XXXIV, 253 (October 1906), p. 272; additional printed 'Testimonial with reference to the Departments of Mechanics and Natural Science', 1858, p. 5, DC Box 91.

11. W. H. Blanch, *The Parish of Camberwell*, 1875, p. 467.

12. DC Box 574.

13. Ms. DC Box 91.

14. 'Alleyn's College of God's Gift 1870', DC Box 92; *Cassell's Family Magazine*, 1880, p. 49.

15. Pamphlet, 'Upper School', 1875, p. 5, DC Box 92.

16. *Interviews*, p. 104.

17. Letter from Carver, GM, 1876, p. 5.

18. BM, 11 March 1873, p. 68; undated ms. DC Box 574.

19. *Times*, 1 August 1881. See also speech of 1875, *A*, III, 17 (October 1875), p. 99.

20. *A*, III, 17 (October 1875), p. 96.

21. Mck, pp. 222–3; Revd E. H. Sweet-Escott, *A*, LVII, 414 (October 1929), p. 301.

22. Ms. speech, pasted into rear of Carver Golden Wedding Album, DC Archives.

23. *Art Journal*, February 1908, p. 60; J. C. L. Sparkes, *Schools of Art, their Origin, History, Work and Influence*, 1884; *The Times*, 19 December 1907.

24. EC, 24 March 1864, p. 19.

25. Op. cit., 1919, pp. 30, 84; Mck, p. 236; *Interviews*, p. 22b; *A*, XXVII, 192 (February 1899), p. 17.

26. Ms., 22 July 1858, DC Box 92.

27. Ms., DC Box 92; cf. *Christian Globe*, 19 July 1879.

28. GM, 21 June 1859.

29. GM, 22 March 1860.

30. Ms., DC Box 91.

31. GM, 8 January 1867, p. 4.

32. EC, 12 Jan 1869, p 4.

33. BM, 11 January, 11 July 1870, p. 3; BM, 13 April 1880, p. 65; BM, 11 July 1870, p. 3.

34. *South London Press*, 5 March 1881.

35. BM, 14 October 1875, p. 197; Mck, p. 471.

36. Ibid., p. 295.

37. Mck, p. 226; EC, 1 October 1863.

38. Ms., post-1864, p. 12, DC Box 92; R. A. Hadden, ed., *Reminiscences of William Rogers*, 1888, p. 194.

39. *The Prince Consort, Principal Speeches and Addresses*, 1862, p. 120.

40. *Lectures on the Results of the Great Exhibition of 1851*, first series, 1852, p. 200. These lectures were Prince Albert's suggestion.

41. Ms., DC Box 92.

42. Ms., '1863', DC Box 92.

43. Ms., '1860', DC Box 92.

44. BM, p. 46; Sp C, p. 133; BM, p. 147.

45. BM, 13 May 1873, p. 106.

46. GM, 14 December 1858.

47. Hadden, p 191.

48. BM, 13 May 1862.

49. Hadden, p. 190.

50. Mck, p. 259.

51. Ms., p. 11, DC Box 91.

52. *School-World*, February 1891, p. 63; *South London Press*, 13 January 1883.

53. Ms., '1863', p. 10, DC Box 92.

54. Ibid., pp. 11, 12, 18, 19.

55. Mck, p. 248.

56. Ibid., p. 278.

57. *A*, XXVI, 189 (October 1898), p. 247.

58. Hadden, p. 80.

59. *The Prince Consort*, 1862, p. 174.

60. Hadden, pp. 134–5.

61. Ibid., p. 198.

62. Ibid., pp. 194, 158–70.

63. Ibid., p 167.

64. Ibid., p.150.

65. Ibid., p. 77; see letter to Lord John Russell, p. 190.

66. Mck, pp. 242–3.

67. GM, July 1862, p. 2; Carver ms., p. 25, DC Box 91.

68. Ms., '1860', and copy of letter from Carver to Rogers, DC Box 91.

69. *Observer*, 22 June 1919.

70. *Interviews*, pp. 27, 31.

71. Hadden, p. 194; Carver ms. post-1864, DC Box 94, p. 12.

72. 'Proposed New College', GM, 4 July 1860, Ex Com, p. 34; cf. GM, 1865, p. 25; engraved plan, DC Box 194.

73. BM, 27 January 1863; 14 April 1863, p. 20; cf. 12 May 1863, p. 28.

74. FC, 28 October 1867, p. 15.

75. BM, 12 May 1863.

76. Appendix A, GM, 11 June 1864, pp. 35–6.

77. GM, Report to EC, 11 June 1864, p. 32.

78. RIBA Drawings Collection, V & A Museum.

79. GM, 1864, p. 76a.

80. Barry to Carver, letter of 28 June 1864: 'we have talked so many times on the subject before'. DC Box 92.

81. 'To the Board of Governors', ms., DC Box 95; GM, 22 March 1859; BM, 14 February 1865, p. 11.

82. GM, 22 January, 27 February 1858.

83. EC, 1867, p. 33.

84. *New Roads and Sites for Building ... to Illustrate a Report*, July 1858, DC, Map Chest, Muniments Room.

85. GM, Supplement, 4 July 1860; GM, 20 April 1863, p. 25.

86. *A*, VII, 44 (October 1879), p. 108.

87. BM, 14 March 1865, p. 23.

88. BM, 16 January 1866.

89. EFC 25 April 1913, p. 50; GM, 6 October 1944, p. 138.

90. EC, 2 June 1870, p. 28; FC, 28 October 1867; *Times*, 15 December 1868.

91. Building contract, 10 July 1866, DC Box 194.

92. Engraving in *The Architect*, April 1870.

93. GM, 27 May 1869.

94. BM 1869, p. 136.

95. Goodall, 'Dulwich College: the Story of a Foundation', *Macmillan's Magazine*, June 1868, p. 131; 'Dulwich in the Seventies', *A*, XXVII, 195 (July 1899), p. 199.

96. BM 1870, p. 32; *A*, XXVI, 186 (May 1898), p. 200.

97. GM, 2 June 1870.

98. FC, 1870, p. 37.

99. Mck, p. 227; undated ms. (?1872), DC Box 91.

100. GM, 1861, pp. 50, 82.

101. GM, 1862, pp. 17–19.

102. EC, 2 June 1870, p. 28.

103. Draft, DC Box 93.

104. GM, Supplement, pp. 5–6.

105. RIBA *Transactions*, 1867–8, p. 263.

106. *The Times*, 27 June 1866; *The Builder*, XXVI, 1328, July 18 1868, p. 522; ground plan and engraving of Great Hall, ibid., pp. 530, 531.

107. A. Barry, *Memoir of the Life and Works of the late Sir Charles Barry*, second edition, 1870, pp. 51–3.

108. M. Seaborne, *The English School*, 1971, II, p. 268.

109. Op. cit., XVI, 11 June 1869, p. 520.

110. Op. cit., pp. 271–3.

111. *Illustrated London News*, XLIV, 1263, 11 June 1864, p. 563, illus. p. 564; RIBA *Transactions*, 1867–8, p. 260.

112. Ibid., pp. 268–9.

113. M. Stratton, *The Terracotta Revival*, 1993, pp. 68–70.

114. *The Seven Lamps of Architecture*, in *Works of Ruskin*, Library Edition, 1903–12, VIII, pp. 50–51; E. M. Barry, *Lectures on Architecture*, 1881, p. 384.

115. J. Mordaunt Crook, in J. Fawcett, ed., *Seven Victorian Architects*, 1976, p. 50.

116. *S Maria della Carità*, to be seen in Canaletto's painting, *The Stonemason's Yard*, 1728, National Gallery.

117. A. Barry, *Memoir...*, first edition, 1867, p. 7.

118. BM, 13 Sept 1870, p. 467.

119. *The Builder*, XXVIII, 1419, 16 April 1870, p. 304; BM, 21 July 1911, pp. 72-73.

120. BM, 1869, pp. 164–5; GM, 22 March 1859.

121. *Sixth Report of the Royal Commission on Scientific Instruction and the Advancement of Science*, 1875, pp. 3, 39; GM, Master's Annual Report, October 1927, p. 52.

122. SC, 22 June 1880, p. 112.

123. I. S. MacNiven, *Lawrence Durrell*, 1998, p 53. Lawrence was at school in Canterbury; Leslie was at Dulwich College, 1931-3; Gerald was schooled at home. The family owned the house 1926-32.

124. Ms., p. 3, DC Box 91.

125. Carver ms., DC Box 91; GM, 1867, p. 124.

126. S&C, 2 July 1872.

127. Hadden, p. 193.

128. *The Times*, 27 June 1866; Mck, p. 250.

129. GM, 16 June 1866.

130. GM, p. 140.

131. GM, 1860, p. 339.

132. 1867; see also GM, 1866, pp. 30, 120.

133. FC, 5 June 1866.

134. BM, 1869, pp. 82-3; EC, 21 March 1871, p. 21.

135. *Times*, 23 December 1868.

136. Op. cit, XVI, 12 February 1869, p. 142; 26 February 1869, p. 173.

137. *City Press*, 16 January 1869.

138. Carver, Memorial to Charity Commissioners, 1869, DC Box 91.

139. Hadden, p. 192.

140. BM, 11 December 1877, p. 180.

141. *Memories*, p. 79.

142. Mck, p. 256.

143. *Interviews*, p. 79.

144. Op. cit., VI, 5, 21 July 1896, pp. 65-6.

145. *Memories*, pp. 71-2; cf. p. 57.

146. Ms., 12 April 1876, DC Box 92.

147. Copy of letter from Young to Sparkes, DC Box 91.

148. Ms., '1876', DC Box 91; *Interviews*, p. 79.

149. DC Box 91.

150. Marshall had enemies among the staff, such as a Modern Languages teacher, E. Passawer, who left soon after to be Secretary of a tramway company in Vienna (*Interviews*, p. 95).

151. *Interviews*, p. 60.

152. Ibid., pp. 79, 90, 95.

153. *Metropolitan*, 13 November 1877.

154. *The Times*, 22 December 1877; 'Marshall Defence Fund', 'Private', DC Box 91; BM, 12 March 1878, p. 12.

155. DC Box 91.

156. BM, 11 December 1877, pp. 173-4.

157. Ms., DC Box 91.

158. Ms., 'Private and confidential', 1877, DC Box 91.

159. DC Box 91; *Report of the Meeting of Head Masters of Schools, held at Dulwich College on December 22nd and 23rd, 1874*, DC Box 305. They discussed: their own constitution, membership and subscriptions; the dangers of 'cramming' for examinations, and the unhealthy competition among schools caused by the Oxford and Cambridge Schools Examination Board publishing lists of successful candidates.

160. Lane figured as a very prominent boy in a report from Carver to the Governors (GM, 1866, p. 33).

161. *Memories*, p. 12.

162. Ibid., p 46; *A*, I, 3 (June 1873), p. 72; see also *A*, XXVI, 198 (October 1898), p. 301.

163. 159 members dined at the twenty-first anniversary in 1894. *Rules* were printed in 1879; the *Year Book* commenced in 1902.

164. Mck, pp. 81, 96; SC, 15 July 1873, p. 159.

165. 'A Dulwich Scandal, First Day', *South London Press*, 4 August 1877.

166. Marshall to Carver, Carver to Marshall, letters, DC Box 91.

167. *A*, III, 15 (June 1875), p. 64.

168. *A*, XII, 80 (December 1884), p. 182; ms. note on Ormiston's filing card for Lane at DC.

169. Carver ms., '1877', DC Box 92.

170. Ms. '1859', DC Box 91.

171. BM, 14 July 1868, p. 47.

172. Draft, no date, DC Box 92.

173. *An Analysis of Abstract of the Accounts of Alleyn's College*, Dulwich, 1877, pp. 3, 6; BM, 11 March 1873, p. 65; BM, 13 January 1880, p. 3.

174. *A*, I, 2 (April 1873), p. 40; I, 3 (June 1873), p 74; Sp C, 30 September 1875, p. 129.

175. BM, 13 January 1880, p. 3.

176. *A*, IX, 54 (March 1881), p. 3; BM, 2 February 1881, p. 21.

177. GM, 1862, p. 148.

178. Farewell testimonial from staff, Carver Golden Wedding Album, DC.

179. Op. cit., 16 January 1869. *A*, XXVII, 192 (February 1899), p. 16.

180. Carver, Ms. summary of 'History of Foundation', p. 5, DC Box 91.

181. BM, 8 December 1868, p. 125.

182. Ms., '1875', DC Box 91.

183. Stipend and fees, BM, 14 July 1868, p. 71; from Annual Accounts in GM: late 1860s roughly £630; 1870s roughly £1,000-2,682.

184. GM, 14 October 1873, p. 206.

185. J. R. Adams, *Dulwich College and the Endowed Schools Commissioners, a Tract for the Times*, 1873, pp. 9, 12, 15.

186. BM, 14 May 1872, pp. 86-7.

187. BM, 11 February 1879, p. 52; EFC, 29 January 1880, p. 20.

188. GM, Audit and EFC, 19 June 1883, pp. 60-1.

189. 'Petition to Council', DC Box 91.

190. EFC, 5 June 1866, p. 7.

191. Adams, p. 52; BM, 1872, p. 91.

192. S&C, 26 March 1872, p. 43.

193. Ormiston, p. 681, lists annual rolls.

194. BM, 1872, p. 91.
195. Mck, pp. 303–4.
196. Ibid., p. 300.
197. BM, 13 July 1875, p. 106.
198. BM, 14 March 1876.
199. BM, 10 October 1876, p. 123.
200. BM, 8 February 1876; GM, February–September 1876.
201. 13 February 1877, p. 26.
202. BM, 16 May 1877; BM, 12 February 1878. £500 in 1879 calculates at around £35,000 in current prices.
203. GM, 1876, letter of 8 February, p. 10.
204. Mck, p. 277.
205. *The History of Dulwich College … showing the Interests and Relations of the Inhabitants of the Parishes … and the proposed alterations of the Endowed Schools Commissioners*, 1873, p. 12.
206. Hadden, p. 192.
207. *Echo*, 29 January 1879.
208. GM, letter of 31 December 1869.
209. E.g., *South London Press*, 12 and 19 February 1881.
210. Mck, p. 282.
211. Ms., post-1864, pp. 2–3, DC Box 94.
212. Memorandum, 5 August 1874, DC Box 91.
213. *A*, XXV, 181 (October 1897), p. 230.
214. Mck, p. 319; note in family papers, DC Box 574.
215. GM, 12 November 1861.
216. DC Box 575.
217. *Hour*, February 1874.
218. Op. cit., 1875, p. 85.
219. BM, 9 March 1875, p. 3.
220. Sp C, 20 January 1879, p. 2; BM, 13 May 1879.
221. *Echo*, 29 January 1879.
222. Sp C, 7 February 1883, p. 13.
223. Carver ms., 4 August 1874, DC Box 91.
224. *Times*, 25 November 1926.
225. Dulwich Education Committee, 1874, DC Box 91.
226. *A*, XIX, 134 (November 1891), p. 25; *A*, XXV, 181 (October 1897), p. 230.
227. BM, January 1883, p. 193.
228. DC Box 92.
229. Resembling the South Block; photos in Carver Golden Wedding Album, DC.
230. Op. cit., p. 236. Eliza's younger sister married the grocer Julius Drewe, for whom Edwin Lutyens designed Castle Drogo in Devon.
231. *A*, XVI, 111 (November 1888), p. 221.
232. DC Box 92.
233. *A*, XI, 73 (November 1883), p. 152; Mck, p. 1.
234. *A*, XXXVI, 268 (July 1908), p. 233.
235. GM, 1859, p. 268.
236. GM, 1862, p. 141.
237. GM, 1863, p. 80; GM, 10 January 1867; GM, 23 November 1867, p. 3; BM, 1869, letter from Governors of 31 December, p. 7.
238. GM, 1868, p. 116.
239. GM, 10 February 1863, p. 10.
240. GM, Agenda for 14 January 1879.
241. EFC, 28 February 1878, p. 41.
242. GM, 23 November 1869, p. 6.
243. Goodall, *Macmillan's Magazine*, June 1868, p. 137.
244. GM, 14 May 1878, p. 80.
245. EFC, 30 September 1880, pp. 160–3.
246. GM, 16 January 1866, p. 21.
247. GM, 1860, p. 365; BM, 10 October 1871, p. 147; BM, 13 April 1880, p. 68.
248. E.g., GM, 1859, p. 255; February 1860, p. 291; EC, 1875, 28 January, p. 17; February 1860, p. 291; EFC, 2 January 1879, p. 2; 30 January 1879, p. 28; 15 March 1879, pp. 79, 81; BM, 13 January 1880, p. 4; EFC, 1882, p. 27. Plane trees and chestnuts at the New College: BM, 29 October 1885, p. 82.
249. GM, 1 October 1868, p. 32.
250. Blanch, *Camberwell*, pp. 411–16; EC, 22 March 1876, p. 2; EC, 1 June 1876, p. 75.
251. Library Edition, III, p. xxviii.
252. Ibid., XXXVI, p. 176, n. 6; VIII, pp. 50–51.
253. *Times*, 26 July 1866, p. 12; Carver, '1865', DC Box 91; Ruskin's letter (whereabouts unknown) is quoted in full in Darby, pp. 329–30.
254. DC Box 574 (photocopy).
255. *Daily Telegraph*, 18 September 1865; Library Edition, XVII, p. 521.
256. 'Fiction, Fair and Foul', Library Edition, XXXIV, pp. 266–7.
257. Mck, p. 250.
258. Library Edition, XXXVII, p. 655, n. Carver's gifts to the Library included Ruskin's *Fors Clavigera* and *Modern Painters* (and a set of Thackeray): Mck, p. 337.
259. *Praeterita*, 1886–9, Library Edition, XXXV, pp. 48–9.
260. BM, 9 October 1866, p. 117.
261. BM, 1873, p. 233.
262. BM, 16 November 1858.
263. BM, 14 March 1871, p. 35.
264. BM, Gallery Report, 1867.
265. BM, 11 March 1873.
266. EC, 29 June 1876, p. 25; BM, 13 July 1880, p. 134.
267. E. Walford, *Old and New London*, 1893, VI, p. 303; *Interviews*, p. 92; Picture Gallery Committee, 15 December 1887, p. 95; EFC, 18 October 1892, p. 56; EFC, 24 July 1894, pp. 57, 67; EFC, 30 April 1895, p. 18; EFC, 21 October 1895, p. 48.
268. Ms. 'History of Foundation', p. 5, DC Box 92.
269. Press cutting, February 1898, Golden Wedding Album, DC, p. 49.
270. Mck, p. 275.
271. *A*, XXXVIII, 205 (October 1900), p. 288; *A*, IX, 54 (March 1881), p. 12.
272. BM, 1876, letter from Carver, p. 5.
273. 'Dulwich College, Examination of the Upper School', 1862.
274. BM, p. 89.
275. BM, 1870, p. 90.

276. BM, 9 July 1872, p. 125.

277. Sp C, 15 July 1873, p. 165.

278. GM, 9 July 1867, p. 68; OCSEB, 1881, p. 160; OCSEB, 1882, p. 123; GM, 9 July 1867, p. 68.

279. *A*, XXXVII, 277 (October 1909), p. 296.

280. BM, 11 March 1873, p. 70.

281. DC Box 92; Charles Voysey published in 1888 his *Dulwich Tracts*.

282. DC Box 443. Voysey was placed 69/72 in the Upper II Form in 1874, but was commended the same year in Class I of the Art Prize at a very young age.

283. GM, 1868, 'Report on holidays'.

284. Sp C, 20 January 1874, p. 16.

285. Sixth Report, p. 39; BM, 1879, pp. 192–3.

286. BM, 10 May 1881, p. 92.

287. BM, 8 October 1877, p. 165; BM, 16 July 1878, p. 108.

288. *Memories*, p. 68; obituary, *A*, LI, 376 (June 1923), p. 190.

289. Letter to Christison, 18 August 1944, DC Box 195; *A*, XLII, 315 (June 1914), p. 274.

290. *A* XVI, 107 (May 1888), pp. 119–20; ibid., 108 June 1888), pp. 136–143; *A New Dictionary of French and English*, 1903; *G & D*, p. 144.

291. 'The Study of the Living Languages', Headmasters Conference pamphlet, December 1876, DC Box 574.

292. EC, April 1875; obituary, *A*, XIV, 89 (February 1886), p. 4.

293. BM, 22 November 1870, p. 534.

294. DC Box 163.

295. *Memories*, p. 45; BM, 10 November 1874, p. 150; Ormiston, p. 55.

296. Carver ordered 20 copies for Governors: BM, 14 March 1865, p. 31.

297. *A*, I, 4 (July 1873), p. 91.

298. *A*, I, 3 (June 1873), p. 73; *A*, XI, 69 (February 1888), p. 28.

299. *A*, I, 5 (October 1873), p. 123.

300. BM, 14 November 1882, p. 157.

301. *A*, XIV, 90–2 (March, May, June 1886).

302. *A*, VI, 37 (October 1878), p. 175.

303. The play was *The Merchant of Venice*: *A*, X, 64 (June 1882), p. 64; Everett in *Memories*, p. 17.

304. *A*, VII, 44 (October 1879), p. 4.

305. Mck, p. 340; *A*, XXVII, 198 (October 1899), p. 301.

306. BM, 14 January 1879, p. 49.

307. BM, 9 January 1877, p. 12; BM, 14 May 1878, p. 80; BM, 11 February 1879, p. 44; BM, 1879, pp. 139–42, 177; BM, 9 December 1879, p. 289; BM, 10 February 1880, p. 31.

308. *A*, II, 7 (February 1874), p. 22; *A*, II, 9 (June 1874), p. 68; BM, 14 December 1880, p. 207; *A*, XVIII, 120 (February 1890), p. 40; *A*, LXIII, 449 (July 1935), p. 227.

309. Letter from McC. Christison, *A*, LX, 429 (March 1932), p. 429; letter to author from Sir Colin Cole, 23 January 1995.

310. Mck, p. 340; *Memories*, p. 87; Treadgold, *Interviews*, p. 104; DC Box 92.

311. Mck, p. 274; P. H. Clifford OA, *South London Press*, 3 March 1883; Mck, pp. 2–3.

312. *Interviews*, pp. 95–6.

313. Mck, p. 273; *A*, XXXV, 269 (July 1907), p. 260 (Alleyn Club dinner); *A*, XXXVII, 277 (October 1909), p. 312 (Carver's speech). See also A. Savours, *The Search for the North West Passage*, 1999; *A*, XIV, 95 (November 1886), pp. 202–7 (obituary of Bedford Pim); Carver mentioned in an Alleyn Club speech a painting shown at the RA (unspecified date) picturing both Pim and Bidgood sledging, *A*, XXXVII, 277 (October 1909), p. 312.

314. *A*, XLII, 312 (February 1914), p. 2; *A*, XLII, 314 (May 1914), p. 140; Wodehouse, 'Huy Day by Day', *Performing Flea*, 1953, p. 207.

315. William Beach Thomas, 'Dulwich College', *Public School Magazine*, March 1898, p. 201.

316. R. L. Green, *A. E. W. Mason*, 1952, p. 16.

317. *Interviews*, pp. 100, 102.

318. *Times*, 31 July 1880.

319. *A*, XXIX, 213 (October 1901), p. 305.

320. *A*, X, 67 (November 1882), p. 166.

321. *Interviews*, p. 98.

322. Shepherd's obituary, *A*, XLVII, 353 (June 1919), p. 201, says he served at the College for 'about twenty years from 1870'.

323. GM, 9 October 1866, p. 96.

324. BM, 12 October 1880, p. 176.

325. BM, 12 October 1880, p. 177.

326. Mck, p. 400.

327. *South London Press*, 17 April 1875; printed prologue in DC Cuttings Book I; BM, 11 March 1879, p. 70.

328. *A*, VII, 40 (February 1879), p. 21; ibid., XI, 69 (February 1883), pp. 20–21.

329. *A*, II, 12 (December 1874), pp. 144–7.

330. Mck, p. 398.

331. Mck, p. 403; GM, 1880, p. 92.

332. Mck, p. 404; 'Memories of the Seventies', *A*, XXVII, 194 (May 1899), p. 141; GM, 12 June 1866, p. 53.

333. S&C, 14 March 1870.

334. 5 November 1863: DC leases, 281.

335. *A*, XVII, 119 (December 1889), p. 238.

336. H. Staunton, *The Great Schools of England*, 1865, p. 504.

337. Sp C, 6 April 1873: Numbers with Mrs Dryland and Mrs Field 13, with Mrs Hawkins 10.

338. BM, 2 February 1881, p. 21.

339. BM, 1871, p. 191.

340. BM, 10 October 1882, p. 138.

341. On Skinner, see J. Physick, *The Victoria and Albert Museum*, 1982, p. 244; A. Burton, *Vision and Accident*, 1999, pp. 152–3, 162, 164; on Thomas, there are several monographs, e.g., R. W. Burnie, *Memoir and Letters of Sidney Gilchrist Thomas*, 1891; see also *A*, LXIX, 482 (February 1941), p. 14.

342. *A*, XXIX, 208 (February 1901), p. 1; *A*, XVII, 115 (May 1898), p. 101; *A*, XXXVI, 266 (May 1908), p. 156.

343. *Mike*, Chapter 29; Edward Robinson, Ormiston, no. 2237; *A*, XXVII, 192 (February 1899), pp. 3–4.

344. *A*, XXXI, 224 (February 1903), p. 46; *A*, LI, 374 (February 1923), p. 5; *A*, XLI, 305 (March 1913), p. 142.

345. *A*, LIII, 389 (July 1925), p. 191; the painting *Old Time Tuition* (see Chapter Five) was presented in his memory in December 1920; *Endurance* diaries of T. L. Orde-Lees and H. McNish ('Chippy').

346. BM, 8 July 1879, p. 154.

347. ODNB; R. L. Green, *A. E. W. Mason*, 1952, passim; *A*, XIII, 82 (March 1885), p. 32. For *As You like It*, see *Memories*, p. 17 (where 1884 is a mistake for 1883).

348. *Public School Magazine*, VIII, p. 47. For identical opinion, see *The Captain*, 1903, p. 221.

349. *Cassell's Family Magazine*, 1880, p. 49; *A*, XXX, 220, July 1902, p. 274.

350. *A*, XXIV, 173 (September 1896), p. 224.

351. BM, 14 February 1882, p. 26; Mck, p. 428; B. Viney, *Dulwich College, A School and its Art*, exhibition catalogue, Dulwich College, 1981.

352. Mck, p. 428.

353. *Memories*, p. 63.

354. 10 August 1944 (DC Box 195).

355. J. Goodall, *Life and Landscape on the Norfolk Broads*, 1886, p. 75.

356. G. Thomson, 'Henry Herbert La Thangue', *Studio*, IX, 1897, p. 164.

357. Mrs L. Birch, *Stanhope A. Forbes ARA and Elizabeth Stanhope Forbes ARWS*, 1906, p. 6.

358. Obituary, *Times*, 23 December 1929.

359. *Speaker*, 11 June 1904, p. 247; J. S. Little, 'H. H. La Thangue', *Art Journal*, n.s., 1893; A. Jenkins, *Henry La Thangue and British Rural Naturalism*, Bolton, 2000; G. Thomson, 'Henry Herbert La Thangue', *Studio*, IX, 1897; *The Man with a Scythe* (RA, 1896), Tate Gallery.

360. Undated letter, DC Box 91.

361. 15 August 1944, DC Box 195.

362. *A*, XL, 30 (July 1912), pp. 231–3.

363. Note in family papers: 'Archbishop Tait proposed to get him a Bishopric but he declined in order to complete his work in establishing Dulwich College as a First Class Public School of which he has been called "The Second Founder"' (DC Box 574).

364. Acts, VII, 18, 'there arose another king over Egypt, who knew not Joseph'.

365. Mck, p. 278.

366. *A*, XXXVI, 277 (October 1908), pp. 295–6.

Chapter Seven

Approximate value of £1 sterling (see Notes to Chapter One): 1885, £74.

1. *G & D*, p. 21; *Memories*, pp. 120–1; Welldon obituary, *A*, LXV, 461 (July 1937), pp. 325–6.

2. The Field Sports Committee, run by the boys, ruled in 1899 that 'every member of the School be allowed to wear a blazer, which shall consist of dark blue serge, with the monogram 'DC' worked in white upon the left breast pocket': *A*, XXVII, 198 (October 1899), p. 314; see also P. G. Wodehouse, 'The Ways We Have – Dulwich', *Public School Magazine*, III, January 1901, p. 28; Smith's speech, *A*, LI, 378 (October 1923), p. 188.

3. BM, 27 June 1885, p. 4; Mck, pp. 363–5; N. Smith, *Dulwich and Beyond: a History of Dulwich College Preparatory School*, 2006, passim.

4. *A*, XIII, 84 (June 1885), p. 105.

5. J. W. Ivimey, *Boys and Music*, 1936, p. 35.

6. C. Tyerman, *A History of Harrow School, 1324–1991*, 2000, p. 364.

7. ODNB.

8. *A*, XLVIII, 360 (October 1920), p. 259; *Boys and Music*, p. 54.

9. *Memoirs*, p. 99.

10. King's College Library, Cambridge, BRA/2/102 (to Henry Bradshaw, 22 February 1880).

11. ODNB.

12. *Interviews*, p. 57.

13. King's College Library, Cambridge (Welldon, II OB/1729/A 14).

14. O. Browning, *Memories of Sixty Years*, 1909, pp. 206–7, 210, 220–1; I. Anstruther, *Oscar Browning*, 1983, passim.

15. See n. 13 above (25 March 1883).

16. Ibid., OB/1/1728/A.

17. *Recollections and Reflections*, 1915; *Forty Years On*, 1935.

18. *Forty Years On*, p. 134.

19. *Interviews*, p. 105.

20. BM, 12 May 1885, p. 34.

21. A. M. Galer, *Norwood and Dulwich Past and Present*, 1890, p. 46.

22. 4 May 1885.

23. *Interviews*, p. 69; cf. Mck, p. 356.

24. C. Tyerman, p. 370; ODNB.

25. 'School Stories', *Public School Magazine*, August 1901, p. 127: 'If you wish to read a really bad school-story, try and get hold of "Gerald Eversley's Friendship"'. (Wodehouse mistakenly believes that Gerald dies the end of the novel, probably confusing it with H. O. Sturgis's *Tim* of 1891, in which one Eton boy who is in love with another, 'passing the love of women', dies of consumption.)

26. *Gerald Eversley's Friendship*, pp. 3, 74, 75, 77, 81.

27. Op. cit., pp. 96–8.

28. Roy Jenkins, *Churchill*, 2001, pp. 19, 140–41; ODNB (Welldon); R. S. Churchill, *Winston S. Churchill*, I, 1966, pp. 111, 140, 323, 324; *The Lyttelton Hart-Davis Letters*, 1978, I, p. 126.

29. *A*, XXXIX, 293 (October 1911), p. 371.

30. W.D. Gibbon, *G & D*, p. 67.

31. *A*, XI, 73 (February 1883), p. 153; text of speech: Mck, pp. 343–52.

32. *A*, XII, 48 (May 1884), p. 86.

33. Acts 9, 36; Mck, p. 353. 'Dorcas' is the Greek version of the Hebrew 'Tabitha'.

34. *Interviews*, p. 103.

35. Ibid., p. 69.
36. *A*, LI, 378 (October 1923), p. 196.
37. Welldon, *Recollections and Reflections*, p. 186.
38. BM, 30 October 1883, p. 97.
39. GM, 1908, p. 135.
40. GM, 1884, p. 5.
41. GM, 16 June 1885, p. 40.
42. *G & D*, p. 46; *Memoirs*, p. 100.
43. Op. cit., pp. 1, 5, 18, 28–9, 35.
44. Mck, p. 406.
45. BM, 29 January 1884, p. 2.
46. *The Nineteenth Century and After*, LXVIII, 401, July 1910, pp. 155-160. See also *Carthusian*, XII, June 1920, p. 430; *Harrovian*, XXXIII, 1920, p. 34. For Mrs Rendall, see *A*, XXXVII, 272 (February 1909), p. 53.
47. *A*, XLVIII, 358 (June 1920), p. 132.
48. *The Complete Angler* was performed in May 1892: *A*, XX, 139 (June 1892), pp. 119–21. The music for the Greek plays has not survived. For *The Frogs*, see *G & D*, p. 135.
49. *Interviews*, p. 76.
50. Postcard from Welldon in reply to an enquiry from McC. Christison, 11 March 1932 (DC Box 52); *A*, XIII, 84 (July 1885), p. 154; *A*, XXII, 197 (October 1894), p. 214. The verses and a translation were published in the *Leisure Hour*, February 1899.
51. *A*, XXIX, 213 (October 1901), p. 327.
52. *A*, XXXIV, 253 (October 1906), p. 276.
53. Ed. E. D. Rendall, *DC Songs*, 1–4.
54. *DC Songs*, 5–8.
55. Mck, p. 355.
56. Mck, pp. 362–3, 368; *Interviews*, p. 6. £2,000 was promised; he needed £20,000.
57. *A*, XII, 48 (May 1884), p. 87; *A*, XXXV, 260 (July 1907), p. 203.
58. Mrs L. Birch, *Stanhope A. Forbes ARA and Elizabeth Stanhope Forbes ARWS*, 1906, p. 6.
59. BM, 18 April 1885, p. 27.
60. Picture Gallery Committee, GM, 5 March 1885, p. 16; BM, 25 March 1884, p. 40; see also Mck, p. 132.
61. *Recollections and Reflections*, p. 166.
62. Op. cit., pp. 2, 230, 7, 9.
63. *A*, XII, 79 (October 1884), p. 86.
64. A. W. P. Gayford, *History of Dulwich College*, second edition, 1967, p. 36n.; *A*, XIV, 91 (May 1886), p. 195; *A*, XXXV, 260 (July 1907), p. 201; *A*, XCI, 601 (Autumn 1963), p. 210.
65. *A*, XXVII, 192 (February 1899), p. 5.
66. *Big Money*, 1931, p. 137; *A*, XXXII, 237 (October 1904), p. 340.
67. *A*, XLIX, 364 (June 1921), p. 364.
68. *A*, LI, 378 (October 1923), p. 196.
69. *A*, LVI, 408 (October 1928), pp. 286–7.
70. *A*, XIII, 86 (October 1885), p. 192. Gilkes (ms. Diary, 1899, p. 7a) wrote that Arnold's speech was 'not a happy one, nor well received', presumably because it did not make enough of the 'Public School' values of the College.

Chapter Eight
Approximate value of £1 sterling (see Notes to Chapter One): 1882, £69; 1886, £75; 1888, £77; 1895, £79; 1898, £77; 1904, £74; 1908, £71; 1910, £70; 1913, £68; 1947, £27; 1971, £10.

1. *G & D*, p. 67; strictly, he applies it to the years 1894–9.
2. Letter from W. R. M. Leake to 'Hudson' (DC Box 227); cf. *G & D*, pp. xiv, 2, 50.
3. A. E. Johnson, *The Captain*, IX, 28, June 1903, p. 221.
4. ODNB; H. W. Nevinson, 'A Master', *Running Accompaniment*, 1936, p. 19.
5. *Interviews*, p. 109.
6. W.D. Gibbon to Mck, ibid., p. 97.
7. H. G. Wells, *The Story of a Great Headmaster*, 1924, pp. 28–9.
8. Mck, p. 530; *G & D*, p. 72.
9. *A*, XIII, 86 (October 1885), p. 182; XIII, 87 (November 1885), p. 246.
10. Nevinson, pp. 18,19, 26.
11. *A*, L, 372 (Oct 1922), p. 251; *G & D*, p. xxviii; 'The Prize Poem', 1901, *Tales of St. Austin's*, 1903, p. 227.
12. *Interviews*, p. 120.
13. Information from Michael Gilkes; W. R. M. Leake's obituary of Mrs Gilkes, *A*, LXIX, 483 (March 1941), p. 115.
14. *God's Gift*, 1981, p. 156.
15. *A*, XC, 598 (Autumn 1962), p. 244.
16. *G & D*, p. xxxi.
17. Ibid., p. xxiv; Mck, p. 533; *A*, XC, 598 (Autumn 1962), p. 244.
18. Op. cit., pp. 141, 145.
19. H.F. Hose, *A*, L, 372 (October 1922), p. 245.
20. *Memories*, p. 100; *G & D*, pp. 115–16, 239.
21. *Interviews*, p. 59; ms. draft of essays for publication, DC Box 227, p. 29.
22. *G & D*, pp. 2, 43, 147.
23. Diary, p. 64; BM, 21 July 1896, p. 3.
24. Diary, pp. 80, 100, 103, 108; P.G. Wodehouse notebook, private collection.
25. *G & D*, pp. 34, 48; BM, 27 July 1900, p. 120.
26. Diary, p. 6; Rehder, *A*, XXXV, 260 (July 1907), p. 296; *G & D*, p. xxxviii; *A*, XXIII, 163 (June 1895), p. 113.
27. BM, 27 Oct 1885, pp. 72–3; Diary, p. 5; Mck, p. 535; *Interviews*, p. 109.
28. *A*, XXX, 220 (July 1902), p. 258.
29. *G & D*, p. 101.
30. Ibid., p. 74.
31. Supplement, *Black and White*, 27 July 1907.
32. Board of Education pamphlet, 'Modern Sides of Public Schools, IV, Dulwich', 1907, p. 9.
33. 'Oxford Letter', *A*, XXII, 152 (March 1894), p. 57.
34. King's College, Cambridge, Library MSS, JTS 2/82.
35. *G & D*, pp. 277–8; letter in DC Box 227.
36. *Interviews*, pp. 47, 93; *G & D*, pp. 72–3.
37. *A*, XLII, 317 (October 1914), p. 380; *A*, LXXX, 551 (September 1952), p. 244.

38. *G & D*, p. 43; H. de Sélincourt, 'The Old Man', *Studies from Life*, 1934, pp. 23–5.
39. *Interviews*, p. 71.
40. *A*, XVII, 114 (April 1889), p. 5.
41. *A*, XXXV, 262, (November 1907), p. 356.
42. BM, 20 Feb 1914, p. 24.
43. Op. cit., p. 184; Gilkes, undated address, DC Box 227; *G & D*, p. 138.
44. Preface to ms. unpublished essays, p. 1, DC Box 227; D. Jasen, *Portrait of a Master*, 1975, p. 19.
45. Diary, pp. 15v, 81.
46. *A*, XVII, 117 (October 1889), p. 167.
47. *Interviews*, p. 87.
48. *A*, XVIII, 123 (June 1890), p. 145.
49. *G & D*, p. 99.
50. *Times*, 1 August 1913.
51. *A*, XXV, 179 (June 1897), p. 146; XXXIV, 251 (June 1906), p. 217.
52. *G & D*, pp. 59, 120.
53. 30 June 1938; Wodehouse, *Performing Flea*, 1953, p. 103.
54. *G & D*, p. 100.
55. 'In Defence of P. G. Wodehouse', *Dickens, Dali and Others*, New York, 1946, p. 230.
56. Diary, p. 130; *G & D*, p. 97.
57. De Sélincourt, *Studies from Life*, p. 26; Alic Smith, *Selected Essays and Addresses*, 1963, p. 28.
58. *The Gold Bat*, 1904, p. 213; *G & D*, pp. xxiii–xxiv.
59. Diary, p. 86. One sermon is printed in *G & D*, pp. 55-60.
60. *A*, LI, 378 (October 1923), p. 203.
61. *A*, XLII, 317 (October 1914), p. 379. *A*, LXXVIII, 539 (November 1950), p. 271; Smith recalls Gilkes's speech as 'simple and charming'.
62. Words by W. H. Bellamy, music by J. L. Hatton; sung at Cambridge by Gilkes, *A*, XXII, 159 (December 1894), p. 314; XXVII, 192 (February 1899), p. 7; *G & D*, p. 129.
63. *G & D*, pp. 3, 401; *Memories*, p. 67; 'Oxford Letter' regrets: *A*, XV, 104 (December 1887), p. 252.
64. McK, p. 534; ms. essay draft warns of the 'great dangers' for older boys of a 'soloist of attractive appearance and a good singing voice'. DC Box 227, p. 26.
65. *Interviews*, p. 87.
66. Diary, p. 17.
67. Ibid., p. 78; BM, 25 July 1899, p. 83; *Interviews*, p. 61.
68. Diary, pp. 8–9.
69. *A*, XXVI, 109 (July 1888), p. 168; *A*, XXXI, 228 (July 1903), p. 226; *A*, XVI, 105 (February 1888), p. 27.
70. Op. cit, p. 2.
71. Op. cit., p. 64.
72. *G & D*, p. 131.
73. Ibid., p. 208.
74. Christ Church, Oxford, Library, MS 413; Christison's grangerised *Alleynian*, XLV (1917), p. 269.
75. *A*, XLI, 309, (August 1913), p. 357.
76. *A*, XIV, 89 (February 1886), pp. 53–4; *A*, XIV, 90 (March 1886), p. 78; *A*, XIV, 91 (May 1886), p. 210.
77. E.g. BM, 25 Oct 1887, p. 61; Gilkes, Annual Report, GM (1891), p. 59.
78. *Interviews*, p. 99.
79. *G & D*, p. 64.
80. *A*, XVI, 105 (February 1888), p. 2; 106 (March 1888), p. 70; XVII, 115 (May 1889), p. 100.
81. *Interviews*, p. 99.
82. Mck, pp. 418–23; *A*, XLII, 312 (February 1914), pp. 50–55.
83. *A*, XXXVI, 265 (March 1908), p. 117; *Interviews*, p. 91. *A*, XXXVII, 272 (February 1909), p. 44.
84. *A*, XXXIII, 240 (February 1905), p. 39; *A*, XXXIII, 241 (March 1905), p. 83.
85. Diary, p 142; *G & D*, p. 64; *A*, XL, 296 (February 1912), p. 5.
86. *A*, LI, 375 (March 1923), pp. 72–5; see also *A*, LXXXI, 554 (March 1952), pp. 56–60.
87. BM, 26 June 1914, p. 78.
88. *A*, XL, 301 (October 1912), p. 306.
89. EFC, 21 July 1899, p. 81; EFC, 8 December 1899, p. 124; EFC, 28 January 1907, p. 11; EFC, March 1913, p. 29.
90. BM, 30 October 1894, p. 81; BM, 5 October 1897, p. 74, f–g.
91. E.g. BM, 15 April 1904, p. 183.
92. BM, 30 October 1888, p. 368.
93. BM, 30 July 1895, pp. 37–8; BM, 29 October 1895, p. 56.
94. EFC, 19 May 1895, p. 40; J. W. Ivimey, *Boys and Music*, 1936, p. 45.
95. BM, March 1888, p. 57.
96. *A*, XXXIII, 242 (May 1905), p. 92.
97. BM, 28 January 1896, n.p.
98. *A*, XVI, 110 (October 1888), p. 210; Diary, p. 17v; Mck, p. 476.
99. BM, 3 December 1895, p. 43a; Diary, p. 58.
100. *Times*, 21 January 1907.
101. *A*, XXX, 220 (July 1902), p. 261; *A*, XXXV, 256 (February 1907), p. 47; Diary, p. 149; BM, 26 April 1907, p. 51.
102. ODNB.
103. EFC, 21 March 1893, p. 221; EFC, 18 July 1893, p. 45.
104. BM, 31 October 1893, p. 63.
105. *G & D*, p. 35; EFC, 22 May 1894, p. 39.
106. *Dulwich History and Romance*, 1922, p. 41.
107. *G & D*, p. 35; BM, 26 July 1901, p. 61.
108. GM, Gilkes's Annual Report, 1912, p. 156.
109. Hall, *Dulwich History*, pp. 39–40.
110. BM, 18 May 1886, p. 53.
111. Diary, p 154.
112. EFC, 18 February 1910, p. 22.
113. ODNB; BM, 10 February 1905, p. 16.
114. BM, 19 July 1912, pp. 121, 157; *A*, LV, 399 (March 1927), p. 309.
115. BM, 11 December 1908, p. 165.
116. *A*, XXXI, 229 (October 1903), pp. 299–300.
117. *A*, XL, 301, (October 1912), p. 315.
118. Op cit, p. 49.
119. *A*, XVIII 123 (June 1890), pp. 155-7; *A*, XXXVIII, 204 (July 1900), pp. 273–4.

120. Diary, p 136.
121. BM, 30 October 1884, p. 84; EFC, 15 April 1890, p. 25.
122. EFC, 20 October 1900, p. 122; EFC, 14 December 1900, p. 150; EFC, 18 July 1901, p. 49.
123. EFC 1908, p. 100; *A*, XXXIV, 249 (March 1906), p. 50.
124. Mck, pp. 516–21; EFC, 1910, p. 53; Mck, p. 521.
125. Diary, p. 128.
126. EFC, 11 March 1910, p. 34; BM, 26 April 1901 p. 36.
127. *A*, XXXII, 232 (February 1904), p. 5.
128. 'Memorial Library, Dulwich College', *The Builder*, LXXXIII, 3125, 27 December 1902, p. 606.
129. GM, 1933, p. 43.
130. *A*, XXXV, 257 (March 1907), p. 87; XXXVIII, 285 (October 1910), p. 285; BM, 21 July 1911, pp. 72–3.
131. BM, 16 July 1909, p. 117.
132. *A*, XXXIII, 244 (July 1905), p. 292.
133. *G & D*, pp. 3, 23.
134. *A*, XIX, 128 (February 1891), p. 2; *Memoirs*, pp. 100,121; *The Caian*, XLIII, 3 (Easter Term, 1935), pp. 82, 93.
135. *Interviews*, p. 105; *G & D*, pp. 54-5; obituary, *A*, XLIV, 335 (December 1916), pp. 340–2.
136. *A*, LXIII, 446 (February 1935), p. 68; A. Smith, *Selected Essays and Addresses*, 1963, p. 26.
137. GM, Gilkes's Annual Report, December 1908, pp. 162–3; *A*, XXXVIII, 202 (May 1900), p. 101.
138. Mck, p. 510; *A*, XXV, 183 (December 1897), p. 314.
139. *A*, XXVII, 301 (Oct 1899), p. 313.
140. XLI, 304 (February 1913), pp. 9–10.
141. *Selected Essays and Addresses*, 1963, pp. 26-7.
142. Obituary, *A*, LXII, 499 (February 1944), pp. 15–16.
143. Obituary, *A*, XCV, 612 (Summer 1967), p. 106.
144. Press cutting, Christison's bound volume of *A*, 1928, p. 370; *A*, L, 371 (July 1922), p. 180.
145. *A*, XXV, 180 (July 1897), p. 168; *A*, XXVI, 186 (May 1898), p. 98; *A*, XXVII, 194 (May 1899), p. 104; *A*, XXVII, 196 (July 1899), p. 168; *G & D*, p. 119.
146. *A*, XXXVIII, 200 (February 1900), p. 107.
147. *A*, XIX, 134 (November 1891 [sic]), p. 247; *G & D*, pp. 54, 78; GM, Gilkes's Annual Report, 29 October 1895, p. 56; GM, Gilkes's annual report, 1899, n.p.; BM, 1901, p. 98.
148. 'Oxford Letter', *A*, XX, 136 (February 1892), pp. 18–19; XXIII, 163 (June 1895), p. 113.
149. *A*, XXXVI, 265 (March 1908), p. 44.
150. OCSEB Report, 1900, p. 101; OCSEB Report, 1887, pp. 4, 118.
151. GM, 1902, pp. 111–15; GM, 1903, p. 117; GM, 1904, p. 167; GM, 1912, pp. 65, 128.
152. OCSEB, 1906, p. 99.
153. GM, 1908, pp. 63, 127–45.
154. GM, Gilkes's Report, 1899, p. 98; Annual Report, 1903, p. 129; GM, Gilkes's Annual Report, 1909, p. 118.
155. *A*, XXXVIII, 280 (Feb 1910), p. 2; J. W. Ivimey, *Boys and Music*, p. 58.
156. GM, 1906, p. 99.
157. Michael Powell, *A Life in Movies*, 1987, p. 92.
158. Paul Jones, *War Letters of a Public-School Boy*, 1918, p. 180.
159. A. Kittermaster, *School Songs &c.*, 1916, pp. 20, 23–6; Diary, p. 413.
160. Letter to author from Christopher Field, 23 February 2007.
161. *A*, LXII, 442 (June 1934), pp. 134-5.
162. *A*, XLII, 317 (Oct 1914), pp. 498, 485.
163. *A*, XLIV, 330 (May 1916), pp. 102–11.
164. *A*, 647 (Autumn 1981), n.p.; ms., DC Box 477.
165. *A*, XLIV, 330 (May 1916), p. 164; reprinted in Wilson Knight, *Gold Dust*, 1968, which includes a tribute to the 'steadfast' Kittermaster in its preface.
166. *A*, XXXIII, 160 (February 1895), p. 4.
167. Stanford's setting of Tennyson's poem memorialised Sir Richard Grenville's famous naval engagement in 1591.
168. *A*, XIII, 83 (April 1885), pp. 70, 72; M. Campbell, *Dolmetsch: the Man and his Work*, 1975, pp. 17–18; *A*, XVI, 107 (May 1888), p. 105.
169. *A*, XXIX, 213 (October 1901), p. 301.
170. *A*, XLVIII, 360 (October 1920), p. 254.
171. *Public School Magazine*, March 1898, pp. 199–206.
172. *A*, LIV, 396 (Oct 1926), p. 723.
173. *Captain*, IX, June 1903, p. 217.
174. *G & D*, p. 184.
175. Hodges, p. 281.
176. *G & D*, p. 3.
177. Richard J. Palmer, 'The Influence of F. W. Sanderson on the development of Science and Engineering at Dulwich College 1885–92', *History of Education*, VI, 2, 1977.
178. *A*, XXV, 189 (October 1897), p. 223.
179. Op. cit., Chapter 24, p. 281.
180. EFC, 16 February 1886, p. 18.
181. Gilkes, ms. draft essays, n.p. (DC Box 227); *A*, XVIII, 126 (November 1890), p. 299.
182. *G & D*, p. 47; BM, 18 January 1887, p. 5.
183. *A*, XVI, 111 (November 1888), p. 259 (the Engine was removed in 1935); BM, 30 October 1888, p. 82.
184. *A*, XVII, 119 (December 1889), p. 259.
185. *G & D*, pp. 16, 18.
186. BM, 26 April 1897, p. 38.
187. Op. cit., 1156, 20 November 1890, p. 1501.
188. BM, 21 October 1890, p. 57.
189. Mck, p 519; *G & D*, pp. 48-9.
190. Op. cit., ed. A .W. Bain, pp. 139–72.
191. Booth, *A*, LIX, 425 (July 1931), p. 294.
192. Diary, p. 8; BM, 26 October 1886, p. 81; obituary, *Times*, 29 April 1935.
193. *Memories*, p. 107.
194. M. E. Barker, 'Gas Mask Development', *Chemical Warfare*, XII, 7, 1926, pp. 11–15; *A*, LXIX, 483 (March 1941), p. 129; Mouat Jones, obituary, *A*, LXXXI, 558 (December 1953).
195. *A*, LXII, 444 (October 1934), p. 360; British Association, press cutting, Christison's bound volume of *A*, 1950, facing p. 165.

196. *A*, XLIII, 324 (July 1915), p. 292.

197. *A*, XXXVI, 266 (May 1908), p. 127; *A*, XXXIV, 253 (October 1906), pp. 284–5; ibid., 254 (November 1906), p. 346; *A*, XXXVI, 264 (February 1908), pp. 16–17; GM, OCSEB, 1905, p. 97.

198. *A*, XIV, 95 (November 1886), p. 201; Diary, p. 17.

199. *A*, XXXVIII, 200, (February 1900), pp. 12–13 ; ibid., 201 (March 1900), pp. 12–16; *A*, XXXIII, 244 (July 1905), p. 281; *A*, XXXI, 229 (October 1903), p. 296; *A*, XXXVIII, 203 (June 1900), p. 167.

200. BM, 1900, p 119; *A*, XXIX, 210 (May 1901), p. 97; XXX, 216 (July 1902), p. 262; XXXI, 228 (July 1903), p. 224.

201. *A*, XV, 101 (July 1887), p. 161; Diary, p. 16v.

202. T. Martin, *Life of Prince Albert*, 1874–80, vol. IV, p. 386; J. R. Piggott, ‘ "A new college worthy of our aspirations and resources": Dulwich College, William Rogers and Alfred Carver and Charles Barry junior', in *Prince Albert and the Development of Education in England and Germany in the 19th century*, ed. K. G. Saur, Munich, 2000.

203. Op. cit., p. 67.

204. *A*, XXI, 147 (June 1893), p. 153; Diary, p. 44; Mck, p. 375.

205. Op. cit., p. 4; *Tales of St. Austin's*, 1903, p. 221.

206. *G & D*, pp. 136–7; *A*, XXIX, 211 (June 1901), p. 162; Diary, p. 106.

207. *A*, XXV, 260 (July 1907), p. 257.

208. *A*, XXXIX, 293 (October 1911), p. 380; GM, Gilkes's Annual Report, 1909, p. 118.

209. ODNB; *Evening News*, 5 September 1913; *Times*, 6 September 1913.

210. (A. F. Thompson) *A*, LXVII, 472 (June 1939), p. 149; *A*, XXXIV, 248 (February 1906), p. 12; see Wodehouse, 'My Friend the Villain', in *A*, XXX, 218 (May 1902), pp. 116 ff.; *A*, LVII, 410 (February 1929), pp. 23–6.

211. *A*, XXX, 218 (May 1902), p. 111.

212. *A*, XXXII, 238 (November 1904) pp. 404–5; *A*, XXXIV, 248 (February 1906), p. 14.

213. *Public School Magazine*, March 1898, p. 206.

214. *A*, XVII, 114 (April 1889), p. 55; *A*, XXXVIII, 287 (December 1910), pp. 447–8; *A*, XXIX, 207 (May 1901), p. 134; ibid, 213 (October 1901), p. 326.

215. *A*, XXIV, 169 (February 1896), p. 5; *A*, XXXI, 224 (February 1903), p. 15; *A*, XXVI, 184 (February 1898), p. 6.

216. *A*, LXXVII, 532 (July 1949), p.118; *A*, XVIII, 124 (July 1890), p. 154; *G & D*, p. 125.

217. *Young Men Magazine*, VI, 6, March 1908; Diary, p. 60. Presidents of the Alleyn Club are listed as a link on the Old Alleynian page at **www.dulwich.org.uk**.

218. *A*, XLI, 310 (November 1913), p. 427; *A*, XXXVIII, 280 (February 1910), p. 5.

219. *Abinger Harvest* (1936), 1953, p. 12.

220. Ms. essays, DC Box 227.

221. *A*, XIV, 94 (October 1886), p. 166.

222. De Sélincourt, *Studies from Life*, p. 28.

223. *A*, XXXVIII, 200 (February 1900), pp. 12–13; *A*, XXXVI,

271 (December 1908), p. 490; *A*, XLI, 311 (December 1913), p. 544; *A*, XXXVIII, 283 (June 1910), pp. 234–9.

224. *Memories*, p 122; *G & D*, p. 36.

225. *A*, LII, 385 (December 1924), p. 277.

226. *A*, XV, 102 (September 1887), pp. 165–7.

227. *A*, XXX, 217 (March 1902), pp. 48–53, 66.

228. *A*, XXXVIII, 286 (November 1910), pp. 43–6.

229. *A*, XL, 299 (June 1912), pp. 183–5.

230. *A*, LII, 382 (June 1924), p. 133; F. A. M. Webster, 'Dulwich College', *Windsor Magazine*, 447, March 1932, p. 498.

231. Ormiston, p. 208; obituary, *Dulwich Year Book*, 69, 1972, pp. 2–3. Letters from Kirby to Colin Hardie, a Fellow of Magdalen College, Oxford, and friend of Bruce McFarlane (OA), DC Box 237.

232. 10 May 1922, letter to H. R. Mill. Scott Polar Research Institute, Cambridge, MS 100/17; D.

233. 'Griff' (A. S. Griffith), *Surrendered. Some Naval Secrets*, 1926, p. 160.

234. *A*, XXXVIII, 287 (December 1910), pp. 472–4.

235. H. Begbie, *Shackleton, a Memory*, 1922, p. 15 (quoting his Form Master, the Revd C. E. C. Lefroy).

236. *A*, XXXVIII, 285 (October 1910), p. 327.

237. *A*, L, 373 (December 1922), p. 317.

238. *Captain*, XXIII, April 1910, pp. 42–3.

239. *A*, XXIX, 215 (December 1901), p. 446; *A*, XXXI, 226 (May 1903), p. 150.

240. Ms. reminiscence, DC Box 477; *A*, XXXVII, 272 (February 1909), pp. 314, 316; Hodges, p. 81; *A*, XXXVIII, 281 (March 1910), pp. 69–71.

241. *A*, XXXVII, 277 (October 1909), p. 302.

242. Ibid., p. 312.

243. *A*, XXXVIII, 281 (March 1910), p. 80.

244. J. R. Piggott, *Shackleton, the Antarctic and Endurance*, 2000, p 93; *A*, XLII, 312 (February 1914), p. 64.

245. *A*, XLII, 317 (October 1914), pp. 374–80; J. E Flecker, *Collected Poems*, 1929, p. 234. Shackleton to Christison, 14 July 1914 (DC Box 459).

246. *A*, XLVI, 344 (February 1918), p. 40; *A*, XLVII, 354 (October 1919), p. 276; obituary, *A*, L, 368 (February 1922), pp. 4–7; *A*, XLVIII, 360 (October 1920), p. 260; 'Sir Ernest Shackleton: a study in Personality', *The Contemporary Review*, CXXI, January–June 1922, p. 325.

247. *A*, XXXIII, 240 (February 1905), pp. 16–17.

248. R. Huntford, *Shackleton*, 1985, pp. 228, 335–6, 341, 359; F. Bamford, *Vicious Circle*, 1965, passim; DC Box 459.

249. Hodges, p. 114.

250. *A*, XXX, 220 (July 1902), p. 277.

251. See the inscription by Wodehouse on a copy of *Pot-hunters*, 1902, J. R Piggott, 'Wodehouse and Dulwich College', in A. Ring and G. Jaggard, eds., *Wodehouse Goes to School*, 1997, p. xxxv. R. McCrum, *Wodehouse: a Life*, 2005.

252. Richard Usborne, *Wodehouse at Work*, 1961, pp. 30–61; Jasen, p. 9; R. McCrum, 2005, pp. 15–40; *Tales of St.*

Austin's (1903) is dedicated '*ad matrem*'; 'In Defence of P. G. Wodehouse', *Dickens, Dali and Others*, p. 230; P. G. Wodehouse, *Over Seventy*, 1957, p. 16; for Wodehouse's schooldays, see also Peter Southern, 'Dulwich Schooldays', J. H. Heineman and D. R. Bensen, *P. G. Wodehouse, A Centenary Celebration*, 1981, pp. 4–7, and Piggott, 'Wodehouse and Dulwich College', passim.

253. BM, Gilkes's Report, 1900, p. 117.

254. *A*, XVII, 198 (October 1899), p. 276; *A*, XXV, 180 (July 1897), p. 114; *A*, XXVII, 194 (May 1899), p. 112; Diary, p. 87; *A*, XXVI, 197 (September 1898), p. 276.

255. 7 March 1946: *Performing Flea*, 1953, p. 135.

256. Jasen, p. 11; Piggott, 'Wodehouse and Dulwich College', pp. xxiii–xxiv; *Daily Mail*, 12 July 1939.

257. Jasen, pp. 18–19; *A*, XXXI, 230 (November 1903), p. 442.

258. Concert Programme, DC Box 765; *Uncle Dynamite*, 1948, p. 64.

259. *A*, XXV, 188 (July 1898), p. 187; *A*, XXXVIII, 204 (July 1900), p. 210.

260. 'Under the Flail', *Public School Magazine*, VI, December 1901, p. 515.

261. *A*, XXXVII, 299 (December 1899), p. 338; *A*, XXVII, 192 (February 1899), p. 9.

262. *A*, XXXIII, 243 (June 1905), p. 199.

263. *Performing Flea*, p. 68.

264. 22 June 1950; 6 July 1951, DC Box 723; Wodehouse 'Box A', DC Box 730.

265. *Performing Flea*, p. 143.

266. *Psmith in the City*, 1910, pp. 26–7.

267. *Mike*, Chapter 17, p. 98; *Head of Kay's*, (1905), p. 50.

268. Mck, p. 437; *A Prefect's Uncle*, (1903), p. 143.

269. 'The Luck Stone' by 'Basil Wyndham' (Wodehouse), *Chums*, XVII, 839, 7 October 1908, p. 72; ibid, 840, 14 October 1908, p. 100.

270. *A*, LXIV, 456 (November 1936), p. 382; *A*, XXXII, 232 (February 1904), p. 9; Mck, p. 410.

271. *A*, XXXIII, 242 (May 1905), p. 143; *A*, XXXVIII, 283 (June 1910), p. 239.

272. *A*, XLV, 336 (February 1917), p. 22.

273. F. MacShane, ed., *Selected Letters of Raymond Chandler*, 1981, p. 49; ed. D. Gardiner and K. S. Wilson, *Raymond Chandler Speaking* (1962), Penguin Books, 1988, pp. 21–2.

274. T. Hiney, *Raymond Chandler*, 1997; obituary, *A*, LXXXVII, 588 (Summer 1959), p. 168.

275. Bodleian Library, Letter from Chandler to Hose, Modern Papers, Dep. Chandler 57, ff. 194–7; reprinted by kind permission of the Estate of Raymond Chandler.

276. 'An Unauthentic Interview', *A*, XXXVII, 273 (March 1909), pp. 68–81; see the letter from Chandler about this piece, ibid., 275 (June 1909), p. 242.

277. *A*, XXXVII, 276 (July 1909), pp. 252–3.

278. 31 March 1959 (DC Box 500).

279. N. de Somogyi, unpublished catalogue, 'Edward Alleyn and the Theatre' exhibition, Wodehouse Library, Dulwich College, 2000.

280. Op. cit., pp. 96–111.

281. *A*, XIX, 132 (July 1891), p. 177; Diary, p. 32.

282. R. F. Harrod, *Life of John Maynard Keynes*, 1951, p.76.

283. *A*, XXIX, 208 (February 1901), p. 6.

284. *A*, XXXI, 224 (February 1903), p. 11.

285. Letter to Christison from G. E. Moore (DC Box 893).

286. S. Legge, *Affectionate Cousins, Thomas Sturge Moore and Marie Appia*, 1980, passim.

287. *A*, XXXI, 225 (March 1903), p. 55.

288. P. Wilkinson, *John Tressider Sheppard*, 1969, p. 3; *A*, LXVI, 407 (July 1938), p. 295; King's College, Cambridge, Library MSS, JTS 1/9.

289. *A*, XXX, 220 (July 1902), pp. 209–16.

290. *A*, XXXII, 238 (November 1904), pp. 407–8; Alic Smith, *Selected Addresses*, pp. xvii–xix, xxiii.

291. Harrod, p. 66, n.

292. *A*, XXIV, 169 (March 1896), p. 64.

293. *A*, XL, 299 (June 1912), pp. 188–9.

294. *A*, XXXIX, 288 (February 1911), p. 18.

295. *A*, LXIII, 449 (July 1935), p. 288.

296. McCrum, p. 390.

297. *A*, LXXIII, 508 (July 1945), pp. 90–1; Wodehouse to Townend, 15 February 1945 (DC Box 723); Wodehouse to Christison, 7 December 1945 (DC Box 405).

298. *A*, LXXII, 500 (April 1944), p. 38.

299. Townend to Wodehouse, 4 March 1952 (Private collection).

300. Op. cit., p. 186.

301. *A*, LXXXV, 518 (March 1947), p. 54; Shawcross to Christison, 22 April 1947 (DC Box 730); McCrum, pp. 414–15; Wodehouse to Townend, 25 December 1950 (DC Box 723); *A*, XCII, 604 (Autumn 1964), p. 220.

302. *A*, LX, 432 (October 1932), p. 387; *Dulwich College War Record*, *1914–19*, 1932, p. 259.

303. E.g., *A*, XLI, 306 (May 1913), p. 224.

304. *A*, XXX, 220 (July 1902), p. 274; *A*, XXXII, 236 (July 1904), p. 207; *A*, XXXIII, 240 (February 1905), pp. 188, 190.

305. Diary, p. 58.

306. *Captain*, IX, June 1903, p. 221. Exhibition, Royal Society of British Artists, 1953.

307. GM, 1914, pp. 92, 110.

308. *A*, XL, 297 (March 1912), p. 87; *A*, XLI, 309 (August 1913), p. 363; *A*, 619 (Autumn 1969), n.p.; DC, Box 693.

309. GM, 1906, pp. 218–19; cf. EFC, 10 April 1908, p 38.

310. Op. cit., (DC Box 282) p. 1.

311. 20 January 1946 (DC Box 723); see also Col. A. F. Marchment, DSO, President of the Alleyn Club, on the 'shabby Brickies' of 1909, *A*, LXXVII, 533 (November 1949), p. 208.

312. BM, 1900, Gilkes's Report, p. 120; *G & D*, p. 390.

313. EFC, 13 September 1907, p. 134.

314. Diary, p. 10.

315. Mck, p. 392; J. W. Ivimey, *Boys and Music*, p. 58.

316. *Captain*, IX, June 1903, p. 217.

317. *Public School Magazine*, VII, Feb 1901, p. 126.

318. *A*, XLII, 317 (October 1914), p. 441; *A*, XL, 296 (February 1912), p. 62.

319. *A*, XLII, 317 (October 1914), p. 485; ibid., 318 (November 1914), p. 492.

320. BM, 30 April, 1909, p. 46.

321. *A*, XL, 300 (July 1912), p. 244; *G & D*, pp. 206, 222; extra allowances were paid to Escott and Hope: see EFC, 17 June 1912.

322. GM, 1914, pp. 88–111.

323. Diary, p. 159.

324. For the *Observer* cutting, see Christison's bound *Alleynian*, DC, June 1914; *Daily Mail*, 15 June 1914.

Chapter Nine

Approximate value of £1 sterling (see Notes to Chapter One): 1895, £79; 1914, £66; 1919, £32; 1920, £28; 1921, £30; 1922, £38; 1923, £39; 1926, £40; 1928, £41; 1930, £43; 1931, £47; 1934, £49; 1939, £43; 1941, £34.

1. Op. cit., passim and pp. 11, 180–1.

2. *A*, XLVII, 354 (October 1919), pp. 226–7.

3. GM, 18 October 1918, p. 90.

4. *A*, XLIII, 322 (May 1915), p. 130.

5. GM, Master's Report, 1914, p. 112.

6. *Daily Telegraph*, 1 August 1928; *A*, LXXV, 521 (October 1947), p. 180.

7. *A*, XLVIII, 360 (October 1920), p. 257.

8. *A*, XLIX, 366 (October 1921), p. 221; *A*, L, 373 (December 1922), p. 313.

9. *A*, LXXXV, 576 (February 1957), p. 4.

10. *A*, LII, 384 (October 1924), p. 203.

11. Press cutting, DC, Christison's bound volume of *A*, 1914.

12. DC Box 32A.

13. *A*, XCV, 616 (Autumn 1968) p. 48; GM, 1914, pp. 133–4.

14. Darby, p. 117.

15. *A*, LVI, 409 (December 1928), p. 426.

16. Hodges, p. 97.

17. GM, Report on Teaching Staff, Sept 1919, n.p.

18. Ibid.

19. *A*, L, 372 (October 1922), p. 314; *A*, XCII, 604 (Autumn 1964), p. 217.

20. *A*, XLVII, 350 (February 1919), p. 33; history of mission: *A*, LI, 374 (February 1923), pp. 72–5; *A*, LI, 378 (October 1923), p. 194.

21. GM, Master's Report, 1914, p. 132.

22. GM, 11 March 1977, pp. 35–6.

23. *A*, XLII, 317 (October 1914), p. 365.

24. *A*, XLIII, 322 (May 1915), pp. 175, 183; press cutting, Christison, bound volume of *A*, 1915, facing p. 179.

25. E.g. *A*, XLIII, 320 (February 1915), passim.

26. *A*, XLIII, 322 (May 1915), p. 121.

27. *A*, XLIII, 327 (December 1915), p. 417.

28. GM, October 1916, p. 95; GM, 19 January 1917, p. 5; GM, Master's Report, 1917, p. 78; *A*, XLV, 348 (November 1918), p. 204.

29. *A*, XLVI, 346 (June 1918), p. 95; GM, 23 May 1919, p. 59; reminiscence: *A*, LXVIII, 478 (June 1940), p. 478; GM, 15 October 1915, p. 116.

30. *A*, XLIV, 328 (February 1916), pp. 14–15; *A*, XLV, 336 (February 1917), frontispiece.

31. PGC, 17 May 1919, p. 49; GM, 1915, p. 144; 16 February 1917, p. 18; 18 May 1917, p. 38.

32. McC. Christison, ed., *Dulwich College War Record, 1914–18*, 1923, pp. 26–7.

33. *A*, XLVI, 344 (February 1917), p. 11.

34. VCs to date: *A*, XLIV, 333 (October 1916), pp. 236–42.

35. *Times*, 1 August 1928.

36. *A*, LVII, 410 (February 1929), p. 19.

37. *A*, L, 1922, 372 (October 1922), p. 255.

38. EFC, 14 March 1919, p. 119; *A*, LXII, 444 (October 1934), p. 399.

39. *A*, LXII, 445 (December 1934), p. 451.

40. *A*, LXV 462 (October 1937), p. 452; *A*, LXV, 463 (December 1937), pp. 535–6; *A*, LXVI, 464 (February 1938), pp 84–6.

41. GM, 3 May 1940, p. 33; *A*, LXVIII, 478 (June 1940), p. 134.

42. Op. cit., p. 16.

43. *Evening Standard*, 22 August 1928.

44. *A*, XLVI, 344 (Feb 1918), pp. 49–50.

45. GM, 19 February 1915, p. 34; GM, 16 February 1916, p. 16.

46. GM, 18 June 1920, p. 60.

47. *A*, XLVII, 353 (June 1919), p. 167; *A*, XLVII, 351 (March 1919), p. 62; *A*, XLVIII, 360 (October 1920), p. 162.

48. GM, 21 March 1919, p. 35.

49. GM, 9 July 1915, p. 88; GM, 1918, p. 71.

50. GM, Report on Teaching Staff, September 1919, n.p.

51. *A*, L, 371 (July 1922), p. 201; *Times*, 2 August, 1922; J. R. Piggott, *Shackleton, the Antarctic and Endurance*, 2000, pp. 51–8.

52. Obituary: *A*, LII, 384 (October 1924), p. 190.

53. M. H. Rosove, (ed.), *Rejoice My Heart, the Private Correspondence of Emily Shackleton and Hugh Robert Mill, 1922–33*, Santa Monica, California, 2007, p. 37.

54. The Royal Academy did not reveal names of purchasers of paintings until the Second World War; F. A. Worsley, *Shackleton's Boat Journey*, 1933, p. 92; E. H. Shackleton, *South*, 1919, p. 165.

55. Op. cit., 14 November 1932.

56. *A*, XLVII, 350 (February 1919), p. 139.

57. Darby, p. 276; GM, 21 September 1923, p. 81.

58. GM, 16 March, 1923, p. 21.

59. *A*, LIII, 386 (February 1925), p. 62.

60. *A*, XCV, 611 (Winter 1967), letter dated 15 November 1966, p. 24; the boat was painted again after 1989, and the name on the bow (originally 'J. CAIRD') lettered by George Marston, the expedition artist, (who sacrificed his oil paints to caulk the boat before the Journey), clearly seen in Frank Hurley's photographs, was followed neither in style nor position.

61. BM, 18 October 1968, p, 82; BM, 14 February 1930, p. 22; painting was again considered, EFC, 24 October 1930, p. 47.

62. *A*, LVI, 409 (December 1928), p. 409; GM, 1936, p. 48.

63. *A*, LII, 382 (June 1924), p. 129.

64. GM, 1915, p. 115.

65. GM, Master's Report, 1929, p. 45; GM, October 1918, p. 81.

66. GM, Master's Report, October 1919, p. 103.

67. GM, 17 October 1919, n.p.

68. *A*, XLVII, 351 (March 1919), p. 62.

69. *A*, LI, 378 (October 1923), p. 196.

70. C. S. Lewis, *Collected Letters*, ed. W. Hooper, Vol. I, 2004, pp. 778–9 (3 November 1928).

71. GM, 17 January 1919, p. 4; GM, 11 July 1919, p. 80.

72. GM, 1915, p. 10: of 633 boys, 173 with fees paid by the LCC; Hodges, pp. 103–4.

73. GM, 14 November 1919, p. 121.

74. GM, 14 June 1918, p. 55; GM, 9 July 1920, p. 67; GM, 10 December 1920, p. 98.

75. GM, March 1923, p. 47; GM, 27 January, 20 February 1920; 20 February 1922, p. 93; 14 May 1923, p. 52; GM, October 1920, p. 87.

76. GM, 1921, p. 22; GM, October 1921, Master's Report, p. 56.

77. GM, 1923, pp. 50, 52, 60; Hodges, p. 109.

78. GM, 1923, pp. 59, 78.

79. GM, Master's Annual Report, October 1924, pp. 41, 45–6.

80. EFC, 20 June 1924, p. 29; GM, 23 October 1924, p. 49; BM, 4 March 1927, p. 13.

81. GM, 17 February 1928, pp. 16–19; *Morning Post*, 2 November 1926; *South London Press*, 22 October 1926.

82. GM, 11 July 1924, p. 35; GM, 10 July 1925, p. 38; GM, 22 October 1926, p. 48.

83. GM, Master's Report, October 1927, p. 59; GM, 1928, pp. 14–17.

84. Op. cit., ed. A. W. Bain, pp. 88, 92, 93.

85. *The Star*, 19 November 1935.

86. GM, 7 July 1916, pp. 81–2.

87. PGC, 29 March 1919, p. 40.

88. EFC, 17 June 1927.

89. ODNB.

90. GM, 1932, p. 5.

91. *A*, XLIX, 362 (February 1921), p. 50.

92. *A*, LVII, 410 (February 1929), p. 66; *A*, LVII, 411 (March 1929), p. 75.

93. *A*, XLVIII, 357 (March 1920), p. 81.

94. *A*, LI, 372 (October 1922), p. 314.

95. Op. cit., 447, March 1932, p. 500.

96. *A*, XLIX, 364 (June 1921), p. 98.

97. Darby, p. 278a; Alick Hamilton, *A*, XCI, 601 (Autumn 1963), p. 216; *A*, LIV, 396 (October 1926), p. 717.

98. *Times*, 25 November 1926.

99. GM, 26 October 1923, p. 90; *Da Capo*, Old Alleynian Music Directory, Dulwich College, 1994, p. 15.

100. GM, Master's Report, 1937, p. 12; *A*, LXXII, 504 (December 1944), p. 126.

101. *A*, LXVII, 473 (July 1939), p. 239.

102. *A*, LVII, 410 (February 1929), pp. 15–17.

103. *A*, LXXIV, 515 (November 1946), p. 155; *A*, LXXVI, 523 (February 1948), p. 53; J. Cobban, *Dulwich Goes to War*, Dulwich College, 1995, p. 8.

104. *A*, LI, 377 (July 1923), p. 383.

105. *A*, LXVII, 471 (March 1939), p. 133; DC Box 373.

106. *A*, XLVIII, 356 (February 1920), p. 120.

107. Hodges, pp. 247–8; GM, Master's Report, 1931, p. 41; *A*, LXVIII, 481 (December 1940), pp. 314–15. Christopher Field, *60 Years On. A Celebration of 60 Years of Scouting at Dulwich College, 1929–59*, Dulwich College, 1989, passim. Hodges says that Smith did not approve of the Scouting movement, but this seems to be contradicted by Styler, as quoted in Field, p. 2. The trek carts feature in the Pathé newsreel for 14 October 1962 showing the Chief Scout opening the 48th Camberwell (OA) troop's headquarters at the Fort on Grange Road, DC, Box 165.

108. GM, 1922. p. 10; GM, 16 February 1923, p. 11; GM, 19 March 1915, p. 47.

109. GM, Master's Report, March 1920; *A*, LIII, 386 (February 1925), p. 1.

110. GM, 12 July 1935, p. 31.

111. GM, Master's Report, March 1919, p. 25; EFC, 19 March 1926, pp. 36, 39; GM, Master's Report, 1927, p. 53.

112. GM, 16 November 1917, p. 92; GM, 14 November 1919, p. 120.

113. EFC, 19 March 1926, p. 12; EFC, 10 May 1929, p. 24; GM, Master's Annual Report, October 1931, p. 43; GM, Master's Report, October 1929, p. 43; BM, 16 February 1930, pp. 16, 43; GM, 14 February 1930, p. 14.

114. *A*, LXX, 491 (October 1942), pp. 215–16.

115. GM, 1931, pp. 27–30; *A*, LX, 432 (October 1932), p. 301.

116. Press cutting, Christison, bound volume of *A*, 1931.

117. GM, 1933, pp. 38–9.

118. GM, 1939, p. 56; *A*, LXXXI, 498 (December 1943), p. 211; *A*, LXVIII, 476 (February 1940), p. 4; drawing, *A*, LXVIII, 477 (March 1940), p. 102.

119. GM, 1937, p. 76.

120. GM, 7 October 1938, p. 72.

121. GM, 3 October 1941, p. 54.

122. GM, 3 February 1939, p. 4.

123. *South London Press*, 9 December 1935.

124. GM, 6 July, 1923.

125. *Times*, 9 April 1926.

126. EFC, 22 March 1929, p. 19; press cuttings, Christison, bound volume of *A*, 1931; *Times*, 24 October 1927.

127. DC Box 723, 9 March 1956; W. Darby, *Dulwich Discovered*, 1966, p. 71.

128. GM, PGC, 9 November 1948, p. 96; PGC, 14 April 1924, pp. 17–18.

129. GM, 9 November 1938; GM, 1939, p. 61; GM, 25 October 1940, p. 82.

130. Op. cit., pp. 68, 70–1, 76.
131. 16 June 1921 (Estate of Michael Powell).
132. *A Life in Movies*, 1986, p. 106.
133. 28 June 1922 (Estate of Michael Powell).
134. Op. cit., p. 92.
135. Ibid., p. 106.
136. Ibid., p. 83.
137. *A*, L, 368 (February 1922), p. 14; on rugby, cf. *A Life in Movies*, p. 77; *A*, L, 371 (July 1922), p. 204.
138. DC *Form and Class Lists*, Midsummer 1922, p. 10.
139. *A*, LII, 385 (December 1924), p. 294.
140. *Independent*, 1 December 2004.
141. DC Box 424 (Letter to Peter Jolly, 14 November 1995).
142. GM, 16 February 1923, p. 38.
143. *A*, XLIX, 362 (February 1921), p. 10; LXI, 436 (June 1933), pp. 178–82; *A*, LXII, 442 (June 1934) pp. 136–8, review by Eric Parsley.
144. EFC, 1934, p. 6; *A*, LXII, 444, (October 1934), p. 316; 'The Cottage', *A*, LXIII, 449 (July 1935), pp. 236–40; *A*, LXVIII, 477 (March 1940), p. 90.
145. G. E. R. Lloyd, *Proceedings of the British Academy*, LXVIII, 1982, pp. 561–77.
146. K. B. McFarlane, *Letters to Friends*, 1940–66, Magdalen College, Oxford, p. xxvi; *A*, LXXXIX, 594 (Summer 1961), p. 158.
147. Alan Bennett, *London Review of Books*, 4 September 1997, pp. 12–15.
148. *A*, LXIII, 450 (October 1935), p. 307.
149. Fletcher's papers are at the University of Reading Library; ms. poems: DC Box 265.
150. *A*, LXII, 443 (July 1934), p. 215; *A*, LXIII, 451 (December 1935), p. 392.
151. *A*, XLIX, 366 (October 1921), p. 251.
152. H. Henderson, 'Tangling with the Langholm Byspale', *Alias MacAlias*, 2004, pp. 381–83.
153. GM, 27 June 1928, p. 50.
154. *A*, LVI, 408 (October 1928), p. 279.
155. *A*, LXXXV, 576 (February 1957), p. 4.
156. *Times*, 31 January 1957, p. 13.
157. Gibbon, *A*, LXXXV, 519 (June 1947), p. 102; Booth, *Evening News*, 24 July 1928.
158. Press cuttings, Christison, bound volume of *A*, 1928, facing p. 353; *A*, LVII, 414 (October 1929), p. 294; *Evening Standard*, 22 October 1931.
159. *DVK*, pp. 43–4.
160. GM, Master's Report, October 1929, pp. 41–3; figures for 1914: Classics, 161; Modern, 140; Science, Maths and Engineering, 229, ibid.
161. GM, September 1934, pp. 37–8; GM, Master's Report, January 1935, p. 30; *Observer*, 5 July 1936.
162. GM, 7 October 1938, p. 74; GM, Master's Annual Report, 1940, p. 75.
163. GM, 14 February 1930, p. 16.
164. *Times*, 6 April 1940.
165. Hansard, 14 March 1928, p. 2064.
166. *Daily Mirror*, 5 June 1928.

167. *A*, LVII, 413 (July 1929), p. 290.
168. GM, September 1934, p. 38.
169. GM, 6 December 1940; GM, 23 December 1940, p. 93.
170. *A*, LIX, 422 (February 1931), p. 83; *A*, LIX, 426 (October 1931), pp. 381–3; *A*, LXI, 439 (December 1933), p. 447.
171. *A*, LXII, 442, (June 1934), p. 118.
172. GM, Master's Report, 1937, p. 12.
173. *A*, LXVI, 464 (February 1938), p. 12.
174. *A*, XLI, 601 (Autumn 1963), p. 136.
175. Cobban, p. 1.
176. Hodges, p. 121; GM, 1938, pp. 65, 76.
177. GM, 22 September 1939, p. 67.
178. GM, 1939, p. 4.
179. GM, 19 May, 1939, p. 33.
180. Ibid, p. 42; GM, 24 November 1939, p. 74; *A*, LXVII, 473 (July 1939), p. 227.
181. Hodges, p. 122; Cobban, p. 5.
182. *Daily Mail*, 28 July 1936.
183. *A*, XVIII, 476 (February 1940), p. 25; GM, General Purposes Committee, 1939, p. 12; GM, 1940, p. 3; GM, 21 March 1941, p. 13.
184. GM, September 1939, p. 84; *Times*, 8 December 1939; photographs: ibid., 7 October 1939.
185. *A*, LXVIII, 480 (November 1940), p. 256; Cobban, pp. 5, 7; D. V. Knight, *DVK*, p. 69; Darby, p. 293.
186. Cobban, p. 5; *A*, XCI, 601 (Autumn 1963), p. 138; GM, 19 July 1940, p. 67; GM, 1940, pp. 51, 76; GM, 19 July 1940, p. 67.
187. GM, 1940, pp. 75, 86; GM, 24 October, 1941, p. 63; GM, 1940, p. 67.
188. Cobban, p. 7; GM, 1940, p. 75.
189. *A*, LXVIII, 480 (November 1940), p. 270; Darby, p 269.
190. H. Saunders, *The Battle of Britain, August–October 1940*, HMSO, 1941, pp. 4–5, 12–13; *A*, LXIX, 486 (October 1941), p. 231.
191. *A*, LXIII, 446 (February 1935), p. 40; *The Last Enemy*, 1946, pp. 13, 35, 37. Hilary says Agazarian was sent down from Oxford for 'breaking up' his College; his obituary says he graduated, *A*, LXIX, 487 (December 1941), p. 314. For Francine Agazarian see L. Jones, *A Quiet Courage*, 1990; for Jack Agazarian, see *The Times*, 1 August, 2007.
192. DC Box 707.
193. GM, 6 December 1940, p. 87; *A*, LXIX, 482 (February 1941), p. 1.
194. GM, 1940, pp. 11–13; GM, 24 January 1941, p. 1; GM, 9 May 1941, p. 23; GM, 18 July 1941, p. 48; GM, 24 October 1941, p. 61.
195. *A*, LXIX, 483 (March 1941), p. 70; *A*, LXIX, 484 (June 1941), p. 228; *A*, LXIX, 486 (October 1941), p. 231.
196. Hodges, p. 126; GM, 1941, p. 21; GM, 25 April, p. 21; *A*, LXIX, 484 (June 1941), p. 131.

Chapter Ten

Approximate value of £1 (see Notes to Chapter One): 1941, £34; 1942, £32; 1943, £31; 1944, 1945, £30; 1949, £24; 1952,

£20; 1953, £19; 1955, £18; 1960, £16; 1962, £15; 1965–67, £13; 1968, £12; 1970, £11; 1972, £9; 1976, £5; 1979–81, £3; 1984, £2.

1. Recalled by Arthur Gayford (see Chapter Nine), *A*, LXXXI, 557 (October 1953), p. 235.

2. *A*, LXXIX, Old Alleynian Section, 1951, p. 10.

3. *A*, XCV, 613 (Autumn 1967), p. 323.

4. Gayford, p. 237; *A*, LXXV, 518 (March 1947), p. 41; DVK, p. 89.

5. A. T. Gregory, *Memoirs*, 2002, p. 28.

6. GM, 21 February 1947, p. 102.

7. *A*, LXXIII, 509 (November 1945), p. 158; cf. GM, 18 May 1945, p. 218.

8. *A*, LXXIX, Old Alleynian Section, 1951, p. 8.

9. GM, 21 July, 1950, p. 21; 1 December 1950, p. 114.

10. *A*, LXXV, 521 (October 1947) p. 178.

11. Op. cit., 12 December 1951.

12. *A*, LXXIX, Old Alleynian Section, 1951, p. 6.

13. GM, 22 February 1942, pp. 11–12; ibid., p. 20; GM, 5 December 1941, p. 76.

14. GM, 2 July 1943, p. 38; £5,000 repaid, see GM, 5 October 1945, p. 246.

15. GM, 6 February 1942, p. 1; ibid., 6 March 1942, p. 15; *A*, LXX, 488 (May 1942), p. 43.

16. *A*, LXXI, 493 (February 1943), p. 4.

17. GM, 3 February 1943, p. 5.

18. *A*, LXXIII, 507 (June 1945), p. 53; LXIX, 482 (February 1941), p. 2; 483 (March 1941), p. 69; GM, 2 July 1943, p. 40; A. T. Gregory, *Memoirs*, 2002, p. 24.

19. Undated, DC, Cuttings Album IV (shelf 1.3).

20. *A*, LXXIV, 513 (June 1946), p. 57.

21. GM, 6 July 1951, p. 178.

22. GM, 3 December 1943, p. 71.

23. GM, 8 March 1943, p. 19.

24. GM, 3 December 1948, p. 104.

25. GM, 18 February 1944, p. 90; cutting in Christison's bound *Alleynian*, LXXII, 499 (February 1944).

26. *A*, LXXIV, 521 (October 1947), p. 177.

27. *A*, XCV, 616 (Autumn 1968), p. 19; *Daily Telegraph*, 18 July 1944; *A*, LXXIX, Old Alleynian Section, 1951, p. 7.

28. *A*, LXIX, 487 (October 1941), pp. 282, 290; *A*, LXX, 490 (July 1942), pp. 96–7; *A*, LXXI, 498 (December 1943), p. 201; *A*, LXXII, 504 (December 1944), p. 125; ibid., 500 (April 1944), p. 26.

29. *A*, LXX, 489 (May 1942), p. 54.

30. *A*, LXIX, 485 (July 1941), pp. 187–8.

31. *A*, LXIX, 486 (October 1941), pp. 242–4; *A*, LXX, 491 (October 1942), p. 172; *A*, 492 (December 1942), p. 244.

32. *A*, LXXII, 499 February 1944), pp. 5–6.

33. *A*, LXXIII, 509 (November 1945), p. 158.

34. *A*, LXXIII, 507 (June 1945), p. 54; *A*, LXXIII, 508 (July 1945), p. 90.

35. *A*, LXXXIII, 568 (July 1955), p. 190; GM, 17 July 1953, p. 166.

36. *A*, 574 (October 1956), p. 194.

37. *A*, LXX, 489 (May 1942), p. 94 & seq.

38. *Times*, 4 January 2003; *Daily Telegraph*, 6 January 2003.

39. *A*, LXX, 471 (October 1942), p. 219.

40. *A*, LXXII, 501 (June 1944), p. 70; *A*, LXXII, 502 (July 1944), p. 87.

41. *A*, LXIX, 483 (March 1941), pp. 74-5; *A*, LXXII, 499 (February 1944), p. 2; *A*, LXXIII, 507 (June 1945), p. 76.

42. *A*, LXXI, 493 (February 1943), pp. 140–41.

43. *A*, LXXV, 520 (July 1947), pp. 135-7.

44. Information from Terry Walsh.

45. GM, 1947, p. 104; *A*, LXXV, 521 (October 1947), p. 179.

46. *A*, LXXIV, 515 (November 1946), p. 160.

47. GM, 18 February 1943, p. 87; ibid., 3 November 1944, pp. 163-4; ibid., 1 December 1944, p. 167; ibid., 18 December 1944, p. 180.

48. 26 January 1945, p. 188; ibid., 16 March 1945, p. 196.

49. GM, 16 March, 1945, p. 214; ibid., 27 July 1945, p. 240.

50. GM, 24 October 1947, p. 33.

51. GM, 26 October 1945, pp. 258-9.

52. GM, 18 May 1945, p. 216.

53. Op. cit., 23 June 1945.

54. GM, 1 March 1946, p. 32; ibid., 12 March 1948, p. 27.

55. DC, shelf A, 1.3.

56. GM, 22 February 1946, p. 11; ibid., 5 April 1946, p. 20; ibid., 4 October 1946, p. 62; ibid., 1 November 1946, p. 71.

57. GM, 27 July 1951, p. 193.

58. *South London Press*, 30 January 1948; *Evening Standard*, 2 October 1947.

59. GM, 21 February 1947, p. 104.

60. *Evening News*, 12 December 1951.

61. *A*, LXXXI, 557 (October 1953), p. 284.

62. GM, 18 May 1945, p. 218; ibid., 22 February 1946, p. 11.

63. *A*, LXXV, 521 (October 1947), p. 176.

64. *South London Press*, 25 September 1953.

65. 22 June 1952. Private collection.

66. *A*, LXXIX, Old Alleynian Section, 1951, pp. 6–8.

67. GM, 24 July 1942, p. 55; ibid., 2 October 1942, p. 62.

68. GM, 18 February 1943, p.87; ibid., 18 May 1944, p. 223.

69. GM, 30 November 1945, p. 279; ibid., 1 March 1946, p. 7.

70. GM, 10 November 1950, p. 102; ibid., 2 February 1951, pp. 133-4.

71. GM, 6 February 1953, p. 117; ibid., 6 February 1953, p. 118.

72. Hodges, p. 153; *A*, LXXXI, 557 (October 1953), p. 237.

73. *A*, LXXXVII, 589 (Autumn 1959), p. 276; LXXVIII, 539 (November 1950), p. 276.

74. *A*, LXXXVII, 589 (Autumn 1959), p. 275.

75. GM, 2 February 1951, p. 129; GPC, 19 April 1952, p. 19; GM, 26 March 1964, p. 165; ibid., 21 January 1972, p. 3; GM, DC Committee, 19 March 1979, p. 43.

76. *A*, LXXX, 547 (January 1952), p. 16.

77. *A*, LXXVII, 533 (November 1949), p. 212.

78. GM, 21 July 1950, p. 67; ibid., 11 May 1951, p. 163; ibid., 18 March 1955, p. 121.

79. Obituary, *A*, 629 (Spring 1973), pp. 5–7; Hodges, p. 138; *A*, LXXI, 493 (February 1943) p. 8; *A*, LXXVII, 532 (July 1949), p. 114.

80. *A*, LXXXVII, 592 (Autumn 1959), p. 255.

81. GM, 3 July 1942, p. 47.

82. *A*, 673 (1998), p. 69.

83. LXXVI (June 1948), p. 52; Coveney, at Dulwich 1945–50, author of *The Image of Childhood* (1967), left to teach at the University of Manchester; *A*, LXXIII, 505 (February 1945), p. 3.

84. *A*, LXXVII, 531 (June 1949), p. 78.

85. *A*, XCV 613, (Autumn 1967), p. 207.

86. Hodges, p. 166.

87. *A*, LXXXIV, 574 (December 1956), pp. 187–8; *A*, XCIV, 611 (Winter 1967), p. 3.

88. *A*, LXXXIV, 575 (December 1956), pp. 257–8; *DVK*, p. 91; *A*, 677 (2002), p. 20.

89. GM, 10 March 1950, p. 31.

90. *A*, XC, 596, (Winter 1960), p. 77.

91. Vellacott in *A*, 592 (Autumn 1960), pp. 161–2.

92. GM, 19 May 1950, p. 39.

93. *A*, LXXIII, 508 (July 1945), p. 93.

94. *A*, LXXXII 559 (February 1954), p. 5.

95. *A*, LXXVI, 523 (February 1948), p. 4.

96. *A*, LXXV, 520 (July 1947), p. 135.

97. *A*, 544 (July 1951), p. 171.

98. *A*, LXXVII 532 (July 1949), p. 115; *A*, LXXIX, 551 (September 1952), p. 196.

99. GM, 3 July 1953, p. 157.

100. *A*, LXXXI, 556 (July 1953), p. 178.

101. *A*, 620 (Winter 1969–70), n. p.; letter of 20 January 1936, DC Box 723.

102. *A*, LXXXV, 576 (February 1957), p. 8.

103. *A*, LXXIV, 516 (December 1946), p. 176.

104. *A*, LXXVII, 531 (June 1949), p. 64.

105. *A*, LXXVII, 533 (November 1949), p. 206.

106. *A*, LXXIII, 509 (November 1945), p. 129.

107. *A*, LXXV, 517 (February 1947), p. 1.

108. *A*, LXXVIII, 536 (March 1950), p. 63.

109. *A*, LXXXVIII, 538 (July 1950), p. 174.

110. Op. cit., pp. 6–8.

111. *A*, LXXXVIII 539 (November 1950), p. 273.

112. Unidentified press cutting, 1951.

113. *A*, 683 (Michaelmas 2005), p. 26; GM, 18 July 1952, p. 72.

114. *A*, LXXXI, 557 (October 1953), p. 283; *A*, LXXVII, 529 (February 1949), p. 8.

115. GM, 23 February 1951, p. 145.

116. GM, 6 October 1944, p. 134.

117. *A*, LXXV, 521 (October 1947), p. 178.

118. GM, 3 February 1956 p. 10; ibid., 23 July 1948, p. 66; ibid., 1 October 1948, p. 76.

119. GM, 11 November 1949, p. 185.

120. GM, 3 February 1950, p. 9; ibid., 1 December 1950, p. 114; BM, 22 Feb 1952, p. 12.

121. GM 1 October 1943, p. 56; ibid., 6 May 1949, p. 136; *A*, LXXXII, 563 (October 1954), p. 279.

122. *A*, LXXIII, 506 (March 1945), p. 29; GM, 9 June 1950, p. 47; ibid., GM, 26 January 1945, p. 186; ibid., 25 February 1949, p. 120.

123. *A*, LXXX, 551 (September 1952), p. 191; *A*, LXXX, 550 (July 1952), p. 125.

124. *A*, LXXXVIII, 538 (July 1950), p. 180.

125. *A*, LXXVI, 528 (December 1948), p. 198.

126. Hodges, p. 141.

127. GM, 3 Feb 1950, p. 9; ibid., 6 July 1951, pp. 185–6.

128. GM, 7 July 1950, p. 61; ibid., 21 July 1950, p. 63.

129. GM, 2 Feb 1951, pp. 129, 132; ibid., 23 Feb 1951, pp. 139–41.

130. *A*, LXXIV, 515 (November 1946), p. 160; *A*, LXXVI, 528 (December 1948), p. 218; GM, 25 February 1949, pp. 120, 125; *A*, LXXX, 551 (September 1952), p. 246.

131. GM, 9 June 1950, p. 59.

132. GM, 2 November 1945, p. 265; *A*, LXXX, 548 (March 1952), p. 42.

133. GM, 30 June 1949, p. 127.

134. *A*, LXIX, 491 (October 1942), p. 156; GM, 27 July 1944, p. 129.

135. *A*, LXXX, 552 (December 1952), p. 257.

136. GM, 10 August 1942, Special Committee, p. 58.

137. GM, 6 October 1944, p. 143.

138. *A*, LXXV 517 (February 1947), p. 35.

139. GM, 22 February 1946, p. 15.

140. GM, 10 May 1957, p. 143; PGC, 14 January 1966, p. 1.

141. GM, 31 May 1945, p. 229.

142. GM, 28 Dec 1944. p. 18; ibid., 27 July 1944, p. 129; GM, 1 February 1949, p. 118.

143. GM, 23 July 1947, p. 167; ibid., 11 November 1949, p. 203; ibid., 27 October 1950, p. 88.

144. GM, 5 December 1946, p. 75.

145. GM, 8 June 1951, p. 173; ibid., 27 July 1951, p.191.

146. GM, 19 December 1952, p. 101; *A*, 619 (Autumn 1969), p. 3.

147. *A*, LXXXI, 554 (March 1953), p. 70; GM, 24 October 1952, p. 80.

148. PGC, 14 March, 1951, p. 150; *The Times*, 12 July 1962.

149. GM, 26 June 1964, p. 84.

150. GM, 24 November 1955, p. 172.

151. GM, GPC, 8 May 1953, p. 147; PGC, 23 January 1953, p. 112; ibid., 27 February 1959, p. 88; ibid., 30 April, 1959, p. 98.

152. GM, 8 May 1953, p. 143.

153. 11 April 1955. Private collection.

154. GM, 25 September 1959, p. 132.

155. *A*, LXXXVI, 586 (October 1958), p. 224; *A*, LXXXVII, 592 (Autumn 1960), p. 248.

156. *A*, XCIV 610 (Autumn 1966), p. 196.

157. Ibid.

158. *A*, XCI, 600 (Summer 1963), p. 213.

159. GM, 26 February 1960, p. 82.

160. N. Earle, Address at Service of Thanksgiving for Ronald Groves, 1991.

161. *A*, XCIV, 610 (Autumn 1966), p. 295.

162. *Notes to Parents*, July 1955.

163. Earle, 1991 (see note 160); *A*, XCIV, 610 (Autumn 1966), p. 196.

164. *A*, XCIV, 608 (Winter 1966), p. 1.

165. *A*, 622 (Autumn 1970), pp. 4–5.

166. GM, 27 February 1951, p. 81.

167. GM, 24 January 1964, p. 14; ibid., 24 September 1965, p. 238.

168. GM, 10 May 1952, p. 137.

169. *A*, XC, 596 (Winter 1962), p. 59.

170. *A*, XCV, 616 (Autumn 1968), p. 50.

171. *A*, LXXXIII, 569 (October 1955), p. 281; GM, 24 February 1956.

172. GM, 10 July 1964, p. 95.

173. GM, 25 September 1959, p. 132.

174. GM, 28 March, 1958 p. 16.

175. *A*, LXXXVI, 585 (July 1958), p. 149; ibid., 586 (October 1958), p. 299.

176. *Notes to Parents*, 1954.

177. GM, 8 May 1956, pp. 23–4; GM, 23 October 1964, p. 118.

178. Groves, *Notes to Parents*, July 1955; GM, 7 May 1954; ibid., 18 March 1955, p. 131.

179. *A*, LXXXV, 578 (May 1957), p. 62.

180. *A*, XC, 596 (Winter 1962), p. 1.

181. GM, 14 November 1958, p. 59; *A*, XCIV 609 (Summer 1966), p. 98.

182. 615 (Summer 1968), n.p.

183. GM, 10 July 1964, p. 94.

184. GM, 1 February 1957, p. 95; ibid., 29 November 1957, p. 118; ibid., 26 March 1964; ibid., 24 September 1964.

185. *A*, XCV, 611 (Winter 1967), pp. 14–18.

186. *A*, XCIV, 608 (Winter 1966), p. 80.

187. *A*, LXXXIV, 572 (May 1956).

188. *A*, XCIV, 608 (Winter 1966), p. 21; *A*, LXXVI, 586 (October 1958), pp. 225–7; Darby, p. 329.

189. *A*, LXXXIV, 572 (May 1956), p. 90.

190. *A*, LXXXVIII, 590 (Winter 1960), p. 83.

191. GM, 26 March 1965, p. 174; ibid., 18 February 1966, p. 14; ibid., 25 March 1966, p. 21.

192. GM, 14 February, 1964, p. 19.

193. Quoted by C. W. Lloyd, *A*, 670 (1995), p. 43.

194. *A*, LXXXVII, 589 (Autumn 1959), p. 197.

195. *A*, LXXXIV, 571 (May 1956), pp. 57–8.

196. *A*, LXXXIV, 574 (December 1956), p. 193; Hodges, p. 126; A. T. Gregory, *Memoirs*, 2002, p. 28.

197. *A*, LXXXIII, 570 (December 1955), p. 320; *A*, LXXXVII, 587 (Winter 1959), p. 1.

198. *A*, LXXXVI, 584 (June 1958), p. 91; ibid., 585 (July 1958), p 197.

199. *A*, LXXXIX 593 (Winter 1961).

200. *A*, LXXX, 576 (Feb 1957), p. 47; ibid., 578 (May 1957), pp. 107, 145.

201. *A*, XCII, 602 (Winter 1964), p. 15.

202. *A*, LXXXVII, 587 (Winter 1959), pp. 13–15; *A*, 589 (Autumn 1959), pp. 193–6; *A*, LXXXVIII, 590 (Winter 1960), pp. 25–8.

203. *A*, XCIV, 610 (Autumn 1966), p. 283; *A*, XCV, 612 (Summer 1967), pp. 115–20.

204. *A*, LXXXIII, 566 (March 1955), p 75; *A*, LXXXV, 576 (February 1957), p. 48.

205. *A*, XC, 598 (Autumn 1962) p. 211.

206. *A*, LXII, 502 (July 1944), p. 76.

207. *A*, 661, Winter 1988–9.

208. *Notes to Parents*, July 1955; December 1956.

209. *Times Educational Supplement*, 11 March 1955; *A*, LXXXIII, 569 (October 1955), pp. 275–6.

210. *A*, LXXXVIII, 590 (Winter 1960), pp. 95–6; *A*, LXXXIX, 593 (Winter 1961), p. 17.

211. *A*, LXXIII, 509 (November 1945), p. 133; *A*, LXXX, 547 (January 1952), p. 35.

212. T. J. Walsh, Memorial Address for Charles Lloyd, 1999; GM, 10 November, 1966, p. 95.

213. *A*, XCV, 613, Autumn 1967, p. 321.

214. *A*, 621 (Summer 1970), pp. 6–8.

215. DC Box 49.

216. GM, 5 December 1969, p. 202.

217. FGP, 18 January 1974, p. 4.

218. Ibid., p. 8; Hodges, pp. 179–80.

219. T. J. Walsh, Memorial Address, 1999.

220. GM, 24 April 1968, p. 41.

221. GM, 28 January 1966, p. 5; ibid., 17 November 1967, p. 198.

222. GM, 15 November 1968, p. 95.

223. FGP, 10 May 1974, p. 40.

224. GM, 15 May 1970, p. 35; ibid., 2 July 1971, p. 158.

225. FGP, 18 January 1974, p. 4.

226. GM, 6 December 1968, p. 99.

227. GM 11 October 1974, p. 90.

228. *A*, 627 (Summer 1972), p. 11.

229. GM, 21 October 1966, p. 86; *A*, 616 (Autumn 1968); GM, 17 October 1969, p. 180.

230. *A*, 616 (Autumn 1968), p. 49; *A*, 619 (Autumn 1969), n. p.; *A*, 627 (Summer 1972), p. 11.

231. GM, 15 July 1966, p. 66.

232. GM, 24 June 1966, p. 50; ibid., 15 September 1972, p. 61.

233. GM, 6 May 1966, p. 36.

234. GM, 10 June 1966, p. 50.

235. GM, 20 October 1967, pp. 191–2.

236. GM, 17 March 1967, p. 139; ibid., 24 May 1968, p 48; ibid., 21 June 1968, p. 57.

237. GM, 26 June 1968, p. 12; ibid., 24 April 1968, p. 40.

238. GM, 21 June 1968, p. 57; report by Roderick Gradidge of the Victorian Society, GM, 6 December 1968, pp. 104–6.

239. GM, 17 September 1972, p. 167; ibid., 15 July 1966, p. 66.

240. FGP, 20 September 1974, p. 72.

241. GM, 17 October 1969, p. 185; *A*, 630 (Spring 1973), p. 11.

242. MRG, 11 October 1974, p. 90.

243. GM, 21 October 1967, p. 87.

244. GM, 18 October 1968, p. 86.

245. GM, 24 October 1947, p. 183; BM, 26 Feb 1960, p. 18; GM, 15 July 1966, p. 64; ibid., 22 June 1967, p. 3; GM, 12 February 1970, p. 16.

246. GM, 20 November 1970, p. 93.

247. *A*, 621 (Summer 1970); *A*, 622 (Autumn 1970).

248. MRG, 1981, p. 83.

249. GM, 19 March 1979, p. 43; MRG, 1974–5, p. 84.

250. DC Committee, GM, 19 March 1979, p. 43.

251. MRG, 1982, p. 86.

252. GM, 7 October 1976, p. 98; MRG, 7 October, 1976, p. 99.

253. GM, 8 December 1978, p. 279.

254. GM, 10 November 1978, pp. 269–70.

255. *Times*, 22 December 1964.

256. *A*, 641 (Autumn 1978), n. p.

257. GM, 17 Feb 1977, p. 23a.

258. DPG Committee, 18 July 1978, p. 233.

259. *A*, 671 (1996), p. 13.

260. *A*, 659 (Spring 1988), n.p.

261. *A*, 672 (1997), p. 2.

262. Ibid., p. 4.

Chapter Eleven

1. Foundation document for Alleyn's College of God's Gift. M 584, DC.

2. Letter from A. C. F. Verity to Praoranuj Chandrasomboon, 20 June 1994, DC.

3. Licence agreement between the Governors of Dulwich College and Dulwich International (Thailand) Ltd, 28 November 1994, DC.

4. Dulwich International College 2004 prospectus, DC.

5. Dulwich College Governors' minutes, November 1997. DC, Clerk's office.

6. Letter from Graham Able to Arthit Ourairat, 28 February 1998, DC.

7. Licence Agreement between DCEL and Dulwich International Ltd, 29 January 2004, DC.

8. DIC Inspection Report written by Graham and Mary Able, 8–15 January, 2005. DC, Master's office.

9. Letter from Arthit Ourairat to Lord George, 4 April 2005, DC; response to Arthit Ourairat from Lord George, 12 April 2005, DC; official letter accepting the termination of the franchise from Graham Able, as Chairman of DCEL, to Arthit Ourairat, 16 May 2005, DC.

10. Letter to DIC parents from Arthit Ourairat, 26 April 2005, DC.

11. Franchise Agreement between Global Education Management Ltd (later GEICC and now Dulwich Management Shanghai Ltd) and DCEL, 21 May 2003. DC, Master's office.

Chapter Twelve

1. The story of this change is very well told in '*Manly and Muscular Diversions – Public Schools and the 19th Century Sporting Revival*' by Tony Money (1997).

2. For Bowden, see Jonty Winch, *England's Youngest Cricket Captain*, 2003.

3. For Douglas and Wells, see *G & D*, pp. 8, 12, 20, 28–30.

4. *Memories*, p. 43.

5. Quoted by Hodges, p. 227.

INDEX

Main references are given in **bold** type, illustrations (by page number) in *italics*.